A History of Seventh day Baptists in West Virginia

Including the Woodbridgetown and Salemville churches in Pennsylvania and the Shrewsbury church in New Jersey

Corliss Fitz Randolph

Alpha Editions

This edition published in 2020

ISBN : 9789354005398

Design and Setting By
Alpha Editions
email - alphaedis@gmail.com

As per information held with us this book is in Public Domain.
This book is a reproduction of an important historical work. Alpha Editions uses the best technology to reproduce historical work in the same manner it was first published to preserve its original nature. Any marks or number seen are left intentionally to preserve its true form.

A HISTORY OF

Seventh Day Baptists in West Virginia

INCLUDING THE WOODBRIDGETOWN
AND SALEMVILLE CHURCHES IN
PENNSYLVANIA AND THE
SHREWSBURY CHURCH
IN NEW JERSEY

BY

CORLISS FITZ RANDOLPH

Chairman of The Committee on Denominational
History of the Seventh Day Baptist
General Conference

Printed for the Author by
THE AMERICAN SABBATH TRACT SOCIETY
(Seventh Day Baptist)
Plainfield, New Jersey
1905

TO
My Father
Whose Patient Precept, Lofty Example, and
Affectionate Encouragement
Have Inspired This Volume.

PREFACE.

THIS volume is the result of an invitation to prepare a historical paper relating to the Seventh Day Baptist South-Eastern Association, for the meeting held at Ashaway, Rhode Island, in August, 1902, in commemoration of the organisation of the Seventh Day Baptist General Conference one hunderd years before. For four years, all the time which could be spared from a very busy life, has been devoted to its preparation.

My first plan was to write a paper which I hoped could be completed in about two weeks. As soon as I began to examine what had been published relating to the subject, however, I found that I should be obliged to consult the original records. As a result, I soon altered my plans, and began the preparation of a more exhaustive treatise, designed to be a classified epitome of all existing records relating to Seventh Day Baptists in Western Virginia, including the Shrewsbury Church of Monmouth County, New Jersey, and the Woodbridgetown Church of Fayette County, Pennsylvaia, and the Salemville Church of Bedford County, Pennsylvania; in short, to supply the material needed for some future historian to write a narrative of these people in story form, occupying about two-fifths the space of this book. At one time I contemplated such a narrative as a suitable introduction to the present work, which long ago grew to proportions such as make that impracticable.

In the pursuit of the plan finally adopted, I have carefully examined, twice, all the records known to be in existence relating to the subject. The site of the Shrewsbury Church, but a few miles distant from Asbury Park, New Jersey—long ago forgotten—I have identified, and visited several times. Besides numerous visits of myself and interested friends to the offices of the Secretary of State, at Trenton, New Jersey; the Secretary of State at Richmond, Virginia; the Clerk of the County Court and the Clerk of the Circuit Court of Harrison County, West Virginia; and the Clerk of the County Court and the Clerk of the Circuit Court of Doddridge County, West Virginia, an extensive correspondence has reached every known or supposed source of desirable information. In one instance, for example, I searched four large metropolitan libraries, and corresponded with the United States War Department, as well as the Department of State, four prominent historical societies, two adjutant generals, and one state historian, besides numerous private individuals, for a period of several weeks, with a net result of less than four full lines of print, and that of very doubtful value. This is a rather rare example, but it shows the care constantly bestowed upon minute details of investigation. In but two instances, both relatively unimportant, were my requests for assistance unheeded. Without such cordial, unanimous co-operation, my task would have been exceedingly difficult.

For much of the more important service thus rendered, due acknowledgment has been made in appropriate connection in the body of the work. The multitude of other friends to whom I am indebted, space forbids me to mention by name. I cannot forbear naming a very few, however. Among these are, Professor Jasper N. Deahl of the West Virginia University, through whose courtesy exceptional privileges in the library of that institution were granted me; Charles H. Greene, Esquire, of Alfred, New York, who generously placed at my disposal his valuable manuscripts upon Seventh

Day Baptist History; and the Honourable Isaiah Bee, M. D., of Princeton, West Virginia, whose personal knowledge of the early Seventh Day Baptist family history of Western Virginia is probably greater than that of any other living person.

However, more than to any one else, and more than to all others, even, I am indebted to my father, Franklin F. Randolph, Esquire, of New Milton, West Virginia, without whose assistance and encouragement, I should have been compelled materially to curtail the plan of the work, if not wholly to abandon it. Possessed of a wide personal acquaintance with the subject, due in no small measure to his official connection with several of the churches, besides other organisations, and a vivid recollection, covering upwards of sixty years of the period treated, together with rich resources of invaluable private papers, among which were those belonging to Samuel Fitz Randolph, the founder of the village of New Salem, in Western Virginia, Jonathan Fitz Randolph, Jepthah Fitz Randolph, and William Fitz Randolph, his great-grandfather, grandfather, father, and uncle, respectively, he has contributed time and labour without stint to the success of the enterprise.

In the selection of illustrations, my sole aim has been to complete the record as far as possible, of which suitable illustrations, of necessity, form an important part.

The maps were all drawn by myself. No attempt was made to draw them to scale, as a sufficient number of familiar landmarks were introduced into each to render accurate measurements unnecessary.

The restorations of buildings and maps long since disappeared, with a single exception, were all made from pencil sketches drawn by myself from available, trustworthy data. Doubtless, they are all faulty in minor details, but in respect to the main features, they are believed to be essentially correct.

In making abstracts directly from the records, I have

endeavoured to preserve the original language of the records, even where the abstract is not a direct quotation.

Certain historical facts have been repeated more or less often, in order to complete groups of related facts.

It should be borne in mind constantly by the reader that, unless specifically stated to the contrary at any given point, this history ends with August 1, 1902.

Due apology is offered the disappointed subscriber for several unexpected delays in the publication of the book owing to unforeseen difficulties beyond the control of the publisher.

The appended list of references is by no means exhaustive. It contains, however, such authorities as are indispensible, or at least representative.

The typographical excellence of the work is due to the unsparing pains of the late Mr. John Hiscox, manager of the publishing house of the American Sabbath Tract Society, whose untimely death is recorded as the last few pages of the book are passing through the press.

I dare not hope that this book has escaped errors of detail—as to fact and date—common to its kind, and I shall be pleased to receive corrections from interested readers.

CORLISS FITZ RANDOLPH.

NEWARK, NEW JERSEY,
December 5, 1905.

AUTHORITIES.

MANUSCRIPT RECORDS.

Shrewsbury and New Salem Churches, 4 vols.
Lost Creek Church, 3 vols.
Middle Island Church, 3 vols.
South Fork of Hughes River Church, 1 vol.
Ritchie Church, 2 vols.
Greenbrier Church, 1 vol.
Roanoke Church, 1 vol.
Conings Church, 1 vol.
Salemville Church, 1 vol.
Copen Church, 1 vol.
West Union Church, 1 vol.
Black Lick Church, 1 vol.
South-Western Association, and Virginia Association, 1 vol.
West Union Academy, 1 vol.

PUBLICATIONS.

History of Monmouth and Ocean Counties (New Jersey). By Edwin Saltus. Bayonne, N. J. 1890.

A History of New Jersey from its Earliest Settlement to the Present Time. By John O. Raum. 2 vols. Philadelphia. 1877.

Historical Collections of the State of New Jersey. By John W. Barber and Henry Howe. Newark, N. J. 1857.

A Gazetteer of the State of New Jersey. By Thomas F. Gordon. Trenton (N. J.). 1834.

Stories of New Jersey. By Frank R. Stockton. New York. 1896.

Official Register of the Officers and Men of New Jersey in the Revolutionary War. By W. S. Stryker. Trenton, N. J. 1872.

Archives of the State of New Jersey. First Series. Vol. xxii. (Marriage Records, 1665-1800). By William Nelson. Paterson, N. J. 1900.

Notes on the State of Virginia. By Thomas Jefferson. Paris. 1784. American edition 1787.

Historical Collections of Virginia. By Henry Howe. Charleston, S. C. 1845.

Chronicles of Border Warfare. By Alexander Withers. Clarksburg, Va. 1831. New edition, by Reuben Gold Thwaites. Cincinnati. 1895.

Notes on the Settlements and Indian Wars of the Western Parts of Virginia and Pennsylvania, from 1763 to 1783 inclusive. By Joseph Doddridge. Reprint. Albany, N. Y. 1876.

Notes on the Early Settlement of the North-Western Territory. By Jacob Burnet. New York and Cincinnati. 1847.

History of West Virginia. By Virgil A. Lewis. Philadelphia. 1887.

The History and Government of West Virginia. By Fast and Maxwell. Morgantown (W. Va.). 1901.

Dyer's Index to Land Grants in West Virginia. Charleston (W. Va.). 1895.

Atlas of Harrison County, West Virginia. Philadelphia. 1886.

Hardesty's Historical and Geographical Encyclopaedia (Counties of Harrison and Marion, W. Va., 1 vol.; and Ritchie and Doddridge, W. Va., 1 vol.). Chicago and Toledo. 1883.

Reports of the Adjutant General of West Virginia. For years 1864 and 1865. Wheeling. 1865-1866.

A History of the Davis Families. By James B. Davis. (Salem, W. Va. 1895).

Genealogy of the Sharpless Family. Descended from John and Jane Sharpless. By Gilbert Cope. Philadelphia. 1887.

Transallegheny Historical Magazine. Quarterly. 1901-1902. Morgantown, W. Va.

West Virginia Historical Magazine. Quarterly. 1901-1905. Charleston, W. Va.

History of Fayette County, Pennsylvania. By Franklin Ellis. Philadelphia. 1882.

History of Monongalia County, West Virginia. By Samuel T. Willey. Kingwood, W. Va. 1883.

AUTHORITIES

History of Preston County, West Virginia. By S. T. Willey. Kingwood (W. Va.). 1882.

William and Mary College Quarterly... Vols. I-XIII. 1892-1905.

Minutes of the Seventh Day Baptist General Conference, from its organisation in 1802 down to 1902. (v. d., v. p.).

Minutes of the Seventh Day Baptist Missionary Society. (v. d., v. p.).

Minutes of the American Sabbath Tract Society. (v. d., v. p.).

Minutes of the Seventh Day Baptist Education Society. (v. d., v. p.).

Minutes of the South-Western and Virginia Associations. (v. d., v. p.).

The Seventh Day Baptist Missionary Magazine. Irregular. Vols. I-II (all published). v. p. 1821-1825.

The Seventh Day Baptist Memorial. Quarterly. Vols. I-III (all published). New York. 1852-54.

The Protestant Sentinel. Weekly. (v. p.). 1830-1839.

The Seventh Day Baptist Register. Weekly. DeRuyter, N. Y. 1840-1844.

The Sabbath Recorder. Weekly. (v. p.). 1844-1902.

Jubilee Papers. Historical Papers Commemorating the Fiftieth Anniversary of the Seventh Day Baptist Missionary Society, and the Centennial of the William Carey Foreign Mission Movement. Alfred Centre, N. Y. 1892.

The Salem Seventh Day Baptist Church. By Rev. Theodore L. Gardiner. Alfred Centre, N. Y. 1892.

A General History of the Baptist Denomination in America, and Other Parts of the World. By David Benedict. 2 vols. Boston. 1813.

History of the Welsh Baptists. By J. Davis. Pittsburgh. 1835.

Materials Toward a History of the American Baptists. By Morgan Edwards. Vol. I. *Pennsylvania.* Philadelphia. 1770. Vol. II. *New Jersey.* Philadelphia. 1792.

A History of the Baptists. By Thomas Armitage. New York. 1887.

A History of the Sabbatarians or Seventh Day Baptists in America. By Henry Clarke. Utica (N. Y.). 1811.

The German Pietists in Pennsylvania. By Julius Friedrich Sachse. Philadelphia. 1895.

History of the Seventh Day Baptist General Conference. By James Bailey. Toledo. 1866.

Autobiography of Rev. Alexander Campbell. Edited by C. A. Burdick, Watertown, N. Y. 1883.

CONTENTS.

		Page
Preface		vii
Authorities		xi
Illustrations		xix
I.	William Davis of Wales	1
II.	The Shrewsbury Church	9
III.	Western Virginia	41
IV.	Frontier Life in Western Virginia	63
V.	The Woodbridgetown Church	73
VI.	The New Salem Church	83
VII.	The West Fork River Church	135
VIII.	The Lost Creek Church	143
IX.	The Middle Island Church	173
X.	The North Fork of Hughes River Church	195
XI.	The South Fork of Hughes River, or Pine Grove, Church	199
XII.	The Ritchie Church	213
XIII.	The Greenbrier Church	229
XIV.	The Roanoke, or West Fork, Church	237
XV.	The Conings, or Bear Fork, Church	241
XVI.	The Salemville Church	245
XVII.	The Copen Church	251
XVIII.	The West Union Church	255

XIX.	THE BLACK LICK CHURCH	261
XX.	THE SOUTH-WESTERN ASSOCIATION	265
XXI.	THE SOUTH-EASTERN ASSOCIATION	281
XXII.	MISSIONARY WORK	313
XXIII.	SABBATH REFORM	331
XXIV.	SABBATH SCHOOLS	335
XXV.	WEST UNION ACADEMY	343
XXVI.	SALEM COLLEGE	367
XXVII.	SLAVERY	383

APPENDIX.

BIOGRAPHICAL SKETCHES.

REV. JOHN DAVIS	397
REV. JACOB DAVIS	398
REV. JOHN DAVIS, 2D	398
REV. LEWIS A. DAVIS	400
REV. PETER DAVIS	401
REV. JAMES BALL DAVIS	403
REV. SAMUEL DAVIS DAVIS	405
REV. JACOB DAVIS, 2D	411
REV. ENOCH DAVID	413
REV. RICHARD CLAYTON BOND	414
SAMUEL FITZ RANDOLPH	415
JEPTHAH FITZ RANDOLPH	418
FRANKLIN FITZ RANDOLPH	419
REV. AZOR ESTEE	420
STEPHEN THOMAS WEST POTTER	422
DANIEL MAXSON BURDICK	422
MOSES HOFFMAN DAVIS	423
REV. DAVID W. LEATH	423
CLYDE FITZ RANDOLPH	424

CLARKE'S ACCOUNT OF THE VIRGINIA
    CHURCHES 426
MINISTERS DESCENDED FROM WILLIAM DAVIS 427
MARRIAGES 428
WILLS, ETC........................ 435

TOMBSTONE INSCRIPTIONS.
    NEW JERSEY 440
    PENNSYLVANIA 440
    WEST VIRGINIA 441
A LIST OF STUDENTS WHO MATRICULATED IN
    ALFRED UNIVERSITY FROM WEST VIRGINIA 447

SEVENTH DAY BAPTIST SOLDIERS.
    REVOLUTIONARY WAR 450
    WAYNE'S WAR 450
    WAR OF 1812.................. 450
    CIVIL WAR.................... 450
    PURCHASERS OF TOWN LOTS AT NEW SALEM 453
INDEX 455
A LIST OF ADVANCE SUBSCRIBERS TO "A HIS-
    TORY OF SEVENTH DAY BAPTISTS IN WEST
    VIRGINIA." 493

ILLUSTRATIONS.

1. SAMUEL D. DAVIS.....................Frontispiece
2. CORLISS FITZ RANDOLPH.........Opposite page xxvi
3. TITLE PAGE OF WILLIAM DAVIS'S BOOK, FACSIMILE......................Page   3
4. MAP OF SHREWSBURY AND VICINITY.........Page 11
5. MAP SHOWING THE ORIGINAL SITE OF THE SHREWSBURY CHURCH. ETC ....Page 13
6. SITE OF THE FORMER VILLAGE OF SQUAN, ADJOINING THE SHREWSBURY CHURCH.................Opposite page 14
7. ORIGINAL RECORD BOOK OF THE SHREWSBURY AND THE NEW SALEM CHURCHES ....Opposite page 18
8. THE "AWFUL SENTENCE OF EXCOMMUNICATION"..............Opposite page 26
9. THE DEED FOR THE SHREWSBURY CHURCH LOT...................Opposite page 28
10. THE SHREWSBURY CHURCH........Opposite page 34
11. INTERIOR OF SHREWSBURY CHURCH, LOOKING TOWARD THE FRONT....Opposite page 36
12. INTERIOR OF SHREWSBURY CHURCH, LOOKING TOWARD THE REAR.....Opposite page 38
13. INSCRIPTION ON STONE TABLET FROM GREAT MOUND AT MOUNDSVILLE ....Page 42
14. THE GREAT MOUND AT MOUNDSVILLE ....Opposite page 44

15. MAP OF EMIGRATION FROM NEW JERSEY AND MARYLAND TO WESTERN VIRGINIA..................Opposite page 46
16. MAP OF DISTRICT OF WEST AUGUSTA, ETC.............................Page 49
17. SURVEYOR'S MAP OF LAND AT NEW SALEM, VIRGINIA, SOLD TO SAMUEL FITZ RANDOLPH...................Page 51
18. HOME OF JESSE FITZ RANDOLPH, AT NEW SALEM................Opposite page 52
19. A WEST VIRGINIA HOME OF THE MIDDLE OF THE NINETEENTH CENTURY ....Opposite page 54
20. MAP OF THE VILLAGE OF NEW SALEM, AS LAID OUT BY SAMUEL F. RANDOLPH. A RESTORATION ....Page 57
21. A LOG SCHOOL HOUSE.............Opposite page 58
22. A QUIET HOUR...................Opposite page 60
23. A HORSEBACK WEDDING...........Opposite page 64
24. A WEDDING GROUP...............Opposite page 66
25. A LOG CABIN....................Opposite page 68
26. MOUNTAIN LIFE..................Opposite page 70
27. WOODBRIDGETOWN CHURCH AND GRAVEYARD ....Opposite page 74
28. SALEM, LOOKING WEST............Opposite page 84
29. SALEM, LOOKING EAST, SHOWING. OIL WELLS IN WEST END.......Opposite page 86
30. THE OLD LOG CHURCH AT NEW SALEM ....Opposite page 100
31. INTERIOR OF OLD LOG CHURCH AT NEW SALEM...................Opposite page 102
32. THE NEW SALEM CHURCH, FRAME BUILDING ....Opposite page 104
33. THE SALEM CHURCH..............Opposite page 106
34. THE PARSONAGE AT SALEM........Opposite page 108

ILLUSTRATIONS

35. Residence of Rev. Charles A. Burdick, at New Salem.......Opposite page 110
36. Rev. Theodore Livingston Gardiner, D. D....................Opposite page 118
37. Jepthah F. Randolph............Opposite page 120
38. Lodowick Hughes Davis..........Opposite page 122
39. Franklin Fitz Randolph........Opposite page 124
40. The Village of Lost Creek.......Opposite page 150
41. Graveyard at Lost Creek, at Site of "Old Frame Meeting House".Opposite page 152
42. Rev. David Clawson..............Opposite page 156
43. Abel P. Bond, Brumfield Bond.................Opposite page 158
44. The Lost Creek Church.........Opposite page 160
45. The Parsonage at Lost Creek.....Opposite page 162
46. Rev. William L. Burdick.........Opposite page 166
47. Graveyard at West Union.......Opposite page 178
48. Log School House at the Mouth of Sugar Camp Run...........Opposite page 180
49. The Middle Island Church......Opposite page 182
50. The Middle Island Church and Parsonage ....Opposite page 184
51. Rev. James Ball Davis...........Opposite page 190
52. The Pine Grove Church.........Opposite page 208
53. The Ritchie Church............Opposite page 214
54. The Parsonage at Ritchie........Opposite page 216
55. Rev. Lely Daniel Seager.........Opposite page 218
56. Rev. Perie R. Burdick..........Opposite page 220
57. Rev. Riley G. Davis..............Opposite page 222
58. Rev. Lewis Fitz Randolph.......Opposite page 230
59. The Greenbrier Church........Opposite page 232
60. Former Residence of Rev. Lewis Fitz Randolph, on Greenbrier Run ....Opposite page 234
61. The Roanoke Church...........Opposite page 238

62. THE CONINGS CHURCH............Opposite page 242
63. THE SALEMVILLE CHURCH AND PARSONAGE ....Opposite page 246
64. REV. GEORGE B. KAGARISE,
    REV. DARWIN C. LIPPINCOTT.......Opposite page 248
65. THE BLACK LICK CHURCH.........Opposite page 262
66. MOSES HOFFMAN DAVIS...........Opposite page 286
67. REV. GIDEON HENRY FITZ RANDOLPH ....Opposite page 288
68. REV. LUCIUS R. SWINNEY,
    REV. URI M. BABCOCK,
    REV. JOHN L. HUFFMAN,
    REV. MAZZINI G. STILLMAN.......Opposite page 292
69. REV. HIRAM P. BURDICK,
    REV. HENRY B. LEWIS,
    REV. CHARLES W. THRELKELD,
    REV. ORPHEUS S. MILLS...........Opposite page 298
70. REV. SANFORD LAFAYETTE MAXSON. Opposite page 304
71. REV. GEORGE W. LEWIS...........Opposite page 306
72. REV. ELLIS ADELBERT WITTER......Opposite page 308
73. MAP SHOWING CHURCHES IN THE SOUTH-EASTERN ASSOCIATION...Opposite page 310
74. REV. JOHN GREENE,
    REV. JOHN DAVIS, OF SHILOH,
       JOHN BRIGHT,
    REV. JOEL GREENE,
    REV. JAMES BAILEY...............Opposite page 320
75. REV. ALEXANDER CAMPBELL,
    REV. STILLMAN COON,
    REV. WALTER B. GILLETTE,
    REV. CHARLES M. LEWIS..........Opposite page 324
76. REV. CHARLES A. BURDICK........Opposite page 328
77. REV. ABRAM HERBERT LEWIS, D. D.
                                    Opposite page 332
78. THE WEST UNION ACADEMY, AS ORIGINALLY BUILT ....Opposite page 344

79. WEST UNION ACADEMY, FROM A
    PHOTOGRAPH TAKEN IN 1902....Opposite page 346
80. CAPTAIN NATHAN DAVIS...........Opposite page 348
81. SAMUEL PRESTON FITZ RANDOLPH..Opposite page 350
82. FRANKLIN F. RANDOLPH,
    PRESTON F. RANDOLPH,
    VIRGINIA F. RANDOLPH,
    ISAIAH BEE,
    LEWIS TOWNSEND DAVIS...........Opposite page 352
83. FACSIMILE OF PROSPECTUS OF
    NORTH - WESTERN VIRGINIA
    ACADEMY ....Page 355
84. PRESTON FITZ RANDOLPH..........Opposite page 356
85. SALEM ACADEMY, FACSIMILE OF
    PROSPECTUS ....Page 359
86. THOMAS H. LOWTHER,
    STILLMAN F. LOWTHER,
    LUTHER F. RANDOLPH,
    DAVIS N. MEREDITH,
    THOMAS B. PEPPER................Opposite page 360
87. STEPHEN THOMAS WEST POTTER,
    DANIEL MAXSON BURDICK,
    AZOR ESTEE......................Opposite page 362
88. TERENCE M. DAVIS,
    CORLISS F. RANDOLPH, .
    GIDEON HENRY F. RANDOLPH,
    LUTHER A. BOND.................Opposite page 368
89. SALEM COLLEGE..................Opposite page 370
90. JESSE FITZ RANDOLPH.............Opposite page 372
91. GEORGE WASHINGTON FITZ RAN-
    DOLPH ....Opposite page 374
92. ESLE FITZ RANDOLPH.............Opposite page 376
93. ALICE CLAWSON GARDINER,
    ELSIE B. BOND,
    CORTEZ R. CLAWSON,
    SAMUEL B. BOND................Opposite page 378

94. PRESIDENT GARDINER AND A GROUP
   OF SALEM COLLEGE STUDENTS....Opposite page 380
95. REV. LEWIS A. DAVIS..............Opposite page 400
96. HOME OF REV. JAMES B. DAVIS,
   NEAR NEW MILTON............Opposite page 404
97. REV. BOOTHE COLWELL DAVIS, D. D. ..Opposite page 406
98. REV. SAMUEL HOFFMAN DAVIS.....Opposite page 408
99. THE HOME OF REV. SAMUEL D.
   DAVIS, NEAR JANE LEW.........Opposite page 410
100. REV. JACOB DAVIS................Opposite page 412
101. REV. RICHARD C. BOND............Opposite page 414
102. THE COMMISSION OF SAMUEL FITZ
   RANDOLPH, AS ENSIGN IN THE
   REVOLUTIONARY WAR...........Opposite page 416
103. THE HOME OF JEPTHAH FITZ RAN-
   DOLPH, AT NEW MILTON.........Opposite page 418
104. FRANKLIN F. RANDOLPH...........Opposite page 420
105. REV. DAVID W. LEATH.............Opposite page 422
106. CLYDE FITZ RANDOLPH.............Opposite page 424
107. THE SOLE REMAINING GRAVESTONE
   IN THE GRAVEYARD AT SHREWS-
   BURY ....Opposite page 440
108. GRAVES OF SAMUEL AND MARGARET
   FITZ RANDOLPH AT SALEM......Opposite page 442
109. REV. DARIUS KING DAVIS..........Opposite page 448

CORLISS FITZ RANDOLPH, son of Franklin and Mary Elisabeth (Fox) Fitz Randolph, was born at New Milton, Doddridge County, West Virginia, July 24, 1863. He is a lineal descendant of William Davis of Wales, the founder of the Shrewsbury-New Salem Church. He is likewise a descendant, in the fourth generation, of Samuel Fitz Randolph, the founder of the village of New Salem, in Harrison County, Virginia,—now West Virginia.

His early education was obtained in the public and private schools of Doddridge and Harrison counties, West Virginia. In 1888, he graduated from Alfred University, at Alfred, New York, with the degrees of B. A., and M. A. From 1896 to 1899, he pursued a course of graduate study at Columbia University, where he held, successively, the following appointments :— University Scholar in Latin, President's University Scholar in Latin, and Drisler Fellow in Classical Philology. Subsequently, he was a non-resident lecturer in the Latin Language and Literature, and in Classical Philology, in Alfred University. In 1903, Alfred University conferred upon him the honorary degree of Doctor of Letters (*litterarum humaniorum doctor*), and in 1904, Salem College conferred upon him the degree of Doctor of Philosophy.

He has long been closely identified with the interests of his *Alma Mater*—Alfred University—of which he has been a trustee since 1895. He has also served as president of the Alfred Alumni Association.

He is a member of the First Seventh Day Baptist Church of New York City. Since 1890, he has been a director of the American Sabbath Tract Society (Seventh Day Baptist), and since 1901, he has been recording secretary of the Sabbath School Board of the Seventh Day Baptist General Conference. In 1903, he succeeded to the chairmanship of the Committee on Denominational History, of the Seventh Day Baptist General Conference, a position held for many years by the late Reverend William Clarke Whitford, D.D., President of Milton College.

CORLISS FITZ RANDOLPH.

CORRECTIONS.

Page 31, line 6 from bottom of page. For *July* read *June*.
Page 37, between lines 25 and 26, insert sub-head MINISTERS.
Page 47, line 12. Omit *Lewis*.
Page 67, line 22. For *door* read *floor*.
Page 78, line 8. For *1809* read *1793*.
Page 85, line 7. For *bettle* read *betle*.
Page 104, line 18 from bottom. For *1793* read *1795*.
Page 107, line 7 from bottom. For *west* read *north*.
Page 110, line 3 of foot-note. For *Nw* read *New*.
Page 176, line 6. For *upwards of* read *nearly*.
Page 203, line 1 of foot-note. For *in* read *is*.
Page 241, last line. For *Clarke* read *Clark*.
Page 252, line 23. For *Clarke* read *Clark*.
Page 256, line 17. For *Ilsand* read *Island*.
Page 256, line 22. For *Ppeston* read *Preston*.
Page 290, line 14 from bottom. For *preceeding* read *preceding*.
Page 291, line 11. For *new* read *news*.
Page 325, line 10 from bottom. For *heardened* read *hardened*.
Page 353, last line but one. For *modelled* read *modeled*.
Page 378, between lines 8 and 9, insert the following:—

FLAVIUS J. EHRET, 1892-1893,
MOSES H. VANHORN, 1894.

Page 404, line 8. For *Northhampton* read *Northampton*.
Page 407, line 10 from bottom. For *Tennesee* read *Tennessee*.
Page 422, line 19. For *Onondago* read *Onondaga*.

I.

WILLIAM DAVIS OF WALES.

WILLIAM DAVIS, so the record runs, was born of respectable parentage in Glamorganshire, Wales, in the year 1663. While conclusive proof is wanting to that effect, it is more than probable that his father was one of four brothers, all of whom were members of the aristocratic Penyfay Church in the county of Glamorgan, a branch of the Baptist church of Swansea. One of these brothers was high sheriff; another, deputy sheriff; a third, recorder of the county of Glamorgan; and the fourth brother, chaplain to the judge in the county town of Cardiff.[1]

William Davis was educated at Oxford University, his parents intending that he should become a clergyman. While at Oxford, he became interested in the doctrines of George Fox, the Quaker, and joined that church. He now left the university, and became a public speaker among the Quakers. He soon afterward sailed for America, with a company of Quakers, to join William Penn's Pennsylvania colony.

He arrived in America in 1684, and seven years afterward, in 1691, he was one of forty-eight persons who separated from William Penn and became followers of George Keith, who was what may be termed a Baptist-Quaker. Some five years later, he again changed his views, and was baptized by Rev. Thomas Killingworth, the pastor of the Baptist Church

---

1. Davis, *Welsh Baptists*, p. 135.

in Cohansey (now Roadstown), New Jersey, and afterward joined the Pennepek Baptist Church, near Philadelphia, of which he was made pastor.[1]

February 17, 1698, he was banished from the Pennepek Church, on account of his un-orthodox views concerning the person of Christ. William Davis maintained that Christ was neither human nor divine, but of a blended nature, like "wine and water in a glass."

He at once went to Upper Providence near Philadelphia upon the invitation of Abel Noble, and learned from him the doctrine of the supremacy of the moral law and the binding force in perpetuity of all its precepts, and the consequent inevitable conclusion that the Seventh Day of the week, the Sabbath of the fourth commandment, was the Sabbath enjoined upon all Christians. He now joined the Seventh Day Baptist organisation in Pennsylvania.

The following year he published a book, entitled *"Jesus the Crucified Man, the Eternal Son of God,"* etc., in vindication of the doctrine for which he was expelled from Pennepek.[2] This provoked a spirited reply from Rev. John Watts, pastor of the Pennepek Church in a book entitled *"Davis Disabled."*[3]

In the latter part of 1699, William Davis returned to Pennepek and there organised a Seventh Day Baptist church from among former Keithians and others in the vicinity, as the first branch of the Providence (Pennsylvania) Church. Thomas Graves gave the church a lot of ground on which they erected a log meeting house. In the year 1700, William Davis baptized six persons in the Pennepek.

---

1. "In 1687 a company of Welsh and Irish Baptists crossed the Atlantic and settled at Lower Dublin, Pa., otherwise called Pemmepeka, Pennepek, or Pennypack, a word of the Delaware Indians which signifies, according to Heckewelder, a 'pond, lake, or bay; water not having a current.'" Armitage, *History of the Baptists*, p. 707.

2. *Issues of the American Press in Pennsylvania*. By Charles R. Hildeburn. No. 86. The Complete title of William Davis's book was as follows: "*Jesus || The Crucified Man, || the || Eternal Son of God, || or, an || Answer || to an Anathema or Paper of || Excommunication, of John Watts, en- || tituled, Points of Doctrine preached & || asserted by William Davis, || wherein the mystery of Christ's Descen- || tion, Incarnation and Crucifixion is || Unfolded, || By William Davis.* [Printed by Reynier Jansen, Philadelphia, 1700]." Cf. Sachse's *German Pietists of Provincial Pennsylvania*. Pp. 162, 164 *et seq*. The fac simile, on the opposite page, of the title page of William Davis's tract is from Sachse's *German Pietists*, p. 165.

3. "There was an order for printing this book dated August 3, 1705, but it was not executed." Benedict, *General History of the Baptist Denomination in America*. Vol. I, p. 582.

JESUS
The Crucifyed Man,
THE
Eternal Son of God.
OR, AN
ANSWER
TO

An *Anathema* or Paper of Excommunication, of *John Wats* eatituled, *Points of Doctrine preached & asserted by* William Davis.

Wherein the Myftry of Chrifts Defcention, Incarnation and Crucifixion is Unfolded.

By *William Davis.*

[PRINTED BY REYNIER JANSEN. PHILADELPHIA, 1700.]

In 1702, George Keith, who had returned to England some time before, again came back to Philadelphia as a full-fledged priest of the Church of England, whose "Society for the Propagation of the Gospel in Foreign Parts," but lately organised in London, had sent him as a missionary to the New World.

His return was the signal for a fierce struggle between Keith and Evan Evans on the one hand: and on the other, Thomas Killingworth, who besides being the ablest Baptist clergyman in Pennsylvania and New Jersey, was also judge of the court at Salem, New Jersey; and William Davis, the pastor of the Seventh Day Baptist Church at Pennepek, who strangely enough now united in common defence.

William Davis published another edition of his book, with a supplement entitled *"George Keith Disabled."*

Keith was now challenged by Killingworth to a joint debate in public, which resulted in a drawn battle.

Evan Evans, who was a former enemy of William Davis, made war upon him with such success that Thomas Graves again joined the Episcopalian Church, and deeded to that church the lot on which stood the meeting house of the Seventh Day Baptists, who had never had a deed for the lot. Deprived of their house of worship the church continued to hold meetings in the houses of the members, but they were badly demoralised and disheartened by their reverses, and little progress was made.

In 1706, William Davis applied for membership in the Seventh Day Baptist Church at Newport, Rhode Island, but complaint from his Pennsylvania brethren preceded him, and his request was denied. The cause of his difference with his fellow church members was due to his eccentric ecclesiastical views, similar in a measure to his views already cited touching the person of Christ, and which, however real and fundamental they appeared to him, were in their last analysis, nothing more than mere differences in the definitions of terms.

On October 12, 1710, William Davis and Elisabeth Brisley, his wife, applied for membership in the Westerly, afterward the First Hopkinton (Rhode Island) Church, which had been organised some two years previously. His wife was immediately received into membership, but the church deferred final action upon his application.

At a church meeting held June 22, 1711, the Westerly Church decided that William Davis had complied with "the rule of Christ," and was therefore eligible to membership in that church. In order, however, to satisfy a group of doubting members, the church presented the case to the Yearly Meeting, at Westerly, July 14, 1711. The Yearly Meeting approved the action of the church, and William Davis became a member of the Westerly Church, in full and regular standing.

This action, however, involved the Westerly Church in an embroilment with Rev. William Gibson, of the Newport Church, together with Jonathan Davis and the brethren in Pennsylvania, which was prolonged until as late as the latter part of the year 1713.

William Davis was invited by the Westerly Church to preach, and in the first part of the year 1713 was authorised by the church to administer the ordinance of baptism.

On March 1, 1714, William Davis requested a letter of recommendation from the church, in order that he might join one of the Seventh Day Baptist churches in England, whither he expected to remove. The church granted his request. His friends, however, were anxious to prevent his going, and circulated a subscription to raise money to compensate him for whatever financial loss he might sustain in abandoning his contemplated removal to England, the object of which was to claim his share in a large estate left him by the death of his father, in Wales. He persisted, however, to the point of going to Newport, ready to embark upon his voyage. At the last moment, he consented to remain; whereupon numberless troubles ensued, some of which found their way into the courts. These difficulties grew, almost if not quite wholly, out of the subscriptions made to induce William Davis to remain in America. The troubles resulted in correspondence on the part of the Westerly Church, with the churches in Newport (Rhode Island), and in New Jersey, Pennsylvania, and London.

Some time during the year 1716, after an ineffectual attempt at reconciliation, the church withdrew its communion from William Davis, with but four dissenting votes. He now decided to leave Westerly, and under date of May 16, 1717, he received a letter signed by twenty-three of his neighbours, testifying to his Christian character, and exonerating him from blame in his litigation and church troubles. This letter became the subject of some spirited correspondence after William Davis had removed to Pennsylvania.

After his removal from Westerly back to Pennsylvania, he suffered a severe loss from fire about the year 1724. This loss, Governor Keith, of the colony of Pennsylvania, ordered made good; but through the secret interference of some enemies of William Davis at Westerly, the order was not carried out.

The whole matter was now dropped, apparently, for a period of twelve years, when we find William Davis again making his home within the bounds of the Westerly Church, in Rhode Island. Under date of October 21, 1734, from his home in Stonington, Connecticut, he wrote a letter of confession to the church, praying for a reconciliation. To this letter, the church replied, under date of November 19, 1734, desiring explanation upon several points named in the letter written by the church to William Davis. Under date of December 16, 1734, he replied to the communication from the church, whereupon he was requested to attend the next church meeting. There is no record of his restoration to membership in the Westerly Church, further than that his name appears as that of a regular attendant at church. Nevertheless, the reconciliation was undoubtedly effected, greatly to the satisfaction of all parties concerned, and to none, doubtless, more than to William Davis himself.

William Davis was married twice. His first wife was Elisabeth Brisley. By her he had four children; viz., Martha, William, John, and Mary. His second wife was Elisabeth Pavior. By her he had seven children; viz., Thomas, Joseph, Lydia, Edward, James, Elisabeth, and William,—the William by his first wife having died.

Soon after the year 1740, a settlement of Seventh Day Baptists was formed in Monmouth County, New Jersey, near the Manasquan River. Perhaps one of the first of this group of settlers was Joseph Maxson, from Stonington, Connecticut.

He sailed from Stonington for the mouth of the Manasquan River, in the fall of 1742. His vessel was caught in the ice in Long Island Sound, and he did not reach his destination until the following spring.

In the fall of 1744, a party of German Sabbath-keepers, consisting of Israel Eckerling, Samuel Eckerling, Alexander Mack, and Rev. Peter Miller, from Ephrata, Pennsylvania, visited their English-speaking, Sabbath-keeping brethren in Monmouth County, New Jersey. They reported that they found there several Sabbath-keepers, who had come to that place a few years before, from Stonington, Connecticut, and from Westerly, Rhode Island. There were also several members of William Davis's family from Pennsylvania. They found fifteen adults in this group of settlers.

Whether William Davis himself had come to Monmouth County, New Jersey, at the time of the visit of this delegation from Ephrata, Pennsylvania, or not, we have no conclusive evidence. At all events, he had come when the group organised itself into a church, at a date not later than 1745.

William Davis, however, had come to his new home in New Jersey, but to die among his children, a large number, if not nearly all, of whom had settled here. His death occurred before the close of the year 1745, when he was eighty-two years of age. His life was a tempestuous one. Its close was peaceful and uneventful, however. But his works ceased not with his death. He may fairly be termed the father of the Shrewsbury Church; whence his followers and descendants scattered to the Piscataway and Shiloh churches in New Jersey, and crowded into the wilderness of Western Virginia, and into Ohio, and afterwards still further westward across the Rocky Mountains to the Pacific Slope.

Seventh Day Baptist descendants of William Davis may be found to-day in the states of Rhode Island, New York, New Jersey, Pennsylvania, Ohio, Illinois, Wisconsin, Iowa, Kansas, Arkansas, California, and in all probability, in other states as well.[1] The churches of the South-Eastern Association, with the exception of the Salemville Church, at Salemville, Pennsylvania,

---

1. A biographical sketch of William Davis, in which he is characterised as an "evangelist," may be found in the *Seventh Day Baptist Memorial*. Vol. II, pp. 101 et seq.

are composed very largely of the descendants of William Davis; and upon the roll of his posterity are to be found the names of upwards of twenty-five Seventh Day Baptist clergymen.

Descendants of William Davis have held positions of honour and trust in almost every walk of life, public and private, business and professional, in war and peace.

II.

THE SHREWSBURY CHURCH.

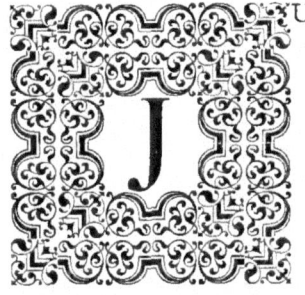

JUST what attracted these Seventh Day Baptists, who settled in Monmouth County, to New Jersey, is uncertain. Some of their number were shipbuilders, and found occupation in that business. Tradition has it that there was a Seventh Day Baptist shipbuilders' yard on the banks of the Manasquan River, owned by the Maxsons. Others appear to have engaged in the manufacture of salt, a business which thrived at the mouth of the Manasquan and up the coast as far as the mouth of the Shark River. Still others engaged in farming, and possibly some were sailors, owning their own boats, and carrying salt, garden vegetables, and farm products to New York City.

The first settlements were at the mouths of the Manasquan and Shark rivers, respectively. Gradually, they extended inward from the shore, until they reached as far as Squankum, and Lower Squankum, south of the Manasquan River. From there they extended northward as far as Deal, which was situated between the present seaside resorts of Long Branch and Elberon. At a somewhat later date, there was a settlement at Clay Pit Creek, an arm of the Navesink, or North Shrewsbury River, near the present village of Navesink. Clay Pit Creek then, as now, was in the town of Middletown. The other Seventh Day Baptist settlements were all at that time in the town of Shrewsbury. That part of Monmouth County is now embraced in the towns of Wall, Howell, Neptune, and Ocean, besides the lower part of the present town of Shrewsbury.

It may be observed in passing, that at the time of which we write, Monmouth County embraced the whole of the present counties of Ocean and Monmouth, and that then the entire county was divided into the two towns of Shrewsbury and Middletown. The present county of Monmouth contains sixteen towns, and Ocean County, eleven.

A little less than four miles from the ocean, on the banks of a little brook, which in dry weather contains no running water, a group of these people built a little village, which, for the lack of a better name, we shall call Squan.[1] In fact there is some evidence that Squan was the name by which the village was actually known, although it was full two and a half miles from the Squan River (contracted from *Manasquan* to *Squan* in much the same way that the cacophonous contraction, *'phone* is obtained from *telephone*).[2]

The little brook on which was situated the village of Squan, was known as the South Branch of Little Brushy Neck (now Cranberry Bog), which in turn, forms what was known then, as now, as the Great Branch. The Great Branch, in its turn, empties into what is now called Wreck Pond, which opens into the sea through Sea Girt inlet, a little more than half way from the mouth of the Shark River to the mouth of the Manasquan River.

Great Branch is very similar to a number of other "branches" along the coast near by, among which are Long Branch and Branchport Creek. Some six or eight miles north of the mouth of Great Branch, are the well known seaside summer resorts of Asbury Park and Ocean Grove.

The book of records of the Shrewsbury Seventh Day Baptist Church, situated at the village of Squan, begins as follows:

"This is a book of records of the settlement and proceedings of the Church of Christ, keeping the commandments of God, particularly the Holy Seventh Day, with the rest of the commandments of God, and believing and practising the Holy Ordinances of the Gospel of Christ

---

1. *Squan* has been incorrectly written *Squam*, by nearly every writer of Seventh Day Baptist history for more than half a century. The editors of the *Seventh Day Baptist Memorial* wrote it *Squam*.

2. *Manasquan* is an Indian name meaning *Squaw-Town*; literally, *an island with an inclosure for squaws.*

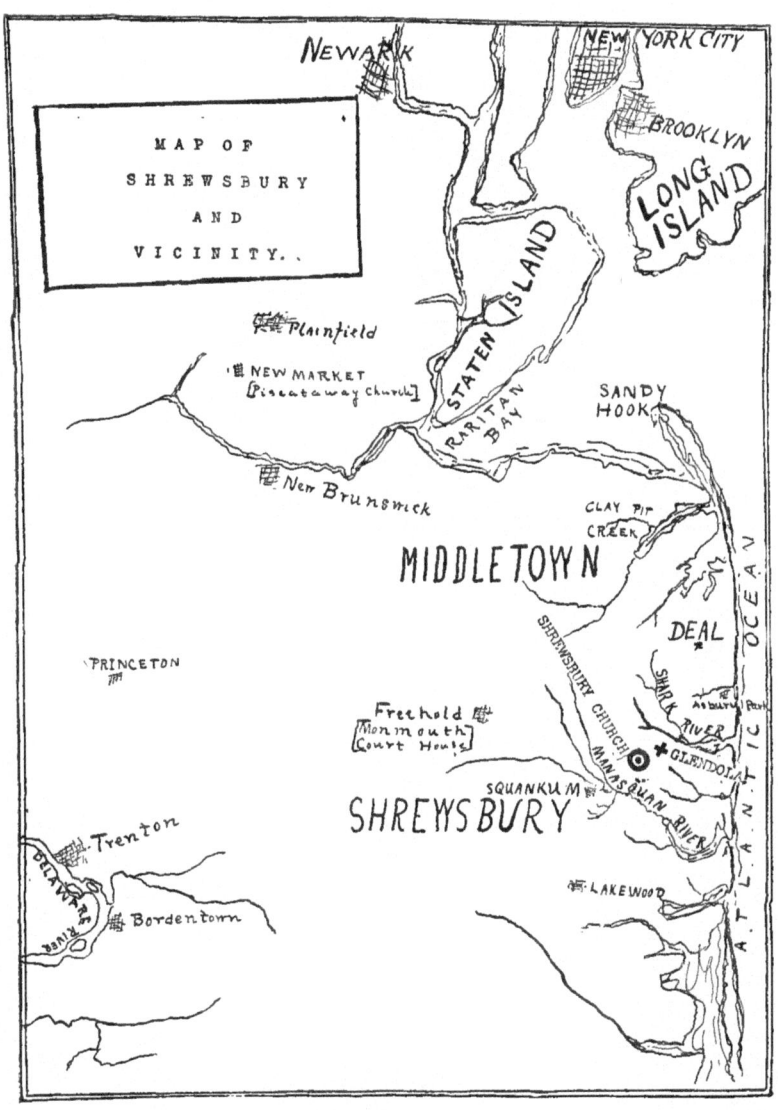

and the Doctrines thereof, inhabiting at Manasquan, Shark River, and places adjacent, in Shrewsbury, in the Province of East New Jersey, &c.

"These first members came from Stonington in New England. This is a list of their names that came and settled as a church:

"WILLIAM DAVIS, an aged minister of the gospel, and formerly an an elder of a church of Christ in Pennsylvania, but sometime since from Stonington, aforesaid,

"JOSEPH MAXSON, a ministering brother in the church aforesaid,
"JOHN DAVIS, a ministering brother in said church,
"THOMAS BABCOCK, a member,
"THOMAS DAVIS, a member,
"WILLIAM BRAND, Junr., a member, and
"JOSEPH DAVIS, a member.

"These are the brethren, there, and the sisters were

"ELISABETH DAVIS, wife of William Davis, the Elder,
"BETHIAH MAXSON, Joseph Maxson's wife,
"ELISABETH DAVIS, John Davis's wife,
"RUTH BABCOCK, Thomas Babcock's wife,
"BETHIAH DAVIS, Thomas Davis's wife,
"ELISABETH BRAND,
"MARY STILLMAN,
"JUDITH DAVIS, wife of James Davis,
"ELISABETH DAVIS, Junr., *alias* Maxson.

"These are the sisters.

"These persons, with others, have from their first settling in this place, endeavoured to uphold the public worship of God at appointed places on the Sabbath Day, with the help of the ministering brethren amongst them, by joining in prayer, reading the Scriptures, preaching, and expounding the Word of God, one to another.

"The persons above named, being in the above noted circumstances, there had been discourse at some times of the need of choosing and appointing persons to the work of the public ministry amongst them, that they might be capable of administering the holy ordinances amongst themselves and to such as may be found willing to join themselves to the Lord, considering it to be their duty so to do.

"In October the eighth [*sic*] month, 1745, Elisabeth Davis, widow, went to sojourn with her son Joseph in Pennsylvania, and Thomas Davis and his family went thither also in March following, in 1746."

It will be observed from the foregoing, that the exact date of the organisation of the Shrewsbury Church is unknown. Certain it is, however, that it was organised long before the end of the year 1745, for we find William Davis, whom, in the preceding chapter, we have styled the father of the church, and who was one of its constituent members, had died before

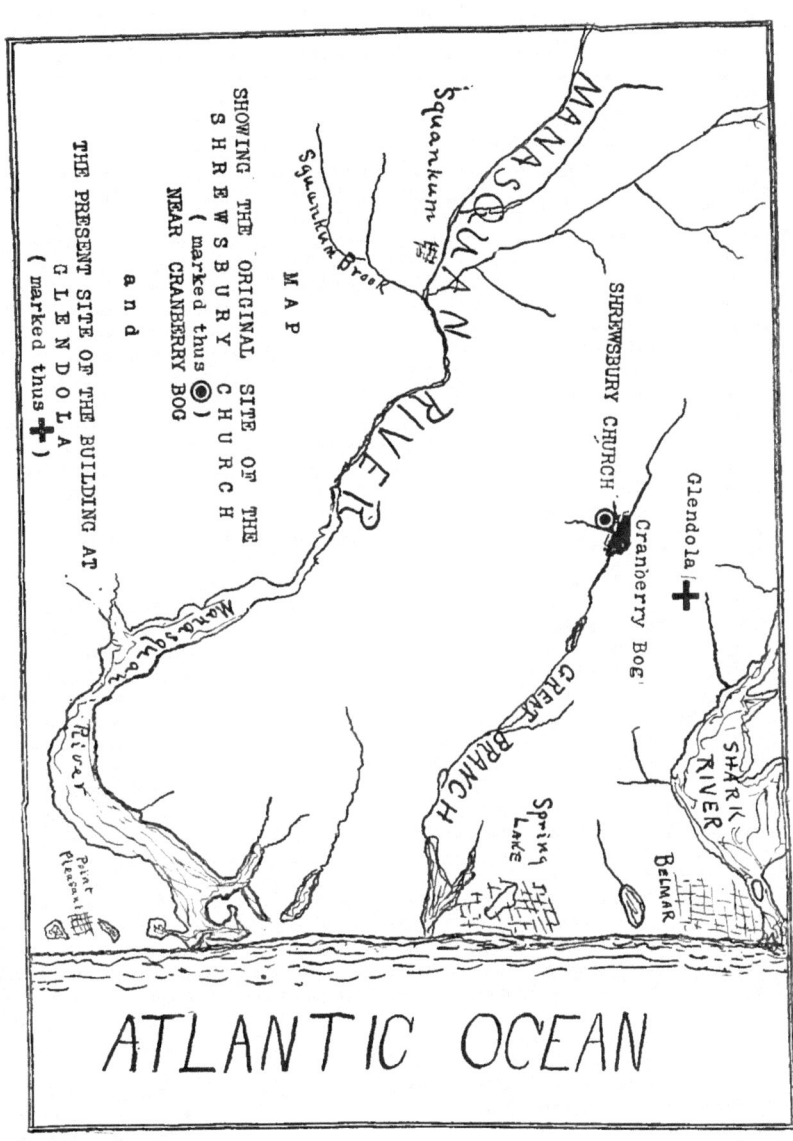

the close of that year. 1745 is generally accepted, however, as the year of the organisation of the church.

The following letter written by the Shrewsbury Church to the church at Westerly, Rhode Island, perhaps at the time of the Yearly Meeting, is of interest at this point. It is noteworthy because of certain details of information it contains concerning their settlement at Shrewsbury, their health, fasting, and the doctrine of feet-washing. It reads as follows:—

SHREWSBURY, 1750.

"The Scattered Remnant of the little flock of Jesus Christ, living at Squan, Squankum, Deal, etc., in Shrewsbury, and at Middletown, all in the Province of East New Jersey; keeping the Commandments of God, particularly that of his holy Seventh Day Sabbath; and believing and practising the faith and ordinances of the Gospel of Jesus Christ, to our well beloved brethren and sisters of the same faith and practise, the church of Christ in Westerly and places adjacent, in the Colony of Rhode Island in New England, Sendeth Christian Salutation: wishing that you may grow in grace and increase in all spiritual wisdom and understanding; that you may walk worthy of your high calling, and be able to bear a faithful testimony to the truth; that you may increase daily, both in members and graces; that you may be steadfast and immovable,—always abounding in the work of the Lord; that you may continue faithful unto death, and, at last, receive a Crown of eternal glory through the merits of Jesus Christ, our Lord, who hath loved us and washed us from our sins in his own blood; to whom, with the Father and the Holy Spirit, be Glory and Dominion, now and ever. AMEN.

"DEARLY BELOVED:

"Although Divine Providence hath set our habitation at so far a distance, one from another, and we have so long neglected this Christian duty of Christian commerce, one with another, by writing; yet we are willing, we hope, to revive this beneficial work, and we desire that you may join with us herein for the future, to improve all suitable opportunities to send one another some lines, that we may know each other's state, and encourage one another in our Christian race; and, in order to it, we shall in this give you a brief account of our present state.

"When Divine Providence had sent us into this remote place we found our disadvantage for want of Gospel ministers from among us; and we had made choice of, and sent to you, and obtained our request in the ordination of our beloved brother John Davis to be our Elder (for which we return God and you thanks): we speedily endeavoured to embody ourselves into a church state, and have endeavoured to maintain the public worship of God, upon his holy Sabbath; and according to our ability and opportunity, to practise the ordinances of the Gospel; and by the grace of God continue it hitherto.

SITE OF THE FORMER VILLAGE OF SQUAN ADJOINING THE SHREWSBURY CHURCH.
(*Site of Church indicated by white circle. Graveyard to right*).
(From a photograph taken in autumn of 1904).

"It hath pleased the sovereign Lord to remove some of our dear brethren and sisters by death, and to receive them to himself: may he give us all that grace to follow them in his time.

"There is about four or five families whose habitations are so near that we may and do endeavour to meet constantly on the Sabbath (may the Lord grant it may be to worship God in truth) and for the rest, though they are scattered more remote, yet we visit one another as often as we conveniently may, and join together in the duties of the Gospel.

"It hath pleased God, by his providence and grace we hope, to add seven to our number; may his grace go on to make the means effectual to add many more in his own time.

"And now, dear brethren, we shall use the freedom to acquaint you with one thing, and do heartily desire to recommend it to your serious and Christian consideration, and that is about the duty of washing one another's feet.[1]

"This is a duty and work which some of us have been long thoughtful and in part persuaded of, even many years before our departing from you; but within the space of some years past, we have conferred and considered more thoroughly about it, and are fully persuaded that it is our duty; and have concluded to and have put it in practise some time since, in the following manner; *viz.*, At the end of the Lord's supper, and before we sing an hymn and go out, the Elder, in imitation of the Lord, takes a towel and girds himself; then he pours water in a basin and begins to wash the disciples' (*viz.*) the brethren's feet, and from him they take it, and the brethren to the brethren, and the sisters to the sisters, they wash one another's feet through the present assembly.

And so dear brethren, we have plainly and simply given you our thoughts and practise in this matter in brief, and desire you to consider

---

1. The practise of feet-washing was continued by this church after its removal to Virginia, but was probably abandoned at some time during the first half of the nineteenth century. The custom was revived afterwards, however, by other churches in West Virginia. The Middle Island Church adopted it about 1870. The Ritchie Church, and probably the Conings church also, practised it for a short time. But it was not looked upon with favour, and it soon fell into disuse again. An incident which occurred about the time of this revival of feet-washing, serves to show another interpretation of the significance of the example of Jesus in washing His disciples' feet. It is as follows: The pastor of one of the New Jersey churches, on one of his visits to West Virginia, was entertained for a short time at the hospitable home of one of the deacons of the New Salem Church. His saintly, and now sainted, hostess asked him for his shoes to polish, and when he hesitated, she said, "I think that is what Jesus meant by his example in washing his disciples' feet, as applied to our conditions of life to-day." She got the shoes to polish. Clarke says: "Some of these [western Virginia] churches, believe in the washing one another's feet, at appointed times, &c. But as the Sabbath and Baptism are their distinguishing tenets, of which I shall say more in its proper place, if the Lord will, it is needless to be more particular as to their doctrines; for those smaller matters are left to each one's conscience, and do not affect Christian charity or fellowship, in case they do not break one of the least of those Ten solemn Precepts, and teach men so, &c." *History of the Sabbatarians*, p. 64.

it, and, when you are come to a result about it, give us your thoughts about it; and, if we are mistaken or out of the way, shew us wherein; and if not, let us all shew that we are the friends of Christ by doing all that he commands us.

Our beloved brother and sister, John and Elisabeth Davis, are designed to come and visit you, who, we trust will be our messengers, with our brother Joseph Stillman, to convey this to you; may God preserve and succeed them in their journey and affairs, and make their company and conversation a blessing, to your and their spiritual good, and send them safe to us again in due time.

"Dear Brethren, pray for us, that we may be preserved from all evil, but especially from sin; that we may be led into all truth and made faithful in every duty and continue steadfast to the end of our race, and at last obtain salvation through Jesus Christ, our Lord, to whom be glory forever. AMEN.

"And so, we commit you to God and to the word of his grace, who is able to build you up and to give you an inheritance among them that are sanctified, and subscribe ourselves your brethren and sisters in the best bonds, ... from our Sabbath meeting at Squan, the 8th of the seventh month, 1750.

ELISABETH BRAND,	THOMAS BABCOCK,
COMFORT DAVIS,	WILLIAM BRAND,
JUDITH MAXSON,	WILLIAM DAVIS,
TACY MAXSON,	SIMEON MAXSON,
	JOSEPH DAVIS,
	MOSHER MAXSON.

"P. S. As to the Scriptures and reasons and motives for, and objections against, washing of feet, we would add in brief what follows:

"*First.* The Scriptures:—John the 13th [chapter] to the end of the 17th verse; Matthew the 28th [chapter] and the 20th verse; John the 15th [chapter] and 14th verse; 1st of Peter 2d and 21st verse; 1st of Timothy 5th and 10th verse.

"*Secondly.* The Reason: 1st. The command of Christ, John 13th and the 15th. Ye ought to wash, etc. 2d. The example of Christ, John 13th and the 15th. I have given you an example, etc. 3dly. The signification: (First) Cleansing from sin, John 13th and 8th, if I wash thee not, etc. (Secondly). Humility and readiness to do the lowest for each other's good, John 13: 13th and 14th verses, etc.

"*Thirdly.* The Motive: (First) To keep in view [?] and represent to our faith our cleansing from sin by Christ, John 13: 8; this was first represented in baptism, but afterwards commemorated in washing of feet. (Secondly). The encouragement of Christ, John 13, verse. Happy are ye, etc.

"*Fourthly and lastly.* The objections against it:

"First objection,—There is but one evidence. Answer:—This reflects on the veracity of the Spirit, and doubts the truth of the Word.

"Second objection,—It's a particular command to the twelve

apostles. Answer:—Pray read, Matt. 28: 19, and compare it with this, etc.

"Third objection,—We don't know how it should be performed, whether by the Elder to the rest, or by each other. Answer:—The direction seems plain, one another's feet, John 13: 14, etc.

"Fourth objection,— ——— [?] be not proper administrators. Answer:—See the qualifications of the worthy widow, 1 Tim. 5: 10, etc.

"Dear Brethren:—Bear with us since we pretend not to instruct you, but to submit these things to your—[?]. Pray, consider them with candour, humility, and love: and the Lord give you understanding.

"Our brother William Brand hath had a long and sore visitation with the Distemper, called the hip-gout, and seemed long near the grave. He desired a day of fasting and prayer on his account which was attended. The Lord was pleased to grant our request, so as to raise him again so that he goes about and does his business. We are at present generally in health, save that some have the fever and ague. We remain, several of us, yet unsettled in our outward affairs, though some of our friends; *viz.*, them at Middletown, have bought some land, and our brother John Davis is about to buy at Squankum, but hath not yet bargained. May the good Lord direct us in this matter as may be most for his and our spiritual good, etc."

At best, records for this period are very meagre. The record book itself, six and a half inches in width, by eight inches in length, and less than an inch in thickness, is bound in pigskin, with its front edges fastened together at either end by means of deerskin strings in place of clasps, after a fashion common for more than a hundred years previous to that time, for certain kinds of bindings. This book was presented to the church, December 26, 1752, more than seven years after the organisation of the church. It is clear that the scant records up to that date, comprising less than six pages of the book, are lacking in very many details..

The record book was presented to the church by John Davis, who "was allowed for it out of the public stock to his satisfaction," and who probably entered the records up to the date of the meeting at which he presented the book to the church.

But now although the church had a record book, very few entries were made until the year 1774, a period of twenty-two years after the record book was provided. The entries made during this period cover less than three pages of the book of records.

But these three pages inform us of the return of Mosher

Maxson and his family from Middletown, and their settling at Manasquan; of the return of Joseph Stillman and his family to New England, and that they took with them letters recommending them to membership in the Westerly Church; of the death of John Davis; and of several accessions to the church, as well as of efforts to reclaim those who had broken their covenant vows.

These last entries made, ten long years of silence elapse. Then on January 2, 1774, the church met "to reconcile differences between brethren and sisters," and to labour with those who had strayed from the fold of the church.

The work of reconciliation was difficult and slow. Some were obstinate, and others were defiant. Accordingly, after carefully considering whether, although the church had the right to excommunicate the recalcitrants at once, it might not be the part of wisdom to wait awhile before taking such drastic measures, it was finally decided that patience had already ceased to be a virtue in at least one case, that of Simeon Maxson, and the church decided "to debar him from having any privilege to this church, till God of His infinite mercy brings him to the truth of Jesus Christ, agreeable to His Holy Word."

In the meantime, Rev. Jonathan Dunham of Piscataway, Rev. Jonathan Jarman of Cohansey (Shiloh), and possibly Rev. John Davis of Trenton, had been visiting this church. Jacob Davis, the son of James Davis, had been baptized and received into the church by Rev. Jonathan Dunham, in the year 1772, and had been licenced by the church to preach. On the 19th of June, 1774, the church gave Jacob Davis a formal call to the Gospel ministry. On the following Christmas day, the church took definite steps to have him ordained, or solemnly set apart to that office.

Soon afterward, probably February 27, 1775, the ordination service took place at the home of Thomas Babcock, conducted by Rev. Jonathan Dunham and Rev. Jonathan Jarman. The formal pledge of the church to support its new pastor, the acceptance of the call by Jacob Davis, and the charge to the candidate, were as follows:

To the church:—

"If it [be] your own free and voluntary choice to require Jacob Davis to be your minister to take the charge and over-sight of you as

ORIGINAL RECORD BOOK OF THE SHREWSBURY AND THE NEW SALEM CHURCHES.

you profess to be the flock of God, and he a shepherd under Christ, do you find a hearty freedom in your minds to receive [him] to be your Elder, Pastor, and Teacher, to rule and govern you according to the Word of God?

"Do you promise and engage to him all the duties of a people to their minister according to the Word of God, such as respect, honour, and reasonable maintenance as far as necessary to enable him to discharge the trust committed to him?

"Is it your desire to endeavour to strengthen his hands and encourage his heart by your prayers for him, and consolatory discourse with him, as occasion may require with a due respect and regard to his correcture, office, and interest?

"Do you look on yourselves [as] bound by the nature of this engagement as far as you are able [to supply him with] such conveniences respecting his living as he may stand in need of to make him profitable to yourselves, and comfortable to himself?

"Which was consented to by the holding up of the hands."

To the candidate:—

"And does the brother, Jacob Davis, heartily and freely accept the request of this church?

"Do you reserve [sic] them as the flock of God, as persons committed to your care and inspection?

"Do you feel love, and Christian love [such] as ought to be in a spiritual shepherd towards his flock?

"Do you look on yourself under this obligation, according to the nature of this engagement to answer all their religious requests as far as your ability will admit?

"Have you entire freedom to administer the ordinances of God to them as to a church of God; to pray with them and for them and endeavour to build them up in the faith?

"Is it your desire and prayer from this time forward, as far as God shall enable you, to be exemplary to them in life and doctrine according to the word of God?

"Do you now give up yourself to the Lord and to them, by the will of God to be their pastor and teacher?

"If so, lift up your [hand]."

The substance of the charge given to Jacob Davis was as follows:—

"Brother Davis, I charge thee before God and the Lord Jesus Christ, that thou take charge of the church of Christ dwelling at Shrewsbury, preach the Word in and amongst them, be instant in season and out of season, administer the holy ordinances amongst them, exhort and rebuke with all long suffering and patience, with meekness and humility of mind, as thou shalt answer the same when thou shalt give up thy account to God at his appearance and kingdom."

In June, 1774, the church adopted the following articles of faith and practise, and covenant:—

"The Church of Christ in Shrewsbury and Middletown in the observation of God's Holy Sanctified Sabbath. First agreed to, the—— [day] of the sixth month, 1774.

"We who desire to walk together in the fear of the Lord, do through the assistance of the Holy Spirit, profess our deep and serious humiliation for our transgressions, and we do also solemnly in the presence of God and of each other, in the sense of our own unworthiness, give up ourselves to the Lord.

"1st. We believe that unto us there is but one GOD, the father, and one LORD, Jesus Christ, Who is the mediator between God and man. We believe the Holy Ghost is the spirit of God.

"2d. We believe all scriptures of the Old and New Testaments, if given by the inspiration of the spirit of God, is the Word of God.

"3d. We believe that the Ten Commandments that were written in the two Tables of Stone by the finger of God, continueth to be the rule of righteousness both to Jews and Gentiles.

"4th. We believe all mankind, in Adam, fell from the estate of perfection in which God made man, and by that fall, Adam brought himself and all his posterity into a state of condemnation.

"5th. We believe that God did appoint His Son before time, and revealed him in time for the salvation of his people.

"6th. We believe that Jesus Christ took human nature, was made under the law, and answered the demands of the law by his holy life and painful death, by which every believer is justified in the sight of God, through sanctification of the spirit and renewing of the Holy Ghost.

"7th. We believe the church triumphant, militant, and invisible, are in regard of their head but one, but different in regard of their situation at present.

"8th. We believe that the church universal is purchased by the precious blood of Christ and supported by His grace and defended by His power.

"9th. We believe the six principles recorded in Hebrews 6: 1-2, to be the rule of faith and practise.

"10th. We believe that the Lord's Supper ought to be administered and received in all Christian churches.

"11th. We believe that all persons thus believing ought to be baptized in water by dipping, or plunging, after confession is made by them of their faith in the above-said things.

"12th. We believe that all Christian churches ought to have church officers in them, as elders and deacons.

"13th. We believe a company of sincere persons being found in the faith and practise of the above-said things may truly be said to be the church of God.

"14th. We give up ourselves unto the Lord and to one another to be guided and governed by one another according to the Word of God.

"15th. We do promise and engage to walk in all holiness, godliness, humility, and brotherly love, as much as in us lies, to render our communion delightful to God, comfortable to ourselves, and lovely to the rest of the Lord's people.

"16th. We do promise to watch over each other's conversation and not suffer sin upon our brother as God shall discover it to us or any of us, and to stir up one another to love and good works, to warn, rebuke, and admonish one another, with meekness, according to the rules left to us of Christ in that behalf.

"17th. We do promise in an especial manner to pray for one another, and for the glory and increase of this church, and for the presence of God in it, and the pouring forth of His spirit on it, and protection over it for His glory.

"18th. We do promise to bear one another's burdens, to cleave to one another, and have fellowship with one another, in all conditions, both outward and inward, as God in His Providence, shall cast any of us into.

"19th. We do promise to bear with one another's weaknesses, failings, and infirmities, with tenderness, not discovering them to any without the church, nor any within, unless according to Christ's rule, and the orders of the Gospel provided in that case.

"20th. We do promise to strive together for the truth of the Gospel and purity of God's word and ordinances, to avoid cause of differences and envying, endeavouring to keep the unity of the spirit in the bond of peace.

"21st. We promise to meet together on the Sabbath Days and other times as the Lord shall give us opportunity, to serve and glorify God in the way of His worship, to edify one another, and to contrive the good of the church.

"22d. We do promise according to our ability or as God shall bless us with the good things of this world, to communicate to our pastor or minister, God having ordained that they that preach the Gospel, should live of the Gospel.

"These and all other Gospel duties we humbly submit unto, promising and purposing to perform, not in our own strength, being conscious of our own weakness, but in the blessed strength of God, Whose we are, and Whom we desire to serve, to Whom be glory, now and forevermore. Amen.

"This is the covenant we now solemnly enter into in the love and fear of God; in testimony and ratification whereof we sign our names.

"THOMAS DAVIS,	JUDITH BABCOCK,
"THOMAS BABCOCK,	TACY DAVIS,
"WILLIAM DAVIS,	ELISABETH MAXSON,
"JOSEPH MAXSON,	EXPERIENCE MAXSON,

"Ephraim Maxson,	Rebekah Davis,
"Nathan Davis,	Ann Davis,
"Thomas Davis, Jun.,	Hannah Smith,
"Jacob Davis,	Elisabeth Babcock,
"Joseph Davis,	Mary Davis,
"James Davis,	Ruth Maxson,
"John Parker,	Penelope Davis,
"James Davis, Jun.,	Lydia Havens,
"William Brand,	Margaret Miller,
"Simeon Maxson,	Experience Babcock,
"Zebulon Maxson,	Mary Maxson,
"William Davis, Jun.,	Elisabeth Brand,
"William Maxson,	Martha Davis,
"Nathan Maxson,	Anna Havens,
"John Davis,	Elisabeth Maxson, Jun.,
"John Maxson,	Marvel Maxson,
"John Brand,	Increase Lippincott."
"Thomas Maxson,	

The church also adopted the following:—

"SHORT ARTICLES PROPER to be read to persons when received into this church, and to be consented to and confessed by the persons so received.

"FIRST.

"Your duty towards your God.

"1st. Do you own God to be your God and only law-giver, the strength of your life, and the life of your souls?

"2d. Do you promise to obey His commands as far as God shall enable you?

"3d. Do you promise to look to Him as your supporter, guider, and director in all things agreeable to His will?

"4th. Do you take His Son, Jesus Christ, to be your king to rule over you and in you and for you, as a prophet to teach you and direct you?

"5th. Do you believe that [by the] atonement that Jesus made by the sacrifice of Himself, that He made satisfaction to God, and by His glorious victory over sin, Satan, death, and the grave, you expect to be a conqueror through Christ, over sin and Satan in this life, and over death and the grave at the resurrection?

"6th. Do you depend upon the atonement of Christ for the salvation of your souls, looking for it in God's way?

"IN THE SECOND PLACE.

"Your duty as a church member in relation to this church in particular.

"1st. That you pray for the growth of the church, and for her peace and safety, and for grace, wisdom, and understanding to be conferred on the ministers thereof.

"2d. That you are constant as far as you can [be] in attending on the public worship of God upon the Holy Sabbath.

"3d. That you shall attend on meetings of conference that are appointed for public consultation of the affairs of the church, and be a useful member in the same.

"4th. That you endeavour as far as God shall enable you to assist in the support of the Gospel in general, and this church in particular.

"IN THE THIRD PLACE.

"Your duty to your brethren as church members.

"1st. You shall live in peace with all your brothers and sisters, and endeavour when opportunity serves to speak about the things of God.

"2d. That you shall watch over your brothers and sisters that you are in communion with; if you see them going astray, you shall endeavour to reclaim them in love and meekness.

"3d. That you shall be willing at all times not only to give reproof, but to take reproof from your brothers and sisters when you go astray yourself.

"4th. That if your brothers or sisters shall offend you in word or action, you shall not divulge it to any brother or sister or any other person, until you have been to the offender and made it known to him; and if he repent, forgive him; and if not, you shall not make it known to those without, but take the Gospel rule.

"5th. That you shall not speak reproachfully of nor backbite your brothers or sisters that you are in communion with.

"6th. That you shall walk honestly towards those that are without, that you give no offence to Jew or Gentile, or the church of God.

"IN THE FOURTH PLACE.

"Of private duties respecting yourselves and families.

"1st. That you search the Scriptures to prove the Word you hear preached, and that you are diligent in reading the Word to yourself and families; that you pray for wisdom and understanding [of] what you read, and the blessing of God on your labour and family.

"2d. That you bring up your children in the nurture and admonition of the Lord, as far as God shall enable you.

"3d. That you watch over your words and actions that your conversation be as becomes the Gospel of Christ, with a holy temper, disposition, and composure of mind, agreeable to the Gospel rule.

"4th. That you shall be courteous and kind in entertaining the poor when called thereunto, as far as your ability will allow.

"5th. And lastly, it is required that you have God's glory in view in all your religious and civil affairs.

"In the name of the Lord Jesus Christ, we receive you into the church, pronounce you a member thereof, partaker of its privileges and subject to its laws and government, agreeable to the Word of God. In token of which I do, in the behalf of this church, give you the right hand of fellowship, praying that what is now done on earth may be confirmed in Heaven."

The foregoing Confession of Faith, etc., remain, unchanged, in use by the Salem (West Virginia) Church, the successor of the Shrewsbury Church, to this day.

The work of discipline and reconciliation proceeded hand in hand. Simeon Maxson was restored to membership, and others were commanded to appear before the bar of the church to answer to charges made against them. To facilitate this work, the church appointed two ruling elders, Joseph Maxson of Middletown, and Thomas Babcock of Shrewsbury.

Simeon Maxson now openly advocated numerous un-orthodox views, particularly concerning the doctrine of eternal punishment. To complicate matters still further, he prayed the church to grant him licence to preach. The church answered him by saying that it thought "it proper to exclude the said Simeon Maxson from communion with the church, till such time as he makes suitable acknowledgment according to the Word of God." Simeon Maxson appealed from this decision, and two months later the church voted to allow him to preach a trial sermon, and if that should be satisfactory doctrinally, he should be allowed to preach until further action by the church. A month afterward he was silenced. He soon acknowledged his doctrinal errors, but declared he would continue to preach. In September, 1776, he was again a subject of consideration by the church, because of his antipathy to war—the War of American Independence then fairly beginning. He had previously been a Quaker, and this fact probably explains not only his dislike of war, but his doctrinal aberrations as well. Afterward, he became reconciled to the church.

Occasionally the church varied the monotony of its business meetings by settling disputes arising from business transactions between its members.

A noted case of this kind was a dispute that arose between Nathan Davis and John Parker. The latter was an indentured servant of the former. The record shows that on April 30, 1775, the church

"VOTED, That John Parker had not clothes sufficient but should have one shirt and one pair of trousers for every-day clothes.

"VOTED, That he have for his freedom suit, a shirt, a jacket, a pair of stockings, a pair of shoes, and new lining in the coat entirely new."

It must not be supposed that John Parker was a negro slave, for he was not. He was one of that numerous class of white people known as "redemptioners." They may be thus described:—

"They were poor people, although often persons of fairly good station and education, who desired to emigrate to America, but who could not afford to pay their passage.

"A regular system was then established, by which a poor person desiring to settle in New Jersey would be brought over free. When one of these emigrants took passage on a ship, he signed a contract which gave the captain of the vessel the right to sell him, as soon as he arrived in America, for enough money to pay his passage. This white man was thus bought, when he reached New Jersey, exactly as if he had been a negro slave; and he was subject to the same rules as those which governed other slaves. Of course, he was made the subject of great imposition; for the captain would naturally desire to get as large a sum of money as possible for each redemptioner, and therefore would be perfectly willing to sell him for a long term.

"The people who owned redemptioners could sell them again if they chose; and it often happened that some of them passed into the possession of several families before they finally served out the term for which they had been sold. All sorts of people became redemptioners, —mechanics, labourers, and even professional men. Among the people who sold themselves into limited slavery there were schoolmasters, and it is stated that at one time the supply of redemptioner schoolmasters was so great that they became a drug in the market."

"It is said that these redemptioners were often treated much more harshly and cruelly than the negro slaves, and any one who assisted one of them to escape was severely punished."

"After a time there were laws made to protect the redemptioners. One of these was, that any person sold after he was seventeen years old could not serve for more than four years; and another provided, that, when a redemptioner's time of service had expired, his master should give him two good suits of clothing, suitable for a servant, one good ax, one good hoe, and seven bushels of Indian corn."[1]

From the foregoing, it will be seen that the dispute between Nathan Davis and John Parker was over the interpretation of the law as to what clothes the latter should have upon the termination of his term of service as a redemptioner.

---

1. From Stockton's *Stories of New Jersey*. Also cf. Gordon's *History of New Jersey*, Raum's *History of New Jersey*, and Barber and Howe's *Historical Collections*.

At one time Thomas Maxson was censured by the church for carrying a couple to the justice of the peace to be married, contrary to law.

Again the church disciplined some of its members for partaking of the "Lord's Supper with the Church of England."

Formal excommunication from the church was no ordinary affair, nor was it to be thought of lightly. On the contrary, it was accounted a public disgrace; and well might it be so considered. A formal letter of excommunication, known as the "Awful Sentence of Excommunication," was drawn up and read before the assembled multitude, at the regular service on Sabbath morning. One of these letters of excommunication, dated July 11, 1778, runs as follows:—

"WHEREAS, Joseph Auger, Elisabeth Auger, and Elisabeth Hampton, members of this church, having been under dealings by this church for some time on the account of breach of Sabbath, and have been cited to our church meeting sundry times, as can be made to appear by the records of this church, they having cast reproach on the authority of this church by not obeying the calls thereof, and still continue to live publickly in the breach of God's law, by Sabbath breaking, week after week; we therefore consulting the volume of God's Word, do look on it to be our abounding duty according to God's Word, to deliver such a one to Satan for the destruction of the flesh that his spirit may be saved in the day of the Lord Jesus, and likewise are exhorted by the same apostle: He that is an heretic after the first and second admonition reject; and our Blessed Lord gave this direction to the church of Christ, concerning one brother with another, [and] says thus: If thy brother trespass against thee, tell him his fault between thee and him alone, and if he hear thee, thou hast gained thy brother, and if he neglect to hear thee, take with thee 2 or 3 more, and if he neglect to hear them, tell it unto the church, and if he neglect to hear the church, let him be unto thee as an heathen man and a publican. Which by consulting these things, we find that such persons after they are regularly proceeded against according to rule and the circumstance of the offenders or of the offender, I do therefore, in behalf of this Church and before this Congregation, in the name of the Lord Jesus Christ, deliver those persons mentioned before by name, to Satan according to the apostle's directions, so thereby depriving them of all the privileges of this Church as a church member, till God of His infinite mercy brings them to the light of his blessed truth in compliance with them. Amen. Which may God grant through Jesus Christ our Lord."

July 11

Whereas Joseph Auger Auger Elizabeth Auger And Elizabeth Hampton, Members of this Church, Haveing ben Under Dealings by this Church for Some Time On the Account of Breach of Sabbath and have ben Cyted To Our Church Meeting Sundry Times As Can be made to Appear by the Records of This Church they Haveing Cast Reproach On Authority of this Church by Not Obeying the Calls Thereof And Still Continues to Live publickly In the Breach of Gods Law by Sabbath Breaking Week after Week We therefore Consulting The Volum of Gods Word Do Look On it to be Our Abounding Duty According to Gods Word to Deliver Such A One To Satan for the Destruction of The flesh that His Spirit May be Saved in the Day of The Lord Jesus and Likewise Are Exhorted by the Same Apposstle he that is An Herent After the first and Second Admonition Reject and Our Blessed Lord gave this Direction to the Church of Christs Concerning One Brother with Another Says thus If Thy Brother Trespass Against the tell him his fault between the and him Alone and if he hear Thee thou hast gained thy Brother and if he Neglect to hear the take with the 2 or 3 more and if he Neglect to hear them

THE "AWFUL SENTENCE OF EXCOMMUNICATION."

In this connection it may be interesting to note that the last recorded official act of the church before it left New Jersey, was the public reading of the "Awful Sentence of Excommunication" of three of its members, on August 16, 1789.

Troublous times beset the Shrewsbury Church. The War of Independence had begun, and the ranks of the Colonial armies claimed the father and sons from many an anxious home. Even the faithful pastor, Rev. Jacob Davis, enlisted as a chaplain. To add to the embarrassment and sorrow of the church, some of its members cast their lot with the royalists, and joined the British army.

At Monmouth Court House, now Freehold, only eight or ten miles distant to the northwest, was fought the celebrated Battle of Monmouth, where Washington administered his stinging rebuke to Lee; and where Molly Pitcher, "a stout, red-haired, freckled-faced young Irish woman with a handsome piercing eye," and but twenty-two years of age, made herself famous for all time by her unique display of bravery.[1]

It was to observe the movements of the British army two days before this hotly contested battle that James Davis, the father of Rev. Jacob Davis, who was pastor of the church at the time of its removal from New Jersey to Virginia, mounted his horse and rode away from his home over to Monmouth Court House, only to return a few hours later fatally wounded by a stray shot from the battle-field, for his grief-stricken family to remove his lifeless body from his faithful horse.

On a line nearly east from Monmouth Court House, and slightly northwest from the village of Squan, at Colt's Neck, some six or eight miles distant, was the home of Captain Joshua Huddy, a terror to the British throughout Monmouth county, who, when captured by the enemy, was wantonly put to death by hanging.

Directly to the eastward, at the mouth of Shark River, some three or four miles distant, the British disembarked one day and burnt the salt works on both sides of the river. At about the same time they burnt the salt works and destroyed the kettles on both sides of the mouth of the Manasquan River, some five or six miles down the coast from Shark River.

---

1. Cf. Raum, *History of New Jersey*. Barber and Howe, *Historical Collections*. Stockton, *Stories of New Jersey*.

Only a short distance away were the "Pines," infested by Indians, pirates, and other robbers, who lived in caves and preyed upon the surrounding country—a constant menace throughout the war.

But the ravages of war were not permitted to stop the advancement of the interests of the church. The pastor, Rev. Jacob Davis, obtained occasional furloughs from his duties as chaplain in the American army, and came home to administer to the spiritual wants of his flock. He preached, conducted communion services, and baptized and received new converts into membership in the church.

Under the zealous leadership of the devoted pastor, in January, 1778, the church opened a subscription for funds with which to complete a house of worship, and "accordingly a quantity of money was collected for that purpose."

The first record concerning a house of worship is dated March 3, 1775, when the church voted to build a meeting house "on the south-east corner of Zebulon Maxson's land lying on one of the branches coming out of the branch commonly known as the Great Branch, the said Zebulon Maxson having given his free consent thereunto."

For this lot which was situated in the little village of Squan, Zebulon Maxson executed the following deed:—

"*To all Christian People to whom these presents shall come*:

"Know ye that I, Zebulon Maxson, of Shrewsbury Township, in the County of Monmouth and Eastern Division of New Jersey, Cordwainer, for and in consideration of love, good-will, and affection which I have and do bear towards my loving brethren, the Seventh Day Baptist Church inhabiting in Shrewsbury Township as aforesaid, I have given, granted, and by these presents do voluntarily of my own free will and accord with the consent of Experience, my wife, give and grant unto the said church or society of people as aforesaid a lot of land for a meeting house lying near the road that goes across the South Branch of Little Brushy Neck, which said land the said Zebulon Maxson lays claim unto by virtue of a deed of sale from David Hall [?], beginning at a heap of stones planted in the earth about thirty links easterly of said road, first running north sixty-three degrees and thirty minutes east two chain and twenty-five links; secondly, south, twenty-six degrees and thirty minutes east two chain and twenty-five links; thirdly, south sixty-three degrees and thirty minutes west two chain and twenty-five links to the brook by the side of the road to where it crosses the said brook; fourthly, north twenty-six degrees and thirty minutes west to where it began, containing eighty-one perches, strict

THE DEED FOR THE SHREWSBURY CHURCH LOT.

measure, to have and to hold the said given and granted premises together with the appurtenances free and clear, freely and heartily by them to be possessed and enjoyed without hurt [?], molestation, interruption whatsoever to them and their heirs forever; and I, the said Zebulon Maxson, for me, my heirs, executors, and administrators do covenant with the said church that before the ensealing and delivery of these presents, I am the true, sole, and lawful owner of the above given and granted premises and have in myself full power and lawful authority to dispose of the same in manner aforesaid, and will forever, by virtue of these presents, hereafter warrant and defend from the lawful claims of all persons whatsoever. In witness hereof I have hereunto put my hand and seal this third day of April, in the year of our Lord God, one thousand, seven hundred and seventy-five.

"ZEBULON MAXSON, [L. S.]"

"Signed, sealed and delivered in the presence of:—
"THOMAS DAVIS, JR.,
"JOHN MAXSON,
"JACOB DAVIS."

The building was ready for the roof by October 27, 1776, when it was voted to proceed with covering it as soon as possible. It was built with a white oak frame, which after standing a century and a quarter, is still firm and solid. It was about thirty feet in length by twenty-five feet in width. On the 8th of August, 1789, the church voted to sell the meeting house and put the proceeds into the treasury of the church.

Four weeks afterward, or on "September the 6th, 1789, then did the body of this church remove from Shrewsbury in order to settle in the State of Virginia. Names: Our Elder, Jacob Davis, with all his family; William Davis, senior; John Davis; Ephraim Maxson; Thomas Badcock [sic]; and Zebulon Maxson; and Benjamin Thorp; with all their families. And on the thirteenth of the same month, set out from the same place these brethren; viz., Simeon Maxson; William Davis, Junior; and William Maxson; with all their families."

The group which started first, appears to have stopped at Clay Pit Creek, in Middletown, for a farewell visit with such friends there as were not going to Virginia, and when joined at that place by the second group which started a week later from Shrewsbury, they all proceeded together on their journey.

Rev. Simeon Babcock, who was about five years of age at the time he accompanied his parents upon this journey, says there were "seven wagons in number." James Davis, who was sixteen years of age when the migration to Virginia took place, and who, also, was one of the company of travellers, says "The train consisted of fifteen wagons." Morgan Edwards, who visited Squan, November 18, 1789, a little more than two months after the departure of the emigrants, says "seventy-two souls" had gone. Still another member of the company, seventeen years of age at the time, says there were ten wagons with seventy souls. The church record shows that ten families started from Shrewsbury.

It is not only possible, but somewhat probable that the original company from Shrewsbury was augmented by recruits from Middletown, and from Piscataway. A daughter of the first William Davis lived at Piscataway, and from this place had started a movement westward, led by Samuel Fitz Randolph, before the Shrewsbury Church started. The different times of starting, as well as the possible several points of starting, make it possible for all the statements of eye witnesses as to the number of wagons and the number of emigrants to be correct.

When the procession was ready to start, the people all assembled in a grove, where their pastor, Rev. Jacob Davis, preached a short farewell sermon for those left behind, after which the travellers partook of refreshments provided for them by their friends, and then started on their long tedious journey, extending more than four hundred miles westward.

The emigrants settled on White Day Creek in what is now Monongalia County, West Virginia. Here they tarried for two years or more, where William Davis died July 15, 1791.

The new settlers were disappointed, however, in their land, which according to Morgan Edwards, was obtained through a man by the name of Reed.[1]

The new comers from New Jersey had friends a few miles away across the Pennsylvania border, north of the Cheat River. Among them was Samuel Fitz Randolph, who

---

[1]. In 1785, Reed and Ford entered lands in Monongalia County aggregating 10,000 acres; in 1786 John Reed entered, in the aggregate, 20,400 acres, on the waters of Big Steer Creek in Monongalia County; and in 1787, he entered an aggregate of 21,200 acres on Ten Mile Creek in Harrison County. Cf., *Dyer's Index to Land Grants in West Virginia*. Charleston, [W. Va.], 1895. Francis Reed owned lands on the West Fork, near the mouth of "Fall Run," as early as 1781; how much earlier is not known.

had a short time before, purchased a tract of land lying on the waters of Ten Mile Creek, a branch of the West Fork of the Monongahela River, some fifty miles beyond White Day Creek. Samuel Fitz Randolph persuaded the dissatisfied settlers at White Day Creek to go and inspect his new purchase, as well as other lands adjacent, consisting largely of five thousand acre tracts. As a result, the new settlers from Shrewsbury purchased farms, and moved to this place, where was laid out the Village of New Salem, on the lands of Samuel Fitz Randolph.

The influences which drew the Shrewsbury Church away from its New Jersey home, as well as a history of the first settlement at New Salem, will be discussed in a subsequent chapter.

A LIST OF THE CONSTITUENT MEMBERS OF THE SHREWSBURY CHURCH.

WILLIAM DAVIS, "an aged minister of the gospel,"
JOSEPH MAXSON, "a ministering brother,"
JOHN DAVIS, "a ministering brother,"
THOMAS BABCOCK,
THOMAS DAVIS,
WILLIAM BRAND, JR.,
JOSEPH DAVIS,
ELISABETH DAVIS, (wife of John Davis the elder),
BETHIAH MAXSON, (wife of Joseph Maxson),
ELISABETH DAVIS, (wife of John Davis),
RUTH BABCOCK, (wife of Thomas Babcock),
BETHIAH DAVIS, (wife of Thomas Davis),
ELISABETH BRAND,
MARY STILLMAN,
JUDITH DAVIS, (wife of James Davis),
ELISABETH DAVIS, JUNIOR, [alias] Maxson.

NOTES CONCERNING THE MEMBERS OF THE SHREWSBURY CHURCH.

(Taken from the Church Records).

"Elisabeth Davis, widow, went in October, 1745, to live with her son Joseph Davis in Pennsylvania."

"Thomas Davis and family went to Pennsylvania in March, 1746."

"John Davis, chosen elder, July 19, 1746."

"Joseph Davis and his family returned to Westerly, he and his wife being recommended there in 1751."

"Thomas Davis and family returned from Pennsylvania in perhaps about two years and settled in Middletown, hard by Clay Pit Creek. Elisabeth Davis, widow, also returned and settled there, where also

Joseph Maxson, husband of Elisabeth Maxson, James Davis, Joseph Stillman, and Mosher Maxson, now live in 1752."

"Mosher Maxson and family returned from Middletown, and settled at Manasquan, April, 1753."

"Joseph Stillman and his family went to settle in New England, he and his wife being recommended to the church in Westerly in September, 1753."

"Nathan Rogers of New London was the first that was baptized here but was recommended to the church in Westerly to be received a member because that was nigher to his habitation."

"The next that were baptized were Simeon Maxson and Comfort Davis, both in one day, and were joined to the church. The next were William Brand and Mosher Maxson, both in a day at Squankum, in the year 1749. The next were Joseph Stillman and Judith Davis alias Babcock at Squan in the year 1749. The next was Tacy Maxson of Squan in the year 1750. Next Joseph Maxson at Middletown, June 22, 1754. Next Anna Havens and Experience Davis, both in a day, July 13, 1754, at Squan."

"Rebecca Brand was the first baptized after brother John Davis's decease, and received as a member of the church, November 11, about the year 1758, Rev. Jonathan Dunham being the administrator."

"Joseph Davis of Middletown was baptized by Joshua Maxson in the year 1760, and received into the church by Rev. Jonathan Dunham."

"Tacy Davis, wife of William Davis; Nathan Davis; John Brand; Tacy Davis (the daughter of William Davis); Elisabeth Davis, were baptized all in a day, by Rev. Jonathan Dunham, and received into the church about the year 1761."

"Ephraim Maxson about the year 1764 returned from New England, where he had been baptized and received into the Westerly Church, and soon after was received as a member of this Church."

"Jacob Davis, son of James Davis, was baptized and received into the church by Rev. Jonathan Dunham in the year 1772."

"Mary Davis, the wife of Jacob Davis was baptized and received into the church June 27, 1773, by Rev. Jonathan Jarman."

"Elisabeth Babcock, Experience Babcock, Ruth Maxson, baptized and received into the church, December 19, 1773, by Rev. Jonathan Jarman."

"Anna Davis, wife of Nathan Davis, baptized and received into the church," (no date).

"Thomas Davis, Junr., baptized and taken into the church by Rev. Jonathan Dunham near the year 1764."

"Elisabeth Hampton, wife of John Hampton, Hannah Smith, wife of Zebulon Smith, both of Shark River; and Penelope Davis, wife of Joseph Davis, of Middletown, baptized and received into the church all in a day, June 19, 1774, by Rev. Jonathan Jarman."

THE FOLLOWING SIGNED THE CHURCH COVENANT WHICH WAS ADOPTED
JUNE, 1774.

THOMAS DAVIS,	JUDITH BABCOCK,
THOMAS BABCOCK,	TACY DAVIS,
WILLIAM DAVIS,	ELISABETH MAXSON,
JOSEPH MAXSON,	EXPERIENCE MAXSON,
EPHRAIM MAXSON,	REBECCA DAVIS,
NATHAN DAVIS,	ANN DAVIS,
THOMAS DAVIS, JUNR.,	HANNAH SMITH,
JACOB DAVIS,	ELISABETH BABCOCK,
JOSEPH DAVIS,	RUTH MAXSON,
JAMES DAVIS,	PENELOPE DAVIS,
JOHN PARKER,	LYDIA HAVENS,
JAMES DAVIS, JUNR.,	MARY DAVIS,
WILLIAM BRAND,	MARGARET MILLER,
SIMEON MAXSON,	EXPERIENCE BABCOCK,
ZEBULON MAXSON,	MARY MAXSON,
WILLIAM DAVIS, JUNR.,	ELISABETH BRAND,
WILLIAM MAXSON,	MARTHA DAVIS,
NATHAN MAXSON,	ANNA HAVENS,
JOHN DAVIS,	ELISABETH MAXSON, JUNR.,
JOHN MAXSON,	MARVEL MAXSON,
JOHN BRAND,	INCREASE LIPPINCOTT.
THOMAS MAXSON,	

"About July 15, 1774, the following were baptized and received into the church by Rev. Jonathan Jarman: James Davis, eldest, James Davis, his son, Joseph Auger, Margaret Miller, Elisabeth Auger (wife of William Auger), Lydia Havens (wife of Jacob Havens), Martha Davis."

"December 4, 1774, John Parker, and Mary Maxson, baptized and received into the church by Rev. Henry Dawson."

"February 27, 1775, Zebulon Maxson, Nathan Maxson, William Maxson, William Davis, and John Davis, baptized and received into the church by Rev. Jonathan Jarman."

"May 14, 1775, John Maxson, and Marvel Maxson, baptized and received into the church by Rev. Jacob Davis."

"August 26, 1775, Margaret Miller, given letter of recommendation."

"September 20, 1777, Increase Lippincott baptized by Rev. Jacob Davis."

"September 27, 1777, Increase Lippincott received into the church by Rev. Jacob Davis."

"April 14, 1778, Thomas Maxson baptized."

"April 14, 1778, Thomas Maxson received into the church by Rev. Jacob Davis."

"April 28, 1781, Joseph Gifford was baptized."

"May 13, 1781, Margaret Newman and Elisabeth Gifford received into the church."

A LIST OF NAMES FOLLOWING THE MINUTES OF MEETING, AUGUST 10, 1783.

WILLIAM BRAND,
THOMAS BABCOCK,
WILLIAM DAVIS,
ZEBULON MAXSON,
EPHRAIM MAXSON,
HENRY LAFFERTY,[1]
NATHAN DAVIS,
WILLIAM MAXSON,
JOHN DAVIS,
SIMEON MAXSON, JUNR.,
JOHN PATTERSON,
JUDITH BABCOCK,
ELISABETH LAFFERTY,[1]
MARVEL DAVIS,
EXPERIENCE MAXSON,
ANN DAVIS,
MARGARET MARTIN,
AMY BABCOCK.

"November 18, 1786, Zebulon Maxson, Anna Maxson, Eamy [Emma or Amy?] Babcock, Sally Patterson, Elisabeth Maxson (daughter of Zebulon), Bethiah Maxson, Prudence Maxson, Lydia Davis, were received into the church."

"December 13, 1786, Thomas Babcock, William Davis, Catharine Davis (wife of William), Hannah Davis, Mosher Maxson, James Maxson, Jacob Davis, Joseph Davis, Samuel Davis, Jesse Maxson, were baptized."

"December 24, 1786, David Davis, Nathan Davis, and William Dennis were baptized."

"December 31, 1786, Susanna Maxson, George Maxson, Experience Maxson, and Mary Davis, were baptized. All young persons."

"January 7, 1787, William Davis, Catharine Davis (wife of William), Mosher Maxson, James Maxson, Jacob Davis, Joseph Davis, Jesse Maxson, Samuel Davis, were received into the church, having been previously baptized."

"January 21, 1787, Ananias Gifford, John Maxson, Hannah Newman, Sarah Gifford, were baptized."

"January 27, 1787, Experience Maxson was received into the church."

"February 5, 1787, Nathan Davis (son of Nathan), and George Maxson, were received into the church."

"February 25, 1787, James Davis, Mary Gifford, and Calvin Harbert were baptized."

"March 10, 1787, William Dennis was received into the church."

"May 13, 1787, Catharine Dennis was baptized."

"June 29, 1787, Anna Dennis was baptized."

"September 1, 1787, Anna Dennis was received into the church."

"June 14, 1789, Gideon Day and Samuel Newman were received into the church."

"September 6, 1789. Then did the body of this church remove

---
1. McLafferty.

THE SHREWSBURY CHURCH, NOW AT GLENDOLA.
(From a photograph taken in 1903).

from Shrewsbury in order to settle in the state of Virginia. Names: Rev. Jacob Davis, with his family; William Davis, Senior; John Davis; Ephraim Maxson; Thomas Babcock; Zebulon Maxson; Benjamin Thorp, with all their families.

"September 13, 1789. Also set out the following from the same place: Simeon Maxson; William Davis, Junior; William Maxson, with all their families."

The next date that appears in the records is May 13, 1792, after the church had settled at New Salem, Harrison County, Virginia. The church there became known as the New Salem Church, to correspond with the name of the new place of settlement.

MEETING HOUSE.

For thirty years the church had no meeting house, but met for worship in the homes of its members in the township of Shrewsbury near the Manasquan and Shark rivers; and in the township of Middletown in the vicinity of Clay Pit Creek. For a time, business meetings and communion services alternated between the two towns.

Upon the whole, however, meetings were more frequently held in Shrewsbury where the larger part of the membership of the church lived, between the Manasquan and Shark rivers. Here the church voted, March 3, 1775, to build a meeting house, which was to be located on the southwest corner of Zebulon Maxson's land, lying on one of the branches coming out of the branch commonly known as the Great Branch, "said Zebulon Maxson having given his free consent thereunto."

But progress was slow. On October 27, 1776, the building had advanced far enough for the roof, and this the church voted to put on as soon as possible. The records of the church also show that in January, 1778, a sum of money was raised for the building of the meeting house.

The building was thirty feet by thirty-two feet, built with a heavy white oak frame, which at the present writing is still in excellent condition.

On the 8th of August, 1789, the church sold the meeting house to a man by the name of Reed, to whom the members also sold their farms; and a few weeks afterward the majority of the families of the church set out "in order to setle in the State of Verginey."[1]

The meeting house now passed into the hands of strangers, and for a period of forty years little is known of its history. About the year 1830, it was used by the Free Methodists as a house of worship, and not long after that date was moved from its original site on what is now known as the Kirby Farm, which is, at the date of this writing, owned by Bartine Newman, Esq., to a point about a mile and a quarter nearly due northeast towards the Shark River, up on top of the hill at the cross roads now known as Glendola, where it served as a Union Chapel, and was used chiefly by the Free Methodists, Baptists, and Universalists. Here it stood for several years without floor or plastering, with many of the clapboards (weatherboards) off, giving free access to the birds and squirrels. The seats consisted of heavy planks or slabs with two holes bored into each end, and into the holes were driven stout wooden pegs a foot and a half long, which served as legs.

In more recent years the meeting house was purchased by the Methodist Protestant Church, turned so that it faces the east instead of the north, and is now used as a house of worship by that church.

Since its last removal, three additions have been made to the meeting house. The first adds about ten feet to the main body of the church in front, allowing a third window to be put in on each side. The second is a tower about ten feet square starting from the ground, at the middle of the front of the main body of the building and terminating in a spire. The third addition, at the rear, not so wide as the main body of the structure, is about ten feet deep, and contains the pulpit and choir box. A gallery extends the entire length of the main part of the building on both sides and across the front.[2]

The original site of the meeting house and the adjoining graveyard is overgrown with briers and bushes. In the

---

1. Sic; verb. et lit.

2. A visit to the site of the old Shrewsbury Church August 2, 1903, by the author of this book, in company with the Reverend Boothe Colwell Davis, D.D., President of Alfred University, is described in the *Sabbath Recorder*, of August 17, 1903, pp. 524-525.

INTERIOR OF SHREWSBURY CHURCH. LOOKING TOWARD THE FRONT.
(After a photograph taken in 1903).

graveyard but a single tombstone remains, that of Hannah Davis, and that is not in its original position.[1]

DEATHS.

"This is a list of the names of them that have been removed out of the world by death:—

"William Davis, the Elder, died at Manasquan in the year 1745.

"Joseph Maxson and his wife died near at a time in the year 1747.

"Ruth Babcock died at Squankum, 1749.

"Elisabeth Davis, wife of John Davis, died at Squan, in April, the year 1751.

"Bethiah Davis died at Middletown, June the 18th, 1754.

"John Davis, the Elder, died at Manasquan, August 18, 1754.

"Elisabeth Davis, wife of William Davis, the Elder, died at Middletown, about the year 1760.

"Judith Davis, the wife of James Davis, departed this life May the 14th, 1773, being the sixth day of the week about 7 o'clock in the morning.

"May the 17th, 1776. Then deceased Brother John Parker.

"May the 20th, 1776. Then deceased Brother John Maxson.

"March, 1777. Brother Joseph Davis departed this life.

"Brother James Davis departed this life June 26, 1778.

"Brother Thomas Davis departed this life February 2d, 1786.

"Anna Havens, the wife of John Havens, departed this life May 10th, 1786.

"Brother Zebulon Maxson departed this life September 8th, 1787."

The following is an abstract from the records of the Church concerning its ministers:—

———— 1745. William Davis, an aged minister at time of organisation.

Joseph Maxson, a ministering brother at time of organisation.

John Davis, a ministering brother at time of organisation.

June 19, 1746. John Davis was chosen elder. Arrangements were made at this meeting to send him to Westerly to be ordained as a minister, and Joseph Maxson was appointed to write a letter to the church at Westerly making known the wishes of the Shrewsbury Church. Five days afterward, John Davis took this letter and set sail for Westerly, where he arrived safely after a week's voyage. Here the letter was read at the Sabbath service on the 12th of July. The

---

[1]. The inscription on this tombstone is as follows:
> Hannah
> Daughr of Nathan
> & Anna Davis died
> March ye 3d 1788
> aged 20 Years
> As you are now so once was I
>   In health and strength now here I lie
> As I am now so you must be
>   Prepare for death and follow me

Westerly Church voted to accede to the request of the Shrewsbury Church; and in the afternoon of the following day, John Davis was solemnly ordained to the sacred duties of the Gospel ministry by Rev. Joseph Maxson, assisted by Rev. John Maxson, and Deacon Clarke.[1]

November 11, 1758. Rev. Jonathan Dunham baptized Rebecca Brand.

———— 1760. Joshua Maxson baptized Joseph Davis of Middletown.

June 27, 1773. Rev. Jonathan Jarman baptized and received into the church Mary, wife of Jacob Davis.

June 19, 1774. Jacob Davis called to the ministry (licenced) by the church. Called to ordination December 25, 1774, when the church voted to send to Piscataway for assistance at the ordination service. On the fourth Sabbath in February he was ordained by Rev. Jonathan Dunham and Rev. Jonathan Jarman.

December 4, 1774. Rev. Henry Dawson baptized John Parker and Mary Maxson.

September 24, 1775. Simeon Maxson, who had virtually been licenced by the church to preach, was silenced because of lack of harmony between him and the church. On December 3d, 1775, he acknowledged to the church that he had been in error concerning certain of his views relating to the Eternal Judgment, but he declared that he would continue to preach despite the vote of silence on the part of the church.

September 8, 1776, Simeon Maxson was debarred from communion on a quadruple charge:

1st. Of non-attendance at church.

2d. The declaration that his brethren and sisters in the church "are the children of the Devil, and his works we do, and that the Devil is our father."

3d. His complaint that the pastor of the church taught carnal war.

4th. His assertion that a visitation of sickness upon the church was due to the fact that the members of the church joined with the carnal war—(the war of the Revolution was then in progress).

July 13, 1783. Simeon Maxson confessed his fault in having spoken against the pastor and thereby "gave satisfaction to the church."

September 14, 1788. A question rose as to whether Henry Lafferty should be silenced or given an extension of licence to preach.[2] It was decided to allow him to continue to preach.

---

1. Cf. *Seventh Day Baptist Memorial*, Vol. II., No. 1, p. 158. Clarke says: "I find by the church records of Hopkinton, that in June 25, 1746, one John Davis was ordained at Westerly by request of the brethren at Shrewsbury, East New Jersey." *History of the Sabbatarians*, p. 27.

2. His name was really McLafferty. He was born in Ireland. He came to America when a boy as a "redemptioner." He spent his time of service at the mouth of the Manasquan River with a salt manufacturer, probably Thomas Babcock, whose daughter Elisabeth afterwards became his wife. He did not accompany or follow the Shrewsbury church to Virginia. He remained at Shrewsbury for a few years and subsequently became the pastor of the Piscataway Seventh Day Baptist church.

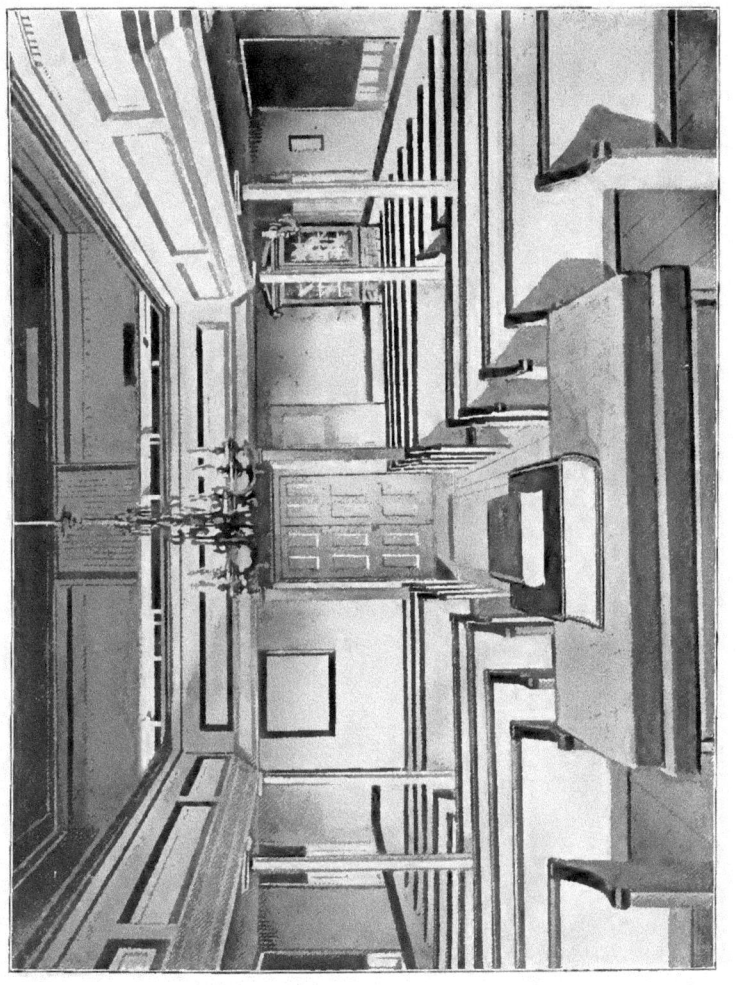

INTERIOR OF SHREWSBURY CHURCH, LOOKING TOWARD THE REAR.
(From a photograph taken in 1903).

July 12, 1789. Gideon Day confessed that a letter of licence to preach, purporting to have been issued by a people on a "branch of Wyoming," which he had presented, was a counterfeit, and that he had told falsehoods concerning it. He was placed under the censure of the church.

RULING ELDERS.

The belief and practise of the church regarding ruling elders varied from time to time. The action of the church on that question at various times was as follows:—

December 25, 1774. "The first thing in consideration is whether it is not thought necessary that there should be ruling elders appointed to take charge in part, of this church, and to endeavour to go to any brother or sister out of the way, to admonish them; and likewise it was thought necessary that some persons should be appointed to this office to assist the person [*sic;* parson is doubtless meant], or minister, and accordingly Brother Joseph Maxson of Middletown, and Thomas Babcock of Shrewsbury, is appointed to this work."

May 14, 1786. Henry Lafferty and John Davis were appointed ruling elders.

DEACONS.

The following record appears concerning deacons of the Shrewsbury Church:—

February, 1752. Thomas Babcock and Thomas Davis were appointed deacons by the church.

June 19, 1774. Ephraim Maxson was chosen deacon.

December 25, 1774. William Davis was chosen deacon.

May 19, 1786. It was voted by the church that Ephraim Maxson be ordained deacon.

October 27, 1786. Ephraim Maxson was ordained deacon, with the assistance of Rev. William Bliss, of Rhode Island.

MODERATOR.

But one moderator of the church is named in the records of the church before it left Shrewsbury, and that is Thomas Davis, who was elected moderator March 3, 1775.

CLERK.

The records of the church do not contain the name of the church clerk until after the church had left Shrewsbury and settled at New Salem, Virginia.

CHURCH MEETING AND COMMUNION SERVICE.

March 3, 1775. The church voted that church meeting

should be held the last First Day of the week in every month, and that communion service should occur on the last Sabbath in November, February, May, and August, respectively.

March 3, 1776. The Quarterly Meeting was changed to the third Sabbath in February, May, and August, respectively; and the Yearly Meeting to the first Sabbath in November.

FAST DAYS.

A day of fasting and prayer was appointed about the year 1750 to relieve William Brand from the gout.

May 11, 1777. The church voted that the Fifth Day of the week preceding communion service, should be a public fast day. This action was doubtless inspired by the troublous times of the American Revolution, which was a very trying period to the Shrewsbury Church.

III.

WESTERN VIRGINIA.

THAT part of Western Virginia, now the state of West Virginia, which is occupied by the Seventh Day Baptists, previous to its occupation by white men, had been the home of the Mound Builders and of the Indians. It lies but a few miles southeast of Moundsville, now one of the prominent towns of West Virginia, which takes its name from a large conical mound at that place. This mound is one of the noted pre-historic monuments of America. When it was opened in 1838, there was found a sculptured stone covered with unknown characters, which J. W. Powell, director of the United States Bureau of Ethnology describes as follows:— "Four of the characters correspond to the ancient Greek, four to the Etruscan, five to the Norse, six to the Gaelic, seven to the old Erse, and ten to the Phoenician." While these characters are generally accepted as the same as those of the Pelasgi and other early Mediterranean people, it is not unlikely that ultimately they will be accepted as a highly refined type of the pictorial or ideographic characters common to the early inhabitants of North America.

This mound is two hundred and forty-five feet in diameter at the base, seventy-nine feet in height, in shape like the frustum of a cone, with a flat apex fifty feet across. Other similar mounds of smaller dimensions have been found in the more immediate vicinity of the Seventh Day Baptists in West Virginia.

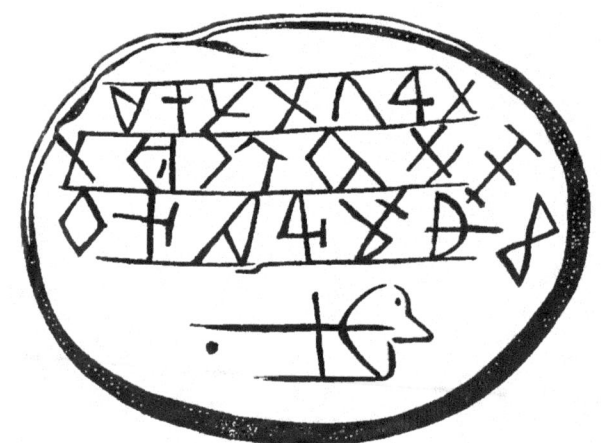

INSCRIPTION ON STONE TABLET FROM GREAT MOUND AT MOUNDSVILLE.

All that part of the state which lies between the Little Kanawha River on the south, and the present site of the city of Wheeling on the north, and bounded on the east by the water-shed which divides the streams flowing west directly into the Ohio River, from those flowing east into the waters of the Monongahela, belonged to the Mingo Indians. The valley of the Monongahela was occupied by the Delawares. Both of these tribes had been subdued by the Six Nations, so that when the Seventh Day Baptists settled here a century and more afterward, they found themselves amid an Indian domination which covered the whole of western New York, western Pennsylvania, and western Virginia as far south as the Tennessee River and westward to the shores of Lake Superior.

The mountainous character of the country with its heavy forests and abundant streams of water, invited game in abundance and made it a favourite hunting ground for many tribes of Indians. Many of the streams, both large and small, retain to this day, names given them by hunters both dusky and pale face, on account of the game which was to be found there. The *Tis-kel-wah* of the Shawnees, which meant "River of Fat Elk," became the *Elk River* of the white hunter. The *Great Kanawha*, as the Delawares called it, meant "The Place of The White Stone." The Delawares called the river on which they lived *Monongahela*, meaning "The River of Caving Banks." Of the smaller streams we have *Meat House Fork, Buffalo Calf, Bear Track, Turkey Track, Turkey Run, Snake Run, Wolf Pen Run, Black Lick, Beach Lick, Raccoon, Hunters Fork, Lick Run, Georges Camp, Turtle Tree*, etc. Curiously enough, Wheeling Creek, which gives its name to the principal city of the state, the Indians called *"Weeling,"* or "The Place of the Skull," from the spherical shape of the adjoining hill.

Into this wild region there came settlers from the colonies of Virginia, Maryland, South Carolina, Pennsylvania, New Jersey, and even from New England.

The first white men who saw the territory of the present state of West Virginia were John Lederer in 1669, and La Salle in the same year. They were followed by an expedition of Governor Spottswood of Virginia, across the Blue Ridge in

1716; and in 1725 John Van Matre, a Dutch trader from New York, visited this region as a fur trader.

The first white man to make his home within the borders of the state was Morgan Morgan, who settled on Mill Creek, in what is now Berkeley County, in 1720. He was followed within a very few years by a large number of other settlers, who very soon found it necessary to make satisfactory arrangements with the Six Nations, upon whose grounds they were encroaching. Accordingly, negotiations were initiated at Lancaster, Pennsylvania, on June 22, 1744, and concluded on July 4, of the same year, whereby the territory lying between the Allegheny Mountains and the Ohio River was peaceably ceded to the English for four hundred pounds sterling.

The first white man to explore that part of western Virginia with which we are immediately concerned, was Christopher Gist, a distinguished surveyor of North Carolina, who was sent out on November 4, 1751, by the Ohio Company to explore lands lying between the Monongahela and the Great Kanawha rivers. On the basis of the survey made by Gist, who reported to the Ohio Company in October, 1752, the Ohio Company petitioned for a grant, which was to include the whole of the territory afterward settled by the Seventh Day Baptists of western Virginia. By the terms of this proposed grant, the Ohio Company was to erect two forts at once and to put three hundred families within its limits; but the French and Indian War put a stop to this.

About 1764 John Simpson, a trapper from the South Branch of the Potomac River, visited the West Fork River at the mouth of Elk Creek, where he erected a cabin and became the first settler in this part of the country. This cabin was the first home of a white man on the present site of the city of Clarksburg, fourteen miles east of the village of Salem in Harrison County. This was but twenty-five years before the Shrewsbury Church abandoned their homes in New Jersey for western Virginia.

In 1770, Colonel George Washington visited the region of the Ohio River for the purpose of locating lands for the veterans of the French and Indian War, who were entitled to land patents under Governor Dinwiddie's proclamation of 1754. He spent a month in surveying upwards of one hundred

THE GREAT MOUND AT MOUNDSVILLE.

thousand acres, when he completed his work and returned home. There exists to-day in the office of the Clerk of the Circuit Court of Harrison County at Clarksburg, a letter, or surveyor's memorandum, of George Washington's, which was offered as evidence in a suit in which the title of some of these lands was in dispute.

When the War of the Revolution broke out in 1775, the first body of troops enlisted for service south of the Potomac River, was a company of western Virginia pioneers. This company was assembled under the command of Captain Hugh Stevenson at Morgans Spring, in what is now Jefferson County, West Virginia. Their flag bore the name of their company, "The Minute Men," and the traditional rattle-snake coiled ready to strike, under which was inscribed the motto "Don't Tread On Me." The centre of the flag was marked in huge letters with the legend "Liberty or Death."

They wore buck tails in their hats and carried tomahawks and scalping knives in their belts. They assembled for departure to the scene of action on the 17th of July, 1775. After attending religious services, and partaking of a repast, they began their march to Boston.

Western Virginia was the scene of many bloody acts in this war, and suffered from the depredations of both the Indians and the British. A careful historian writes,

"How many West Virginians served during this war we do not know, but certain it is that the founders of our state [West Virginia] were represented on almost every battlefield of the Revolution . . . . . Of all the American States, West Virginia stands, in point of service, next to the original colonies."

Two years after the close of the Revolutionary War, the village of Clarksburg was established at the junction of Elk Creek with the West Fork of the Monongahela River. Morgantown was established in the same year. In this year began a renewal of hostilities on the part of the Indians, which continued for ten years afterward, until General Wayne, popularly known as "Mad Anthony," was put in command, and waged a vigorous campaign, which was known in local annals as "Wayne's War." General Wayne's command included Captain Coburn's company, recruited, partly at least, from Harrison county, Virginia, which carried upon its roll some of the members of the Seventh Day Baptist Church at New Salem.

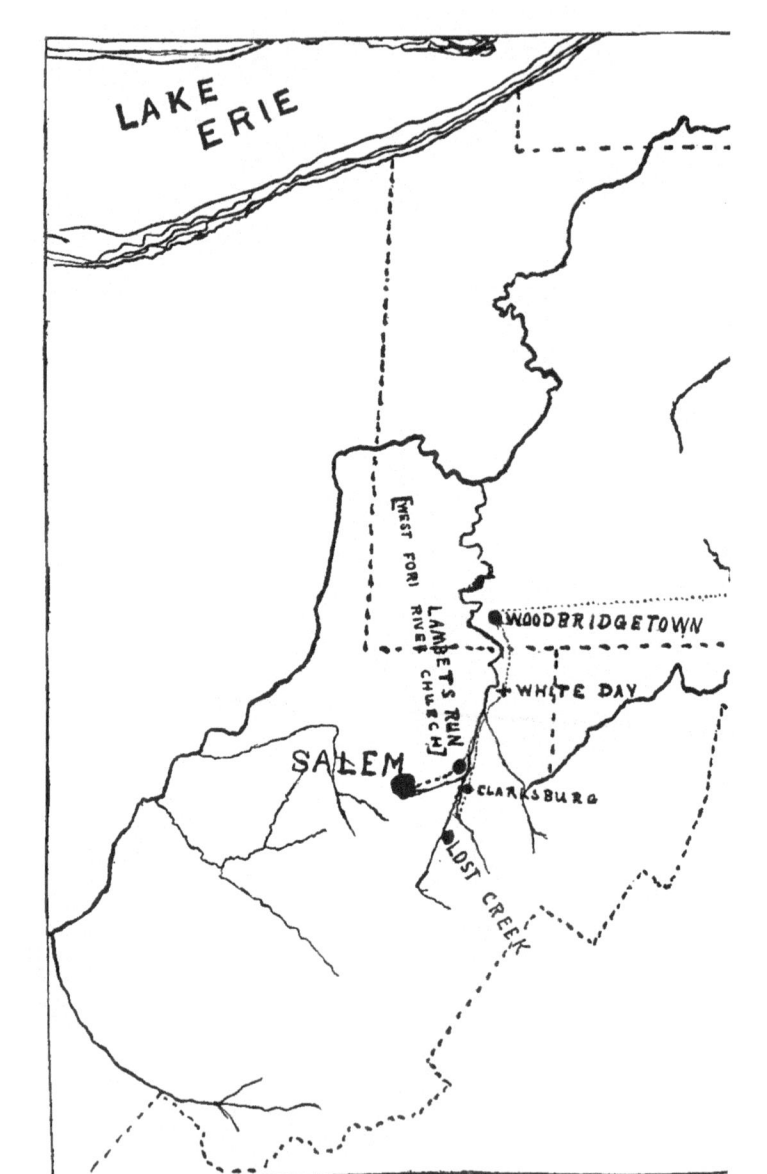

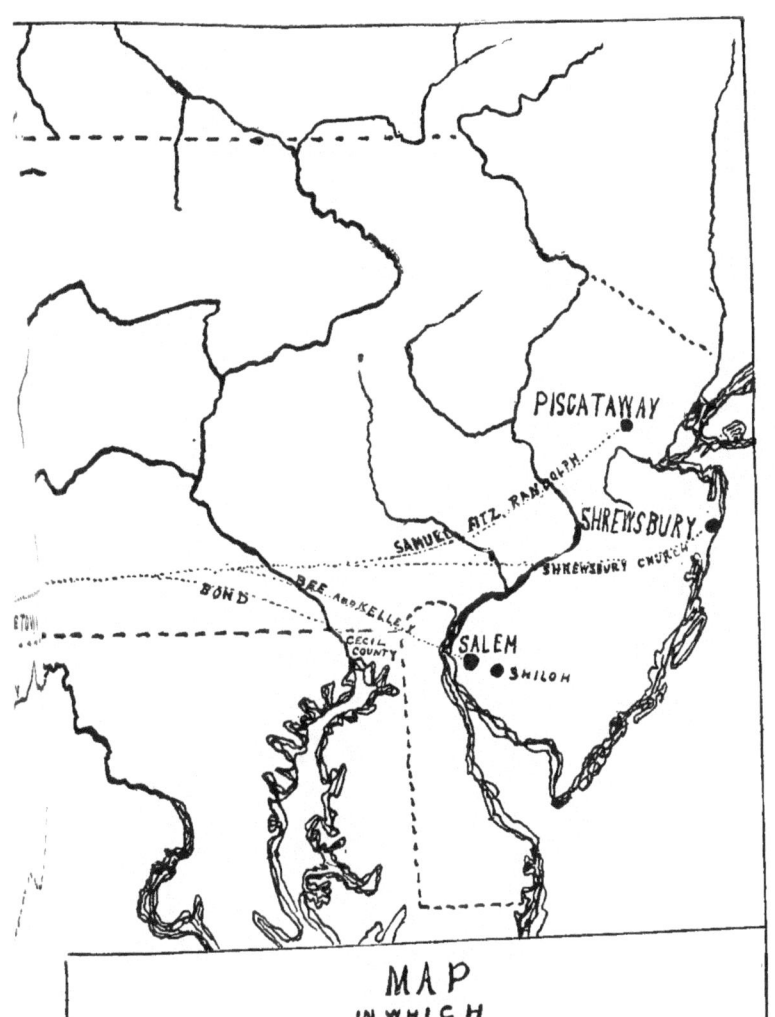

Doddridge County, almost within the sound of the bell of the Middle Island Church.[1]

In 1789, when the Shrewsbury Church started for New Salem, the number of counties comprising the present state of West Virginia had increased to nine, which, at the time West Virginia was organised as a state and admitted into the Union in 1863, had reached fifty in number. At the present time there are fifty-five counties in the state. The counties in which Seventh Day Baptist churches are now located, or have been located, number six as follows:— Braxton, Doddridge, Gilmer, Harrison, Lewis, and Ritchie; but the church membership has extended into the counties of Barbour, Lewis, Monongalia, Roane, Upshur, Webster, and Wood, besides.

As previously stated, the territory occupied by the Seventh Day Baptist churches of West Virginia all lies between the Ohio River on the west, and the Monongahela River with its branches on the east. A deed for this territory was made by the Six Nations of Indians to William Trent and others, November 3, 1768, twenty-one years previous to the setting out of the Church from Shrewsbury, Monmouth County, New Jersey, for the state of Virginia, in September, 1789.[2]

This church gives us no record of its history from that time until the 13th of May, 1792, nearly three years afterward. In the meantime, they had in all probability gone in a very leisurely manner, through Pennsylvania, stopping at various places with friends and acquaintances, and possibly some of their number settling in the southwestern part of the present county of Fayette, Pennsylvania, in the vicinity of the Woodbridgetown Seventh Day Baptist Church of that county. Thence they crossed over the Cheat River into western Virginia, some settling for the time being on White Day Creek in Monongalia County, and later the most of them making their way across the Monongahela, following up the West Fork of that river, thence up the Ten Mile Creek branch of the West Fork River to the head waters of the Middle Fork of Ten Mile Creek. Here lay a tract of land which had been surveyed on the 20th of January, 1786, for Joseph Swearingen, the son of

---

1. This discovery was made by James E. Robinson about the year 1885.

2. This deed relinquished certain claims set up by the Indians subsequent to the Treaty of Lancaster, under date of July, 1744.

Catharine Swearingen,[1] whose husband, John Swearingen, had been adjudged owner of this land by the commissioners appointed for adjusting the claims to unpatented lands in the District of West Augusta, comprising the counties of Monongalia, Yohogania, and Ohio[2] and who had issued to John

---

1. Catharine Swearingen was registered as a slave holder from Spring Hill Township, Fayette County, Pennsylvania, prior to 1803, in conformity with the requirements of a law passed in 1780. Ellis, *History of Fayette County, Pennsylvania*, p. 128.

2. In October, 1776, the General Assembly of the Commonwealth of Virginia fixed the boundaries of the District of West Augusta as follows:—
"Beginning on the Allegheny Mountain, between the heads of Potowmack, Cheat, and Greenbrier rivers [said to be Haystack Knob, now at the north-east corner of Pocahontas County] thence along the ridge of mountains which divides the waters of Cheat River from those of Greenbrier, and that branch of the Monongahela River, called the Tyger's [Tygart's] Valley River to Monongahela River, thence up the said river and the West Fork thereof, to Bingerman's [Bingamon] creek, on the north-west side of said fork, thence up the said creek to the head thereof, thence in a direct line to the head of Middle Island Creek, a branch of the Ohio, and thence to the Ohio, including all the said waters of said creek, in the aforesaid district of West Augusta, all that territory lying to the northward of said boundary, and to the westward of the States of Pennsylvania and Maryland, shall be deemed, and is hereby declared, to be within the DISTRICT OF WEST AUGUSTA."..*History of Monongalia County, West Virginia*. By Samuel T. Willey, Kingwood, W. Va. 1883. Pp. 47-48.

By the same act which created the District of West Augusta, the boundaries of the counties of Ohio, Yohogania, and Monongalia, were fixed as follows:—

"And to render the benefits of government, and the administration of justice, more easy and convenient to the people within the said district [West Augusta]:—

"*Be it therefore enacted by the authority aforesaid*, That from and after the 8th day of November [1776] next ensuing, all that part of said district [of West Augusta] lying within the following lines; to wit, Beginning at the mouth of Cross Creek, thence up the same to the head thereof, thence eastwardly to the nearest part of the ridge which divides the waters of the Ohio from those of the Monongahela, thence along the said ridge to the line which divides the county of Augusta from the said district, thence with the said boundary to the Ohio, thence up the same to the beginning, shall be one distinct county, and be called and known by the name of OHIO;

"And all that part of the said district [of West Augusta] lying to the northward of the following lines; *viz*., Beginning at the mouth of Cross Creek, and running up its several courses to the head thereof, thence south-eastwardly to the nearest part of the aforesaid dividing ridge between the waters of the Monongahela and the Ohio, thence along the said ridge to the head of Ten Mile Creek, thence east to the road leading from Cat Fish Camp to Red Stone Old Fort, thence along the said road to the Monongahela River, thence crossing the said river to the said fort, thence along Dunlap's old road to Braddock's road, and with the same to the meridian of the head fountain of Potowmack, shall be one other distinct county, and be called and known by the name of YOHOGANIA COUNTY;

"And all that part of the said district [of West Augusta] lying to the northward of the county of Augusta, to the westward of the meridian of the head fountain of the Potomack, to the southward of the county of Yohogania, and to the eastward of the county of Ohio shall be one other distinct county, and shall be called and known by the name of the county of MONONGALIA." *Ibidem*, pp. 50-51.

(3)

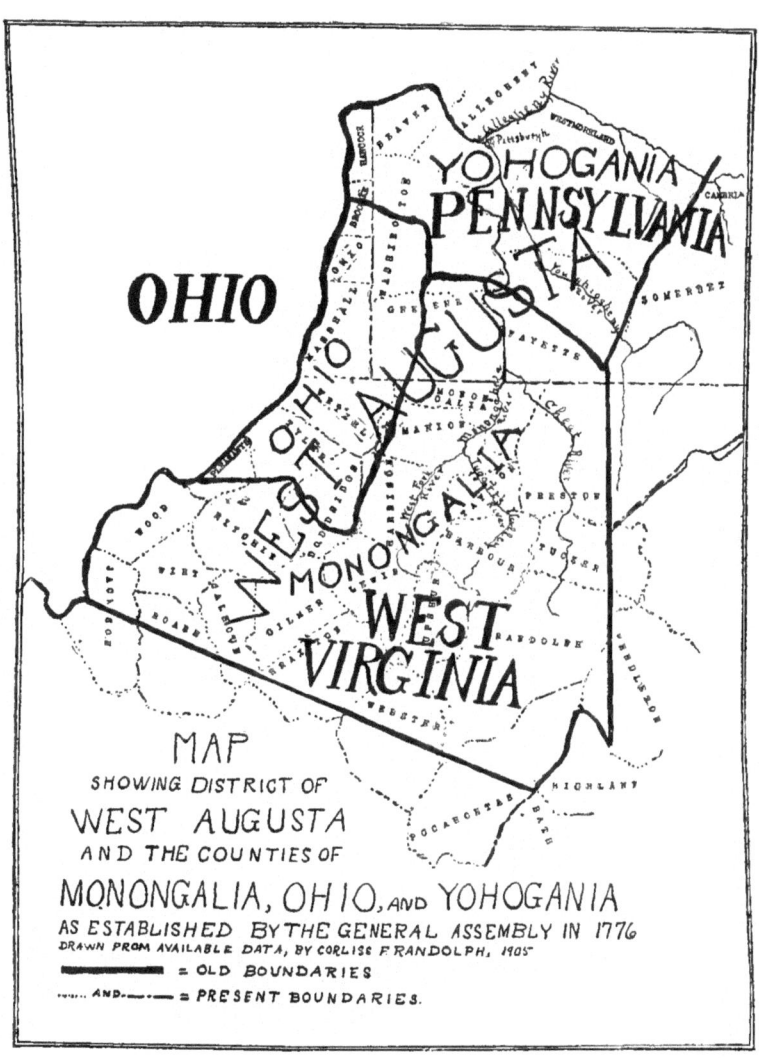

Swearingen a certificate of right of residence.[1] Of this tract of four hundred acres, two hundred and fifty-six acres, extending for a mile and a half along the valley and embracing the most of the present village of Salem,[2] was sold in turn by Catharine Swearingen on the 26th of November, 1790, to Samuel Fitz Randolph of Fayette County, Pennsylvania, who bonded himself in the sum of one hundred and thirty-two pounds, ten shillings, and five pence, Virginia money, for its payment.[3]

Samuel Fitz Randolph, himself a Seventh Day Baptist of Puritan descent, had formerly resided in the town of Piscataway, Middlesex County, New Jersey, where he was born in October, 1738. After service in the Revolutionary War as ensign in the Second Regiment of Militia of Sussex County, New Jersey, he had become interested in lands in Pennsylvania. This was probably due to the influence of Major Benjamin Stites of Redstone, Fayette County, Pennsylvania, who in the winter of 1786, visited New York, where Congress was at that time in session, for the purpose of purchasing a tract of land lying between the two Miamis in Ohio.

---

1. "We, the Commissioners for adjusting the claims of unpatented lands in the counties of Monongalia, Yohogania, & Ohio, hereby certify that John Swearingen, Sen'r., is entitled to four hundred acres of land in Monongalia County, on Ten Mile Creek, a branch of the West Fork, at Nicholas Carpenter's Camp, in the right of residing & making corn in said county before the year 1778.

"Given under our hands, at Colo. John Evans's, this 25th day of April, 1781. "*Teste*. WM. MCCLEERY, *Cl'k*.

"JOHN P. DUVALL,
"JAMES NEAL,
"WM. HAYMOND."

"*Memorandum.*

"This certificate cannot be entered with the Surveyor after the 14th day of July, 1781."

"Entered May the 1st., 1781."

2. Settlement had been made at New Salem, under the name of Carpenter's Camp, (and near by it was Hezekiah Davisson's) as early as 1772. Clearly, Davisson's settlement was made merely for entry or pre-emption rights, as he entered several thousands of acres of land in that vicinity. Carpenter entered but a few hundreds.

3. The tract of land sold to Samuel Fitz Randolph was surveyed January 20, 1786, for Joseph Swearingen, heir of John Swearingen.

The boundaries were as follows: "Beginning at a poplar on the north bank of said [Ten Mile] Creek, and running thence S 3 W, 105 poles crossing the creek to a poplar; S 46 W, 140 [poles] to a gum; N 50 W, 148 [poles]to a white oak; S 79 W, 232 [poles] to a poplar; N 20 W, 86 [poles] crossing the creek to a hickory; N 70 E, 88 [poles] to a white oak; N 84 E, 396 to the beginning. Variation 30 min. east."

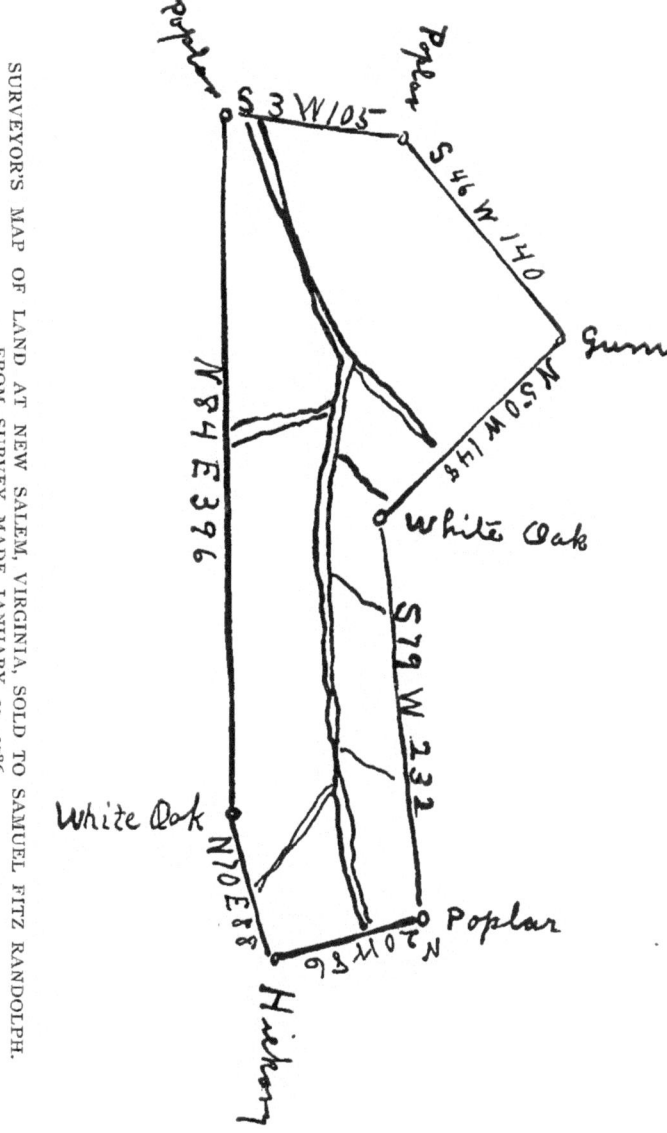

SURVEYOR'S MAP OF LAND AT NEW SALEM, VIRGINIA, SOLD TO SAMUEL FITZ RANDOLPH. FROM SURVEY MADE JANUARY 20, 1786.

He interested John Cleves Symmes,[1] a representative in Congress from New Jersey, whose aid he solicited in his efforts to effect his proposed purchase.[2] Symmes became so favourably impressed with the reports of this country, that he visited it himself and purchased a million acres of land lying between the Great and Little Miamis.[3] Symmes soon afterard sold ten thousand (10,000) acres to Major Stites, who led the first party, some eighteen or twenty in number, to settle at the mouth of the Little Miami, in November, 1788.[4] Other parties followed, starting a movement from New York, New Jersey, and New England, by way of the *Redstone Country,* to this section.[5] It was this movement which drew the little Church of Shrewsbury into its current and carried it along as far as the *Redstone Country,* whence it was deflected south into Virginia.

Sometime before the departure of the church from Shrewsbury, Samuel Fitz Randolph had purchased of Mary Hodgson three hundred acres of land situated on Yellow Creek of Armstrong Township of Westmoreland County, Pennsylvania. This purchase was effected on the 16th of April, 1785, and the land lay a little to the north .of *Redstone.* On November 21, 1785, he purchased eight hundred acres of land to be selected by himself from a tract of five thousand acres owned by Robert Martin, situated in the town of Northumberland in the county of Northumberland, Pennsylvania. The Northumberland tract, from the description contained in the deed, evidently was entirely virgin forest; while upon the three hundred acres in the south-western part of the state, had been built a dwelling house and several farm buildings, and the land was at least partly under cultivation. Here he went to make his home sometime between November 21, 1785, and November 26, 1790. At the time of his purchase

---

1. John [Cleves(?)] Symes made an entry settlement on the Cheat River in 1774, but afterward assigned the claim.

2. John Cleves Symes was appointed a judge of one of the courts of the North-West Territory, January 6, 1787. He was again appointed to a similar position, August 20, 1789. Cf. Burnet's *Notes on the Early Settlement of the North-Western Territory.* pp. 38 and 40.

3. He first applied for two million (2,000,000) acres. Cf. *ibidem,* p. 490.

4. For the essential documents in this grant, cf. *ibidem,* pp. 481-496.

5. The *Redstone Country* was a general name for what is now the south-western corner of Pennsylvania, and the northern part of West Virginia. *Redstone,* proper, corresponds to what is now Brownsville, Pennsylvania.

HOME OF JESSE FITZ RANDOLPH, AT NEW SALEM.
(*Son of Samuel Fitz Randolph*).
(From a photograph taken in 1900)

of the land at New Salem, he was beyond question a resident of Fayette County, Pennsylvania.

Although the Six Nations had formally relinquished all claim to western Virginia in 1768, they continued their depredations until the summer of 1795. It appears that immigration from New York, New Jersey, and the southwestern part of Pennsylvania, into western Virginia and Ohio, had excited anew the jealousy of the Indians, who became more than ordinarily troublesome in the fall of 1791. Accordingly three detachments of soldiers, aggregating nearly five hundred regulars, were sent to the defence of these settlers.

The new settlers on Ten Mile Creek built for themselves a block-house within the limits of the present village of Salem, and protected themselves as best they could against unexpected attacks of the savages. They were, however, outside of the usual trails of the Indians, who seemed disposed to follow the larger water courses; and as Salem is at the crown of the water-shed which sends its waters on the one hand west directly into the Ohio, and on the other hand east into the waters of the Monongahela, it does not seem to have been threatened by large bodies of Indians, except on rare occasions. Twice, however, our colonists were in great peril. Once was on the occasion of a trip made by Nicholas Carpenter from the *Redstone Country* to Marietta with a drove of cattle, when a band of Indians who had crossed the Ohio from the mouth of the Little Kanawha and were moving towards the settlements on the West Fork River, on striking the trail of Carpenter's cattle, were drawn aside from the real purpose of their expedition. This was in September, 1791. The other occasion was in July, 1794, when there were two attacks made upon the settlement of the West Fork River. Soon after this time, General Wayne advanced upon the Indians' country, his force being augmented from time to time by volunteers from among the settlers, among whom were included some from the New Salem settlement, as previously recorded.

In the summer of 1795, occurred the last invasion of this country by the Indians, when they murdered three or four victims, took three prisoners, and returned to their towns in time to surrender their captives to General Wayne. Wayne's treaty with the Indians at Greenville on August 3, 1795, forever freed north-western Virginia from Indian terrors.

When it is remembered that this part of north-western Virginia was the theatre of the action of the celebrated Indian chief Tecumseh, who is said to have been born on Hackers Creek near the mouth of Jesse's Run, only twenty or thirty miles distant from the Ten Mile settlement; that here was the scene of the activities of Logan and Girty; that Cornstalk, the renowned king of the Northern Confederacy of Indians, conducted many of his bloody campaigns in this region; and when we remember, too, that New Salem was but a short distance from the scenes of such wanton murders of friendly Indians by cruel white men, as the murder of Logan's family by Daniel Greathouse and Joshua Baker;[1] of the Bald Eagle by Jacob Scott, William Hacker, and Elijah Runner; and that of Captain Bull, the Delaware chief of the Indian village of Bulltown, on the Little Kanawha, by William White, William Hacker, and probably Jesse Hughes, John Cutright, and others; not to mention still others equally well known in the annals of border warfare, we can appreciate to a slight extent, at least, the dangers with which this country abounded at the time when the settlement was made at Nicholas Carpenter's Camp on Ten Mile Creek. The new settlers were by no means strangers, however, to the perils and treacherous methods of Indian warfare. Their former homes in New Jersey had been situated almost literally upon the very battlefields of the Revolution, where the Indians had sustained their well-earned reputation for the violation of all the laws of warfare among civilised nations.

Although the new-comers built a blockhouse—the common type of fort for protection against the Indians,—there is no available evidence that the Indians did their new pale-face neighbours any harm. On the other hand, the evidence all seems to be to the contrary. Dr. Isaiah Bee of Princeton, West Virginia, a great-grandson of both the William Davises who emigrated from Shrewsbury, says that his great-grandfather, William Davis, called "Greenbrier Billy," from Greenbrier Run the name of the stream on which he settled in

---

1. This murder was long ascribed to Michael Cresap, who it is now known, was innocent of the charge.

A WEST VIRGINIA HOME OF THE MIDDLE OF THE NINETEENTH CENTURY.
(The Home of Jepthah F. Randolph, 1847-1874).
(After a pencil sketch by Corliss F. Randolph).

Virginia, in contra-distinction from the other William Davis who was called "Jarsey Billy," told him (Dr. Bee) then a lad of eight or nine years, that "an Indian chief said to the people at the fort at New Salem, that they were so careless that they (the Indians) could have killed them all, had they wanted to do so. But as they wore shoes and coats, the Indians knew they were from Pennsylvania or New Jersey and were friends. Had they worn moccasins and hunting shirts, they would not have left one alive in the fort." Dr. Bee further states that he himself remembers an old lady by the name of Childers, *nee* Richards, of Meat House Fork, saying that she stood on a stump and saw the Indians scalp her father. This incident, together with others recorded by such authorities as Withers in his *Chronicles of Border Warfare*, and Drake in his *Aboriginal Races of North America*, shows that the Indians were active in their bloody pursuits in the locality of the Seventh Day Baptists even after their arrival at their new homes. Fear of the Indians caused them all to build their cabins in a cluster near to their blockhouse, and when they went out to labour in their fields, they all went together after the custom prevailing in frontier settlements, taking turns in doing each other's work. There is a tradition that at one time a detachment of soldiers occupied the fort at New Salem in defence of the settlers; although this tradition is unsupported by available documentary evidence, it is none the less likely that it is true, as it is an established fact that the village of New Salem was represented in the company of Captain Coburn, an Indian fighter and scout of local reputation, who it will be remembered fought under General Wayne at the Battle of Fallen Timbers on the Maumee.

Within a few years after the arrival of John Simpson at the mouth of Elk Creek, he was followed by a considerable number of settlers, among whom were many famous Indian fighters. One of these was Daniel Davisson, who held the title for the land upon which the greater part of the city of Clarksburg now stands. His wife was a niece of Aaron Burr, whose political intrigues formed upon the beautiful Island of Blennerhassett in the Ohio River, some eighty miles to the west of Clarksburg, are so conspicuous in the early history of the Government of the United States.[1]

Others came attracted by the natural resources of the country. Among these was Nicholas Carpenter from *Redstone*, now Brownsville, in the south-western corner of Pennsylvania, where he had extensive grazing lands for cattle. Without disposing of his *Redstone* lands, he established a home at Clarksburg; and when Harrison County was organised in 1784, he became one of the county's first two coroners, and a member of the first county court. When the town of Clarksburg was established by an act of the General Assembly of the Commonwealth of Virginia, passed in October, 1785, Nicholas Carpenter became one of its first trustees.[2]

About the time that Nicholas Carpenter came to Clarksburg, he established a camp fourteen miles west of Clarksburg on the Middle Fork of Ten Mile, which he called *Nicholas Carpenter's Camp*. Carpenter's name is perpetuated by a tiny stream in the village of Salem, close by the Seventh Day Baptist Church, which to this day is known as Carpenter's Run.

This camp was established probably for hunting and trapping, for the country abounded in game, such as buffalo, elk, deer, bear, wolves, wild turkeys, and numerous smaller game,[3] also for prospecting and surveying; and as a station on the road to the Ohio River, for Nicholas Carpenter was a trader in cattle and other commodities. In fact it was on one of his trips in driving cattle to Marietta, in September, 1791, that he lost his life at the hands of the Indians who attacked his party and tomahawked both him and his son.

---

1. Joseph Johnson, a distinguished governor of Virginia, from 1852 to 1856, locally reputed to have been a natural son of Aaron Burr, lived at Bridgeport, five miles east of Clarksburg, whither he removed in company with his mother, from New York, in 1801, until his death on February 27, 1877, in the 92d year of his age.

2. In 1797, the *American Gazeteer*, published in Boston, by Jedidiah Morse, says that Clarksburg "contains about 40 houses, a court house and jail." Cf. *Transallegheny Historical Magazine*. Vol. I., No. 1, p. 106.

3. "As late as 1825, buffalo were killed near the source of the Tygarts Valley River. In 1843, elk were killed on a branch of the Cheat River, near where the town of Davis now stands; they did not wholly disappear from the present boundaries of West Virginia until some fifteen or twenty years afterward." *Transallegheny Historical Magazine*. Vol. I., No. 2, p. 200.

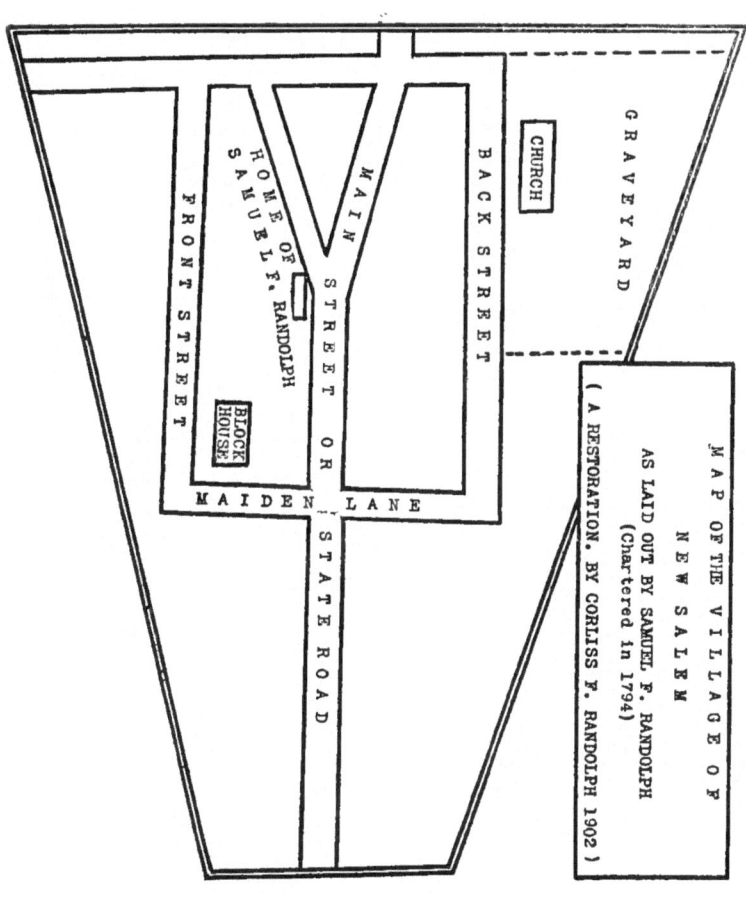

Carpenter established his camp on the tract of land which, as has been pointed out, was conveyed by the heirs of Joseph Swearingen to Samuel Fitz Randolph on the 26th of November, 1790. Samuel Fitz Randolph continued as a resident of Fayette County, Pennsylvania, where he remained an active member of the Seventh Day Baptist Church of Woodbridgetown, Pennsylvania, of which church he and his wife were two of the four constituent members at its first organisation November 8, 1789; and did not remove to his new home in Virginia, until, according to the records of that church, after May 10, 1792.

Samuel Fitz Randolph laid out a part of his land purchased from Joseph and Catharine Swearingen into streets and lots in the form of a town. The town was somewhat in the form of a sort of truncated triangle, with its base to the west, and its apex to the eastward. The town contained five streets,—a main street running nearly east and west, with two others parallel to it, and two shorter streets at the west end of the town running parallel to each other and at right angles to the main street. The lots were divided into two classes: "in" lots and "out" lots, the former fronting on the streets, the latter bordering on the boundaries of the town away from the streets.

A block-house was erected near the centre of the town, where the inhabitants could take refuge in times of danger from the Indians.

The church and graveyard were located on the hillside at the northern terminus of the longer cross street, which was the further west, but a few rods from the home of the founder, Samuel Fitz Randolph.

The town was established by an act of the General Assembly of the Commonwealth of Virginia, as appears from the following extract from its Session Laws for 1794; viz.,

"CHAPTER 44.—AN ACT FOR ESTABLISHING SEVERAL TOWNS.
"Passed December 19, 1794.

"BE IT ENACTED BY THE GENERAL ASSEMBLY, That the lots and streets as the same are already laid off on the lands of Samuel Fitz Randolph, in the County of Harrison, shall be, and are hereby established a town, by the name of 'New Salem,' and John Patterson, John Davis, Samuel Lippincott, James Davis, Zebulon Maxson, Benjamin Thorp, Thomas Clayton, William Davis, Jacob Davis, George Jackson,

A LOG SCHOOL HOUSE.
(After a photograph taken in 1882).

and John Haymond, gentlemen, constituted and appointed trustees thereof."

"Sec. 9.—The trustees of the said towns, respectively, or a majority of them, are empowered to make such rules and orders for the regular building of houses therein as to them shall seem best, and to settle and determine all disputes concerning the bounds of the said lots.

"Sec. 10.—If the purchaser of any lot in either of the said towns, shall fail to build thereon within the time limited for that purpose by their respective deeds of conveyance, the trustees of the said town may thereupon enter into such lot, and sell the same again, and apply the money for the benefit of the inhabitants of the said town.

"Sec. 11.—In case of the death, resignation, or removal out of the county of one or more of the trustees of the said towns respectively, the vacancy thereby occasioned shall be supplied by the remaining trustees or a majority of them; and the person so elected, shall have the same power and authority as if he had been particularly named in this act."

"COMMONWEALTH OF VIRGINIA:—

"I, D. Q. EGGLESTON, Secretary of the Commonwealth of Virginia, certify that the foregoing is a true copy of an Act passed by the General Assembly of Virginia, December 19, 1794, entitled *An Act For Establishing Several Towns,* of record in this office.

"Given under my hand, at Richmond, this 5th day of December, 1902, A. D.

"D. Q. EGGLESTON,
"Secretary of the Commonwealth."

Of the foregoing trustees, William Davis, John Davis, Jacob Davis, Zebulon Maxson, and Benjamin Thorp, were of those who in September, 1789, had set out from their homes in Shrewsbury, New Jersey, "in order to settle in the State of Virginia."

Just why Samuel Fitz Randolph called this village *New Salem* is not wholly certain. There is a well defined tradition that it was so-called for *Salem,* in the southern part of New Jersey, with which Samuel Fitz Randolph, as well as some of the members of the Shrewsbury Church, may have been more or less intimately connected, on account of family ties; and the present writer is inclined to accept that as the true explanation, but conclusive documentary evidence in support of that theory is not available.[1]

Here in the town of New Salem, the new settlers made

---

[1]. There is a village by the name of New Salem in the township of Menallen, in Fayette County, Pennsylvania, which was laid out into a village of sixty lots on August 17, 1799, by David Arnold. Why it was called New Salem is not known. Ellis, *History of Fayette County, Pennsylvania,* p. 658.

their homes for the purpose of security from the Indians. In the meantime, they selected and purchased farms in the vicinity which they cleared and tilled as best they could under the circumstances, since the necessity previously pointed out, for mutual protection from their red-faced foes, which required them when they went out to do their farm work, to go in groups of several each, working one another's farms in successive order, naturally militated greatly against the best interests of the crops.

As soon as they felt that it would be safe to do so, they moved to their farms. Then they began to extend the limits of their settlement over a larger range of country. The Middle Fork of Ten Mile Creek was occupied from its very head to its mouth at the West Fork River. Several of its tributaries, as well as Lamberts Run which flows into the West Fork a short distance further up the West Fork River towards Clarksburg, supplied homes for several of the families of the new immigration.

Some passed west of New Salem to Long Run, Buckeye Run, Buckeye Fork, and Middle Island Creek down three or four miles below the site of the present town of West Union; then still further west across Arnolds Creek, to the North Fork of Hughes River, near the site of the present village of Pennsboro.

To the south of New Salem, they took their way up Pattersons Fork over to Greenbrier Run, and the head waters of Buckeye Creek; thence on to Meat House Fork, and beyond to the South Fork of Hughes River. To the north and northwest of New Salem, they penetrated the deep forests of Robinsons Fork and Flint Run.

Thus from the West Fork River at the mouth of Ten Mile Creek and Lamberts Run, there ran a chain of Seventh Day Baptist homes, practically unbroken, across a belt of country from two to ten miles in width and some forty miles in length, or more than half the distance from the West Fork of the Monongahela River to the Ohio River.

The settlement on the South Fork of Hughes River was detached, geographically, from this belt, but it covered several square miles.

On Elk Creek, which flows into the West Fork River at

A QUIET HOUR.
(From a photograph taken in 1900)

Clarksburg, was another settlement at what it now known as Quiet Dell, situated at a distance of some five miles from Clarksburg; and ten miles south of Clarksburg was the settlement on Lost Creek, which afterwards extended to Hackers Creek on the south and south-east of Lost Creek.

This stream of immigration brought with it the Davises, the Maxsons, the Babcocks, the Thorps, the Brands, and the Claytons, from the Shrewsbury Church. They were either accompanied or followed by the Randolphs from Piscataway, New Jersey; the Bonds from Maryland and Pennsylvania; the Bees and Kelleys from the vicinity of Salem, New Jersey; and the Suttons, the Lippincotts, the Van Horns, the Kennedys, the Williamses, the Loofboros, the Battens and others from various points in New Jersey and Pennsylvania.

These people came into a goodly heritage. The surface formation of the country was hilly. It lay at an altitude of from some seven hundred feet, to about thirteen hundred feet above the level of the sea. The ground was covered by an unbroken forest of heavy building timber of the best quality in great variety. The soil was fertile, and the mineral resources vast. Land could be had at from a few cents to a dollar or two an acre.

The new settlers purchased large farms ranging in size from two or three hundred to several thousands of acres. Samuel Fitz Randolph already held lands in Pennsylvania aggregating eleven hunderd acres; and without disposing of them he made an initial purchase at New Salem of two hundred and sixty-six and a half acres. Three brothers, Nathan, Joseph, and William Davis, purchased a tract of twenty thousand acres of land of the original patentee at the rate of twenty-three cents an acre. It was on a part of this purchase that the present town of West Union in Doddridge County was laid out.

The forests were soon converted into grazing lands upon which were produced fatted cattle that were the envy of the cattle markets of the large cities of the Atlantic seaboard. Gradually the timber markets opened up, and the forests of pine, oak, ash, and yellow poplar, with a fair sprinkling of black walnut and wild cherry were converted into valuable merchandise.

Then later, the boundless wealth of coal and oil was

discovered, so that within the past decade there has been poured into the coffers of the farmers of this region a stream of money aggregating, literally, many millions of dollars, of which our Seventh Day Baptist friends have had a generous share, and, as a result, have become a most prosperous people.

NOTE. In the preparation of this chapter the author has consulted freely, besides the authorities already cited, the following: *History of West Virginia.* By Virgil A. Lewis. Philadelphia. 1887; *The History and Government of West Virginia.* By Fast and Maxwell. Morgantown (W. Va.). 1901; *Chronicles of Border Warfare.* By Alexander Withers. Clarksburg, Va. 1831; *Historical Collections of Virginia.* By Henry Howe. Charleston, South Carolina. 1845; *Notes on The State of Virginia,* with additions. By Thomas Jefferson. 1801; *et al.*

IV.

FRONTIER LIFE IN WESTERN VIRGINIA.

HE Reverend Dr. Joseph Doddridge, a physician and Episcopal clergyman of Wellsburg, Virginia (now West Virginia), wrote a book which he published in 1824, entitled, *Notes on the settlement and Indian wars of the western parts of Virginia and Pennsylvania, from the year 1763 until the year 1783, inclusive, together with a view of the state of society, and manners of the first settlers of the western country.* Although this book was reprinted in 1876, it is very scarce; and as it contains much that is of interest in this connection, as showing the manners and customs of the frontier life into which the Shrewsbury Church projected itself, when it left its home in New Jersey and sought a new home in the mountain fastnesses of western Virginia, the present writer has quoted somewhat freely from several chapters of Dr. Doddridge's most excellent, if somewhat plain and blunt book. In this connection, it should be observed that although Dr. Doddridge gives the year 1783 as his latest date on the title page, the last chapter of his book records events which occurred in the year 1793, four years after the Shrewsbury Church went to that region.[1]

---

1. Communication with the outside world was difficult as the postal service was very limited. Of the five hundred and ten (510) post offices in the United States in 1797, there were eight within the present territory of West Virginia, and the one nearest to New Salem was the post office at Morgantown. *American Gazeteer.* Cf. *Transallegheny Historical Magazine.* Vol. I. No. 1, p. 111. But "a mail route was established in Monongalia County as early as 1794." *Ibidem.* Vol. 1. No. 2, p. 125.

The conditions, together with the manners and customs of life as set forth by Dr. Doddridge may then fairly be accepted as typical of those which greeted our pilgrims upon their arrival at New Salem. The book records its author's own personal observations, thus stamping his evidence as first hand and wholly authentic.

WEDDING CUSTOMS.

Of *Wedding Customs in Western Virginia,* Dr. Doddridge observes the following:—

"For a long time after the first settlement of this country, the inhabitants in general married young. There was no distinction of rank, and very little of fortune. On these accounts the first impression of love resulted in marriage; and a family establishment cost but a little labour, and nothing else. A description of a wedding from the beginning to the end, will serve to show the manners of our forefathers, and mark the grade of civilisation which has succeeded to their rude state of society in the course of a few years. At an early period, the practise of celebrating the marriage at the house of the bride began, and, it should seem, with great propriety. She also has the choice of the priest to perform the ceremony.

"A wedding engaged the attention of a whole neighbourhood; and the frolic was anticipated by old and young with eager expectation. This is not to be wondered at, when it is told that a wedding was almost the only gathering which was not accompanied with the labour of reaping, log-rolling, building a cabin, or planning some scout or campaign.

"In the morning of the wedding-day, the groom and his attendants assembled at the house of his father, for the purpose of reaching the mansion of his bride by noon, which was the usual time for celebrating the nuptials, which for certain must take place before dinner.

"Let the reader imagine an assemblage of people, without a store, tailor, or mantua-maker, within an hundred miles; and an assemblage of horses, without a blacksmith or saddler within an equal distance. The gentlemen dressed in shoe-packs, moccasins, leather breeches, leggins, linsey hunting-shirts, and all home-made. The ladies dressed in linsey petticoats, and linsey or linen bed-gowns, coarse shoes, stockings, handkerchiefs, and buckskin gloves, if any. If there were any buckles, rings, buttons, or ruffles, they were the relics of old times; family pieces, from parents or grand-parents. The horses were caparisoned with old saddles, old bridles or halters, and pack-saddles, with a bag or blanket thrown over them; a rope or string as often constituted the girth, as a piece of leather.

"The march, in double file, was often interrupted by the narrowness and obstructions of our horse-paths, as they were called, for we had no roads; and these difficulties were often increased, sometimes by the good, and sometimes by the ill-will of neighbours, by falling trees, and

A HORSEBACK WEDDING.
(1887).

tying grapevines across the way. Sometimes an ambuscade was formed by the wayside, and an unexpected discharge of several guns took place, so as to cover the wedding company with smoke. Let the reader imagine the scene which followed this discharge; the sudden spring of the horses, the shrieks of the girls, and the chivalric bustle of their partners to save them from falling. Sometimes, in spite of all that could be done to prevent it, some were thrown to the ground. If a wrist, elbow, or ankle happened to be sprained, it was tied with a handkerchief, and little more was thought or said about it.

"Another ceremony commonly took place before the party reached the house of the bride, after the practise of making whiskey began, which was at an early period; when the party were about a mile from the place of their destination, two young men would single out to run for the bottle; the worse the path, the more logs, brush, and deep hollows, the better, as these obstacles afforded an opportunity for the greater display of intrepidity and horsemanship. The English-fox-chase, in point of danger to the riders and their horses, is nothing to this race for the bottle. The start was announced by an Indian yell; logs, brush, muddy hollows, hill and glen, were speedily passed by the rival ponies. The bottle was always filled for the occasion, so that there was no use for judges; for the first who reached the door was presented with the prize, with which he returned in triumph to the company. On approaching them, he announced his victory over his rival by a shrill whoop. At the head of the troop, he gave the bottle first to the groom and his attendants, and then to each pair in succession to the rear of the line, giving each a dram; and then putting the bottle in the bosom of his hunting shirt, took his station in the company.

"The ceremony of the marriage preceded the dinner, which was a substantial back-woods feast, of beef, pork, fowls, and sometimes venison and bear-meat, roasted and boiled, with plenty of potatoes, cabbage, and other vegetables. During the dinner the greatest hilarity always prevailed, although the table might be a large slab of timber, hewed out with a broadaxe, supported by four sticks set in auger holes; and the furniture, some old pewter dishes and plates; the rest, wooden bowls and trenchers; a few pewter spoons, much battered about the edges, were to be seen at some tables. The rest were made of horns. If knives were scarce, the deficiency was made up by the scalping knives, which were carried in sheaths suspended to the belt of the hunting shirt.

"After dinner the dancing commenced, and generally lasted till the next morning. The figures of the dances were three- and four-handed reels, or square sets and jigs. The commencement was always a square four, which was followed by what was called jigging it off; that is, two of the four would single out for a jig, and were followed by the remaining couple. The jigs were often accompanied with what was called cutting out; that is, when either of the parties became tired of the dance, on intimation the place was supplied by some one of the company without any interruption of the dance. In this way a dance was often continued till the musician was heartily tired of his situation. Towards the latter part of the night, if any of the company, through weariness, attempted to conceal themselves, for the purpose of sleeping, they were hunted up, paraded on the floor, and the fiddler ordered to play, 'Hang on till to-morrow morning.'

"About nine or ten o'clock, a deputation of the young ladies stole off the bride, and put her to bed. In doing this, it frequently happened that they had to ascend a ladder instead of a pair of stairs, leading from the dining- and ball-room to the loft, the floor of which was made of clap-boards, lying loose, and without nails. . . . . . As the foot of the ladder was commonly behind the door, which was purposely opened for the occasion, and its rounds at the inner ends were well hung with hunting shirts, petticoats, and other articles of clothing, the candles being on the opposite side of the house, the exit of the bride was noticed but by few. This done, a deputation of young men in like manner stole off the groom, and placed him snugly by the side of his bride. The dance still continued; and if seats happened to be scarce, which was often the case, every young man, when not engaged in the dance, was obliged to offer his lap as a seat for one of the girls; and the offer was sure to be accepted. In the midst of this hilarity the bride and groom were not forgotten. Pretty late in the night, some one would remind the company that the new couple must stand in need of some refreshment; black Betty, which was the name of the bottle, was called for, and sent up the ladder; but sometimes black Betty did not go alone. I have many times seen as much bread, beef, pork, and cabbage, sent along with her, as would afford a good meal for a half a dozen hungry men. The young couple were compelled to eat and drink, more or less, of whatever was offered them."

"It often happened that some neighbours or relations, not being asked to the wedding, took offence; and the mode of revenge adopted by them on such occasions, was that of cutting off the manes, foretops, and tails of the horses of the wedding company."

"On returning to the infare, the order of procession, and the race for black Betty, was the same as before. The feasting and dancing often lasted for several days, at the end of which the whole company were so exhausted with loss of sleep, that several days rest were requisite to fit them to return to their ordinary labours."

Notwithstanding Dr. Doddridge's declaration that these customs so vividly depicted by him were rapidly passing at the time of his writing, many of them existed in a more or less modified form down to a quarter century ago.[1] Doubtless

---

1. About the middle of the second half of the nineteenth century, "horseback" weddings were much in vogue in some parts of this country. The bride and groom, accompanied by one or more other couples, all mounted on horseback, the usual mode of conveyance at that time, travelled to the home of some clergyman, often without previous notice to him, and without dismounting, were married in the public highway, the clergyman standing by the roadside in front of his home. Sometimes the clergyman was overtaken as he travelled along the

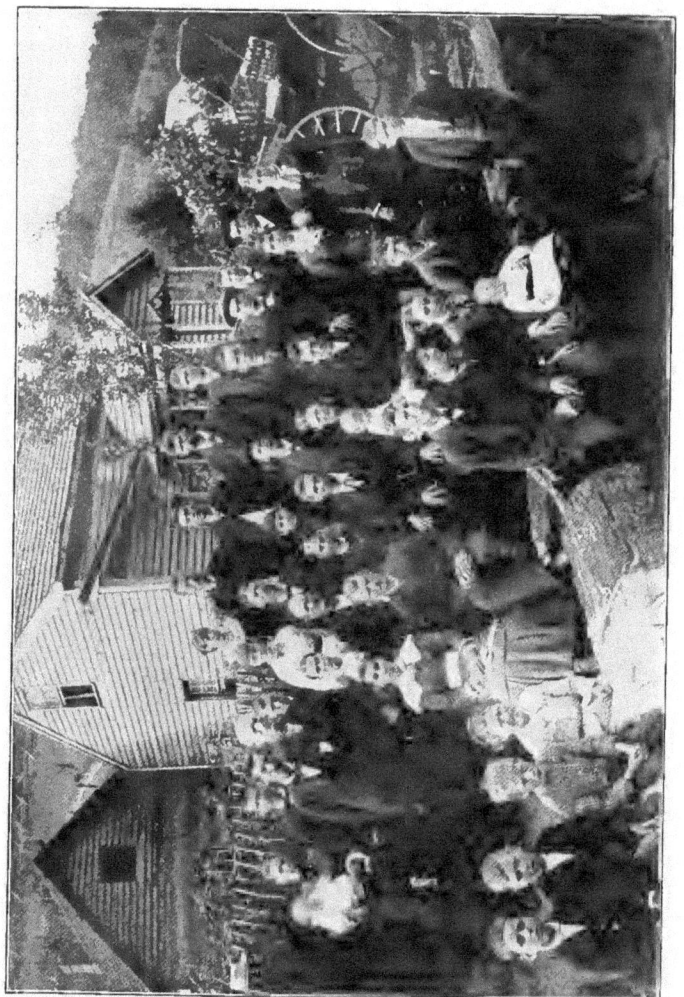

A WEDDING GROUP.
(From a photograph taken about 1885).

many distinct traces of them may be found even to-day in the more remote parts of that country.

In continuing, Dr. Doddridge gives the following description of

THE HOUSEWARMING.

"I will proceed to state the usual manner of settling a young couple in the world.

"A spot was selected on a piece of land of one of the parents, for their habitation. A day was appointed shortly after their marriage for commencing the work of building their cabin. The fatigue party consisted of choppers, whose business it was to fell the trees and cut them off at proper lengths. A man with a team for hauling them to the place, and arranging them, properly assorted, at the sides and ends of the building, a carpenter, if such he might be called, whose business it was to search the woods for a proper tree for making clapboards for the roof. The tree for this purpose must be straight grained and from three to four feet in diameter. The boards were split four feet long, with a large frow, and as wide as the timber would allow. They were used without planing or shaving. Another division was employed in getting puncheons for the floor of the cabin; this was done by splitting trees, about eighteen inches in diameter, and hewing the faces of them with a broadaxe. They were half the length of the door they were intended to make. The materials for the cabin were mostly prepared on the first day and sometimes the foundation laid in the evening. The second day was allotted for the raising.

"In the morning of the next day the neighbours collected for the raising. The first thing to be done was the election of four corner men, whose business it was to notch and place the logs. The rest of the company furnished them with the timbers. In the meantime the boards and puncheons were collecting for the floor and roof, so that by the time the cabin was a few rounds high the sleepers and floor began to be laid. The door was made by sawing or cutting the logs in one side so as to make an opening about three feet wide. This opening was secured by upright pieces of timber about three inches thick through which holes were bored into the ends of the logs for the purpose of pinning them fast. A similar opening, but wider, was made at the end for the chimney. This was built of logs and made large to admit of a back and jambs of stone. At the square, two end logs projected a foot or eighteen inches to receive the butting poles, as they were called, against which the ends of the first row of clapboards was supported.

---

road, and under the friendly shade of some nearby tree, the marriage service took place. Often the horseback weddings were regarded as a sort of adventure, when the bride and groom were likely to be accompanied by a dozen or more couples. At other times it was resorted to as a means of economy, and to avoid display, when the bride and groom were accompanied by but a single couple, or were wholly unattended, members of the family of the officiating clergyman, or of some nearby neighbour, acting as witnesses.

The roof was formed by making the end logs shorter until a single log formed the comb of the roof, on these logs the clapboards were placed, the ranges of them lapping some distance over those next below them and kept in their places by logs, placed at proper distances upon them.

"The roof and sometimes the floor were finished on the same day of the raising. A third day was commonly spent by a few carpenters in leveling off the floor, making a clapboard door and a table. This last was made of a split slab and supported by four round legs set in auger holes. Some three-legged stools were made in the same manner. Some pins stuck in the logs at the back of the house supported some clapboards which served for shelves for the table furniture. A single fork, placed with its lower end in a hole in the floor and the upper end fastened to a joist, served for a bedstead, by placing a pole in the fork with one end through a crack between the logs of the wall. This front pole was crossed by a shorter one within the fork, with its outer end through another crack. From the front pole, through a crack between the logs of the end of the house, the boards were put on which formed the bottom of the bed. Sometimes other poles were pinned to the fork a little distance above these, for the purpose of supporting the front and foot of the bed, while the walls were the supports of its back and head. A few pegs around the walls for a display of the coats of the women, and hunting shirts of the men, and two small forks or buck's horns to a joist for the rifle and shot pouch, completed the carpenter work.

"In the mean time masons were at work. With the heart pieces of the timber of which the clapboards were made, they made billets for chunking up the cracks between the logs of the cabin and chimney, a large bed of mortar was made for daubing up those cracks; a few stones formed the back and jambs of the chimney.

"The cabin being finished, the ceremony of house-warming took place, before the young couple were permitted to move into it. The house-warming was a dance of a whole night's continuance, made up of the relations of the bride and groom, and their neighbours. On the day following the young couple took possession of their new mansion."

In the chapter on

"LABOUR AND ITS DISCOURAGEMENTS,"

Dr. Doddridge says:—

"The necessary labours of the farms along the frontiers, were performed with every danger and difficulty imaginable. The whole population of the frontiers huddled together in their little forts, left the country with every appearance of a deserted region; and such would have been the opinion of a traveler concerning it, if he had not seen, here and there, some small fields of corn or other grain in a growing state.

"It is easy to imagine what losses must have been sustained by our first settlers owing to this deserted state of their farms. It was not the full measure of their trouble, that they risked their lives, and often lost

A LOG CABIN.
(From a photograph taken in 1902.)

them, in subduing the forest, and turning it into fruitful fields; but compelled to leave them in a deserted state during the summer season, a great part of the fruits of their labours was lost by this untoward circumstance. Their sheep and hogs were devoured by the wolves, panthers, and bears. Horses and cattle were often let into their fields, through breaches made in their fences by the falling of trees, and frequently almost the whole of a little crop of corn was destroyed by squirrels and raccoons, so that many families, and after an hazardous and laborious spring and summer, had but little left for the comfort of the dreary winter.

"The early settlers on the frontiers of this country were like Arabs of the desert of Africa, in at least two respects; every man was a soldier, and from early in the spring, till late in the fall, was almost continually in arms. Their work was often carried on by parties, each one of whom had his rifle and everything else belonging to his war dress. These were deposited in some central place in the field. A sentinel was stationed on the outside of the fence, so that on the least alarm the whole company repaired to their arms, and were ready for the combat in a moment. Here, again, the rashness of some families proved a source of difficulty. Instead of joining the working parties, they went out and attended their farms by themselves, and in case of alarm, an express was sent for them, and sometimes a party of men to guard them to the fort. These families, in some instances, could boast that they had better crops, and were every way better provided for the winter than their neighbours. In other instances their temerity cost them their lives.

"In military affairs, when every one concerned is left to his own will, matters are sure to be but badly managed. The whole frontiers of Pennsylvania and Virginia presented a succession of military camps or forts. We had military officers, that is to say, captains and colonels, but they, in many respects, were only nominally such. They could advise but not command. Those who chose to follow their advice did so, to such an extent as suited their fancy, or interest. Others were refractory, and thereby gave much trouble. These officers would lead a scout, or campaign. Those who thought proper to accompany them did so, those who did not remained at home. Public odium was the only punishment for their laziness or cowardice. There was no compulsion to the performance of military duties, and no pecuniary reward when they were performed.

"It is but doing justice to the first settlers of this country to say, that instances of disobedience of families and individuals to the advice of our officers, were by no means numerous. The greater number cheerfully submitted to their directions with a prompt and faithful obedience."

The following interesting extracts are made from Dr. Doddridge's chapter on

"THE MECHANIC ARTS.

"My reader will naturally ask where were their mills for grinding grain? Where their tanners for making leather? Where their smith shops for making and repairing their farming utensils? Who were their carpenters, tailors, cabinet workmen, shoemakers, and weavers? The answer is, these manufacturers did not exist, nor had they any tradesmen, who were professedly such. Every family were under the necessity of doing every thing for themselves, as well as they could.

"The hominy block and hand mills were in use in most of our houses. The first was made of a large block of wood about three feet long, with an excavation burned in one end, wide at the top, and narrow at the bottom, so that the action of the pestle on the bottom threw the corn up to the sides toward the top of it, from whence it continually fell down into the centre. In consequence of this movement, the whole mass of the grain was pretty equally subjected to the strokes of the pestle. In the fall of the year, while the Indian corn was soft, the block and pestle did very well for making meal for johnny cake and mush, but were rather slow when the corn became hard.

"The sweep was sometimes used to lessen the toil of pounding grain into meal. This was a pole of some springy elastic wood, thirty feet long or more; the butt end was placed under the side of a house, or a large stump; this pole was supported by two forks, placed about one-third of its length from the butt end so as to elevate the small end about fifteen feet from the ground; to this was attached, by a large mortise, a piece of a sapling about five or six inches in diameter, and eight or ten feet long. The lower end of this was shaped so as to answer for a pestle. A pin of wood was put through it at a proper height, so that two persons could work at the sweep at once. This simple machine very much lessened the labour, and expedited the work. I remember that when a boy I put up an excellent sweep at my father's. It was made of a sugar tree sapling. It was kept going almost constantly from morning till night by our neighbours for several weeks.

"In the Greenbrier country, where they had a number of salt-petre caves, the first settlers made plenty of excellent gun powder by the means of these sweeps and mortars.

"A machine, still more simple than the mortar and pestle, was used for making meal, while the corn was too soft to be beaten. It was called a grater. This was a half circular piece of tin, perforated with a punch from the concave side, and nailed by its edges to a block of wood. The ears of corn were rubbed on the rough edges of the holes, while the meal fell through them on the board or block, to which the grater was nailed, which, being in a slanting direction, discharged the meal into a cloth or bowl placed for its reception. This to be sure was a slow way of making meal; but necessity has no law.

"The hand mill was better than the mortar, and grater. It was made of two circular stones, the lowest of which was called the bed stone, the upper one the runner. These were placed in a hoop, with a

MOUNTAIN LIFE.

spout for discharging the meal. A staff was let into a hole in the upper surface of the runner, near the outer edge, and its upper end through a hole in a board fastened to a joist above, so that two persons could be employed in turning the mill at the same time. The grain was put into the opening in the runner by hand."

"Our first water mills were of that description denominated tub mills. It consisted of a perpendicular shaft, to the lower end of which an horizontal wheel of about four or five feet diameter is attached, the upper end passes through the bedstone and carries the runner after the manner of a trundle head. These mills were built with very little expence, and many of them answered the purpose very well.

"Instead of bolting cloths, sifters were in general use. These were made of deer skins in the state of parchment, stretched over a hoop and perforated with a hot wire.

"Our clothing was all of domestic manufacture. We had no other resource for clothing, and this, indeed, was a poor one. The crops of flax often failed, and the sheep were destroyed by the wolves. Linsey, which is made of flax and wool, the former the chain and the latter the filling, was the warmest and most substantial cloth we could make. Almost every house contained a loom, and almost every woman was a weaver.

"Every family tanned their own leather. The tan vat was a large trough sunk to the upper edge in the ground. A quantity of bark was easily obtained every spring, in clearing and fencing the land. This, after drying, was brought in and in wet days was shaved and pounded on a block of wood, with an axe or mallet. Ashes was used in place of lime for taking off the hair. Bear's oil, hog's lard and tallow, answered the place of fish oil. The leather, to be sure, was coarse; but it was substantially good. The operation of currying was performed by a drawing knife with its edge turned, after the manner of a currying knife. The blacking for the leather was made of soot and hog's lard.

"Almost every family contained its own tailors and shoemakers. Those who could not make shoes, could make shoepacks. These, like moccasins, were made of a single piece of leather with the exception of a tongue piece on the top of the foot. This was about two inches broad and circular at the lower end. To this the main piece of leather was sewed, with a gathering stitch. The seam behind was like that of a moccasin. To the shoepack a sole was sometimes added. The women did the tailor work. They could all cut out and make hunting shirts, leggins and drawers."

"There was, in almost every neighbourhood, some one whose natural ingenuity enabled him to do many things for himself and his neighbours, far above what could have been reasonably expected. With a few tools which they brought with them into the country, they certainly performed wonders. Their plows, harrows with their wooden teeth, and sleds, were in many instances well made. Their cooper ware, which comprehended everything for holding milk and water, was generally pretty well executed. The cedar ware, by having alternately a white and red stave, was thought beautiful. Many of their puncheon floors were very neat, their joints close and the top even and smooth. Their looms, although heavy, did very well. Those who could not exercise these mechanic arts, were under the necessity of giving labour, or barter, to their neighbours in exchange for the use of them, so far as their necessities required.

"An old man in my father's neighbourhood had the art of turning bowls, from the knots of trees, particularly those of the ash. In what way he did it, I do not know: or whether there was much mystery in his art. Be that as it may, the old man's skill was in great request, as well turned wooden bowls were amongst our first rate articles of household furniture."

"A small depression on the surface of a stump or log and a wooden mallet, were his [Dr. Doddridge's father's] instruments for straightening a gun barrel when crooked. Without the aid of a bow-string he could discover the smallest bend in a barrel. With a bit of steel, he could make a saw for deepening the furrows, when requisite. A few shots determined whether the gun might be trusted."

V.

THE WOODBRIDGETOWN CHURCH.

THE Book of Records of the Woodbridgetown Church begins as follows:—

"This is a record of the proceedings of the first Seventh Day Baptist Church of Christ on the waters of Georges Creek, keeping the commandments of God, particularly God's Holy Seventh Day Sabbath, with the rest of the commandments of God, believing and practising the Holy Ordinances of the Gospel of Christ [and] the doctrines thereof; inhabitants of the western waters of the State of Pennsylvania, agreed and concluded upon by some members belonging to a Church of Christ in the State of New Jersey, township of Piscataway of the same Faith and Order, with their consent, we said members, with the assistance of Elder Jacob Davis, late from New Jersey, and Elder Woodbridge of the State [of] Pennsylvania, Fayette County, Georges Township, met, on the eighth of November, in the year of our Lord one thousand seven hundred and eighty nine met together at a meeting appointed to consult religious matters, and then agreed that there should be a church constituted at Georges Creek, Fayette County, State aforesaid, the next May ensuing. At the same [meeting] Stephen Dunham was appointed to make a minute of the same, but appointment was adjourned to the sixth day of June following.

"June the 6th day one thousand seven hundred and ninety, we, the said members, met according to adjournment and was constituted into a church, Elder Jacob Davis being Administrator and Deacon Maxson, present.

"We, who desire to walk together in the fear of the Lord, do through the assistance of the Holy Spirit, profess our deep and sincere humiliation for our transgressions and we do also solemnly in the presence of God and of each other in the sense of our own unworthiness, give up ourselves to the Lord and to one another by the will [of] God."

Then follow twenty-two articles of faith, similar in spirit and form to those of other Seventh Day Baptist churches of that time. These in turn are followed immediately by the following:—

"This is the covenant we now solemnly enter into, in the love and fear of God, in testimony and ratification whereof we sign our names:—

"SAMUEL WOODBRIDGE, [Elder],
"STEPHEN DUNHAM, [Clerk],
"SAMUEL FITZ RANDOLPH,
"MARGARET FITZ RANDOLPH,
"JOHN MORRIS,
"JOHN PATTERSON,
"ANNE WOODBRIDGE,
"JONATHAN PRESTON,
"ELISABETH BRAND,
"OBED MEREDITH,
"SALLY PATTERSON,
"LEAH STURGIS,
"JAMES DUNN,
"CORNELIUS WILLIAMS,
[Dr.] "JOE BACON,
"MARY GRIFFIN,
"RHODA BACON."

Following this list of names, appear three more articles of faith, the first of which treats, at some length, of marriage and the duties of married life. The second asserts belief in the use of hymns in public and private worship. The third and last declares that "a lawful oath is a part of religious worship and a confirmation of truth and ending of all strife."

From the fact that John Morris was received into the church by baptism and laying on of hands on the 6th of June, 1790, the day of the formal organisation of the church and that all of the others whose names follow his in the list appended to the articles of faith were received into the church afterward, it would appear that the original temporary organisation effected November 8, 1789, consisted of but four members; viz., Samuel Woodbridge, Elder; Stephen Dunham, Clerk; Samuel Fitz Randolph; and his wife, Margaret Fitz Randolph.

On the 8th of August, 1790, John Patterson was received into the church by letter and on that date he was called by the church "to the trial of his gifts" and at the same time given leave to go and make a visit to the people of the Glades, to

WOODBRIDGETOWN CHURCH AND GRAVEYARD.
(From a photograph taken in 1903).

preach while there, and not to preach again abroad without the leave of the church.

On the same day it was decided that the communion service should be held on the third Sabbath in September, December, March, and June, respectively; and Samuel Fitz Randolph and John Patterson were appointed a committee to procure paper for a church book and wine for communion.

On September 2, following, the church took formal action to the effect that, in the case of necessary absence from home of any member of the church, the other members were authorised to proceed with business, a question of considerable importance in a church of seven members.

On December 19, 1790, the church permitted John Patterson "to go to Besentown to preach, and not to preach any more abroad without the leave of the church, but to preach among the members at home when there is a door open." In the following January he was given "leave to preach when and where a door should be opened, for the space of six months." On July 17, 1791, he was "licenced to preach the gospel of Jesus Christ wherever a door shall be open to him without any limitation, provided he continues sound in the faith and practise. At the same time Elder Samuel Woodbridge was appointed to write his licence."

This church appears to have been made up of former members of the Piscataway Church, and converts to the Sabbath, largely from a local Baptist church.[1] The church does not appear ever to have been a strong one and it is of importance mainly because it was a sort of door-way through which the emigrants from New Jersey and certain parts of Pennsylvania passed to western Virginia and Ohio, and other parts west.

Rev. Samuel Woodbridge was the first pastor and it was from him that the locality and church took its name. It afterward became the church home of Rev. Enoch David, a well-known clergyman of his time among Seventh Day

---

1. Rev. Samuel Woodbridge was the second pastor of the Mount Moriah Baptist Church of Fayette County, Pennsylvania. He accepted the call to this pastorate as early as March 1, 1786. Cf. Ellis, *History of Fayette County, Pennsylvania.* Philadelphia, 1882. P. 578.

Baptists.[1] It was through his grandson, Mr. Francis Kildow of Berea, West Virginia, that the records of the church were preserved and passed into the hands of the present writer in the spring of 1902.

The last entry in the book of records is dated August, 1844, and records a visit of Richard C. Bond to the church in April preceding. During the course of his visit he preached five times, administered the Lord's Supper, and, in the following August, visited the church again, preaching several sermons and receiving into the church Richard C. Bond, Jr.

There is also recorded, on the 9th of March of the same year, the dismissal, by letter, of Benjamin F. Bond and Richard C. Bond, who removed to Rock County, Wisconsin Territory.

On the 13th of January, 1793, arose the question of building a meeting house, but the subject was laid upon the table until the next meeting. On the 12th of April, 1795, Samuel Woodbridge, John Shacklett, and John Clauson were appointed a committee to increase the subscription sufficiently to cover the cost of the proposed meeting house. The house was built of logs with its cracks chinked with clay mortar. It was heated with a stove.

At a meeting held in March, 1800, a report was made to the church to the effect that a "penal bill" had been granted Isaac Griffin, Esq., and Nathan Martin, to compel Samuel Woodbridge or his heirs to make a deed for one-half acre of ground to the Seventh Day Baptist Church "where the meeting house stands in Mifflintown," later called Woodbridgetown, in honour of Samuel Woodbridge.

Whatever difference may have existed between the church and Rev. Samuel Woodbridge must have been amicably adjusted before the death of the latter, for Rev. John Davis of Shiloh, New Jersey, who visited the Woodbridgetown Church in 1821, says that this church had a house of worship and a graveyard at Woodbridgetown; that adjoining it, there was a lot of six acres of land left the church by Rev. Samuel Woodbridge, for a parsonage, but that Rev. Samuel Wood-

---

1. "Other preachers were John Corbly, —— Stone, —— Mayberry, and Thomas Hersey, who was chaplain of a regiment in the war of 1812. William Brownfield preached there sometimes." Ellis, *History of Fayette County, Pennsylvania*, p. 578.

bridge's widow was to have the use of this land, however, until the church had a settled pastor.[1]

CLERKS.

The church records also show the following:— That on November 8, 1789, Stephen Dunham was elected clerk of the church. May 22, 1796, Owen David was elected to the same office. Benjamin F. Bond was appointed clerk on May 17, 1840. The last entry made in the record book, under date of April, 1849, is signed by Jonathan Bond, *Clerk, pro tem.*

No record appears, however, from December 28, 1810, to August 4, 1830.

DEACONS.

The deacons of the church were as follows:—

James Dunn, chosen on trial September 9, 1792, and dismissed from the church August 15, 1805, apparently to join the French Creek Seventh Day Baptist Church. Rev. Samuel Woodbridge was instructed to ordain him formally to the office of deacon, however, before his departure.

John Shacklett was chosen deacon, March 12, 1801. A record appears, however, under date of November 24, 1809, indicating that John Shacklett was at that time deceased, and had left a bequest of five pounds to the church.

On February 23, 1832, Jonathan Bond was chosen deacon. In the following May, he was ordained by Rev. Joel Greene.

MINISTERS.

Rev. Samuel Woodbridge, one of the constituent members, continued an active minister at least until near the time of his death, July 15, 1814.

On August 8, 1790, John Patterson was called by the church "to a trial of his gifts," and on the 16th of the following January he was given full licence to preach for a period of six months. At the end of this period, Rev. Samuel Woodbridge was instructed to write John Patterson's licence to preach, the licence to be without limitation so long as the holder should continue sound in the faith. About a year and a half afterward the church voted that preparatory to his

---

1. Cf. *Last Will and Testament of Rev. Samuel Woodbrige*, at the end of this chapter.

ordination, he should preach a series of sermons on the following subjects:—
  I. Doctrine of the Trinity,
  II. The Old and New Testaments,
  III. The Commandments of God.
  IV. The six principles of Christ as found in Hebrews, chapter VI.
  V. Baptism and the Lord's supper.

In the year 1809, Rev. Enoch David divided the ministerial care of the church with Rev. Samuel Woodbridge.

Lewis Sammons, who had been received as a member previously from a First Day Baptist church, was licenced on the 16th of September, 1838, to preach the gospel for one year.

In May, 1840, the licence was renewed for one year, and a year later it was renewed without limitation. But in December, 1842, he was excommunicated from the church for abandoning the Sabbath.

The church records show the following visits from ministers from other chcurches of the denomination:—

August, 1830, Rev. Lewis A. Davis,
February, 1832, Walter B. Gillette (not yet ordained),
April, 1832, Rev. Peter Davis,
May, 1832, Rev. Lewis A. Davis,
June, 1832, Rev. Joel Greene, on his way to Virginia,
July, 1832, Rev. Joel Greene, on his return from Virginia,
Winter of 1832-33, Rev. Alexander Campbell,
Winter of 1834, Rev. Stillman Coon,
May, 1835, Rev. Stillman Coon,
April, 1839, Rev. Joel Greene,
February, 1844, Richard C. Bond,
April, 1844, Richard C. Bond.

MEMBERSHIP IN SUPERIOUR BODIES.

It was not until the year 1832, that the Woodbridgetown Church became a member of the General Conference, at its annual session held at Brookfield, New York, beginning September 6.

When the South-Western Association was formed in 1839, the Woodbridgetown Church became one of its constituent members. It was also admitted to membership in the Virginia Association in 1851.

A LIST OF MEMBERS OF THE WOODBRIDGETOWN CHURCH.

Names.	Date Received.
SAMUEL WOODBRIDGE, *Elder,*	Nov. 8, 1789,

THE WOODBRIDGETOWN CHURCH

STEPHEN DUNHAM, *Clerk*,	Nov. 8, 1789,
SAMUEL FITZ RANDOLPH,	Nov. 8, 1789,
MARGARET FITZ RANDOLPH,	Nov. 8, 1789,
JOHN MORRIS, (by baptism),	June 6, 1790,
(Dismissed, Nov. 13, 1790),	
(" Nov. 11, 1792),	
JOHN PATTERSON, (by letter),	Aug. 8, 1790,
ANN WOODBRIDGE, (by letter),	Aug. 8, 1790,
JONATHAN PRESTON, (by baptism),	Oct. 30, 1790,
(Dismissed Nov. 13, 1790),	
ELISABETH BRAND, (by letter),	June 18, 1791,
OBED MEREDITH, (by letter from the First Day Baptist Church),	Mar. 20, 1792,
SALLY PATTERSON, (by letter),	June 14, 1792,
LEAH STURGUS, (by letter from the First Day Baptist Church at "Conotoway"),	June 14, 1792,
JAMES DUNN, (by letter from Piscataway),	Aug. 9, 1792,
(Dismissed, Aug. 15, 1805),	
CORNELIUS WILLIAMS, (from First-Day Baptist Church without a letter),	Sept. 9, 1792,
(Dismissed, June 9, 1804, to New Salem, Va.),	
RHODA BACON,	Sept. 9, 1792,
MARY GRIFFIN, (admitted to communion),	Jan. 13, 1793,
JOB BACON, (admitted to communion),	Mar. 10, 1793,
OWEN DAVID, (by letter from Piscataway),	Apl. 12, 1795,
JOHN CLAYTON,	
JOHN SHACKLETT, (by baptism),	Sept. 3, 1796,
ANN MARTIN, (by baptism),	Mar. 17, 1797,
LOIS DAY, (member in church),	Feb. 9, 1798,
JEHU JOHN,	Feb. 9, 1798,
ELISABETH JOHN, (wife of Jehu),	Feb. 9, 1798,
ELISABETH DAVID,	Feb. 9, 1798,
RACHEL DRAKE,	June 15, 1798,
(Dismissed, May 24, 1799),	
NAOMI DAVID,	June 15, 1798,
ABRAHAM WELLS, (baptized),	Sept. 15, 1798,
ANN WELLS, (wife of Abraham, baptized),	Sept. 15, 1798,
ABRAHAM MARTIN, (baptized),	Dec. 1798,
NATHANIEL MARTIN,	Mar. 20, 1801,
ELISABETH SHACKLETT,	Mar. 20, 1801,
ANN MUNDY,	Mar. 20, 1801,
BARBARA TAYLOR,	Mar. 20, 1801,
HANNAH DAVIS, (by letter from First Day Baptist Church of Mt. Moriah),	Sept. 1, 1809,
MARY PEIRMAN, (by baptism),	Oct. 12, 1810,
MARY WOODBRIDGE, (by baptism),	Oct. 12, 1810,
JONATHAN BOND,	Aug. 4, 1830,
NAOMI BOND,	Aug. 4, 1830,

Daniel David,	Aug. 7,	1830,
Jane David,	Aug. 7,	1830,
(Removed to Ohio, 1835),		
Nancy Nicholson,		
Francis Nicholson, (by baptism),	Apl. 1,	1832,
Joseph Watkins, (letter from First-Day Baptist Church),	June 16,	1832,
(Removed to Ohio, 1835),		
Sarah Watkins, (wife of Joseph. Letter from First-Day Baptist Church),	June 16,	1832,
(Removed to Ohio, 1835),		
William David,	June 16,	1832,
(Removed to Ohio, 1835),		
Isaac David and wife,	July 31,	1832,
(Removed to Wisconsin),		
Ebenezer David,	May	1835,
Penelope David,	May	1835,
Mary Hall,	May	1835,
(Removed to Iowa),		
John Kildow,	—— — 1837 or	1838,
Lewis Sammons, (from First Day Baptist Church),	Apl.	1838,
Joseph David, (baptized)	———	1838,
Mary Ann David, (wife of Joseph. From First Day Baptists),	———	1838,
Benjamin F. Bond,	Apl. 7,	1839,
(Dismissed Mar. 9, 1844, to Rock Co., Wis.),		
Frances Bond, (his wife),	Apl. 7,	1839,
David Dunn,	Apl. 7,	1839,
Charlotte Dunn, (his wife),	Apl. 7,	1839,
Sarah Dunn,	Apl. 7,	1839,
Richard C. Bond, Jr.,	Aug.	1844,
Jane Jones,	———	1850.

DEATHS.

ELISABETH DAVID, departed this life August 20, 1833. Aged 60 years, 2 months, 2 days.

REV. SAMUEL WOODBRIDGE, departed this life July 15, 1814.

NANCY NICHOLSON, departed this life February 22, 1834, in the 58th year of her age.

MARY GRIFFIN, departed this life May 25, 1835, in the 79th year of her age.

JOHN KILDOW, died February 9, 1839.

MRS. FRANCES W. BOND, died June 17, 1843, (wife of Benjamin F. Bond).

DANIEL G. W. DAVID, died May 7th, 1861, in the 94th year of his age.

LAST WILL AND TESTAMENT OF REV. SAMUEL WOODBRIDGE.

Recorded in the office of Register of Wills, Will Book No. 1, Uniontown, Pennsylvania.

"IN THE NAME OF GOD AMEN—

I SAMUEL WOODBRIDGE of Fayette County and State of Pennsylvania, Georges township, Mifflin Town, being well in body and of a sound mind and memory, blessed be God for all his favours through Christ his dear Son—, I do make and publish this my last will in the following manner, that is to say, after all my debts is paid—

"I will and bequeath unto my wife Anne Woodbridge all my real and personal estate during her natural life—provided she gives my mother Mary Woodbridge one feather bed and beding and a room with a fier place in it and fierwood and board during her natural life—.

"Likewise at the death of my wife Ann Woodbridge I impower her to dispose of my moveables at her pleasure. And if she makes know will I bequeath them to Woodbridge Oliphant and Julit Oliphant after they come of age—to be equally divided.

"I will unto my mother, Mary Woodbridge, provided she outlives my wife, Ann Woodbridge, the former privileges above mentioned to her and five pound per year and her fier wood cut and holed to my house, said five pounds is to buy her cloaths or what she may think best, to be paid by my executors or by my niece Sarah Oliphant who is to have possession of my estate. After the death of my wife, Ann Woodbridge, and at the death of said Sarah Oliphant, it is to be divided equally between her children—Woodbridge Oliphant & Julit Oliphant.

"Again after my death I bind either of the above mentioned persons that may possess my real estate to give when demanded of them, or either of them, to my sister's children, Elisabeth Brown, who died last year in New York, an in lot and out lot in Mifflin town, two to each child as they are laid out in the Plot of said town.

"I likewise will one half acre of land on which the meeting house stands, and an out lot, to the Seventh Day Baptis Church now metting at Mifflin town as it is laid off in the town plot to a pepole holding the following doctrins—

"*First*, The Doctrine of the Holy Trinity.

"*Second*, The fall of Man.

"*Third*, Recovery only by Christ's Holy Life and painfull death.

"*Fourth*, The doctrin of regeneration.

"*Fifth*, Perseverence of Saints.

"*Sixth*, The ten commandment law Recorded in Exd. 20 as a rule of life and practise— The Seventh day Sabbath as a day of rest from servile labour.

"*Seventh*, Belivers baptism only by dipping.

"*Eighth*, The eternal happiness of the Saints in heaven and the torments of the wicked in hell.

"I likewise will to Hanah Merideth, daughter of Davis Merideth, one lot containing one quarter of an acre fronting Anon street, North West side of said street, adjoining the land of James Tate—

"I likewise appoint Cornel Zeadock Springer [and] John Oliphant excutors, and my wife, Ann Woodbridge, executrix to this my last will,

"As witness my hand and seal this twentieth day of August, 1799—

"SAMUEL WOODBRIDGE (SEAL)

"Witness present
    "DAN. W. DAVID, 13th October 1814.
    "SAMUEL COOLEY, 30th Sept. 1814,
    "JEHU JOHN."

VI.

THE NEW SALEM CHURCH.

ROM the time the Shrewsbury Church left its old home in New Jersey, in September, 1789, until after its arrival at New Salem, Virginia, the church records are wholly silent, save for the death of William Davis, at White Day Creek, July 15, 1791.

The records begin anew as follows:—

"May the 13, 1792.

"The Church met in conference at New Salem, where the Church, or part of them, is now embodied; this being the first opportunity of coming under regular discipline in church order since we left New Jersey."

Henceforth the church abandoned the name of "Shrewsbury," and was known, first as the "New Salem," and afterward as the "Salem," Church, its present name.

Not all the company that originally set out from New Jersey, came to New Salem. Death had claimed some on the way, and others had selected homes by the wayside. Some had settled on the West Fork of the Monongahela River, a little south of the mouth of Ten Mile Creek, where a small stream known as Lamberts Run enters the West Fork River, at a distance of less than twenty miles from New Salem.

As early as June 28, 1793, a request was presented to the New Salem Church by these settlers at the mouth of Lamberts Run, to be organised into a separate church. This request was granted, and the West Fork River Church resulted, only to go crashing into oblivion a few years afterward, over the precipice of "open communion."

Soon after coming to its new home, the New Salem Church was called upon to mourn the loss by death of its pastor, Rev. Jacob Davis, who in the summer of 1793, went away on a missionary journey to Fayette County, Pennsylvania, where he was taken sick and died, July 17, of that year. He was buried in the graveyard adjoining the Seventh Day Baptist meeting house at Woodbridgetown.

Rev. Isaac Morris soon joined the West Fork River Church. On March 8, 1795, by vote of the church, Rev. John Patterson became pastor of the New Salem Church. At short intervals, Joseph Davis, Mosher Maxson, and Zebulon Maxson were all licenced to preach; and in 1801, John Davis was ordained pastor by Rev. Samuel Woodbridge of the Woodbrigetown church, and Rev. John Patterson. Two years afterward, Rev. John Patterson was debarred from communion because of a lack of loyalty to the church.

Meantime the church was kept busily occupied in dealing with members who were summoned before the bar of the church for petty, as well as for more serious, breaches of church discipline, besides performing the functions of the court of a justice of the peace. Business differences were regularly taken to the church, and members whose opinions of their respective pugilistic powers led them astray, were threated with the "awful sentence of excommunication," which appears in the records as late as November, 1822. At one time, the church ordered William Davis to make one hundred and sixty fence rails for one of his brethren, and Thomas Badcock (*sic*) was instructed not to pay a bill presented by James Maxson.

On July 8, 1798, Thomas Maxson and Jesse Maxson called upon the church to pass judgment upon the merits of a horse trade in which they were the principals. On another occasion, a member was denied the privileges of the church because he "hath challenged Salem Settlement in general for fighting, and the world at large." Again George Maxson brought complaint against several of his own brothers, concerning some business transactions, and the latter were

SALEM. LOOKING WEST.
(From a photograph taken about 1900).

ordered, each, to pay the former, three bushels and ten quarts of corn.

The second church meeting held at New Salem was called "to settle some business between Brother William Maxson and Mosher Maxson; and it was agreed that William Maxson return the slait [sic] to Mosher Maxson and pay twenty-eight shillings, and Mosher to return the ax and bettle rings to William Maxson."

The church quickly recognised the need of a house of worship in its new home, and soon took steps preparatory to building one. On June 13, 1795, the size and style of house were agreed upon, and a committee appointed to superintend its erection. Whether such a house was built or not does not appear from the records. At all events, on January 10, 1796, the church instructed the deacon to arrange for Thomas Babcock's house for a place of worship, and in case of failure to procure that, to obtain John Davis's. On August 9, 1801, the church voted to try to buy the house in which they met for worship, and offered fifty dollars ($50.00) for it. Either this offer was rejected, or the church after a little reflection, preferred to build a new house, for a week later, on August 16, the church voted to build a meeting house on the lower side of the burying ground.

Upon their arrival at New Salem, the new settlers had erected their cabins about a block-house, which they built for their mutual protection, a common kind of defence on the frontier in those times, but soon after Wayne's victory over the Indians, at the Maumee, in 1794, all danger from the savages passed away, and the settlers began to scatter to Buckeye Creek, Buckeye Run, Flint Run, Middle Island Creek, Meat House Fork, Greenbrier Run, Cherry Camp, Halls Run, etc.; so that before many years had passed, the New Salem Church, in order to accommodate the various groups of its members, some of whom were situated several miles distant from New Salem, maintained church services at Middle Island (now West Union), on Greenbrier Run, and on Halls Run. At Middle Island and on Greenbrier Run, log meeting houses were built. Business meetings were held in all three places, in turn with the village of New Salem. It is probable that communion service was likewise held at all these places.

In the meantime, the Bonds from Cecil County, Maryland, had arrived and settled on Lost Creek and Hackers Creek. They were joined by other members of the New Salem church, and in 1805, the Lost Creek Church was organised.

Rev. Peter Davis was received into the New Salem church sometime between August 16, 1807 and December 28, 1815, licenced to preach in 1819, and ordained as a duly accredited minister in December, 1823, at Middle Island, by Rev. John Davis and Rev. John Greene. Rev. John Greene, in company with Deacon Zaccheus Maxson, of Truxton, New York, at this time was on a missionary visit to the churches in western Virginia. Rev. Lewis A. Davis was ordained on January 15th, following, by Rev. John Davis and Rev. John Greene.

Previous to the visit of Rev. John Greene and Deacon Zaccheus Maxson, several missionary visits had been made to the New Salem and Lost Creek churches. In the winter of 1818-1819, Rev. Amos R. Wells, of Hopkinton, Rhode Island, and Rev. Samuel Davis, of Shiloh, New Jersey, had visited them. In the following summer, that of 1819, Rev. Amos R. Wells visited them again, and then once more in the summer of 1820. In 1821, Rev. John Davis and Deacon John Bright, both of Shiloh, New Jersey, visited these churches; and in the winter of 1821-1822, Rev. John Greene made them his first visit. These visits strengthened and encouraged both churches greatly.

Rev. Peter Davis engaged in pastoral work along with Rev. John Davis. Rev. Lewis A. Davis engaged in missionary work, giving his time largely to the interests of the Virginia churches for the first two or three years, and then transferring the field of his activity to the churches in Ohio, where he and his wife, Rebecca, transferred their membership from the New Salem Church to the Pike Church in 1833.

For a few years about this time, the New Salem Church enjoyed a season of great prosperity. From the Quarterly Meeting in November, 1829, until the Quarterly Meeting in February, 1830, a period of three months, seventy-two souls were added to the church.

In 1831, the Middle Island Church was organised with twenty-nine members drawn from the membership of the New Salem Church, and others soon followed. This church was

SALEM LOOKING EAST, SHOWING OIL WELLS IN WEST END.
(From a photograph taken in autumn of 1904).

located at Lewisport (now West Union), and included not only those who lived in that immediate vicinity, but those, also, who had settled on the Meat House Fork of Middle Island Creek. These settlers lived at a distance of from four to eight miles from Lewisport, and included the numerous Bee families, who with the Kelleys had come from near Salem, New Jersey.

The first book of records of the New Salem Church closes with the minutes of the church meeting held April 11, 1834, and contains the history of the church for a period of eighty-nine years.

A new record book was purchased, and the first entry made under date of February 10, 1833, fourteen months before the date of the final entry in the old book.

The over-lapping of records was due to some of the troubles which overtook the church about this time and pursued it for a period of twenty years; and at two different times shook it to its foundations. These troubles which appear to have been more or less closely related, seem to fall into three classes, as follows:—

Doctrinal, organic, and personal.

First. DOCTRINAL. Rev. Peter Davis had aroused distrust as to his orthodoxy as early as 1825, by the public avowal of certain beliefs concerning the immortality of the soul. For this, he was cited to appear before the bar of the church; and pending his trial, was barred from communion. After a space of nearly two years, the trouble was amicably adjusted by a joint committee of the New Salem and Lost Creek churches, which after listening to an exposition of his views, could find nothing unscriptural in them, whereupon the charges were dismissed, and he was restored to full communion with the church.

Again in 1834, a group of the membership living on Greenbrier Run, including Rev. Peter Davis and Ezekiel Bee, refused to abide by the covenant of the church, and declared themselves in favour of open communion. This defection caused anxiety for a time, but it finally subsided, and was forgotten in the excitement of more threatening events.

Second. ORGANIC. Early in the year 1834, complaint was made to the church, in church meeting, that two of its members had taken unlawful possession of the church book, and that a third member had circulated "a superscription to divide the church." At a subsequent meeting, the two members charged with seizing the church book were excommunicated. It was further decided that the third offender "should be dealt with for taking an active part in the division of the church."

The church was now in a state of chaos, and unable to decide for itself what its organic status was. It called in a committee, composed of members of the Lost Creek and Middle Island churches, which decided that although the seceding party was in possession of the records, it not only did not represent the original organisation, but it did not even have any accepted or legal standing, whatever, and could be treated only as a body of seceders. The decision of the joint committee was not satisfactory, and the church appealed to the General Conference, convened for its annual session at DeRuyter, New York, in September, 1834. The General Conference referred the questions involved to a special committee, consisting of William B. Maxson, Martin Wilcox, Daniel Coon, Joel Greene, and John Whitford. This committee reported as follows:—

"From sundry communications, it appears that a serious and unhappy difficulty exists in the Salem, Va., church, which in the opinion of the committee, is calculated to injure, if not to prostrate the interest and influence of the churches of our connection in that section of the country; and to us it appears that the difficulty is of a character which would render it very difficult to render them efficient aid by any written communications. We therefore, suggest to the General Conference, the propriety of sending two capable brethren to assist them in reconciling their difficulties, and restoring to them peace and good order; and that a letter be directed to be written to them, entreating them to desist from uncharitable and harsh proceedings, and advising them of the appointment of the committee to visit them."

The General Conference adopted the report of the special committee, and appointed as the committee to visit the New Salem Church, Joel Greene and Nathan V. Hull, with Alexander Campbell as alternate for Joel Greene.

But one member of the committee, Rev. Joel Greene, was able to visit Virginia, in accordance with the appointment of the General Conference. He was assisted in his duties, however, by Rev. Stillman Coon, who was at that time labouring among the Virginia churches.

At the annual session of the General Conference held in September, of the following year at Hopkinton, Rhode Island, Rev. Joel Greene, reported as follows:—

"The undersigned, one of the committee appointed last session to visit several Seventh Day Baptist churches in Virginia, beg leave to report that we have visited those churches, accompanied and assisted by Brother Stillman Coon, our missionary in that quarter, and after a very laborious and protracted investigation of the case of the New Salem Church, had the happiness to see those difficulties which so afflicted them and the friends of Zion in that country entirely removed and settled, the church again united and promising to live peaceably and usefully in the world.

"JOEL GREENE."

Third. PERSONAL. Disagreements and difficulties between individual members, were constantly brought before the church for adjustment; but for the most part, they in no way disturbed the equilibrium of the church. Nevertheless at about the time of the difficulties just described, several things conspired to make one of these personal difficulties an event of portentous importance.

With the establishment of the village of New Salem by the General Assembly of Virginia, and the attendant appointment of several members of the New Salem Church as trustees of the village, came a gradual recognition of the civil courts as the proper medium for the adjustment of business differences; and gradually disagreements growing out of business transactions ceased to be brought to the church for settlement. The growth of sentiment in favour of this new order of things was greatly facilitated by the fact that several members of the church were elected to the office of justice of the peace, in whose courts many of these cases were tried. Jonathan Fitz Randolph and Nathan Davis were two of the more prominent members of the church holding this office. It naturally followed, then, that even the more simple legal technicalities and formalities, such as are accepted as a mere matter of course by the average citizen of to-day, were more or less confusing to the minds of the many to whom such things were wholly new and strange, and it required several decades for them to become thoroughly acquainted with the new *régime.*

Along with the advent of the courts, with their more formal methods of transacting business, came a demand on the part of the more progressive business men of the church, that the business of the church should be conducted upon business principles, and that the church records should be made more complete, and more accurate. Complete the records never had been; and hazy, ambiguous, and indefinite they often were. The minutes of church meetings were originally written upon loose bits of paper, which were taken home by the clerk of the church and laid away to be transcribed at his convenience. Often they were mislaid, and the records written up from memory several weeks or months afterwards, or not transcribed at all. More often than otherwise, the minutes were not approved formally, by the church. This loose condition of the records was aggravated by the fact that the business meetings were held in different neighbourhoods by turn, several miles apart, necessitating several clerks *pro tempore*, who often acted for but a single day.

These facts will, at least partly, explain the fundamental causes of the troubles, the general details of which follow; troubles which again threatened the stability of the New Salem Church, and which not only brought that church into unpleasant relations with the Lost Creek Church, and the South-Western Association, but finally compelled the New Salem church to repudiate its second book of records, covering a period of upwards of thirteen years, as, in certain vital respects, entirely untrustworthy, and to confess itself wholly unable ever to correct the errors satisfactorily.

A careful study of the records has been made by the present writer, and untrustworthy as these records are, he believes that the essential facts in the controversy are set forth in this chapter.

At a business meeting of the church held on May 20, 1831, Joshua G. Davis preferred certain charges to the church against William F. Randolph. These charges grew out of a suit at law, before Nathan Davis, Esquire, a justice of the peace, in which both Joshua G. Davis and William F. Randolph were concerned. At the next business meeting of the church, all but one of the charges were dismissed. This charge was afterward referred to a committee of nine members, of which Rev. Peter Davis was chairman. This committee reported that in

THE NEW SALEM CHURCH

their opinion, an apology was due from William F. Randolph. This he declined to make, and, according to the record, on August 19, 1831, was debarred from communion.[1] After one or two further unsuccessful attempts to adjust the difficulty, William F. Randolph was excommunicated from the church, May 13, 1832. The affair remained in *statu quo* until August 9, 1835, when William F. Randolph appeared before the church and made a satisfactory acknowledgment. He was accordingly restored to membership, and the incident was considered closed.

On May 19, 1837, William F. Randolph called the attention of the church to the lack of completeness of the record concerning the dealings of the church with him.

Accordingly, the church requested Rev. Stillman Coon, who was labouring among the churches in western Virginia at that time, and Abel Bond of the Lost Creek Church, to examine the records and report to the church.

This committee rendered its report eleven months afterward, April 20, 1838, as follows:—

"To the New Salem Church; Dear Brethren:— Your Committee appointed to examine the records of the proceedings of the church in the case of the deal with William F. Randolph, beg leave to report, [that] after careful examination, we are utterly unable to ascertain the nature of the complaint preferred against him by Joshua Davis, neither anything definite of the travissing [*sic*] the case; only that a committee was appointed to act upon it, who brought him in guilty of something indefinable, upon which he was excommunicated.

"It is our opinion that every subject taken up in church meeting, should be distinctly stated, as also every act of the church thereon, and in this manner carried on to the book, so that any person reading can understand it; and we believe any church greatly in fault, that suffers their clerk to remain negligent of this duty, and now if the records can be so rectified as to make the case appear in its true colours, we would advise that it be done.

"Yours in the Gospel,
"Stillman Coon,
"Abel Bond."

The church now appointed a committee of five members, with Rev. Peter Davis as chairman, to correct the records. The report of this committee was unsatisfactory, and was not

---

[1]. This record, it will be observed further on in this chapter, was afterward discredited by the church itself.

adopted. Then followed three more abortive attempts to correct the records.

In the meantime, William F. Randolph had been admitted to membership in the Lost Creek Church, March 8, 1840, with the result that the New Salem Church, on November 19, 1840, voted to inquire of the Lost Creek Church as to the regularity of its action. For, according to the records of the New Salem Church, William F. Randolph had been excommunicated a second time on February 14, 1840, some three weeks before the date of his admission to membership in the Lost Creek Church.

After a lengthy correspondence, covering about a year, the New Salem and Lost Creek churches referred the difference between the two churches to a committee of six, consisting of two members of the South Fork of Hughes River Church (formerly members of the New Salem Church), one member of the New Salem Church, and three members of the Lost Creek Church. The New Salem and Lost Creek churches bound themselves to abide by the decision of the committee.

This committee promptly set about its work, and on December 16, 1841, reported as follows:—

"THE REPORT OF THE JOINT COMMITTEE APPOINTED BY THE LOST CREEK AND NEW SALEM CHURCHES.

"December 6, 1841.

"Agreeable to the former arrangements of the New Salem and Lost Creek churches, the Committee appointed to adjust the difficulty existing between the two churches in regard to the reception of Bro. Wm. F. Randolph, met and the grounds of dissatisfaction were presented, which was the receiving of an excluded member into the Lost Creek Church. In answer to the above complaint, preferred against us by the Salem Church, we, the Lost Creek Church, consider we are justifiable in receiving Bro. Randolph, both in point of legality and necessity.

"*1st.* It was legal because we know of no circumstances that should debar him from the privileges of the connection; and

"*2nd.* We understand that the doors of the Salem Church were open for him to come in. The Committee jointly agree that the grounds of dissatisfaction with the Lost Creek Church were not of such a nature as they supposed. By comparing the dates of the records, we find that he was received before the case was re-acted upon by the Salem Church, and Bro. Randolph set back. The Committee, therefore,

"*Resolve,* That by comparing and examining the records, that the

THE NEW SALEM CHURCH

minutes of Feb. 1840, so much as relates to Bro. Randolph, should be transferred to the minutes of the May meeting, where they seem to belong.

"And we certify that the differences between the two churches are hereby amicably settled.

"Given under our hands this the day and date above written.

"JOSHUA S. DAVIS,
"LODOWICK H. DAVIS,
"EZEKIEL BEE,
"ABEL BOND,
"LEVI H. BOND,
"ELI BOND.
"*Committee.*

From this report, it will be seen that the trouble between the two churches was due to gross inaccuracies in the records of the New Salem Church. The Lost Creek Church, as its records showed, instead of admitting William F. Randolph to membership some three weeks after he had been excommunicated from the New Salem Church, really had admitted him to membership while he was a member in good standing in the New Salem Church, and more than two months before the New Salem Church voted to excommunicate him.

Thus the differences between the New Salem and Lost Creek churches were amicably adjusted, but the relations between William F. Randolph and the New Salem Church were more strained than ever.

The original charge presented to the church by Joshua G. Davis against William F. Randolph, had never been recorded. After having been lost for ten years, it was found among the papers of Joshua G. Davis after his death, and presented to the church, August 19, 1841, and ordered placed on record, more than a year after William F. Randolph had been excommunicated from the New Salem Church the second time.

On January 13, 1842, four weeks after the report of the joint committee of the New Salem and Lost Creek churches had been presented, correcting an error of date in the records of the New Salem Church, the church itself recorded the proof of another error, by declaring that William F. Randolph had not been debarred from communion, August 19, 1831, for refusing to comply with a recommendation of the committee considering his case, as the committee in question *had made no report on that date.*

The New Salem Church now appointed another committee to settle its differences with William F. Randolph, and two more efforts were made within four months to settle the difficulty, but without avail.

On the 18th day of October, 1843, William F. Randolph carried the case to the South-Western Association, at that time in session at Lost Creek, Virginia.

The Association appointed a committee, consisting of Rev. Thomas B. Brown and Benjamin Franklin Bond, to take the case into consideration. The committee drafted a report, which was submitted to the New Salem Church, December 21, 1843. The church protested that the association had overstepped its constitutional jurisdiction in taking up the case. This action by the church was displeasing to several of its members, who had hoped that through the intercession of the association, an amicable adjustment of the whole unfortunate affair might be reached. As a result their disappointment was bitter, and in the heated condition of feeling then prevalent, disruption again threatened the church.

The committee appointed by the association in 1843, failed to report to that body, which at its annual session held at Jackson Centre, Ohio, in October, 1844, appointed another committee to take the matter under consideration. This committee consisted of Rev. Joel Greene and Lewis Bond. They were empowered to add another member to the committee, if they deemed it necessary.

The new committee reported to the association at its next annual session, held with the New Salem Church, beginning October 8, 1845. The consideration of the report, which was hotly discussed, occupied the attention of the association for the greater part of each of two consecutive days, when, goaded almost to desperation, that body peremptorily took the following drastic action:—

"*Whereas,* Difficulties of a withering nature are existing in the Association, growing out of action in the affair of dealing in the case of William F. Randolph, which are injuring our influence and usefulness in the vineyard of our Lord, and investigation seems impracticable under existing circumstances; therefore

"RESOLVED, That this Association close and settle this matter, to be considered as finally settled from this time forward, and that papers that may be in the hands of individuals, or elsewhere, relating

THE NEW SALEM CHURCH 95

to the affair (not including dockets of the Association or churches, already recorded), be burned, and that it shall be a disorderly act of any individual or individuals, ever to move, either in the Association or elsewhere, the matter, and be dealt with accordingly as disorderly persons, and that we mutually forgive each other anything that may have been a cause of hard feelings, and strive for the future to cultivate brotherly love."

Radical as the action of the association was, all parties concerned bowed in meek submission. Four weeks after the final adjournment of the association, the New Salem Church met, purged its records of condemnation of members who, as individuals, were parties to the controversy, restored William F. Randolph to full fellowship with the church, and in accordance with the action of the association, *"passed a resolution that all the papers in the church docket and elsewhere not being a matter of record, pertaining to the case, be burnt, and the matter be finally settled from this day forward, and any individual stirring up anything pertaining to the case, either directly or indirectly, or make any move thereabout in the church, or elsewhere, hereafter, shall be considered an offender, and dealt with accordingly."*[1]

For one year longer, or until November 15, 1846, the record book in use for the past fourteen years, nearly, continued in use. On this date, a special business meeting of the church was called, upon the request of Rev. Peter Davis, Lodowick H. Davis, and Jonathan F. Randolph, when the following action was taken and recorded in a new book:—

"*Whereas,* Unfavourable difficulties have occurred in the Seventh Day Baptist Church at New Salem, from some derangement in the church record, and doubting that they can ever be properly revised or arranged or corrected; we therefore

"RESOLVE, To lay them by in safe keeping, commencing anew to try to keep a correct record, resolving in the future to discharge our duty to God and each other, as He has required us in His Word, leaving all past difficulties that have ever occurred in the church, considering it a breach of the covenant in any member to mention past difficulties to the disturbance of any member of the church, resolving to keep strict gospel order, as a Gospel-organised church, at least as far as we can.

"RESOLVED, That we procure a new book for the use of the church."

---

1. Quoted from the records of the New Salem Church.

Thus was finally laid away the second book of records of the New Salem Church, a book whose false and discredited contents kept the church in a state of internal dissension for a period of thirteen years, disturbed the peaceful relations of the New Salem Church with at least two of its sister churches, and claimed the attention of the South-Western Association for three consecutive years. Its records, however, whose inaccuracies and careless entries none but the pen of the Recording Angel can ever blot out, have passed into history. In fact, they are history; and when read aright in the larger sense, they portray the most awful struggle in the eventful history of the New Salem Church during the more then a century and a half that has elapsed since it was constituted in 1745.

Rev. John Davis, so long the pastor of the church, passed to his eternal reward, June 22, 1842, and Rev. Peter Davis, who for many years had performed the most of the duties of the pastor of the church, now assumed sole charge.

The old hewed log meeting house had undergone extensive repairs, and many alterations had been made. But it was dark, gloomy, and forbidding at best.

The business meetings and communion services were held at New Salem, but monthly meetings were held on Greenbrier Run, Meat House Fork, and Buckeye Run.

In 1850, Rev. Azor Estee began his labours among the churches in western Virginia, and the New Salem Church received its share of his ministrations. In 1856, Rev. David Clawson came, and finally determined to make his home there permanently, devoting his time for the most part, to the needs of the New Salem and Lost Creek churches. But death soon claimed him, and he passed to his eternal reward, March 6, 1860. His last resting place was chosen in the graveyard adjoining the Old Frame Meeting House at Lost Creek, where his grave is marked by a suitable monument, bearing a record of his earthly labours, erected by the New Salem and Lost Creek churches, jointly.

About this time, Rev. Peter Davis, who was still the acknowledged pastor of the New Salem Church, declined to officiate at the communion service, which he held had been "fulfilled and had passed away," and for that reason was no longer binding. As a result, the communion service was omitted for a few times; but it was soon resumed, since the new doctrine, as held by the pastor, did not find favour with the church. After a year or two, however, the pastor, weighed down by the infirmities of advancing years, and still adhering to his newly-found views concerning the communion service, was relieved of his active duties. He received, nevertheless, a vote of respect, confidence, and esteem from the church, which he had served so long and so faithfully.

Thus harmlessly died away the last ripple of doctrinal excitement that disturbed the serenity of the church.

In 1858, a new house of worship had been completed, and a commendable spirit of activity in church work prevailed among the members of the church.

The first years of the second half of the nineteenth century had witnessed a wave of educational enthusiasm, which culminated in the West Union Academy, sweep over the church. When it subsided a few years afterward, and the West Union Academy was abandoned, several of the young people who had been students of the defunct academy, members of the New Salem Church, went away to Alfred Academy, now Alfred University, at Alfred, New York.

The Civil War soon followed, bringing in its wake ruin and subsequent depression, as the church was on the border over-lapped by the activities of both armies.

In 1866, Rev. Walter B. Gillette made his first visit to West Virginia as a missionary. His coming was a God-send to all the churches there, but especially so to the New Salem Church. In 1870, he again visited this field, and assisted in the organisation of the Ritchie and Greenbrier churches, both of which drew from the membership of the New Salem Church. The Greenbrier Church was constituted almost wholly of members of the New Salem Church.

Rev. Charles A. Burdick came upon the West Virginia field as a general missionary in October, 1870, soon after the close of the labours of Rev. Walter B. Gillette. He established his residence and headquarters at New Salem, and when a few years afterwards he engaged in educational work, the house of worship of the New Salem Church served as the building in which he conducted his select school at New Salem.

Ever since 1854, when he was called to serve the church as its assistant pastor, Rev. Samuel D. Davis had ministered to the church from time to time. Jacob Davis, Lewis F. Randolph, and Judson F. Randolph had been licenced to preach, and had participated in the pastoral work of the church. Jacob Davis and Lewis F. Randolph were both ordained and set apart to the work of the Gospel ministry, each after a satisfactory term of probation as a licentiate.

The church was sadly in need of a pastor who could give his entire time and strength to the work, but financial weakness was a strong barrier to such a plan. In April, 1876, however, Rev. Samuel D. Davis entered upon a term of service as pastor of the church, giving his entire time to the duties of his office, at a salary of four hundred dollars a year. This was the first time the church had ever employed a pastor, upon a stated salary, to give his entire time to church work. He served the church most satisfactorily in this manner, for a period of three years; but the church ran steadily behind in its finances. After the close of Rev. Samuel D. Davis's pastorate, Rev. Uri M. Babcock was engaged as pastor, four members making themselves personally responsible for his salary for one year. During the second year of his term of service, the finances of the church became so badly involved, that he resigned to accept a call to the pastorate of another church.

For a period of several years, now, the church struggled against a strong tide of discouragement. It was embarrassed because of strained relations with a sister church, occasioned by a series of unfortunate misunderstandings, which became the subject of consideration at the hands of the General Conference. Members living at a distance from New Salem removed their membership to churches nearer home. Among these was the faithful clerk of the church, Franklin F. Randolph, who had kept the records for a period of twenty-eight years, and who in storm and sunshine alike, the mountainous roads often all but impassable, had ridden on horseback or, as was often necessary, had traveled on foot from his home ten miles away at New Milton, to attend the business meetings of the church.

But the dawn of a brighter day was at hand. Again the

interest of the Seventh Day Baptists in West Virginia in education was becoming aroused, and the long-cherished plan of establishing a denominational school at Salem began to take definite shape; with the result that in the spring of 1889, Salem Academy, soon afterward changed to Salem College, was opened under the temporary leadership of Rev. John L. Huffman, who was at that time serving the New Salem Church as its pastor. A president was soon obtained for the college, in the person of Rev. Sanford L. Maxson, the principal of Albion Academy, at Albion, Wisconsin.

In 1890, Rev. Theodore L. Gardiner became pastor of the church, which soon afterward entered upon a period of unprecedented prosperity.

During the year 1891-1892, the church became a corporate body, for the first time in its history, its legal business having been done previously by a board of trustees appointed by the courts.

The first of August, 1902, finds the church with a new brick house of worship of modern design, and a well appointed parsonage with commodious grounds; the church itself prospering spiritually and financially under the efficient leadership of its zealous pastor, Rev. Ellis A. Witter.

COMMUNION SERVICE; AND QUARTERLY AND YEARLY MEETINGS.

On July 12, 1746, the church voted that on the third Sabbath in September following, there should be a communion service, and that after that, communion service should occur once in two months, beginning with the last Sabbath in October, "that being the day of communion in Westerly," Rhode Island, whence the church had come.

At the same time, it was voted that church meeting be held at the place of communion service, on the Third Day of the week before communion. Not having a meeting house, the church met for worship at the homes of its members, in turn, where communion service and church meeting were held likewise.

The church meeting was afterward changed from the Third Day to the Fifth Day, of the week, for the convenience of the members living at Middletown.

March 3, 1775, the church voted that church meeting should be held the last First Day of the week in every month, and that communion service should occur the last Sabbath in November, February, May, and August respectively.

One year afterward, March 3, 1776, the Quarterly Meeting was changed to the third Sabbath in February, May, and August. The November meeting, which was also the Yearly Meeting of the church, was changed to the first Sabbath of the month, in order to escape, if possible, the bad weather that marked the end of autumn and the beginning of winter, and thereby secure as large an attendance as possible from Middletown.

On December 28, 1815, a quarter of a century and more after the church had left Shrewsbury to settle in Virginia, a discussion arose as to whether the Quarterly Meetings should be continued or not. It was finally decided that they should be continued, and that they should be held at William Davis's on Middle Island.

On May 14, 1819, the church voted that the Quarterly Meetings should alternate between William Davis's on Middle Island, and George Davis's near New Salem, and that church meetings should be held on the First Day of the week preceding communion service.

On August 16, 1822, it was voted that the Yearly Meeting should be held on the third Sabbath in September following, at New Salem.

During the next thirty-seven years the records are silent concerning the Quarterly Meeting. But during that time, it gradually came about that the Quarterly Meetings were all, or practically all, held at New Salem; and the church meetings were held on the Sixth Day of the week preceding communion, thus merging the church meeting into the Quarterly Meeting.

On August 19, 1859, the New Salem Church received a communication from the Lost Creek Church, suggesting that the two churches unite in a joint Yearly Meeting, and stating that the date for holding the Yearly Meeting at Lost Creek had been changed from the second Sabbath in August to the second Sabbath in September, as the latter date was that of the regular communion service.

The New Salem Church acquiesced in the proposed union, but named the third Sabbath in August as the date for the

THE OLD LOG CHURCH AT NEW SALEM.
(After a pencil sketch by Corliss F. Randolph).

THE NEW SALEM CHURCH

Yearly Meeting, when it should be held at New Salem, as that date coincided with that of the August Quarterly Meeting.

On May 19, 1865, the New Salem Church took the following action:—

"*Whereas*, We believe it would add to the interest of our church meetings, and promote the cause of the Redeemer by having preaching before entering into business; therefore

"RESOLVED, That our business meetings on each quarterly occasion, be opened by a short sermon."

This practise was carried out for a time, but it gradually fell into disuse. Aside from this, and the fact that the church meetings were finally changed from the Sixth Day, to the First Day, of the week preceding communion service, the Quarterly Meeting has been practically unchanged for a full half century.

FAST DAYS.

After the removal of the church to New Salem, the following records appear concerning fast days:—

November 18, 1819. The church appointed the following Third Day of the week as a day of fasting and prayer, the meeting to be held at the home of Jonathan F. Randolph.

July 17, 1829. The third Sabbath in August following, was set apart as a fast day.

MEMBERSHIP IN SUPERIOUR BODIES.

Association in New Jersey.[1]

At a meeting of the New Salem Church held July 13, 1794, the following action was taken:—

"The first thing came under consideration was whether we should send meeting-goers to the Association to New Jersey, or whether we should only send letters. Agreed to send letters annually, and meeting-goers, when there is opportunity."

The foregoing action, it will be observed, is dated eight years before the organisation of the Seventh Day Baptist General Conference.

General Conference.

The Seventh Day Baptist General Conference at its annual session held with the church at Cohansey (now

---

1. This "Association in New Jersey" was doubtless the Yearly Meeting, which in 1788 had been in existence for several years. Bailey conjectures that it dates back to 1734. It is represented at the present time by the Yearly Meeting of the Seventh Day Baptist Churches of New Jersey and New York City. Cf. Bailey's *History of the Seventh Day Baptist General Conference*, pp. 24 *et. seq.* Toledo, Ohio, 1866.

Shiloh), New Jersey, beginning September 10, 1807, in addition to the annual circular letter addressed *"to our well beloved brethren and sisters of the same faith and order of the Gospel, who are scattered up and down in the United States of America,"* took the following action:—

"VOTED, That the letter for opening the correspondence with our brethren in the Western parts of America, be left to the care and inspection of the church at Cohansey."

As the result of the invitation contained in the letter provided for in the foregoing action, Rev. John Davis, the pastor of the New Salem and Lost Creek churches, appeared at the next annual session of the General Conference, held with the church at Hopkinton, Rhode Island, beginning September 8, 1808, as the representative of these churches, bearing a petition from them both for membership in the General Conference. Their request was granted, and the New Salem, as well as the Lost Creek Church, has maintained its membership in that body continuously ever since.

In its application for membership in the General Conference, the New Salem Church reported a total membership of thirty-eight. This, it will be remembered, was after the organisation of the West Fork River and the Lost Creek churches, both of which drew largely from the parent church.

Western Association.

At its regular quarterly business meeting held May 19, 1837, the New Salem Church voted to request admission to membership in the recently organised Western Association. The communication addressed by the church to the association at its annual session held with the church at Alfred, New York, beginning June 28, 1837, was received too late to be considered at that session. But at the next annual session, the application was presented, and the church admitted to membership. The application for membership showed an aggregate number of seventy-seven members of the church at that time. That was a few years after the organisation of the Middle Island Church, which was composed almost, if not quite. wholly of former members of the New Salem Church.

South-Western Association.

The newly organised South-Western Association, composed of the churches of Virginia and Ohio, besides that of

INTERIOR OF OLD LOG CHURCH AT NEW SALEM.
(After a pencil sketch by Corliss F. Randolph).

Woodbridgetown, Pennsylvania, met for its first annual session (at which its organisation was concluded), with the Lost Creek Church, August 7, 1839. The New Salem Church, although in the throes of internal dissension, took a prominent part in the formation of the new association.

Virginia Association.

When, in 1850, the South-Western Association voted to separate into two bodies, the Virginia and the Ohio associations, with the Ohio River as the boundary separating the two organisations, the New Salem Church at once swung into line, and remained an active, loyal member of the Virginia Association, until the latter collapsed, and by the mutual consent of the churches composing it, dissolved, in 1855.

Eastern Association.

Immediately after the dissolution of the Virginia Association, the New Salem and Lost Creek churches, which, despite occasional differences and friction between themselves, have always been drawn together by a strong, common bond of sympathy and mutual protection, at once made application for membership in the Eastern Association at the annual session of that body, held with the church at Shiloh, New Jersey, in May, 1856, and sent Rev. Samuel D. Davis, as a joint delegate, to bear the petitions of both churches. These petitions at once precipitated a spirited debate upon the reputed attitude of these churches toward the question of slavery, a subject which is treated in a subsequent chapter of this book. The petitions of both churches, however, were finally granted.

Two years afterward, the New Salem Church appointed a committee to consider the propriety of withdrawing from membership in the Eastern Association, so unpleasant had the slavery discussion become. Through the intervention, however, of Rev. David Clawson, who had recently come among the Virginia churches from New Jersey, no further action was taken. The church, nevertheless, maintained a position of dignified silence until 1867, after the hateful question of human slavery in the United States of America had passed into history, at the awful price of the Civil War.

Active communication was now resumed with the Eastern Association by the New Salem Church until after the organisation of the

South-Eastern Association.

In the organisation of the South-Eastern Association in January, 1872, at Lost Creek, the New Salem Church took the initial steps; and it has maintained an influential position in the affairs of the association ever since.

MEETING HOUSES OF THE NEW SALEM CHURCH.

After the arrival of the church at its new home at New Salem in western Virginia, it reverted to the plan originally followed in New Jersey of holding its meetings for worship and business in the homes of its members.

On the 12th of April, 1795, the church considered the propriety of erecting a house of worship. On the 10th of May, following, it was determined to build a meeting house in the following autumn. Two months afterward, in June, it was determined to build a house, twenty-four feet long by twenty feet wide, and that a foundation should be laid for galleries. The meeting house was to be covered with a cabin roof, and the deacons were instructed to keep a strict account of every man's work, so that each one should do an equal part.

Straightway, there arose a question as to the authority of the church to allow churches of other denominations to worship in the new meeting house, but on the 11th of July, 1793, after a spirited discussion, it was voted that the church had authority to prohibit other societies from using the meeting house.

Whether this house was never completed, or whether it was destroyed by fire soon after its completion, does not appear from the records. At all events, we find that on January 10, 1796, the deacons of the church were instructed to try to obtain permission to use the house of Thomas Babcock for worship, and in the event of failure to secure that, the house of John Davis was to be used for that purpose.

On August 9th, 1801, the church voted to try to buy the house in which meetings were held, and voted to pay fifty dollars ($50) for the house and lot.

A week afterward, August 16th, the church voted to build a meeting house on the burying ground, twenty-eight feet long by twenty-two feet in width, with galleries. Nathan Davis and Thomas Clayton were appointed trustees to have

THE NEW SALEM CHURCH.
(Frame Building).

charge of the work, and for their services they were to receive four shillings and sixpence a day and "find themselves."

Nathan Davis moved away to his farm at Lewisport (now West Union, in Doddridge County); and on November 8, 1801, William Davis, the clerk of the church, was appointed to assist Thomas Babcock in superintending the erection of the building. On August 12, 1804, the church appointed a day on which to meet and settle with the trustees for their services.

On the 19th of May, 1820, Nathan Davis and Jesse Davis were appointed to wait upon the venerable founder of the village of New Salem, Samuel Fitz Randolph, and get the deeds for the meeting house and grave yard lots. The deeds were executed by Samuel Fitz Randolph for "in lot" number 26, under date of September 5, 1803, and by Nathan Davis for "in lot" number 27,[1] under date of March 14, 1811, these lots embracing the church yard and grave yard.

This meeting house was built of hewed logs. In the middle was a chimney with a double fireplace to supply heat. The crevices between the logs were filled with sticks and clay mortar. After it had been completely renovated, and at least three new windows and one new door added, it was described by Rev. Thomas E. Babcock, who visited it in 1853, as follows:—

"The Meeting House is an ancient looking structure of hewed logs. There is a gallery in it, which, however, seems to have fallen into disuse. The gloomy aspect of the house is, perhaps, too true an index to the condition of the church. It is a sad picture, to see a church that has stood the vicissitudes of more than a century, feebly struggling for existence."

On the 14th of June, 1839, Jonathan F. Randolph, Peter Davis, and Jepthah F. Randolph, who had been appointed a committee to examine the meeting house, reported to the church "that there had better be two new logs put in the west end, and all the old chunking knocked out clean, and then fill up all the cracks with stone, lime, and sand; weatherboard [clapboard] the west end; cut a window in the south side on the left of the door, as well as one in the east end, and one in the west end; ceil it all below the joists; make a stairway;

---
1. "In lot" number 27, had been conveyed to Nathan Davis, Sr., by Samuel Fitz Randolph, by a deed bearing date, February 13, 1796..

throw out the chimney and put in a stove; lay the upper floor down snug; make seats; repair the gable ends, etc."

The church as thus repaired served until 1857, when at a meeting held on the 15th day of May, it was voted to erect a frame building, forty-six feet long by twenty-eight feet wide, and twelve feet from the floor to the ceiling, with a vestibule ten feet deep. This building was completed and dedicated on the 19th of August, 1858, the dedicatory sermon being preached by Rev. David Clawson. The total net cost of the new building was eight hundred dollars ($800.00).

The frame building served as a house of worship until 1899, when on the 13th of August of that year, the church gave instructions to its building committee to remove the old meeting house and proceed to erect upon the same site, where the old log house had also stood, a new edifice, to be constructed of brick. On the 30th of December, 1900, the old building was sold to Jesse F. Randolph, one of the members of the church, for the sum of fifty dollars ($50.00), with the understanding that it was to be torn down and taken away. The new church was completed at a cost of seven thousand dollars ($7,000.00), and dedicated at the time of the annual session of the South-Eastern Association, which met with the church at Salem, in May, 1901. The dedicatory sermon was preached by the Reverend Abram Herbert Lewis, D.D., of Plainfield, New Jersey, the Corresponding Secretary of the American Sabbath Tract Society, and Editor of the *Sabbath Recorder*.

As the people began to go out from New Salem, soon after its settlement, to settle at various points in the surrounding country, they formed various other little settlements, ranging in distance from three or four miles, to ten or twelve miles, from New Salem, and the meeting house. These little groups found it practically impossible to attend church at New Salem with any regularity, and consequently began to hold Sabbath services in their own settlements, using the homes of various ones of their number as meeting places.

In the early days, such services were held at Lewisport (now West Union), and on Greenbrier Run, Halls Run, and Lamberts Run. In the course of time, stated meetings of the church were held at these places.

THE SALEM CHURCH.

As these settlements grew, they began to feel the need of houses of worship in their midst, and the need was met in some places by the erection of meeting houses which were the property of the church.

The first of these meeting houses to be built was at Lewisport, where three brothers, Nathan, Joseph, and William Davis had purchased twenty thousand (20,000) acres of land and settled for their homes. Here upon a little bluff, only a stone's throw from the very verge of the banks of the Middle Island Creek, a rude log meeting house was erected, and a grave yard established upon the lands of Joseph Davis. This was probably built some time during the first decade of the nineteenth century, and was doubtless a crude affair of round, unhewed logs, with a cabin roof. After a few years, this gave way to another log structure, which too had fallen into decay, not many years after the first quarter of the century had passed.

After the organisation of the Middle Island Church at Lewisport was finally consummated in 1832, the New Salem Church relinquished all claim to the property in favour of the Middle Island Church. The latter church obtained legal title to the meeting house lot and grave yard from Joseph Davis, the former owner of the land, under date of March 31, 1858. The Middle Island Church still retains possession of this property, all of which is now used as a grave yard, where are buried several members of early Seventh Day Baptist families who lived in that locality.

Another meeting house was built on Greenbrier Run, on the hillside across the valley, about opposite the house in which John Williams lived for some thirty years.

This meeting house was a very small building of hewed logs, with a cabin roof; and a chimney, with an open fireplace in the north-east corner of the single room of the interior. The building faced the west, and stood on the land of John Sutton, who made a deed for it, in 1841, to Jonathan F. Randolph and Peter Davis, as trustees of the New Salem Church. The lot was seventeen and a half rods long by eleven rods wide, and was surveyed on the 31st of January, 1841, by William F. Randolph.

This lot was sold and a new one purchased of Rev. Peter

Davis, a mile or two further up Greenbrier Run. The new lot was in turn exchanged for one a few rods further up on the hillside, and the log house first built on the lot obtained from John Sutton was moved to the new location. The building was enlarged by a "Yankee-frame" (plank) addition, and then stood until about 1880, when the present house of worship of the Greenbrier Church was erected. The old meeting house was then torn down, and the logs used for building a barn on the farm of Jesse Clark, one of the deacons of the Greenbrier Church.

At a business meeting of the New Salem Church, held on November 18, 1870, it was voted that the house and lot on Greenbrier Run belonging to the New Salem Church, be conveyed by deed to certain trustees for the use of the Greenbrier Church, which had been organised on the 24th of the preceding September, inasmuch as forty-three of the forty-six members of the new church had been members of the New Salem Church.

Owing to delay occasioned by legal technicalities and other causes, it was not until the first of March, 1880, that the New Salem Church formally relinquished all right and title to the property in favour of the Greenbrier Church.

The foregoing are all the houses of worship ever owned by the New Salem Church, after its removal to western Virginia.

Although as early as November 11, 1804, the church voted to hold meetings on Halls Run, no meeting house was ever built in that locality by the New Salem Church.

The church maintained services at different other places, some, at least, of which were as follows:— For many years on the Meat House Fork of Middle Island Creek, at the present location of the Middle Island Church; and for several years, each, on Buckeye Run, Long Run, and Flint Run; but at none of these places did the New Salem Church build a meeting house. When the present house of worship of the Middle Island Church was built, half of the church lot was donated by Jepthah F. Randolph, one of the deacons of the New Salem Church, and he and his family, as well as other members of the New Salem Church living in that vicinity, contributed liberally toward the cost of the building.

At all these outlying stations where the New Salem

THE PARSONAGE AT SALEM.

Church maintained services, with the exception of Lewisport and Greenbrier Run, dwelling house and school houses were, for the most part, used for places of meeting for religious service.

The logs of the old meeting house torn down at New Salem in 1857 to make room for the new frame building, were sold to Elmore B. Hursey, Esq., for the sum of twenty-five dollars ($25.00), and removed to a point on the other side of the valley about half a mile distant from the site where the meeting house stood, and left to lie on the ground until they decayed and disappeared.

The logs of the meeting house at Lewisport, decayed and disappeared from view half a century ago.

The old frame meeting house at New Salem, as already related, was sold to Jesse F. Randolph, Esq., one of the active members of the church, for the sum of fifty dollars ($50.00), with the express understanding that he should demolish it.

The old school house in which meetings were held on Meat House Fork, and which stood by the roadside almost directly in front of the present house of worship of the Middle Island Church, on completion of the new building, was sold at public auction to Jepthah F. Randolph for the sum of four dollars ($4.00), and removed by him to his home half a mile away and converted into a farm building. This old school house, together with the old log meeting house on Greenbrier Run, which was removed to the farm of Jesse Clark, are the only survivors of the old buildings used by the New Salem Church as houses of worship, with the exception of the Old Township Hall at New Milton, a mile and a half distant from the present house of worship of the Middle Island Church. This still stands near its original site, but has been converted into a farm building.

PARSONAGE.

There is no record of any action on the part of the church to provide its pastor with a home at any time during its sojourn of nearly half a century in New Jersey.

The first action taken by the church toward providing a home for any one performing ministerial labour among them was on the 14th of May, 1824, when the church voted to raise money by subscription to build a home for Rev. John Greene at Quiet Dell, on Elk Creek. Quiet Dell was the home of Abel

Bond, one of the prominent members of the Lost Creek Church. His was the first Seventh Day Baptist home within the bounds of the New Salem and Lost Creek churches reached by the missionaries sent to western Virginia from the churches in the north and east; at the same time it constituted a central point from which they could work to advantage within the bounds of both churches.

Apparently, however, the house was not completed in time to be used until the second visit of Alexander Campbell, in the summer of 1834. Even then it appears to have been built almost, if not quite, wholly, by Abel Bond, himself. Campbell says,

"That good man, Deacon Abel Bond, had built a nice little house in his spacious yard, during my absence, for the accommodation of whoever might be their future missionary. He said to me (my wife and son of five years being with me):—'The new house [which] I have built is your own home while you choose to occupy it; but you will take your meals with my family.' The house was furnished with a good bed, chairs, and a writing table, with plenty of stationery."

Whether the New Salem Church really contributed to the cost of this little home for missionaries at Quiet Dell, or not, it is nevertheless true that the vote taken on the 14th of May, 1824, is all the action of that church recorded looking toward a home for any one performing ministerial labour within its bounds for almost, if not quite, a round century after its arrival at New Salem.[1]

On the 2d of November, 1890, a call was extended to Rev. Theodore L. Gardiner, at that time pastor of the church at Shiloh, New Jersey, to become the pastor of the New Salem Church at a stated salary, besides a suitable home. Two or three weeks afterward, it was announced that the call had been accepted, and action was taken looking toward the erection of a parsonage. A year later the parsonage was practically completed. The total cost of the pastor's home, including land, house, and barn, was sixteen hundred dollars ($1,600.00).

MINISTERS.

The following is an abstract from the records of the

---

1. When Rev. Charles A. Burdick closed his labours in West Virginia, and arranged to remove from the state, he offered his residence at New Salem, near the meeting house, to the Nw Salem Church for use as a parsonage. Although the offer met with favour, it was finally decided not to accept it.

RESIDENCE OF REV. CHARLES A. BURDICK AT NEW SALEM.
(After a photograph taken in 1890).

THE NEW SALEM CHURCH

church concerning its ministers, including pastors and other ordained ministers of the church, as well as members licenced to preach:—

May 11, 1794. Rev. Isaac Morris was dismissed to join the West Fork River Church.

December 14, 1794. A request was presented from the West Fork River Church for assistance to excommunicate Rev. Isaac Morris. "Agreed to send them a letter directing them to take the Gospel rule, according to their articles [of faith]."

March 8, 1795. Rev. John Patterson was given pastoral care of the church.

January 10, 1796. Joseph Davis applied for, and received, a call "to improve his gift in the work of the Gospel."

May 13, 1798. Joseph Davis was silenced until further action of the church.

November 14, 1798. Zebulon Maxson was given a call to preach, and Joseph Davis "was given liberty to exhort."

June 8, 1800. The church deferred the ordination of Zebulon Maxson till the first Sabbath in July, on account of "disappointment of help."

August 10, 1800. Mosher Maxson was invited "to improve his gift in preaching, in this church."

November 10, 1800. Mosher Maxson was authorised "to improve his gift in preaching amongst all the churches of the same faith and order."

———— 1801. Sometime between January 11, and May 10, of this year, Rev. Samuel Woodbridge and Rev. John Patterson ordained John Davis as a Gospel minister.

August 9, 1801. Zebulon Maxson was licenced to preach. The church clerk was instructed to write the certificate of licence, and affix the names of all the members present at the meeting to it.

May 5, 1802. Mosher Maxson was silenced, because he held that the "conviction of the soul was the gift of the Holy Ghost."

May 16, 1802. Licence was restored to Mosher Maxson, who had "made satisfaction to the church."

May 9, 1803. Fellowship and communion were withdrawn from Rev. John Patterson, because "he fellowshipped with First Day Baptists." It was voted that Joseph Davis be permitted "to improve his gift in exhortation or in doctrine within the church, till further orders."

November 21, 1819. Licence was granted to Peter Davis "to go into the world and preach the Gospel."

February 18, 1821. Licence was granted to Lewis A. Davis "to go forth to preach the Gospel."

August 16, 1822. The ordination of Peter Davis was deferred until the next church meeting.

August 15, 1823. It was voted that Peter Davis should be ordained the third Sabbath in October following.

November 14, 1823. Peter Davis, not having been ordained in October, in accordance with action of the church on August 15, for lack of ministerial help, it was voted that Rev. John Davis perform the ordination the third Sabbath in December, alone, "if no ministerial helpers be present."

November 19, 1824. "It also came under consideration that Elder John Davis wishes a letter of dismission. Laid over till next church meeting."

November 18, 1825. Rev. Peter Davis was charged with preaching a new doctrine, which the church did not approve. He was debarred from communion, and a committee appointed to admonish him by letter, and cite him to the next church meeting.

February 17, 1826. The committee appointed to communicate with Rev. Peter Davis in behalf of the church, reported that the letter had been written. But as he was not present, the church deferred further action until the next church meeting.

May 18, 1827. Because the church was informed that Rev. Peter Davis supposed that the church did not understand certain doctrinal views which he held, the church appointed a committee of seven members, five from the New Salem Church and two from the Lost Creek Church, to meet with the church at New Salem on the Fifth Day of the week before the third Sabbath in August following, to give him a hearing.

August 16, 1827. The committee appointed to consider the doctrinal views of Rev. Peter Davis, met. He appeared before them and presented an exposition of his belief concerning the immortality of the soul, which met the approval of the committee, who recommended that the church restore him to his former full standing in the church. Apparently the church adopted the recommendation of the committee.

November 19, 1830. It was voted that William Babcock "continue to improve as an evangelist in this society until further orders, and that he have liberty to exercise his gifts wherever he may think proper."

May 20, 1831. The church took the following action:—

"RESOLVED, That Brother Ezekiel Bee improve in the way of preaching within the bounds of this church."

May 20, 1831. Rev. John Davis entered complaint that the Lost Creek Church had debarred him from communion. A committee was appointed to visit the Lost Creek Church and inquire into the cause of such action.

August 19, 1831. The church voted that Ezekiel Bee be licenced "to go forth to preach the Gospel."

November 18, 1831. The church voted that William Babcock and Ezekiel Bee be licenced to preach. Asa Bee was "called on trial" to the ministry.

February 12, 1832. Asa Bee was licenced "to go forth to preach the Gospel."

(7)

April 11, 1834. Ezekiel Bee, Asa Bee, George J. Davis, and Peter Davis "denied the government of the church, and expressed a wish for free communion."

July 21, 1833. Lewis Bond was granted licence to preach.

June 20, 1834. Amaziah Bee was accorded the privilege of preaching.

May 7, 1835. Amaziah Bee was deprived of the privilege of preaching.

January 11, 1847. "Peter Davis was appointed elder [*sic*]." (The record doubtless should read "pastor" instead of "elder").

February 16, 1855. Rev. Samuel D. Davis was appointed pastor for one year.

September 19, 1858. Rev. David Clawson was appointed pastor.

November 18, 1859. Jacob Davis was appointed to labour in the New Salem and Lost Creek churches.

May 18, 1860. Levi Stalnaker was granted licence to preach.

November 16, 1860. Rev. Peter Davis was excused from the active duties of the pastorate of the church; and Rev. Samuel D. Davis was invited to be present and officiate at Quarterly Meetings.

November 20, 1863. Licence was granted Jacob Davis to preach.

May 20, 1864. Judson F. Randolph and Lewis F. Randolph were licenced to preach.

August 19, 1865. Jacob Davis was ordained to the Gospel ministry. Rev. Samuel D. Davis conducted the ordination service.

May 18, 1866. The church accepted the resignation of Rev. Samuel D. Davis as pastor, and Rev. Jacob Davis was appointed to act as pastor for a period of one year. Rev. Samuel D. Davis was appointed assistant pastor for the same period.

May 20, 1870. Lewis F. Randolph was requested to preach, or provide some one in his stead, every Sabbath for one year at Salem, except when the church should arrange otherwise. At the same time, the church expressed its gratification that Rev. Walter B. Gillette had been sent to labour upon the West Virginia field under the auspices of the Seventh Day Baptist Missionary Society, and urged that he be kept upon that field for a full year.

September 24, 1870. Lewis F. Randolph, who had been called to ordination as a Gospel minister by the New Salem Church, was solemnly consecrated to the duties of that office, at the request of the New Salem Church, by the council which met at Greenbrier to organise a church at that place. The ordination services took place in connection with the organisation of the Greenbrier Church.

November 18, 1870. Rev. Jacob Davis was appointed to labour with the Greenbrier Church, preaching there in accordance with the regular appointments established at that place before the organisation of the Greenbrier Church.

May 19, 1871. Rev. Jacob Davis was engaged for the ensuing year to spend about one-sixth of his time in pastoral work in the church, preaching two Sabbaths in each month at New Salem, but preaching the first Sabbath of the month at such places as his judgment might dictate.

August 14, 1874. Rev. Charles A. Burdick was requested to join the pastor in officiating at "Quarterly Meetings, monthly meetings, and other services of the church, until other arrangements should be made."

April 16, 1876. Rev. Samuel D. Davis was elected pastor of the church, with the understanding that he give his entire time to his pastoral duties, at an annual salary of four hundred dollars ($400.00).

March 30, 1877. Rev. Samuel D. Davis was re-elected pastor for the ensuing year.

May 17, 1878. Rev. Samuel D. Davis was re-elected pastor for the ensuing year.

February 14, 1879. Rev. Samuel D. Davis offered his resignation as pastor. The resignation was laid upon the table, and a committee was appointed on ways and means of paying the pastor's salary, and to recommend an available candidate for that office.

April 6, 1879. The committee on ways and means reported that it had arranged with Rev. Samuel D. Davis to continue his pastorate to June 1, following, giving one-half his time to the duties of his office, from April 1. The committee was instructed to engage Rev. Charles M. Lewis as pastor. If he should not be available, other names were suggested to the committee from which they might select a pastor.

May 16, 1879. Rev. Samuel D. Davis presented his report as pastor for the year ending April 1, previous. In his report he offers his resignation as follows:—

"The experience of the past year has impressed me more and more with the fact that we need a live man on the field over which our large and interesting church is scattered, who could, untrammeled, spend his time and strength in building up the church. Hoping this want will be supplied, I now tender my resignation to take effect on the first day of June, 1879."

The resignation was accepted. In his report, he further states that through the liberality of Luther F. Randolph and Daniel Fillmore F. Randolph, he had been able to secure the services of Rev. Charles M. Lewis, for some time, for revival work within the bounds of the church.

August 15, 1879. The committee on ways and means reported that the four surviving members of the committee,—Lodowick H. Davis, Richard Ford, Preston F. Randolph, and Jesse F. Randolph—(the fifth member, Jepthah F. Randolph, had died on the 19th of the preceding July), would become personally responsible for the salary of the pastor for one year, and that an arrangement had been effected with Rev. Uri M. Babcock, whereby he would become pastor of the church about the first of the following November.

November 19, 1880. Rev. Uri M. Babcock accepted the call of the church to continue as its pastor for another year.

May 20, 1881. Rev. Uri M. Babcock offered his resignation to take

THE NEW SALEM CHURCH

effect at the close of the annual session of the South-Eastern Association, which was to convene on the Fifth Day of the following week. The resignation was reluctantly accepted.

August 18, 1882. The church extended a vote of thanks to Rev. Samuel D. Davis for his services rendered to the church since it had been without a pastor. He was requested to continue his services, and the church pledged contributions for his support.

February 20, 1885. Presley Chedester was granted licence to preach within the bounds of the church for one year. He was requested to preach once a month at the school house on Buckeye Run.

May 15, 1885. The church took action designed to encourage Marshall L. Chedester to enter the ministry.

February 19, 1886. The licence of Presley Chedester to preach within the bounds of the church, was continued for another year. Again on the 18th of February, 1887, his licence to preach was extended until the next Quarterly Meeting, at which time, May 20, 1887, his licence was again renewed, and he was requested to preach for the church at Salem, on the second Sabbath in each month for the following six months. Finally on November 18, 1887, the licence was made permanent "to preach the Gospel wherever a door of usefulness is open to him."

November 18, 1887. The church appointed a committee "to take such steps as in their opinion would be best calculated to secure a pastor at an early date."

November 18, 1887. Boothe C. Davis was granted licence to preach the Gospel "wherever a door of usefulness might be open to him."

February 19, 1888. The church voted to employ Rev. John L. Huffman to give one-fourth of his time to pastoral work in the church, at the rate of one hundred dollars ($100.00) a year, until more satisfactory arrangements could be made. The following resolution was adopted by a unanimous vote:—

"RESOLVED, That we hereby express our heartfelt thanks to Elder Samuel D. Davis for his faithful services and pastoral care of the church, in the years past, and ask that he still make the church his special care, and give it such needed services as he may be able."

June 18, 1888. The church extended a call to Rev. Ira L. Cottrell to become its pastor at a salary of five hundred dollars ($500.00) a year.

August 17, 1888. Rev. Ira L. Cottrell declined to accept the call of the church to become its pastor. The committee was instructed to continue its search for a pastor.

August 16, 1889. Pursuant to the recommendation of the committee, the church voted that Rev. Sanford L. Maxson be employed "as pastor at a salary of four hundred dollars ($400.00) per year." Under the direction of the committee, he had already entered upon his duties as pastor about July 20th, immediately preceding the date of this meeting.

August 30, 1890. Rev. Sanford L. Maxson presented his resignation at the regular Sabbath morning service, to order to devote his entire time to his duties as president of Salem College.

September 7, 1890. The church accepted the resignation of its pastor, Rev. Sanford L. Maxson, and extended a call to Rev. Oscar U. Whitford to become its pastor.

September 21, 1890. The clerk of the church reported that Rev. Oscar U. Whitford had declined to accept the call of the church to become its pastor. The church now extended a call to Rev. Lucius R. Swinney.

October 12, 1890. The church received a communication from Rev. Lucius R. Swinney, declining the call of the church to become its pastor. The committee was instructed to continue its search for a pastor.

November 2, 1890. The church extended a call to Rev. Theodore L. Gardiner to become its pastor at an annual salary of five hundred dollars ($500.00), and a home. At the regular Quarterly Meeting of the church, which occurred on the third Sabbath in November, the church received a communication from Rev. Theodore L. Gardiner accepting this call.

August 19, 1892. Rev. Theodore L. Gardiner presented his resignation as pastor of the church, by means of the following communication:—

"Salem, West Virginia, August 19, 1892.

"To the Salem Seventh Day Baptist Church; in regular business meeting assembled;

"DEAR BRETHREN:—It is well known to most of the membership that your pastor has received an urgent call to accept the presidency of Salem College, to give his entire time to that work. Nothing but the great importance of that work, as it relates to all our people in West Virginia, would induce me to consider it for a moment, since it involves the necessity of resigning this pastorate. But the circumstances are such that it seems to be my duty for the present at least, to accept their call to the school work. This I do with great reluctancy, and not without many misgivings.

"I have decided, however, to accept that work for *one year only,* with the privilege of making final decision later in the year, as to whether I accept it as a permanent work. Some months will elapse before I can fully settle the question as to the future. Meantime, I am willing to do all of the Sabbath preaching that I am able to do for the church, until such time as the church may find it convenient and feasible to settle another as my successor.

"I, therefore, do hereby ask the church to release me as their pastor, my resignation to take effect, August 31, 1892.

Respectfully, and with great regard,

"THEODORE L. GARDINER."

The resignation was accepted, and the offer to preach on Sabbath, as a supply, was likewise accepted. In return for his services in preaching, he received the privilege of occupying the parsonage free of charge.

February 17, 1893. Samuel Hoffman Davis "was granted licence to preach the Gospel wherever a door of usefulness is open to him."

March 26, 1893. The church extended a call to Rev. John L. Huffman to become pastor of the church. On April 16, 1893, a communication was received from Rev. John L. Huffman, accepting the call of the church to become its pastor, at a salary of five hundred dollars ($500.00) annually, and the use of the parsonage, from July 1, 1893. He further stipulated that the engagement should continue indefinitely, but that it should cease upon three months notice given by either party.

May 19, 1893. A communication was received by the church from Rev. Arthur E. Main, corresponding secretary of the Seventh Day Baptist Missionary Society, stating that that society had appropriated one hundred ($100.00) a year toward the support of a pastor of the Salem Church.

August 24, 1894. The church granted the pastor leave of absence to enable him to engage in evangelistic labour, for a period not to exceed four months. The church was not to be responsible for his salary during his absence; but he was to occupy the parsonage, in return for the use of which he was to engage Rev. Theodore L. Gardiner, the president of Salem College, to preach at the Sabbath morning service.

November 16, 1894. The clerk of the church was instructed to inform the Seventh Day Baptist Missionary Society that the church was willing to endeavour to meet its own expenses for the ensuing year.

December 15, 1894. Rev. John L. Huffman's leave of absence was extended, at his request, until the 1st of the following April, if in his judgment, circumstances should so require. A committee was appointed to arrange with Rev. Theodore L. Gardiner to preach for the church, during the pastor's continued absence.

May 25, 1895. Rev. John L. Huffman presented the following letter:—

"To the Salem Seventh Day Baptist Church;

"DEAR BRETHREN:—I hereby offer my resignation as pastor of this church, to take effect the 30th day of June, 1895. My reasons for doing so are,

"*First,* The great demands on the part of our people at the present time for evangelistic work, and my especial adaptation to that kind of work, and my desire to engage in such work while I am able.

"*Second.* I do so, hoping that you may get some one to serve you as pastor, who may be better able to succeed in building up the cause of God among you.

"J. L. HUFFMAN."

June 9, 1895. At a special meeting of the church, the pastor withdrew his resignation, at the urgent request of the church, and he was granted leave of absence for a period of one year, from the first of the following July. The church engaged Rev. Theodore L. Gardiner to occupy the pulpit and to perform such pastoral labour as he might be able. For this service, he was to receive two hundred dollars for the year, and have the use of the parsonage besides.

August 18, 1895. Darwin C. Lippincott "was licenced to preach the Gospel as opportunity is presented."

December 28, 1895. Rev. John L. Huffman again offered his resignation, to take effect April 1, 1896. At a church meeting, held on the 14th of the following February, the resignation was accepted, and a committee appointed to take steps to obtain his successor.

March 29, 1896. The church extended a call to Rev. Lely D. Seager to become its pastor, at a salary of four hundred dollars ($400.00) a year, and the use of the parsonage. The call was accepted, and the church acceded to the request of its new pastor that he be allowed to wait until the following fall to move his family to Salem.

November 20, 1896. The church accepted the resignation of the pastor, Rev. Lely D. Seager, to take effect January 1, 1897, and appointed a committee to obtain another pastor.

September 12, 1897. The church extended a call to Rev. George W. Lewis, of Hammond, Louisiana, to become its pastor at a salary of four hundred dollars ($400.00) a year, and the use of the parsonage. The call was accepted, and the new pastor entered upon his labours on the first of the following November. In the meantime, the church had invited Riley G. Davis, a licentiate of the Greenbrier Church, attending Salem College, to occupy the pulpit, until the arrival of the pastor.

November 13, 1898. Flavius J. Ehret was granted licence to preach "wherever a door of usefulness was open to him to do so."

February 12, 1899. The church took action encouraging Aldis L. Davis to make preparation to enter the Gospel ministry.

July 2, 1899. Rev. George W. Lewis presented his resignation as pastor, urging as the reason for this action, the ill health of his wife, and of his parents. The church regretfully accepted the resignation to take effect the 20th of the following August, and appointed a committee to obtain a new pastor.

August 13, 1899. The church adopted the following recommendation of the committee on pastor :—

"That Rev. Theodore L. Gardiner take pastoral charge, temporarily, until a permanent pastor be secured, and that he have at the rate of two hundred and fifty dollars ($250.00) per year, and the use of the parsonage, for the benefit of himself and such supply as he may see fit to employ. The church may not terminate this arrangement until at least three months' notice thereof be given."

October 2, 1899. Samuel B. Bond, who had previously been a member of the Lost Creek Church, by which he had been licenced to preach, was received into the membership of the Salem Church, and his licence to preach continued.

May 12, 1901. Rev. Theodore L. Gardiner presented his resig-

REV. THEODORE LIVINGSTON GARDINER, D. D.

THE NEW SALEM CHURCH

nation as acting pastor, to take effect at the close of the spring term of the college year, in the following month. The resignation was accepted.

May 25, 1901. The church extended a call to Rev. Ellis A. Witter to become its pastor. On June 22, following, a communication was presented to the church from him, in which he stated the conditions upon which he would accept the call, which were accepted, as follows:

"*First.* The term of service shall be indefinite, but not less than three years; and three months notice shall be given by either party wishing to terminate the agreement, after three years. Service shall begin about the 1st of October next.

"*Second.* The church shall pay him six hundred dollars ($600.00) per year, and give him the use of the parsonage. It shall also pay him half of his expense in moving to this place."

The deacons were instructed to make arrangements for the services of the church, pending the arrival of the pastor. On October 26, 1901, at the Sabbath morning service, Rev. Ellis A. Witter, his wife, and two daughters, were received into membership of the church, and his term of service as pastor began. It continues at the date of this writing, August 1, 1902.

RULING ELDERS.

After the removal of the church to New Salem, the church records show the following action regarding ruling elders:—

November 11, 1798. Jacob Davis was appointed a ruling elder.

August 11, 1799. The church voted that the office of ruling elder was not scriptural, unless they were ordained ministers of the Gospel.

November 16, 1799. After a protracted discussion of the subject, it was voted that laymen should be appointed to the office of ruling elder, and John Davis was appointed ruling elder. The church voted further that he should be ordained, for the purpose of administering the ordinances of the church. He was also granted licence to preach.

June 8, 1800. The ordination of John Davis as a ruling elder, which was to have taken place on this date, was postponed till the first Sabbath in July, for lack of necessary official assistance.

August 10, 1800. Jacob Davis was appointed an elder.

May 14, 1819. George J. Davis, of Greenbrier, was appointed a ruling elder. On the same day, Simeon Maxson was appointed a ruling elder, on Middle Island.

August 16, 1822. It was voted that the office of ruling elder should be abolished.

DEACONS.

The following records appear relating to the deacons of the New Salem Church:—

January 11, 1795. Zebulon Maxson was chosen deacon on trial.

May 10, 1795. The church on this date recognised two deacons, but their names are not given.

August 9, 1795. It was voted that Zebulon Maxson should be ordained deacon, at the first opportunity.

February 12, 1797. It was again voted that Zebulon Maxson should be ordained deacon at the first opportunity.

August 11, 1799. Jacob Davis was chosen deacon.

August 10, 1800. Simeon Maxson was appointed deacon.

November 8, 1801. Samuel Lippincott was appointed deacon.

April 10, 1802. Simeon Maxson and Samuel Lippincott were ordained deacons, by Rev. John Davis, and by Thomas Maxson, deacon of the West Fork River Church.

June 19, 1818. Peter Davis was chosen deacon.

February 20, 1824. William F. Randolph and Jacob Maxson were appointed deacons.

May 20, 1831. John Sutton was appointed deacon.

May 12, 1833. Jonathan F. Randolph and Amaziah Bee were appointed deacons.

June 12, 1836. The church accepted the resignation of Amaziah Bee as deacon.

February 12, 1844. Jonathan F. Randolph resigned his office as deacon.

February 12, 1844. Lodowick H. Davis was appointed deacon.

November 17, 1855. Jepthah F. Randolph was appointed deacon, to serve in connection with Lodowick H. Davis.

May 18, 1866. Judson F. Randolph was appointed deacon, to serve in connection with the present deacons (Lodowick H. Davis and Jepthah F. Randolph).

May 18, 1867. Rev. Samuel D. Davis and Rev. Jacob Davis solemnly set apart by ordination, Lodowick H. Davis, Jepthah F. Randolph, and Judson F. Randolph, to the duties of their office as deacons, by prayer, laying on of hands, extending the right hand of fellowship, and a charge as to the duties of their office.

August 19, 1871. Lloyd F. Randolph was ordained to the office of deacon.

November 8, 1887. Frederick M. Swiger was appointed deacon.

February 20, 1888. Frederick M. Swiger was ordained to the office of deacon.

March 19, 1892. Flavius J. Ehret, a deacon in the Ritchie Church was received into the New Salem Church as a member and authorised to continue his functions as a deacon.

May 7, 1899. Stillman F. Lowther, M. Wardner Davis, and Martin Van Buren Davis were appointed deacons, and ordained to that office on the 17th of the following June.

MODERATORS.

After the last record was made before the church deserted its New Jersey home, no mention is made of a moderator until February 18, 1831, when, after due deliberation, the church voted to have a permanent moderator, and Ezekiel Bee was

elected at once, to that office. How long he acted in that capacity, the records do not state explicitly.

Business meetings of the church were held in various places, such as on Halls Run, Greenbrier Run, Meat House Fork, and at Lewisport, as well as at other places perhaps, in order to bring the various groups of the membership living at points too remote to attend such meetings at the village of New Salem conveniently, into vital contact with the business interests of the church. Consequently, it was by no means convenient for the moderator and clerk to attend all, or any large proportion, of the church meetings. As a result, some one who happened to be present at any given meeting, was elected moderator for the day.

Then again, after it became the practise to hold the business meetings of the church at the village of New Salem, only, it was the custom to appoint, with greater or less frequency, as moderator for the day, some visiting minister, or some prominent lay member of another church, who happened to be present. This was looked upon as a sort of honour, which it was the privilege of the church to bestow upon a guest. Such action was doubtless inspired in part also, by a realising sense of ignorance, on the part of the members of the church, of parliamentary usage.

In this way, the records of the church show that James Bailey, David Clawson, Azor Estee, Walter B. Gillette, Charles A. Burdick, and Charles M. Lewis, presided over the business meetings of the church. Some of these, particularly David Clawson and Charles A. Burdick, acted as moderator almost continuously for a year or more at a time.

Previous to 1840, the following named persons served as moderator *pro tempore*:— Asa Bee, Amaziah Bee, Peter Davis, and James Bailey.

During the next decade, the following names appear:— Amaziah Bee, Peter Davis, Lodowick H. Davis, Jesse J. Davis, George J. Davis, and George Ford.

From 1850 to 1859, inclusive, Azor Estee, Lodowick H. Davis, Jepthah F. Randolph, Jesse J. Davis, David Clawson, and John LaForge F. Randolph, all occupied the moderator's chair, *pro tempore*.

During the next ten years, are found the following named

moderators *pro tempore*:— Samuel D. Davis, Lodowick H. Davis, and Judson F. Randolph.

During the following ten years, 1870-1879, Lloyd F. Randolph, Walter B. Gillette, Charles A. Burdick, Moses H. Davis, Jacob Davis, Charles M. Lewis, Samuel D. Davis, and Jepthah F. Randolph, were all elected to the the chair for the day.

In the absence of any record to the contrary, it is fair to assume that Ezekiel Bee was regarded as the permanent moderator from the date of his election in 1831, till he severed his connection with the New Salem Church, August 30, 1844, in order to become a member of the Middle Island Church.

The church then seems to have been without a permanent moderator until November 17, 1848, when George J. Davis appears to have been elected to that office.

In order to lessen the burdens imposed by the official duties of the moderator, George J. Davis, the office of assistant moderator was created, on November 17, 1854, and George Ford was elected to fill it. On the 14th of February, 1862, on account of his advanced age, the church relieved George J. Davis from serving as moderator; and George Ford, the assistant moderator, succeeded to the office of moderator. George J. Davis died February 10, 1868.

On the 17th of February, 1865, Lodowick H. Davis was elected assistant moderator.

August 15, 1879, the church voted to elect a moderator annually, beginning with the next regular church meeting, and on the 14th of the following November, George Ford was elected moderator for one year.

November 19, 1880, Lodowick H. Davis was elected moderator. He was succeeded on February 17, 1882, by Lloyd F. Randolph, who served continuously for many years, being re-elected from year to year.

On February 19, 1898, W. Franklin Davis was elected moderator for the ensuing year, and at the expiration of that period, he was re-elected and has served down to the date of this writing, August 1, 1902.

CHURCH CLERKS.

For a period of fifty years and more, the records of the Shrewsbury and New Salem Church fail to show the name of

LODOWICK HUGHES DAVIS.

the church clerk, as the minutes of church meetings are unsigned, and mention of the name of the clerk is not otherwise made. The records contain the name of the clerk, for the first time, January 10, 1796. That record and subsequent ones are as follows:—

January 10, 1796. William Davis was discharged as clerk of the church, and Mosher Maxson was appointed in his stead.

November 8, 1801. William Davis appears again as clerk; and also on May 9, 1803.

July 15, 1804. Joshua Davis was appointed clerk.

January, 1828. John Sutton was appointed clerk, probably for the day only.[1]

August 12, 1832. Jesse Davis was appointed permanent clerk to serve co-ordinately with Joshua Davis. On this date, Jonathan F. Randolph and John Sutton were appointed to supervise the beginning of the new book of records.

February 10, 1833. The name of Jesse J. Davis appears as clerk.

April 14, 1835. The church accepted the resignation of Joshua Davis as clerk, and John Sutton was appointed to serve in his stead, along with Jesse J. Davis.

May 15, 1836. Jepthah F. Randolph was chosen permanent clerk.

May 19, 1843. The resignation of Jepthah F. Randolph as clerk of the church was accepted.

December 7, 1843. William B. Davis was appointed assistant to the clerk, Jesse J. Davis.

May 18, 1855. Franklin F. Randolph was appointed assistant to the clerk, William B. Davis.

May 20, 1864. Franklin F. Randolph was elected clerk, inasmuch as the duties of that office had fallen upon him, wholly, since August 15, 1855.

On November 16, 1883, Franklin F. Randolph served the New Salem Church as clerk for the last time, as he had joined the Greenbrier Church on the 22d of September previous. In recognition of his twenty-eight years of faithful service as clerk, the church adopted the following resolution, offered by Rev. Samuel D. Davis:—

"*Whereas*, Brother Franklin F. Randolph has served this church for twenty-eight years as secretary, in all of which time he has been faithful and efficient; therefore,

RESOLVED, That we wish to place on record our heartfelt thanks to him, under God, for this self-sacrificing service."

---

1. An entry made under date of May 20, 1831, may indicate that at Middle Island (Lewisport), another record book was kept by Nathan Davis. If such a record book did exist, the present writer has been unable to find it.

Although he served as clerk at the church meeting on the 16th of November, 1883, the last record entered in his handwriting is that under date of August 17, 1883.

November 16, 1883. Alexander F. Randolph was elected clerk.

February 15, 1884. Alexander F. Randolph declined to serve as clerk, and Marshall L. Chedester was elected in his place.

May 18, 1888. Marshall L. Chedester presented his resignation as clerk. The church accepted it, and Preston F. Randolph was elected to that office, and has served continuously up to the present time.

CHURCH MEMBERS.

This is a list of names of members of the New Salem Church, as they appear in the church records, from the date of the arrival of the church at New Salem, down to the close of the year 1845.

This list and a similar list in the chapter on the *Shrewsbury Church* contain all the names of members of the church, which appear in the records for a full hundred years.

In the absence from the records, of a formal list of names of the members of the church, the names are given as they appear in the records from time to time, as follows:—

December 24, 1792. WILLIAM MAXSON and MOSHER MAXSON are named as the principals in a dispute, regarding their private business affairs.

June 28, 1793. ISAAC MORRIS and "DEACON" MAXSON were appointed to represent the New Salem Church at the organisation of the West Fork River Church.

May 11, 1794. REV. ISAAC MORRIS was given a letter of recommendation to join the West Fork River Church. The church also settled business affairs involving JACOB DAVIS, SIMEON MAXSON, WILLIAM DAVIS, JAMES MAXSON, and THOMAS BABCOCK.

September 14, 1794. JOHN DAVIS, SAMUEL FITZ RANDOLPH, and SIMEON MAXSON were appointed to represent the church at a business meeting of the West Fork River Church.

December 20, 1794. JOSEPH DAVIS (son of James), and AMY LIPPINCOTT (wife of Samuel Lippincott), were received into the church.

January 11, 1795. JOHN PATTERSON and his wife, SARAH, were received into the church, by letter from the church at Georges Creek, (the Woodbridgetown, Pennsylvania, Church).

March 12, 1797. The names of CORNELIUS SUTTON and BENJAMIN THORP are recorded as members of the church.

August 14, 1797. The name of GEORGE MAXSON appears as a member of the church.

September 10, 1797. JAMES DAVIS and REBEKAH, his wife, are recorded as members of the church.

FRANKLIN FITZ RANDOLPH.
(From a photograph taken in 1888).

October 14, 1797. JOHN DAVIS, JONATHAN DAVIS, and ELISABETH BALL, were all baptized.

January 14, 1798. JOEL DAVIS, son of William, was baptized and received into the church.

July 8, 1798. THOMAS MAXSON, JESSE MAXSON and JAMES MAXSON are recorded as members of the church.

March 24, 1799. JOHN BERTLY was baptized.

June 8, 1800. JOHN MAXSON and MARY FITZ RANDOLPH were received into the church.

May 10, 1801. MARGARET DAVIS, wife of Philip Davis; and NANCY DAVIS, wife of Samuel Davis, were baptized and received into the church.

June 14, 1801. The following were baptized and received into the church:—
  PETER HALL,
  JOSHUA DAVIS,
  GEORGE DAVIS,
  CONTENT DAVIS,
  ELISABETH DAVIS,
  SALLY DAVIS,
  HANNAH DAVIS.

July 19, 1801. The following were baptized and received into the church:—
  SAMUEL LIPPINCOTT,
  MARY MAXSON,
  HANNAH DAVIS, wife of Joseph Davis.

August 16, 1801. The following were received into the church:—
  THOMAS CLAYTON,
  ELISABETH CLAYTON, wife of Thomas Clayton,
  DAVID FITZ RANDOLPH,
  MARY FITZ RANDOLPH, wife of David Fitz Randolph,
  CHARITY MAXSON,
  AMY DAVIS.

October 15, 1802. JAMES HILL was baptized and received into the church.

May 9, 1803. On this date, the following named members were all present at a church meeting, and had their names affixed to a certificate of licence to preach, granted by the church to Joseph Davis:—
  Rev. JOHN DAVIS,
  ZEBULON MAXSON,
  NATHAN DAVIS, *Senior*,
  NATHAN DAVIS, *Junior*,
  SAMUEL FITZ RANDOLPH,
  THOMAS CLAYTON,
  JAMES DAVIS,
  REBEKAH DAVIS,
  GEORGE DAVIS,

JOSEPH DAVIS,
JOSEPH DAVIS AND WIFE,
JESSE F. RANDOLPH,
RICHARD BOND, *Senior*,
MARY BOND,
RICHARD BOND, *Junior*,
PETER HALL,
SAMUEL DAVIS,
ELISABETH CLAYTON,
DELILAH FITZ RANDOLPH,
MARGARET FITZ RANDOLPH,
NANCY DAVIS,
SIMEON MAXSON,
ELISABETH MAXSON,
WILLIAM DAVIS, *Clerk*.

October 5, 1805. MARY BOND was baptized and received into the church by Rev. John Davis.

Oct. 5, 1805—May 11, 1806. At some time between these two dates, the following joined the newly organised Lost Creek Church :—

RICHARD BOND, *Senior*,
RICHARD BOND, *Junior*,
GEORGE DAVIS,
MARVEL DAVIS,
MARY BOND.

August 16, 1807—December 28, 1815. At some time between these two dates, PETER DAVIS was received into the church by the laying on of hands.

January 4, 1817. JACOB DAVIS, SARAH DAVIS, and ELISABETH DAVIS were received into the church by Rev. John Davis.

May 15, 1818. The following were received into the church by Rev. John Davis :—

MARY DAVIS, daughter of Rev. John Davis,
MARY MAXSON, daughter of Simeon Maxson,
MARVEL MAXSON, daughter of Zebulon Maxson,
PARMELIA MAXSON, daughter of Zebulon Maxson.

April 17, 1819. The following were received into the church by Rev. John Davis :—

GEORGE J. DAVIS, son of William, of Greenbrier,
ASENATH HUGHES,
LEAH HUGHES,
HANNAH HUGHES,
RACHEL SUTTON.

April 18, 1819. The following were received into the church :—

DUDLEY HUGHES, son of Jonathan,
WILLIAM HUGHES, son of Jonathan,
JONATHAN HOWELL,

CATHARINE DAVIS, wife of George J. Davis,
ANNA DAVIS.

May 14, 1819. ABIGAIL HUGHES, wife of Jonathan Hughes, was received into the church.

May 15, 1819. The following were received into the church:—
JONATHAN HUGHES,
MARTIN HUGHES, son of Jonathan,
WILLIAM F. RANDOLPH, son of Jonathan,
ELISABETH HUGHES, daughter of Jonathan Hughes.

June 20, 1819. The following were received into the church by Rev. John Davis:—
PHINEAS DAVIS,
RHULANAH DAVIS,
STEPHEN DAVIS,
JESSE DAVIS,
GAMBLE SHANNON.

July 18, 1819. The following were received into the church by Rev. John Davis:—
ELISABETH DAVIS, wife of William Davis, of Greenbrier,
JOHN SUTTON,
WILLIAM DAVIS, son of "Bottom William,"
RACHEL DAVIS,
VIENNA DAVIS,
CHARITY LEVENSTON (LIVINGSTON?).

August 21, 1819. The following were received into the church by Rev. John Davis:—
BETSEY DAVIS, wife of James Davis,
SYLVESTER DAVIS,
LYDIA DAVIS,
JEPTHAH DAVIS,
ELISABETH HOWELL,
KEZIAH DAVIS,
LYDIA BROWN,
EXPERIENCE DAVIS,
JANE DAVIS,
JACOB MAXSON, son of Simeon,
REBEKAH MAXSON,
JOSHUA DAVIS, son of William,
CATHARINE DAVIS, wife of Joshua,
SAMUEL F. RANDOLPH, (son of Jesse?),
JOHN LOOFBORO,
LEWIS DAVIS.

September 19, 1819. The following were received into the church:—
EZEKIEL BROWN,
TACY BROWN,
ELISABETH DAVIS, wife of "Bottom William,"
ELISABETH DAVIS, wife of William, son of Nathan.

November 20, 1819. CONTENT DAVIS was received into the church by Rev. John Davis.

March 19, 1820. JOHN DAVIS, son of Rev. John Davis, was baptized and received into the church by Rev. John Davis.

August 18, 1820. LEAH STUTTLER is recorded as a member of the church.

October 21, 1820. TACY DAVIS was received into the church.

May 17, 1821. JAMES JARVIS was received into the church by Rev. John Davis.

May 17, 1822. EPHRAIM BEE was received into the church by Rev. John Davis.

May 15, 1824. EXPERIENCE BROWN was baptized by Lewis A. Davis and received into the church by Rev. John Davis.

1829-1830. The following is "a list of those received into this church from the Quarterly Meeting, November, 1829, until the February [Quarterly] Meeting, 1830":—

>REUBEN D. SUTTON,
>DRUSILLA SUTTON,
>ABSOLOM A. DAVIS,
>POLINA DAVIS,
>JOSHUA S. DAVIS,
>HANNAH DAVIS,
>WILLIAM BABCOCK,
>DAVID HUGHES,
>JANE FITZ RANDOLPH,
>JESSE J. DAVIS,
>AMOS DAVIS,
>ZIBA DAVIS,
>JOHN MAXSON,
>MARY MAXSON,
>GIDEON MAXSON,
>ELISABETH MAXSON,
>LEVI B. MATTHEW,
>JOHN W. MATTHEW,
>LEVI DAVIS,
>JANE ELIZA DAVIS,
>DEBORAH SUTTON,
>LEVI SUTTON,
>DAVIS SUTTON,
>ASA BEE,
>JOSIAH BEE,
>JOHN D. BEE,
>PRISCILLA DAVIS,
>HULDA DAVIS,
>EHUD DAVIS,
>GEORGE J. SUTTON,
>ELEANOR SUTTON,
>ELIONA DAVIS,

Sophia Davis,
John Kelley,
Sophia Kelley,
Amaziah Bee,
Rhoda Bee,
Ezekiel Bee,
Jonathan Fitz Randolph, *Senior*,
Elisabeth Fitz Randolph,
Lurana Davis,
William B. Davis,
Martha Davis,
Charlotte Davis,
Mary Josephine Davis,
David Davis, *Senior*,
Lydia Davis,
Elias B. Davis,
Delilah Davis,
Robert Alexander,
Lydia Maxson,
James Maxson,
Lucinda Howell,
Maria Ann Howell,
Washington Howell,
Content Shannon,
William J. Davis,
John S. Davis,
Esther Davis,
Calvin Davis,
James Davis, *Senior*,
Luther Davis,
Madison Davis,
Phiathata Davis,
John Knight,
Solomon Sayres,
William S. Davis,
Sophia Davis,
Mary Davis,
Lewis Davis,
Edith Davis,
Asenath Davis.

1830. The following were received into the church in this year, after the Quarterly Meeting in February:—

"Squire" Davis,
James Shannon,
Jepthah Fitz Randolph,
Mary Hughes,
Laban Davis.

1831. The following were received into the church during this year :—

>Lodowick H. Davis,
>Peter W. Davis,
>Ann Davis.

August 19, 1831. On this date, the Middle Island Church presented a letter containing the names of those members of the New Salem Church who had joined the recently organised Middle Island Church. They were as follows:

>William G. Davis,
>Elias L. Davis,
>Ephraim Bee,
>James Davis,
>Gamble Shannon,
>Jonathan Howell,
>Simeon Maxson,
>Jacob Maxson,
>George W. Howell,
>Calvin Davis,
>James M. Davis,
>James Maxson,
>Elisabeth Howell,
>Lydia Davis,
>Phiathata Davis,
>Mary Howell,
>Maria A. Howell,
>William J. Davis,
>James Shannon,
>Content Shannon,
>Elisabeth Davis,
>Solomon Sayres,
>Experience Davis,
>John Knight,
>Mary Knight,
>William S. Davis,
>Lewis Bond,
>Elisabeth Davis,
>Keziah Davis.

August 19, 1831. On this date, letters of dismissal were granted the following :—

>Robert Alexander,
>Luther Davis,
>Sylvester Davis.

February 12, 1832. Letters of dismissal were granted the following :—

>Nathan Davis,
>Jane Davis,
>Lewis Davis,

MARY DAVIS,
EDITH DAVIS,
SAPPHIRA DAVIS, wife of William S. Davis,
MARY MAXSON,
JOSHUA DAVIS,
CATHARINE DAVIS,
WILLIAM BABCOCK,
ASENETH BABCOCK,
MARY HUGHES.

August 16, 1833. Letters of dismissal were granted REV. LEWIS A. DAVIS, and his wife, REBECCA, to join the church at Pike, Ohio. On the same date, the following were also received into membership in the church:—

NANCY BROWN,
CHARLOTTE DAVIS,
HENRY JONES,
HESTER JONES,
JANE SUTTON.

August 9, 1835. A letter of dismissal was granted to ASA BEE.

April 20, 1838. The name of ELISABETH FRASURE appears in the minutes of the church meeting of this date.

May 17, 1839. The name of BENJAMIN DAVIS appears in the minutes of the business meeting of this date.

August 21, 1841. MARTHA BEE, wife of Jonathan Bee, was baptized, and on the following day was received into the church.

April 16, 1842. MARY ANN KELLEY, daughter of John Kelley, was baptized and received into the church.

May 21, 1842. LUCINDA DAVIS, daughter of Rev. Peter Davis, was received into the church. She had been baptized some years previously.

November 18, 1843. ABIGAIL KELLEY and JEMIMA DAVIS were received into membership in the church.

August 15, 1844. A letter of recommendation was granted JOSEPH JEFFREY and his wife, TACY, to join the Middle Island Church.

————— 1845. The following were received into membership in the church:—

GEORGE FORD,
POLINA FORD,
RICHARD FORD,
EMILY FORD,
JOEL H. DAVIS,
CHARLES G. DAVIS,
MARGARET DAVIS,
JESSE D. DAVIS.

January 11, 1845. The following were received into the church on this date:—

ZEBULON DAVIS,
CATHARINE MAXSON,

SARAH DAVIS,
CHARLOTTA DAVIS.

March 30, 1845. DEBORAH F. RANDOLPH, wife of Jepthah F. Randolph, received a letter to join some other church of the same faith and order. The letter was not used, however.

May 15, 1845. The name of INGABY BEE appears in the minutes of a business meeting held on this date.

August 9, 1845. The following were received into the church on this date:—

JAMES HYATT,
THEODORE DAVIS,
DORINDA DAVIS.

December 15, 1845. The following is a list of members received into the New Salem church on this date, at a meeting held on Buckeye Run:—

THOMAS FORD,
MARGARET DAVIS,
JOEL DAVIS,
CHARLES G. DAVIS,
GEORGE FORD,
RICHARD FORD,
IRA C. DAVIS,
EHUD DAVIS,
EMILY FORD,
EMILY DAVIS,
POLINA A. DAVIS,
ELISABETH FORD,
ELISABETH DAVIS,
JANE DAVIS,
PHOEBE DAVIS.

BAPTIZED.

June 24, 1843. Mary Ann F. Randolph, Esther F. Randolph, and Ezra F. Randolph were all baptized at New Salem.

July 1, 1843. Harriet, wife of Isaac F. Randolph, was baptized.

October 14, 1843. Catharine, wife of Gideon Maxson; Sally Hughes, and Jemima Davis were all baptized by Joshua Hill, at New Salem.

December 9, 1844. Charles G. Davis, Richard Ford, Elisabeth Randolph, Mary Randolph, and Elisabeth Davis were all baptized by Richard C. Bond. On the following day Emily Davis was baptized also.

December 14, 1844. Phoebe Davis, Ira Davis, and Ehud Davis were baptized at New Salem by Richard C. Bond.

December 15, 1844. George Ford, Emily Ford, Elizabeth F. Davis, Joel Davis, Jane Davis, Polina Davis (daughter of William B. Davis), Charlotte Davis (daughter of Absolom Davis), were all baptized on Buckeye Run, by Richard C. Bond.

THE NEW SALEM CHURCH

December 22, 1844. Zebulon Davis was baptized on Greenbrier Run.

December 29, 1844. Lemuel Davis was baptized on Meat House Fork.

January 4, 1845. Elisabeth Sutton was baptized at New Salem.

January 4, 1845. Annetta Maxson was baptized on Greenbrier Run.

January 25, 1845. Stephen Davis, Neely Jeffrey, Isaiah Bee, and Rhoda Davis were baptized on Middle Island Creek.

February 2, 1845. Theodore Davis and Jesse Davis were baptized at New Salem.

DEATHS.

"This is a list of the names of them that have been removed out of the world by death:—

"Brother WILLIAM DAVIS departed this life at White Day, July 15, 1791.

"Our dearly beloved brother and elder, JACOB DAVIS, departed this life, July the 17th, 1793.

"Sister TAYSEY (TACY) DAVIS, the widow of William Davis, departed this life, the 1st of June 1795.

"Brother EPHRAIM MAXSON departed this life, September 10, 1795, at Salem.

"Sister EXPERIENCE MAXSON departed this life, October the 20th, 1795.

"Brother JOEL DAVIS, the son of William, departed this life, June 1, 1798.

"Our aged brother, SIMEON MAXSON, departed this life, February 26, 1802, at Salem.

"BENJAMIN THORP departed this life, April 15, 1804.

"Brother NATHAN DAVIS departed this life on—[date wanting].

"Brother DUDLEY HUGHES departed this life, May the 14, 1820.

"Sister AMY DAVIS departed this life, October the 14, 1820.

"Brother JESSE DAVIS, departed this life, December 22, 1824.

"Brother WILLIAM DAVIS, called "JARSEY" BILLY, departed this life, April 10, 1840.

"Sister CONTENT, consort of Joshua G. Davis, departed this life, July 27, 1840.

"Sister SALLY, consort of Elder Peter Davis, departed this life, January 10, 1842.

"Sister MARY JOSEPHINE, consort of Ziba Davis, departed this life, March 1, 1842.

"Brother Elder JOHN DAVIS, pastor of this church, departed this life, June 22, 1842.

"Sister ABIGAIL, consort of Jonathan Hughes, departed this life, July 1, 1842.

"Sister JANE, consort of Jonathan F. Randolph, departed this life, April 24, 1843.

"Sister RACHEL, consort of William F. Davis, departed this life, May 21, 1843.

"WILLIAM DAVIS, known as "GREENBRIER BILLY," departed this life, January 6, 1845.

"Sister BETSEY, consort of William Davis ["Greenbrier Billy"], departed this life, January 6, 1845.

VII.

THE WEST FORK RIVER CHURCH.

HE records of this church have long since disappeared. The only documentary sources of information now available are the records of the New Salem Church; a single letter addressed to the General Conference under date of July 23, 1808, by the hand of Thomas Maxson, clerk of the church; and the reply of the General Conference to the church.

The West Fork River Church was located at or near the mouth of Lamberts Run, a small stream which flows into the West Fork of the Monongahela River from the west, some six or eight miles north of Clarksburg, and but a short distance south of the junction of Ten Mile Creek with the West Fork of the Monongahela River. Here there settled Thomas Maxson, a prosperous farmer from Shrewsbury, New Jersey. He rapidly improved his farm, built a brick dwelling house with brick out buildings, and gathered around him a small company, consisting of his son Timothy, with his wife, Anna; William Vanhorn, and his wife, Virginia, and perhaps others.

On June 25, 1793, these settlers presented a petition to the New Salem Church to send delegates to attend the organisation of a church on the West Fork of the Monongahela. The petition was granted and Isaac Morris and Ephraim Maxson were sent as such delegates, and the organisation was effected with a membership of five souls.

The membership, which was never large, had in 1808

increased to a total enrollment of sixteen, since the organisation of the church, of whom one had been excommunicated, two dismissed to other churches, and one deceased, leaving an actual membership at that time of but twelve. Although they then had hope of growth, the church soon went into a decline and gradually became extinct.

On May 11, 1794, Rev. Isaac Morris received a letter of dismissal from the New Salem Church to join the West Fork River Church, and on December 14, following, the New Salem Church received a request from the West Fork River Church for assistance to excommunicate Isaac Morris. The New Salem Church replied by letter, directing the West Fork River Church to follow the gospel rule as laid down in their articles of faith and practise.

Presumably, however, the West Fork River Church, for some unexplained reason, found itself unable to take final action without further advice and assistance, for on September 14, 1794, there was a special business meeting of the New Salem Church to consider the propriety of sending delegates to a church meeting of the West Fork River Church. It was decided to send such delegates, and three were appointed; viz., Rev. John Davis, Samuel Fitz Randolph, and Simeon Maxson. The purpose of sending these delegates to the church meeting at West Fork River, is not specifically stated, but it may be assumed fairly, that it related to the matter presented to the New Salem Church by the West Fork River Church, only four months before.

On June 13, 1795, the New Salem Church received a request from the West Fork River Church to send the pastor of the New Salem Church to ordain an elder and deacon. The New Salem Church granted the request, but stipulated that the West Fork River Church should secure other assistance, presumably from the Woodbridgetown Church, as that church, next after the New Salem Church, was the nearest Seventh Day Baptist church.

On September 9, 1798, James Maxson received a letter of dismissal from the New Salem Church to join the West Fork River Church; and on November 10, 1799, Joseph Davis, Sr., was granted a letter of dismissal by the New Salem Church to join the West Fork River Church.

On February 14, 1802, the New Salem Church voted to ask the West Fork River Church to send Rev. William Davis to assist in ordaining two deacons, and if he were not available, to ask for Deacon Thomas Maxson of that church. These deacons were ordained on April 10, following, by Rev. John Davis of the New Salem Church, and Deacon Thomas Maxson of the West Fork River Church.

On May 9, 1803, after having debarred Rev. John Patterson and his wife, Sarah, from communion "for joining fellowship with the First Day Baptist Church" of which he had assumed charge, the New Salem Church took the following significant action:—

"We do renounce communion with all Seventh Day [Baptist] Churches that do give toleration and full fellowship with First Day Churches, and we appoint James Davis and Samuel Davis as messengers to the West Fork [River] Church."

The records of the New Salem Church contain nothing further concerning the West Fork River Church, and all fraternal intercourse between the West Fork River Church and other Seventh Day Baptists appears to have lapsed until in 1808, the New Salem, Lost Creek, and West Fork River churches all applied for membership in the Seventh Day Baptist General Conference and sent Rev. John Davis jointly, as a delegate to the annual session of the General Conference, held in September of that year, at Hopkinton, Rhode Island.

The applications of the New Salem and Lost Creek Churches were acted upon favourably, but that of the West Fork River Church was denied because it held open communion with First Day Baptists.

The correspondence is as follows:—

"JULY 23d, 1808.

"We, the Seventh Day Baptist Church who reside on the West Fork of the Monongahela [River], Harrison County, State of Virginia, received a request from the Eastern Churches to obtain the knowledge of the number of [Seventh Day] Baptists [here], and further to join in a Conference with them.

"We rejoice to learn that the work of God is a-carrying on amongst you. We do send our christian salutation to all our brethren and sisters in the bonds of the gospel of Jesus Christ. We join you in your motion. If we can be accepted, we shall acquaint you of our faith and order.

"We believe in the doctrine of election, of the final perseverence of the saints, of the resurrection of the dead, and eternal judgment.

"Further, we do hold a full fellowship with the First Day Baptists, and send these lines as children to our father in the gospel, looking for an answer; as in the multitude of counsel, there is safety.[1]

"This Church was constituted in the year of our Lord, 1793, of five members. At the present time [there are] twelve members; one excommunicated; two dismissed; one deceased.

"Religion appears to be [at a] low ebb at present, though we have hopes of an addition to this church.

"So we bid you farewell. Though we should never see each others' faces, in time may we be prepared by grace to meet in the world above.

"By order of the Church,
"THOMAS MAXSON, *Clerk.*"

To this the General Conference made reply:—

"To the Seventh Day Baptist Church residing on the West Fork of the Monongahela River:—

The Elders, Messengers, and Brethren, composing the Sabbatarian General Conference, now sitting at Hopkinton, State of Rhode Island, to the Seventh Day Baptist Church, on the West Fork of the Monongahela River, Harrison County, State of Virginia, *Sendeth Greeting*:—

DEAR BRETHREN: We feel ourselves under the greatest obligation imaginable, to adore and praise the name of our God, for his unbounded love and goodness manifested to a sinful world, that he has not left us to perish in our iniquities, he being not willing that any should perish, not willing that the numerous posterity of Adam, who were made sinners by his transgressions, and who were not active in that transgression, should thereby inevitably and eternally perish; therefore He sent his only begotten Son into the world to seek and to save that which was lost, to put away sin by the sacrifice of himself, who through the Eternal Spirit, offered himself without spot unto God, a sacrifice of a sweet smelling savour, acceptable unto the father, whereby we are redeemed from under the curse of the law; so that we are no more to be condemned for Adam's transgressions, for as by the offence of one, many were made sinners, even so by the righteousness of one, many were made righteous; as likewise saith the Prophet, "this proverb shall no more be heard in Israel, that the fathers have eaten sour grapes and the children's teeth are set on edge, but the soul that sinneth, shall die,"—thus we behold the loving kindness of the Lord; notwithstanding we were all included under sin, yet He had mercy upon all.

"But behold, the goodness of God did not stop here, for Christ

---

1. Benedict says that the West Fork River Church admitted First Day Baptists to membership. *General History of the Baptist Denomination in America.* Benedict. Boston 1813. Vol. II, p. 421.

came into the world not only to make an atonement for sin, but He came a light into the world, to lighten every man that cometh into the world, to preach the Gospel to the poor, to bind up the broken-hearted, to preach deliverance to the captives, and recovering of sight to the blind; to set at liberty them that are bruised; to preach the acceptable year of the Lord; and likewise the day of vengeance of our God, wherein He will pour out his fury upon all them that will not have this man to reign over them—and further, He has burst the bars of the grave, and risen a victorious conqueror over all our enemies, and is now seated at the right hand of God, making intercession for us; and has laid a foundation of eternal salvation, and has left exceeding great and precious promises, even eternal life, for all that believe in and obey him—He has likewise sent the Holy Spirit into the world, not only to convince the world of sin, of righteousness, and of judgment, but likewise to lead and guide us into all truth, even into the ways of Holiness; and now dearly beloved, may not these contemplations stimulate our hearts to love him supremely, above all other objects, and lead us to true and swift obedience to all his Holy requirements.

"O, dear Brethren, let us lift up our heads and rejoice, because we know that our Redeemer liveth, and shall be alive for ever more; we know that He liveth because he is yet inspiring his servants to lisp forth the sound of his glorious Gospel; we know that He liveth because He has been refreshing our souls as with the dews of heaven, while we have been sitting down together in our present annual meeting—we rejoice, dear Brethren, that the Lord has given us this one opportunity more of meeting with our beloved Brethren from foreign lands, to sit down together to commemorate the dying love of a Saviour; we sit down under His banner with great delight, and His fruit is sweet to our taste; we rejoice that the Lord has put into the heart of our beloved brother, John Davis, from your country, and has enabled him to travel seven hundred miles, to join with us in so good a cause, whose coming was to us like the coming of Titus, and we pray God to return him, as well as all the rest of our brethren, safe in His own due time, and we hope if it may be consistent with the will of God, that the coming of some of you may in a future time, give us the like cause to rejoice.

"We rejoice that the Lord is building up His churches in the western country, that the desert is blossoming like the rose, etc. We rejoiced at the reception of a brotherly letter from you, wherein we find an account of the rise, and the present number of your church, together with a short account of your faith and order; you say you hold the doctrines of election, and final perseverance of Saints, which doctrines we also hold; that is, we hold that all those saints who finally persevere, will compose God's elect, so perhaps we should not wrangle much about that, although we have known of some who hold that God has from eternity unconditionally elected a part of Adam's race for glory, and that He has unconditionally and eternally reprobated all the rest to misery; and tell the people 'they must do, and they cannot do, that they must go to God for salvation, and they cannot, etc., but these things being contradictions in term, and therefore mere nonsense, we pass it by, and hope better things of you.

"But further, you inform us that you hold a full communion with the First Day Baptists. Dear Brethren, we do not blame you for loving christians of any denomination, for we find it more than we can do to avoid it, nay, we do not wish to avoid it, would to God we could love them even out of that error, for we find many sweet and comfortable hours in joining with our First Day brethren, in the worship of our God; yet, for the sake of good order and discipline in God's house, we think it necessary to take up the cross in that one point, that is, to withhold our external fellowship, in token that we do not fellowship that error.

"Now we know that the sweetest part of religion is the internal work of grace and the love of God, shed abroad in the heart, which is the essence of charity. Now, all this, Brethren, we wish you to maintain with your First Day brethren, as saith the apostle, above all things put on fervent charity, which is the bond of perfectness; this we say is the sweetest part of religious fellowship, yet for the well ordering of God's house, He has seen fit to appoint external rules and ordinances; and it is in these alone that we wish you to withhold your communion, and that from no other motive but that of love. We think that you would readily grant that to come round the table of the Lord, to eat the bread and drink the wine, without the love of God in the heart, would be but a dry morsel. And do you think they can reasonably be grieved with you when that outward part is all you withhold from them? So likewise we hope you will not be grieved with us, while we inform you that your liberty herein has exceeded the bounds of our external fellowship, although we love you still, hoping that you will upon further consideration discover the impropriety of that liberty and retract therefrom, upon which we know not but you will stand in full fellowship with this Conference, if it should be your desire.

"But we consider it not consistent to be in full fellowship with those out of the church, whose practise is such as we could not receive into the church, and if we receive First Day members into the church, and allow them the liberty of working on the Seventh Day, it would not be a consistent chain of discipline to deal with others for taking the same liberty; and if we cease to deal with members for the nonobservance of that solemn, delightful, and necessary command of God, it would soon become a matter of indifference in the eyes of posterity; who would naturally act as worldly interest and temporal convenience should dictate, so that it is beyond a doubt if such a practise was universally adopted, that in a short time the observation of the Seventh Day Sabbath, would be nearly or totally extinct; that this would be the case is evident not only from the nature of things, but likewise from all the instances of the kind which has happened within the circle of our acquaintance. So we hope you will see the propriety of our conduct and put on charity for us.

"So dear Brethren, we commend you to God and the world of his grace, which is able to build you up and give you an inheritance among them that are sanctified. AMEN.

"SEPTEMBER 11th, 1808."

The Conference minutes of the following year state that no report was received from the West Fork River Church, and nothing appears from it afterwards.[1]

So far as the present writer has been able to ascertain, the West Fork River Church is the only one of this group of churches in which the doctrine of open, or free, communion ever obtained a footing firm enough to menace its integrity.

The West Fork River Church, doubtless, carried its practise of open communion to a much greater length than merely admitting their First Day friends to the communion service and inviting them to participate in the Lord's Supper. This, undoubtedly, opened the way to a much closer affiliation with members of non-Sabbath-keeping churches.

It is somewhat doubtful, however, if Benedict's statement (see note on p. 138) to the effect that First Day Baptists were admitted to membership, is correct; as the source of his information, probably, was the foregoing correspondence, published at that time in the minutes of the Seventh Day Baptist General Conference.

The Shrewsbury Church at one time censured one of its members for partaking of the communion with the Church of England, but that offence appears to have been sporadic.

After the removal of the church to western Virginia, however, the only trouble over the communion in that church arose from the position taken by the pastor, Rev. Peter Davis, to the effect that the Lord's Supper was akin to the Mosaic Ceremonial Law, and had been fulfilled and passed away. Few, if any, of the members of the church sympathised with his views, however, and the equipoise of the church was in no wise disturbed.

The West Fork River Church now rapidly declined, and

---

1. The author is under obligations to Rev. Samuel D. Davis, of Jane Lew, West Virginia, for much of his information concerning this article.

in a short time those who had not left the Sabbath, had become members of the Lost Creek Church.

A PARTIAL LIST OF MEMBERS OF THE WEST FORK RIVER CHURCH.

THOMAS MAXSON, *Deacon* and *Church Clerk*,
TIMOTHY MAXSON, son of Thomas,
ANNA MAXSON, wife of Timothy,
WILLIAM VANHORN,
VIRGINIA VANHORN, wife of William,
ISAAC MORRIS, *Elder*,
JAMES MAXSON,
JOSEPH DAVIS, SR.,
WILLIAM DAVIS, *Elder*.

VIII.

THE LOST CREEK CHURCH.

HE original records of the Lost Creek Church, which was organised October 27, 1805, have all disappeared. On the 9th of March, 1855, William F. Randolph, a member of the Lost Creek Church, was instructed, by order of the church, to make an abridged transcript of the records as they existed at that time. This transcript is the oldest record now in possession of the church. On the title page of the book containing the transcript, is the following inscription:—

"Summary transcript of the original record of the institution and proceedings of the Seventh Day Baptist Church at Lost Creek, Harrison County, Virginia. Written 1857."

This book contains, as a sort of preface, four pages of explanatory remarks by the transcriber, reciting the history of his work and the manner in which he did it. It runs as follows:—

"The following is an abridged transcript of the rise and transactions of the Seventh Day Baptist Church at Lost Creek, Harrison County, Virginia, inscribed in compliance with an order of the church, passed March 9, 1855.

"The writer here would say that it was with a considerable degree of reluctance that he engaged in the work, under various considerations;

"*First.* Because he is aware that there is a liability, even with much faithfulness and care, in condensing writings, of not giving every feature contained in the original in its clear light.

"*Secondly.* Because the proper execution of such a work necessarily required more time, labour, and attention, than could be given at one period by the writer, pressed as he is almost continually under a multiplicity of cares at home and abroad.

"*Thirdly.* On account of inability to do the work in a fair legible manner, because of a disabled hand.

"These embarrassments combined have made the work far more burdensome and tedious than it might have been under favourable circumstances. But, yet, however, notwithstanding these impediments, the need of the work, and the call of the brethren for me to engage in it has made the task rather a pleasant duty, whenever opportunity was found to engage in it, though but a few hours at a time.

"The writing was commenced, and the most of it done, in the winter of 1855 and 1856, but not finished until February, 1857.

"The Articles of Faith, Covenant, and Duty, found on pages 2 to 8 partly inclusive, are copied entire. The small amount of other matter on pages 2 and 8 is also given about in full. The abridgment begins with page 9.

"The original record shows that the business meetings were almost uniformly opened and closed with prayer, frequently accompanied with reading or singing, sometimes both. They show also that a moderator was frequently appointed at church meetings. These parts of the record are altogether omitted in this edition, yet the writer has endeavoured to notice every meeting mentioned in the original, giving distinctly the nature and extent of business done at each.

"Names of members are given, commencing with page 72, showing the time of reception, baptism, etc., as far as the original record shows, or [as] such matters otherwise come to my knowledge. Considerable, however, is wanting to make this information full, the old writings being somewhat short in this respect.

"On page 115, a list is started giving the time of decease of members as far as found in the old book, with some others collected. This list, I think, should be filled out without delay as far as practicable.

"An alphabetical index will be found in the fore part of the book, giving names of members, with other persons, and subjects of matter contained in the book (though this index, with the arrangement of references to pages connected, has taken considerable time and care, and perhaps there may yet be room for improvement) [which] may prove to be beneficial, not only in saving time by readily pointing to subjects and matter, but also by saving the book from that wear and defacement which is the consequent result of much handling the leaves of any volume.

"Commencing with page 9, running forward over part of the 30th page, will be found the substance of the business matter recorded in the old book, covering the time from June, 1806, to March, 1844. That part from page 30 to page 38 never having been embodied in a book has come into my hands at a distance from the church, at various periods, on loose memorandum papers.

(9)

"Here it may be well to remark that, although much care and pains have been taken to make this a faithful, clear, condensed copy, and I feel to hope it is very near if not entirely so, yet as I have worked alone, which is rather an ill-convenient way of compiling writings, and far from being the readiest way of detecting errors, it may therefore be, upon examination with help, that matter may be found lacking, or out of place.

"This would seem probable, not only on account of the crowded and frequently interrupted circumstances under which the work has been executed, but more particularly, because of the detached names, that the embodied part of the original record is found in the old book, but few leaves in that being paged, and much of the matter standing scattered in irregular, interspersed parcels through the book.

"I would suggest, therefore, that the church either examine the work as a body, or appoint two or more members to compare this summary with the original record and papers, and report to the church at some future time before the new copy is received [i. e., accepted]. Such an examination seems necessary, not only because errors or omissions, if any, may thereby be detected and the copy thus perfected; but also because if such steps are not taken, heavy and undesirable responsibilities must rest upon your humble compiler, who has done the work unaided under unfavourable circumstances, but with little suitable opportunity to look over it. I hope, therefore, that these measures will be carried out by the church.

"Some 23 pages are used as an index; other matter now written occupies about 50 pages, giving the Articles, the Rise and Doings of the church for more than fifty years, leaving, I believe, rather more than half of the book yet blank; which, with proper handling, may serve as record paper yet for many years to come.

"With these remarks I submit the book to the brethren, at whose call the work has been done, concluding by mentioning the propriety of properly entering and preserving future records. The saying that 'What is worth doing at all, is worth doing well' is probably true, and will apply to putting down and keeping records as well as other matters of business.

"From the little experience I have had in looking over old manuscripts, I find that ill-convenience is often given from poor ink having been used, as well as from [the] imperfect handling and preserving [of] record books and papers.

"I would suggest the propriety, therefore, of the church instructing her clerk not to attempt to spread business matter upon the regular record book at the time of transacting it; but then on a memorandum paper or book, and shorly afterwards, at his own convenience, always using good ink, in a short but explicit manner, enter it in the regular book, reading it at the next meeting for approval.

"This course, properly pursued, may prove to be an advantage to those who may follow after, if not to the present acting brethren.
"WM. F. RANDOLPH."

The records proper of the church as transcribed, begin as follows:—

"Harrison County, State of Virginia, October 27, 1805, the Seventh Day Baptist Society on Lost Creek was formed into a church, comprising the following members:—

"RICHARD BOND, SR.,
"RICHARD BOND, JR.,
"WILLIAM VANHORN, JR.,
"CORNELIUS WILLIAMS,
"GEORGE DAVIS,
"MOSES HUFFMAN,
"MARY BOND,
"MARY BOND,
"MARVEL DAVIS,
"AMY DAVIS.

"These were the constituent members. Within the next six weeks the following additional members joined the church:—

"ABEL BOND, SR.,
"MARY DUNAWAY,
"WILLIAM VANHORN, SR.,
"JOHN DUNAWAY,
"SARAH VANHORN, (wife of William, Sr.),
"SARAH VANHORN, (wife of William, Jr.),
"ELISABETH HUFFMAN.

"Cornelius Williams was chosen Ruling Elder; Abel Bond, Sr., Deacon, and Moses Huffman, Clerk.

"The Church Covenant was as follows:—

"The Church of Christ on Lost Creek, in the observance of God's Holy Sanctified Seventh Day-Sabbath, first agreed to: We, who desire to walk together in the fear of the Lord, do, through the assistance of His Holy Spirit, profess our deep and serious humiliation for our transgressions. And we do also solemnly, in the presence of God and each other, in the sense of our unworthiness, give up ourselves to the Lord."

The Articles of Faith were twenty-two in number. These, in turn, were followed by "Short Articles, proper to be read to persons when received into this Church, and to be consented to, and confessed, by the persons so received."

These "Short Articles" consisted of six interrogations, concerning personal duty to God, four statements of duty as to church members in relation to the church, six statements of duty in relation to brethren as church members, and five statements of private duty.

The Lost Creek Church was formed of a group of

Seventh Day Baptists who settled on Lost Creek, and the neighbouring streams of Hackers Creek and Elk Creek, early in the nineteenth century.

In the early part of its history, the church was made up, for the most part, of the Bonds, who had come from Cecil County, Maryland, and the VanHorns, Williamses, and others, who had embraced the Sabbath in the south-western part of Pennsylvania, through the influence of the Woodbridgetown Seventh Day Baptist Church. These were joined by other families from time to time, from New Salem, and from Woodbridgetown, as well as from points in Maryland and New Jersey. Among these were the Huffmans, Loofboros, Forsythes, etc.

In July, 1806, the church decided to build a meeting house, but the exact location was not determined upon until November 29, 1807. The building appears to have been completed in December, 1809.

At the session of the General Conference held with the church at Hopkinton, Rhode Island, in September, 1808, the Lost Creek Church, together with the New Salem Church, was admitted to membership in that body. Both churches were represented by Rev. John Davis, who was in attendance upon Conference that year.

Three years afterward, the church addressed the following letter to the General Conference:—

"Lost Creek Church, Harrison County, State of Virginia,
July the 6th, 1811.

"DEARLY BELOVED BRETHREN IN CHRIST:—

"We send you our Christian salutation in the Lord. Grace, peace, and mercy, from God the Father, and our Lord Jesus Christ be unto you all who look and long for His appearing the second time, without sin, unto salvation.

"DEAR BRETHREN: We thank you for your good will and brotherly love in sending us the letters of your Conference, and [we] greatly desire to keep up a correspondence with you by letter, if no more.

"Elder John Davis says that he would have been with you this fall, if he had not to move to the Ohio State.

"You ask the reason why his name was not in our letter to Cohansey. We can render no reason, only neglect, at this time; for we thought it was [in the letter]. He expects to move to the Ohio State to join and take the care of a church of about 18 members there, this fall.

"Dear Brethren: We have received six members, and excommunicated two, since our last letter to you. Our number at present is thirty-one.

"May God of his infinite mercy and for Christ's sake, increase our faith and number, and bless you with all spiritual blessings in heavenly places; and finally accept of you and us in the Beloved, is the prayer of your brothers and sisters in the Lord.

"John Davis, *Elder,*
"Cornelius Williams, *Ruling Elder,*
"Abel Bond, *Deacon,*
"Moses Huffman, *Clerk.*

"N. B. We beg you would overlook our weakness and bad writing, and pray for us that the word of the Lord may have free course, and be glorified, even as it is with you, and that we may be delivered from unreasonable and wicked men—for all men have not faith—and the Lord direct your hearts into the love of God, and into the patient waiting for Christ. AMEN.

"M. H.

"To the Conference at Rhode Island. [In care of]
"Mr.'s John Davis, *Elder,* or Jacob West,
"Cohansey, West New Jersey.
"To be left at Bridge Town Post Office."

The church addressed the General Conference again in 1818, as follows:—

"Lost Creek, 1818.

"Esteemed Brethren:—

"Having taken a deliberate view of the subject of the Missionary Society as proposed by a circular letter, communicated through the medium of Brother Manning Dunn, we most cordially acquiesce in the utility of the measure, conceiving the sole object to be no other than to supply those that are destitute of the Gospel, and to promote the cause of true religion; and earnestly hope, if adopted, that we shall shortly experience something of the cordial efforts, resulting from so benevolent an institution.

"From a conception that our situation calls loud for your earliest attention, as being situated in a very remote part, and destitute of such teachers as can be profitable or received, we do most fervently wish you, in your wisdom, may select and send forth to our relief a teacher whose superiour ability, external deportment, and innate virtues, are such as will secure confidence, and adorn the doctrine of God, our Saviour. Let him be furnished with such a recommendation in addition, as will remove every doubt of his being an impostor, as we have been much imposed on by men of that description, which hath brought reproach on the Sabbatarian societies in this quarter. Let his system embrace a belief that he hath been called to preach to sinners, for such we are. And being useless to multiply words, we, nearly as sheep without a shepherd, submit our case to your better judgment, to do for us as may seem meet in your eyes.

"And now, dear Brethren, we submit you to God, who is able to build you up, and give you an inheritance among them that are sanctified; that we, with you all, may experience an unmeasurable flow of divine love, is the earnest prayer of your brethren and sisters whose names are hereunto annexed.

"WILLIAM VANHORN,	ELISABETH HUFFMAN,
"THOMAS VANHORN,	SARAH DAVIS,
"JOHN FORSYTHE, *Clerk*,	J. W. LOOFBORO,
"WILLIAM WILLIAMS,	MARY LOOFBORO,
"JACOB DAVIS,	D. W. LOOFBORO,
"SARAH VANHORN, SR.,	RICHARD BOND, SR.,
"SARAH FORSYTHE,	MARY BOND,
"SARAH DAVIS,	ABEL BOND, JR.,
"SARAH VANHORN, JR.,	SARAH BOND,
"SARAH VANHORN, YE 3D,	RICHARD BOND, JR.,
"LOIS VANHORN,	MARY BOND,
"ZURAH KENNEDY,	RICHARD BOND, *Minor*,
"PRUDENCE BOND,	MARGARET BOND,
"THOMAS BOND,	ELI BOND,
"AMELIA BOND,	REUBEN BOND,
"SARAH BOND,	JAMES KENNEDY.

"BRETHREN: Let the following insertion be a sufficient apology for the subscribers' names all appearing in the same handwriting,— this being a copy of the original, which was sent to me this day, with a request that I should copy and direct to whomsoever I might think proper, lest the original should miscarry, and this possibly might arrive safe.

"ABEL BOND, SR.,
"ELISABETH BOND.

"Clarksburg, Harrison County, Virginia.
"July ye 12th, 1818.

"The above-signed (with only one exception) are heads of families, and a considerable number more of a similar sentiment reside within the vicinity of the Lost Creek Church, that had not an opportunity of seeing this letter; all of whom have rising families of the Seventh-day order.

"Although we are not in opulent circumstances, yet we feel willing to contribute something toward the support of a teacher, who, in addition to the foregoing requisite qualifications, can stand forth bold as a lion in support of the Fourth Commandment, as there is uncommon pains taken by some teachers of different orders to inform a belief that it is by no means binding, and exert every faculty to obliterate, if possible, the observance of that most prominent command, which, indeed hath led some of our youths to query, whether or no we were not in an error.

"DEAR BRETHREN: How are such teachers to account for their conduct at the great and decisive day of Acc'ts? But we must leave them to see to that.

"While we most earnestly desire an interest in your most fervent petitions that we may be enabled, through divine grace, to trace the remaining steps of our days in stability and firmness, that we, with you all, may be found included in the happified number at the last, that shall receive the approbatory sentence of 'Well done, good and faithful servants, enter ye into the joy of your Lord,' is the earnest prayer of your affectionate brethren and sisters. ADIEU.
"ABEL BOND.
"In behalf of the Lost Creek Church.
"Addressed
"*To the Elders and Messengers composing the Sabbatarian General Conference to be held in East Jersey.*
"*To be left in the Post Office at Brunswick.*
"*To the immediate care of the Rev. Manning Dunn.*
"CLARKSBURG, VA., JULY 26."

Rev. John Davis was pastor, not only of the New Salem Church, but of the Lost Creek Church as well.

In November, 1810, Moses Huffman and Cornelius Williams were called to improve their gift of exhortation and preaching in the society at their own convenience, and a year afterward, Hamilton Goss was invited to preach for the church once a month.

Early in 1811, the meeting house was burnt down by accident, and the church decided to build again; this time on the land of William VanHorn, who agreed to make the church a deed for a lot of one acre.

In 1815, some trouble arose between Rev. John Davis on the one hand, and various members of the church on the other. This continued to agitate the church at irregular intervals for a period of some fifteen years, and at times it interfered materially with its spiritual welfare. Indeed, the trouble was far reaching, and extended not only to the uttermost bounds of the Lost Creek and New Salem churches, but to the Mad River Seventh Day Baptist Church in Ohio, where Rev. John Davis had spent some time, after which he had returned to Virginia. The exact nature of the charges against him are not wholly clear from the records, but they were of such a nature that his personal character was impeached. Apparently, however, he succeeded in clearing himself of the charges in a satisfactory manner.

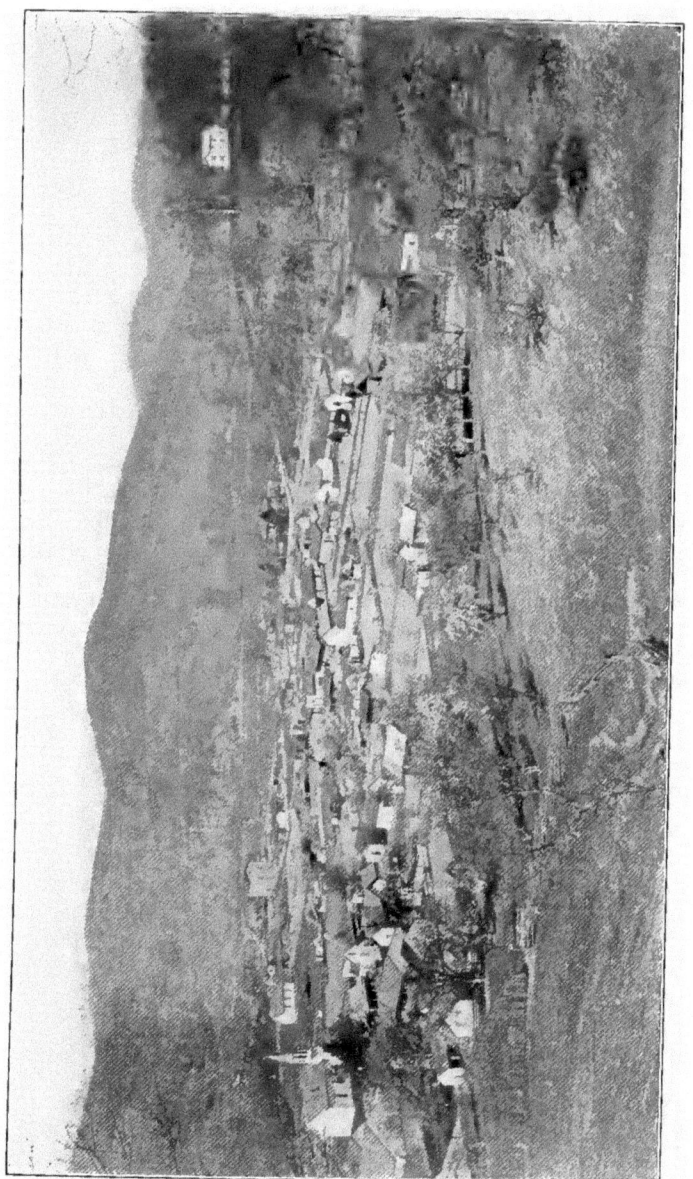

THE VILLAGE OF LOST CREEK.

As early as in September, 1815, a question arose about free communion with the First Day Baptists. Two years afterward, the question came to the fore-ground again, but at neither time did the church take action favouring free communion.

Early in the year, 1821, a controversy waged over Calvinism, a question which divided the church into two opposing factions. The controversy continued until a business meeting of the church held April 29, following, which was attended by Rev. John Davis and Deacon John Bright, both of the Cohansey (Shiloh), New Jersey, Church. These two brethren were requested by the church to take the question in controversy under consideration, and advise the church what course to pursue.

They decided upon new articles of faith, which they submitted to the church on December 2, following. The report was acceptable to all, and on the 30th of the same month, the new articles of faith were adopted and signed by the members of the church.

In October, 1819, William Williams was called, along with Abel Bond, to improve his gifts in the church, at his convenience, in exhorting or preaching. Williams soon displeased some of the church, and in the following April, the church considered the advisability of revoking his licence, but it was finally decided to allow it to stand for the remainder of the year for which it was originally granted. At the end of the year the church refused to renew the licence, but finally rescinded its adverse action.

William Williams continued to preach with more or less regularity, until in March, 1830, when a question arose as to whether he should be ordained, or continue to preach as a licentiate.

After careful consideration of the question, the church declined to ordain him, but instructed the clerk of the church to send him a formal licence to preach. Again in January, 1831, the church decided by a vote of twenty-five to thirteen, not to call Williams to ordination.

Williams now became an issue, and that question together with others soon created a division in the church. A small minority, in face of the strong opposition of the rest of the church, vigorously advocated a change in the polity of the church, so that on June 20, 1831, "after mature deliberation, for the sake of harmony and to obviate a difficulty under which we have long laboured, and for other reasons, a large majority submitted to the requisition of the minority, and granted their request."

This concession did not avail, however, and the minority under the leadership of Williams seceded from the church, seized the meeting house, and organised the *Second Seventh Day Baptist Church of Lost Creek.*

The new church at once ordained Williams, and in September, 1834, applied for admission to the General Conference, at the session of the Conference held at DeRuyter, New York.

The General Conference acted upon the application by referring it to a committee, which made the following report:—

"Respecting the request of the 2d S[eventh] D[ay] B[aptist] Church on Lost Creek, we would respectfully suggest, that, agreeably to a resolution of the General Conference, which requires of any church, wishing to become a member of this Conference, [that] they forward to the Conference a copy of the articles of faith, upon which said church is constituted, it would not be expedient to grant this request, at this time, as the above condition has not been complied with; but that the brethren who may be appointed to visit the church, in New Salem, visit these brethren also, investigate the circumstances of their organisation, and ordination of brother Williams, and act in behalf of this General Conference, as in their wisdom they may deem expedient; and that a letter be written to them apprising them thereof."

At the next annual session of the General Conference, held with the church at Hopkinton, Rhode Island, in September, 1835, the report of this committee appears in the following record:—

"Eld. Joel Greene of the committee appointed to visit the churches of New Salem and Lost Creek, reported as follows:—

"'The undersigned, one of the committee appointed last session to visit several Seventh Day Baptist churches in Virginia, beg leave to report that we have visited those churches, accompanied and assisted by br. S. Coon, our missionary in that quarter. . . . . .

"'We also visited the 2d Seventh Day Baptist Church on Lost Creek, and after a careful examination of their Articles of Faith, their discipline, &c.,

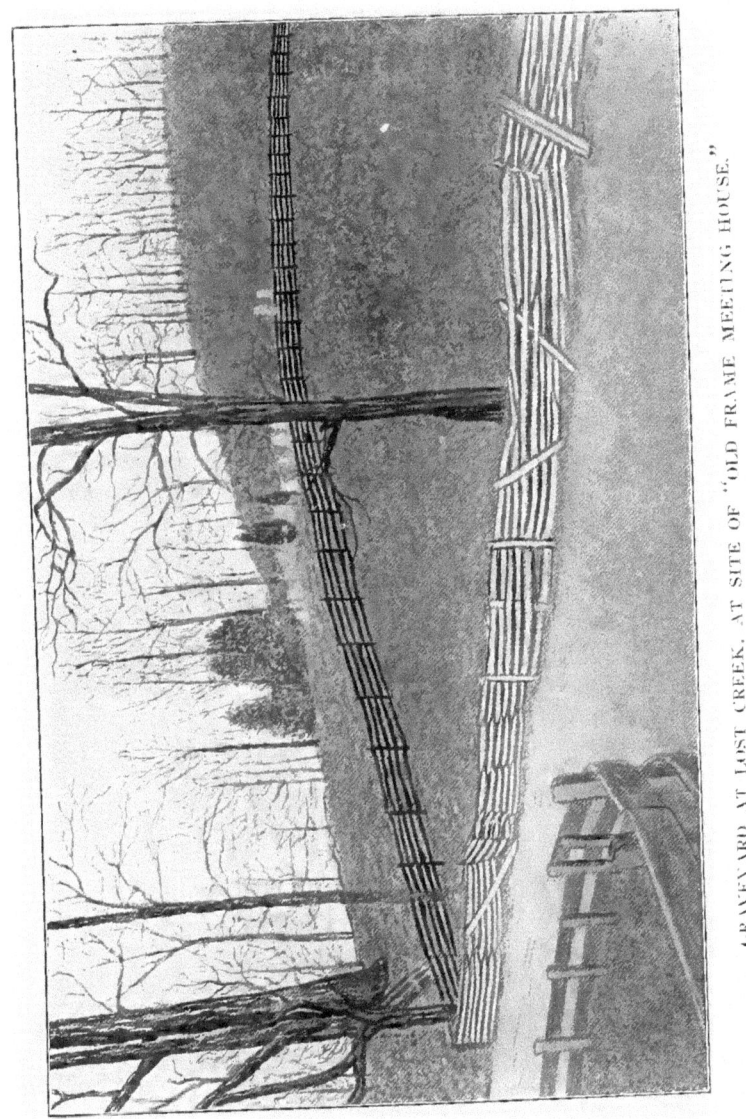

GRAVEYARD AT LOST CREEK, AT SITE OF "OLD FRAME MEETING HOUSE."

"'RESOLVED, That we do not recognise the rectitude of the motives which led to their separation from the 1st Seventh Day Baptist Church on Lost Creek.

"'RESOLVED, That the circumstances attending the ordination of Wm. Williams, are, in the opinion of the committee, such as to forbid the validity of said ordination being admitted by the conference.

"'RESOLVED, That in the opinion of the committee it is inexpedient to grant their request for admission to this body.
"JOEL GREENE."

The new church was left in quiet possession of the old meeting house, the old church holding services, first at the home of one of its members, and afterwards at the "school house by Elisabeth VanHorn's."

Under the sagacious leadership of Rev. Joel Greene, who, as we have seen, was on a visit to Virginia at that time, it was decided to build a new meeting house; and on July 23, 1832, the church took formal action to that effect, voting "to build a frame meeting house at the old burying ground on Mr. Bassel's premises." This is the building that for many years was known in all that region of country round about as the "Frame Church." Of its erection, Rev. Joel Greene relates as follows:—

"This was done with [such] unanimity, liberality, and celerity, as to do honour to the church and disarm opposition. In a short time, the larger portion of the dissenters retraced their steps, resumed their walk with the church, and the community rejoiced in a rather extensive revival of religion, bringing increased strength to the church, and benefit to the cause of religion generally."

These were days of stormy trial for the church, nevertheless. The new church continued its existence with a handful of members, for several years. Finally becoming weary, themselves, of the division and consequent strife, on April 10, 1835, they presented a petition to the old church praying for admission to that church. The petition was rejected, and the new church gradually died away.

On May 24, 1834, a request was presented to the Lost Creek Church asking it to undertake to settle certain matters of difference between individual members of the New Salem Church. This the Lost Creek Church declined to do, on the ground that the New Salem Church had not made due effort to settle the difficulties itself. After the New Salem Church should have made proper effort to settle these difficulties and then failed, the Lost Creek Church expressed a willingness to lend its aid.

In the end, the Lost Creek Church became involved in this trouble itself, through receiving William F. Randolph into its membership, under the circumstances set forth in the chapter on the history of the *New Salem Church*.

On March 3, 1844, Samuel D. Davis and Abel B. Bond were called to improve their "talents within the bounds of this church." On the same day, Abel Bond, 2d., was appointed a committee to correspond with Rev. Thomas B. Brown and ascertain what his travelling expences would be during his travels in Virginia.

On December 9, 1849, Rev. Azor Estee and his wife were received into membership from the church at Petersburgh, New York. He had come upon the field in the capacity of a general missionary among the churches in Virginia, and when some six months afterward the establishment of an academy among these churches came to be seriously considered, under the leadership of William F. Randolph and Rev. Azor Estee, the Lost Creek Church pledged its moral and financial support to the enterprise.[1]

June 9, 1854, Rev. Samuel D. Davis was appointed pastor of the church. He continued to act in that capacity for several years, a part of the period dividing his time between the Lost Creek and New Salem churches.

On May 11, 1856, the church voted to ask admission into the Eastern Association, and appointed Rev. Samuel D. Davis a delegate to that body. This application precipitated a spirited discussion of the Slavery Question, which is described in the subsequent chapter on *Slavery*.

On March 13, 1857, Lewis Bond and his wife were received into the membership of the church. They were the two remaining members of the North Fork of Hughes River Church, in which Lewis Bond had been ordained a deacon and licenced to preach. He was received into the Lost Creek Church upon the same footing he occupied as a member of the North Fork of Hughes River Church.

On the same day, Naomi Kildow, formerly a member of

---

1. Cf. chapter in this book on the *West Union Academy*.

the defunct Woodbridgetown Church, and a descendant of Rev. Enoch David, was made a member of the Lost Creek Church.

Also upon this date, action was taken preparatory to securing the services of Rev. David Clawson, as pastor of the church.

On September 10, 1858, a committee was appointed to confer with a like committee from the New Salem Church for the purpose of making the arrangements necessary to secure Rev. David Clawson as the pastor of the two churches jointly. The negotiations were successful, and on March 11, 1859, a brief synopsis of the theological views of David Clawson were presented and recorded as follows:—

"Synopsis of views presented by Elder David Clawson to the Brethren of the Lost Creek Church on their extending to him a call to preach to them, as his sentiments, what he understands to be the basis of the views, doctrines, and organisation of said church, as also a brief outline of the doctrines and sentiments he expects to hold forth; [*viz.*],

"THAT ALL men are under obligation to keep all the commandments of God, as given at Sinai. See Exodus XX. 1-17; Matthew V. 17, etc.

"THAT ALL men are justly included under sin and its consequences, of condemnation, and un-reconciliation of God for their disobedience and enmity to that law.

"THAT THE Gospel is a glorious scheme or plan of God's own devising, originating in his love and the effect of His wisdom, to save man from all the consequences of sin by reconciling them to himself in Christ Jesus, his Son, who died for our sins.

"IT IS TRUE (or sincere) living (or active) faith, and that only, that does secure to any, pardon, justification, and eternal life. And all that thus believe have that pardon, justification, and life. (See John III, 39).

"ALL THAT have faith to feel that sin is exceedingly sinful and are ready to confess it with full purpose of heart to forsake it. (1st John I, 9).

"THAT SUCH confession is set forth in all, each, and every ordinance of the Gospel, and is, on the part of the believer, a solemn declaration of his faith in, and submission to, our Lord Jesus Christ. The union of believers thus manifesting their faith in and for Christ and his cause, is what composes, or constitutes a Gospel church.

"THAT SUCH union is enjoined by Christ for the benefit of his people, and to present through him his truth to the world."

He came upon the field and entered upon his work with earnestness and zeal, but the two churches he came to serve were not to enjoy his labours long, for he was soon called away to the better world, and on March 8, 1860, the church recorded the following resolution:—

"RESOLVED, That while we would desire to bow in submission to the divine will we deeply mourn the removal of our beloved Elder David Clawson from our midst by death, and we heartily recommend the widow of our beloved Elder to the sympathies and charity of both this and the New Salem Church."

Upon the death of Rev. David Clawson, Rev. Samuel D. Davis was again called to the pastorate of the church. He accepted the call and continued as pastor, assisted from time to time by Rev. Jacob Davis and Lewis F. Randolph, until the 1st of January, 1869, when he resigned of his own free will on account of ill health, and relinquished the work for a short time.

The Civil War threw its clouds over the Lost Creek Church in common with the other churches in Virginia, and when after the formation of the State of West Virginia, and the formal adoption of its constitution on June 20, 1863, the local civil authorities saw fit to use the house of worship of the Lost Creek Church as a suitable place in which to conduct an election on December 10, 1863, the church made the following protest:—

"RESOLVED, That we deeply regret that there is a township election to be held at our Church House on the 11th of this month, believing, as we do, that the house of God should be used only for religious purposes.

"WHEREAS, The foregoing resolution expresses the feelings of all our members, together with the fact that there is a good school house in sight of the Church suitable for the occasion, therefore,

"RESOLVED, That we humbly ask the Commissioners to change the place of holding the election to the school house or some other suitable place, and that Brothers William Batten and William Kennedy be a committee to visit them and present to them a copy of the foregoing resolution."

On the 12th of March, 1864, the committee appointed to visit the Election Commissioners, reported that while they had not succeeded in preventing the holding of the election in the meeting house on the 11th of December preceding, they had obtained a promise to the effect that elections would be held elsewhere in the future.

March 9, 1866, the church took action as follows con-

REV. DAVID CLAWSON.

cerning a recent visit of Rev. Walter B. Gillette to West Virginia:—

"WHEREAS, We believe the faithful, though short, labours of Elder Gillette were well received and highly appreciated by our people and friends generally, therefore,

"RESOLVED, That we tender to him our sincere thanks for the same, and that the clerk forward to him a copy of the foregoing resolution."

Action was taken from time to time as to ways and means whereby Rev. Samuel D. Davis and Rev. Jacob Davis could be actively employed for more of their time in the work of administering to the needs of the Lost Creek and New Salem churches, not forgetting to visit the isolated members of these churches, many of whom lived at a great distance from the immediate bounds of these churches.

In the summer of 1867, Samuel D. Davis and Jacob Davis made a trip to Shelbyville, Tennessee, to visit Dr. William J. Gordon, a member of the New Salem Church.[1] At the business meeting of the Lost Creek Church, held September 13, 1867, Rev. Samuel D. Davis presented a report of this trip to the Lost Creek Church as follows:—

"Lost Creek, West Virginia, September 13, 1867.
"To the Brethren composing the Seventh Day Baptist Church at Lost Creek;

"DEAR BRETHREN :—

"Having been appointed by you at your last church meeting to go on a short missionary tour to Tennessee; in compliance with your arrangement, I left my home on the 16th day of June, 1867, having previously received at the hands of your committee, Hiram N. Davis, who was appointed to solicit funds for said Mission, $99.00, and proceeded to New Salem. On my way, I called on Randolph Davis, who swelled the mission fund to $100.00.

"On arriving at New Salem, I was joined by Brother Jacob Davis, and at 4 P. M., we left the friends of New Salem for Shelbyville, Tennessee, where we arrived on the evening of the 18th, and met with Doctor William J. Gordon, who was in waiting at that point to receive us.

"The next day, we went with him to his lovely home in the beautiful hills of Middle Tennessee. In this section we remained nearly two weeks, visiting and preaching to large, increasing, and attentive congregations, when we decided (having asked wisdom from

---

1. Dr. William J. Gordon, who was a member of the New Salem Church died at Shelbyville, Bedford County, Tennessee, August 21, 1875.

above) that under all the circumstances, our work in that section, for the present, was ended, Doctor Gordon concurring in the decision.

"Owing to the extreme hot weather, and brother Jacob's bad health, we only preached in this section eleven sermons.

"We found Doctor Gordon to be a man of high standing in his neighbourhood, and a firm and an able contender for the faith once delivered to the saints; his wife, an accomplished lady and a Seventh Day Baptist in principle and practise; the people of his neighbourhood, sociable, affable, and hospitable, and we hope our labours among them were not in vain in the Lord.

"On our return, we called on our brethren in Jackson Centre, Ohio, and preached four sermons for them. They are in a destitute condition, having no minister except Elder S. Babcock, who is superannuated. They seemed much refreshed with our visit.

"I returned to my home on the 9th day of July, having been absent twenty-four days, travelled fifteen hundred and seventy-two miles, preached nine sermons, and made twenty-four visits.

"Travelling expenses, $59.20; incidental expenses, $15.00. We received of friends in Tennesee $7.00, of the brethren and friends in Ohio $14.50, which we divided equally, making [us each] $10.75. Total amount money received, $110.75. Total amount of expenses, $74.20. Money received over expenses, $36.55.

"All of which we respectfully submit.

"S. D. DAVIS."

At the next church meeting after the one at which the foregoing report was presented, Jacob VanHorn, of the church at Welton, Iowa, and Simeon Babcock and Hezekiah M. Stout of the church at Jackson Centre, Ohio, appeared with a request that Rev. Samuel D. Davis should visit their respective churches, and engage for a time in evangelistic work. The church voted to leave the matter to the discretion of Samuel D. Davis.

In the year 1870, the church undertook the erection of a new house of worship, to be built of brick. This was carried through to a successful accomplishment, and the Lost Creek Church was provided with the best house of worship of any of the churches of the South-Eastern Association, and one of the best be found at that time in central West Virginia.

At the end of the year 1874, Rev. Samuel D. Davis finally resigned the pastorate of the church, and was succeeded by Rev. Charles A. Burdick, who for several years had been engaged in missionary work in West Virginia.

Charles A. Burdick was followed, successively, by Lucius

ABEL P. BOND.

BRUMFIELD BOND.

R. Swinney, John L. Huffman, Lely D. Seager, William L. Burdick, and Mazzina G. Stillman.

In October, 1880, the church purchased a parsonage, and in 1887, for a second time, the church lost its house of worship by fire. The loss was promptly repaired.

With the establishment of Salem College in 1889, the Lost Creek Church began to suffer a decline in its resident membership, several families moving away to Salem in order to give their children the advantages offered by the new school. The church, however, is in a flourishing condition at the present time, and the outlook for its future prosperity and usefulness is bright.

QUIET DELL AND HACKERS CREEK.

From the very beginning of its existence up to within a few years of the date of this writing, the Lost Creek Church has maintained a preaching station at Quiet Dell, situated on Elk Creek, some ten miles from Clarksburg, and about an equal distance from Lost Creek Station.

This was the home of Abel Bond, Sr. His home was the first stopping place of missionaries sent to Virginia from the north and east, as they came on horseback up the West Fork River from the Woodbridgetown Church.

Here were entertained Rev. Amos R. Wells, from Hopkinton, Rhode Island; Rev. John Davis and Deacon John Bright, of Shiloh, New Jersey; Rev. John Greene, from DeRuyter, New York; Rev. Alexander Campbell, of DeRuyter, New York; and others. Here a home was built in the corner of the yard of Abel Bond for the use of Alexander Campbell and his family upon their second visit to this field.

Here, Abel Bond established a grist and saw mill, run by water power from Elk Creek, and for many years the place was known as Bond's Mills. With the exception of one or two short intervals, the mills remained in the hands of the Bond family until about the year 1880, when they passed into other hands forever, and after a few years became neglected, and went to ruin.

In later years, the most spirited member of the Lost Creek Church at Quiet Dell was Dudley H. Davis. He interested himself greatly in church work, and was the superintendent for several years of a flourishing Sabbath School at

Quiet Dell. But physical infirmities overtook him which prevented his taking part in public meetings, and the interests at Quiet Dell languished, and have finally almost wholly died out from deaths and removals.

Other important interests of the church have been for a great many years on Hackers Creek, where another one of the Bond families located, some ten or twelve miles away from Lost Creek Station. The interests there are represented at the present time by the family of Mr. Boothe Bond and his brother, Levi D. Bond.

MEETING HOUSES.

The Lost Creek Church has had four houses of worship. On July 20, 1806, the church voted to build a log meeting house twenty-two feet wide by twenty-eight feet in length on the land of Richard Bond. This building served the church for a house of worship for several years, and was then accidentally burnt.

On February 22, 1811, it was decided to replace the burnt house with another log building slightly smaller than the first, the new house to be twenty-six feet long and twenty-two feet wide. The church also decided to change the site, and place the new building on the land of William VanHorn, who agreed to give the church a deed to a lot of one acre.

The second house was used by the church, until the seceding body, known as the Second Seventh Day Baptist Church of Lost Creek, was formed, when the new church seized the house of worship, and as a result, the old church was compelled for a time to worship in the private houses of its members and in a school house that was near by.

Instead of trying to regain possession of the house of worship, the church wisely decided to build a new meeting house, this time a frame building, at the old burying ground on the farm of Mr. Bassel. The church took action to this effect, on July 23, 1832. This building, when completed, was called the "Frame Church," and was known by that name far and wide so long as it stood.

On the 11th of March, 1870, a committee was appointed to select a site for a new church edifice, submit a plan for the proposed building, and recommend whether it should be a frame or brick building.

THE LOST CREEK CHURCH.

On the 8th of the following April, the committee reported that it had selected as a site for the new house of worship, a lot of land containing a trifle more than two acres belonging to Samuel Cookman, and situated on the east side of the turnpike leading from Clarksburg to Weston, at a cost of $157.57. The committee likewise submitted a plan providing for a building fifty feet in length by thirty-eight feet in width, and recommended that it be built of brick. They submitted estimates for both brick and frame work, however. The former at $2,503.60, and the latter at $2,191.40.

The report of the committee, with its recommendations, was adopted. Title was taken the same day to the new site. Moses H. Davis was appointed to solicit funds for the building, and a building committee was appointed. The work was completed as directed, at a total cost of $4,300.00, as reported to the church on December 12, 1872. It was formally dedicated on January 14, 1872.

On the preceding day, Sabbath, an affecting farewell service was held in the Old Frame Meeting House. Rev. Samuel D. Davis preached a sermon, using as his text, Exodus XXXIII, 15. He was followed by Rev. Abram Herbert Lewis, who used the same text.

At the dedication service, on the next day, the order of exercises was as follows:—

Singing.
Presentation of Bible, in behalf of the donor, Rev. Walter B. Gillette.
Reading of Scriptures, by Rev. Charles A. Burdick.
Hymn No. 903, from the Christian Psalmody, "The perfect world, by Adam trod."
Prayer, by Rev. Lewis F. Randolph.
Hymn No. 905, from the Christian Psalmody, "Great King of Glory, Come."
Sermon, from II Chronicles II, 4, by Rev. Abram Herbert Lewis.
Collection to apply upon debt of church.
Delivery of keys of the new edifice, by the Building Committee.
Dedicatory Prayer, by Rev. Samuel D. Davis.
Charge to Trustees and Church, by Rev. Charles A. Burdick.
Benediction, by Rev. Abram Herbert Lewis.

In the evening, after the dedication service of the day, Moses H. Davis and William B. VanHorn were ordained deacons of the Lost Creek Church.

On the following day, the Second Day of the week, the

organisation of the South-Eastern Association was effected at Lost Creek, and on the following Sixth Day of the week, there was organised within the bounds of the Lost Creek Church the West Fork (now called the Roanoke) Church, in what was then called "Sabbatarian Valley." Here the Lost Creek Church had recently completed a neat frame building to be used as a house of worship by those members of the church living in that vicinity.

On December 24, 1876, Moses H. Davis was directed by the church, to advertise for bids for the "Old Frame" structure, and sell it, and on March 4, 1877, it was sold to Clinton H. Davis for thirty-five dollars ($35.00).

On the night of September 24, 1887, the Lost Creek Church, for a second time, had the misfortune to have its house of worship destroyed by fire. The walls, however, were for the most part left standing, and not so seriously damaged but that they could be repaired without tearing them wholly down.

The church immediately rallied to the work of rebuilding. On the day following the fire, a business meeting of the church was held on the church lot, and a committee, consisting of Charles N. Maxson, Boothe Bond, Levi B. Davis, and Wardner Davis, was appointed to solicit funds. A committee was appointed to superintend the work of repairing, and still another committee was appointed to secure a suitable place in which the church could meet for worship until the repairs could be completed.

The repairs were completed at a cost of $1,671.90, and the edifice was re-dedicated at the annual session of the South-Eastern Association, held with the Lost Creek Church, in May, 1888. The dedicatory sermon was preached by the pastor, Rev. John L. Huffman.

GRAVEYARDS.

When the Old Frame Church was abandoned, the lot, which had been used for many years as a graveyard, remained in the possession of the church, and continued to be used as a burying ground.

On March 12, 1897, Lloyd R. Kennedy and Clinton H. Davis were appointed a committee to confer with Lloyd Stout, the owner of a piece of land lying across the public highway

THE PARSONAGE AT LOST CREEK.

from the Brick Church, and ascertain upon what terms it could be obtained for a graveyard. On the 9th of the following April, the committee reported that an option had been secured upon a plot of about two acres at the rate of sixty-six and two-thirds dollars ($66.67) an acre. The action of the committee was approved and it was ordered to proceed with the actual purchase of the ground. Accordingly, on June 10, 1898, the committee reported to the church that the new graveyard, purchased at an aggregate cost of one hundred and thirty-eight dollars and seventy-five cents ($138.75), was paid for, and the deed for it passed to the church.

PARSONAGE.

For three quarters of a century the Lost Creek Church had no home for its pastor, unless the house built at Quiet Dell on the premises of Abel Bond for the use of Rev. Alexander Campbell might be so called. This is described in the chapter on the *New Salem Church* and as intimated there, was probably largely, if not wholly, built by Abel Bond himself.

On September 5, 1880, Loman J. Kennedy, W. H. Ferris, William P. Bond, Dudley H. Davis, and Boothe Bond, were appointed a committee to select a site for a parsonage, to select a plan, and report the probable cost of such a building to the church.

On the 18th of the following October, the committee recommended the purchase of the unfinished house of Thomas A. Davis, at Lost Creek Station. The report of the committee was adopted, and the committee was instructed to purchase the house and have it completed. It was empowered to raise the money by subscription to pay for the house.

On the 11th of November, 1883, the last payment on the parsonage was reported as made, and an unencumbered title passed to the church. The total cost of the parsonage was upwards of six hundred dollars ($600.00).

PASTORS.

Rev. John Davis was the early pastor of the Lost Creek, and as early as 1811, he was reported to Conference as the elder of that church, although he was a member of the New Salem Church. He probably visited the church quite frequently, especially on the occasion of Communion Service and other special services.

On June 20, 1806, the church decided to have Communion Service three times a year, the last Sabbath in March, July, and November, respectively. The Sixth Day of the week preceding the Communion Service was to be a day of prayer and fasting. They also decided to have a Yearly Meeting the first Sabbath in October, which was conducted by the Lost Creek Church alone until in the year 1859, when on the 10th of June of that year the church appointed a committee to visit the New Salem Church and invite it to unite with the Lost Creek Church in this service. The committee carried out the instructions of the church, and the proposed arrangement was effected.

The First Day of the week before Communion Service was the time for the regular business meetings of the church.

The church had Ruling Elders for a time, but this arrangement proved unsatisfactory, and on November 20, 1820, the office was abolished.

Much of the preaching from Sabbath to Sabbath, however, was done by the licentiate members of the church, and by roving clergymen of too questionable a character to entitle them to be called itinerant ministers. These men usually professed to be Seventh Day Baptists until their true colours were uncovered. The church was frequently deceived in this manner. As early as 1811, one Smith, of doubtful reputation, claiming to come from New Jersey, appeared among them.

On November 24, 1811, the church voted to request Hamilton Goss to preach for them once a month.

About the year, 1811, Rev. John Davis moved to the state of Ohio, and connected himself for a time with the church at Mad River. He then returned to Virginia, when difficulties arose involving him with several of the members of the Lost Creek Church, but he continued to minister to its wants.

On July 6, 1817, Abel Bond was instructed by the church to write to the General Conference soliciting ministerial aid, and in the November following, similar action was taken.

In common with the New Salem Church, the Lost Creek Church was visited from time to time by ministers from other parts of the denomination. Amos R. Wells, Joel Greene, John Davis of Shiloh, New Jersey, Alexander Campbell, and others, came from time to time. But their stay was always short.

As early as April 4, 1824, Rev. Lewis A. Davis began to preach for the church. He continued preaching without any official connection with the church, until June 3, 1827, when he accepted a call previously extended to him to become pastor of the church.

On March 6, 1831, Rev. Peter Davis of the New Salem Church, was solicited to attend the Quarterly Meetings (communion services) of the Lost Creek Church.

On March 3, 1844, Abel Bond, 2d, was appointed to correspond with Rev. Thomas B. Brown concerning a trip to Virginia.

As early as June 5, 1845, Samuel D. Davis was licenced to preach, and occupied the pulpit quite regularly for several years.

On December 9, 1849, the church appointed a committee to confer with a similar committee from the New Salem Church, regarding a proper division of the services of Rev. Azor Estee, who had recently come upon the Virginia field, and who with his wife joined the Lost Creek Church upon that date. But his services were soon claimed for the newly established Academy at West Union.

On June 9, 1854, Rev. Samuel D. Davis was appointed pastor of the church for a period of one year. At the expiration of this time, he was re-elected, and continued as pastor of the Lost Creek Church, dividing his labours a part of the time, with the New Salem Church, until on December 11, 1868, when on account of ill-health, he declined a call from the church to continue as it pastor.

In the meantime, Rev. David Clawson was employed jointly by the Lost Creek and New Salem churches, from a time early in the year 1858, until his death, which occurred about two years afterward, to labour within the bounds of the two churches.

Rev. Jacob Davis of the New Salem Church was invited on March 8, 1860, to preach for the Lost Creek Church on the second Sabbath in each month. On March 13, 1863, he was invited to preach for the church at his convenience, and the members were solicited to contribute to his support.

On September 8, 1865, when Rev. Samuel D. Davis received his annual call to the pastorate for the ensuing year, Rev. Jacob Davis, and Lewis F. Randolph and his brother Judson, the last two of whom were licentiate members of the New Salem Church, were all invited to labour in the church during the following year.

On June 8, 1866, a committee was appointed to confer with a like committee from the New Salem Church to arrange with Samuel D. Davis and Jacob Davis to give more time to pastoral work in the two churches, so that every member of each church "should be reached as often as once in six months."

After Rev. Samuel D. Davis had declined on account of impaired health to serve the church longer as pastor, arrangements were concluded with Rev. Jacob Davis on January 8, 1869, to become pastor of the church until the second Sabbath in March, 1870. Rev. Samuel D. Davis was also invited "to preach when his health will permit, and he may think the cause demands."

The salary paid the pastor in those days was small. At one time Samuel D. Davis and Jacob Davis were voted an annual salary of seventy-five dollars ($75.00) each for their labours with both the Lost Creek and New Salem churches. And on March 12, 1869, arrangements were completed for the employment of Rev. Jacob Davis "to give his entire time, beginning with the first Sabbath in February, 1869, to March 15, 1870, to the work of the church, for the sum of two hundred and fifty dollars ($250.00)." And Rev. Jacob Davis lived at Greenbrier, twenty miles away!

On March 11, 1870, Rev. Samuel D. Davis was again chosen pastor. He presented his last report as pastor to the church, March 13, 1874, and Rev. Charles A. Burdick, who had been employed by the Missionary Board as a general missionary upon the West Virginia field for several years past, accepted a call, December 5, 1875, to become his successor.

Rev. Charles A. Burdick served as pastor nearly two years, and then resigned to give his attention to other interests in the State of New York.

REV. WILLIAM L. BURDICK.

On August 5, 1877, Rev. Lucius R. Swinney was elected pastor. He served for a period of nine years, and then resigned to accept the pastorate of the church at DeRuyter, New York.

On September 5, 1886, Rev. John L. Huffman was elected pastor. He remained with the church until he resigned to accept the pastorate of the Salem Church. His resignation was accepted March 13, 1891, and on the 23d of the same month, Rev. Lely D. Seager was elected his successor.

On February 4, 1893, the church accepted the resignation of Rev. Lely D. Seager, who soon after assumed the pastoral charge of the Ritchie Church.

On June 9, 1893, the Lost Creek Church extended a call to Rev. William L. Burdick to become its pastor. He accepted the call and remained until August, 1895. He was succeeded by Rev. Mazzini G. Stillman, who began his labour with the church in January, 1896.

Rev. Mazzini G. Stillman presented his resignation July 26, 1902, when it was accepted by the church.

LICENCED TO PREACH.

Concerning licence to preach the records of the Lost Creek Church show the following:—

November 18, 1810. Moses Huffman and Cornelius Williams were given licence to preach within the bounds of the church, at their convenience.

March 31, 1811. Richard Bond was disciplined by the church for having given a letter of recommendation to one Mr. Smith, a preacher from New Jersey, without the consent of the church.

October 3, 1819. William Williams and Abel Bond were licenced to preach within the bounds of the church.

November 8, 1819. Moses H. Ailes and Davis Loofboro were both licenced by the church to preach for a period of one year. The licences of both were probably renewed, although there is no record of such action, save that in the year 1828, Davis Loofboro voluntarily resigned his licence.

March 14, 1830. The church voted a formal licence to William Williams who was a candidate for ordination. The church felt that it could not ordain him, and reluctantly voted to grant him a certificate of licence. Afterward, when William Williams and his followers had seceded from the church and set up a new organisation, he was ordained by the new church.

April 10, 1835. Licence was granted Richard C. Bond to preach, in case that he should feel it to be his duty to do so. This licence was apparently for preaching within the bounds of the church, for on March 8, 1840, he was granted licence to preach wherever he might be called.

September 5, 1842. The church voted to request the South-Western Association to ordain Richard C. Bond at its annual session to be held with the church at Port Jefferson, Shelby County, Ohio in the following month of October. The request was presented to the association, which referred it to the Presbytery of the association. The Presbytery made a favourable report, and on the First Day of the week, October 16, the ordination took place. The ordination sermon was preached by Rev. Lewis A. Davis, at that time an elder in the Port Jefferson Church. The consecrating prayer was offered by Rev. Peter Davis of the New Salem Church. The charge was delivered by Rev. Lewis A. Davis, and the right hand of fellowship was extended by Rev. Joshua Hill of the Port Jefferson Church.

December 17, 1843. Samuel Davis Davis was granted licence to preach within the bounds of the church, and on March 3, 1844, licence was granted Abel D. Bond. The licence of Samuel Davis Davis was continued from year to year, until at the time of its renewal on September 7, 1849, he was requested to take his ordination into consideration. He hesitated about accepting ordination at that time, however. [Nevertheless, at the annual meeting of the South-Western Association, held with the church at Lost Creek, beginning the 11th of the following October, the Lost Creek Church presented a petition that he be ordained. Owing to the fact, however, that there was but one ordained minister present, Rev. Peter Davis, who was in feeble health, and consequently felt unable to conduct such a service, the ordination was postponed. The Presbytery of the association, which but a few years before, had examined Bethnel C. Church and Richard C. Bond, appears to have dissolved and wholly disappeared.] At a meeting of the church, January 27, 1850, after having given his consent, the church instructed Rev. Azor Estee, who was at that time dividing his labours between the Lost Creek and New Salem churches, to make the necessary arrangements for the ordination. [Accordingly on the 11th of May following, he was solemnly set apart to the sacred duties of a minister of the Gospel, at a service held with the Lost Creek Church, and conducted by Rev. Azor Estee and Rev. Peter Davis, who wrote and signed a formal certificate of ordination and presented it to the candidate.]

June 14, 1850. Licence was granted Joshua S. Davis to preach the gospel wherever a door of usefulness might be opened.

THE LOST CREEK CHURCH

June 14, 1856. Levi Stalnaker was licenced to preach for a period of one year. On March 13, 1857, this licence was renewed for a period of one year.

March 13, 1857. Lewis Bond, formerly a member of the North Fork of Hughes River Church, which had declined and gone out of existence, who had been ordained there as a deacon and licenced to preach, applied for membership in the Lost Creek Church. He was accepted as a deacon and a licentiate of the Lost Creek Church.

December 12, 1873. Lewis Bond was granted licence to preach.

December 11, 1874. Albert Shock, who had been previously a licentiate member of the Middle Island Church, but had now joined the Lost Creek Church, had his licence to preach recognised by the Lost Creek church.

September 10, 1897. Moses H. VanHorn was called "to the improvement of his gift," and invited to preach once a month.

Samuel B. Bond was licenced to preach the Gospel, at some time previous to October, 1899.

On September 13, 1901. S. Orestes Bond and Austin O. Bond were licenced by the church to preach.

At some time previous to the withdrawal of Jacob Davis to join the New Salem Church, he had been licenced to preach, by the Lost Creek Church. This licence was continued by the New Salem Church, by which he was afterward ordained, as will be observed by consulting the chapter on the *New Salem Church.*

DEACONS.

A few weeks after the organisation of the church, Abel Bond was appointed deacon. He was the only deacon of the church until July 21, 1811, when William VanHorn was appointed to serve as deacon in the absence of Deacon Bond. And on the 1st of November, 1813, William VanHorn was made a deacon, with Abel Bond, by permanent appointment. The records also show the following:—

March 2, 1823. John Forsythe was appointed assistant deacon, to serve along with Deacon Bond, who was now serving alone again. And on September 5, 1830, Abner Batten succeeded John Forsythe as deacon, since the latter intended to remove to the State of Ohio.

December 3, 1838. Levi H. Bond was appointed assistant deacon. He served until March 10, 1848, when William Kennedy was appointed deacon in the stead of Levi H. Bond, who for several years had been recognised as a deacon in full standing, but who was now leaving the country. The church now, as for several years previous to this time, had three deacons, Abel Bond, Sr., and Abner Batten still serving.

June 8, 1855. John J. VanHorn was appointed deacon.

March 13, 1857. Lewis Bond, who had previously served as a deacon of the North Fork of Hughes River Church, was admitted as a member and deacon into the Lost Creek Church.

March 10, 1865, Levi Bond was appointed a deacon of the church, and on June 8, 1866, the church voted that on the second Sabbath of the following September the deacons of the church should be ordained. As no record of the ordination of deacons appears before this date, it is doubtful if any of the deacons had ever been ordained by the church previous to this time.

December 8, 1871. Moses H. Davis and William B. VanHorn were chosen deacons by the church. Arrangements were made to have them ordained at the meeting called for the organisation of the South-Eastern Association, which was held with the church at Lost Creek, beginning the 15th of the following January.

February, 1873. Deacon Holly Welcome Maxson was received into the membership of the church by letter from the Seventh Day Baptist Church at Cussewago, Pennsylvania. As he had already been ordained a deacon, he was received into the Lost Creek Church as such.

March 9, 1888. Charles N. Maxson was chosen a deacon of the church.

December 11, 1891. Boothe Bond and Levi B. Davis were chosen deacons. Boothe Bond declined, however, to accept the appointment, and Luther A. Bond was elected in his place on the 2d of January following. The new deacons were ordained on January 3, 1892.

MODERATOR.

The name of no moderator appears in the records of the church until March 8, 1861, when William Kennedy was elected moderator for the day. Then appear the following names successively:—

June 7, 1861,	Ebenezer Bond,
September 13, 1861,	William Kennedy,
December 13, 1861,	Walter Fields McWhorter,
September 12, 1862,	William Batten,
March 13, 1863,	William Batten,
June 12, 1863,	William Kennedy,
December 10, 1863,	William Kennedy,
March 12, 1864,	William Kennedy,
September 9, 1864,	Thomas B. Davis,
March 10, 1865,	William Kennedy,
June 9, 1865,	William Batten.

On the 8th of September, 1865, the church voted that the

THE LOST CREEK CHURCH

term of office of certain officers of the church, the moderator included, should be one year. The name of the permanent moderator does not appear, however, until on September 11, 1868, when Hiram N. Davis was elected moderator for one year. He was re-elected annually until September 11, 1874, when Holly Welcome Maxson was elected to succeed him. On September 5, 1875, Charles N. Maxson was elected moderator, and he served as such until September 11, 1891, when he was succeeded by S. Orlando Davis, who has served continuously to the date of this writing, August 1, 1902.

CHURCH CLERK.

The following is a complete transcript from the record as regards the appointment of church clerk:—

December 18, 1805. Moses Huffman chosen clerk.

March 4, 1814. John Forsythe chosen clerk.

March 2, 1823. Levi H. Bond appointed clerk in place of John Forsythe.

September 4, 1831. Thomas B. Bond appointed assistant clerk.

December 3, 1838. Richard C. Bond appointed clerk.

December 4, 1842. Richard C. Bond released from clerkship, and Abel Bond, Jr., appointed in his stead as assistant clerk.

March 10, 1848. Jacob Davis appointed assistant clerk.

March 7, 1851. Joshua S. Davis appointed assistant clerk.

June 15, 1851. Jacob Davis resigned his clerkship, and L. Bond, Jr., appointed to fill his place.

December 12, 1857. Moses H. Davis appointed assistant clerk.

March 8, 1860. Levi B. Davis appointed assistant clerk in place of Moses H. Davis.

March 10, 1865. Moses H. Davis appointed clerk in place of Levi Bond resigned.

September 7, 1866. Moses H. Davis appointed clerk, and Levi B. Davis assistant clerk, for another year.

March 7, 1875. Luther A. Bond elected assistant clerk.

October 31, 1882. Luther A. Bond made clerk in place of Levi B. Davis resigned.

September 7, 1884. Marcellus Berkeley Davis made assistant clerk.

September 11, 1891. Charles A. F. Randolph made assistant clerk.

September 8, 1893. Owen T. Davis elected assistant clerk.

September 10, 1897. Marcellus Berkeley Davis elected assistant clerk.

MEMBERSHIP IN SUPERIOUR BODIES.

The Lost Creek Church became a member of the General Conference in 1808, along with the New Salem Church. In 1837, it was admitted to membership in the Western Association, at the annual session of that body, held with the church at Alfred, New York.

When the old South-Western Association was organised in 1839, the Lost Creek Church was one of its constituent members. And when the Virginia Association was constituted in 1851, the Lost Creek Church became one of the constituent members of that body, likewise.

After the dissolution of the Virginia Association, the Lost Creek Church, along with the New Salem Church, became a member of the Eastern Association in 1865, where its presence precipitated a rancorous discussion, which is treated in full in the subsequent chapter on *Slavery*. In 1858, the Lost Creek Church withdrew from the Eastern Association.

When the South-Eastern Association was constituted in 1872, the Lost Creek Church was one of the most prominent factors in its organisation, and has maintained that position to the present time.

IX.

THE MIDDLE ISLAND CHURCH.

THE Middle Island Church as originally organised was situated at Lewisport, now a part of the village of West Union, in Doddridge County on Middle Island Creek.

Here the New Salem Church had erected a house of worship several years before, for the use of several families living in that vicinity who were members of that church. A graveyard had been established on a plot of ground adjoining the church yard.

On the 19th day of August, 1831, there was presented to the New Salem Church a list of twenty-nine names of individuals who had joined the Middle Island Church. The New Salem Church approved this action, and on that date, and likewise at a meeting held in February following, granted letters of dismissal to others who wished to join the new church at Middle Island.

A permanent organisation was not consummated, however, until a later date, as will be observed from the following certificate:—

"This is to certify [to] all whom it may concern that the Seventh Day Baptist Church at Middle Island was this day organised according to [the] rules and regulations of the Seventh Day Baptist Denomination.

July 15th, 1832.

"JOHN DAVIS,
"JOEL GREENE,

"Elders."

At the time the permanent organisation of the church was effected, Gamble Shannon was called to the office of deacon, and Ephraim Bee was elected clerk.

It was voted that the quarterly meetings should be held on the Sixth Day of the week before the first Sabbath in the months of February, May, August, and November.

At the regular quarterly business meeting of the church in November, following the organisation, there was presented to the church a controversy which had arisen between Ephraim Bee and Nathan Davis. This dispute shook the infant church to its foundations, and planted the seeds of trouble for years to come. So serious was it that at the regular meeting in February next, Ephraim Bee was relieved of his duties as clerk of the church until the unfortunate difference should be adjusted.

Nathan Davis was a justice of the peace, and before him had been tried a suit at law in which Ephraim Bee and one William I. Lowther were the principals. Decision was rendered against Ephraim Bee, and a judgment entered for the sum of nine dollars ($9.00). The latter charged partiality on the part of the court in favour of Lowther, and the matter was taken to the church.

The church referred the whole matter to a committee, which after a careful review of the case, acquitted the justice of the peace of any charge of bias, and decided that due acknowledgment should be made him by his accuser. The committee further recommended that the suggestion of the accused justice be followed, to the effect that the case be tried again *ab initio*, before another justice.

Upon their request, letters of dismissal were granted to a considerable number of the leading members of the church, in February, 1835. The records of the church were committed to safe keeping in the hands of William J. Davis, and the church went into a state of lethargy for a period of more than nine years.

There was a called meeting of the church held August 30, 1844, and the active work of the church resumed. At this time Ezekiel Bee was received into the membership of the church, and invited to become its pastor. Five months afterward the invitation was accepted, and he became one of its leading spirits for several years, or until he severed his connection to become a member of the newly organised South Fork of Hughes River Church.

On January 31, 1845, the Articles of Faith were abandoned, and none were adopted in their stead until after the second revival of the organisation of the church nearly twenty years afterward. It was likewise voted on May 2d following, to revise the covenant of the church, and a committee was appointed for that purpose. The committee consisted of Ezekiel Bee, Josiah Bee, Amaziah Bee, and Joseph Jeffrey. On August 1, 1845, they presented their report which was adopted as follows:—

"We, the Seventh Day Baptist Church at Middle Island, do covenant and agree to give ourselves to the Lord and to each other by the will of God; to watch over and pray for each other as the Lord by his grace may enable us; and to be faithful and punctual in attending to Sabbath and church meetings; and to be mutual according to our abilities in contributing to defray such expences as may necessarily devolve upon us; and strive, as much as in us lies, to live peaceably with all men: and further agree that, if any one or more of our brethren trespass against us, we will strictly adhere to the rule given us by our Saviour in Matthew XVIII, 15-16-17; and to take the Scriptures for the rule of our faith and practise."

At the meeting at which the new covenant was adopted, steps were taken toward obtaining a deed from the New Salem Church for the lot owned by that church at Lewisport. After some delay occasioned by doubt as to the proper course of procedure, the deed was obtained in the name of William J. Davis, Joshua J. Davis, Joseph Jeffrey, Amaziah Bee, and Ezekiel Bee, as trustees. A new fence was built around the graveyard, but the old log church which had already disappeared was never replaced. The meetings of the church were held for the most part in the homes of its members, as follows:— Joseph Jeffrey, near Lewisport; William J. Davis, on Rock Run;[1] Amaziah Bee, at the mouth of Sugar Camp Run, on Meathouse Fork; Ezekiel Bee (lower farm), some distance below the mouth of Sugar Camp Run; and Stephen T. Davis, still further down Meathouse Fork toward Lewisport. Meetings were held frequently at the school house at the mouth of Sugar Camp Run, within a few steps of the site

---

1. Known as "Rock Run Billy" Davis.

of the present house of worship of the Middle Island Church. This school house was built of hewed logs, and was one of the first school houses built in that part of the country. As early as 1845, the church had voted to hold its quarterly meetings alternately at Middle Island and Meathouse Fork.

For upwards of forty years, the only pastor recognised by the records of the church was the one already mentioned, Ezekiel Bee. October 31, 1845, he was called to ordination. At the business meeting of the church held August 7, 1849, he received from the church the following credentials:—

"Doddridge County, Va.

"Know all persons whom it may concern, that we the Seventh Day Baptist Church of Middle Island have legally appointed Brother Ezekiel Bee pastor of our church, and thereby authorising him to administer and officiate in all the ordinances of the Gospel in our church and elsewhere, as circumstances may require.

"May the 4th, 1849.

"J[OSEPH] JEFFREY, *Clerk.*"

At a church meeting held January 5, 1851, the following delegates were appointed to attend the convention called to meet with the New Salem Church for the organisation of the Virginia Association, at the time of the division of the South-Western Association into the Virginia and Ohio associations; *viz.*, Ezekiel Bee, Joseph Jeffrey, Amaziah Bee, Joshua J. Davis, William J. Davis, Alfred N. Davis, Neely D. Jeffrey, Stephen T. Davis, and Samuel Polan.

At a business meeting of the church held March 9, 1854, the following questions were propounded:—

"*1st.* Is it proper and right for a brother when he is grieved with a brother, to absent himself from the church and neglect to take Gospel measures to remove difficulties and restore peace and good feeling, and thereby promote union and prosperity?

"In answer to the above question, the members present voted that it was not proper nor right that a brother when grieved with a brother should neglect to take Gospel measures to remove difficulties.

"*2d.* Is it our duty as christians to deal and traffic in intoxicating liquors, thereby promoting vice and immorality?

"Voted not our duty.

"*3rd.* Is it the privilege of the christian in carrying out his profession to drink of the intoxicating draught with habitual drinkers, using it as a beverage?

"Voted not the christian's privilege.

"*4th.* Can we as christians be justified in retaining as members those brethren who have gone into the ways of the world, using profane language, and engaging in vain amusements, and combating, without calling for reformation?

"Voted to the above question that we should call for reformation."

Twelve years afterwards, these questions were ordered expunged from the minutes of the church; but they are interesting in the light of existing conditions implied by them, and also as marking a certain type of activity in the career of their author, Ezekiel Bee,—a type of activity which was very marked afterwards in his connection with the South Fork of Hughes River, or the Pine Grove, Church.

The church had already entered upon troublous times, for previous to the meeting of March 9, 1854, no meeting had been held for nearly two years; and after this meeting none was held for a period of almost four years, and then no business was transacted beyond that of organising for the day, and appointing Stephen T. Davis permanent clerk.

Nearly nine years now elapsed before any further record appears.

On August 10, 1866, an unsuccessful attempt was made to transact business; and three weeks afterward, August 31, 1866, a meeting was held at the home of William J. Davis, on Rock Run, when "The remaining few resolved to revive the church," and the church entered upon another stage of its existence, which although more or less uneven has continued without intermission up to the present time.

Previous to the revival of the church in 1866, the following had served as officers of the church:—

Name.	Term of Service.
DEACONS.	
GAMBLE SHANNON,	Chosen July 15, 1832.
JOSIAH BEE,	Chosen for one year, May 1, 1846.
	Chosen for one year, August 6, 1847.
CLERKS.	
EPHRAIM BEE,	1832, 1835.
JOSEPH JEFFREY,	1834, 1844—1852.
EZEKIEL BEE,	Temporarily, 1848.
STEPHEN T. DAVIS,	1852, 1858—1866.
MODERATORS, (Appointed for the day only).	
JOSEPH JEFFREY,	1835, 1844.
AMAZIAH BEE,	1845, 1846, 1847, 1848, 1849, 1850, 1852, 1858.
EZEKIEL BEE,	1845, 1850, 1852.

JOSIAH BEE,	1846, 1848, 1851.
JOHN D. BEE,	1846.
STEPHEN T. DAVIS,	1847, 1849, 1851.
WILLIAM J. DAVIS,	1849.
AZOR ESTEE,	1851.
ALFRED N. DAVIS,	1854.

PASTOR.

EZEKIEL BEE. Called to ordination, October 31, 1845. Appointed pastor, May 4, 1849.

TREASURER.

There is no record of a treasurer, nor of the need of any money, except as follows:—

"Fee for recording deed to lot at Lewisport. [Amount not given.]
"Cost of fencing graveyard at Lewisport. Thirty Dollars."

MEETING HOUSE.

During the first thirty-four years of its existence, the church made no palpable effort to provide itself with a house of worship. Presumably the desire to possess the lot and graveyard at Lewisport formerly owned by the New Salem Church, was inspired by such a hope. But apparently no attempt was ever made to realise that hope.

February 4, 1848, Nathan Davis submitted a proposition to the church offering to give the church a site for a house of worship just across the creek in the newly organised village of West Union, which had been laid out on the lands of Nathan Davis, and made the county seat of Doddridge County. Doddridge County was formed from parts of Harrison, Lewis, Ritchie, and Tyler counties by an act of the General Assembly of Virginia, passed on the 4th day of February, 1845. The interests of the new village and county were promoted largely by members of the Middle Island and New Salem churches, and it was but natural that there should be a desire on their part for the Middle Island Church to locate in West Union. But for some cause, the offer was rejected. Nathan Davis, together with his brothers William and Joseph, had purchased twenty thousand (20,000) acres of land here in 1807 at the rate of twenty-three cents an acre, and at the time of the organisation of the Middle Island Church and for many years after, their holdings continued large. It was Joseph Davis who conveyed the lot for a meeting house and graveyard to the New Salem Church at Lewisport.

GRAVEYARD AT WEST UNION. WHITE CIRCLE SHOWS SITE OF OLD MEETING HOUSE.

MEMBERS.

At a meeting of the New Salem Church held August 19, 1831, there was presented the following list of members of the New Salem Church who had joined the Middle Island Church:—

>EPHRAIM BEE,
>LEWIS BOND,
>CALVIN DAVIS,
>ELIAS L. DAVIS,
>ELISABETH DAVIS, (1),
>ELISABETH DAVIS (2) .
>EXPERIENCE DAVIS,
>JAMES DAVIS,
>JAMES M. DAVIS,
>KEZIAH DAVIS,
>LYDIA DAVIS,
>PHIATHATA DAVIS,
>WILLIAM G. DAVIS,
>WILLIAM J. DAVIS,
>WILLIAM S. DAVIS,
>ELISABETH HOWELL,
>GEORGE W. HOWELL,
>JONATHAN HOWELL,
>MARIAH A. HOWELL,
>MARY HOWELL,
>JOHN KNIGHT,
>MARY KNIGHT,
>JACOB MAXSON,
>JAMES MAXSON,
>SIMEON MAXSON,
>SOLOMON SAYRES,
>CONTENT SHANNON,
>GAMBLE SHANNON,
>JAMES SHANNON.

On the day that the foregoing list of names was presented to the New Salem Church, that church granted letters of dismissal to the following, presumably to join the Middle Island Church:—

>ROBERT ALEXANDER,
>LUTHER DAVIS,
>SYLVESTER DAVIS.

On the twelfth of February next, the New Salem Church granted letters to the following also, presumably to join the Middle Island Church:—

>ASENETH BABCOCK,
>WILLIAM BABCOCK,

CATHARINE DAVIS,
EDITH DAVIS,
JAMES DAVIS,
JOSHUA DAVIS,
LEWIS DAVIS,
MARY DAVIS,
NATHAN DAVIS,
SAPPHIRA DAVIS, wife of William S. Davis,
MARY HUGHES,
MARY MAXSON.

The following additional names appear in the records prior to the revival of the organisation in 1866:—

AMAZIAH BEE,
EZEKIEL BEE,
ISAIAH BEE,
INGABY BEE,
JOHN D. BEE,
JOSIAH BEE,
PRISCILLA BEE,
ALFRED N. DAVIS,
LEMUEL DAVIS,
ELISABETH DAVIS, wife of Stephen T. Davis,
KATHARINE DAVIS,
RHODA DAVIS,
SARAH ANN DAVIS,
STEPHEN T. DAVIS,
DELIA ANN JEFFREY,
JOSEPH JEFFREY,
NEELY D. JEFFREY,
TACY JEFFREY,
JEMIMA KELLEY,
KEZIAH POLAN,
SAMUEL POLAN.

RE-ORGANISATION AND SUBSEQUENT HISTORY.

On the last day of August, 1866, there was a business meeting called at the home of William J. Davis on Rock Run, when "the remaining few resolved to revive the church." Joseph Jeffrey acted as moderator for the day. Prayer was offered by Amaziah Bee. Stephen T. Davis served as clerk. Amaziah Bee was given licence "to preach the Gospel for the term of six months."

Other business meetings were held at the home of William J. Davis on September 19, 1866, and October 19, 1866, respectively. On the Sixth Day of the week before the first

LOG SCHOOL HOUSE AT THE MOUTH OF SUGAR CAMP RUN.
(A Restoration).

Sabbath in December, 1866 (November 30), a business meeting was held at the home of Joseph Jeffrey, near West Union. At this meeting James B. Davis was received as a member and given licence to preach, for one year. This was the last business meeting of the church held in the neighbourhood of its original location.

Several members of the church still lived at or near West Union, and retained their membership in the Middle Island Church, until the organisation of the West Union Church, in 1888, when such of them as were still living, became constituent members of that church.

The majority of the members of the Middle Island Church, however, lived at New Milton, on the Meat House Fork of Middle Island Creek, some seven miles above West Union. There also lived at New Milton several families which still retained their membership with the mother church at New Salem. These together with the members of the Middle Island Church, and other Sabbath keepers residing in that vicinity, had maintained worship on the Sabbath for several years, meeting sometimes in private houses, sometimes in school houses, and sometimes in the Township Hall. Many of these families were several miles apart, and lived on Red Lick Run, Wolf Pen Run, Sugar Camp Run, and Lick Run, besides the main stream of Meat House Fork, into which the others flowed.

These people all united in building a house of worship for their common use, near the banks of the Meat House Fork of Middle Island Creek, at the mouth of Sugar Camp Run, on the line dividing the farms of Jepthah F. Randolph and Amaziah Bee, both of whom contributed land for the site of the new meeting house.

The Middle Island Church held its first business meeting in the new building, on the Sixth Day of the week, September 5, 1867. At this meeting, James B. Davis, who had previously been appointed a committee for that purpose, presented an *exposé* of faith, which was adopted. This meeting was also marked by the report of a council which met that day to pass upon the qualifications of James B. Davis, who had been called to ordination by the church. The council recommended his ordination.

The church was now fairly launched upon its new period of existence, which dates from the very middle of its period of seventy years of history embraced in this book. The fortunes of the church during the second period have ebbed and flowed, but the church has maintained a continual active life.

MEETING HOUSES.

The Middle Island Church existed for thirty-five years without a house of worship. The second one of the log cabins erected at Lewisport, by the New Salem Church, on the lot given it by Joseph Davis, was already crumbling into ruin when the Middle Island Church was originally organized. The church met, for worship and business meetings alike, in the homes of its members at Lewisport; on Rock Run; and on Meat House Fork in the Township Hall at New Milton, and the school house at the mouth of Sugar Camp Run.

A few years previous to 1830, the Bee family, consisting of the widow of Asa Bee, with several of her children, settled on the Meat House Fork of Middle Island Creek, securing the proprietary right practically to all the land from about half a mile above the mouth of Red Lick Run, to the mouth of Georges Camp, embracing a strip of land some four miles in length, and half a mile, more or less, in width. This family included Asa (2d), Ezekiel, and Amaziah, all Seventh Day Baptist clergymen; besides Ephraim, Josiah, and John Davis, all active members of the Middle Island and New Salem churches.

The Bee family was soon followed by the family of John Kelley, which, like the Bee family, came from near Salem, New Jersey, and emigrated thence to western Virginia after the Shrewsbury Church had taken up its home at New Salem. Two of the sons of John Kelley, Nathan and Asa, married and settled, the former on Lick Run, and the latter on Sugar Camp Run. A sister of Nathan and Asa married Samuel Polan, who embraced the Sabbath and settled on Meat House Fork.

Here also came Jepthah Fitz Randolph, who had left New Salem in the spring of 1845 and gone to Milton, Wisconsin; but after a single summer spent there, became dissatisfied and returned to Virginia, where he determined to settle on Meat House Fork, and called the post office which he established

THE MIDDLE ISLAND CHURCH.

and kept in his house, New Milton, after Milton, where he had spent the summer in Wisconsin.

Two or three other families also settled here, including that of James Ball Davis, who had lived for some time previously in Ohio.

Some of these families were about equally distant from the Middle Island Church at West Union (formerly Lewisport), and the New Salem Church, and consequently did not remove their membership from the New Salem Church. The latter church maintained a preaching station at Meat House Fork, and when the question of building a new house of worship was agitated by the Middle Island Church, the members of both churches living on Meat House Fork evinced a keen interest in the matter, with the result that the Middle Island Church was removed bodily to New Milton. The members of the New Salem Church for the most part continued their membership with the mother church, many of them until death. A good sized group of these members of the New Salem Church transferred their membership to the Middle Island Church, March 5, 1887. At the present time, there are but two or three members of the New Salem Church living on Meat House Fork.

Previous to October 17, 1865, subscription papers had been circulated for funds for the erection of a house of worship near the old school house at the mouth of Sugar Camp Run, where the people living in the neighbourhood had so often met for worship. On that date a meeting was called at the old school house, of all parties interested. At this meeting a building committee was appointed, consisting of Stephen T. Davis, Samuel Polan, Jepthah F. Randolph, James B. Davis, and William Jeffrey. This committee was really an executive committee with plenary powers. William Jeffrey soon moved away to Kansas, and at a meeting held January 28, 1866, Amaziah Bee and Franklin F. Randolph were added to the committee; and Stephen T. Davis and Franklin F. Randolph were elected chairman and secretary, respectively, of the committee. Both had acted in these respective capacities at the first meeting. Amaziah Bee, Jepthah F. Randolph, and James B. Davis were appointed trustees.

Samuel Polan was elected treasurer of the committee;

Amaziah Bee, collector; Jepthah F. Randolph, general agent; and Stephen T. Davis, assistant general agent.

The committee agreed to let a contract for the new building, and make themselves responsible personally for its cost. To this end, they drew up and executed a bond, making themselves responsible, each to all the others, to bear equally the expence involved in the undertaking.

On September 20, 1866, the contract for the building was awarded to Dennis Carder, for the sum of two hundred and five dollars ($205.00) and the work proceeded. By the terms of the contract, the building was to be completed by January 1, 1867. The time was afterward extended to February 1, 1867.

The original plan for the building contemplated a rude sort of structure called, in local parlance, a "Yankee frame," with the walls made of boards one and a half inches in thickness placed perpendicular, and nailed at the top to a transverse plank running lengthwise of the building, on which to lay the joists. At the lower end, the boards were nailed to the sill. The joints in the walls were to be covered by strips half an inch in thickness and two or three inches wide, extending from the eaves to the sill. This was a style of building much in vogue in that country at that time.

As the work progressed, the plans were changed, however, resulting in a substantial building, weatherboarded (clapboarded) without, and ceiled within, at a cost, when completed, of about six hundred and fifty dollars ($650.00).

The work had reached a stage sufficiently near completion, for the Middle Island Church to hold its regular Quarterly Meeting, September 5-7, 1867, in the new house of worship. But the building was not entirely completed until sometime during the summer of 1870.

The meeting house was used as it was originally contemplated, not only by the Middle Island Church, but by the Salem Church also, for the use of its members living in that vicinity. The Salem Church maintained a regular monthly service here until March, 1885, when nearly all the members of the Salem Church in the neighbourhood, joined the Middle Island Church.

This monthly service of the New Salem Church, when not

THE MIDDLE ISLAND CHURCH AND PARSONAGE.

conducted by the pastor, was led by Jepthah F. Randolph, a deacon of the New Salem Church, until his death in 1879.

The above mentioned building is the one still used by the Middle Island Church for a house of worship. The old log school house which originally stood near the site of this meeting house, and which was used as a house of worship for many years, was sold at public auction to the highest bidder, after the erection of the meeting house. It was purchased by Jepthah F. Randolph for the sum of four dollars ($4.00), and removed to his farm, where it has been in use ever since as a farm building.

At a business meeting of the Middle Island Church held March 1, 1878, a committee was appointed to stake off a site upon which to build a house of worship on the lot at West Union (formerly Lewisport), given to the New Salem Church, probably about 1810, by Joseph Davis for a churchyard and graveyard; but at the request of the New Salem Church, which never held a legal title to this property, Joseph Davis conveyed it to the Middle Island Church by a deed dated March 31, 1848. The above mentioned committee reported to the church on April 7, 1878, that a location for a meeting house had been staked off, according to the instructions of the church. Here the matter dropped and the project was not revived again until in 1889, when the newly organised West Union Church desired to build a house of worship. It was decided, however, that a more suitable location could be found elsewhere.[1]

The deed for the lot at West Union runs as follows:—

"THIS INDENTURE made the 31st day of March, in the year One Thousand Eight Hundred and Forty-eight, between Joseph Davis and Hannah, his wife, of the county of Doddridge, and State of Virginia, of the one part, and we, Joshua J. Davis, William J. Davis, Ezekiel Bee, and Amaziah Bee, trustees, in behalf of the Seventh Day Baptist Church on Middle Island, all of the county and state aforesaid, of the other part,

"*Witnesseth*, That the said Joseph Davis and Hannah, his wife, for and in the consideration of the sum of Fifty Dollars, to them in hand paid, the receipt whereof is hereby acknowledged, has granted, bargained, sold, assigned, enfeoffed, released, and confirmed, and by these presents grant, bargain, sell, alien, enfeoff, release, and confirm unto the above named trustees, their heirs, and assigns forever, for the

---

1. See chapter on the *West Union Church*.

use of the Seventh Day Baptist Church on Middle Island all that piece or parcel of ground that the Seventh Day Baptist Meeting House formerly stood on, near the Middle Island Bridge, adjoining lands deeded by the above named Joseph Davis to Samuel Chana; and the lines of said lot or parcel of land run as follows: Beginning at a Stone, No. One; thence sixteen poles to a Stone, No. Two; thence ten poles to a Stone, No. Three; thence sixteen poles to a Stone, No. Four; thence to the beginning containing one acre, to have and to hold the above described tract or parcel of land unto the above named trustees, their heirs, and assigns for use of the above named church forever, with all appurtenances, and they the said Joseph Davis and Hannah, his wife, themselves, their heirs, do covenant that they will forever warrant and defend the above described tract or parcel of land from themselves, their heirs, and assigns, and not otherwise, unto the above named trustees, their heirs and assigns forever.

"In testimony whereof the aforesaid Joseph Davis and Hannah, his wife, have hereunto set their hands and fixed seals the day and year first above written.

his
"JOSEPH x DAVIS," [Seal].
mark

her
"HANNAH x DAVIS," [Seal].
mark

"Signed and sealed
in the presence of us.
"JOSEPH JEFFREY,
"THO. S. NEELY.

"DODDRIDGE COUNTY COURT:—

"We, Joseph Jeffrey, Thomas S. Neeley, Justices of the Peace in the County aforesaid, and State of Virginia, do hereby certify that Joseph Davis, party to a certain deed bearing date 31st March, 1848, and hereto annexed, personally appeared before us in our County aforesaid, and acknowledged the same to be his act and deed and desired us to certify the same acknowledgment to the Clerk of the County Court in order that the said deed may be recorded.

"Given under our hands this the 31 day of March, 1848.
"JOSEPH JEFFREY, [Seal].
"THOS. S. NEELY," [Seal].

"DODDRIDGE COUNTY COURT:—

"We, Joseph Jeffrey, Thomas S. Neely, Justices of the Peace in the County aforesaid and State of Virginia, do hereby certify that Hannah Davis, the wife of Joseph Davis, party to a certain deed bearing date the 31st March, 1848, and hereunto annexed, personally appeared before us in our County aforesaid, and being examined by us privately and apart from her husband and having the said deed fully explained to her, the said Hannah Davis acknowledged the same to be her act and declared she wished not to retract the same, and had willingly signed the same.

"Given under our hands this 31st day of March, 1848.
"JOSEPH JEFFREY, [Seal],
"THO. S. NEELY," [Seal].

"DODDRIDGE COUNTY COURT CLERK'S OFFICE, APRIL 14, 1848:

"This deed of bargain and sale from Joseph Davis and wife to Joshua J. Davis and others, was this day presented in the Clerk's Office aforesaid, and the same was admitted to record.

"*Teste.* S. P. F. RANDOLPH, *Clk.*"
"*Copy Teste.* LUTHER E. KILE, *Clerk.*"

Recorded in Deed Book No. 1, Page 286.

The deed for the lot where the present house of worship stands is as follows:—

"THIS DEED made this 31st day of October in the year 1865, between Amaziah Bee and Rhoda, his wife, Jepthah F. Randolph and Deborah, his wife, of the County of Doddridge and State of West Virginia, of the first part, and James B. Davis, Jepthah F. Randolph, and Amaziah Bee, Trustees, and their successors in office for the Seventh Day Baptists on the Meat House Fork of Middle Island Creek of the county and state aforesaid, of the second part,

"*Witnesseth,* That the said parties of the first part for and in consideration of the sum of one dollar, to them in hand paid, the receipt whereof is hereby acknowledged, do grant unto the said parties of the second part a certain lot of land for the use and benefit of the aforesaid Seventh Day Baptists, said land being situate on the Meat House Fork of Middle Island Creek, in the County and State aforesaid, and bounded as follows; to wit, Beginning at a small sycamore near the lower end of Jepthah F. Randolph's farm, and running thence N 64 E 136 feet, N 14 W 144 feet, S 74 W 100 feet, S 12 E 165 feet, to the beginning, containing about 72 square poles with all the appurtenances, with covenants of general warranty.

"Witness the following signatures and seals.

"AMAZIAH BEE, [Seal],
"RHODA BEE, [Seal],
"JEPTHAH F. RANDOLPH, [Seal],
"DEBORAH F. RANDOLPH." [Seal].

"W. VA., DODDRIDGE COUNTY, TO WIT:—

"I, A. B. PARKS, a Justice of the Peace for the county aforesaid in the State of West Virginia, do hereby certify that Amaziah Bee and Rhoda, his wife, whose names are signed to this deed bearing date on the 31st day of October, 1865, have acknowledged the same before me in my county aforesaid, and the said Rhoda being examined by me privily and apart from her husband, and having the deed aforesaid fully explained to her, declared she had willingly executed the same and does not wish to retract it.

"Given under my hand this 1st day of Nov., 1865.

"A. B. PARKS, J. P.,
"In New Milton Township."

"WEST VA., DODDRIDGE COUNTY, TO WIT:—

"I, A. B. PARKS, a Justice of the Peace for the county aforesaid in the State of West Virginia, do hereby certify that Jepthah F. Randolph, and Deborah, his wife, whose names are signed to this deed bearing date on the 31st day of October, 1865, have acknowledged the same before me in my county aforesaid, and the said Deborah being examined by me privily and apart from her husband, and having the deed aforesaid fully explained to her, declared she had willingly executed the same, and does not wish to retract it.

"Given under my hand this 13th day of Nov. 1865.

"A. B. PARKS, *Justice.*"

PARSONAGE.

Some time in the spring of 1901, while a series of revival meetings was in progress at the church under the leadership of Rev. Judson G. Burdick, who was in the employ of the Board of Managers of the Seventh Day Baptist Missionary Society, the question of building a parsonage was broached. The church had just accepted the resignation of its pastor, Rev. David W. Leath, and a call had been extended to Rev. Darwin C. Lippincott, with whom the question of a suitable home for his family would enter largely into consideration when he made his final decision as to accepting the call.

At a special business meeting of the church held April 26, 1901, it was decided to purchase additional land adjoining the church lot, on which to build a parsonage. On July 17, 1901, Rhoda Bee (widow of Amaziah Bee), Thomas W. Noble and Keziah Noble, his wife, executed a deed to the Middle Island Church, for seven and a half acres of land adjoining the church lot, for the consideration of five hundred dollars ($500.00).

Already on June 30, 1901, the church had appointed a parsonage building committee, consisting of Rev. Darwin C. Lippincott, Ezekiel B. Kelley, Abner J. Davis, Varnum B. Lowther, and Linville B. Davis.

Rev. Darwin C. Lippincott was appointed chairman, Ezekiel B. Kelley, treasurer of the committee, and Franklin F.

THE MIDDLE ISLAND CHURCH

Randolph, clerk. The committee was instructed to build a parsonage, and was clothed with power necessary to do so.

The committee immediately entered upon its duties, and in a few months the parsonage, together with a barn and other like accessories, was completed at an aggregate cost of some fifteen hundred dollars ($1,500.00).

GRAVEYARDS.

In addition to the graveyard at West Union owned by the church, there is another within a short distance of the present house of worship, originally given for that purpose by John Davis Bee, probably. At the present time, the owner of adjoining land surrounding this graveyard is Franklin F. Randolph, from whom the church purchased an additional half acre adjoining the graveyard to be added to the original graveyard, at a cost of twenty-five dollars ($25.00). The deed for this addition was executed May 10, 1897.

PREACHING STATIONS.

As early as January 1, 1845, the Middle Island Church decided to hold its Quarterly Meetings at Middle Island and Meat House Fork, alternately. Probably there was no other preaching stations maintained by the church until after its re-organisation in 1867. Since the re-organisation, preaching stations have been maintained at various times by the church, on Long Run, the Bear Fork of Cove Creek (where the Conings Church is now situated), Rock Run, Hughes Fork of Buckeye Creek, and Lick Run. Lick Run is the only one of these stations still maintained by the Middle Island Church. The interests at other points mentioned are cared for by other churches.

PASTORS.

The first pastor of the Middle Island Church, under its re-organisation, was Rev. James B. Davis, who was called to that trust, September 4, 1868. He served the church for four years. Then followed an *interim* of two years and a half, during which the church had no recognised pastor, when Rev. James B. Davis was again chosen pastor for one year from March 6, 1874; and again on March 4, 1881, he was chosen pastor for one year.

From February 28, 1879, Rev. Lewis F. Randolph conducted the Quarterly Meetings for two years.

Rev. Hiram P. Burdick was called, on October 30, 1887, to the pastorate, giving one-half of his time to the Middle Island Church and half of it to the Greenbrier Church.

For a year from January 26, 1890, Rev. John L. Huffman conducted the Quarterly Meetings.

On March 6, 1891, Rev. Marcus E. Martin was chosen pastor, and continued to give part of his time to the church, until May 1, 1899, when Rev. David W. Leath began his labours as pastor. David W. Leath served for two years and was succeeded on July 1, 1901, by Rev. Darwin C. Lippincott, who has continued in that capacity to the date of this writing, August 1, 1902. Darwin C. Lippincott, while a student in Salem College, had previously done service for the church during the period of 1893 to 1896.

Rev. James B. Davis, from the time of the re-organisation of the church, up to the day of his removal from the bounds of the church in 1890, preached once a month and conducted Quarterly Meetings in the absence of any one else to officiate, whether he was pastor or not.

Amaziah Bee, a licentiate member of the church, also from the date of the re-organisation for a period of some twenty years, or until failing health forbade his continuing longer, preached for the church as often as once a month. He often supplied some preaching station besides.

Beginning with December, 1898, Samuel A. Ford, a licentiate member of the church, preached for the church once a month for two or three years.

In connection with the foregoing, it should be borne in mind that the church has never had a pastor who has given his entire time to the church. The pastor has either been some one devoting a part of his time to ministerial work, preaching once or twice a month for a mere nominal salary, and dependent upon daily labour upon a farm for his living; or he has divided his time with one or more other churches.

LICENCED TO PREACH.

The records of the church show that the following were licenced to preach:—

August 31, 1866. Amaziah Bee was licenced to preach for a period of six months.

REV. JAMES BALL DAVIS.

March 1, 1867. Amaziah Bee was licenced "to preach when and where a door may open."

November 10, 1866. James B. Davis was licenced to preach for one year.

September 3, 1869. Granville H. Davis was licenced to preach within the bounds of the church for one year.

September 8, 1872. Albert Shock was licenced to preach "when and where a door may be opened."

March 17, 1893. Alvin M. Davis was granted licence to preach for one year, "when and where an opportunity may offer and a door of usefulness may be opened."

September 2, 1898. Samuel A. Ford was granted licence to preach "wherever opportunity affords."

March 2, 1900. William L. Davis was granted licence to preach "wherever opportunity offers for one year."

March 1, 1901. The licence of William L. Davis was renewed for one year.

March 1, 1867. James B. Davis was called by the church to ordination; and on September 5, 1867, a council met with the Middle Island Church to consider the expediency of the ordination. The council was composed of the following members:—

From the New Salem Church:—

Lodowick H. Davis,
George Ford,
Richard Ford,
Jesse Clark,
Lloyd F. Randolph,
Fenton F. Randolph.

From the Lost Creek Church:—

William Kennedy,
Moses H. Davis,
Walter Fields McWhorter.

From the Middle Island Church:—

Amaziah Bee,
Stephen T. Davis.

The council recommended the ordination of the candidate. The ordination service was deferred, however, until early in the year, 1868, when it was conducted by Rev. Samuel D. Davis, of the Lost Creek Church, and Rev. Jacob Davis, of the New Salem Church. In the meantime, James B. Davis had been licenced by the church on December 6, 1867, "to preach the Gospel of Christ when and where a door may open."

DEACONS.

The records of the church show that deacons were chosen and ordained as follows:—

January 4, 1867. Amaziah Bee was chosen deacon. He was relieved of this office on March 4, 1870.

March 4, 1870. Walter Fields McWhorter and William Buckeye Davis were chosen deacons by the church, and were ordained on the following day.

September 1, 1876. Johnson J. Lowther was chosen deacon, and was ordained, December 2, following.

August 7, 1881. Charles L. Polan was chosen deacon. He was ordained on the 3d of the following September.

September 6, 1889. John A. Polan was chosen deacon, and ordained on December 7, following.

MODERATORS.

Until 1889, the church never had a standing moderator. The presiding officer was appointed for the day only, on which he served. The regular business meetings occurred four times a year, at the time of the Quarterly Meeting, or communion service.

During a period of twenty-three years, one hundred and twenty-one business meetings were held, of which one hundred and two were presided over by fourteen different members of the church; sixteen were presided over by members of other churches; and of three, the presiding officers are not named.

The venerable Joseph Jeffrey, who had been one of the mainstays of the church during the first period of its existence, presided over four of the first five meetings of the second period.

Rev. James B. Davis presided over forty-one meetings, extending over a period of eighteen years. The following table serves to show these officers, together with the years in which they served, and the number of times each served:—

Names.	Years in which they served.	Times served.
Amaziah Bee,	1867-71,	12
Granville H. Davis,	1868-71,	4
James B. Davis,	1870-84, 1886-88,	41
William B. Davis,	1871-72, 1879,	3
Stephen T. Davis,	1875-78, 1881,	6
Joseph Jeffrey,	1866-67,	4
Archibald W. Kelley,	1884-86, 1889,	7
John Leeson,	1882-83,	2
Johnson J. Lowther,	1876,1879-80,1882-83,1885-86,	12
Walter Fields McWhorter,	1869-70, 1875,	3

---
1. Known as " Billy Buckeye."

Names.	Years in which they served.	Times served.
John A. Polan,	1874,	1
Samuel Polan,	1869,	1
Franklin Fitz Randolph,	1887-1889,	5
James E. Willis,	1880,	1
		105

Non-members of the Middle Island Church, who on the occasion of visits to the business meetings of the church, were, out of courtesy, appointed moderator for the day.

Names.	Years in which they served.	Times served.
1Charles A. Burdick,	1872-1874,	5
2Hiram P. Burdick,	1888,	4
3Jesse Clark,	1887,	1
4Samuel D. Davis,	1887, 1889,	2
5John L. Huffman,	1889,	1
6Abram Herbert Lewis,	1868,	1
7Lewis F. Randolph,	1877,	1
		15

On December 6, 1889, the church elected Franklin F. Randolph permanent moderator for a term of one year, and year by year he has been re-elected to that office up to the present time.

CHURCH CLERKS.

At the church meeting held August 31, 1866, when it was determined to resuscitate and reorganise the church, Stephen Thorp Davis, who had been elected church clerk, August 26, 1852, served as clerk again. For the next three meetings held September 14, 1866; October 19, 1866; and November 30, 1866; Amaziah Bee acted as clerk.

At the next meeting held January 4, 1867, James Ball Davis was elected clerk for the day. The minutes of the meetings held March 1, 1867; and May 31, 1867, are attested by Stephen Thorp Davis, as clerk.

James Ball Davis then served as clerk until September 4, 1868, when Charles L. Polan was elected to that office perma-

---

1. General missionary on the West Virginia Field.
2. Pastor of the Middle Island and Greenbrier churches, jointly.
3. A deacon in the Greenbrier Church.
4. An ordained minister in the Salem Church.
5. Pastor of the Salem Church.
6. Representative of the American Sabbath Tract Society.
7. An ordained minister in the Greenbrier Church.

nently. He continued to serve as clerk of the church until February 29, 1884, when he resigned and Linville Bee Davis, the present clerk, was elected in his stead.

On September 4, 1885, John A. Polan was elected assistant clerk. He, too, remains in the service, as originally elected.

MEMBERSHIP IN SUPERIOUR BODIES.

The Middle Island Church was admitted to membership in the General Conference at the annual session of the latter body, at Brookfield, New York, beginning September 6, 1832.

There is no record of membership of the church in the Western Association, and none of membership in the old South-Western Association. But upon the organisation of the Virginia Association in 1851, the Middle Island Church appears as one of its constituent members.

Upon the dissolution of the Virginia Association, the Middle Island Church remained without associational connection until the organisation of the South-Eastern Association in 1872, when the church became a constituent member of the new body, with which it has always remained in harmony.

X.

NORTH FORK OF HUGHES RIVER CHURCH.

DOUBTLESS, the records of the North Fork of Hughes River Church were never more than extremely meagre; and whatever there may have been, have long since disappeared from view and been forgotten.

As a natural consequence, the story of the church must be woven from mere fragments, gathered from sources as widely scattered, as they are strangely diversified.

The church is really but a memory today, and that memory, reluctant and sluggish at best, is taxed to its utmost to recall anything of the history of the church; for there are but mere fleeting, elusive touches, here and there, to serve as landmarks whereby such a memory may be compelled to yield up its secrets.

The material for the following very brief history of the church has been gathered principally from letters written by Rev. Charles A. Burdick to the *Sabbath Recorder*, while he was engaged in missionary labour in West Virginia; from the *Autobiography of Alexander Campbell;* from the minutes of the Seventh Day Baptist General Conference; from the minutes of the old South-Western Association, as well as the Virginia Association; from the records of the Lost Creek Church; from the *Sharpless Genealogy;* and from various other sources, including the memories of people now living.

The result is by no means satisfactory, but it is the best that can be secured from available trustworthy material.

This church centres around the history of one man, Lewis Bond, who was born in Cecil County, Maryland, February 16, 1780. He was one of a family of fifteen children. His father, Richard Clayton Bond, was born in the same county in 1727 or 1728.

About the year 1800 or 1801, Richard Clayton Bond emigrated with some six of his children, to that part of Harrison County in West Virginia, now included in the bounds of the Lost Creek Church. Here he died in the year 1819.

Lewis Bond, who was about twenty years of age when his father moved to western Virginia, was married October 15, 1805, to Lydia John, of Fayette County, Pennsylvania, daughter of John John and Elisabeth David, the daughter of Rev. Enoch David of the Woodbridgetown Church.

In 1813, Lewis Bond with his family removed to Brookville, Indiana. In 1816, some three years before the death of his father, he returned to western Virginia, and settled on the head waters of the North Fork of Hughes River, about five miles above the present village of Toll Gate, which is a few miles west of the present village of West Union in Doddridge County, and not far from the present village of Pennsboro in Ritchie County.

Lewis and Lydia Bond had eleven children. They were as follows:—

ALFRED J., married Pamela Allen.

EDWIN PASSMORE, (M. D. and Rev.), married Louisa John.

ETHELBERT D. (M. D. and surveyor).[1] Married daughter of Captain Nathan Davis. Lived at West Union, Doddridge County, Virginia.

BENJAMIN FRANKLIN, married Frances Nicholson, and, for his second wife, Adelia Coon. Adelia Coon was the daughter of Rev. Stillman Coon, of Milton, Wisconsin.

REBECCA E., married William P. Bond.

THOMAS, died in an insane asylum.

CASSANDRA, married Simeon Bond.

RICHARD C., married Eliza Bliven.

MARY ANN, married Thomas Boothe Bond.

LYDIA, married Daniel D. Kildow.

---

1. Ethelbert D. Bond was the surveyor who laid out the village of West Union, the county seat of Doddridge County, when it was established by an act of the General Assembly of the Commonwealth of Virginia, passed in February, 1845. He was also one of the leading spirits in establishing the West Union Academy, as related in the chapter on the *West Union Academy*.

At his home on the North Fork of Hughes River, Lewis Bond was visited by the missionaries sent to western Virginia by the Missionary Board in its early operations, as related in a subsequent chapter on *Missions*.

As a result of one of the visits of Alexander Campbell in 1833, a church was organised here in that year, consisting of some eight or nine members, of whom four were Lewis Bond and his wife, and his son Ethelbert and his wife. The remaining members of the church were, in all probability, other members of Lewis Bond's family.

Lewis Bond was appointed deacon and ordained to that office. He was also licenced to preach, and served for many years as the pastor of the church. His son Ethelbert D. Bond was the clerk of the church.

In 1837, the church became a member of the Western Association, which had been but recently organised, at its annual session held with the church at Alfred, New York, in June of that year. At that time the North Fork of Hughes River Church consisted of nine members and for the past year, had neither increased nor decreased in membership. In its communication to the Western Association requesting membership in that body, the church said, "We desire your prayers for us, a small branch, that we may extend as the watered tree, far and wide."

By virtue of its membership in the Western Association, the North Fork of Hughes River Church became a member of the General Conference. But there is no record of the church ever having reported directly to Conference.

When the South-Western Association was organised in 1839, the North Fork of Hughes River Church was one of its constituent members, and its deacon and pastor, Lewis Bond, presided as moderator at the first annual session of that association. He was also honoured with the appointment as delegate from that association to the next annual session of the Western Association.

In 1839 the North Fork of Hughes River Church reported a membership of seven. With the exception of the years 1841 and 1842, the church reported regularly to the South-Western Association until 1845, when it reported for the last time. When the Virginia Association was organised in

1851, by the division of the South-Western Association into the Virginia and the Ohio associations, the North Fork of Hughes River Church was extinct.

On March 13, 1857, Lewis Bond and his wife, Lydia, applied for membership in the Lost Creek Church, as they had moved to Quiet Dell in the bounds of the Lost Creek Church. They were accepted as members of the Lost Creek Church, and Lewis Bond was continued as a deacon and a licentiate in that church. He died April 14, 1867.

XI.

SOUTH FORK OF HUGHES RIVER, OR PINE GROVE, CHURCH.

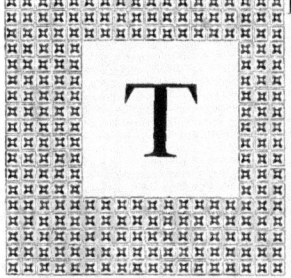

THE records of this church begin as follows:—

"JANUARY THE 25TH, 1842.

"*Whereas*, We, the Seventh Day Baptist Church of the South Fork of Hughes River do deem it our indispensible duty to show to the rising generation a statistical account of the rise and progress of this church to the present date, [the following record is made]:—

"By the preaching of the Gospel and perusing the Word of God, we saw it to be our indispensible duty to follow our Saviour into the liquid grave; and in the year 1833, there were immersed by Elder Peter Davis, nine; namely,

"GEORGE STARKEY,
"SARAH STARKEY,
"DECATUR LOWTHER,
"JONATHAN C. LOWTHER,
"JOHN C. STARKEY,
"REBECCA LOWTHER,
"MARGARET LOWTHER,
"MARY LOWTHER,
"DORINDA LOWTHER.

"By carefully and prayerfully perusing the Bible, we saw that we were living in violation of the Fourth Precept of the Decalogue by observing the First Day of the week for the Sabbath in preference to the Seventh, which we clearly discovered to be a violation of God's moral government of the universe.

"*Whereupon,* Being determined to follow God in all His fast requirements contained in His Word, upon the first Seventh Day [of the week] in June, 1834, we changed our practise from the observance of the First Day of the week, to the Seventh, for the Sabbath.

"Upon the 13th day of July, 1834, we were constituted a church by Elder Peter Davis, upon the Word of God; being truly convinced that all scripture is given by inspiration of God and is profitable for doctrine, for reproof, for correction, for instruction in righteousness, that the man of God may be perfect, thereby furnished unto all good works, agreeable to the constitution to which our names are annexed, which reads thus:—

"CONSTITUTION.

"JULY THE 13TH, 1834.

"We who have heretofore been convinced of the error of our ways and the folly of sin, and the kindness and love of a Saviour to a dying world, and thereby have been made willing to follow our Lord and Saviour Jesus Christ in all of his requirements, do therefore this day covenant together to watch over each other for good and serve each other in love, and take the Word of God for the rule of our faith and practise.

"GEORGE STARKEY,
"DECATUR LOWTHER,
"JONATHAN C. LOWTHER,
"JOHN C. STARKEY,
"REBECCA LOWTHER,
"MARGARET LOWTHER,
"SARAH STARKEY,
"MARY LOWTHER,
"DORINDA LOWTHER."

This church originally composed, wholly, of the members of two families who were converts to the Sabbath, sprang into existence through the labours of Rev. Alexander Campbell, who had visited Lewis Bond on the North Fork of Hughes River, not far from the present village of Pennsboro. While there, Alexander Campbell held a series of revival meetings, and as a result there were some conversions to the Sabbath. After his departure to Quiet Dell, one of the preaching stations of the Lost Creek Church, a local clergyman by the name of Tichnell, of the Methodist Episcopal church, challenged any one, who would, to discuss the Sabbath question publicly. Contrary to the Reverend Mr. Tichnell's expectation, Alexander Campbell returned and accepted the challenge. The debate was attended by a large audience, many of them coming from a distance of several miles. Among the throng were those who embraced the Sabbath and were organised into the South Fork of Hughes River Seventh Day Baptist Church.

For a period of five years, the church no more than held its own. On May 7, 1839, Asa Bee was received into membership, and soon afterward assumed the leadership of the church. Others joined the church, some, like Asa Bee, coming from other Seventh Day Baptist churches; and others, like the original members, were converts to the Sabbath.

For the first thirty-four years of the history of the church, its records, never very full, are extremely meagre. From June 17, 1860, to February 12, 1868, no record whatever appears. For many years the proceedings of the business meetings of the church were kept a profound secret, and members who violated this secrecy were subjected to severe discipline.

Many perplexing questions arose respecting doctrine and church polity. These questions involved articles of diet and manner of dress as well as church control of family government and discipline. In short here an attempt was made to apply the provisions of the Mosaic law governing the domestic life of the early Hebrews to American Seventh Day Baptists, in the middle of the nineteenth century of the Christian Era, irrespective of the changed conditions of modern civilisation and radically different racial instinct, to say nothing of the profound differences between the Christian and Hebrew religions. The result, as might have been expected, was a grotesque failure.

On February 28, 1842, Asa Bee and Joshua S. Davis were appointed a committee to "make a thorough examination of scriptural evidence and intuitive reasons why we keep our church meetings secreted from the world," and report at the next church meeting.

March 23, 1851, it was voted to submit the following questions to the Virginia Seventh Day Baptist Association, at its next session, to be held at Middle Island at the house of Jepthah F. Randolph:—

"1. What is our duty toward christian professors of other denominations?

"2. Is it christian duty to hold any office whatever under the political government?"

On August 15, 1852, the church voted to submit the following questions to the association:—

"1. What is our duty in supporting the ministers of the gospel?

"2. Is it right for professors to marry un-professors?"

March 20, 1853, it was voted that communion service be

held once in twelve months "on the fourteenth day of the first Jewish month"; *i. e.*, on the evening of the Passover.

April 3, 1859, Rev. Asa Bee announced that the church was "not organised according to the will of God," and presented the following questions for consideration:—

"1. Who among us are elders?
"2. What is their office?
"3. The office of Bishop.
"4. Who are elderly women; *i. e.*, female elders, and their office?
"5. Young men and their office.
"6. Young women and their office.
"7. Children and their office."

Taken all in all, although the church for the greater part of its existence, was under the leadership of Asa Bee and his brother Ezekiel, both of whom were men of marked mental ability, as well as men of sincerity of purpose, such questions as the foregoing, taken in connection with such interpretation of Holy Writ as gave rise to such queries, were bounteously fruitful of discord.

In 1870, this spirit of dissension resulted in a split in the South Fork of Hughes River Church, and the organisation of the Ritchie Church. This precipitated a life and death struggle between the two opposing churches. The Ritchie Church received recognition at the hands of the Seventh Day Baptist General Conference, as well as at the hands of the South-Eastern Seventh Day Baptist Association, when the latter was organised in 1871.

The mother church steadily lost ground, and when after a decade had passed after the organisation of the Ritchie Church, the Pine Grove Church (as the South Fork of Hughes River Church came to be called) gave one of its members, Alpheus A. Meredith, permission to distribute among its membership, tracts containing the doctrines of the Seventh Day Adventists, its doom was sealed. Two years afterward, on February 22, 1883, ten members were excommunicated for affiliating with the Seventh Day Adventists; and the book of records of the South Fork of Hughes River, or Pine Grove, Church passing into the hands of one of the excommunicated members, was closed forever, although a few more meetings were held before the final absorption of the remaining few members into the Ritchie Church, as described in the next chapter.

DISTINCTIVE TENETS OF FAITH AND PRACTISE. [1]

This church, in its effort to promote simplicity of life, placed a premium upon lack of personal adornment and beauty, and almost upon discomfort. Dress, particularly that of the women, was made after certain uniform patterns, approved if not prescribed by the old men of the church. The result was attire often so ungainly and grotesque as not only to make the wearers objects of ridicule, but to incite them to rebellion against ecclesiastical authority as well, so that they were often excommunicated from the church for violating the rules of prescribed fashion in dress as laid down by the councils of the church. This one thing, perhaps more than anything else, retarded the growth and prosperity of the church.

Rules for dress in which the dead must be clothed, even to minute directions as to the style of the coffin and the material of which it was to be constructed, were established.

In the event of marriage, the *trousseau* of the bride and the dress of the groom were described in the code of the church. Both were to be arrayed in white, all except their shoes or boots. The bride should not wear a cap, nor any other article of ornament.

Certain rules relating to courtship were prescribed and insisted upon by the church, with the result that infractions of them were the subject of frequent disciplinary action by the church.

Parental control of children was transferred to the church, and on many an occasion, the church was called upon to consider the complaints of parents concerning unruly sons and daughters.

In their effort to follow the mandates of the Mosaic law, the flesh of swine as food, was placed under ban. Mutton and beef tallow took the place of lard in cooking. A few of the more well-to-do used olive oil.

If a father died, his family was committed to the care of the church, and his property to the supervision of its elders.

---

[1]. This brief statement of "*Distinctive Tenets of Faith and Practise*," in based upon personal statements made to the present writer, by former members of this church.

"Investigating meetings" were frequently held. These lasted continuously from early in the morning until late in the afternoon, the people coming and going constantly; some for purposes of consultation, others for refreshments, and others for the performance of duties at home. Subjects of all kinds were discussed, from female underwear to doctrines of eternal damnation and endless happiness.

Great stress was laid upon the word *"peculiar"* in the following and similar passages from the Bible:—

"The Lord hath chosen thee to be a *peculiar* people unto himself, above all the nations that are upon the earth." Deut. XIV, 2.

"And the Lord hath avouched thee this day to be his *peculiar* people." Deut. XXVI, 18.

"But ye are a chosen generation, a royal priesthood, a holy nation, a *peculiar* people." 1 Peter II, 9.

By *"peculiar,"* they understand that something bizarre, grotesque, or odd was meant.

To the idea of a *"peculiar"* people, they added the many warnings of the Bible against mingling with the world. The result was that, in their minds, God's chosen *peculiar* people must in no sense identify themselves with the world, even in that which pertained to food and clothing, and other habits of life common to everybody.

These strange doctrines of the South Fork of Hughes River Church were not only extremely Puritanical,—ultra-Puritanical,—but Puritanism gone grotesquely mad.

MEMBERSHIP IN SUPERIOUR BODIES.

The South Fork of Hughes River Church was one of the constituent members of the South-Western Association at the organisation of that association in 1839; and when the South-Western Association was divided into the Ohio, and Virginia associations, the South Fork of Hughes River Church became a constituent member of the Virginia Association at its organisation in 1851.

When the South-Eastern Association was organised in 1872, the South Fork of Hughes River Church did not apply for membership. The steps which finally led up to a formal application of this church for membership in that association, and the process by which it was merged into the Ritchie Church, are set forth in the next chapter of this book under the sub-title, *"Consolidation of the South Fork of Hughes River, or Pine Grove, Church with the Ritchie Church."*

The South Fork of Hughes River Church became a member of the General Conference by virtue of its membership in the South-Western Association, in 1839. On account of the doctrinal differences between this church and the other churches of the denomination, however, it gradually drifted away from the General Conference, and for a good many years before its final dissolution, it had really withdrawn from fellowship with, not only the General Conference, but all other Seventh Day Baptist organisations.

PASTORS.

Rev. Peter Davis, who baptized the constituent members of the church and organised them into a church, visited them from time to time as often as his duties with the New Salem Church and the distance of the new church from his home on Greenbrier Run would permit. Other ministers, also, visited the church from time to time. Of these, Asa Bee, and his brother Ezekiel Bee, were doubtless the most frequent visitors.

Asa Bee, who had previously moved into the neighbourhood, was received into this church, May 7, 1839. On January 24, 1842, he was called to the pastorate of the church. He accepted the call for a period of six months. On the 29th of the following August, he was elected pastor for an indefinite period, and served in that capacity until his death. He was generally known as "The Elder," and is constantly called by that name in the records of the church.

On March 22, 1857, the church granted Asa Bee the privilege of inviting Ezekiel Bee, at that time living on Meat House Fork of Middle Island Creek, but who expected to locate, in the near future, within the bounds of the South Fork of Hughes River Church, to labour with the church at such times as might be most expedient.

June 21, 1868, Ezekiel Bee became the pastor of the church.

Marcus E. Martin was called to become the assistant pastor of the church for a term of one year from March 19, 1876, at a salary of fifty-two dollars ($52.00) a year. Previous to this time, the pastor had served without pay.

On the 16th of June, 1878, Ezekiel Bee requested the church to appoint a committee to look for a pastor. The church complied with the request, and on the 14th of July following, Alpheus A. Meredith became pastor and served until October 1, 1880.

LICENCED TO PREACH.

On December 24, 1843, the church voted that Joshua S. Davis be granted licence to preach, and appointed Asa Bee to write the licence and deliver it to the candidate. The licence runs as follows:—

"May 11, 1844.

"*Know all men to whom these may be presented,* That we, the Seventh Day Baptist Church of Christ, on the South Fork of Hughes River, of Ritchie County, and State of Virginia, do authorise our Brother Joshua S. Davis to go forth and preach the Gospel of the Blessed Lord and Saviour, and to perform all the duties required of him in the Gospel.

"Signed in behalf of the church by

"ASA BEE, *A Preacher of the Gospel.*

"Recorded this fifth day of October, 1845."

In addition to the foregoing, the church granted licence to preach as follows:—

June 21, 1868. Job Meredith was appointed to exhort and labour publicly in this church.

December 20, 1874. Marcus E. Martin was licenced to preach for six months.

May 16, 1875. Alpheus A. Meredith was licenced to preach till the next Quarterly Meeting.

June 20, 1875. John Ehret was licenced to exhort.

April 7, 1878. Alpheus A. Meredith and Marcus E. Martin were ordained to preach.

July 14, 1878. Zebulon Bee was licenced to preach for a term of six months.

December 21, 1879. Zebulon Bee's licence was renewed for one year.

DEACONS.

The records of the church contain the following entries concerning deacons:—

"November 25, 1844. Jesse M. Lowther appointed deacon.

"December 21, 1851. Jesse M. Lowther released from serving as deacon, at his own request.

"March 21, 1858. After considering whether the church had need of a deacon, it was decided affirmatively, but the selection of some one to fill that office was deferred.

"June 21, 1868. Jonathan C. Lowther appointed deacon.

"September 19, 1869. Jonathan C. Lowther was released from serving as deacon, and Hezekiah D. Sutton appointed in his stead.

"October 31, 1881. John Ehret appointed assistant deacon for six months.

"December 18, 1881. Jonathan C. Lowther, who had again been appointed deacon, was released from further service at his own request."

MODERATORS.

The moderator was known by various terms; as "moderator," "foreman," and "president."

With the exception of a single meeting, Asa Bee served as moderator from May 7, 1839, to January 25, 1841, when Joshua S. Davis was elected permanent moderator. How long Joshua S. Davis served in this capacity is not known, but he was succeeded, presumably, by Asa Bee, for the latter was relieved from that office at his own request, on February 12, 1860, and Jonathan C. Lowther appointed in his stead. From this time forward, we find the following alternating with each other in serving as "moderator for the day":— Rev. Ezekiel Bee, Job Meredith, Alpheus A. Meredith, and Marcus E. Martin.

Davis N. Meredith was appointed permanent moderator on November 15, 1874, and on the 3d of January following, John Ehret was appointed assistant moderator.

Ezekiel Bee appears as moderator for the last time, on March 17, 1878. On June 22, 1879, Davis N. Meredith was released from further services as moderator, and on the 20th of the following month, John Ehret was appointed as his successor, and presumably served until the final disintegration of the church.

CHURCH CLERKS.

Although the church was organised in June, 1834, no records of the business meetings of the church were kept until May 7, 1839, when Joshua S. Davis was appointed clerk for the day. He was re-appointed from meeting to meeting, alternating from time to time, with Jonathan C. Lowther and Asa Bee, until November 30, 1840, when Jonathan C. Lowther was appointed standing clerk of the church.

The record concerning the organisation of the church was written by Asa Bee, from loose papers in possession of various members of the church, and approved by the church at a business meeting held August 29, 1842.

Jonathan C. Lowther served as clerk of the church until May 29, 1843, when he vacated the office. His brother Jesse M. Lowther succeeded him by appointment under date of July 6, 1844, and served until his death, November 15, 1855.

The next clerk under permanent appointment, of whom there is a record, was Josiah Bee, appointed June 22, 1873.

On April 7, 1878, Jonathan C. Lowther again became permanent clerk of the church, and apparently served until the date of the last record in the book, February 22, 1883.

Asa Bee, Jr., was appointed assistant clerk March 20, 1853. How long he served does not appear.

During the various interims between the terms of office of the different permanent clerks, several members of the church acted as clerk temporarily. Among these were Otho P. Zinn, Jonathan C. Lowther, Zebulon Bee, William Jett, and Davis N. Meredith.

MEETING HOUSES.

For many years after its organisation, the church held its meetings for worship and business alike in private houses, the homes of its members.

On March 23, 1851, the church adopted the following resolution:—

"RESOLVED, That we put up a frame [meeting house], thirty feet long and twenty feet wide, one story, thirteen feet high, with a partition of three leaves at or near the middle of the house, to be raised and let down at pleasure; with two doors, one in the end designed for a school room, the other door in the other end of the house by the side of the pulpit, it [the pulpit] also being in the other end. Four twelve-light windows in the school room, [the panes of glass to be] 8"x10", one in each end of the house, and one on each side of the door in the end. Three windows in the other room, one in each side with twelve lights [each pane of glass to be] 8"x10", and one over the pulpit with nine lights, 8"x10" each, in size.

The building was completed in less than two years, as will be observed from the following action of the church, under date of December 19, 1852:—

"Being compelled to hold our meetings in private houses heretofore for the want of a more suitable place, but now blessed of God with a house prepared for that purpose,

(13)

THE PINE GROVE CHURCH.

SOUTH FORK CHURCH

"RESOLVED, *Therefore,* That we meet at the frame school house in the Pine Grove to hold all our public meetings hereafter."

The lot on which this building was erected was purchased of Asa Bee, but the church did not receive a deed for it until May 21, 1871, when trustees were appointed by the church to receive the deed for the church lot and graveyard.

The church used this building, which served the double purpose, for a long while, of meeting house and school house, until 1875. On October 17 of that year, the church voted to build anew, and on the 28th of the next November, the dimensions were fixed as follows:—

> "House to be twenty-six feet wide, by thirty-six feet long, thirteen feet in height to the square, and to have two aisles and two doors. The ceiling overhead to be left to the building committee as to whether it shall be arched or not."

The church committed this work to a building committee with power, and gave it two years in which to complete the work. The work appears to have been completed about as planned, with the exception of the seating, which was not finished until November, 1880.

The meeting house and graveyard of the Pine Grove Church passed into the possession of the Ritchie Church after the consolidation of the two churches.

SCHOOL.

As previously set forth, the first meeting house erected by the church was designed for use as a school house, as well as a house of worship. This of course antedated the public free school system, which was not inaugurated here until after the events of the Civil War had separated West Virginia from the Old Dominion.

The school was under the strict management of the church, and at times, at least, members of the church were commanded by that body to prepare themselves for teaching at some specified future time.

MEMBERS.

A list of members of the South Fork of Hughes River, or Pine Grove, Church, compiled from the records of the church, with the date of admission, or the date when the name first appears, is as follows:—

BEE, ALBERT, son of John D.,	June 20,	1875,
BEE, ALLEN, appears as a member,	April 7,	1878,
BEE, ALMIRA, dau. of Asa,	February 25,	1850,
BEE, ANGELINA, dau. of Ezekiel,	————	1857,
BEE, ARTHUR G., son of Ezekiel,	————	1857,
BEE, ARTHUR G., JR.,	———— 1881 or	1882,
BEE, ASA,	May 7,	1839,
BEE, ASA, JR.,	March 2,	1850,
BEE, AZOR ESTEE, son of John D.,	————	1857,
BEE, A. Z.,	———— 1881 or	1882,
BEE, B. WILSON, son of Ezekiel,	November 15,	1874,
BEE, CHARLES W.	December 22,	1872,
BEE, CORDELIA,	————	1857,
BEE, C. R., appears as a member,	June 19,	1881,
BEE, ELMA,	———— 1881 or	1882,
BEE, ELISABETH, wife of Zebulon,	January 19,	1856,
BEE, ELISABETH, dau. of Ezekiel,	————	1857,
BEE, ELISABETH ANN,	January 14,	1876,
BEE, ELISABETH,	January 14,	1876,
BEE, EUDOLPHEUS, son of Ezekiel,	January —,	1875,
BEE, EZEKIEL,	February 12,	1868,
BEE, EZEKIEL, JR.,	———— 1881 or	1882,
BEE, HANNAH, wife of Asa,	May 7,	1839,
BEE, HANNAH, wife of Jeremiah,	July 12,	1857,
BEE, INGABY, wife of John D.,	————	1857,
BEE, IRA., son of John D.,	Nov. or Dec.,	1872,
BEE, JERUSHA,	———— 1881 or	1882,
BEE, JOEL, son of John D.,	————	1857,
BEE, JOSIAH, son of Ezekiel, appears as member,	June 22,	1873,
BEE, JOSIAH, JR.,	———— 1881 or	1882,
BEE, JOHN NELSON,	———— 1881 or	1882,
BEE, KOSANNAH,	November —,	1872,
BEE, LEAR V.,	November —,	1872,
BEE, LOAMI, son of Asa,	March 2,	1850,
BEE, LUHAMA, dau. of John D.,	————	1857,
BEE, MARY A.,	April 26,	1868,
BEE, MARY,	January 14,	1876,
BEE, OLIVE E., dau. of Zebulon,	April 26,	1868,
BEE, OZINA M., dau. of Zebulon,	January —,	1875,
BEE, PERDILLA, wife of J. Nelson Bee,	January 14,	1876,
BEE, PRISCILLA, dau. of B. Wilson Bee,	March 23,	1850,
BEE, PRISCILLA, dau. of Asa,	———— 1881 or	1882,
BEE, SALLY,	November —,	1872,
BEE, SEDILLA, dau. of Ezekiel,	April 26,	1868,
BEE, STEPHEN,	———— 1881 or	1882,
BEE, ZEBULON, son of Asa,	January 19,	1856,
BOND, EMELINE wife of Richard E.,	July —,	1869,

SOUTH FORK CHURCH

BOND, LUTHER H., son of Richard E.,	July —,	1869,
BOND, MARTHA, dau. of Richard E.,	————	1857,
BOND, RICHARD E.,	April 26,	1868,
COLLINS, CYNTHIA, appears as a member,	February 22,	1883,
COLLINS, SYLVESTER,	—— 1881 or	1882,
DAVIS, ARZANDER,	June 21,	1868,
DAVIS, DANIEL W.,	January 21,	1876,
DAVIS, DORINDA, 2d wife of Ziba,	April 13,	1850,
DAVIS, DORINDA, dau. of Joshua S.,	————	1857,
DAVIS, FRANCIS M.,	January 21,	1876,
DAVIS, HANNAH, wife of Joshua S.,	July 6,	1843,
DAVIS, ISAIAH B., son of Stephen,	June 21,	1868,
DAVIS, JOHNSON, son of Ziba,	February 25,	1850,
DAVIS, JOSHUA S.,	July 6,	1843,
DAVIS, LEANDER,	June 21,	1868,
DAVIS, LEMUEL, son of Joshua J.,	February 25,	1847,
DAVIS, PHILOTHETA, dau. of Ziba,	February 25,	1850,
DAVIS, PHINEAS R., son of Lemuel,	April 26,	1868,
DAVIS, RHODA, wife of Lemuel,	February 25,	1847,
DAVIS, SABRINA, dau. of Ziba,	March 23,	1850,
DAVIS, TALITHA, dau. of Ziba,	————	1857,
DAVIS, ZIBA,	April 13,	1850,
EHRET, ELISABETH,	March 21,	1875,
EHRET, HANNAH M.,	————	—,
EHRET, JOHN,	April 26,	1868,
EHRET, WILLIAM F.,	————	1857,
GOODWIN, E. A.,	January,	1875
GOODWIN, HENRY H.,	Nov. or Dec.,	1872,
HALBERT, PRINE,	—— 1881 or	1882,
HOFF, ERI,	March 18,	1881,
HOFF, MALINDA,	—— 1881 or	1882,
JETT, WILLIAM, name appears,	March 21,	1875,
JONES, JOSHUA E.,	March 21,	1875,
KELLEY, AI G., son of Ezekiel,	June 21,	1868,
KELLEY, CATHARINE L.,	June 21,	1868,
KELLEY, ESTELLA, wife of Ezekiel,	July 12,	1857,
KELLEY, EZEKIEL,	————	1857,
KELLEY, RUANNA,	————	1857,
LOWTHER, CATHARINE R.,	April 26,	1868,
LOWTHER, CELINA,	————	1857,
LOWTHER, DECATUR, son of Elias,	Constituent	member,
LOWTHER, DORINDA, dau. of Elias,	Constituent	member,
LOWTHER, ELIAS, name appears as a member,	May 7,	1839,
LOWTHER, EMZA M., wife of Jonathan C.,	February 21,	1850,
LOWTHER, JESSE M., son of Elias,	July 6,	1843,
LOWTHER, JONATHAN C., son of Eilas,	Constituent	member,
LOWTHER, LUCINDA, wife of Jesse M.,	August 31,	1844,

LOWTHER, MANDANE, dau. of Jesse M.,	————	1857,
LOWTHER, MARGARET,	Constituent	member,
LOWTHER, MARY,	Constituent	member,
LOWTHER, REBECCA, dau. of Jonathan C.,	Constituent	member,
LOWTHER, SIMILDE J., dau. of Jesse M.,	————	1857,
LOWTHER, SOPHRONIA, dau. of Jonathan C.,	————	1857,
LOWTHER, STILLMAN F., son of Jesse M.,	April 26,	1868,
LOWTHER, THOMAS H., son of Jesse M.,	————	1857,
LOWTHER, WILLIAM W.,	April 26,	1868,
MARTIN, MARCUS E.,	April 26,	1868,
MEREDITH, ALPHEUS A., son of Job,	April 26,	1868,
MEREDITH, DAVIS N., son of Job,	March 16,	1873,
MEREDITH, EDITH, (nee Pepper), wife of Davis N.,	December 19,	1880,
MEREDITH, ELMINA, dau. of Job,	————	1857,
MEREDITH, HARRIET, dau. of Job,	————	1857,
MEREDITH, JANE, dau. of Job,	———— 1881 or	1882,
MEREDITH, JOB,	November 3,	1844,
MEREDITH, JOHN,	———— 1881 or	1882,
MEREDITH, MARSHALL, son of Job,	————	1857,
MEREDITH, MARY ANN, wife of Job,	November 3,	1844,
PRITCHARD, MARY, appears as a member,	December 21,	1851,
RICHARDS, ISAAC H.,	January 21,	1876,
RICHARDS, JOHN W.,	January 21,	1876,
STALNAKER, LEVI, name appears,	June 20,	1869,
STARKEY, GEORGE,	Constituent	member,
STARKEY, JOHN C.,	Constituent	member,
STARKEY, REBECCA,	December 21,	1840,
STARKEY, SARAH,	Constituent	member,
SUMMERVILLE, ROSANNA,	April 7,	1878,
SUTTON, DORINDA, dau. of Hezekiah D.,	January —,	1875,
SUTTON, FRANCIS M., son of Hezekiah D.,	January —,	1875,
SUTTON, HANNAH J., wife of Hezekiah D.,	June 21,	1868,
SUTTON, HEZEKIAH D.,	————	1857,
SUTTON, LOVEY J., dau. of Hezekiah D.,	April 26,	1868,
SUTTON, MARTIN, son of Hezekiah D.,	April 26,	1868,
ZINN, ADELINE, dau. of Otho P.,	————	1857,
ZINN, ANGELINA, dau. of Otho P.,	————	1857,
ZINN, ELISABETH, dau. of Otho P.,	————	1857,
ZINN, NANCY, wife of Otho P.,	September 22,	1850,
ZINN, OTHO PRESTON, (died May 31, 1857),	September 22,	1850,

XII.

THE RITCHIE CHURCH.

HE records of the Ritchie Church begin as follows:—

"In 1834 there was an organisation of S[eventh] D[ay] B[aptist] members on the South Fork of Hughes River in Ritchie County, brought together by Elder Peter Davis, which run for a season; but in the course of time, it came under the leadership of some who taught obedience to the Ceremonial Law, and enforced on the church, contrary to the faith of the Denomination, abstinence from certain meats, peculiarities of dress, and urged that the church should be governed by elders exclusively; which led to dissatisfaction with a number of the membership, and members of other churches moving into the bounds of the church, and several received baptism who could not conscientiously unite with said church; and at different times efforts being made for a reconciliation and all failing, it was thought (after prayerful consideration) that it was best to move toward an organisation that would be in unison with the Denomination.

"Accordingly, there was a call made for the brethren to meet at Brother Ziba Davis's on the seventh day of August, 1870."

Besides other visitors, this meeting was attended by Rev. Walter B. Gillette, who at that time was visiting the churches in West Virginia under the direction of the Seventh Day Baptist Missionary Society. Rev. James B. Davis of the Middle Island Church was also in attendance, as were nineteen others who expressed a desire to become members of the proposed new church.

Rev. James B. Davis acted as chairman of the meeting, and William Jett was made clerk.

A committee was appointed to draft a constitution and by-laws for the government of the church.

An invitation was extended to all of the Seventh Day Baptist churches in West Virginia, except the Pine Grove (formerly the South Fork of Hughes River) Church, from which the majority of the members of the new church seceded, to send delegates to meet in council with the seceding brethren on the Sixth Day of the week before the third Sabbath in September, at nine o'clock, A. M.

Another meeting was held on August 22, at which the committee appointed at the previous meeting for that purpose, presented a report embodying a constitution and by-laws for the government of the church. The report was adopted.

In accordance with the invitation extended on the 7th of August preceding, a council, composed of delegates from the Middle Island, New Salem, and Lost Creek churches convened on September 16, 1870, to consider the request of the Ritchie brethren to be organised into a church.

The delegates in attendance were as follows:—
From the Middle Island Church:—
    REV. JAMES B. DAVIS,
    GRANVILLE H. DAVIS,
    WILLIAM B. DAVIS,
    ABSOLOM DAVIS.
From the New Salem Church:—
    REV. JACOB DAVIS,
    JEPTHAH F. RANDOLPH,
    LEWIS F. RANDOLPH,
    JESSE CLARK,
    JUDSON F. RANDOLPH,
    LLOYD F. RANDOLPH,
From the Lost Creek Church:—
    REV. SAMUEL D. DAVIS,
    REV. WALTER B. GILLETTE,
    JOHN M. BATTEN.
From the Seventh Day Baptist Missionary Society:—
    REV. WALTER B. GILLETTE.
From the Ritchie brethren:—
    WILLIAM JETT,
    WILLIAM F. EHRET,
    ZIBA DAVIS,
    STEPHEN C. DAVIS,
    LEVI STALNAKER.

The council organised by electing Rev. Samuel D. Davis, moderator; Jepthah F. Randolph, secretary; and Lewis F. Randolph, assistant secretary.

THE RITCHIE CHURCH.

THE RITCHIE CHURCH

After some discussion, the council decided to organise a church; and, to that end, accepted the *exposé* of faith, and the church covenant previously adopted by the temporary organisation of August 22, preceding.

At the session of the council held in the afternoon of the same day that the council first convened, the formal organisation of the church took place. The sermon was preached by Rev. Samuel D. Davis, after which recognition was accorded the members of the new church by the imposition of hands and prayer by Rev. Jacob Davis and Rev. Walter B. Gillette, followed by the right hand of fellowship given by the members of the council.

On the following day, Sabbath, John Ehret and Ziba Davis were ordained deacons, and baptism was administered to one candidate for church membership.

CONSTITUENT MEMBERS.

JOSIAH BEE,
EZEKIEL KELLEY,
WILLIAM F. EHRET,
SARAH A. EHRET,
JOHN EHRET,
ELISABETH EHRET,
ZIBA DAVIS,
DORINDA DAVIS,
WILLIAM JETT,
SOPHRONIA E. JETT,
JANE DAVIS,
RICHARD BOND,
EMELINE BOND,
LEVI STALNAKER,
DORINDA STALNAKER,
JACOB EHRET,
JOANNA EHRET,
JEMIMA DAVIS,
LUTHER H. BOND,
JEREMIAH BEE,
STEPHEN C. DAVIS,
THOMAS N. GRIBBLE,
TALITHA C. GRIBBLE,
TACY JANE BEE,
M. HOMER MORRISON,
MARY MORRISON.

This list was made up as follows:—

11 from the Pine Grove Church,

6 from the Lost Creek Church,
4 from the New Salem Church,
2 from the Middle Island Church,
1 from the First Day Baptists,
2 baptized, not members of any church previously; total, 26.

MEMBERSHIP IN SUPERIOUR BODIES.

The Ritchie Church was a constituent member of the South-Eastern Association, at its organisation in 1872. It was received into the General Conference, at the annual session of the latter body, held with the church at Adams Centre, New York, in September, 1871.

MEETING HOUSES AND PARSONAGE.

At the outset, the newly organised Ritchie Church clearly perceived the significance of the step they had taken, and lost no time in taking the preliminary measures necessary for providing themselves with a house of worship. On the 22d of October, 1870, a committee was appointed to select a suitable site, and erect upon it a house of worship.

This committee proceeded with its work by careful stages, receiving additional instructions from time to time. January 27, 1871, it received authority from the church to purchase a lot suitable for a burying ground. Accordingly a lot was purchased adjoining the burying ground of the mother church.

On the 14th of May, 1871, the church voted to accept an offer from Richard Bond, one of the members of the church, to give half an acre of land to the church upon which to build a house of worship. This site was situated "on the upper end of A. M. Wade's farm," on Otter Slide, a small stream flowing into the South Fork of Hughes River, a short distance above Berea.

The committee now proceeded with the active work of erection, and reported to the church, July 10, 1874, that the new house of worship had arrived at the stage of completion required of the committee, and asked to be discharged. The request was granted, and the interior of the house, which had not been finished, remained in that state until on April 9, 1881, when the church voted to finish it, and appointed a committee for that purpose. The committee completed its work, and the finished house of worship was dedicated on the First Day of

THE PARSONAGE AT RITCHIE.

the week following the second Sabbath in January, 1882. The dedicatory service was conducted by Rev. Lewis F. Randolph, at that time pastor of the church. The dedicatory sermon was preached by Rev. Lucius R. Swinney. On February 10, 1882, the committee reported the completed building paid for.

On the 20th of August, 1896, the church purchased of Rev. Lely D. Seager, the house and lot at that time occupied by him, lying in the bend of the South Fork of Hughes River, just below the mouth of Otter Slide Creek. This property was purchased for a parsonage, and remains the property of the church, to be used for that purpose.

On October 24, 1897, the surviving members of the original Pine Grove, or South Fork of Hughes River, Church, met and organised for the transaction of business. They then proceeded to make a formal transfer of the property of that church, consisting of the meeting house and the lot upon which it stood, and a graveyard, to the Ritchie Church. The Pine Grove Church then adjourned, *sine die,* leaving the Ritchie Church in possession of the two houses of worship, as well as the two graveyards.

PASTORS.

On the day of the organisation of the church, September 16, 1870, the church called as its pastor Rev. James B. Davis, his term of service to begin on October 22, following. James B. Davis lived at New Milton, near the Middle Island Church, and visited the Ritchie Church once a month, preaching on Sabbath and visiting for a day or two preceding Sabbath and a day or two afterward. He served the church faithfully in this manner until November 24, 1871, when he severed his connection with the church.

The church was now left without a pastor, and on April 21, 1872, it invited Levi Stalnaker, a lay member of the church, who had previously been licenced to preach, to supply the pulpit. He accepted the invitation, and continued to act as a pulpit supply until June, 1874. On the 12th of that month, the church completed an arrangement with Rev. Jacob Davis, of Greenbrier, to become its pastor, visiting the church once a month. He served as pastor of the church in this way until July 9, 1875. He served a second term from July 7, 1876 to

July 13, 1877. He then visited the church at frequent intervals until the fall of 1880.

On the 10th of October, 1880, Rev. Lewis F. Randolph, of Greenbrier, accepted a call to become the pastor of the church, devoting about half of his time to that work. This relation was continued harmoniously until May 11, 1883, when he terminated his relations with the church to accept a call to the pastorate of the Second Hopkinton Church of Rhode Island.

June 3, 1883, the Ritchie Church extended a call to Rev. Samuel D. Davis of Jane Lew to visit the church once a month. The call was accepted, but at the end of four months, he declined to serve longer, as the church was at too great a distance from his home to be reached easily.

On the 18th of May, 1884, the church extended a call to Rev. Charles W. Threlkeld, at that time of Alfred, New York, to become the pastor of the church. He accepted the call and began his labours with the church in the following October. He remained with the church for one year.

Rev. Amos W. Coon, of Alfred, New York, was invited by the church, on April 4, 1886, to visit that field. He accepted the invitation and subsequently received a call to become the pastor of the church. He declined to accept the call, but remained and preached for the church for several months.

On the 8th of October, 1886, Rev. Henry B. Lewis was called to the pastorate of the church. This call was accepted, dating from March 1, 1887. He remained with the church until August of the following year, when he relinquished the work on account of ill health.

On October 12, 1888, a call was extended to Rev. Horace Stillman of Ashaway, Rhode Island. This call was declined, and on January 11, 1889, a call was extended to Rev. Orpheus S. Mills, who accepted the call and soon afterward entered upon his pastoral labour in the church. He remained with the church for a period of two years.

On the last day of April, 1892, the church extended a call to William H. Brown of Missouri to become its pastor. The call was accepted, and he soon afterward began his labours with the church. The relation was summarily terminated by the church, August 26, following, because Mr. Brown

REV. LELY DANIEL SEAGER.

had accepted, and taught, the doctrines of the Seventh Day Adventists.

The church now extended a call to Rev. John L. Huffman, to become its pastor, but he was not available. On November 7, 1892, a call was extended to Rev. Lely D. Seager, who was at that time pastor of the Lost Creek Church, to become the pastor of the church. The latter accepted the call, and remained with the church for six years. He was succeeded by Riley G. Davis, a licentiate member of the Greenbrier Church, and at that time a student in Salem College. Mr. Davis entered upon his new duties the first of June, 1899, and on the 22d of October following, he was called to ordination by the Ritchie Church. The ordination took place November 25, 1899. The following clergymen were present and participated in the ordination service:— Theodore L. Gardiner, the president of Salem College, who conducted the public examination of the candidate and preached the ordination sermon; Darwin C. Lippincott, the acting pastor of the Salem Church, who offered the consecrating prayer; and David W. Leath, the pastor of the Middle Island, Greenbrier, and Black Lick churches, who delivered the charge of office to the candidate.

LICENCED TO PREACH.

Levi Stalnaker received licence to preach, at the hands of the church, October 22, 1870. By action of the church, this licence expired November 13, 1874. It was renewed again January 9, 1890.

April 11, 1884, the church recommended to Miss Ozina M. Bee that she "improve her gift."

August 4, 1901, George Amos Brissey and Erlow Sutton were both granted licence to preach for one year. On July 11, 1902, this licence was renewed for one year, for both.

July 7, 1883, the church took the following action:—

"*Whereas,* It has come to our hearing that Sister Experience F. Randolph has decided to prepare herself for the ministry, therefore,

"RESOLVED, That we most heartily approve of her decision, and we promise her our sympathies and prayers."

DEACONS.

On the day of the organisation of the church, John Ehret and Ziba Davis were chosen deacons, and the following day they were ordained to the solemn duties of that office. John Ehret severed his connection with the Ritchie Church, however, on January 17, 1873, in order to return to the mother (the Pine Grove) church.

Asa F. Randolph received a call to become a deacon, July 10, 1874, and was ordained on the 10th day of the following October, at the hands of Rev. Charles A. Burdick and Rev. Jacob Davis.

October 8, 1880, Elisha J. Maxson was chosen to serve as an acting deacon. He was never ordained, and was relieved of the office on May 11, 1883, having rendered acceptable service to the church during the emergency.

On the 13th of May, 1887, Flavius J. Ehret was chosen deacon, and was ordained in the following July at the time of the regular Quarterly Meeting.

Eudolpheus J. Bee was chosen as an assistant deacon, January 19, 1892; but he was not ordained.

April 8, 1892, Joshua S. Bond was chosen deacon; and August 26, 1892, Ellsworth F. Randolph was called to the same office. They were both ordained July 15, 1894.

Elva Maxson was elected deacon, October 22, 1899. He was solemnly consecrated to that office on the 25th of the following November, at the same time that Riley G. Davis was ordained to the work of the Gospel ministry.

MODERATORS.

Rev. James B. Davis, of the Middle Island Church, was present at the first meeting, called August 7, 1870, at the house of Ziba Davis to consider the propriety of organising a new church, and presided as moderator.

The second meeting, held the 22d of August, was presided over by Ziba Davis.

Rev. Samuel D. Davis presided as moderator over the council which met September 16, 1870, to organise the church.

On October 22, 1870, at the first business meeting of the church after the organisation was completed, William F. Ehret was elected moderator. He served in that capacity until his death, nearly ten years afterward.

On July 12, 1880, Flavius J. Ehret succeeded to the office of moderator, made vacant but a few months previous to that time, by the death of his father. He served until he severed

REV. PERIE R. BURDICK.
(Formerly Rev. Experience Fitz Randolph).

his connection with the Ritchie Church, nearly twelve years afterward, to join the Salem Church.

On April 8, 1892, Ellsworth F. Randolph was elected moderator and he continues to serve in that capacity at the date of this writing, August 1, 1902.

CHURCH CLERKS.

October 22, 1870, at the first business meeting of the church after its organisation, William Jett was elected church clerk. He served until January 7, 1881, when he presented his resignation to the church, but served until the following October, thus completing eleven years of faithful service.

Ellsworth F. Randolph was elected clerk, October 7, 1881. He in turn, was succeeded by his brother, Alva F. Randolph, September 5, 1884. The latter served until October 8, 1886, when he too, resigned. On January 7, 1887, Emza F. Randolph was elected his successor, and served until October 12, 1888, when she also resigned.

On October 28, 1888, Leonard F. Jett became clerk, and has served continuously to the present time.

THE CONSOLIDATION OF THE SOUTH FORK OF HUGHES RIVER AND THE RITCHIE CHURCHES.

The Pine Grove Church, as the mother church, was deeply grieved at the threatened rupture in the church, and on the 28th of August immediately preceding the meeting of the council on September 16, 1870, when the Ritchie Church was organised, appointed a committee to make an effort to effect a reconciliation with the aggrieved members, and report at a meeting of the church to be held two weeks afterward. The efforts of the committee were abortive, and the Ritchie Church was organised as related in the preceding part of this chapter.

No further official action was taken toward bringing about a union, until at a business meeting held February 22, 1876, the Ritchie Church received the following communication:—

"We, the Seventh Day Baptist Church of the South Fork of Hughes River, believing that two churches in close proximity, so nearly of the same faith and order, is not fraternal, and

"*Whereas,* Our influence and strength would be much greater in promulgating the truth of God to a gainsaying world,

"WE, THEREFORE, Propose a unity, admitting on our part that we did not act wisely with respect to Christian courtesy, as further experience has taught us. But our honest convictions are that this did not justify a withdrawal on your part.

"WE, THEREFORE, Propose to receive to our fellowship, all who are in good standing in your church, upon the acknowledgment on the part of those who withdrew from our church, that the above named withdrawal was wrong; and what we mean by this is, that we may become satisfied by a hearty vote on their part, in connection with the rest of their brethren, for the adoption of this paper.

"We would respectfully ask an answer with respect to your action on the above propositions at your earliest convenience.

"D. N. MEREDITH, *Chairman.*"

To this letter, the Ritchie Church responded as follows:—

"February 22, 1876.

"Response of the Ritchie Seventh Day Baptist Church to proposition for consolidation or unity, presented by the Seventh Day Baptist South Fork of Hughes River Church, for the union between the two churches:—

"*1st.* RESOLVED, That we accept your proposition with the appended resolutions and explanations as hereinafter stated, and are willing to meet you at such time and place as may be agreeable to yourselves to take into consideration such final measures as may be deemed necessary to effect the proposed union, so as to make it pleasant to all concerned.

"With reference to the several points made in your communication to us, the following action was taken:—

"*1st.* On the point of the existence of two churches of kindred faith so near each other, being unfriendly to Christian influence, and wanting in "fraternal" appearance to those about us, it was

"RESOLVED, *Unanimously,* That we adopt the clause or item as presented by you.

"*2d.* On the proposition that the two churches become a "unit" it was

"RESOLVED, 'Yes, heartily,' if it can be done on Christian and Gospel principles.

"*3d.* On your statement that you did not act wisely in reference to Christian courtesy toward us, it was

"RESOLVED, That we receive with gratification said admission.

"*4th.* On the point of your grief with us for our withdrawal from your church, we have this to say:—

"That while we frankly acknowledge that we might have erred in rashness and unkindness, in the *manner* of our procedure, and we do *now* think it would have been better had we waited *longer* before taking the responsible step of a new organisation, nevertheless, we do at the same time hope that you will not too *sternly* hold us to a wrong intention, when we freely tell you that it is true that in-cautiousness on your part had its influence; but that was not all which induced us to take the step we did. But it was from a real conviction on our part

REV. RILEY G. DAVIS.

that there were honest differences as to some Gospel orders in the church,—and those not likely soon to be harmonised.

"And further that a number of brethren and sisters standing outside of the church, and who were not willing to unite with your church as it was, and who were anxious to effect such an organisation as would at the [same] time allow them to become identified with the Seventh Day Baptist Denomination, had its influence on us in favouring such a course, and particularly as that consideration had for a long time been very dear to us, and which we thought we were not likely to secure if we remained with you. With these explanations, we hope that we may be restored to your confidence, after you shall become satisfied that as a church, we harmoniously and unanimously respond to your proposition of unity, which were the facts in the case.

"*5th.* In response to your proposition to receive to fellowship such of our members as were in fellowship with you once, on certain conditions specified by you, we *are willing to that;* PROVIDED, That nothing in the proposed *union* should so be understood or construed as to deprive us of the final privilege of being as we now are; [*viz.,*] a church in fellowship with the Seventh Day Baptist Denomination.

"APPENDAGES.

"*1st.* RESOLVED, That the following be presented to our brethren at Pine Grove as points of vital importance to our future growth and prosperity as a people, and points which we should be anxious to have adopted if the union should take place :—

"*1st Item.* That there should be on the part of all, great care not to chafe and worry each other, on matters of conscientious and honest differences, and in these respects to do nothing contrary to the law of love.

"*2d Item.* That there be a mutual agreement to stand in connection with the Seventh Day Baptist Denomination, and be organised on a plan agreeing with the sentiments and usages of our people which we are satisfied has been a great strength and encouragement to us, by delegations to them, and from them to us.

"*3d Item.* That while it is not our wish to undervalue or discard our present ministry among us, we would wish as near as we can, to have a settled minister, [from] among ourselves, or from abroad, which shall give to us faithful and efficient pastoral aid, and that we would be willing to do what we could, consistently, toward the support of such labourers.

"The foregoing was unanimously adopted as a whole by the church and ordered to be transmitted to you.

"WILLIAM JETT, *Secretary.*"

One week afterward, February 29, 1876, the foregoing communication from the Ritchie Church was presented at a business meeting of the South Fork of Hughes River Church. Rev. Charles M. Lewis, who was engaged at that time in missionary work in West Virginia, was present in company with William F. Ehret and his son, Flavius J. Ehret, of the Ritchie Church. The mother church voted to hold a union business meeting with the Ritchie Church, but no record appears of such a meeting.

April 7, 1876, the Ritchie Church took the following action:—

"*Whereas,* We desire to cultivate the spirit of brotherly love with our Pine Grove brethren, therefore,

"RESOLVED, That we hereby express our willingness to unite with them in Sabbath School and social worship, meeting with them at their house of worship one-half of the time, and at our place of worship on Otter Slide the other half, and we also instruct our clerk to forward a copy of this preamble and resolution to them and request them to give us an answer in time to organise by the first Sabbath in May.

"VOTED, That as to-morrow is our communion season, we invite the members of the South Fork of Hughes River Church, who may be present and who are members in good standing with them, to partake with us."

To this the following reply was received:—

"June 18, 1876.

"The Seventh Day Baptist South Fork [of Hughes River] Church, in reply to the request of the Ritchie Church to combine and attend the Sabbath Schools and meetings of Otter Slide and Pine Grove, would respectfully say we think it is not best *now*. Members of our Sabbath School are not favourable to it, and we fear it would not have a good effect.

"We ask you to pardon our slothfulness in the making of this reply. We did not intentionally disregard your request, but have neglected it until our regular church meeting.

"H. H. GOODWIN, *Clerk.*"

On the 4th of August, 1878, the Pine Grove Church took the following action:—

"*Whereas,* The success of the cause of Christ depends largely on a united work (for union means strength), and feeling the weakening influence of a divided church, and knowing that division does not harmonise with the Word of God; therefore,

"RESOLVED, That we as a church do not hold meetings at Pine Grove during the time of the Quarterly Meetings of the Otter Slide [the Ritchie] Church, and that as many of us as feel free to do so, attend their meetings when convenient, and endeavour by associating with them both in private and in public, to so manifest love for them as to break down the division."

On July 20, 1879, the Pine Grove Church again took action, as follows:—

"RESOLVED, That the Sabbath School in unison with the Ritchie Church stand as it does till the present session is out."

Once more, on February 1, 1880, the Pine Grove Church, after an exhaustive discussion of the subject, decided not to unite its Sabbath School with that of the Ritchie Church for the following summer.

But on October 8, 1880, at a business meeting of the Ritchie Church, the superintendent of the Sabbath School presented a communication from the Pine Grove Church, inviting the Ritchie Sabbath School to unite with the Pine Grove Sabbath School for the following summer.

To this the Ritchie Church made reply as follows:—

"October 8th, 1880.
"TO THE PINE GROVE CHURCH:—
In reply to your proposed union, we would say,

"*Whereas*, We believe it to be detrimental to the cause of God to unite the Sabbath Schools, and then separate the meetings, therefore,

"RESOLVED, That we are willing to unite the Sabbath Schools on the following terms:—

"That Sabbath Schools and meetings [both] unite. That is, the Sabbath School [shall meet] half the time with us, and when it is with us, for there to be no meeting at Pine Grove, but for the meetings to be at our place; and when the Sabbath School is at your place, we will have no meeting, but let it be at your place. And that we have the Sabbath School at our place at the time of our Quarterly Meetings, and you have it at your place at the time of your Quarterly Meetings."

This reply was presented to a business meeting of the Pine Grove Church, held December 19, 1880, when the terms of the union as set forth by the Ritchie Church were accepted, and a union Sabbath School and meetings were decided upon.

At the session of the South-Eastern Association held at New Salem, West Virginia, beginning May 29, 1879, there appeared representatives of the Pine Grove Church, who expressed a desire of the church to unite with the association, and a committee was appointed for the purpose of conferring with the Pine Grove Church and deciding upon conditions of union. This committee was continued the following year for the same purpose. At the session of the association held with the Middle Island Church, beginning May 26, 1881, the committee made a final report to the effect that a majority of the members of the Pine Grove Church were not in favour of uniting with the association.

Nevertheless, two years later, at the session of the association held at Lost Creek, beginning May 24, 1883, the Pine Grove Church presented a petition for membership in the association. This petition was referred to a special committee, who reported as follows:—

"Your Committee to whom was referred the petition of the Pine Grove Church, would respectfully report the following:—

"After carefully considering the matter in the light of all the facts within our reach, we recommend that the church be received into the association on these conditions; viz.,

"*1st.* That two mistakes of fact in their communication to this body be corrected.

"*2d.* That the Pine Grove Church shall be understood to agree, by coming into the association, to take the very earliest practicable steps to bring about a consolidation with the Ritchie Church,—steps that shall duly recognise the fact that the latter church is and has always been a regularly organised Seventh Day Baptist Church.

"*3d.* That all personal difficulties that have existed or may now exist on the part of persons concerned in the union of these churches, shall, in the exercise of mutual Christian forbearance, be forever dropped.

"A. E. MAIN,
"G. J. CRANDALL,
"O. D. SHERMAN,
"Committee."

The report of the committee was adopted.

The first move made toward bringing about the union of the two churches as provided in the foregoing report, was made by the Pine Grove Church, as appears from the following communication, received by the Ritchie Church at its regular business meeting, October 12, 1883:—

"October 12, 1883.
"TO THE RITCHIE SEVENTH DAY BAPTIST CHURCH;
"DEAR BRETHREN:—

"The Pine Grove Seventh Day Baptist Church appointed H. D. Sutton, A. G. Bee, and John Ehret as a committee to confer with your church in regard to a consolidation of the two churches.

"Done by order of the Pine Grove Church, at a regular church meeting on the 23d of September, 1883.

"A. G. BEE, *Clerk."*

The Ritchie Church promptly appointed a committee of three, consisting of Asa F. Randolph, Flavius J. Ehret, and

William Jett to confer with the committee from the Pine Grove Church, and report at the next regular meeting.

On the 27th of the following January, the committee rendered the following report:—

"Ritchie Church House, Berea, Ritchie County, West Virginia.
"January 24th, 1884.

"The Joint Committee of Consolidation of the Pine Grove and Ritchie Churches met as per agreement. Elder John L. Huffman was appointed clerk.

"The Joint Committee unanimously agreed upon the following terms of consolidation of the Pine Grove and Ritchie churches in harmony with the advice of the association:—

"1. That all feelings of animosity be dropped, forgiven, and go into oblivion, and that we cultivate a spirit of love for each other.

"2. That the property now held by each church shall be the property of the consolidated church, and that either property shall not be disposed of without the unanimous consent of the church.

"3. That the persons who are now trustees of the Pine Grove Church shall be recognised as trustees of the Ritchie Church, to whom shall be entrusted the property now entrusted to them by the Pine Grove Church.

"4. That the Ritchie Church shall not be responsible for any debts or claims that may be against the Pine Grove Church at the time of the consolidation. Neither shall the persons who are now members of the Pine Grove Church be responsible for any debts or claims that may be against the Ritchie Church at the time of consolidation.

"5. That the meetings of the [consolidated] church, including the Sabbath School, shall alternate monthly, holding its sessions first in one house and then in the other.

"6. That by virtue of this consolidation all persons in the Pine Grove Church, considered by that church to be in good standing, shall be recognised as such, and become members in good standing in the Ritchie Church, and thus the Pine Grove Church being a part of the Ritchie Church ceases to exist as a separate organisation.

"JOHN L. HUFFMAN, *Clerk.*

"We submit the foregoing and recommend its adoption by the church.

"ASA F. RANDOLPH,
"FLAVIUS J. EHRET,
"WILLIAM JETT,
"Committee."

This report was adopted by the church by a unanimous vote, and the church fixed upon February 9, following, as the day upon which the formal merging of the two churches into one body, should take place at the house of worship of the Ritchie Church. Rev. John L. Huffman was present at this service and conducted it by request of the Ritchie Church, at the Pine Grove Meeting House.

Almost a full year previous to the final consolidation, however, a large number of the prominent members of the Pine Grove Church deserted that church and affiliated themselves with the Seventh Day Adventists, who had recently organised a church in that vicinity.

May 13, 1887, there was presented to the Ritchie Church a communication purporting to come from the Pine Grove Church. The Ritchie Church declined to consider the letter, as the Pine Grove Church had passed out of existence more than three years before that date.

Again, about two years afterwards, Marcus E. Martin organised a church designed to be a sort of successor to the Pine Grove church, and seized the house of worship, which had belonged to the Pine Grove Church. The move proved abortive, however.

The remaining members of the Pine Grove Church, who were now members of the Ritchie Church, met and held a business meeting on October 24, 1897, for the purpose of complying with the laws of the state of West Virginia, in making a legal transfer to the Ritchie Church of the real estate that had been the property of the Pine Grove Church. This was literally the last meeting of the Pine Grove Church, and on the 7th of October, 1898, a report was made to the Ritchie Church, that the real estate of the Pine Grove Church had been legally transferred to the Ritchie Church, in testimony whereof a deed duly executed and recorded in the office of the Clerk of Ritchie County was presented to the meeting, and the union was finally complete.

XIII.

THE GREENBRIER CHURCH.

HE first book of records of the Greenbrier Seventh Day Baptist Church begins as follows:—

"A few of the members of the New Salem Church residing on Greenbrier Run and in its vicinity, held a meeting on Greenbrier Run, August 14, 1870, to consider the propriety of organising a new church in the above mentioned neighbourhood."

This meeting occurred during a visit of Rev. Walter B. Gillette to West Virginia, and he was in attendance upon this occasion. The meeting passed a resolution to the effect that in the opinion of those present, a church should be organised on Greenbrier Run; and appointed a committee consisting of Lewis F. Randolph, and Jesse Clark to visit the members of the New Salem Church in that vicinity, and ascertain their views on this subject.

In about a week the committee, in accordance with instructions given at the time of its appointment, reported directly to the New Salem Church, at its regular church meeting, held on the Sixth Day of the week before the third Sabbath in August, 1870, to the effect that some forty-five individuals had expressed a desire to be formed into the proposed new church on Greenbrier Run.

Accordingly, the New Salem Church invited the Lost Creek and Middle Island churches to appoint delegates to meet in council with delegates from the New Salem Church, on Greenbrier Run on the 23d of September following, for the purpose of considering "the propriety of organising a church in that neighbourhood."

The council met on the day appointed with the following accredited delegates in attendance:—

From the New Salem Church:—
    Rev. Jacob Davis,
    Lodowick H. Davis, *Deacon*,
    Jepthah F. Randolph, *Deacon*,
    George Ford,
    Lloyd F. Randolph,
    Franklin F. Randolph.

From the Lost Creek Church:—
    Rev. Walter B. Gillette,
    Rev. Samuel D. Davis,
    Eli Bond,
    George Paugh,
    Francis M. Kildow,
    Austin VanHorn.

From the Middle Island Church:—
    Rev. James B. Davis,
    William B. Davis, *Deacon*,
    Sylvanus Davis,
    Granville H. Davis,
    Alvin H. Davis,
    John A. Polan.

The following members of the Ritchie Church were present and invited by the council to occupy seats in that body:—

    Ziba Davis, *Deacon*,
    Levi Stalnaker,
    Josiah Bee.

The council organised by electing Rev. Walter B. Gillette, chairman; and Franklin F. Randolph, clerk.

After due deliberation, the council agreed that there ought to be a church on Greenbrier Run, and voted to proceed with the work of organisation in the afternoon of the same day.

At the afternoon session, the organisation was effected with forty-six constituent members.

At the request of the New Salem Church, Lewis F. Randolph, after passing a satisfactory examination at the hands of the council, was ordained to the work of the Gospel ministry, Rev. Walter B. Gillette preaching the ordination sermon the following day,—Sabbath.

These meetings of the council were held in an old log meeting house erected on Greenbrier Run by the New Salem Church for the use of its members in that vicinity.

REV. LEWIS FITZ RANDOLPH.

Rev. Peter Davis, who lived near by, bowed with the infirmities of age, was waited upon by a committee consisting of all the Seventh Day Baptist clergymen of West Virginia in attendance upon the meetings of the council, and invited to attend and assist in the organisation of the new church, the committee offering to carry him to and from the meeting in his chair. But his physical disabilities were so great that he was compelled to decline to accept the invitation.

Of all the churches in western Virginia organised wholly or in part from the membership of the New Salem Church, there has been none toward which the New Salem Church has ever shown a more tender, affectionate regard.

Greenbrier was the home of Rev. Peter Davis and his son-in-law, Rev. Jacob Davis; the former of whom was for so many years, the beloved pastor of the church. The latter who had been for some years the pastor of the New Salem Church, and who continued to minister to its spiritual wants, was held in no less high regard. This relation was less that between sisters, than that between mother and daughter. Indeed, for many years, the latter relationship was openly avowed,—a relationship which inured to the good of both churches, who entertained none but the best feelings for each other. They rejoiced in each other's prosperity, and shared the cup of sadness and sorrow, each with the other.

MEMBERSHIP IN SUPERIOUR BODIES.

The Greenbrier Church was a constituent member of the South-Eastern Association, at its organisation in 1872; and it became a member of the General Conference at the annual session of the latter body at Southampton, Illinois, in September, 1872.

HOUSE OF WORSHIP.

Immediately upon the organisation of the Greenbrier Church, the New Salem Church, which had many years before provided a house of worship on Greenbrier Run for the use of such of its members as lived in that vicinity, offered this house and lot to the new church. This offer was gratefully accepted, but owing to certain legal technicalities, the title did not pass to the Greenbrier Church until several years afterward.

In the mean time, as early as December, 1872, the church appointed a committee to take steps initiatory to the erection of a new house of worship. It was not until some five years afterward, however, or January, 1878, that the committee was instructed to proceed with the erection of the building.

Two months later, March 22, 1878, the committee reported that a contract had been let for the construction of the new meeting house.

The new house of worship was completed and dedicated on March 28, 1880, the dedicatory sermon being preached by Rev. Lucius R. Swinney, at that time pastor of the Lost Creek Church.

The total cost of the new building can not readily be obtained, as considerable labour, as well as material upon which no price was placed, was contributed.

The new house was built upon the lot given the church by the New Salem Church, very nearly upon the exact site of the old building, which was of logs with a plank addition. It has been described in fuller detail in the chapter upon the *New Salem Church.*

PASTORS.

Rev. Jacob Davis was chosen the first pastor of the Greenbrier Church, and served from December, 1870, to May, 1871, when he was succeeded by Rev. Lewis F. Randolph, who served until March, 1873, and then resigned to accept the pastorate of the church at Marlboro, New Jersey.

In the following September, Rev. Jacob Davis was requested "to preach and hold such other meetings as he may deem best;" and in June, 1874, he was chosen pastor for a period of six months, and again in March, 1877, for one year.

In March, 1878, Rev. Lewis F. Randolph having returned to Greenbrier, he and Rev. Jacob Davis were both requested to attend Quarterly Meetings and to preach at other times as they might think best.

In December, 1880, Rev. Lewis F. Randolph was chosen pastor again, and served in that capacity until May, 1883, when he resigned to accept the pastorate of the Second Hopkinton Church, of Rhode Island. In June, 1883, Rev. Jacob Davis was asked by the church to conduct Quarterly Meetings until a pastor could be obtained.

In June, 1885, Rev. Samuel D. Davis was employed by the church to serve as pastor for a period of one year.

THE GREENBRIER CHURCH.

In November, 1887, Rev. Hiram P. Burdick, of Hartsville, New York, was engaged as pastor for a term of one year.

In March, 1890, Rev. Marcus E. Martin accepted a call to the pastorate of the church, and continued to serve in that capacity until the end of December, 1893.

In March, 1894, Riley G. Davis, a licentiate member of the church, was asked to supply the pulpit; and in March, 1898, four years afterward, Samuel Albert Ford, a licentiate member of the Middle Island Church, was invited to preach, at his convenience.

In May, 1899, Rev. David W. Leath became pastor of the church, and served for two years, when he was succeeded by Rev. Darwin C. Lippincott.

LICENCED TO PREACH.

On June 25, 1880, the church expressed its best wishes to James E. Strother, one of its members, in view of his expressed desire to enter the Gospel ministry; and invited him to engage in active labour in the church and Sabbath School, and expressed a willingness to grant him licence to preach, when he should have exhibited due ability to do so. No further record relating to this subject appears, however.

March 25, 1892, Riley G. Davis was granted licnece to preach, for a term of six months. At the expiration of this period, his licence was renewed for one year, then again for another year, and on December 27, 1895, it was made permanent by renewing it for an indefinite period.

September 23, 1892, licence to preach was granted Alfred N. Meek for a period of one year. At the expiration of this time it was renewed for another year, but no further record appears concerning his licence.

DEACONS.

Judson F. Randolph, one of the constituent members of the church, had been ordained to the office of deacon by the New Salem Church, before the organisation of the Greenbrier Church; and at the time the Greenbrier Church was organised, he complied with the request of the new church to serve it, also as a deacon.

April 21, 1876, Jesse Clark was called by the church to

the office of deacon, and on the 21st of June following, he was ordained to that office.

On the 22d of March, 1889, Cornelius S. Davis and Cornelius R. Davis each received a call from the church to become a deacon; and September 29th, following, they were both ordained.

Again, September 27, 1901, Milton Clark and Daniel P. Strother were elected deacons, and on the first Sabbath in the following November, they were set apart to that office by ordination.

MODERATORS.

At the first church meeting, held September 24, 1870, after the organisation of the church, Rev. Lewis F. Randolph was elected moderator for a term of one year.

On September 22, 1871, Rev. Jacob Davis was elected moderator, and served for a term of five years, until September 22, 1876, when Rev. Lewis F. Randolph was again elected. Lewis F. Randolph served until his departure to Rhode Island in May, 1883, but no successor appears to have been elected until the following September, when Judson F. Randolph was elected for a term of one year.

Franklin F. Randolph was elected moderator September 19, 1884, and was re-elected annually for two successive years.

September 23, 1887, John J. Davis was elected for one year; at the expiration of that period, Judson F. Randolph was elected and served until September 22, 1892, when Riley G. Davis was elected for one year.

September 22, 1893, John F. Randolph was elected moderator, and served until September 27, 1901, when Rev. Darwin C. Lippincott was elected in his stead.

CHURCH CLERKS.

Upon the completion of the organisation of the church in 1870, Ethelbert J. Davis was elected clerk, and served in that capacity until September, 1875, when Judson F. Randolph succeeded him for a term of one year.

On September 22, 1876, Ethelbert J. Davis was again elected clerk, and served continuously until December 23, 1898, when he was a second time succeeded by Judson F. Randolph, who served until September 27, 1901, on which date Oris O. Stutler became clerk.

FORMER RESIDENCE OF LEWIS FITZ RANDOLPH, ON GREENBRIER RUN.
(Built by his father, William Fitz Randolph).

CONSTITUENT MEMBERS.

Jacob Davis,
Jemima Davis,
Jesse J. Davis,
Huldah Davis,
Sally C. Davis,
Delia G. Davis,
Jesse Clark,
Charlotte Clark,
Marvel Clark,
Lucy A. Clark,
Effilee Clark,
Fenton R. Clark,
Milton Clark,
Judson F. Randolph,
Mary E. Randolph,
Jonathan F. Randolph,
Elisabeth Ann Randolph,
Charlotte Hutson,
Lucinda Strother,
Oliver C. Strother,
Daniel P. Strother,
James E. Strother,
Rosella Strother,
Mary J. Strother,
Love C. Strother,
Ethelbert J. Davis,
Alcena J. Davis,
Lewis F. Randolph,
Elisabeth Jane F. Randolph,
Amaziah Flint,
Joshua J. Davis,
Cornelius Maxson,
Catharine L. Maxson,
Gideon Maxson,
Charles B. Bonnell,
Rhulana Bonnell,
Francis M. Davis,
Adolphus A. Davis,
Mary Ann Davis,

JOHN F. RANDOLPH,
ANN HUGHES,
SARAH STUTTLER,
MELISSA F. RANDOLPH,
ALMEDA DAVIS,
MARY FLINT,
SALATHIEL DAVIS.

XIV.

ROANOKE, OR WEST FORK, CHURCH.

ON December 2, 1871, there was a meeting at the home of Reuben Hevener, in what was called "Sabbatarian Valley" (now known as Roanoke), Lewis County, West Virginia, to consider the propriety of taking steps looking toward the organisation of a Seventh Day Baptist church at that place.

This council met by order of the newly-organised South-Eastern Association, which had met with the church at Lost Creek, on the preceding Second Day of the week, and completed its organisation. It may be interesting to note that this is the only church in West Virginia organised directly by the association. All others have been organised by the churches directly, without regard to associational supervision.

The following persons were in attendance:—

    REUBEN HEVENER,
    ABIGAIL H. HEVENER,
    JOHN C. BOND,
    BETSEY BOND,
    ANN E. BOND,
    SAMUEL D. BOND,
    MARY E. HEVENER,
    FLORIN L. BOND,
    MANSFIELD M. HEVENER.

Rev. Samuel D. Davis was also present and participated in the deliberations.

Reuben Hevener was appointed moderator, and John J. Hevener, clerk.

It was agreed that a church ought to organised in the neighbourhood, and the Lost Creek Church, of which almost, if not quite all, of those present were members, was requested to take steps to organise such a church at an early date.

On the following day another meeting was held, when John C. Bond, John J. Hevener, and Samuel D. Bond were appointed to attend such a council as the Lost Creek Church might call to consider the propriety of organising the church as requested.

On the receipt of this petition for the organisation of a new church, the Lost Creek Church referred it to the South-Eastern Association. The association appointed a council, consisting of three delegates from each church in the association. This council met in the new house of worship erected for the use of these Seventh Day Baptists living at Roanoke, on the afternoon of the Sixth Day of the week, January 19, 1872.

The following delegates were present:—

From the Lost Creek Church:—
    REV. SAMUEL D. DAVIS,
    LEVI B. DAVIS,
    MOSES H. DAVIS.
From the New Salem Church:—
    REV. CHARLES A. BURDICK.
From the Greenbrier Church:—
    REV. JACOB DAVIS.
From the Middle Island Church:—
    GRANVILLE H. DAVIS.

Moses H. Davis was chosen moderator of the council, and Rev. Charles A. Burdick, secretary.

After some discussion of the question in hand, the council voted to proceed with the work of organising the new church.

After consultation with such of the prospective members of the new church as were present, a covenant and articles of faith were agreed upon and adopted.

On the following day, Sabbath, Rev. Charles A. Burdick preached a sermon, after which the following persons formally accepted the articles of faith and signed the covenant:—

    REUBEN HEVENER,
    ABIGAIL H. HEVENER,
    SAMUEL D. BOND,
    JANE C. BOND,
    MARY E. HEVENER,

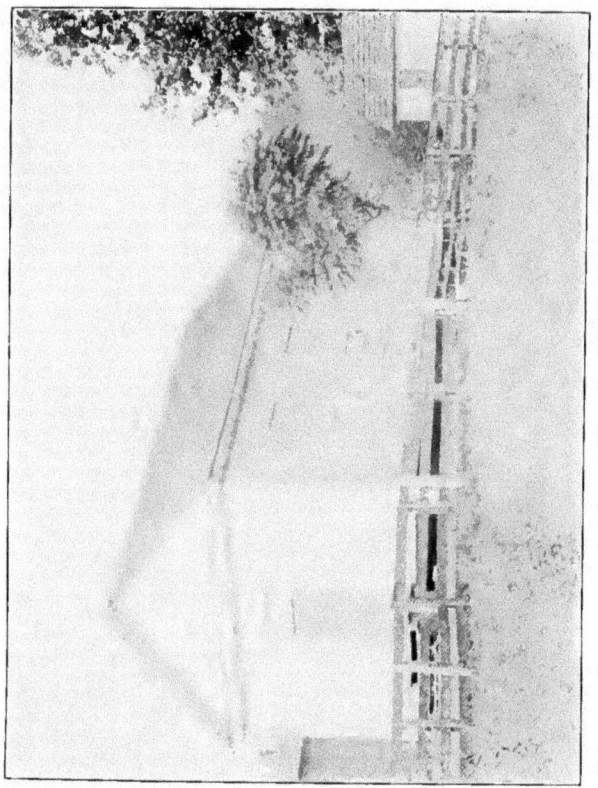

THE ROANOKE CHURCH.

ANN ELIZA BOND,
ELISABETH S. BOND,
AMANDA J. HEVENER,
ELISABETH BOND,
FLORIN L. BOND.

At a business meeting held in the evening after the Sabbath, of the same day, Samuel D. Bond and Reuben Hevener were chosen deacons; Rev. Samuel D. Davis, pastor; and John J. Hevener, clerk of the church.

On the following day, the newly chosen deacons were duly ordained.

MEMBERSHIP IN SUPERIOUR BODIES.

This church was received into membership in the South-Eastern Association, at the first annual session of the association, held with the Middle Island Church, at New Milton, West Virginia, in June, 1872.

At the annual session of the General Conference, held with the church at Southampton, Illinois, in the following September, the West Fork (Roanoke) Church became a member of the General Conference.

MEETING HOUSE.

But a short time before the organisation of the church, these people had built for their use, a neat frame building to be used as a house of worship, which has served their purpose up to the present time.

PASTORS.

Rev. Samuel D. Davis, who was chosen pastor at the time of the organisation of the church, served until November, 1874. After an *interim* of a year, during which time the church had been without a recognised pastor, he was again pastor for a short time.

In November, 1877, Rev. Lewis F. Randolph, who had been visiting the church, coming from his home on Greenbrier Run, was made pastor for a year.

In May, 1879, Marcus E. Martin was called to the pastorate of the church, and served in that capacity for some three years.

Again in May, 1882, Rev. Samuel D. Davis was chosen pastor and served until November 6, 1885, when he resigned. He continued to visit the church, however, at intervals of two or three months until February 6, 1891, when he was once more recognised as pastor, and served until May 4, 1894. He then finally resigned the charge because of physical infirmity.

On November 7, 1895, Rev. Mazzini G. Stillman was called to the pastorate of the Roanoke and Lost Creek churches, jointly. He entered upon his term of service, January 1, 1896, and at the date of this writing, August 1, 1902, remains in the service.

At no time in its history has the church had a pastor who has given his entire time to the church. A part of this period he has given one-fourth of his time. At other times he has preached once in two weeks, once a month, or attended the Quarterly Meetings of the church.

LICENCED TO PREACH.

Marcus E. Martin was licenced to preach, May, 1879; and in compliance with a call from the church to ordination, he was ordained February 6, 1880.

Ahva John Clarence Bond was licenced by the church, November 3, 1899, to preach "wherever duty might call."

MODERATORS.

For several years the church appointed its moderators from meeting to meeting, until in May 1880, Samuel D. Bond was appointed moderator for nine months. He still serves the church in that capacity.

CLERKS.

John J. Hevener, who was chosen clerk at the time of the organisation of the church, served until May 1, 1874, when he resigned, and Abigail H. Hevener was appointed in his stead. She served for two years, and upon her resignation in May, 1876, Mansfield M. Hevener was elected in her stead, and has served continuously ever since.

NAME.

The name chosen at the time of the organisation was the SEVENTH DAY BAPTIST CHURCH ON THE WEST FORK RIVER. In November, 1882, the name was changed to the ROANOKE SEVENTH DAY BAPTIST CHURCH, to correspond to the name of the post office recently established in the neighbourhood.

XV.

CONINGS, OR BEAR FORK, CHURCH.

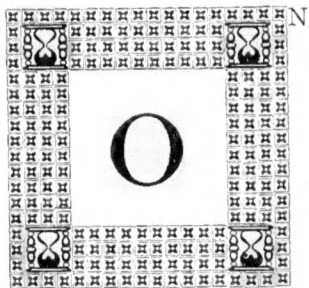ON June 26, 1881, there was a meeting of Seventh Day Baptists residing on the Bear Fork of Cove Creek, in Gilmer County, to consider the propriety of organising a Seventh Day Baptist church in their midst. Of those present, fourteen were ready to enter into such an organisation.

At an adjourned meeting, held the same day, Rev. James B. Davis, who was present and acted as chairman of both meetings, was appointed to draft articles of faith, and a covenant.

Another meeting was held July 22, 1881, when the proposed covenant was presented and pronounced satisfactory. On the 23d of September, 1881, another meeting was held which was attended by Rev. Samuel D. Davis, who presided. Arrangements were completed at this meeting for calling a council of the churches of the South-Eastern Association.

On the 21st of October, following, the council convened at the Boyce School House, on Bear Fork, and organised by appointing Rev. Marcus E. Martin, moderator; and Franklin F. Randolph, clerk.

Prayer was offered by Rev. Lewis F. Randolph.
The following delegates were in attendance:—
From the New Salem Church:—
    FRANKLIN F. RANDOLPH.
From the Greenbrier Church:—
    REV. LEWIS F. RANDOLPH,
    JUDSON F. RANDOLPH,
    FENTON R. CLARKE.

From the Middle Island Church:—
  REV. JAMES B. DAVIS,
  STEPHEN T. DAVIS,
  JOHN A. POLAN.
From the Ritchie Church:—
  ASA F. RANDOLPH,
  ELISHA J. MAXSON,
  LUTHER H. BOND.
From the West Fork (Roanoke) Church:—
  REV. MARCUS E. MARTIN,
  FLORIN LEE BOND,
  MANSFIELD M. HEVENER.
From the Lost Creek Church:—
  FRANCIS M. KILDOW.

After careful deliberation, the council decided to proceed with the organisation of the new church. The covenant and articles of faith, previously prepared, were approved. William Flesher was chosen deacon.

On the following day, Sabbath, October 22, the formal exercises incident to the organisation of the church, and to the ordination of the newly chosen deacon, were conducted. These services were conducted by Rev. James B. Davis and Rev. Lewis F. Randolph. Rev. James B. Davis preached the sermon.

The following were the constituent members:—
  REBECCA ANN FLESHER,
  WILLIAM H. FLESHER,
  JABEZ SPURGEON,
  CHRISTINA SPURGEON,
  CHARLES J. SPURGEON,
  MARY E. ADAMS,
  JOSHUA C. SPURGEON,
  EMILY E. SPURGEON *Lasure*,
  ANDREW J. LASURE,
  ARY LASURE.

NAME.

When the church was organised, it adopted as its name, THE BEAR FORK SEVENTH DAY BAPTIST CHURCH. On July 27, 1888, by vote of the church, it was changed to THE CONINGS SEVENTH DAY BAPTIST CHURCH.

MEMBERSHIP IN SUPERIOUR BODIES.

At the annual session of the South-Eastern Association, held with the Ritchie Church, beginning May 25, 1882, the

THE CONINGS CHURCH.

Bear Fork Church, upon its application, was received into the membership of the association.

Just when the church was received into the General Conference, the records, neither of the church nor the General Conference, state. No recognition is given the church in the Conference minutes until 1889. That year the church wrote a letter to the General Conference, apparently assuming that it was already a member of that body, and the letter seems to have been received by the General Conference upon that basis. But the recording secretary of the General Conference, in making up the statistical tables for that year, having found no previous record of the church, apparently assumed that the church had just been organised that year (and recorded it so), and consequently assumed that it likewise became a member of Conference in that year.

HOUSE OF WORSHIP.

As early as April 21, 1882, the church took initial steps toward building a house of worship. It was not until March 4, 1883, however, that the building committee, consisting of Jabez Spurgeon, William H. Flesher, and George W. Brissey, were instructed to proceed with the erection of a log house for a house of worship, upon a lot given for that purpose by Jabez Spurgeon. A few months afterward, the house was completed.

In the mean-time the church held its meetings in the Boyce School House, and in the homes of its members.

PASTORS.

At the time of the organisation of the Bear Fork Church, the Middle Island Church had for some time been maintaining a preaching station at that point, and Rev. James B. Davis of the Middle Island Church, visited the neighbourhood with more or less regularity, and conducted religious services.

On the 21st of April, 1882, seven months after its organisation, the church extended a call to Rev. Marcus E. Martin to become its pastor. He accepted the call and served the church until July 28, 1884, when he requested the church to dismiss him because he had ceased to observe the Sabbath of the Bible.

The church was then without a recognised pastor for a period of nearly seven years. In the mean time it enjoyed the temporary services of such ministers as were available for that purpose. At one time, Rev. Samuel D. Davis visited the church at intervals of three or four months for a period of a year or more.

Beginning with January 1, 1891, Rev. Orpheus S. Mills, who at that time was pastor of the Ritchie Church, assumed pastoral charge of the Bear Fork Church, also, giving it one-fourth of his time. He closed his term of service March 1, 1892.

Rev. Lely D. Seager became the next pastor, and remained with it until February 1, 1889, giving one-fourth of his time to the Conings Church, as the Bear Fork Church was now called, and three-fourths to the Ritchie Church.

Rev. Riley G. Davis became the next pastor, upon conditions similar to those of his predecessor, and remains the pastor at the date of this writing, August 1, 1902.

DEACON.

William H. Flesher, the only deacon the church has ever had, was ordained at the organisation of the church, October 22, 1881.

MODERATOR.

For a period of one year dating from January 29, 1883, the church had a permanent moderator, William H. Flesher. Before that time and afterwards, the moderator was appointed for the day, and was usually the pastor, or such other minister as might happen to be present.

CLERK.

Charles J. Spurgeon was the first clerk, and began his term of service with the first meeting held preliminary to the organisation of the church. Just how long he was clerk is not wholly clear from the records. He was excommunicated from the church July 27, 1883, for forsaking the Sabbath. At that time he had not attended the meetings of the church for more than a year.

Joshua C. Spurgeon was elected clerk of the church January 29, 1883, but Rev. Marcus E. Martin, who had been acting in that capacity for some time, continued to keep the records until July 28, 1884, since which time, they have been kept by Joshua C. Spurgeon.

XVI.

THE SALEMVILLE CHURCH.

THE Salemville Seventh Day Baptist Church had its origin in a German Seventh Day Baptist church, whose history may be briefly sketched as follows:—

In the year 1708, as a result of the revolt from the State Church of Germany, due to an irresistable longing for a greater degree of spirituality, Andrew Mack with others who sympathised with him, organised, at Schwartzenau, a church of the order known as the German Baptist Brethren, or Dunkers, or Dunkards. Although Andrew Mack was their first minister, the church did not regard him as its founder.

A storm of persecution immediately broke over their heads, and they were driven to Wittgenstein. They rejected all creeds of human origin and accepted the Gospel of Jesus Christ as their only rule of faith and practise. Persecution still raged, and they sought an asylum in America, settling near Germantown, Pennsylvania, where they organised their first church in this country in 1723. Among the early settlers was Christopher Sauer, who was the first printer in America to print the Bible in an American tongue.

Conrad Beissel was one of those who had fallen a victim to the persecution in Germany, and had been compelled to flee from his native land for safety. He was a mystic, born at Eberbach in the Palatinate in 1690, and learned the trade of a baker. He was fond of music and became a violinist of no mean ability. He studied theology at Halle, after which he was exiled in 1720, for holding Pietistic and Inspirational views, and settled at Germantown, Pennsylvania. In the following year, he became a hermit at Mill Creek, Lancaster County, Pennsylvania, where he remained until 1724, when he returned to Germantown and accepted baptism at the hands of the Dunkers. He soon offended the Dunkers by his advocacy of celibacy and the observance of the Seventh Day of the week as the Sabbath. In May, 1725, he founded the sect of Seventh Day Dunkers, or German Seventh Day Baptists. He again became a hermit in 1732; this time on the Cocalico River. Here his adherents followed him, and in 1735 he founded the mystic *Order of the Solitary*, and established the celebrated settlement at Ephrata, Pennsylvania, at whose head he remained until his death in July, 1768. Here he put into practise many of his theories, religious as well as socialistic and communistic. The members, comprising both men and women, adopted a peculiar dress, resembling somewhat that of the Capuchins, or White Friars, and the men wore long beards. Celibacy was encouraged, but marriage was not prohibited. Property was held in common, although private ownership was not forbidden. Many of the members were well educated. A printing press was set up, and a number of works in both English and German were published, some of them very beautifully made, and now highly prized.

After the Battle of Brandywine, in the War of the Revolution, these monastic buildings were thrown open for the care of the wounded, and one hundred and fifty American soldiers were buried in the German Seventh Day Baptist Cemetery at Ephrata.[1]

After the death of Conrad Beissel, Peter Miller succeeded to the leadership, and various branches were established; one in York County, in 1758; another at Snow Hill, Franklin County; and in 1763, one at Salemville, Bedford County, which still continues under the leadership of John S. King and David C. Long, as elders. These were all in the state of Pennsylvania.

At the first annual session of the Seventh Day Baptist South-Eastern Association, in 1872, the corresponding secre-

---

1. The wadding used by the American soldiers for their guns, in the Battle of Brandywine, was of unbound Seventh Day Baptist hymn books printed in the German language.

THE SALEMVILLE CHURCH AND PARSONAGE.

tary of that body reported correspondence between himself in behalf of the association and Jacob Long of Salemville, Pennsylvania, representing the German Seventh Day Baptists of Pennsylvania. Arrangements were made for the correspondence to be continued.

In 1876, at the request of the German Seventh Day Baptists of Salemville, Rev. Lester C. Rogers, at that time in the service of the American Sabbath Tract Society, visited them in behalf of Sabbath reform, and was cordially received and assisted in his labours by Rev. David C. Long, one of the clergymen of the church at Salemville. In writing of this visit, David C. Long says:—

"We are loth to have Bro. Rogers leave us. We are thankful to God for his able ministry, and also to our kind brethren who have spared him from other fields for our good. May the Lord reward you for your kind help to us through him! We hope this display of feeling for us by our English [-speaking] Seventh-day Baptist Brethren, may, under God's blessing, more closely identify us with you in the great work of Sabbath reform."

These people were visited subsequently by various other Seventh Day Baptist clergymen, including Rev. Arthur E. Main and Rev. Libbeus M. Cottrell. In 1882, Rev. Samuel D. Davis visited them and conducted a series of successful revival meetings.

Previous to the visit of Rev. Lester C. Rogers, Rev. Walter B. Gillette had visited these people on his way home from one of his visits to western Virginia.

The church at Salemville became divided because of certain differences of opinion, and on December 23, 1885, fourteen of its members left the mother church and, at a meeting held at the home of Noah Blough, organised themselves into the Salemville Seventh Day Baptist Church. Rev. Samuel D. Davis was present and assisted in the organisation.

MEMBERSHIP IN SUPERIOUR BODIES.

At the annual session of the South-Eastern Association, held with the Middle Island Church, at New Milton, West Virginia, in May, 1886, the Salemville Church was received into membership in that body. In the following September, it was received into the General Conference, at the annual session of that organisation, at Milton, Wisconsin.

HOUSE OF WORSHIP.

At the time of organisation, the church being without a house of worship, it arranged to worship in private houses, the homes of its members, for an indefinite length of time.

On the 12th of March, 1886, a building committee was appointed, consisting of Jacob B. Kagarise, George B. Kagarise, Noah Blough, and Wilson Kagarise. They obtained subscriptions on the spot, aggregating one hundred and eighty-seven dollars ($187.00). The committee proceeded at once to build, and on the 26th of the following September, the new house of worship was pronounced complete, at a total cost of eleven hundred dollars ($1100.00), of which four hundred dollars ($400.00) was yet unpaid. The members of the committee assumed personal responsibility for the debt, and three days later, September 29, 1886, the edifice was dedicated, Rev. Samuel D. Davis preaching the dedicatory sermon.

The remaining debt was paid by contributions from the Seventh Day Baptist Missionary Society, and by friends from other churches, so that all obligations incurred on account of the new building were cancelled by December 8, 1888.[1]

PASTORS.

Rev. George B. Kagarise was elected pastor on the day of the organisation, and served in that capacity until his death on September 10, 1893. In the mean time the church was visited occasionally by Rev. Samuel D. Davis, who after the death of Rev. George B. Kagarise was called to the pastorate of the church, on September 17, 1893. The pastor visited the church at the time of the Quarterly Meetings (communion services), and remained for a week or two, the distance of the church from his home at Jane Lew, West Virginia, being too great to permit more frequent visits. He resigned the pastorate June 14, 1895.

Rev. Lely Daniel Seager became the next pastor, beginning his term of service in September, 1895. He, too, was a visiting pastor, with his home at Berea, West Virginia, where he was at the same time serving the Ritchie Church as its resident pastor. On June 19, 1896, he resigned as pastor, and the church called Darwin C. Lippincott, a student of

---

1. A commodious and comfortable parsonage has been erected since the date of the above writing, August 1, 1902.

REV. GEORGE B. KAGARISE.

REV. DARWIN C. LIPPINCOTT.

Salem College, Salem, West Virginia, to serve in a manner similar to that of his immediate predecessors. Beginning with July, 1897, however, he became the resident pastor of the church. On September 28, 1897, Edward B. Saunders, an evangelist in the service of the Seventh Day Baptist Missionary Society, began a series of evangelistic meetings at Salemville, which continued for a period of four weeks, and resulted in several additions to the membership of the church.

On September 11, 1898, the church called its pastor, Darwin C. Lippincott, to ordination, and the 28th of the following January was fixed upon as the date for the ordination service, when the following clergymen were present to assist; viz., Rev. Mazzini G. Stillman, pastor of the church at Lost Creek; Rev. Theodore L. Gardiner, of the New Salem Church; and Rev. Oscar U. Whitford, of Westerly, Rhode Island, corresponding secretary of the Seventh Day Baptist Missionary Society.

Rev. Darwin C. Lippincott terminated his term of service as pastor of the church, September 10, 1899. The church was now without a pastor for more than a year, Jerome Kagarise supplying the pulpit from time to time. He was a member of the German Seventh Day Baptist Church, near by.

On November 4, 1900, the church extended a call to John H. Wolfe to act as pastor for a period of six months, and on the 10th of March, 1901, called him to ordination. He declined ordination, however, as he wished to pursue his studies at Alfred University. On the same day, March 10, 1901, the church extended a call to Rev. David W. Leath to become its pastor from the first day of the following June. The call was accepted, but at the end of a year's service, he closed his connection with the church, and sought other fields of labour, and the church was left without a pastor.

LICENCED TO PREACH.

John H. Wolfe was licenced to preach, March 6, 1892.

DEACONS.

At the time of the organisation of the church, Jacob B. Kagarise and David E. Rice were elected to the office of deacon.

On the 11th of March, 1888, it was voted that John Wolfe, Sr., be recognised as a deacon.

At the annual session of the South-Eastern Association,

held with the Salemville Church in May, 1902, Charles C. Wolfe was, on the 18th day of that month, ordained deacon. All the clergymen in attendance at the association, assisted in the ordination service.

CHURCH CLERKS.

Noah B. Blough was elected the first clerk of the church on the date of its organisation, December 23, 1885.

On January 21, 1887, George C. Long was elected clerk.

Amos D. Wolfe was elected to the office of clerk for a term of three years from September 4, 1892, and has been re-elected continuously ever since.

CONSTITUENT MEMBERS OF THE SALEMVILLE CHURCH.

GEORGE B. KAGARISE, *Elder,*
SUSAN KAGARISE,
DAVID E. RICE,
BARBARA RICE,
NOAH B. BLOUGH,
LEANNAH BLOUGH,
JACOB B. KAGARISE,
WILSON S. KAGARISE,
JENNIE KAGARISE,
ESTHER WALTER,
CHARLES F. SHRINER,
NANCY SHRINER,
JEREMIAH GROWDEN,
BARBARA GROWDEN.

XVII.

THE COPEN CHURCH.

IN the month of September, 1887, a petition was drawn up by a few Seventh Day Baptists residing on Copen Run, Braxton County, West Virginia, and presented to the churches of the South-Eastern Association, praying for these churches to send delegates to sit in council, on Copen Run, the evening after the second Sabbath of the following November, and, if, in the judgment of the council, it seemed wise to do so, to organise the petitioners into a Seventh Day Baptist Church.

The petition ran as follows:—

"To the S[eventh] D[ay] B[aptist] Churches of the S[outh] E[astern] Association, Greeting:

"DEAR BRETHREN:—

"We, the undersigned, have covenanted together to ask that you will, with delegates and ministers, meet us in council on Copen Run, Braxton County, West Virginia, on the evening after the second Sabbath in November next, to consider the propriety of organizing a S[eventh] D[ay] B[aptist] church at this place.

"Respectfully yours in Christ,

"CINDRILLA SHOCK,
"A. SHOCK,
"W. L. WILDMAN,
"MARY E. WILDMAN,
"SALLY C. WILDMAN,
"EMILY A. WILDMAN,
"MARY G. WILDMAN,
"BIRD WILDMAN,
"U. C. SHOCK,

"Virginia Shock,
"W. T. W. Davis,
"S. B. Davis,
"N. C. D. Bond,
"Clara Shock,
"W. A. Gochenour."

In accordance with the petition, on November 12, 1887, delegates from the several churches met as follows:—

From the New Salem Church:—
Rev. Samuel D. Davis.
From the Lost Creek Church:—
Rev. John L. Huffman.
From the Middle Island Church:—
Nathan Kelley,
John A. Polan.
From the Ritchie Church:—
Asa F. Randolph,
Elisha J. Maxson.
From the Greenbrier Church:—
Rev. Hiram P. Burdick,
Riley G. Davis,
Ethelbert J. Davis,
G. Wise Clarke.
From the Bear Fork, Conings, Church:—
Jabez B. Spurgeon,
Joshua C. Spurgeon.

The council was called to order by Rev. Samuel D. Davis, and prayer was offered by Rev. John L. Huffman.

Rev. Hiram P. Burdick was elected chairman, and Ethelbert J. Davis, secretary, of the council.

The following resolution was adopted:—

"RESOLVED, That we believe that the time has come when the good of the cause of Christ and the best interests of God's people in this vicinity, demand the organisation of a Seventh Day Baptist Church here; and further, that we proceed to organise such a church to be known as the Copen Seventh Day Baptist Church, of the persons whose names are attached to the petition calling for the council."

Pursuant to the foregoing resolution, the following named individuals were declared organised into a church:—

William L. Wildman,
Mary E. Wildman,
Emily A. Nettie Wildman,
Sally C. Wildman,
Cora Bird Wildman,

MARY WILDMAN,
WAITMAN T. WILLEY DAVIS,
LOUISA BELL DAVIS,
ALBERT SHOCK,
CINDERILLA SHOCK,
URIAH C. SHOCK,
IVA VIRGINIA SHOCK,
CLARA ETHEL SHOCK,
WILLIAM ALONZO GOCHENOUR.

Articles of faith and practise were adopted similar to those of other Seventh Day Baptist churches.

The following officers were chosen:—

ALBERT SHOCK, *Moderator,*
URIAH C. SHOCK, *Clerk,*
WAITMAN T. WILLEY DAVIS, *Treasurer,*
WILLIAM L. WILDMAN, *Deacon.*

The following service was then conducted for the purpose of ordaining the newly appointed deacon:—

Prayer. By Rev. Hiram P. Burdick, accompanied by the imposition of hands.
Charge to the Candidate. By Deacon Asa F. Randolph.
Charge to the Church. By Rev. Samuel D. Davis.

The book of records of the church contains, in addition to the minutes of the council of organisation, the minutes of but six business meetings of the church. The first appears under date of November 13, 1887, the day following the date of the organisation; the last, May, 1891.

On November 13, 1887, the church voted to hold weekly service for worship on Sabbath morning, and invited Rev. Samuel D. Davis to attend their Quarterly Meetings.

On February 10, 1888, the church took initial steps toward uniting with the churches of other denominations in the neighbourhood in building a union meeting house. But nothing appears to have come of the action.

After the organisation of the church, there were added the following members:—

N. CLAYTON D. BOND,
SARAH CATHARINE HITT,
JENNIE STEELE, (joined August 8, 1890).

MEMBERSHIP IN SUPERIOUR BODIES.

On May 11, 1888, the church voted to request admission to the South-Eastern Seventh Day Baptist Association; and at the annual session of that body, held with the Lost Creek Church in May following, the request was presented and granted. The church continued to be recognised as an active member of the association as late as its annual session in 1896.

At the annual session of the General Conference held at Leonardsville, New York, in August, 1888, the Copen Church became a member of the General Conference. The church has not been represented at Conference, by delegate or otherwise, since 1890.

OFFICERS.

The officers elected at the time of the organisation, continued in office, and Rev. Samuel D. Davis was the only pastor of the church.

RECORDS.

The records of the Copen Church are at the date of this writing in the hands of Albert Shock, of Burnsville, West Virginia.

XVIII.

THE WEST UNION CHURCH.

N the 28th of September, 1888, a council convened at West Union, Doddridge County, West Virginia, at the call of a number of Sabbath-keepers in that vicinity, to consider the propriety of organising a Seventh Day Baptist church at that place. The following delegates were present:— Rev. Samuel D. Davis and Preston F. Randolph, from the New Salem Church; Rev. Hiram P. Burdick from the Middle Island and Greenbrier churches; Rev. James B. Davis and Johnson Joseph Lowther, from the Middle Island Church; and Mrs. Laura Ford and Rev. John L. Huffman, from the Lost Creek Church.

Rev. Samuel D. Davis was elected chairman, and Festus P. Ford, secretary, of the council.

The following resolution was adopted:—

"RESOLVED, That it is the opinion of this council that the interests of the cause of God would be better advanced by organising a Seventh Day Baptist church in the vicinity of West Union, West Virginia, and we now recommend that the brethren and sisters living in this vicinity proceed at once to organise such a church."

A committee to draft articles of faith and a covenant, in order to carry out the object of the foregoing resolution, was appointed. The council then adjourned until the following day at 10:30 o'clock A. M., when it again met.

An *exposé* of faith and practise, and a covenant were presented by the committee and adopted. The church was then organised with the following constituent members:—

FESTUS P. FORD,
E. JANE FORD,
S. PRESTON DAVIS,
KATE DAVIS,
EMMA J. DAVIS,
JAMES FORD,
TALITHA W. FORD,
SEPTIMIUS ARDVERN FORD,
SAMUEL L. FORD,
LAURA A. FORD,
LILLIE M. FORD,
N. VICTORIA HUSTED,
DELIA ANN JEFFREY,
MELISSA DAVIS,
C. LATON FORD.

The constituent membership was drawn almost wholly from the New Salem and Middle Ilsand churches.

On the following day a business meeting of the church was called, at which the following officers were elected:—

JAMES FORD, *Moderator,*
KATE DAVIS, *Clerk,*
S. PPESTON, DAVIS, *Treasurer,*
REV. SAMUEL D. DAVIS, *Pastor.*

Festus P. Ford and Samuel L. Ford were ordained deacons, and Experience Davis and Ollie Sullivan were received as members, and a constitution adopted at this meeting. The name was also selected as follows:—THE SEVENTH DAY BAPTIST CHURCH OF WEST UNION, WEST VIRGINIA.

The public school house, known as the Rock Run School House, was used as a house of worship; and, on the 19th of April, 1889, a committee was appointed to find a suitable lot on which to erect a meeting house, and report at the next business meeting of the church, when the committee reported progress and was continued.

At a meeting held on the 18th of October, following, the committee reported that they had secured an option on a lot belonging to Franklin Maxwell just east of the old Seventh Day Baptist graveyard, but on the other side of the public road from it, at West Union, and recommended its purchase. The recommendation of the committee was adopted, the lot was purchased, and the following trustees appointed:— Gamble S. Davis, Herman Davis, Septimius Ardvern Ford, Festus P. Ford, and Samuel L. Ford.

On the 18th of April, 1890, the church called Rev. Marcus E. Martin as pastor of the church for six months. The call was accepted, and service began at once.

On the 20th of September, 1890, a committee of five was appointed to solicit funds for the purpose of building a house of worship. On the 17th of October following, the soliciting committee reported subscriptions aggregating two hundred and ninety-three dollars and fifty cents ($293.50). A building committee was then appointed to proceed to build and complete the meeting house.

At the same meeting the pastor, Rev. Marcus E. Martin, was invited to continue his labours with the church for another year.

On the 18th of January, 1891, the committee appointed to close the purchase of the lot for the house of worship reported that he had not yet succeeded in obtaining the deed for it. On the same day the building committee reported that they had decided to build a meeting house forty-five feet long by thirty feet wide, and that they had made a contract for the necessary timber for the frame, and were awaiting the delivery of the deed for the lot.

On the 19th of the following April, the committee reported to the church that they had been unable to obtain the deed as yet, but had reason to hope that it would be delivered soon. The building committee reported that they had done nothing, pending the delivery of the deed.

On the 10th of January, 1892, Rev. Marcus E. Martin received and accepted a call to continue his labours as pastor of the church for another year.

On the 15th of May, 1892, the committee on purchase of the lot, reported that a deed had been received and the lot paid for.

Rev. Marcus E. Martin discontinued his pastoral relations with the church at the end of the year 1892, and Rev. Samuel D. Davis accepted a call to visit the church once a month during the following year.

On the 13th of April, 1894, the church held its last business meeting, at which delegates were appointed to the association and the clerk was directed to write a letter to the association.

Some of the families composing the membership of the church moved away about this time and left the organisation too weak to sustain itself. The most of the membership, accordingly, was transferred to other churches, principally the New Salem and Middle Island churches.

The lot purchased upon which to erect a house of worship, was sold by order of the Circuit Court of Doddridge County, and the proceeds applied toward the liquidation of the debts of the church.

It is a cause of sincere regret that the West Union Church, the second, and it may almost fairly be called the third, attempt to establish a Seventh Day Baptist church at West Union, should result in so signal a failure.

West Union, like Salem, is one of those strategic points, which give strength, stability, and character to any religious denomination, and especially to one whose test of fealty is as critical as that of the Seventh Day Baptists.

The village of West Union was laid out on the lands of Captain Nathan Davis, a soldier of the War of 1812, and an influential member of the New Salem Church.

He exerted his influence, to the utmost, to have the Middle Island Church erect a house of worship in West Union, at the time that village was established by act of the General Assembly of Virginia, in 1845, offering to contribute generously for that purpose; but without avail. Afterward the West Union Academy was established at West Union, but it was short-lived, and when the Middle Island Church was finally resuscitated and re-organised, it had to be removed to New Milton, several miles away, in order to keep it alive.

MEMBERSHIP IN SUPERIOUR BODIES.

At the annual session of the South-Eastern Association held with the church at Salem, in May, 1889, the West Union Church was, upon its petition, received into membership in that body; and in the following August, at the annual session of the General Conference, at Alfred, New York, the church became a member of the General Conference also.

RECORDS.

The records of the church are now in the care of Samuel L. Ford, one of the deacons of the defunct church. His Post Office address is West Union, West Virginia.

THE WEST UNION CHURCH

MODERATOR.

On September, 30, 1888, at the first business meeting of the church held after its organisation, James Ford was elected moderator. His death on the 31st of December following, left the office vacant, and on the 19th of April, 1889, his son Septimius Ardvern Ford was elected in his stead.

At a later date, some-time before January 10, 1892, Gamble S. Davis became moderator, and continued in that office until the dissolution of the church.

CLERK.

Miss Kate Davis, the only clerk of the church, was elected on September 30, 1888, at the first business meeting held after the organisation of the church.

A LIST OF THE NAMES OF THE MEMBERS OF THE WEST UNION CHURCH, TOGETHER WITH THE DATE OF THEIR RECEPTION.

FESTUS P. FORD,	Constituent member,
E. JANE FORD,	Constituent member,
KATE DAVIS,	Constituent member,
JAMES FORD,	Constituent member,
TALITHA W. FORD,	Constituent member,
MISS E. J. DAVIS,	Constituent member,
SAMUEL L. FORD,	Constituent member,
LAURA A. FORD,	Constituent member,
S. ARDVERN FORD,	Constituent member,
LILLIE M. FORD,	Constituent member,
S. PRESTON DAVIS,	Constituent member,
DELIA ANN JEFFREY,	Constituent member,
MRS. N. VICTORIA HUSTED,	Constituent member,
C. LATON FORD,	Constituent member,
MELISSA DAVIS,	Constituent member,
OLLIE SULLIVAN,	September 30, 1888,
EXPERIENCE DAVIS *Polan*,	September 30, 1888,
BENJAMIN KINNEY,	September 30, 1888,
C. C. DAVIS,	April 28, 1889,
GAMBLE S. DAVIS,	June 9, 1889,
ALWILDA DAVIS,	July 20, 1889,
HARMON DAVIS,	July 20, 1889,
MARY D. DAVIS,	July 20, 1889,
XENIA DAVIS *Holtz*,	July 20, 1889,
CECELIA DAVIS,	July 20, 1889,
MELVINA DAVIS *Furby*,	July 20, 1889,
IRENE BELLE DAVIS *Ford*,	July 21, 1889,
SYLVANUS DAVIS,	January 18, 1890,

WILLIAM DAVIS,	January 18,	1890,
ELI R. DAVIS,	May 10,	1890,
OKEY S. DAVIS,	May 10,	1890,
NEWTON DAVIS,	May 10,	1890,
ANDERSON DAVIS,	February 23,	1893,
MAGGIE E. DAVIS,	July 9,	1893,

XIX.

THE BLACK LICK CHURCH.

IN response to a request from members of the New Salem, Greenbrier, West Union, and Middle Island churches residing in the vicinity of Black Lick Run, near Long Run Station, in Doddridge County, a council composed of delegates from the New Salem, Lost Creek, Greenbrier, Middle Island, Ritchie, and West Union churches, met at the Trough School House, near the mouth of Black Lick Run, on the evening after the Sabbath, January 20, 1894, to consider the feasibility of organising a Seventh Day Baptist church at that place.

The following delegates were in attendance from their respective churches:—

New Salem:—
    Rev. John L. Huffman,
    Darwin C. Lippincott.
Lost Creek:—
    Rev. John L. Huffman,
    Rev. William L. Burdick.
Greenbrier:—
    Rev. Marcus E. Martin,
    Ethelbert J. Davis,
    Alfred N. Meek,
    Riley G. Davis.
Middle Island:—
    Johnson Joseph Lowther,
    Archibald W. Kelley,
    John A. Polan,
    Samuel A. Ford.

Ritchie:—
    JOSHUA BOND,
West Union:—
    SYLVANUS DAVIS.

The council organised by electing Rev. John L. Huffman, moderator, and Rev. William L. Burdick, secretary.

After a general discussion of the question in hand, it was voted to organise a church. Accordingly a constitution, articles of faith and practise, and a covenant were adopted.

On the following morning, the organisation of the church was completed by the election of the following officers:—

    ALFRED N. MEEK, *Moderator,*
    GERTRUDE COTTRILLE, *Secretary,*
    SYLVANUS DAVIS, *Treasurer.*

It was voted to recognise Cornelius S. Davis as a deacon, since he had been ordained previously to that office by the Greenbrier Church.

The organisation sermon was preached by Rev. John L. Huffman, after which Rev. Marcus E. Martin gave the right hand of fellowship to the members of the new church, and the work of the council was completed.

MEMBERSHIP IN SUPERIOUR BODIES.

At the annual session of the South-Eastern Association held at Roanoke, West Virginia, beginning May 17, 1894, the Black Lick Church was received into the association; and at the annual session of the Seventh Day Baptist General Conference held at Brookfield, New York, in September, 1894, the church became a member of that body also.

HOUSE OF WORSHIP.

The Black Lick Church after its organisation united with the Baptist Church in the same neighbourhood, in building a house of worship on the Buckeye Fork of Middle Island Creek, at the mouth of Black Lick Run. This building the Black Lick Church continues to use.

PASTORS.

At a business meeting of the church held April 20, 1894, Alvin M. Davis, Darwin C. Lippincott, and Rev. Marcus E. Martin were each cordially invited to preach for the church when convenient to them.

On January 18, 1895, Rev. Marcus E. Martin, Darwin C.

THE BLACK LICK CHURCH.

Lippincott, and Riley G. Davis were invited to preach to the church at their convenience.

On the 17th of April, 1897, Rev. Marcus E. Martin was called to the pastorate of the church, and continued to serve in that capacity for two years.

On the 14th of July, 1899, the Black Lick Church united with the Middle Island and Greenbrier churches in calling Rev. David W. Leath, who was already upon the field, to the pastorate of the three churches, his term of service to date from May 1, 1899. He served the three churches in this manner for two years, and was succeeded by Rev. Darwin C. Lippincott, who entered upon his duties May 1, 1901.

LICENCED TO PREACH.

Alvin M. Davis was licenced to preach for one year, April 20, 1894. This licence was renewed for another year, January 18, 1895, and on January 17, 1896, licence was granted him for an indefinite period.

DEACONS.

Cornelius S. Davis, one of the constituent members of the church, had been ordained previous to the organisation of the Black Lick Church, by the Greenbrier Church, of which he was then a member. The Black Lick Church recognised him as a deacon from the time of its organisation.

Theodore Davis was chosen deacon April 20, 1894, and was ordained to that office on Sabbath Day, July 21, 1894.

MODERATORS.

At the time of the organisation of the church, Alfred N. Meek was elected moderator. He was succeeded after his term of service had expired by Alvin M. Davis, who still occupies that office.

CLERKS.

At the time of the organisation of the church, Gertrude Cottrille was elected clerk. She was succeeded on January 18, 1895, by Sylvanus Davis, the present clerk.

CONSTITUENT MEMBERS.

SYLVANUS DAVIS,
ELIZABETH A. DAVIS, wife of Sylvanus,
ALFRED N. MEEK,
LUCETTA MEEK,
JOHN J. DAVIS,

николаi I. Davis,
Sarah E. Cottrille,
Nancy Davis,
Delilah Davis,
May M. Hutson,
Delia L. Hutson,
Addie Cottrille,
Gertrude Cottrille,
Gladie Davis,
Jean Davis,
Alvin M. Davis,
Theodore Davis,
Marvel Davis,
Lora Davis,
Ananias Davis,
Charlotte Davis,
Zania Davis,
Cornelius S. Davis,
Hannah Davis,
Leda Davis,
Polina S. W. Davis,
Arthur Davis,
Victoria Davis,
Maria Davis,
Ananias R. Davis,
Elijah Davis,
Nancy E. Davis,
Loverna Beatrice Davis,
Artilla Davis.

XX.

THE SOUTH-WESTERN ASSOCIATION.

HE Seventh Day Baptist General Conference at its annual session held with the First Hopkinton Church, of Rhode Island, in September, 1835, took the following action:—

"RESOLVED, That a committee of six be appointed to draft a plan for the new arrangement of Conference and prepare a complete system, for the consideration of Conference, and that brethren Orson Campbell, Alexander Campbell, Joel Greene, Amos R. Wells, Nathan V. Hull, and Ebenezer Davis be said committee."

This committee at the same session of the General Conference, rendered a report, which was adopted as follows:—

"That upon mature reflection, we deem it expedient that the Seventh Day Baptist churches in the United States, form themselves into three associations, which may properly be denominated the Eastern, Middle, and Western associations, which shall hold sessions in each year, a little prior to the sitting of the General Conference; and we would suggest the appointment of twelve delegates, to sit in the Conference, from each of the several associations.

"And that the churches in Rhode Island, New Jersey, and Connecticut, form the Eastern; and the churches east of Alleghany County, New York, and west of the Hudson River, form the Middle; leaving to the choice of the churches of Berlin, Petersburgh, and Schenectady, to attach themselves either to the Eastern or Middle, as they wish; and that all the churches including Alleghany [County], on westward and south, form the Western.

"ALEXANDER CAMPBELL,
"Secretary of Committee."

In accordance with the foregoing action of the General Conference the churches in western Virginia were included in the territory covered by the Western Association. Accordingly at the annual session of the Western Association, held with the Second Alfred Church, at Alfred, New York, in June, 1837, the Lost Creek and North Fork of Hughes River churches in Virginia, made application for membership in that body, and were duly accepted. The New Salem Church sent an application also, but it arrived too late for action at that session of the association. However, at the next annual session of the association, held with the church at Clarence, Erie County, New York, in June, 1838, the request was formally presented, and granted.

Before the next annual meeting of the Western Association, the churches of western Virginia, south-western Pennsylvania, and the state of Ohio, had organised themselves into the South-Western Association, which upon application, was admitted into the General Conference, at its annual session, held with the First Brookfield Church, at Brookfield, New York, in September, 1839. Joel Greene and James H. Cochran represented the South-Western Association at this session of the General Conference.

This organisation was the outgrowth of a convention of Seventh Day Baptist churches of Ohio and Virginia, held at Lost Creek, Virginia, February 23, 1839, apparently under the leadership of Rev. Joel Greene, who at that time was engaged in missionary labour among the churches of western Virginia.

After prayer by Rev. Peter Davis, the convention organised by appointing Lewis Bond, moderator, and Lewis A. Davis, secretary. After Joel Greene had stated the object of the convention, it was voted that measures be taken to form an association, and Lewis A. Davis, Lewis Bond, and Levi H. Bond were appointed a committee to draft a constitution to be presented at the next meeting with such resolutions as might be thought advisable. The convention met on the following day, when the report of the committee was called for, and the following resolutions presented by them were unanimously adopted:—

"1. RESOLVED, That the location and circumstances of the Seventh Day Baptist churches in this country, in our opinion, render it desirable and expedient that an association be organised.

"2. RESOLVED, That we respectfully solicit our brethren of the Western Association to send us a number of brethren, to sit with us in council, and if thought proper, to assist in the organisation of an association, and that the time of our meeting be fixed on the 7th day of August next.

"3. RESOLVED, *Unanimously,* That we feel under great obligations to the Missionary Society for the aid hitherto afforded us, and that we solicit a continuance of their fostering care, and we solemnly pledge ourselves to use our best exertions to co-operate with them to sustain the interest of the Redeemer's kingdom in this country by supplying the Gospel, in the hope that at a future time we may be able to contribute our share to send the Gospel to those who may be dependent as we are now.

"4. RESOLVED, That Abel Bond, Levi H. Bond, Gamble Shannon, Lewis Bond, and Lewis A. Davis, be a committee to correspond with the Executive Committee of the S[eventh] D[ay Baptist] Missionary Society in behalf of the churches in reference to the prospects of future supplies of missionary helps, etc., in this country.

"5. RESOLVED, That the secretary of this convention revise the minutes of its proceedings and forward the same to the editor of the *Protestant Sentinel* for publication.

"6. RESOLVED, That this convention adjourn to meet at this place, on the Fourth Day of the week before the second Sabbath in August next, at 10 o'clock A. M., and that Brother L. A. Davis deliver an introductory discourse on that occasion; Bro. Lewis Bond [to be] his substitute in case of failure."

Before adjournment, the date of the First Annual Session was fixed for August 7, 1839, and the place of meeting was Lost Creek; at which time and place the association convened, and the introductory discourse was preached by Lewis Bond, after which the association organised for business by appointing Lewis Bond, moderator, and James Bailey and Richard C. Bond, clerks.

Seven churches appeared as members of the association. Those of Virginia were:— The New Salem, Lost Creek, North Fork of Hughes River, and South Fork of Hughes River. Those of Ohio were:— The Pike, and Temperance Reform Pike churches, both of Clark County. From Pennsylvania, was the Woodbridgetown Church of Fayette County. These seven churches represented a total membership of two hundred and seventy-one [271].

James Bailey appeared as a delegate from the Central Association, and James H. Cochran from the Western. Lewis Bond was appointed delegate to the Western Association with Peter Davis as his alternate; and James Bailey delegate to the Central Association. Joel Greene and James H. Cochran were appointed delegates to the General Conference from this association. Apparently the seeds of the discord, which was finally to destroy the organisation, appeared in this first annual convention, for we find that the two churches at Pike sent communications which were referred to a committee, whose report was adopted but not permitted to be entered upon the minutes.

The constitution which was adopted was as follows:—

"*Art.* 1. This association may be composed of such churches of the Seventh Day Baptist order, as are now located in the states of Virginia, Ohio, and the church in Fayette County, Pennsylvania, and such other churches as may from time to time be received by the association at its annual sessions; and shall be known by the name of the 'SEVENTH DAY BAPTIST SOUTH-WESTERN ASSOCIATION.'

"*Art.* 2. This association shall hold an annual meeting at such time and place as shall be agreed on at the preceding annual meeting and shall be composed of the elders and delegates from the several churches of which it is composed.

"*Art.* 3. A discourse shall be delivered at the opening of each session of the association, after which a moderator, one or more secretaries, and a treasurer, shall be chosen.

"It shall be the duty of the moderator to preserve order during the deliberations of the association; and he shall have a casting vote in case of an equal division.

"The secretary shall keep a record of the transactions of the association at its annual meetings, and shall record the same in a book, to be provided for that purpose, which shall be presented at the annual meetings of the association, together with all valuable papers belonging to the association, and shall deliver the same to his successor.

"*Art.* 4. All resolutions shall be presented in writing, and no resolution or motion shall be put by the moderator, or debated by the members of the association, unless said resolutions shall have been seconded.

"All resolutions or motions shall, in ordinary cases, be decided by a majority of the members of the association; but in all cases, when requested, they shall be decided by the churches; *i. e.,* the delegates of each church shall give but one vote, which shall be decided by a majority of its representatives.

"*Art.* 5. This association shall choose annually, a corresponding secretary, whose duty it shall be to correspond with other associations, with the General Conference, and with every other body whereby the cause of truth may be advanced; and shall submit his correspondence to the examination of the association at its annual session.

"*Art.* 6. This association shall not interfere with the internal concerns of the churches of which it is composed, so as to infringe on their independence; but shall act as an advisory council when necessary. In case any church shall depart from the faith, or become corrupt in practise, this association may inquire into such defect, and labour with them; and if they cannot be reclaimed, they may be dropped from the association.

"*Art.* 7. All elders not examined and ordained by the Presbytery of the General Conference, or this association, shall be examined by a committee appointed by the association, before they are admitted as members thereof.

"*Art.* 8. This association shall, at its annual meetings, appoint a number of delegates (the number to be agreed on annually) to represent this association and to represent it to the General Conference at its meetings.

"*Art.* 9. No alteration shall be made to these articles, unless such alterations shall have been presented at a preceding annual meeting and approved by a majority of the churches represented."

The Second Annual Session of the South-Western Association was held at New Salem, Virginia, beginning August 20, 1840. The introductory discourse was preached by Lewis Bond, in the absence of Ezekiel Bee who had been appointed for that purpose.

The association organised with Lewis Bond as moderator, and Henry R. Stillman and Jepthah F. Randolph as secretaries. Stillman Coon appeared as a delegate from the Western Association. The churches reporting were as follows:— Lost Creek, New Salem, South Fork of Hughes River, and North Fork of Hughes River, in Virginia; Woodbridgetown of Pennsylvania; Pike and North Hampton of Ohio. The last named was known the year before, as the Temperance Reform Church of Pike. The grievances presented the preceding year by two Ohio churches were, at this session, referred to a committee, who reported that, in their belief, a committee should be appointed to labour to effect a reconciliation, either in person or by writing, and Rev. Stillman Coon and Lewis Bond were named as such committee. Lewis Sammons was appointed a delegate to the Western Association, and William F. Randolph as his alternate. The association adjourned to meet with the church at North Hampton in Pike Township, Clarke County, Ohio, at 10 o'clock A. M., on the Fifth Day of the week before the second Sabbath in October, 1841.

The Third Annual Session of the South-Western Association convened at the time and place appointed, and the introductory sermon was preached by Lewis A. Davis, after which the association organised for business by the appointment of John Forsythe as moderator and Lemon Lippincott and John Babcock as clerks. The following churches reported:— From Virginia; New Salem and Lost Creek. From Ohio; Pike and North Hampton. The Woodbridgetown Church, of Pennsylvania, made no report. The South Fork of Hughes River, and North Fork of Hughes River churches, in Virginia, also failed to report.

Aside from the discord existing among the Ohio churches there appears to have been entire harmony and union throughout the sessions of the association, for the report of the committee on the state of religion expresses gratitude for the harmony and union apparent in most of the churches.

At this session of the association, Bethuel C. Church presented himself as a candidate for ordination, when the association took the following action:—

"RESOLVED, That we believe that he [Bethel C. Church] ought to be ordained and that the case be referred to the Presbytery of this association, who shall examine and ordain him if they think proper."

At this early date the temperance question received consideration, as is shown by the following preamble and resolution, which were unanimously adopted:—

Whereas, Intemperance is a prolific source of evil, moral and physical; therefore,

"RESOLVED, That this association sustain the cause of temperance as advocated by its friends in the United States."

Joshua Hill was appointed a delegate to the General Conference for the ensuing year.

The Presbytery evidently took favourable action upon the question of the ordination of Bethuel C. Church, for, at the close of the association, he was ordained. The ordination sermon was preached by Lewis A. Davis.

The Fourth Annual Session met according to appointment, with the church at Port Jefferson, Ohio, on October 13, 1842. The introductory sermon was preached by Joshua Hill. Simeon Babcock was appointed moderator, and William F. Randolph and Richard C. Bond, secretaries.

Reports were presented from the Lost Creek and New Salem churches, in Virginia; and the North Hampton Church, of Ohio. The Woodbridgetown Church, of Pennsylvania; the South Fork of Hughes River, and the North Fork of

Hughes River churches, of Virginia; and the Pike Church, of Ohio, failed to report. The following churches of Ohio were admitted as members of the association:— Port Jefferson, Jackson Centre, Sciota, and Stokes. Lewis A. Davis was appointed delegate to the Western Association, with Joshua Hill as his alternate.

Through a committee, a claim was presented for missionary work within the bounds of the association. Joshua Hill was appointed an agent to preach upon the Sabbath question whenever a suitable opportunity should offer.

While the report of the committee on the state of religion shows that there was a commendable degree of union existing among the churches, it appears that the Pike Township Church had voted itself out of the association, and a committee consisting of Rev. Peter Davis and L. D. Ayres was appointed to "visit, inquire the cause, and admonish the brethren of said church, and report to the next association."

The Lost Creek Church presented a request for the ordination of Richard C. Bond. This request was referred to the Presbytery, which acted favourably upon it, and the ordination took place on the First Day of the week, the last day of the session. The ordination sermon was preached by Rev. Lewis A. Davis, the consecrating prayer was offered by Rev. Peter Davis, and the charge to the candidate was given by Rev. Lewis A. Davis. The right hand of fellowship was offered by Rev. Joshua Hill. The benediction was pronounced by Richard C. Bond.

The Fifth Annual Session of the association convened at Lost Creek, Virginia, October 18, 1843. The introductory sermon was preached by Richard C. Bond, after which the association organised with Joshua Hill as moderator, and Jonathan Bond and Benjamin Franklin Bond as secretaries. The following churches reported:— Lost Creek, New Salem, North Fork of Hughes River, and South Fork of Hughes River, from Virginia; Woodbridgetown, from Pennsylvania; North Hampton, Port Jefferson, Sciota, Jackson Centre, and Stokes, from Ohio. The church of Madison Township, Jay County, Indiana, was admitted to membership in the association.

The committee appointed the previous year to inquire into

the cause of the withdrawal of the Pike Church from the association, rendered a report, which was adopted, and the church dropped from the association.

A petition was presented by William F. Randolph, which set forth that the New Salem Church had difficulties existing in it and that it refused to have these difficulties adjusted. The subject of this petition was prominent throughout this session of the association, and a committee, consisting of Rev. Thomas B. Brown and Benjamin Franklin Bond, was finally appointed to inquire into these difficulties and report upon them.

Notwithstanding the dissensions within the organisation itself, and within some of the churches of which the association was composed, the report of the committee on the state of religion was a very hopeful one, and Sabbath reform and Sabbath observance were especially emphasised.

The association met for its Sixth Annual Session with the church at Jackson Centre, Shelby County, Ohio, October 9, 1844. Rev. Joshua Hill preached the introductory sermon, Richard C. Bond was elected moderator, and Eli Forsythe and James Hill, clerks.

The missionary committee reported that Richard C. Bond had laboured among the churches since February last, under an appointment from the Missionary Association, that he had spent one hundred and twenty-two days, travelled fifteen hundred and seventeen miles, and preached eighty-nine sermons.

A plan for missionary operations for the coming year was adopted, recommending that the association be divided into two districts, with the Ohio River as the dividing line, and that the churches in each district be requested to raise money to support a missionary. An executive committee in each district was appointed to carry out the plan.

The following churches reported to the association:— North Hampton, Port Jefferson, Jackson Centre, and Stokes, of Ohio; Lost Creek, and North Fork of Hughes River, of Virginia. The New Salem, and South Fork of Hughes River churches, of Virginia, failed to report; as did the Sciota Church of Ohio; the Madison, Indiana, Church; and the Woodbridgetown Church, of Pennsylvania.

The committee which had been appointed the preceding

year to inquire into the difficulties existing in the New Salem Church, failed to make a report, and Rev. Joel Greene and Lewis Bond were appointed a new committee, and requested to report at the next annual meeting of the association.

Richard C. Bond was appointed a delegate to the General Conference and Lewis A. Davis was appointed a delegate to the Western Association. It was also voted that the association should be divided, making the Ohio River the line of division, and that the division should take effect after the next annual session.

The Seventh Annual Session of the South-Western Association, according to previous appointment, convened with the New Salem Church, October 8, 1845. The introductory sermon was preached by Rev. Richard C. Bond, after which the association organised by the appointment of Rev. John Davis as moderator and Isaac F. Randolph, secretary. The following churches reported:— Lost Creek, New Salem, and North Fork of Hughes River, of Virginia; and the Jackson Centre and Port Jefferson churches, of Ohio. The South Fork of Hughes River Church, of Virginia, made no returns, nor did the Woodbridgetown Church, of Pennsylvania. The North Hampton, Sciota, and Stokes churches of Ohio, and the Madison Church of Indiana, also failed to report.

Richard C. Bond was appointed agent for preaching on the Sabbath question for the ensuing year.

Concerning the difficulties previously reported as existing within the New Salem Church, drastic action was taken by the association and the incident apparently closed.

The Eighth Annual Session of the association was held with the Jackson Centre Church, and began on the 8th of October, 1846. The introductory sermon was preached by Rev. Joshua Hill. Rev. Simeon Babcock was appointed moderator, and Eli Forsythe and James Hill, secretaries. The following churches reported to the association at this session:— Lost Creek and New Salem, of Virginia; Jackson Centre, Stokes, Port Jefferson, North Hampton, and Sciota, of Ohio. The report of the committee on the state of religion shows that religious conditions were at a low ebb throughout the association. The action taken two years before, dividing the association, was rescinded, as repugnant to the feelings of the body. Missionary work received prominent attention at the hands of the association, which resolved itself into a missionary body, and each member was requested to pay quarterly at the rate of one cent, or more, per week to support the missionary work of the association. Each church was to be provided with a treasurer for this fund, and the treasurers were appointed by the association. Rev. Joshua Hill was appointed an agent to lay this subject before the churches and, if possible, secure favourable action by them. The treasurer of each church was expected to visit and solicit subscriptions from the members of his respective church.

The Ninth Annual Session was held with the church at Lost Creek, Harrison County, Virginia, beginning the 4th day of October, 1847. In the absence of Rev. Joshua Hill, who had been appointed to preach the introductory sermon, Samuel D. Davis preached from Psalm CXIII, "Behold how good and how pleasant it is for brethren to dwell together in unity," *etc.*

Eli Bond was appointed moderator, and William F. Randolph and Joshua G. Babcock, secretaries. The following churches reported:— Lost Creek, and New Salem of Virginia; Jackson Centre, Stokes, North Hampton, and Sciota of Ohio. The South Fork of Hughes River, and North Fork of Hughes River churches, of Virginia; the Port Jefferson Church, of Ohio; the Woodbridgetown Church, of Pennsylvania; and the Madison Church, of Indiana made no report.

The association adopted the following resolution:—

"RESOLVED, That the Seventh Day Baptist Missionary Association, in its efforts to propagate the Gospel in foreign lands, is entitled to the warmest sympathies and vigorous support of our entire denomination; that we anxiously commend the mission in China to the prayers and liberalities of the churches; and that we especially request the ministers and the churches of this association to adopt the plan recommended by Walter B. Gillette in the *Sabbath Recorder* of February 25, 1847."

The association met for its Tenth Annual Session with the church at Jackson Centre, Shelby County, Ohio, on the 12th day of October, 1848, at 10 o'clock A. M. The introductory sermon was preached by Rev. Joshua Hill. Joshua Hill was elected moderator, and Eli Forsythe and Benjamin Clement, secretaries. The following churches submitted annual reports:— Lost Creek, and New Salem, of Virginia; and North Hampton, Port Jefferson, Sciota, Jackson Centre, and Stokes, of Ohio. The South Fork of Hughes River, and North Fork of Hughes River churches of Virginia; the Woodbridgetown Church of Pennsylvania; and the Madison Church of Indiana all failed to report. The report of the committee on the state of religion set forth that the churches of Woodbridgetown, Pennsylvania; and Madison, Indiana, were believed to have become extinct by deaths and removal of families to more western parts. The tone of the committee's report is, nevertheless, upon the whole a confident and encouraging one.

The action of the previous year recommending the adoption of a plan for regular contributions for missionary work, seems to have failed for lack of co-operation of the churches. Vigorous resolutions were adopted, however, commending the work of the Seventh Day Baptist Missionary Association and the American Sabbath Tract Society, and endorsing the *Sabbath Recorder*.

A resolution was adopted, strongly condemning secret societies, on the grounds that "their real tendency is anti-Christian and that they are dangerous to the true interests of society."

The minutes of the association as published in the *Sabbath Recorder*, of November 2, 1848, are accompanied by a letter from Rev. Samuel Davisson, who says that while the attendance from the churches of Ohio was good, there was but one delegate from the churches in Virginia, and there were but two ordained ministers in attendance belonging to the association. The only other ordained minister in the association, Rev. Lewis A. Davis, having become physically incapacitated for professional duties, had removed to another part of the state. Rev. Samuel Davisson speaks in high terms of the apparent zeal and good spirit, both of the clergy and laymen, and commends the efforts made by the association to have missionary work done, and explains that the association has been badly hampered because of the restricted financial resources of its church membership. Of the ministers, he says nothing but praise. Lewis A. Davis had exhausted himself physically, by riding, practising as a physician, and labouring beyond his strength as a preacher of the Gospel in a comparatively new country, and had left his field of labour because he did not know how to deny urgent applications, even when he knew they were taxing him beyond his strength. Rev. Samuel Davisson called attention to the fact that while there were several men licenced to preach, there was but one ordained minister, Rev. Peter Davis, among the churches in Virginia. He also believed that the association should be divided, as had been previously proposed, for the reason, that as it now existed, it was really two associations holding biennial meetings, instead of one holding annual meeting.

The Eleventh Annual Session of the association convened with the church at Lost Creek, Virginia, on the 11th day of October, 1849, at eleven o'clock A. M. The introductory discourse was preached by Samuel D. Davis. Rev. Peter Davis was appointed moderator, William F. Randolph, clerk, and Jacob Davis, assistant clerk. The following churches reported to the association:— Lost Creek and New Salem of Virginia; and North Hampton, Jackson Centre, and Stokes of Ohio. The South Fork of Hughes River and North Fork of Hughes River churches of Virginia, and the Port Jefferson and Sciota churches of Ohio made no report.

Rev. Peter Davis, on the second day of the session, resigned his office as moderator, on account of the infirmities of age, and James Simpson was appointed in his place. The question of dividing the association, with the Ohio River as the dividing line, was again raised, but was left over until the next annual session, and all the churches of the association were requested to present their views on the subject at that time.

The report of the executive committee on missions showed that Benjamin Clement had laboured a few weeks among the churches of Ohio and that the committee had corresponded with Rev. Azor Estee of Petersburgh, New York, and had arranged with him to come and engage in missionary work within the bounds of the association. The report of the committee was adopted and the corresponding secretary was instructed to communicate with Rev. Azor Estee and request him to come upon the field at once.

The Lost Creek Church requested the ordination of Samuel D. Davis to the work of the gospel ministry, but as there was but one ordained minister in attendance, Rev. Peter Davis, and he preferred to have assistance in the work, the ordination was deferred until another time.

The Twelfth Annual Session of the association was held with the church at Jackson Centre, Shelby County, Ohio, beginning October 10, 1850, at eleven o'clock A. M.

Rev. Azor Estee, who had been appointed to preach the introductory sermon, was not present at the meeting, and his place was filled by Rev, Rowse Babcock. The association organised with Rev. Rowse Babcock as moderator, and Eli Forsythe and Joshua G. Babcock, clerks.

It was voted that the association should be divided, with the Ohio River as the dividing line, and that the part lying north of the Ohio should be called the Ohio Seventh Day Baptist Association. It was further decided that the aims and work of the Ohio Association should be similar to those of its predecessor, the South-Western Association.

Strong temperance ground was taken by the association and a vigorous protest made against war and secret societies. The work of the Sabbath Tract Society was endorsed. The following churches reported at this association:— Lost Creek, New Salem, and South Fork of Hughes River, of Virginia; North Hampton, Port Jefferson, Jackson Centre, and Stokes, of Ohio; and Woodbridgetown of Pennsylvania, the latter reporting a membership of five. The North Fork of Hughes River Church, of Virginia; and the Sciota Church, of Ohio, failed to report.

Rev. Lewis A. Davis, who two years before was reported as incapacitated for ministerial work, was in attendance upon the association, in which he took an active part, and the association recommended that the executive committee engage him as a missionary.

THE VIRGINIA ASSOCIATION.

The churches of western Virginia met on April 14, 1851, with the Middle Island Church, at a house belonging to Jepthah F. Randolph, on the Meat House Fork of Middle

Island Creek,[1] at the mouth of Wolf Pen Run, and organised themselves into the Virginia Association.

The new association met for its First Annual Session with the church at New Salem on the fourth day of September, 1851, at 10 o'clock A. M. Rev. Azor Estee preached the introductory sermon. Samuel D. Davis was appointed moderator, Jacob Davis and Jepthah F. Randolph, secretaries, and George J. Davis, treasurer. The following churches reported to the association:— Lost Creek, New Salem, Middle Island, and South Fork of Hughes River. The church at Woodbridgetown, Pennsylvania, was received as a member of the new body. The following topics were presented for discussion:—

"Is it Christian duty to hold any office whatever under the political government?"

"What is our duty as Christians with respect to the subject of war?"

"What is our duty with respect to using and trafficing in intoxicating drinks?"

"What is our duty as Christians with respect to American Slavery?"

"What is our view of the doctrine of Christian Equality?"

"Is it consistent with our Christian profession to unite with secret societies?"

The following resolution was adopted:—

"RESOLVED, That we approve the enterprise now in progress of establishing a High School at West Union and recommend its support and patronage to all the members of our denomination."

This is the first appearance of the subject of education in the minutes of these associations.

The Second Annual Session of the Virginia Association was held with the church at Lost Creek on the 2d day of December, 1852, at 11 o'clock A. M. Ezekiel Bee preached the introductory sermon. Ezekiel Bee was appointed moderator, Jepthah F. Randolph and Moses H. Davis, secretaries, and George J. Davis, treasurer. The following churches

---

1. This was not the residence of Jepthah F. Randolph, but was an unoccupied dwelling house on his farm. The house subsequently was occupied by the following:— Mrs. Jane Childers, Joshua Wright, Asa F. Randolph, Tillman H. Burcher, Elhanan W. Davis, and William H. H. Davis. The house was built by Josiah Bee. It was used at one time as the temporary home of Rev. Alexander Campbell, while he conducted a series of revival meetings in a grove near by.

reported:— Lost Creek, New Salem, Middle Island, South Fork of Hughes River, and Woodbridgetown.

The action taken at the previous session as regards the proposed academy at West Union, was repeated at this session in even stronger terms.

The Third Annual Session of the Virginia Association convened at New Milton, Doddridge County, Virginia, on the second day of September, 1853, at 12 o'clock M.[1] The introductory sermon was preached by Rev. Samuel D. Davis. Samuel D. Davis was appointed moderator; Jepthah F. Randolph, secretary; Moses H. Davis, assistant secretary; Ezekiel Bee, treasurer; and Asa Bee, corresponding secretary.

The following churches reported:— Lost Creek, New Salem, Middle Island, and South Fork of Hughes River. The report of the committee on the state of religion was an encouraging one.

The association met for its Fourth Annual Session with the church on the South Fork of Hughes River in Ritchie County, Virginia, September 21, 1854, at 11 o'clock A. M. The introductory sermon was preached by Rev. H. W. Babcock of the Western Association. Samuel D. Davis was appointed moderator, and Jepthah F. Randolph and Asa Bee, Jr., clerks. Reports were presented from the following churches:— Lost Creek, South Fork of Hughes River, Middle Island, and New Salem. The thirty-five cents which was reported in the treasury the preceding year, was reported still in the treasury. The report of the committee on the state

---

1. The following is a copy of the invitation sent to the Western Association requesting that delegates be sent to this session of the Virginia Association:—

"*The churches of The Seventh Day Baptist Virginia Association to the churches of the Western Association of the same faith and order:*

"DEAR BRETHREN:—

"We request a delegation from your association to meet with us at our next annual anniversary, which is to be held on the Meat House Fork Creek, Doddridge County, Virginia, on the Sixth Day of the week before the first Sabbath in September, 1853.

"We very much need your help and prayers. Come over and help us. The fields are already white for harvesting and the labourers are few.

"Yours in Christian love.

"Written by order of the Association.
"JEPTHAH F. RANDOLPH,
"*Cor. Sec.*"

"Feb. 9, 1853."
"Directed to Rev. T. E. Babcock,
"Independence,
"Allegany County, N. Y."

of religion indicated that religion was at a low ebb and presaged the announcement contained in the *"Sabbath Recorder"* January 24, 1856, as follows:—

"THE VIRGINIA ASSOCIATION.

In compliance with the resolution of the Virginia Association, Brother William F. Randolph forwards to us the following:—

"'On the 23d of September, 1855, the last day of the annual session of the late Seventh Day Baptist Virginia Association held at Lost Creek, the representatives of the churches comprised in that body, after much deliberation upon the apparent deleterious effects of inharmonious views and movements evinced at past meetings of this body and seeing little or no prospect under existing circumstances of the cause being any better advanced in the future by continuing the present order of things, it was, therefore,

"'RESOLVED, That we mutually dissolve the compact which the several churches of this body entered into when forming the association.'"

The minutes of this association for the last two years of its life are not to be found. They were probably destroyed when the organisation was dissolved, owing to their very unpleasant character.

The meetings of the last session of the association became so stormy, that it was generally agreed that they should not be held in a house of worship. The body accordingly met for its last meeting in the barn of William Kennedy, one of the deacons of the Lost Creek Church.

XXI.

THE SOUTH-EASTERN ASSOCIATION.

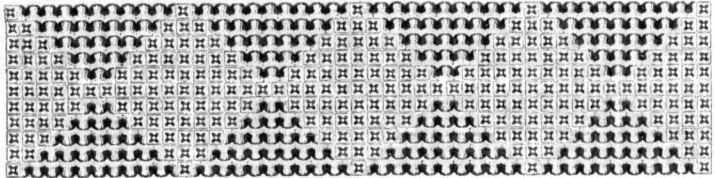AT the annual session of the Eastern Association held in Shiloh, New Jersey, in May, 1856, Rev. Samuel D. Davis appeared as a delegate from the New Salem and Lost Creek churches of Virginia, bearing a petition from those churches for admission to the Eastern Association.

This request was granted after a spirited discussion of the relation of these churches to slavery, only one dissenting vote being cast, that of Alfred B. Burdick. At its next annual session, the Eastern Association addressed a communication to the Lost Creek Church upon the subject of slavery; whereupon that church severed its relations with the association. The Lost Creek Church remained without connection with any association until the organisation of the South-Eastern Association in 1872.

The New Salem Church, while not formally severing its connection with the Eastern Association, maintained an attitude of silence after the withdrawal of the Lost Creek Church from that association, making no report after 1858 until 1867, when it resumed its annual reports. The revived relation continued until after the organisation of the South-Eastern Association, when it amicably severed its relations with the Eastern Association and became a potent factor in the new organisation.

None of the other Virginia (now West Virginia) churches formed an associational connection from the time of the dissolution of the old Virginia Association until the organisation of the South-Eastern Association, which all the churches in West Virginia joined, except the old South Fork of Hughes River Church, then known as the Pine Grove Church.

On May 19, 1871, at a regular business meeting of the New Salem Church, it took the following action; viz.,

"RESOLVED, That this church invite our sister churches in West Virginia to appoint delegates to meet with delegates of this church at our house of worship in New Salem on the First Day [of the week] after the third Sabbath in August, 1871, at 8 o'clock A. M. to consider the propriety of organising an association of said churches, and, if thought advisable, to draft a constitution for such an organisation to be submitted to the churches for their approval or rejection."

This council met, as contemplated, at New Salem, August 20, 1871, and adopted the following constitution which was afterward approved by the churches:—

"CONSTITUTION.

"*Article* 1. This association shall be called THE SOUTH-WESTERN SEVENTH DAY BAPTIST ASSOCIATION, and shall be composed of such Seventh Day Baptist churches of West Virginia as may adopt this constitution, and such other churches in harmony with the objects of this association as may hereafter be received by vote of the association.

"*Article* 2. The objects of this association shall be to promote the piety, order, and increase of the churches belonging to it, the Sabbath cause, and the cause of our Lord Jesus Christ generally in the world.

"*Article* 3. There shall be an annual meeting of delegates appointed by the several churches united in this association, to transact its business affairs, and to carry into operation all its objects.

"*Article* 4. In the business meetings of this association, the churches composing it shall be represented as follows; *viz.*, One delegate for each church as a church, and one additional delegate for every ten members of the church.

"*Article* 5. The officers of this association shall be a moderator, who shall preside at all its business meetings; a recording secretary, who shall keep a faithful record of the proceedings of the association, preserve all valuable papers of the association, and deliver all such records and papers to his successor in office; an assistant recording secretary; a corresponding secretary, who shall conduct the correspondence; and a treasurer, who shall keep all the funds of the association, pay out the same on proper orders, keep an exact account of all receipts and disbursements, and transmit to his successor in office all funds in his possession. The corresponding secretary shall make an annual report of all the correspondence conducted by him; and the treasurer shall make a careful annual report of all funds received and paid out, and of the present state of the treasury.

"*Article* 6. It shall be the duty of each church composing this body to correspond with it by letter annually, stating, so far as it may think proper, its condition; and especially report the number of additions, deaths, dismissions, and rejections during the year; its present whole number of members, and the names of the officers of the church. Also to state the condition of its Sabbath Schools, the number of scholars and teachers, and the name of the superintendent of each.

"*Article* 7. The association may, if it see proper, at any annual meeting, appoint an executive committee of three or more members, one of whom shall be the moderator, for the more efficient prosecution of any of the objects of the association. Such committee, if appointed, shall make a report of its proceedings at the next annual meeting.

"*Article* 8. This constitution may be revised or amended at any annual meeting of this association by a two-thirds vote of the members."

The council appointed September, 1872, as the date for effecting a complete organisation, but the following preamble and resolution were adopted by the Lost Creek Church, September 8, 1871:—

"*Whereas*, We think that the interests of the contemplated association of our churches demand a completed organisation earlier than September, 1872, and also that it is desirable [that] it should communicate with the other S[eventh] D[ay] Baptist associations at their next meetings, therefore,

"RESOLVED, That this church respectfully request our sister churches to appoint, if in their judgment they deem best, the number of delegates provided for by the constitution, to meet with the Lost Creek Church on the Fifth Day [of the week] before the second Sabbath in December, 1871, to organise under the constitution referred to the churches for adoption, and that they be requested to make known their action in the matter to the clerk of the Lost Creek Church."

The invitation of the Lost Creek Church was accepted, but the date of the meeting was afterward changed to the Second Day of the week, January 15, 1872, on the day following the dedication of the new brick house of worship of the Lost Creek Church.

The introductory sermon was preached by Rev. Abram Herbert Lewis, who had come to Lost Creek to attend the dedication of the new church. Rev. Charles A. Burdick was elected moderator for the session; Moses H. Davis, clerk; and Franklin F. Randolph, assistant clerk.

The constitution previously adopted by the council which

had met at New Salem in August preceding, was read, and adopted, except that the name of the new organisation was changed from the SOUTH-WESTERN SEVENTH DAY BAPTIST ASSOCIATION, to the SOUTH-EASTERN SEVENTH DAY BAPTIST ASSOCIATION.

The corresponding secretary, Moses H. Davis, was instructed to inform the other associations that the new organisation had been consummated, and request that they send delegates to the first annual session of the South-Eastern Association, to be held with the Middle Island Church, at New Milton, beginning on the Fifth Day of the week before the fifth Sabbath in the following June.

A petition was received from a group of members of the Lost Creek Church living in "Sabbatarian Valley," some ten or twelve miles away from Lost Creek, that they be organised into a church. The association, accordingly, appointed delegates to form a council to consider this request. The council met a few days afterward, and organised the West Fork (now Roanoke) Church.

The association instructed its corresponding secretary to open correspondence with the church at Jackson Centre, Ohio, inviting it to become a member of the association; and with the German Seventh Day Baptists at New Enterprise, Pennsylvania, with a similar purpose, if it should be found that they were in doctrinal harmony with the association.[1]

At the First Annual Session, the West Fork Church applied for admission, and the application was granted.

Although an invitation had been extended by vote of the body at the time of organisation, to the church at Jackson Centre, Ohio, to join this association; it was not until two years afterward when, at the annual session held with the church at Lost Creek, beginning on May 28, 1874, that Hezekiah M. Stout appeared from the Jackson Centre Church and presented a letter to the association, in which the invitation previously extended to the church at Jackson Centre to join the association, was accepted.

---

1. The minutes of this first meeting of the South-Eastern Association may be found in the *Sabbath Recorder*, under date of January 25, 1872.

At the annual session in 1872, the corresponding secretary reported that he had opened correspondence with Jacob Long of Salemville, Pennsylvania, representing the German Seventh Day Baptists of Pennsylvania, in which it appeared that, because of their want of organised church regulations, they were unable to enter officially into correspondence, but expressed a willingness to do so as individuals. Accordingly Jepthah F. Randolph was requested by the association to open an unofficial correspondence with these Sabbath-keepers; and, at the next annual session, he presented correspondence which had passed between himself and David C. Long of New Enterprise, Pennsylvania. It does not appear, however, that the German Sabbath observers of Pennsylvania were ready to accept the Seventh Day Baptist articles of faith and church polity, until several years afterward.

At the first session, the introductory sermon was preached by Rev. Samuel D. Davis. Rev. Charles A. Burdick presided as moderator. The recording secretaries were Preston F. Randolph and Franklin F. Randolph. The corresponding secretary was Moses H. Davis. Rev. George E. Tomlinson appeared as delegate from the Eastern and Central associations, and Rev. Darius K. Davis was present as delegate from the Western and North-Western associations. These delegates were warmly welcomed, and formally invited to participate in the deliberations of the body.

Rev. Lewis F. Randolph had been appointed a delegate to represent the South-Eastern Association at the other associations whose sessions had already been held, but he was prevented from doing so on account of illness in his family.

It may be noted in this connection that Rev. George E. Tomlinson made a profound and lasting impression not only upon our own people, but upon those of other denominations as well, so that on the occasion of his untimely death, four years afterward, expressions of grief and sympathy were called forth from a number of the prominent members of the Methodist Episcopal Church, a neighbour of the Middle Island Church, at New Milton.

The question of Sabbath reform received marked attention at this meeting, and provision was made for the Sabbath question to be presented in the non-Sabbath-keeping neighbourhood of Hunters Fork, a few miles distant, at some convenient time during the sessions of the association.

The report of the committee on the state of religion was a conservative but hopeful one. The subject of education received special attention. The total membership of the churches of the association for that year, including the West Fork Church, numbered four hundred and thirty-three (433).

The Second Annual Session of the association convened with the church at New Salem on the Fifth Day of the week, May 29, 1873, at 10 o'clock A. M. The introductory sermon was preached by Rev. James Bailey. All of the churches were represented both by letter and by delegates. Rev. Charles A. Burdick again presided over the association as its moderator. The recording secretaries were Preston F. Randolph and Franklin F. Randolph. The corresponding secretary was Moses H. Davis. Rev. James Bailey appeared as delegate from the North-Western Association and Rev. Asa B. Prentice from the Central Association. The report of the executive committee showed that a Sabbath School institute had been conducted at Salem on the Sixth Day, and First Day of the week, respectively, September 20, and 22, 1872, by Rev. Lewis A. Platts, corresponding secretary of the Sabbath School Board of the Seventh Day Baptist General Conference, assisted by Deacon Isaac D. Titsworth of New Market, New Jersey. The report of the committee on Sabbath Schools speaks strongly in favour of Sabbath School work. The report of the committee on education again exhibits a marked degree of interest in that question. The question of Sabbath reform was given prominence on account of the recent labours within the bounds of the association, of Rev. James Bailey, the lecturing agent of the American Sabbath Tract Society.

Rev. Jacob Davis was appointed delegate to visit the other associations. The report of the committee on obituaries records the death of Rev. Peter Davis on March 4, 1873. He was one of the original company of Sabbath-keepers, who emigrated to New Salem, from Shrewsbury, New Jersey.

The association convened, for its Third Annual Session, with the church at Lost Creek, May 28, 1874, at 10 o'clock A. M. The introductory sermon was preached by Albert Shock, a licentiate member of the Middle Island Church. Rev.

MOSES HOFFMAN DAVIS.

Samuel D. Davis was moderator, Rev. Charles A. Burdick and Dudley H. Davis were the recording secretaries, and Jepthah F. Randolph was corresponding secretary. Letters were presented from the following churches:— New Salem, Lost Creek, Middle Island, Ritchie, and West Fork. No letter was presented from Greenbrier, although it, in common with other churches, was represented by delegates. Hezekiah M. Stout appeared as a representative of the church at Jackson Centre, Ohio, and presented a letter accepting the invitation previously extended to that church by the association, to become a member of this body. He was cordially welcomed and the church at Jackson Centre formally made a member of the association.

The executive committee reported that a Sabbath School institute had been held at Lost Creek the preceding August, with Rev. Lewis A. Platts, the secretary of the Sabbath School Board of the Seventh Day Baptist General Conference, as its conductor.

The report of the special committee of two, appointed at the session the year before, to consider the question of a denominational school, excited considerable interest, inasmuch as the committee presented a dual report, or more properly speaking, two reports, one from each of the two members of the committee. These reports were in turn referred to another special committee, with instructions to report at this session. This committee, after careful consideration of the subject, rendered a report, which, while recognising the importance of schools for higher education, considered the conditions within the association such as not to warrant any specific action by that body looking toward establishing such a school. At this session of the association, Rev. George B. Utter appeared as a delegate from the Eastern Association, Rev. Amos W. Coon from the Central, Rev. Nathan V. Hull from the Western, and Rev. James C. Rogers from the North-Western. Rev. Charles A. Burdick was appointed a delegate to attend the sessions of the sister associations for that year.

The Fourth Annual Session of the association was held with the church at Jackson Centre, Ohio, beginning on the Fifth Day of the week, May 27, 1875, at 10 o'clock A. M. The introductory sermon was preached by Rev. Simeon H. Babcock. Moses H. Davis presided as moderator, Simeon H. Babcock and Franklin F. Randolph were the recording secretaries, and Jepthah F. Randolph acted as corresponding secretary. Letters were presented from the following churches:— New Salem, Lost Creek, Greenbrier, Middle Island, Ritchie, and Jackson Centre. The West Fork Church was not represented either by letter or by delegate.

Rev. Abram H. Lewis appeared as a delegate from the Eastern Association, Rev. Julius M. Todd from the Central, Rev. John L. Huffman from the Western, and Rev. Samuel R. Wheeler from the North-Western. The report of the committee on the state of religion deplored the want of pastoral and missionary labour, but stated that harmony prevailed throughout the churches. Rev. Samuel D. Davis was sent as a delegate to the other associations.

The Fifth Annual Session of the association was held with the church at Greenbrier, West Virginia, beginning on the Fifth Day of the week May 25, 1876, at 10 o'clock A. M.

The introductory sermon was preached by Rev. Jacob Davis. In the absence of the officers who had been elected the year before for this session, Rev. Charles A. Burdick was elected moderator, Moses H. Davis and Franklin F. Randolph, recording secretaries, and Preston F. Randolph, corresponding secretary.

Letters were presented from all the churches, and all except the Jackson Centre Church, were represented by delegates.

Rev. Lewis A. Platts appeared as a delegate from the Eastern Association, Rev. Stephen Burdick from the Central, and Rev. Thomas R. Williams from the Western.

The reports of the various committees, while recognising certain failures and weaknesses, nevertheless, all, either tacitly or avowedly, disclaimed any cause for discouragement.

Rev. James B. Davis was sent as a delegate to the other associations.

The Sixth Annual Session of the association was held with the Middle Island Church, at New Milton, West Virginia, beginning May 24, 1877, at 10 o'clock A. M.

The introductory sermon was preached by Rev. Samuel D. Davis. Rev. James B. Davis was moderator, Franklin F.

REV. GIDEON HENRY FITZ RANDOLPH, LATE MISSIONARY TO SHANGHAI, CHINA.
(A native of New Salem).

Randolph and Moses H. Davis, recording secretaries, and Asa F. Randolph, corresponding secretary.

Reports were presented from the Lost Creek, West Fork, Greenbrier, Middle Island, New Salem, and Ritchie churches. No report was presented from the Jackson Centre Church.

Rev. James R. Irish appeared as a delegate from the Eastern Association, Rev. J. Bennett Clarke from the Central, Rev. Lucius R. Swinney from the Western, and Rev. Oscar U. Whitford from the North-Western.

The report of the committee on resolutions approved the action of the Missionary Society, in seeking to re-inforce the China Mission; spoke appreciatively of the missionary work of Rev. Lewis F. Randolph within the bounds of the association; and pledged the support of the association to the American Sabbath Tract Society, in the various lines of its work.

Representatives who were present from the Pine Grove Church (the old South Fork of Hughes River Church, in Ritchie County, West Virginia,—not a member of the association) were invited to an honorary seat in the body.

The committee on obituary notices reported the death of Deacon William Kennedy of the Lost Creek Church, who, as a child, came to Lost Creek from within the bounds of the Woodbridgetown Church, in Fayette County, Pennsylvania.

Rev. Lewis F. Randolph was sent as a delegate to the other associations.

The Seventh Annual Session of the association was held with the church at Lost Creek, beginning on the Fifth Day of the week May 23, 1878, at 10 o'clock A. M.

The introductory sermon was preached by Rev. Lewis F. Randolph, who presided as moderator. The recording secretaries were Preston F. Randolph and Luther A. Bond. Jacob Davis was corresponding secretary.

Reports were presented from all the churches. Rev. David H. Davis appeared as a delegate from the Eastern Association, Rev. Darius K. Davis from the Central, Rev. Uri M. Babcock from the Western, and Rev. Henry B. Lewis from the North-Western.

The executive committee reported that a Sabbath School institute had been held with the Greenbrier Church under the leadership of Rev. Lucius R. Swinney, Milton S. Davis, and Moses H. Davis.

The committee on Sabbath Schools reported an active, appreciative interest in the Sabbath Schools of the association, but deplored the fact that not all of them continued their sessions throughout the year.

The committee on education re-iterated the oft-repeated recognition of the need of higher education and expressed the hope that opportunities for such education might materialise at New Salem.

On account of financial embarrassment, no delegate was sent to the other associations that year.

The Eighth Annual Session of the association was held with the church at New Salem, West Virginia, beginning May 29, 1879, at 10 o'clock A. M. The introductory sermon was preached by Rev. Lucius R. Swinney, who presided over the association as its moderator. The recording secretaries were Charles N. Maxson and Festus P. Ford. Franklin F. Randolph acted as corresponding secretary. The following churches were represented by letter and delegates:— Lost Creek, New Salem, Middle Island, Greenbrier, Ritchie, and West Fork. Rev. Arthur E. Main appeared as a delegate from the Eastern Association, Rev. Joshua Clarke from the Central, Rev. Oliver D. Sherman from the Western, and Rev. Elston M. Dunn from the North-Western. The executive committee reported that they had carried out the recommendation of the association of the preceeding year in regard to Sabbath School work, and that institutes had been held at Lost Creek, Quiet Dell, and Middle Island. The basis of the work of these institutes was the Chautauqua Normal Course, Number One.

The committee on Sabbath Schools reported a growing interest in almost every Sabbath School of the association and noted that the Pine Grove and Ritchie Sabbath Schools had united during the year. The committee commended highly the work of the institutes and believed that much good had been accomplished by them. The committee on the state of religion reported an aggregate of thirty-four additions to the membership of the various churches.

The report of the committee on education emphasised the

need of secondary school privileges in the association, but pointed to the disagreement and opposition to such a movement developed in the session six years before, and expressed the opinion that there was no hope for such a school under existing circumstances.

In adopting the report of the committee on resolutions, the association emphasised the importance of the Sabbath School, deprecated the use of so much space in the *Sabbath Recorder* for the single question of the Sabbath, and advised that more room be given to denominational and general religious new and to the building up of the denomination and all that relates to Christian life and doctrine, besides urging that more of its best writers should contribute to the columns of the *Sabbath Recorder* with greater frequency. The association pledged itself anew to temperance reform work; and because of its influence upon the growth and prosperity of our people as a denomination, the continuance of the annual associations was recommended; and all Sabbath-keeping churches in full sympathy and fellowship with the denomination were urged to remain in vital connection with their respective associations.

The following members of the Pine Grove Church were present and participated in the proceedings of the body:— Alpheus A. Meredith, Jonathan C. Lowther, and Zebulon Bee. Jonathan C. Lowther expressed the desire of the Pine Grove Church to become connected with the association, and Rev. Lucius R. Swinney, Rev. Lewis F. Randolph, and Rev. Jacob Davis were appointed a special committee to confer with a committee from the Pine Grove Church, and, if possible, decide upon conditions of union, and report at the next session. The Pine Grove Church was requested to represent itself at the next session by letter, delegate, and *exposé* of faith.

It was voted that the minutes of the association for this year should not be printed in pamphlet form, but that their publication should be requested in the *Sabbath Recorder*. Moses H. Davis of the Lost Creek Church was sent as a delegate to the other associations.

The Ninth Annual Session of the association was held with the church at Greenbrier beginning on the Fifth Day of the week, May 27, 1880, at 10:30 o'clock A. M. Rev. Lewis

F. Randolph preached the introductory sermon. Moses H. Davis presided over the association as its moderator. The recording secretaries were Charles N. Maxson and Jesse F. Randolph. Rev. Lucius R. Swinney acted as corresponding secretary.

The following churches were represented:— Lost Creek, New Salem, Middle Island, Greenbrier, Ritchie, and West Fork. Rev. Theodore L. Gardiner was present as a delegate from the Eastern Association, Rev. Julius M. Todd from the Central, Rev. Abram Herbert Lewis from the Western, and Rev. George W. Burdick from the North-Western. The executive committee reported that plans had been made for Sabbath School institute work during the year, but illness had interfered with their being carried out. The association, through its committee on resolutions, recommended that a plan of systematic benevolence be adopted; pledged its hearty support to the American Sabbath Tract Society and its work, especially to the *Sabbath Recorder;* and expressed a painful anxiety concerning the apparent dearth of candidates for the Gospel ministry.

The committee to confer with the Pine Grove Church made a report to the effect that, while in their opinion there was a strong tendency toward a union of the Pine Grove Church with the association, they did not believe that union was feasible at present; but recommended that the Pine Grove Church be requested to continue to send delegates to the association as in the past. The committee was continued with instructions to continue its work along the line of the directions given the preceding year.

Reports from four of the churches showed an aggregate of thirty accessions during the year. The committee on education again exhibited anxiety concerning a denominational school, but expressed the opinion that the only school privileges practicable would be those of a graded public school at New Salem. The people were urged to increase their patronage of Alfred University. Preston F. Randolph was sent as a delegate to the other associations.

For its Tenth Annual Session, the association convened with the church at Middle Island on the Fifth Day of the week, May 26, 1881, at 10 o'clock A. M. The introductory

REV. LUCIUS R. SWINNEY. REV. URI M. BABCOCK.
REV. JOHN L. HUFFMAN. REV. MAZZINI G. STILLMAN.

sermon was preached by Rev. James B. Davis. The moderator was Rev. Uri M. Babcock. Charles L. Polan and Franklin F. Randolph were recording secretaries, and Moses H. Davis, corresponding secretary. The following churches were represented by letter or delegate, or both:— Lost Creek, New Salem, Middle Island, West Fork, Ritchie, and Greenbrier. Rev. Sherman S. Griswold appeared as a delegate from the Eastern Association, Rev. Alexander Campbell from the Central, Rev. Ira Lee Cottrell from the Western, and Rev. Simeon H. Babcock from the North-Western.

The executive committee reported that a Sabbath School institute had been held with the Ritchie Church in July of the preceding year. The usual strong stand was taken on the temperance question; the support of the association was pledged to foreign missions, and to the "envelope system" of systematic benevolence.

The minutes of the association were ordered printed in connection with the minutes of the Seventh Day Baptist General Conference.

The committee to confer with the Pine Grove Church reported that a majority of the members of that church were not in favour of union with the association.

On account of financial disability, no delegate was sent to the other associations this year.

The association met for its Eleventh Annual Session with the church at Ritchie on the Fifth Day of the week, May 25, 1882, at 10 o'clock A. M. The introductory sermon was preached by Rev. Lucius R. Swinney. The officers of the association were:— Rev. Lewis F. Randolph, moderator; Rev. Lucius R. Swinney and Preston F. Randolph, recording secretaries; and Preston F. Randolph, corresponding secretary.

Letters were read from the Lost Creek, New Salem, Middle Island, Ritchie, Greenbrier, and West Fork churches. A petition was received from the Bear Fork Church, recently organised, asking for admission into the association. The request was granted.

Rev. Leander E. Livermore appeared as a delegate from the Eastern Association, Rev. Joshua Judson White from the Central, Rev. Hiram P. Burdick from the Western, Rev.

George M. Cottrell from the North-Western, and Rev. Arthur E. Main from the Seventh Day Baptist Missionary Society.

The reports of the committees on education, Sabbath Schools, and state of religion were all of a hopeful tone. Rev. Lucius R. Swinney was sent as a delegate to the other associations.

The Twelfth Annual Session of the association convened with the church at Lost Creek on the Fifth Day of the week, May 24, 1883, at 10 o'clock A. M. The introductory sermon was preached by Rev. Jacob Davis. The moderator was Preston F. Randolph; the recording secretaries, Corliss F. Randolph and Charles N. Maxson; and the corresponding secretary, Levi B. Davis. The following churches were represented:— New Salem, Ritchie, Middle Island, Roanoke, Lost Creek, and Bear Fork.

The delegates from the other associations were:— Rev. Oliver D. Sherman from the Eastern, Rev. Herman D. Clark from the Central, Rev. James Summerbell from the Western, and Rev. George J. Crandall from the North-Western. Rev. Arthur E. Main appeared in the interest of the Seventh Day Baptist Missionary Society, and Rev. Lewis A. Platts in the interest of the American Sabbath Tract Society.

The executive committee reported that a Sabbath School institute had been held at Salem. The committee on education again expressed its regret at the want of facilities for higher education within the bounds of the association, and recommended that our people avail themselves of the opportunities offered at Alfred University and Milton College.

A petition was received from the Pine Grove Church asking for admission into the association. This was referred to a special committee consisting of Rev. Arthur E. Main, Rev. Oliver D. Sherman, and Rev. George J. Crandall, who rendered the following report:—

"Your committee to whom was referred the petition of the Pine Grove Church, would respectfully report the following:—

"After carefully considering the matter in the light of all the facts within our reach, we recommend that the church be received into the association on these conditions; *viz.,*

"*1st,* That two mistakes of fact in their communications to this body be corrected.

"*2d,* That the Pine Grove Church shall be understood to agree, by coming into this association, to take the very earliest practicable steps to bring about a consolidation with the Ritchie Church,—steps that shall duly recognise the fact that the latter church is and has always been a regularly-organised Seventh Day Baptist Church.

"3d, That all personal difficulties that have existed or may now exist on the part of persons concerned in the union of these churches shall, in the exercise of mutual Christian forbearance, be forever dropped."

The report of the committee on the state of religion was a very hopeful one. Rev. Samuel D. Davis was sent as a delegate to the other associations.

The association convened for its Thirteenth Annual Session with the church at Greenbrier on the Fifth Day of the week, May 29, 1884, at 10 o'clock A. M. The introductory sermon was preached by Rev. Samuel D. Davis, who also presided as moderator. Franklin F. Randolph was recording secretary, and Corliss F. Randolph, corresponding secretary. The churches were all represented by letter and delegate, except the Bear Fork Church. Rev. Horace Stillman was present as a delegate from the Eastern Association, Rev. J. Bennett Clarke from the Central Association, Rev. Nathan Wardner from the North-Western Association. Rev. Arthur E. Main, corresponding secretary of the Seventh Day Baptist Missionary Society, acted as delegate from the Western Association, in the absence of the appointed delegate.

The committee on the state of religion reported three revival meetings within the year, and an increase of fifty in the membership of the churches of the association.

The delegate and alternate appointed to attend the other associations being unable to go, Rev. Arthur E. Main and Holly Welcome Maxson, a deacon of the Lost Creek Church, were requested to act in that capacity.

The Fourteenth Annual Session of the association was held with the church at Salem, beginning on the Fifth Day of the week, May 28, 1885, at 10 o'clock A. M. The introductory sermon was preached by Rev. Charles W. Threlkeld. Jesse F. Randolph presided over the association as moderator. The recording secretaries were Charles N. Maxson and Moses H. Davis, and the corresponding secretary, Flavius J. Ehret.

All the churches were represented either by letter or delegate, or both, with the exception of the Bear Fork Church.

The delegates from the other associations were as follows:—
Rev. Benjamin F. Rogers from the Eastern, Rev. Orville D.
Williams from the Central, Rev. Leander E. Livermore from
the Western, and Rev. William H. Ernst from the North-
Western. Rev. Arthur E. Main, corresponding secretary
of the Seventh Day Baptist Missionary Society, and Rev. J.
Bennett Clarke, general agent of the American Sabbath Tract
Society, were also present. Rev. Leander E. Livermore
represented the Seventh Day Baptist Education Society.

The committee on obituaries reported the death of Rev.
Jacob Davis, who had been an active minister of the Gospel
for more than twenty years.

The report of the committee on the state of religion,
though brief, was hopeful. A custom, which had been growing for several years, of the preparation of essays for presentation at the association, is found in vogue at this session.

Charles N. Maxson was appointed delegate to the other
associations, but was unable to act.

The Fifteenth Annual Session of the association was held
with the Middle Island Church, at New Milton, beginning at 10
o'clock A. M. on the Fifth Day of the week, May 27, 1886.
The introductory sermon was preached by Rev. Lucius R.
Swinney. Charles N. Maxson presided as moderator. The
recording secretaries were Preston F. Randolph and Flavius
J. Ehret; the corresponding secretary, Franklin F. Randolph.
Each session of the association began with a period of devotional exercises. All the churches of the association were
represented by letter or delegate.

Rev. Lewis F. Randolph appeared as a delegate from the
Eastern Association, and also in behalf of the Seventh Day
Baptist Missionary Society. The Central Association was represented by Rev. Stephen Burdick. The delegate from the
Western Association was Rev. James E. N. Backus, who
also represented the interests of the American Sabbath Tract
Society, and the Seventh Day Baptist Education Society. The
delegate from the North-Western Association was Rev. John
L. Huffman.

A petition was presented from the Seventh Day Baptist
Church at Salemville, Bedford County, Pennsylvania, by Rev.
George B. Kagarise, a delegate from that church, asking for

admission into the association. After a careful examination of the articles of faith and the covenant of the church, and finding them in essential harmony with the other churches of the association, the church at Salemville was received as a member of the association.

Loyalty and support were pledged by the association to the publications of the American Sabbath Tract Society, especially the *Sabbath Recorder* and the *Outlook*. Evangelistic work on the part of the denomination was discussed at length and warmly approved. A Sabbath School institute was conducted by Preston F. Randolph during the session of the association.

The association failed to send a delegate to the other associations because the delegate appointed for that purpose had moved beyond the bounds of the association, and the alternate had not been notified of that fact in time for the latter to attend.

The Sixteenth Annual Session of the association was convened with the Ritchie Church at Berea at 10 o'clock A. M. on the Fifth Day of the week, May 26, 1887. The introductory sermon was preached by Rev. Samuel D. Davis, the moderator. The recording secretaries were Franklin F. Randolph and Alva F. Randolph. The corresponding secretary was Jesse F. Randolph.

The following churches were represented:— Ritchie, Middle Island, Salem, Greenbrier, Roanoke, and Lost Creek. Rev. Judson G. Burdick was present as a delegate from the Eastern Association, Rev. Julius M. Todd from the Central, Rev. J. Bennett Clarke from the Western, and Rev. Alexander McLearn from the North-Western. Rev. Judson G. Burdick represented the interests of the Seventh Day Baptist Missionary Society, and Rev. J. Bennett Clarke those of the American Sabbath Tract Society.

A noteworthy feature of the report of the committee on resolutions was a resolution which strongly urged Seventh Day Baptists to remain within the bounds of already well established churches and not to go to non-Sabbath-keeping communities for homes.

The report of the committee on education noted, with satisfaction, the increased interest on the part of the young people in education and urged the association to encourage the establishment of a college-preparatory school within the bounds of the association. Rev. John L. Huffman, Jesse F. Randolph, and Rev. Henry B. Lewis were appointed a committee to canvass the educational situation and to take such steps as they might deem practicable for the establishment of such a school.

The report of the committee on the state of religion showed that five of the eight churches of the association had held revival meetings within the year, that two new pastors had been settled within the association; and that, although three more pastors were yet needed, there was a commendable Christian spirit existing throughout all the churches.

A Sabbath School institute was conducted on the afternoon of the second day of the session.

The report of the committee on Sabbath Schools showed that there were seven Sabbath Schools within the association, with a total membership of three hundred and sixty-nine (369).

Charles N. Maxson was sent as a delegate to the other associations.

The Seventeenth Annual Session of the association was held with the church at Lost Creek, beginning on the Fifth Day of the week, May 24, 1888, at 10 o'clock A. M. The introductory sermon was preached by Rev. George B. Kagarise of Salemville, Pennsylvania. Rev. Henry B. Lewis presided as moderator. The recording secretaries were Charles N. Maxson and Luther A. Bond. The corresponding secretary was Rev. John L. Huffman.

The churches in the association were all represented by delegates except the Bear Fork Church. The West Fork Church had changed its name to that of the ROANOKE SEVENTH DAY BAPTIST CHURCH. Rev. Joseph C. Bowen appeared as a delegate from the Eastern Association, Rev. William C. Daland from the Central, Rev. Orpheus S. Mills from the Western, and Rev. John T. Davis from the North-Western. Rev. Gideon Henry F. Randolph, who was soon to go as a missionary to Shanghai, China, was present and represented the interests of the Seventh Day Baptist Missionary Society.

The report of the committee on education voiced an imperative demand for a denominational school within the

REV. HIRAM P. BURDICK.   REV. HENRY B. LEWIS.
REV. CHARLES W. THRELKELD. REV. ORPHEUS S. MILLS.

bounds of the association. The special committee, appointed the previous year to canvass this situation, reported as follows:—

First. That they were fully satisfied that the time had come when there should be such a school.

Second. That Salem was a suitable place for its location.

Third. That they were of the opinion that sufficient money could be raised within the bounds of the association to secure the grounds and erect such buildings as would be suitable for present use.

Fourth. They recommended that a committee be appointed, which should take steps at once to ascertain the amount which could be raised by subscription; and if a sufficient amount should be secured so that no debts should be incurred, to make the necessary arrangements and secure a suitable location and erect the buildings.

The report was adopted, and in accordance with the recommendation, a committee was appointed consisting of the following members:— Rev. John L. Huffman, Rev. Samuel D. Davis, Jesse F. Randolph, George W. F. Randolph, Charles N. Maxson, Ethelbert J. Davis, Franklin F. Randolph, Flavius J. Ehret, and Samuel D. Bond.

The report of the committee on the state of religion was full of confidence and hope. The Copen Church, which had been organised in Braxton County, West Virginia, in the preceding November, was, upon its petition, received into the association.

The committee on institute work reported that a Sabbath School institute had been held with the Middle Island Church the preceding September. The session of the association was marked by the dedication of the church at Lost Creek, which had been rebuilt after a disastrous fire.

Rev. Henry B. Lewis was sent as a delegate to the other associations.

For several years there had been a growing tendency to minimise the routine work of the association and thereby give more time to devotional services. That was especially true of this session.

The association convened with the church at New Salem on the Fifth Day of the week, May 23, 1889, at 10 o'clock A. M. for its Eighteenth Annual Session. The introductory sermon was preached by Rev. Samuel D. Davis. The moderator was Rev. John L. Huffman; the recording secretaries, M. Wardner

Davis and Franklin F. Randolph; the corresponding secretary, Rev. Orpheus S. Mills.

All of the churches of the association were represented. The West Union Church, at West Union, Doddridge County, was, upon its application, received into the association. Rev. Theodore L. Gardiner appeared as a delegate from the Eastern Association, Rev. Experience R. Burdick from the Central, Rev. George W. Burdick from the Western, and Rev. Fred F. Johnson from the North-Western.

The interest of this session of the association seems to have been centred very largely around the report of the special committee on schools appointed the previous year. This committee reported that they had secured pledges to the amount of nearly five thousand dollars ($5,000.00), including a lot of five acres of land at the west end of the village of Salem, valued at one thousand dollars ($1,000). A stock company under the name of Salem Academy had been organised and incorporated in accordance with the laws of the state of West Virginia, and in harmony with the requirements of the Seventh Day Baptist Education Society. The charter was for an academy, with the privilege of extending it to that of a college as soon as circumstances warranted. The contract had been let for the erection of a two-story frame building, forty-five feet by sixty feet, which was to be completed by the 15th of the following November.

Already a school had been organised with Rev. John L. Huffman as acting principal, assisted by three other teachers. There was an enrollment of eighty-four pupils. The committee felt that the prospect for the school was even better than they had had reason to expect.

The report of the committee on the state of religion pointed out that eight of the ten churches embraced within the association, had enjoyed revival meetings during the past year, that there had been an increased activity in religious work within the bounds of all the churches, and that the number of churches composing the body had been increased from five at its formation in 1872, to ten at this time.

Rev. George B. Kagarise was sent as a delegate to the other associations.

The Nineteenth Annual Session of the association was

held with the church at Greenbrier beginning on the Fifth Day of the week, May 29, 1890, at 10 o'clock A. M. Rev. Marcus E. Martin preached the introductory sermon. The moderator was Charles N. Maxson; the recording secretaries, M. Wardner Davis and Flavius J. Ehret; the corresponding secretary, Franklin F. Randolph.

Letters were read from the following churches:— Lost Creek, Salem, Greenbrier, Middle Island, Ritchie, Roanoke, Copen, Conings, and West Union. Rev. Oscar U. Whitford was present as a delegate from the Eastern Association, Rev. Byron E. Fiske from the Western, and Rev. Elston M. Dunn from the North-Western. Rev. John L. Huffman presented the interests of the South-Western Association.

The committee on Sabbath School institutes reported that an institute had been held in October preceding, with the Ritchie Church.

The committee on resolutions recognised the importance of the work of the Seventh Day Baptist Missionary Society; took strong temperance ground; and recognised the prosperity of Salem College, and urged its hearty support.

The committee on the state of religion reported an active religious interest and a net increase of fifty-one in the membership of the churches of the association.

The question of changing the time of holding the sessions of the association came up and was referred to a special committee, whose recommendation was adopted as follows:—

"That, when this association adjourns, it adjourns to meet on [the] Fifth Day [of the week] before the fourth Sabbath in October, 1891, providing the other associations change the time of holding their sessions; if not, at our usual time."

The work of the Young People's Society of Christian Endeavour received special recognition at this session of the association.

Rev. John L. Huffman was sent as a delegate to the other associations.

The association convened for its Twentieth Annual Session with the Middle Island Church at New Milton on the Fifth Day of the week, May 28, 1891, at 10 o'clock A. M. The introductory sermon was preached by Rev. Sanford L. Maxson. Rev. Theodore L. Gardiner presided as moderator, with Preston F. Randolph and Festus P. Ford as recording secretaries.

The corresponding secretary was Luther A. Bond. Communications were presented from nearly all the churches of the association.

Rev. Alexander McLearn was present as a delegate from the Eastern Association, Rev. Clayton A. Burdick from the Central, Rev. Joshua Clarke from the Western, and Rev. Asa G. Crofoot from the North-Western. Rev. Arthur E. Main and Rev. and Mrs. David H. Davis appeared as representatives of the Seventh Day Baptist Missionary Society.

The report of the committee on resolutions, as adopted, pledged the hearty support of the association to the missionary work of the denomination and recognised the imperative demand for the re-inforcement of the medical department of the Shanghai (China) Mission. It strongly endorsed Sabbath reform, took advanced temperance ground, and urged the loyal support of Salem College.

The report of the committee on the state of religion was very brief, and deplored the lack of religious spirit throughout the association. Special interest this year, as for the past two years, centred around the cause of education. The committee on education reported that Salem Academy had changed its name to that of Salem College to correspond with its courses of study, that the faculty of the college had been enlarged and otherwise strengthened, and that certain pledges amounting to from five hundred dollars ($500.00) to seven hundred dollars ($700.00) had been secured for the next succeeding four years for current expenses. There were about one hundred students enrolled in the institution; four courses of study besides music and art were taught. In short, Salem College was fairly launched upon its career. For some years past there had been a growing custom of having special services during the association, representing the different interests of the denomination. This year is found an hour devoted to each of the following:— Women's work, missionary work, publishing interests and Sabbath reform, young people's work, and educational work.

The Twenty-first Annual Session of the association was held with the Ritchie Church beginning on the Fifth Day of the week, May 26, 1892, at 10 o'clock A. M. The introductory sermon was preached by Rev. Samuel D. Davis, who presided as moderator. The recording secretaries were Rev. Theodore L. Gardiner and Ray F. Randolph; the corresponding secretary, Franklin F. Randolph.

The following churches were represented:— Ritchie, Greenbrier, Roanoke, Middle Island, Salem, Lost Creek, West Union, and Conings. Rev. Oliver D. Sherman represented the Eastern Association, Rev. Alphonso Lawrence the Central, and Rev. Samuel R. Wheeler the North-Western.

All of the denominational interests were recognised in the report of the committee on resolutions. The work of the American Sabbath Tract Society as well as the work of the Seventh Day Baptist students of Morgan Park (Chicago) Theological Seminary received special notice.

The report of the committee on the state of religion indicated a low ebb of spiritual life. The report of the committee on education was devoted almost wholly to the work of Salem College and the encouraging outlook for that institution.

Rev. Theodore L. Gardiner was sent as a delegate to the other associations.

The association was convened for its Twenty-second Annual Session with the church at Lost Creek on the Fifth Day of the week, May 25, 1893, at 10 o'clock A. M. The introductory sermon was preached by Rev. Lely D. Seager, who presided as moderator. The recording secretaries were Festus P. Ford and Preston F. Randolph, and the corresponding secretary, Moses H. VanHorn. Letters were read from the Salem, Roanoke, Lost Creek, Conings, Middle Island, West Union, and Greenbrier churches.

Rev. Lewis F. Randolph appeared as a delegate from the Eastern Association, Rev. Lucius R. Swinney from the Central, Rev. George P. Kenyon from the Western, and Rev. Stephen Burdick from the North-Western.

The report of the committee on resolutions endorsed the position previously taken by the association concerning missionary work and Sabbath reform work, and the study of the Bible. It also commended the work of the Home Department of the Sabbath School. The attempt previously made to change the time for the meeting of the association having failed, it was now voted that the time be changed to the Fifth Day of the week before the last Sabbath, but one, in May, provided the other associations would take corresponding action.

The report of the Sabbath School committee, while commending the condition of the Sabbath Schools and the excellent work that they were doing, deplored the neglect of institute work. The report of the committee recommended an earnest effort to secure the attendance at the Sabbath School of more of the adult members of the church.

The report of the committee on education was a lengthy one, being in reality an epitome of the history of Salem College for the past year. It closed with a strong appeal to the friends of the college for financial help.

The committee on the state of religion reported revival meetings in most of the churches during the year, resulting in upwards of fifty additions to the church membership of the association.

The association sent Rev. Lely D. Seager as a delegate to the other associations.

The association convened for its Twenty-third Annual Session with the church at Roanoke on the Fifth Day of the week, May 17, 1894, at 10 o'clock A. M.

The introductory sermon was preached by Darwin C. Lippincott, a licentiate member of the Salem Church. The moderator was Samuel B. Bond; the recording secretaries, Luther A. Bond and Flavius J. Ehret; the corresponding secretary, M. Wardner Davis.

Letters were read from the Roanoke, Salem, Ritchie, Conings, Lost Creek, Greenbrier, Black Lick, Middle Island, and Copen churches.

Rev. Frank E. Peterson was present as a delegate from the Eastern Association, Rev. Asa B. Prentice from the Central, Rev. Mordecai B. Kelly from the Western, and Rev. Eugene H. Socwell from the North-Western.

On application from that church, the Black Lick Church, near Long Run, in Doddridge County, West Virginia, which had recently been organised, was received as a member of the association. The report of the committee on resolutions, while re-iterating former utterances upon the questions of temperance, missionary work, and Sabbath reform, emphasised the need of systematic, reverent study of the Bible.

The report of the committee on education was full of grati-

REV. SANFORD LAFAYETTE MAXSON.

tude for the successful work of Salem College, and pledged it the heartiest support of the association. The sum of five hundred dollars ($500.00) was raised at the association toward liquidating the debt of the college.

This session of the association was note-worthy for the prominent part taken in it by the young people; the moderator being a young man, a student of Salem College; and the committee-work, as well as the other parts of the work of the association, was performed largely by young people.

Rev. Samuel D. Davis was sent as a delegate to the other associations.

The association convened for its Twenty-fourth Annual Session with the church at Salem on the Fifth Day of the week, May 16, 1895, at 10 o'clock A. M. The introductory sermon was preached by Rev. William L. Burdick. The moderator was Moses H. VanHorn; the recording secretaries, Samuel B. Bond and Flavius J. Ehret; and the corresponding secretary, M. Wardner Davis.

Letters were read from the following churches:— Lost Creek, Roanoke, Ritchie, Middle Island, Black Lick, Salem, and Greenbrier.

Rev. Benjamin F. Rogers was present as a delegate from the Central Association, Rev. Sylvester S. Powell from the Western, and Rev. Darius K. Davis from the North-Western. Rev. Oscar U. Whitford was present as a representative of the South-Western Association, and also in the interest of the Seventh Day Baptist Missionary Society.

The report of the committee on resolutions appears to have laid special emphasis upon the desirability of an earnest, evangelistic spirit, and a steady spiritual growth. The report of the committee on education centred about Salem College, and the discussion of the report emphasised the difference between utilitarian training and a purely academic education, and also the superiourity of denominational schools over schools under control of the state.

The committee on the state of religion deplored defections from the Sabbath because of business interests.

Rev. Marcus E. Martin was sent as a delegate to the other associations.

The Twenty-fifth Annual Session of the association was

held with the church at Greenbrier, beginning on the Fifth Day of the week, May 21, 1896, at 10 o'clock A. M. The introductory sermon was preached by Riley G. Davis, a licentiate member of the Greenbrier Church. John H. Wolfe presided as moderator. Samuel B. Bond and Miss Beatrice Lowther acted as recording secretaries. The corresponding secretary was Mrs. Iva Randolph *Rosier.*

The following churches were represented:— Salem, Ritchie, Salemville, Roanoke, Lost Creek, Black Lick, Middle Island, and Greenbrier. Rev. Judson G. Burdick was present as a delegate from the Eastern Association, Rev. J. Allison Platts from the Central, and Rev. Willard D. Burdick from the North-Western. The appointed delegate from the Western Association not being present, Miss Susie M. Burdick acted in that capacity. The American Sabbath Tract Society was represented by Rev. Abram Herbert Lewis, and the Seventh Day Baptist Missionary Society by Edward B. Saunders.

The report of the committee on resolutions urged a higher state of religious activity; that greater prominence be given Sabbath reform in our evangelistic work; and that denominational work as a whole, should receive the support of our people.

The committee on the state of religion, while rejoicing over successful revival meetings in several of the churches, deplored the fact that but three of the churches of the association had pastors and that a large part of the church membership were without pastoral care. An increase of nineteen in the membership was reported.

The report of the committee on Sabbath Schools was hopeful.

Darwin C. Lippincott was sent as a delegate to the other associations.

The Twenty-sixth Annual Session of the association was held with the church at Salemville, Pennsylvania, beginning May 27, 1897, at 10 o'clock A. M. The introductory sermon was preached by Rev. Mazzini G. Stillman. Flavius J. Ehret presided as moderator. Mazzini G. Stillman and Ahva J. C. Bond were recording secretaries. Mrs. Marcella Stillman acted as corresponding secretary.

There were eight churches represented by letter or dele-

REV. GEORGE W. LEWIS.

gate, as follows:— Salem, Ritchie, Middle Island, Greenbrier, Black Lick, Lost Creek, Roanoke, and Salemville.

Rev. Oliver D. Sherman was present as a delegate from the Eastern Association, Rev. Orpheus S. Mills from the Central, Rev. William L. Burdick from the Western, and Rev. Theodore J. VanHorn from the North-Western. Rev. Abram Herbert Lewis represented the South-Western. Rev. Oscar U. Whitford was present as a delegate from the Seventh Day Baptist Missionary Society, Rev. Abram Herbert Lewis from the American Sabbath Tract Society, and Rev. Boothe C. Davis from the Seventh Day Baptist Education Society.

The report of the committee on resolutions, while strong regarding denominational interests, was in no sense noteworthy.

The committee on the state of religion reported a number of revival meetings and a very steady spiritual growth in most of the churches.

Riley G. Davis was sent as a delegate to the Eastern, Central, and North-Western associations, and Samuel B. Bond to the Western.

The Twenty-seventh Annual Session of the association was convened with the Middle Island Church on the Fifth Day of the week, May 19, 1898, at 10 o'clock A. M. The introductory sermon was preached by Darwin C. Lippincott. The association was presided over by Ernest F. Randolph as moderator. Xenia E. Bond and Beatrice Lowther were recording secretaries; and Rev. Mazzini G. Stillman, corresponding secretary.

The following churches were represented:— Lost Creek, Greenbrier, Salem, Black Lick, Roanoke, Middle Island, Salemville, and Ritchie.

The delegates from the other associations were as follows:— Rev. Martin Sindall from the Central, Rev. James L. Gamble from the Western, Rev. D. Burdette Coon from the North-Western and South-Western. No delegate was present from the Eastern Association.

The report of the committee on Sabbath Schools notes as a cause of encouragement, that in nearly all the churches reporting revivals, the increase in church membership was largely from the Sabbath Schools.

The committee on the state of religion reported several revival meetings with additions to the membership in growth and spiritual power, and reported five churches as having pastors.

The report of the committee on resolutions recommended and urged upon the people the practise of some plan of systematic giving for denominational work.

Flavius J. Ehret was sent as a delegate to the other associations.

The Twenty-eighth Annual Session of the association was held with the Ritchie Church, at Berea, beginning on the Fifth Day of the week, May 18, 1899, at 10 o'clock A. M. The introductory sermon was preached by Riley G. Davis. Avah John Clarence Bond presided as moderator; Xenia E. Bond and Flavius J. Ehret acted as recording secretaries, and M. Wardner Davis, as corresponding secretary.

Letters were read from all the churches. Rev. Herman D. Clarke was present as a delegate from the North-Western Association, Rev. Clayton A. Burdick from the Central, Rev. Willard D. Burdick from the Western, and Rev. Oscar U. Whitford from the Eastern. Edward B. Saunders was present in the interest of the South-Western Association. Rev. Abram Herbert Lewis, corresponding secretary of the American Sabbath Tract Society, was also present. Rev. Oscar U. Whitford represented the Seventh Day Baptist Missionary Society.

The report of the committee on Sabbath Schools showed that ten Sabbath Schools had been maintained in the Association during the past year.

The report of the committee on the state of religion showed that the resident membership of the churches in the association numbered five hundred and eighty, a net loss of seventeen during the year.

The work of the committee on education was confined to an Educational Hour, conducted by Rev. Theodore L. Gardiner, president of Salem College. Rev. Boothe C. Davis, president of Alfred University; Rev. Oscar U. Whitford, corresponding secretary of the Seventh Day Baptist Missionary Society; Rev. Abram H. Lewis, corresponding secretary of the American Sabbath Tract Society; and Rev. Theodore

REV. ELLIS ADELBERT WITTER.

L. Gardiner, president of Salem College, took part upon the programme.

Rev. Theodore L. Gardiner was sent as a delegate to the other associations.

The Twenty-ninth Annual Session of the association was held with the church at Lost Creek beginning on the Fifth Day of the week, May 17, 1900, at 10 o'clock A. M. The introductory sermon was preached by Rev. David W. Leath, and was followed by an address by the moderator, Roy F. Randolph. The recording secretaries were Xenia E. Bond and Flavius J. Ehret. Samuel B. Bond acted as corresponding secretary.

Letters were read from the Lost Creek, Greenbrier, Conings, Salem, Salemville, Berea, Black Lick, Roanoke, and Middle Island churches.

The Eastern Association was represented by Rev. Samuel H. Davis, the Central by Dr. Herbert C. Brown, the Western by Rev. James G. Mahoney, the North-Western by Rev. Sanford L. Maxson, and the South-Western by Rev. Oscar U. Whitford. The Seventh Day Baptist Missionary Society and the American Sabbath Tract Society were represented by their corresponding secretaries, Rev. Oscar U. Whitford and Rev. Abram H. Lewis, respectively. The Seventh Day Baptist Education Society was represented by Rev. Theodore L. Gardiner, president of Salem College; and by Rev. Boothe C. Davis, president of Alfred University.

The report of the committee on Sabbath Schools, and that of the committee on the state of religion contained nothing note-worthy.

The report of the committee on resolutions urged a greater consecration to Christ, a more active service, and a more liberal giving for the salvation of lost men. It also pledged the support of the association to the missionary work recently initiated in British Central Africa. At this session of the association, the sum of two hundred and five dollars ($205.00) was pledged toward liquidating the debt of Salem College. Rev. Mazzini G. Stillman was sent as a delegate to the other associations.

The Thirtieth Annual Session of the association convened

with the church at Salem on the Fifth Day of the week, May 16, 1901, at 10 o'clock A. M.

The introductory sermon was preached by Rev. Darwin C. Lippincott. It was followed by an address by the moderator, Aldis L. Davis.

The recording secretaries were Flavius J. Ehret and Dora Gardiner. The corresponding secretary was Samuel B. Bond.

The following churches were represented:— Salem, Lost Creek, Ritchie, Middle Island, Greenbrier, Black Lick, and Conings.

The delegates from the other associations were as follows:— Rev. Leon D. Burdick from the Eastern, Rev. John T. Davis from the Central, Rev. Lester C. Randolph from the Western, and Rev. Ellis A. Witter from the North-Western.

By request of that body, Rev. Theodore L. Gardiner appeared as a delegate from the South-Western Association.

Rev. Judson G. Burdick represented the Seventh Day Baptist Missionary Society; Rev. Abram Herbert Lewis, the American Sabbath Tract Society; Rev. Boothe C. Davis, the Seventh Day Baptist Education Society. Rose Palmborg, M. D., medical missionary to Shanghai, China, was also present.

The committee on the state of religion shows twenty-seven accessions to the membership of the churches of the association during the year.

The committee on education conducted a special educational service on the second day of the association, in which the following speakers took part:— Rev. Boothe C. Davis, president of Alfred University; Rev. Theodore L. Gardiner, president of Salem College; Rev. Ellis A. Witter, and Rev. Lester C. Randolph.

On the last day of the session, a special service was conducted, dedicating the new house of worship of the Salem Church. Rev. Abram Herbert Lewis preached the dedicatory sermon; and Rev. Boothe C. Davis, Rev. Theodore L. Gardiner, and Rev. Samuel D. Davis assisted in the service.

Moses H. VanHorn was sent as a delegate to the other associations.

The association met for its Thirty-first Annual Session with the church at Salemville, Pennsylvania, on the Fifth

THE SOUTH-EASTERN ASSOCIATION

Day of the week, May 15, 1902, at 10 o'clock A. M. The introductory sermon was preached by William L. Davis. S. Orestes Bond presided as moderator. The recording secretaries were Harold Stillman and Charles C. Wolfe. Rev. Mazzini G. Stillman acted as corresponding secretary.

The following churches were represented:— Salem, Lost Creek, Middle Island, Greenbrier, Black Lick, Ritchie, Conings, Roanoke, and Salemville.

Rev. George B. Shaw was present as a delegate from the Eastern Association, Rev. William C. Daland from the Central, Rev. William C. Whitford from the Western, and Rev. George W. Hills from the North-Western. The South-Western Association was not represented. Rev. Theodore L. Gardiner represented the American Sabbath Tract Society; Rev. Ellis A. Witter, the Seventh Day Baptist Missionary Society; and Rev. Arthur E. Main, the Seventh Day Baptist Education Society.

The report of the committee on the state of religion showed a net increase of eighteen in the membership of the churches of the association. The ordination of Charles C. Wolfe, who had been chosen as a deacon of the Salemville Church, took place in the afternoon of the last day of the session. Rev. Theodore L. Gardiner, Rev. William C. Daland, Rev. Mazzini G. Stillman, and Rev. George B. Shaw took part in this service. Ahva J. C. Bond was sent as a delegate to the other associations.

The South-Eastern Association, unlike its predecessors, the old South-Western and the Virginia associations, was built upon a substantial foundation. As a legitimate result, denominational spirit has been fostered and developed, community of interest has been accentuated, and structural solidarity has been established and maintained.

To this end, doctrinal discussions have been avoided, and church embroilments sedulously guarded against; and the concrete results place the wisdom of such a course beyond the pale of doubt.

The number (five) of churches originally composing the association, has, from time to time, been increased by seven in all; *viz.*, Roanoke (West Fork); Jackson Centre, Ohio; Conings (Bear Fork); Salemville; Copen; West Union; and

Black Lick. Of these the Jackson Centre Church, for reasons of convenience to itself, has become a member of the North-Western Association; and the West Union and Copen churches have become extinct. The others all preserve their identity, and the most of them maintain a state of normal activity.

Not only that, but the original churches have grown, not merely in numbers, but in organisation and power, both spiritual and material.

The greatest result accomplished by the association has been the establishing and maintaining of Salem College, whose history is discussed in a subsequent chapter of this book.

The South-Eastern Association has before it a most promising future; and it likewise has the ability and desire to fulfill these promises.

XXII.

MISSIONARY WORK.

ALTHOUGH situated at a remote distance from other Seventh Day Baptist churches, the new settlers in Virginia struggled hard to keep in close touch with the rest of the denomination.

In the year 1808, Rev. John Davis attended the annual session of the General Conference, held with the church at Hopkinton, Rhode Island, as the representative of both the New Salem and Lost Creek churches, and had expected to attend the annual session of the General Conference at the same place three years afterward, but his plans changed, upon his determination to remove to the state of Ohio.

In the spring of 1817, Manning Dunn, a licentiate member of the Piscataway Church, made a visit to the Virginia churches.

At the annual session of the General Conference held with the church at Hopkinton, Rhode Island, in September, 1817, a plan for missionary work to be undertaken under the general direction of the General Conference was submitted, which was adopted the following year, at the annual session held with the church at Berlin, New York, in September. A board of managers was elected. Rev. William Satterlee, Rev. Amos R. Wells, and Rev. William B. Maxson were recommended by the General Conference to be employed to do missionary work for the following year. To Rev. Amos R. Wells was assigned the task of making a missionary journey to New Jersey, Pennsylvania, western Virginia, and Ohio.

He made his first visit to the Virginia field in the following winter, (1818-19), accompanied by Rev. Samuel Davis, of the church at Salem, New Jersey. There appears to be no record of this visit, further than some general references to it in the report by Rev. Amos R. Wells, of his second visit a few months afterward, in the summer of 1819.

On his second visit, Rev. Amos R. Wells was unaccompanied. He reached Lost Creek about the 10th of July. Since his visit the preceding winter, he says "the Lord has been carrying on his good work, in a manner, before this, unknown in these parts, particularly within the bounds of the New Salem Church."

Here he spent some three weeks in faithful missionary labour, and in the first part of August, he regretfully pursued his journey toward the Mad River Church in Ohio. After remaining there as long as he felt that he had time to remain, he returned, contrary to his previous plans, through Virginia. He conducted more meetings, after which several candidates for baptism presented themselves. In all he baptized thirty-five persons in Harrison County, Virginia, during this visit.

On the 23d of May, 1820, for a third time, Rev. Amos R. Wells again set his face toward western Virginia, as, doubtless not without purpose, he remarks in his journal of this tour, "to go forth facing a frowning world, and a tempting Devil," etc.

He further says:—

"With considerable difficulty, and much fatigue, I arrived at Brother Abel Bond's, in Harrison County, Virginia, the Sixth Day [of the week], it being the 25th of August. I staid in this county nine days, in which time I travelled upwards of one hundred miles, attended a Methodist camp-meeting two days, and one church meeting, tried to preach ten times, baptized two persons, and administered the communion."

On the 4th of September, he set out for the Salem and Shiloh churches in New Jersey, where he arrived on the ninth day, after travelling three hunrdred and forty miles in dry hot weather, on horseback. After spending a week there, he proceeded to Piscataway in order to attend the annual session of the General Conference. On his way to Virginia, he had gone through New York State, visiting among other churches, those at Petersburgh, DeRuyter, Scott (where he assisted

William B. Maxson to organise a Seventh Day Baptist church), and Alfred. He also visited French Creek in Pennsylvania, and from that point, he started on the 7th of August on his way to Virginia accompanied by "a young man by the name of Cornwall . . . who wished to travel on account of his health." His companion not only visited Virginia with him, but also accompanied him to New Jersey.

On this journey he received the following contributions in Virginia:—

From Seventh Day Baptists on Lost Creek	$ 8 00
From Jonathan Bond at Lost Creek	1 00
From Simeon Maxson, of the New Salem Church	2 00
From Nathan Davis, of the New Salem Church	1 00
From Samuel Fitz Randolph, of the New Salem Church	1 00
From Jesse Fitz Randolph, of the New Salem Church	50
Total	$13 50

The total amount collected on the entire trip of three months and a half, was forty-one dollars and eighteen cents ($41.18).

On the 2d of April, 1821, Rev. John Davis, pastor of the church at Shiloh, New Jersey, accompanied by John Bright, a deacon of the same church, set out for a missionary tour through Pennsylvania, Virginia, Ohio, and Indiana.

Like the missionaries who had preceded him, Rev. John Davis visited the old Woodbridgetown Church, which for several years had been so sadly on the decline that it was at a very low ebb. Here he preached three times, besides twice on Georges Creek, and once at New Geneva on the Monongahela River, at the mouth of Georges Creek. On the 20th of the month he arrived at Abel Bond's. For the next eight or nine days, he visited within the bounds of the Lost Creek Church. He preached nine times, and baptized four individuals.

He next went to New Salem, and spent the same length of time with that church, preaching an equal number of times, but he records no baptisms there.

Both churches expressed gratitude that missionaries had been sent among them, and hoped that the practise would continue.

On the 7th of May, he set forward on his journey to Ohio and Indiana, still accompanied by Deacon Bright, where he was to visit former members of the Shiloh and Piscataway churches. They did not return by way of Virginia.

During their visit with the Lost Creek Church, Rev. John Davis and Deacon John Bright were invited to sit in judgment upon the articles of faith of that church, as the church was divided at that time upon the doctrine of Calvinism. They rendered a report, after taking a due length of time to consider the questions at issue, which was read at a business meeting of the Lost Creek Church on December 2, 1821. The report gave satisfaction to all.

In Virginia, Rev. John Davis received the following contributions:—

At Lost Creek:—

John Forsythe	$ 2 00
William VanHorn	1 00
Abner Batten	50
Mary Bond (widow)	50
Cornelius Williams	25
Jacob Davis	1 00
Davis Loofboro	50
Collection	3 18

At New Salem:—

Jesse F. Randolph	50
Simeon Maxson	2 00
James Graves	50
Nathan Davis, Esq.	1 00
Mrs. Jane Davis	50
George J. Davis	12½
Jesse Davis	25
Total	$13 80½

At Woodbridgetown, Pennsylvania:—

Mrs. Woodbridge	$1 00

At New Geneva, Pennsylvania:—

Mrs. Nicholson	$5 00

On December 6, 1821, Rev. John Greene started from his home at DeRuyter, New York, on a missionary tour through the western parts of New York, and in the states of Pennsylvania and Virginia. He reached Woodbridgetown on the 12th of January, where he stopped at Isaac Griffin's, whose wife was a Seventh Day Baptist. Here he remained for two days, and preached once.

Despite the extremely unpropitious weather, he started on the 15th of the month for Abel Bond's, where he arrived the next day. After a day's rest, in company with Rev. John Davis, whose home was near that of Abel Bond, and Levi Bond, he started for New Salem, eighteen miles distant, where he was warmly greeted. Here he staid for ten days, visiting the widely scattered membership of that church, and preaching twelve times.

On the 28th of January, he returned to Lost Creek, where he remained for eight days, visiting from house to house, and preaching nine times, besides baptizing one person.

Both the New Salem and Lost Creek churches were greatly pleased at this coming of Rev. John Greene, and prayed that the visits of missionaries might continue.

On the 6th of February, he set out on his return trip home. He first proceeded to Woodbridgetown, where he remained three days, during which time, he visited the members of the church, and preached four times. On February 11, he departed from that place.

During this visit, he received the following contributions:—

New Salem:—
James Davis	$ 25
Dea. Simeon Maxson	3 50
Nathan Davis	1 00
William Davis	25
John Howell	25
William Davis, Esq.	50
George J. Davis	50
Widow Maxson	25
Jesse Fitz Randolph	1 00
Jesse Davis	25
Joshua Davis	25
William Davis	25

Lost Creek:—
Collection	$10 82
Widow Bond	50
Thomas B. Bond	25
Dea. Abel Bond	75

Total for New Salem and Lost Creek	$20 57
Also received at Lost Creek for Magazines	$4 63

Woodbridgetown:—
Mrs. Griffin	$ 50
Eliza Griffin	75
Mrs. David	51

Mrs. Nicholson 1 00
Mr. Dunaway 1 00

Total $3 76

On the 9th of November, 1821, almost a full month before Rev. John Greene had set out on his tour on which he visited Virginia, Rev. Amos R. Wells had once more set out on a missionary tour, on which he was to visit the churches of New Jersey, Pennsylvania, Virginia, Ohio, Indiana, and New York State.

On the 12th of February following, he reached Isaac Griffin's near Woodbridgetown, only to learn that Rev. John Greene had finally departed on his way home that morning.

Rev. Amos R. Wells remained over night at Mr. Griffin's, and the next day proceeded on his journey, at that time planning to return by way of Woodbridgetown. He arrived at the home of Abel Bond on February 14.

He remained with the Lost Creek and New Salem churches about a month and a half. He found the people "as they had ever been, very kind." A good fraternal spirit existed in the churches, which were apparently in a flourishing condition.

Rev. Amos R. Wells attended thirty-nine meetings in Virginia, and received two new members into the Lost Creek Church, who had previously been baptized.

As heretofore stated, Rev. Amos R. Wells had originally intended to return by way of Woodbridgetown, and thence go to New York State. But after reaching Virginia, and carefully considering every thing, he decided to visit the Mad River Church in Ohio, whence he was prevailed upon to go on to Indiana. And on the 2d of April, in company with Jacob Maxson, he proceeded on his journey.

While in Virginia, Rev. Amos R. Wells received the following contributions:—

Lost Creek Church:—
Mrs. Mary Loofboro ....$ 25
Davis Loofboro   25
Mary Bond (widow)   50
James Kennedy   37
Ichabod Davis   25
Cornelius Williams   25
Elijah Williams   13

New Salem Church:—

Jesse Davis ....$	25
Samuel Fitz Randolph	50
Jesse Fitz Randolph	1 00
Joshua Davis	50
Jonathan Fitz Randolph	50
William Davis, Greenbrier	50
Peter Davis, Greenbrier	20
George J. Davis, Greenbrier	25
Nathan Davis, Middle Island	1 00
Deacon Simeon Maxson, Middle Island	3 50
Betsey Hughes, Middle Island	50
Total for two churches $10 70	

Besides the foregoing, he acknowledges the receipt of one pair of woolen socks from "Mrs. Randolph," of New Salem.

Again on the 18th of November, 1823, Rev. John Greene set out from his home at DeRuyter, New York, on a missionary tour through the western part of New York, and through Pennsylvania and Virginia.

On the 12th of December, 1823, he arrived at John Dunaway's, near Woodbridgetown, Pennsylvania. Here he remained until the 16th of December, when he resumed his journey to Virginia. He reached Abel Bond's on the following day. Here he found a call to go to Middle Island, one of the settlements within the bounds of the New Salem Church, to assist in the ordination of Peter Davis to the work of the Gospel ministry. Accordingly, on the 19th of December, in company with several members of the Lost Creek Church, he set out for Middle Island, or Lewisport (now West Union). He preached on the Sabbath; and on the following day, he assisted in the ordination service, preaching a sermon, using as a text, II Corinthians v, 20.

Rev. John Greene continued for some time in this region labouring within the bounds of the Lost Creek and New Salem churches. On the 15th of January he assisted in the ordination of Lewis A. Davis to the work of the Gospel ministry. On this occasion, the candidate preached a discourse, after which Rev. John Greene also preached, taking as a text, I Timothy III, 15. The same day, he baptized John La Forge F. Randolph.

After having laboured in this region for a period of thirty-two days, and preached forty times, Rev. John Greene started from Abel Bond's on his return trip, on the 19th of January, followed by the blessings and prayers of the Virginia people. On the 21st, he arrived at Isaac Griffin's, Esq., where he remained for three days, and preached three times, and then proceeded homeward.

On this visit, Rev. John Greene received the following contributions from the people in Virginia:—

Mrs. Bond	$ 1 00
Milan Stout	25
Anna Bond	45
Rachel Bond	50
Dea. Abel Bond	62½
Mrs. Dicks	50
Collection at Lost Creek	3 54½
Cornelius Williams	25
Elijah Williams	12½
Nathan Davis, Esq.	1 50
Jesse Davis	50
Dea. Simeon Maxson	4 00
Jonathan Howell	37½
Jesse Davis	25
Stephen Davis	50
George J. Davis	25
Jesse Fitz Randolph	1 00
Mrs. Randolph	50
Lewis A. Davis	50
Sally VanHorn	1 00
Jacob D. Maxson	25
James Clendennon	50
Thomas VanHorn	25
William VanHorn	47½
Total Amount received in Virginia	$19 09½

At its annual meeting held with the Piscataway Church, October, 1828, the Missionary Society voted to employ Rev. Joel Greene for the entire year following, and directed that he spend three months of this time in the states of Virginia, Indiana, and Ohio, and at French Creek, Pennsylvania. His report the following year shows that he travelled for ten months and two days, but does not state whether he visited Virginia or not.

The Missionary Society, at its annual meeting held with the church at Alfred, New York, in September, 1830, adopted a report of its committee on arrangements, recommending the

REV. JOHN GREENE.   REV. JOHN DAVIS, OF SHILOH.
JOHN BRIGHT.
REV. JOEL GREENE.   REV. JAMES BAILEY.

employment of a missionary for six months of the ensuing year, in the vicinities, respectively, of Hayfield and Woodbridgetown, Pennsylvania, and Lost Creek and New Salem, Virginia; and Rev. William B. Maxson was appointed to occupy that field. But at the annual meeting of the society, held with the church at Petersburgh, New York, the following year, in September, 1831, Rev. William B. Maxson reported that he had not performed the labour assigned him. Then the society voted to send a missionary to that field for four months of the following year.

At the next annual meeting of the Missionary Society, held with the church at Brookfield, New York, in September, 1832, Rev. Joel Greene presented a report showing that he had laboured upon the Virginia field for four months and a half, and had collected forty-eight dollars and ninety-one cents ($48.91).

At the annual meeting of the Missionary Society, held with the church at Shiloh, New Jersey, in September, 1833, the executive committee reported that during the preceding year, the committee had sent Rev. Alexander Campbell to Virginia as a missionary for a term of six months. And that his work had been so successful, and the solicitations of the Virginia people for his return so great, that the committee had re-appointed him indefinitely, subject to the approval of the society. And although the last report from him showed that he was in rather feeble health, the committee had not seen fit to recall him. Before the next annual session of the society, however, he had finished his labours on the Virginia field.

For his first visit to Virginia, Rev. Alexander Campbell started from his home at DeRuyter some time during the fall of 1832. When he reached Uniontown, Pennsylvania, he stopped at the home of Colonel Oliphant, whose wife was a daughter of Rev. Samuel Woodbridge, and was herself a member of the Woodbridgetown Church. Here he was heartily welcomed. He visited until the next day, when he proceeded to Woodbridgetown, which was several miles distant, in company with Jonathan Bond, of Woodbridgetown, whom Mrs. Oliphant had invited to Uniontown to meet her distinguished guest.

He remained at Woodbridgetown for some time,

preaching evenings and visiting during the day. He found a church of about fourteen members, including five or six families. He began holding meetings in a school house, but in order to accommodate the growing congregations, the meetings were soon afterward removed to the meeting house, which was soon crowded to its utmost capacity. He says, "The people in that vicinity had been so long fed with election and fore-ordination that they were almost starved to death. I think I never was in another such a hot-bed of rank Calvinism." He found three families of the Woodbridgetown Church to be Calvinists, who appeared to lay more stress upon the teachings of John Calvin, than upon those of the Master.

In this connection, a letter addressed to him by one of the members of the Woodbridgetown Church, soon after one of his visits there, will throw a strong sidelight upon the theology of the church. The letter runs as follows:

"NEW GENEVA, 2ND MO., 19TH, 1834.

"MY DEAR BROTHER CAMPBELL:—

"Perhaps we do not disagree in sentiment so much as in words. When we were conversing together about doctrine, I could not recollect some passages of Scripture concerning the chosen people of God, which have since recurred to my mind, and which I wish to mention to you; *viz.*, Acts XIII, 48; Acts XVIII, 10; Acts IV, 15; Eph. I, 4; Eph. V, II; Matt. XXV, 34; Matt. II, 25, 26, I Peter I, 2; John XVII, 9; Rom. VIII, 22, 24, 30, 32, 39; I Cor. I, 26, 27, 28.

"But the time would fail me to enumerate all the passages which teach me that the Lord has a chosen people. I have not since our conversation, had occasion to change my opinion, but [to] all men, *plain* and *clear,* salvation is all of the *free* distinguishing grace of God, for by grace are ye saved, through faith, and that not of yourselves. It is the gift of God, not of works, lest any man should boast; Eph. II, 8, 9.

"I am now very low; I never expect to see you again in this world. I was taken the Sabbath eve after I saw you, and have been confined to bed ever since.

"Now that I am about to enter upon the realities of an eternal world, I know that I have not believed in cunningly devised fables, but I hope I have built upon the Rock of Ages. I feel that I am the chief of sinners, and Christ came to save such; and I trust He will save me from my sins, and wash me, and cleanse me in his blood. I trust I shall be justified by what He has done and suffered in the *days of his flesh* when he did *hang upon the tree,* from *all things,* from which I could not be justified by the Law of Moses, even the righteousness of God, which is by faith of Jesus Christ, unto all, and upon all them that believe; Rom. III, 22.

"When I spoke to you of justification by the righteousness of Christ, I did not mean that we might live an unholy life; nor that we are justified by it in the eyes of men. Good works are evidences to them of our justification. But in the eyes of a pure and holy God, no righteousness will cover us but the perfect righteousness of Christ.

"Give my love, my kindest and best remembrances to Brother John Greene, Brother Joel Greene, Sister Greene, Brother Gillette, Sister Campbell, Brother John Davis, and Brother John Bright of New Jersey; and all the brethren who love the Lord Jesus Christ in sincerity. I trust and hope we shall soon meet in that blessed world, where we shall no more sin nor sorrow, and where all tears shall be wiped from our eyes.

"Beloved, now are we the sons of God, and it doth not yet appear what we shall be; but we know that when He shall appear, we shall be like him, for we shall see him as he is; I John III, 2. O, blessed state which I long to enjoy. I should love to see you all in the flesh, but it is far better to depart and be with Christ.

"I am glad to hear that so many young men of our connection are inspired with the missionary spirit. I hope they will not be led away into what are called new measures (though many of them are old extravagant ones). I hope that none will go so far as to whip children to make them submit to God. But I am persuaded better things of you, my dear brethren.

"Though I thus speak, we should be careful not to be cold, nor too hot. I pray the Lord to guide you in a right medium [*sic*].

"*6th Day, 21st.* I will stop where you said you did:— That none but the regenerate are saved, and the unregenerate, or unbelievers, perish, because they will not believe. But we know that they must be born again. I will go no further than this.

"I must bid you all adieu, my dear brethren; I hope to meet you in that heavenly rest, there to sing praises, to all eternity, to the Lamb that was slain for sinners.

"From your unworthy sister (I trust in Christ).
"NANCY NICHOLSON."
"To ELD. A. CAMPBELL."

Owing to want of time, Alexander Campbell was obliged to hasten away to Virginia, before he had really completed the work that he had so well begun here. He says, "I am somewhat of the opinion that if I could have staid three months in the place, we might have had a flourishing church in Woodbridgetown at this time" (1880).

From Woodbridgetown, he proceeded to Abel Bond's, at Quiet Dell. He at once began active labours with the Lost Creek Church, which he found in a state of discouragement. Here he introduced with great success, the "conference meetings," which have been so widely known among the Virginia churches ever since.

After about seven weeks of unceasing activity at Lost Creek, he went to Greenbrier, where the New Salem Church had one of its meeting houses, and where the pastor of the church, Rev. Peter Davis, lived. He arrived there late in the afternoon of the Sixth Day of the week, and on the following day, began a series of meetings on Greenbrier Run.

While on this visit, he made a trip to Ohio, going as far as Woodsfield, the county seat of Monroe County. On this trip he preached five times.

After his return from Ohio, he spent some time again on Greenbrier Run and at New Salem, after which he proceeded to Lost Creek. Early in March, he left the home of Abel Bond on his homeward journey, accompanied for several miles by Abel Bond and others. He reached home early in April.

In a short time he received notice from the Missionary Board of another appointment to the Virginia field, and requesting that he proceed to the field at his early convenience. He reached Abel Bond's about the first of July, 1833, four months after he had started for home from his first visit. Abel Bond had built a house in his own door yard for the missionary, who on this visit was accompanied by his wife and a five-year-old son. His second coming was received with great joy, and he was given a princely reception by the Virginia people. He remained until the late autumn, labouring with the Lost Creek and New Salem churches, and going in all directions to preach wherever the numerous calls led him.

During one of these visits to Virginia, he went to visit Lewis Bond, who lived on the North Fork of Hughes River, not far from the present village of Pennsboro. Here he held some meetings, and organised the North Fork of Hughes River Church, of seven members, composed of Lewis Bond and his family, and possibly two or three converts to the Sabbath. Here also occurred a debate on the question of the day of the Sabbath, between Alexander Campbell and a clergyman of the Methodist Episcopal Church, Tichnell by name. As the outcome of this debate, two families by

REV. ALEXANDER CAMPBELL.   REV. STILLMAN COON.
REV. WALTER B. GILLETTE.   REV. CHARLES M. LEWIS.

the name of Lowther and Starkey embraced the Sabbath, and were organised into the South Fork of Hughes River Church.

Many of the meetings conducted by Alexander Campbell during the summer of 1834, were held in groves, the meeting houses being too small to accommodate the crowds which attended. Some of these meetings continuing several days, took on something of the character of the camp meetings of that time.

One of these meetings was held in a grove on Meat House Fork at the mouth of Wolf Pen Run, almost upon the very spot where once stood the famous "Meat House," built by the early hunters in which to store their game, and from which the Meat House Fork of Middle Island Creek took its name. Here came people from all the surrounding country, as far away as Greenbrier, New Salem, Lewisport, and other places. The people came in rough, heavy farm wagons, prepared to remain several days, many of them sleeping in wagons, or other hastily improvised resting places. A single house near by accommodated the evangelist and his family, besides several of the women in attendance upon the meetings. The meetings were held in a grove of hard maples and white oaks, with logs and split slabs for seats.

In these meetings, Rev. Alexander Campbell knew neither Jew nor Gentile, Pharisee nor Sadducee, Arminian nor Calvinist,—only saints and sinners. Methodists, First Day Baptists, all were welcome alike. The religion which he preached was for all mankind. His tall, gaunt physique was strikingly commanding, and his strong penetrating voice, which carried far out into the grove to the furthermost part of his congregation, and a sharp piercing eye, gave him a personality well designed to inspire terror in the heart of the most heardened sinner, forcibly reminding him of the Judgment and the wrath to come. He was a veritable John the Baptist crying out in the wilderness "Behold the Lamb of God, which taketh away the sin of the world." And he cried not without effect, for men and women came in troops, with tears and groans, crying aloud for mercy.

In the late fall, he again bade Virginia farewell, and returned to his home in DeRuyter, New York. But his works he left behind him, and half a century afterward, when he returned to the field of his former labours, for a short visit as a delegate to the South-Eastern Association, the memory of him and his mission of years long gone by revived with an irresistible power, and profoundly impressed those of his former acquaintances who yet remained, as well as their children, and the children of the multitudes of his friends passed away, but who had left their oft-repeated story of the marvellous work of this venerable missionary behind, as a sacred heritage to those who should come after them.[1]

The executive committee of the Missionary Society, at the annual meeting of the society, held with the church at DeRuyter, New York, in September, 1834, reported that Rev. Alexander Campbell had finished his labours on the Virginia field, and recommended that a missionary be stationed at Lost Creek for the following year. The report of the committee was adopted. The executive committee secured the services of Rev. Stillman Coon, of Independence, New York, to visit the Virginia field. At the next annual session of the society, he reported that he had been engaged in missionary work six months and four days, during the preceding year. The most, if not all, of this time was undoubtedly spent in Virginia. One of the most important features of his work on this mission was the assistance he rendered Rev. Joel Greene, who had been sent to Virginia by the General Conference, in order, if possible, to bring about an amicable settlement of certain difficulties that existed in the New Salem Church, and to look into the circumtances attending the organisation of the 2d Seventh Day Baptist Church of Lost Creek, and the regularity of the ordination of William Williams of that church to the Gospel ministry.

At the annual meeting of the Missionary Society held with the church at Hopkinton, Rhode Island, in September, 1835, the executive committee was instructed to obtain the services of Rev. Lewis A. Davis, for the Virginia field. For several years past, Lewis A. Davis had been employed by the society as a missionary in Ohio and Indiana, and had rendered satisfactory service there. He declined the appointment to the Virginia field, however, and the executive committee employed Rev. John Davis of the New Salem Church to perform what

---

1. Cf. *Autobiography of Rev. Alexander Campbell*, pp. 37-62 et 261-270.

labour he could in the short time given him after the receipt of his notification.

During the next three years, Rev. Joel Greene appears to have been upon the Virginia field, more or less of the time. In 1839, he assisted in organising the South-Western Association at Lost Creek, and was one of the delegates from that association to the General Conference, at its annual session at Brookfield, New York, in September, 1839.

Late in the summer or early in the fall of 1839, James Bailey, then a young man of about twenty-six years of age, made a journey from his home in New York State to Virginia for his health. On his way thither, he was ordained at Scott, New York, at the request of the Missionary Society. He remained in Virginia for about a year, and did considerable missionary work during his stay.

From about this time forward for many years, the Missionary Society apparently took but little interest in the Virginia field.

The report of the Board of Managers of the Missionary Association, submitted to the association at its annual session held with the church at Plainfield, New Jersey, in May, 1845, shows that at some time during the preceding year, Rev. Azor Estee had made a short visit to the Virginia field, and that during the year just closing, Richard C. Bond had held an "itinerancy" upon this field.

About the year 1849, Rev. Azor Estee returned to Virginia at the solicitation of the New Salem and Lost Creek churches to become the pastor of the two churches jointly. But in the end he gave the most of his time and energy to the promotion of the interests of the West Union Academy, until his return to his home at Petersburgh, New York.

About the year 1858, Rev. David Clawson came to this field, but was little more than settled as the pastor of the Lost Creek and New Salem churches, and fairly started in his work, when he was removed by the hand of death.

In 1856, an acrimonious discussion was precipitated in the Eastern Association, by the application of the Lost Creek Church for membership in the association. This lasted over a period of several years, and in the end, together with the events of the Civil War, created an alienation on the part of the Virginia churches from the rest of the denomination, that lasted for many years.

In 1866, Rev. Walter B. Gillette made a visit to the churches of West Virginia, under the auspices of the "American Missionary Association."

In April, 1870, accompanied by his wife, he made another trip to West Virginia, under the auspices of the Missionary Board, or Board of Managers of the Seventh Day Baptist Missionary Society, remaining upon the field for a period of six months. During this summer, he visited generally within the bounds of the churches, which were situated in Harrison, Doddridge, and Ritchie counties, besides visiting a number of lone Sabbath-keepers in Upshur and Gilmer counties. He assisted in the organisation of the Ritchie and Greenbrier churches, and the ordination of Lewis F. Randolph, a licentiate of the New Salem Church, to the Gospel ministry.

It had been hoped that Rev. Walter B. Gillette would be sufficiently well pleased with the outlook for work in West Virginia, to be willing to remain there permanently, as Messrs. C. Potter, Jr. & Co. (a firm composed of Charles Potter, Jr. and J. Frank Hubbard, engaged in the manufacture of printing presses), of Plainfield, New Jersey, had offered to contribute the sum of six hundred dollars ($600.00) a year, toward sustaining a missionary on this field. But he felt that he was physically unable to stand the strain of the labour involved, and decided to relinquish the work.

Accordingly, in October, 1870, Rev. Charles A. Burdick, who had previously accepted a call from the Missionary Board to go to West Virginia, arrived upon the field, and at once entered upon active work. He purchased a home and soon settled down to a firm steady tread, and in less than a year, the initial steps had been taken for the organisation of an association of the churches in that state. He devoted himself largely to the fundamental interests of the field with a view to obtaining permanency of results. He strove to bring about improved methods of church order and business, to improve the quality of church music, and to establish a higher standard for the Sabbath Schools. He closed his labours under the auspices of the Missionary Board on the 20th of November,

REV. CHARLES A. BURDICK.

1874, and devoted himself to a strong personal effort to meet the needs prevalent in the association for higher education.

During the four years that he was in the service of the Missionary Board, Charles A. Burdick had assisted in the successful organisation of the South-Eastern Association, and the organisation of the West Fork (now Roanoke) Church. The business methods of the churches of the association had been greatly developed; the interest in Sabbath Schools, as well as their efficiency, greatly increased; and the value of the church, as an organisation, magnified. The Lost Creek Church had completed an excellent, new house of worship. The interest in higher education had grown, and through his influence, several young people from the association had gone to Alfred University. The field was now ripe for an advance step in higher education, and it was to that work that he addressed himself when he severed his connection with the Missionary Board. An account of his efforts in this direction will be found in the subsequent chapter of this book on the *West Union Academy*.

During his connection with the Missionary Board, while he was on the West Virginia field, Charles A. Burdick received from the Board for salary and expenses, the sum of three thousand two hundred and seventy-eight dollars and eighty-two cents ($3,278.82). For other objects, the Missionary Board contributed to the West Virginia field, during this period, one hundred and seventy-five dollars ($175.00). The Missionary Board received from the West Virginia field during this same period, the sum of two hundred and seventy-nine dollars and sixty-three cents ($279.63).

In response to a call from the Missionary Board, Rev. Charles M. Lewis visited the West Virginia field for missionary work, beginning about the 1st of March, 1875. He remained in West Virginia until about the 20th of May following.

He visited this field again, beginning work on the 29th of October, 1875, and closing April 20, 1876. Since his second visit the Missionary Board has, upon different occasions, sent evangelists into West Virginia for work. In the spring of 1896, Rev. Edward B. Saunders made his first visit to West Virginia as an evangelist. The second was made in September, 1897, and the third in the summer of 1899. In the spring, summer, and fall of 1901, Rev. Judson G. Burdick spent about eight months in evangelistic work upon this field.

For many years past the Missionary Board has wisely done all it could to encourage individual churches to employ pastors, sometimes a group of two or three churches employing one pastor jointly. To this end the Missionary Board has contributed liberally. In fact the Lost Creek Church is the only existing church of the South-Eastern Association which has not received assistance in this way.

The pastors, missionary and others, of West Virginia have done a great deal of evangelistic work during the past quarter of a century. Rev. Samuel D. Davis, who has served several of the churches as a missionary pastor, has also done a great deal of general missionary work, but his personal relationship with all the churches in this association, has long been such that his missionary work has been, after all, pastoral work of the best sort.

XXIII.

SABBATH REFORM.

ABBATH reform in western Virginia received its greatest impetus at the time of Rev. Alexander Campbell's missionary tours among the churches there. As related elsewhere, the organisation of the South Fork of Hughes River Church was due to a debate upon the Sabbath question, between Rev. Alexander Campbell and a local Methodist Episcopal clergyman. As a result of the debate, there were several converts to the Sabbath, who were the constituent members of that church.

Although the South Fork of Hughes River Church ceased to exist as a church at the time it was merged into the Ritchie Church, it must not be forgotten that many other Seventh Day Baptist churches have received accessions to their membership, respectively, from the group of converts to the Sabbath, of whom the church was originally composed.

In the winter of 1868, Rev. Abram Herbert Lewis, travelling agent of the American Sabbath Tract Society, visited West Virginia. He reached Lost Creek on the 20th of February. After assisting for a week in a revival meeting which he found in progress there, he went to the South Fork of Hughes River, where he remained another week. He then returned to Lost Creek, by way of New Milton, where he stopped four days, reaching Lost Creek on the 10th of March. Here he remained a few days, and on the 16th proceeded to Clarksburg, where he lectured on the Sabbath question for three evenings in the county court house. He then returned to Lost Creek, and on the 20th went to New Salem, where he remained until the 23d, when he went to West Union, and he lectured upon the Sabbath in the county court house, of Doddridge County, on the evenings of the 23d and 24th. On the 25th of March, he left for home. During the whole of this visit, he was engaged in preaching or lecturing, speaking often upon the Sabbath question. At other times, he spoke upon temperance, always upon some theme of general interest. He scattered Sabbath literature freely wherever he went.

This visit was highly appreciated by the West Virginia people. The Lost Creek Church took action, March 13, 1868, as follows: —

"*Whereas*, The labours of the Lecturing Agent of the American Sabbath Tract Society, A. H. Lewis, are thus far highly appreciated by us; therefore,

"RESOLVED, That we return thanks to Almighty God, and to the Society under Him, for sending Bro. Lewis among us, and that we will try, as far as God may give the ability, to contribute to the aid of the Society, and that a copy of this resolution be forwarded by our clerk to said Society."

In May following, a petition was drawn up, signed by nearly thirty of the more prominent members of the Lost Creek Church, and forwarded to the American Sabbath Tract Society, praying that it return the agent to that field. The report of the corresponding secretary of the society for that year, shows that this petition "represented that there was pressing need of more labour in that section, that the prospect for good results were never brighter, that two persons had embraced the Sabbath since the agent left, and many others were halting between two opinions, and that the subject was being agitated outside our own people, and that this had been brought about by the labours of Eld. Lewis when there."

Accordingly, Rev. Abram Herbert Lewis returned to West Virginia, arriving at Lost Creek on the 10th of July. He remained upon this field until the 1st of September. During this time, he conducted forty-four public services, and distributed about seventy-five thousand pages of Sabbath tracts.

Of this second visit, in his report to the Executive Board of the American Sabbath Tract Society, he wrote as follows:—

"It seemed best to revisit, as far as possible, these points previously visited, and as many new ones as could be reached. The churches at

REV. ABRAM HERBERT LEWIS, D.D.

Lost Creek and New Salem are each surrounded by a set of outposts, from five to thirty miles distant from the central points, where the houses of worship are situated. In a few instances, these posts are held by a single family; at other points there are enough Sabbath-keepers to allow of occasional Sabbath services. Our people at these points are firm Sabbath-keepers, and hold influential positions in social and business relations; hence the First Day people are easily induced to attend any religious services held under the patronage of the Seventh Day Baptists. The presence of our people and the tracts, which are always eagerly taken, keep the interest alive, and nourish the truth when the public meetings are over. The Sabbath-keepers, who are thus isolated, are also much strengthened and encouraged by such labours. In each place (with a single exception) I preached at least twice; usually three to five times. In this way, eight new fields were visited, and six others revisited."

Toward the expences of this work during the year, the West Virginia churches contributed three hundred and thirty-seven dollars, and thirteen cents ($337.13).

In the spring of 1873, Rev. James Bailey spent about two months in West Virginia just preceding the annual session of the South-Eastern Association, in the interest of Sabbath reform, under the auspices of the American Sabbath Tract Society. He lectured twelve times upon the Sabbath question, besides preaching several times. He was assisted by Rev. Samuel D. Davis of the Lost Creek Church.

He was admirably equipped for such work in this particular field, for a year's residence in western Virginia when a young man, had given him a personal acquaintance with the people there that was of great value to him now.

At the time of the first annual meeting of the South-Eastern Association with the Middle Island Church, at New Milton, in 1872, there was considerable interest manifested in the Sabbath question, and arrangements were made for Rev. George E. Tomlinson, who was present as the delegate from the Eastern Association, to speak upon that subject at the school house on Hunter's Fork of Buckeye Creek, where a large, appreciative audience composed almost wholly of non-Sabbath-keepers greeted him.

Beginning in the latter part of August, 1890, Rev. J. Bennett Clarke, then in the service of the American Sabbath Tract Society, spent some time in West Virginia, in the interest of the work in which the Society was at that time engaged.

He was not promoting Sabbath reform by lecturing and distributing tracts among non-Sabbath-keepers, so much as he was striving to arouse in Seventh Day Baptists an interest in Sabbath reform to such an extent that they would support adequately the aggressive work in which the society was engaged.

If the work done in Sabbath reform in western Virginia seems meagre as to efforts as well as results, it is because other phases of denominational work have been accentuated out of proportion, rather than that Sabbath reform has been neglected or ignored.

The emphasis placed upon evangelistic labour and the magnitude of its results have always carried with them the idea of Sabbath reform as well, and the inequality of results is due there, as elsewhere, to problems inherent in the subject of Sabbath reform, not found in evangelistic work, pure and simple.

XXIV.

SABBATH SCHOOLS.

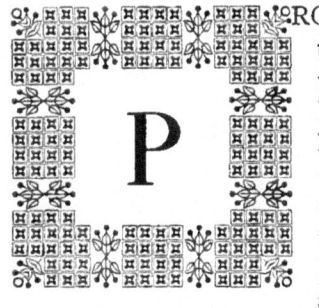ROBABLY the first of the churches to begin Sabbath School work, was that of the South Fork of Hughes River Church, afterward popularly known as the Pine Grove Church. Comparatively early in its history, it organised a Sabbath School for the study of special topics of the Bible. This was probably as early as 1842.

Sabbath Schools did not become very general, however, until the latter part of the '60's. Preston F. Randolph was the most active of the pioneer workers in the Sabbath School movement in West Virginia. In connection with his work of teaching private "select" schools, after his return from Alfred University, he organised and conducted Sabbath Schools, and at the same time, he did much to introduce music into the Sabbath School as well as church services.

When Rev. Charles A. Burdick came upon that field as a missionary, he strongly seconded the efforts already making for better Sabbath Schools. He instituted a number of classes in normal methods for Sabbath Schools, and organised Sabbath School teachers' meetings.

Soon after his arrival, two or three Sabbath School institutes were held at New Salem and Lost Creek, a part of which, at least, were attended by Rev. Lewis A. Platts, and Deacon Isaac D. Titsworth, both of the Piscataway Church in New Jersey, and both of whom were experienced workers in the Sabbath School.

Sabbath School institutes were conducted by a committee

of the South-Eastern Association, until a very recent date. Rev. Lucius R. Swinney, the pastor of the Lost Creek Church for several years, and Dudley H. Davis, of Quiet Dell, were two spirited Sabbath School workers, and contributed generously of valuable time to the success of the institutes thus held, in various parts of the association.

Except in a very few instances, the churches have exercised little direct control over their respective Sabbath Schools, from the time of their organisation, originally, down to the present time. The latter have been, to all intents and purposes, wholly independent organisations within the former; but the churches have fostered the Sabbath Schools as the surest and most natural means of promoting the growth of the church.

The South Fork of Hughes River (Pine Grove) Church, doubtless, was an exception to the general rule. For although its records contain very little about its Sabbath School, it is equally true that, in order to maintain the greatest possible degree of secrecy concerning the business affairs of the church, much, even, of its more important proceedings was never recorded. Moreover, the close supervision it exercised, not only over all its church affairs, but over its individual members as well, is convincing evidence of its direct government of its Sabbath School.

Authentic records of Sabbath School work in West Virginia are defective and unsatisfactory in the extreme. The following brief sketches about several of the schools have been compiled partly from records, but for the most part, from the statements of older members of their respective Sabbath Schools, and while trustworthy in the main, they doubtless contain errors of detail. They are as follows:—

NEW SALEM.

In the year 1868, a class of children was organised at New Salem, by Preston F. Randolph, for the study of the Bible. Among the few adults who were in regular attendance were, Phineas F. Randolph, and his wife, Marvel, who came with their grand daughter, Columbia Jeffrey; Fenton F. Randolph, and Emily, his wife; Phineas Chapin F. Randolph, and Margaret, his wife; Lloyd F. Randolph; and Mary Davis, the

(21)

widow of Silas C. Davis. These parents came because of their interest in their children, who together with Walton and Belle, children of Daniel and Nancy F. Randolph; and Lafayette Sutton, made up the class of children.

Preston F. Randolph served as superintendent for the most of the time, when his duties as a teacher of public and select schools did not call him away from New Salem, till about the year 1890. During such absences, Jesse F. Randolph, Terence M. Davis, and Lodowick H. Davis, took the place of the superintendent.

Since 1890, the following have served as superintendents:— Cora F. Randolph *Ogden*, Ernest F. Randolph, Flavius J. Ehret, M. Wardner Davis, Cortez R. Clawson, Moses H. VanHorn, Stillman F. Lowther, Dora Gardiner, Beatrice Lowther, and Samuel B. Bond.

The original class was composed of about fifteen members. The present enrollment numbers nearly one hundred.

LONG RUN.

About the time of the organisation of the Sabbath School at New Salem, a similar school was organised by Preston F. Randolph at the home of Richard Ford on Long Run, for the benefit of a group of members of the New Salem Church who lived in that locality, among whom, besides that of Richard Ford, were the families of the following:— Milton S. Davis, Nathan J. Davis, and Cornelius S. Davis. After a few years, the interests here languished, and such as finally survived, were transferred to other fields.

BUCKEYE RUN.

At a somewhat later date, a Sabbath School was organised on Buckeye Run, where another group of members of the New Salem Church lived. This finally absorbed the surviving interest in the Sabbath School on Long Run.

In the earlier days, the leading spirits in the Sabbath School on Buckeye Run, were the families of the following:— Lodowick H. Davis, William B. Davis, James Ford, and George Ford. A library was procured for the Sabbath School through the influence of Rev. Walter B. Gillette, which a few years afterward, when the Sabbath School on Buckeye

Run had been out of existence for several years, was transferred to the Middle Island Sabbath School, through the influence of Thomas Edgar Davis, a former pupil of the Buckeye Sabbath School, which was sometimes known as the "Grant Sabbath School."

After a few years, however, the Sabbath School was again revived with Stillman F. Lowther as its superintendent, and it has been maintained to the present time.

LOST CREEK.

On the occasion of one of the visits of Rev. Abram Herbert Lewis to West Virginia, probably in 1868, he organised a Sabbath School at Lost Creek, which after his departure, was left under the leadership of Moses H. Davis as superintendent.

Among others who have served as superintendent, were Albert R. Jones, Charles N. Maxson, Luther A. Bond, and Marcellus Berkeley Davis.

Among the leading spirits in the early history of the Sabbath School, were William Kennedy, Eli Bond, Levi Bond, Jesse Davis, Joshua Davis, George Paugh, Boothe Bond, and Brumfield Bond, with their respective families.

The present membership is a little short of one hundred.

QUIET DELL.

For many years the Lost Creek Church maintained a Sabbath School at Quiet Dell, on Elk Creek, where Rev. John Davis and Deacon Abel Bond, whose home for so many years was the home of all missionaries to western Virginia, lived in earlier days. This Sabbath School was conducted, for the most part, under the spirited leadership of Dudley H. Davis, whose home was at Quiet Dell. This school was composed of a group of members of the Lost Creek Church living at that place; it gradually fell into decay and was abandoned several years ago.

MIDDLE ISLAND.

There was a Sabbath School organised at the Middle Island Church as early as 1868. Probably the first superintendent was Franklin F. Randolph. The Sabbath School was composed, for the most part, of the following named, with their respective families:— Rev. James B. Davis, Jepthah F. Randolph, Amaziah Bee, Samuel Polan, Nathan Kelley, Asa

Kelley, Franklin F. Randolph, Granville H. Davis, William H. H. Davis, and Abner J. Davis.

The long list of superintendents includes, besides Franklin F. Randolph, the following:— Rev. James B. Davis, Abner J. Davis, Luther F. Randolph, Albert Shock, Daniel Fillmore F. Randolph, Clementina M. Davis, Anderson H. Davis, Walter Fields McWhorter, Johnson J. Lowther, James E. Willis, Corliss F. Randolph, Archibald W. Kelley, Iseus F. Randolph, Linville B. Davis, Esle F. Randolph, Manville O. Polan, William L. Davis, Charles Compton Davis, Eva Noble, and Roy F. Randolph.

The present membership numbers about thirty-five.

About the year 1870, a Sabbath School library, such as was published at that time for the purpose of the American Tract Society, was procured, through the influence of Rev. Walter B. Gillette. A few years afterward, a library which had belonged to the defunct "Grant Sabbath School" on Buckeye Run, was secured for the Middle Island Sabbath School, through the agency of Thomas Edgar Davis, a former member of the "Grant Sabbath School."

SOUTH FORK OF HUGHES RIVER (PINE GROVE).

According to the best available information, this Sabbath School had its beginning as early as 1842. Its chief promoters were Asa Bee, Sr., Joshua S. Davis, and Jonathan C. Lowther.

Jonathan C. Lowther, the first superintendent, served in that capacity for many years.

The enrollment, never large, was at first about ten. The average attendance during the entire term of its existence was probably about twelve.

The school was finally merged into the Ritchie Sabbath School.

RITCHIE.

The Ritchie Sabbath School was organised soon after the organisation of the Ritchie Church in 1870. The active promoters of the new organisation were Asa F. Randolph, William F. Ehret, William Jett, and Levi B. Stalnaker.

The first superintendent was Levi B. Stalnaker. He was succeeded, in turn, first by William F. Ehret, and then by William Jett. The following is an incomplete list of the superintendents since that time:— Alva F. Randolph, Orpheus S. Mills, Ellsworth F. Randolph, Luther Brissey, Calphurnia F. Randolph *Meathrell,* Clyde Ehret, Elva Sutton, and Erlow Sutton.

The present enrollment is upwards of sixty.

GREENBRIER.

The Greenbrier Sabbath School was organised, probably, about the year 1867, by Preston F. Randolph.

Among the superintendents have been the following:— Rev. Lewis F. Randolph, Ethelbert J. Davis, Judson F. Randolph, John F. Randolph, Festus P. Ford, Riley G. Davis, Mrs. Marcus E. Martin, Fenton R. Clark, Milton Clark, Fenton Williams, Lewis B. Stuttler, Frank W. Williams.

The leading spirits in the organisation of the school included Rev. Jacob Davis, Jesse Clark, Lewis F. Randolph, Judson F. Randolph, and others.

At the present time the enrollment numbers about thirty.

ROANOKE.

The Roanoke Sabbath School was organised April 14, 1872, soon after the organisation of the Roanoke Church.

The superintedents have been as follows:— John J. Hevener, Mansfield M. Hevener, Festus Kelley, Ina Hevener, B. Wilson Bee, Ahva J. C. Bond, and Samuel D. Bond.

At the organisation of the school, the enrollment numbered twenty. At the present time, it is upwards of thirty.

CONINGS (BEAR FORK).

The Conings (Bear Fork) Sabbath School was organised about the time of the organisation of the Conings (Bear Fork) Church in 1881.

The more prominent members were, John Leeson, Mary Ann Leeson, Thomas Leeson, Nancy Ellen Leeson, William H. Flesher, Eliza Jane Flesher, Rebecca Ann Flesher, J. L. Flesher, Sigourney Flesher, Jabez Spurgeon, Christina Spurgeon, Charles Spurgeon, A. J. Lasure and wife, Joshua C. Spurgeon, and Emily Spurgeon.

The first superintendent was John Leeson. Other superintendents have been William H. Flesher and Joshua C. Spurgeon.

At the time of organisation the enrollment numbered about twenty. The largest enrollment was twenty-five.

The Sabbath School was conducted through the summer season only. Some three or four years ago, it was discontinued altogether.

SALEMVILLE.

This Sabbath School was organised in March, 1887. Among those active in establishing it were, Rev. George B. Kagarise, George C. Long, Amos D. Wolfe, Charles F. Shriner, and others.

The first superintendent was Wilson Kagarise. The following have likewise served in that capacity:— John Wolfe, Sr., Noah B. Blough, Abraham W. Walter, Amos D. Wolfe, George E. Negley, Charles C. Wolfe, George C. Long, and Jerome Kagarise.

In the earliest history of the school, its membership numbered about eighty. The present enrollment is about forty-five.

WEST UNION.

The West Union Sabbath School was organised April 20, 1889. Gamble S. Davis, Festus P. Ford, Lillie M. Ford, Septimius A. Ford, Emma Davis, Samuel L. Ford, and Laura A. Ford, were the leading members.

Festus P. Ford was the first and only superintendent during the four years and a half of the existence of the school.

The membership in the beginning was about eighteen. The largest enrollment was thirty.

The school was discontinued in September, 1893.

COPEN.

The Copen Sabbath School was organised and maintained during some two or three consecutive summers, about the time of the organisation of the Copen Church in 1887.

The officers were: Albert Shock, superintendent; William L. Wildman, assistant superintendent; Uriah C. Shock, secretary; and Waitman T. W. Davis, chorister. Albert Shock, William L. Wildman, and Iva Virginia Shock, were among those who served as teachers.

The average membership was about nineteen. The school was discontinued in 1889.

BLACK LICK.

The Black Lick Sabbath School was organised in the year 1891, with the Trough School House as the place of meeting. The chief promoters were Sylvanus Davis, Mrs. Sarah E. Cottrille, and her daughter Gertrude Cottrille. The enrollment at first numbered twenty-one.

The first superintendent was Gertrude Cottrille. Others who occupied that office were Alfred N. Meek, Sylvanus Davis, Mrs. Marcus E. Martin, Nancy J. Davis, and Samuel A. Ford.

This school was open during six months of the year, only. In the late fall and winter months, the weather was too severe for regular attendance. The school has not been open since 1899. At the time the school was discontinued, the average attendance was twenty-two.

XXV.

WEST UNION ACADEMY.

THE first formal meeting of the Seventh Day Baptists of which we have any record, for the purpose of considering the educational interests of this association, was held at New Salem, Virginia, December 4, 1850.

Previous to this time, Dr. Ethelbert Bond, John S. Davis, and Samuel Preston F. Randolph, all brothers-in-law, and all living at West Union, the county seat of Doddridge County, some thirteen miles west of New Salem, had purchased, jointly, at a cost of three hundred dollars ($300.0), a house and lot in West Union for school purposes;[1] and Rev. Azor Estee, at that time labouring as a missionary among the churches in Virginia, had secured the services of Stephen Thomas West Potter of Scott, New York, as a teacher. The minutes of the meeting referred to above, are as follows:—

"A council of the Seventh Day Baptist friends convened for the purpose of consulting the religious and educational interests of the denomination. The meeting being opened by prayer, and the objects thereof stated, Lodowick H. Davis was called to the chair and William F. Randolph appointed secretary.

---

1. This property was purchased of Henry M. Miller, who had used it for a private school himself. The deed for it was not executed, however, until January 18, 1856, when he and his wife, Elizabeth, made the deed directly to John S. Davis, Lodowick H. Davis, Samuel Preston F. Randolph, Joseph Jeffrey, and David D. Davis, as trustees of the West Union Academy. Two hundred and fifty dollars ($250.00) was finally made the purchase price, instead of three hundred dollars ($300.00) as originally agreed. The property is designated as "lot No. 4 on the north side of Wood Street" in the town of West Union. The adjoining lot, No. 5, was deeded to Joseph Jeffrey as president of the board of directors of the West Union Academy, by Nathan Davis and Jane, his wife, under date of October 21, 1853.

"1. RESOLVED, That we approve the course pursued by Elder Azor Estee in obtaining a teacher for the purpose of starting a high school at West Union; that we feel encouraged by his success in engaging Mr. Potter, of New York, and the progress made thus far in organising the school.

"2. RESOLVED, That we will use our best exertions and influence, and our wealth as far as may be consistent, for the erection of an academy at West Union, which we deem indispensably necessary for the advancement of education in western Virginia.

"3. RESOLVED, That A. Estee, Lodowick H. Davis, Isaac F. Randolph, John Maxson, John L. F. Randolph, and Jepthah F. Randolph be a committee to draft and mature as far as practicable a general plan of operation for carrying forward the enterprise, and that it be their duty to inquire of the present proprietors of the school property at West Union and others what their wishes are with regard to erecting a more extensive building. Also to prepare and circulate a subscription for obtaining funds for that purpose, and use their best endeavours to secure united and efficient action in the matter, and report their progress to the next meeting.

"Adjourned to meet again at this place on [the] First Day [of the week] after the fourth Sabbath in this month.

"By consultation afterwards the adjourned meeting was postponed until January 13, 1851."

At the meeting of the council held at New Salem, January 13, 1851, the committee appointed at the previous meeting reported in favour of building an academy at West Union and presented a plan for accomplishing the object. The report was adopted by the council, and William F. Randolph and John S. Davis were appointed a committee to secure a charter from the General Assembly of Virginia.

On February 16, following, the committee previously appointed made further report. The committee on a charter was urged to proceed with its work with all practicable speed.

John S. Davis, Rev. Azor Estee, Lodowick H. Davis, and Jepthah F. Randolph were appointed a committee "to use further effort in raising funds to carry forward the enterprise."

Three days later, February 19, William F. Randolph, of the committee on charter, forwarded to Richmond, the capital of the state of Virginia, a copy of the draft of charter which had been presented to the council and adopted by that body January 13, 1851. Apparently it reached Richmond too late for consideration before the adjournment of the General Assembly, for on December 26, 1851, it was copied a second

THE WEST UNION ACADEMY: AS ORIGINALLY BUILT.
(After a pencil sketch by Franklin F. Randolph).

time and forwarded to Richmond. It provided that the capital stock should be divided into shares of fifteen dollars each with a minimum aggregate of one thousand dollars, ($1,000.00), and a maximum aggregate of twenty thousand dollars ($20,000.00). On the 16th of the next April, the following charter was passed:—

"AN ACT TO INCORPORATE THE WEST UNION ACADEMY IN THE COUNTY OF DODDRIDGE.

"Passed April 16th, 1852.

"1. BE IT ENACTED BY THE GENERAL ASSEMBLY, That for the purpose of establishing a seminary of learning in the town of West Union in the County of Doddridge, it shall be lawful to open books for receiving subscriptions to the amount of twenty thousand dollars, in shares of fifteen dollars each; the said books to be opened at West Union, under the direction of William F. Randolph, Ethelbert Bond, John S. Davis, Ezekiel Bee, Joseph Jeffrey, Abel P. Bond, and Eliona Davis, or any four of them, and at such other places and at the direction of such other persons as the said commissioners or any four of them may appoint.

"2. Whenever seventy shares of the said stock shall be subscribed, the subscribers, their executors, administrators, and assigns shall be and are hereby incorporated into a company by the name and style of 'The West Union Academy;' by which name they shall have perpetual succession, may sue and be sued, contract and be contracted with, and have, use, and alter a common seal, with power to purchase, take, and hold lands, tenements, goods, chattels, and moneys for the use and benefit of such academy.

"3. A general meeting of the stockholders for the election of a board of trustees shall be held in the town of West Union as soon after the subscription of the said forty shares as shall be convenient, at such time and place as the said trustees or a majority of them may appoint, and annually thereafter.

"4. Two weeks notice at least shall be given of all general meetings of the stockholders, and notice to be given in such manner as the trustees may appoint; and to constitute a quorum, a majority of the shares subscribed must be represented, but a less number may adjourn from day to day until a quorum be obtained. And in all such general meetings each stockholder may in person or by proxy give the following vote on the stock held by him, to wit: One vote for each share of said stock not exceeding six; one vote for every two shares of said stock over six and not exceeding twelve; and one vote for every four shares over twelve and not exceeding twenty-four; and one vote for every ten shares exceeding twenty-four.

"5. The affairs of said corporation shall be managed by a board of trustees consisting of five persons, to be elected by the stockholders in general meeting, and to continue in office one year, or until their successors be appointed, any three of which trustees shall be a quorum for the transaction of business.

"6. The trustees or a majority of them shall choose by a ballot, a president, secretary, and treasurer, and such other officers, teachers, agents, or servants as they shall deem necessary, and shall have power to make such contracts as they may consider conducive to the interests of the academy, and to require the subscribers to the stock of the academy to pay in the stock, by them severally subscribed, to the treasurer at such times and in such installments as they shall specify: *provided,* that the said trustees shall not sell or dispose of any real estate belonging to said academy, unless the consent of a majority of shareholders be first had and obtained at some general meeting thereof.

"7. The treasurer shall receive all moneys accruing to the academy and property delivered to his care, and shall pay or deliver the same to the order of the board. Before entering upon his duties he shall give bond, with security in such penalty as the board may direct, made payable to the trustees for the time being and their successors, and conditions for the faithful discharge of his duties, under such rules and regulations as may be adopted by the board, and it shall be lawful for the said trustees to obtain a judgment for the amount thereof, or any special delinquencies incurred by said treasurer, on motion, in the Circuit Court of Doddridge County, against the said treasurer and his securities, his or their executors or administrators, upon giving ten days notice of said motion, and in case any stockholder shall fail to pay any subscription or installment due from him or her to said academy, when thereto required as here-in-before provided for, after notice to the subscriber or such requisition, the same may be recovered in any Court of Record in Doddridge County, in like manner and on like notice.

"8. The said board of trustees may supply vacancies in their own body and make such by-laws, rules, and regulations respecting the affairs of the corporation, as they may approve, not inconsistent with the constitution and laws of this commonwealth or of the United States, but a majority of the stockholders at any general meeting may amend, alter or repeal such by-laws, rules, and regulations, or any of them.

"9. The president shall preside over the proceedings of the trustees, and in his absence a chairman *pro tempore* may be chosen to preside at such meeting. The said trustees shall keep a full and fair record of their proceedings in a suitable book to be provided for the purpose, the record of the proceedings of each meeting to be signed by the chairman, or chairman *pro tempore.*

"10. The capital stock of said seminary shall be deemed personal estate, and shall pass and descend in the same manner, and shall be transferable on the books of such seminary in such form as the by-laws shall prescribe; and any debt which any stockholder may owe

WEST UNION ACADEMY.
(From a photograph taken in 1902).

said academy being arrearages upon his stock, shall constitute a lien upon the same until such debt is paid.

"11. Extra meetings of the stockholders may be convened at any time by order of the board of trustees, or by any number of stockholders holding together twenty shares of stock or more. Notice of such meetings to be given in the manner here-in-before prescribed.

"12. This act shall be in force from its passage."

"STATE OF VIRGINIA, CITY OF RICHMOND; *To wit,*

"I, George W. Mumford, Clerk of the House of Delegates and Keeper of the Rolls of Virginia, do hereby certify that the foregoing is a true copy of an act passed by the General Assembly of Virginia on the 16th day of April, 1852. Given under my hand this 30th day of September, 1852.

"GEORGE W. MUMFORD,
"C[lerk of the] H[ouse of] D[elegates] and Keeper of the Rolls of Virginia."

Through an error of the engrossing clerk of the House of Delegates the required number of shares of stock was made "seventy" instead of "forty." This together with another verbal error arising from the same cause, necessitated amendments to the charter which were passed by the next General Assembly as early as January 13, 1853. These amendments altered the word "seventy" in the second section to "forty," and the word "trustees" in the third section became "commissioners."

The charter and amendments as finally passed were drawn by Benjamin W. Jackson, and differed materially as to details from the draft first approved by the council.

On June 20, 1853, George J. Davis, Joseph Jeffrey, John S. Davis, Lodowick H. Davis, Stephen T. Davis, Samuel Preston F. Randolph, and Jepthah F. Randolph, stockholders, met at West Union for the purpose of considering the interests of the academy. Upon an examination of the book of subscriptions for stock, it was found that enough stock had been subscribed for to enable the organisation of the corporation to proceed. Accordingly, they issued a call for the stockholders to meet at West Union on the 8th of July following for that purpose. Owing, however, to the scant attendance of stockholders at that time, it was not until August 12, 1853, that the organisation was effected. On that date, the following named stockholders were present:— John S. Davis, Lodowick H. Davis, Jepthah F. Randolph, Neeley D. Jeffrey, William

Batten (also as proxy for Abraham Batten), Peter F. Randolph (also as proxy for Isaac F. Randolph), Samuel Preston F. Randolph, Stephen T. Davis, William J. Davis, Joseph Jeffrey, Richard Ford, David D. Davis, George J. Davis, and William F. Randolph (also as proxy for Jonathan F. Randolph).

John S. Davis, Lodowick H. Davis, Samuel Preston F. Randolph, Joseph Jeffrey, and David D. Davis were elected the first Board of Trustees. The stockholders with their respective shares were as follows:—

WILLIAM F. RANDOLPH,	7	Shares,
PETER F. RANDOLPH,	1 2-3	Shares,
ISAAC F. RANDOLPH,	3 1-3	Shares,
JESSE F. RANDOLPH,	3 1-3	Shares,
JONATHAN F. RANDOLPH,	3 1-3	Shares,
JEPTHAH F. RANDOLPH,	3 1-3	Shares,
SAMUEL PRESTON F. RANDOLPH,	3 1-3	Shares,
ELIONA DAVIS,	3 1-3	Shares,
JOHN S. DAVIS,	5	Shares,
RICHARD FORD,	1 2-3	Shares,
GEORGE FORD,	1	Share,
LODOWICK H. DAVIS,	2	Shares,
GEORGE J. DAVIS,	1	Share,
DAVID D. DAVIS,	2	Shares,
STEPHEN T. DAVIS,	2	Shares,
WILLIAM J. DAVIS,	2	Shares,
NATHAN DAVIS,	4 1-3	Shares,
JOSEPH JEFFREY,	1 2-3	Shares,
WILLIAM BATTEN,	3 1-3	Shares,
ABRAHAM BATTEN,	1 2-3	Shares,
THOMAS BOND,	1 2-3	Shares,
ABEL P. BOND,	1 2-3	Shares,
AMAZIAH BEE,	2	Shares,

60 2-3 Shares at $15,—$910

These shares of stock were taken to cover subscriptions previously made to the academy.

Thus it will be observed that from the time of the first meeting at New Salem for the purpose of organising a school, more than two years had elapsed before the organisation under the charter was completed.

At about this time it appears that there was some thought of inviting the general public to take stock in the institution,

CAPTAIN NATHAN DAVIS.

and make it undenominational. It was decided, however, not to do so, but to keep the school as it had been from the beginning, wholly under Seventh Day Baptist control.

In the meantime the material business affairs of the school had progressed as if the academy had been incorporated from the beginning.

March 16, 1851, subscribers to stock had been obtained as follows:— William F. Randolph, Jonathan F. Randolph, Jesse F. Randolph, Jepthah F. Randolph, Richard Ford, George Ford, Eliona Davis, Lodowick H. Davis, Stephen T. Davis, William J. Davis, Nathan Davis, George J. Davis, John S. Davis, and Samuel Preston F. Randolph. On the above mentioned date, these subscribers all met at West Union. There were present, also, Rev. Azor Estee, Stephen Thomas West Potter, Dr. John LaForge F. Randolph, and other friends of the school, who were invited to participate in the deliberations of the day.

At this meeting it was voted to accept the offer of Dr. Ethelbert Bond, John S. Davis, and Samuel Preston F. Randolph, the owners of the building and lot then used for school purposes, as follows:—

"*That,* Inasmuch as the present owners had paid three hundred dollars for the property, they would sell it for school purposes for that sum with interest on what they had already paid toward it. John S. Davis offered to subscribe seventy-five dollars, and Samuel Preston F. Randolph fifty dollars, respectively, of the amount to the capital fund of the institution."

The offer accepted, a board of eight directors was elected in accordance with the terms of the form of charter adopted by the council January 13, 1851. The directors were as follows:— John S. Davis, William F. Randolph, Nathan Davis, Joseph Jeffrey, Samuel Preston F. Randolph, Lodowick H. Davis, Stephen T. Davis, and William J. Davis. They were instructed to be governed by the terms of the charter as agreed upon by the council.

Stephen Thomas West Potter and Rev. Azor Estee were requested to assist the directors in their duties. Rev. Azor Estee was appointed solicitor and collector.

On the evening of the same day, the directors held a meeting, at which the following members were present:— John S.

Davis, William F. Randolph, Nathan Davis, Lodowick H. Davis, Samuel Preston F. Randolph, and Stephen T. Davis. Stephen Thomas West Potter presented a plan for a building, two stories high, thirty-six feet long and twenty-six feet wide, to be erected adjoining or near the present school house. The plan was adopted and the board took the following action:—

"RESOLVED, To commence building as soon as practicable, but being doubtful of the present subscribed funds being sufficient to finish fully, it was thought best only to erect, inclose, lay the floors and finish one room for the present."

Nathan Davis, Samuel Preston F. Randolph, John S. Davis, and William F. Randolph were appointed a building committee.

On April 30, 1851, Eliona Davis signed a contract for erecting the new academy building "in a workmanlike manner, embracing the following items; *viz.*, Making the shingles, framing, finishing the roof and gables and weather-boarding, windows and door-frames, painting steeple, sash, putting in windows, doors, laying the upper and lower floors, and plastering one room eighteen by twenty-six feet" for the sum of two hundred and twenty-five dollars ($225.00).

On February 26, 1852, the agent, Samuel Preston F. Randolph, rendered a statement showing that the contractor had been allowed one hundred dollars and seventy-three cents ($100.73) for extra work, and six dollars and thirty-seven cents ($6.37) for disbursements, leaving an unadjusted claim of fifty dollars ($50.00) for extra work on the cupola. The agent further said that the contract was not completed, for want of lumber.

The total cost of the buildings and grounds was eight hundred and twenty-seven dollars and thirteen cents ($827.13). This included the original house and lot at three hundred dollars ($300.00); the cost to erect the new building, four hundred and sixty-two dollars and thirteen cents ($462.13); and an additional lot purchased of Nathan Davis for sixty-five dollars ($65.00).

On the twenty-eighth of August, 1853, the directors authorised Samuel Preston F. Randolph to rent the old school house to the best advantage.

At a meeting of the directors held September 13, 1854,

SAMUEL PRESTON FITZ RANDOLPH.

Samuel Preston F. Randolph was instructed to make such improvements on the academy as he might deem best, and he was further instructed to rent both the school house and academy as opportunity might offer.

The directors at a meeting held April 22, 1855, set nine hundred dollars ($900.00) as the lowest price they could accept for the property of the corporation, and authorised Jepthah F. Randolph to sell it, if opportunity offered.

On August 8, 1856, a sale was closed, whereby the entire property was sold by Jepthah F. Randolph as agent to Isaiah Bee for one thousand dollars ($1,000.00). On March 16, 1860, the General Assembly of the Commonwealth of Virginia passed bill No. 449, introduced by Samuel Preston F. Randolph, one of the directors of the academy and at that time representing Doddridge County in the lower house of the General Assembly. The act runs as follows:—

"*Be it enacted by the General Assembly*, That the sale of the real estate belonging to the corporation styled the West Union Academy of Doddridge, including the academy buildings and appurtenances, heretofore made by the trustees of said academy, shall be and the same is hereby legalised, and the conveyance of said property made by them is hereby confirmed and ratified; provided, however, that nothing herein contained shall be construed to impair or destroy any lien or claim against said property at the time of said sale. And a general meeting of the stockholders of said corporation shall be called in the manner presented by the charter of said company to decide how the proceeds of the sale aforesaid shall be disposed of. But if it be found impossible to convene such meeting, then the trustees shall settle up the affairs of said corporation as may be deemed best for the interest of the stockholders. This act shall be in force from its passage."

On December 18, 1863, the trustees of the West Union Academy met at Joseph Jeffrey's near West Union to close up the business of the corporation of The West Union Academy. The following trustees were present:— Joseph Jeffrey, Jepthah F. Randolph, Lodowick H. Davis, and Stephen T. Davis.

Jepthah F. Randolph presented written assignments for all the outstanding stock of the corporation save that held by himself. By vote of the trustees, the assignments were all accepted, and the stock all accordingly transferred to Jepthah F. Randolph into whose hands the entire remaining business of the West Union Academy was committed, and the corporation passed out of existence. The records were left with Franklin F. Randolph, of New Milton, West Virginia, who had for two years been the secretary of the corporation, "for reference for all concerned."

The history of the school itself was of a spasmodic character. It is probable that after the original building was purchased by Dr. Ethelbert Bond, John S. Davis, and Samuel Preston F. Randolph, it was not used for school purposes until the arrival of Stephen Thomas West Potter from Scott, New York, who as stated previously, was secured through the efforts of Rev. Azor Estee.

Mr. Potter taught two terms of school during the winter of 1850-51, and the following spring. At the close of the second term, he left and did not return. During the summer of 1851, Miss Esther F. Randolph, daughter of William F. Randolph, one of the trustees of the academy, taught a term of seventeen weeks.

In the following autumn (1851), Rev. Azor Estee opened school in the new building. This was probably the most prosperous year of the life of the institution. It was not only well patronised by the people of the town, regardless of denominational affiliation, but students came from a large number of Seventh Day Baptist families located at New Milton, Greenbrier, New Salem, and various other localities within the bounds of the Seventh Day Baptist churches of Virginia. Many of these students boarded themselves, and Rev. Azor Estee conducted a club of twenty-six members, besides his own family, at a cost of seventy-two cents a week for each member.

Apparently, a term was taught the following summer (1852), by Ezra F. Randolph, a brother of Miss Esther F. Randolph, who had taught in the summer of 1851. During the year 1852-53, the school seems to have been taught by two brothers, Benoni Israel and Robert Alexander Jeffrey, sons of Joseph Jeffrey, one of the trustees of the academy.

In the meantime, William F. Randolph had been appointed corresponding secretary, and instructed to open correspondence to secure a suitable teacher for the school. As a result of his efforts, Daniel Maxson Burdick of Little Genesee, New York, was secured and was upon the ground by the 20th of June, 1853. As he arrived later than he had expected, he

FRANKLIN F. RANDOLPH.   PRESTON F. RANDOLPH.
VIRGINIA F. RANDOLPH.
ISAIAH BEE.   LEWIS TOWNSEND DAVIS.
(A group of West Union Academy students).

found a school already in progress in the village in the county court house, taught by a Baptist clergyman. The trustees, nevertheless, tendered him the academy, rent free, and he opened a school with some twenty pupils, with a promise of about seventy for the following term. He was, however, called home by sickness in his family, and although he promised to return, he found on his arrival at home that it would be impossible for him to do so, and so abandoned the enterprise. This was undoubtedly the last tangible effort of the trustees to conduct a denominational school in the buildings.

Apparently from the time of Daniel Maxson Burdick's departure in the late summer or autumn of 1853, there was no school conducted in the buildings, as it was hoped he would return, until the first of the following June, when the property was rented to one H. T. Hays, who continued to hold possession until June 6, 1855, paying a rent of forty dollars ($40.00) a year. Hays was not a Seventh Day Baptist, and probably conducted a subscription (select) school for the benefit of the children of the village. The buildings then appear to have stood idle until the 8th day of August, 1856, when the entire property was sold and passed into the possession of Isaiah Bee, who taught two terms of school in the academy, when it ceased to be used for school purposes. During the Civil War it was used as a hospital by the Union Army. Later the cupola was removed, and the building was transformed into a dwelling house. It is now the comfortable home of the daughter of one of Rev. Azor Estee's former school patrons.

The academy was organised and established mainly through the joint efforts of Rev. Azor Estee and William F. Randolph, the latter of whom was its largest stockholder and its leading spirit throughout the entire period of its active history. He, together with his father, Jonathan F. Randolph; his uncle, Jesse F. Randolph; his brothers, Jepthah F. Randolph, Peter F. Randolph, Samuel Preston F. Randolph, and Isaac F. Randolph; his brothers-in-law, John S. Davis and Eliona Davis; and his son-in-law, Richard Ford; held a preponderence of the stock.

The academy was modelled largely after the North-Western Virginia Academy situated at Clarksburg, twenty-seven miles east of West Union, and fourteen miles east of New Salem.[1] The North-Western Academy was originally incorporated by an act of the General Assembly of the Commonwealth of Virginia, passed December 31, 1787, as a branch of William and Mary's College, under the name of the Randolph Academy, so called in honor of Governor Edmund Randolph, who was one of the original trustees. Its first principal was Rev. George Towers, a graduate of Oxford University, England. It was re-incorporated as the North-Western Virginia Academy, in 1842; and in 1866 passed into the public school system, and survives to-day as the most excellent public high school of the city of Clarksburg, West Virginia. The North-Western Virginia Academy was patronised to some extent by Seventh Day Baptists after the West Union Academy was closed and perhaps before the latter was established.

A prospectus of the North-Western Virginia Academy marked in the handwriting of William F. Randolph, is in existence at the present time, filed away among the surviving papers of the West Union Academy. This prospectus embodies what are well known to have been William F. Randolph's ideals for the West Union Academy.

The fundamental weakness of the West Union Academy was the fact that while it was undertaken as a denominational school for which there was a crying need, it was also undertaken as a financial enterprise which was expected to pay handsome dividends to the stockholders. When these financial hopes were not fulfilled and the real character of the situation dawned upon the promoters of the enterprise, they became disappointed and discouraged. Those who could have supported it as a philanthropic institution refused to do so, and those who would have done so, were unable.

Nevertheless, the West Union Academy was by no means wholly a failure. Of its students, there went later to Alfred, New York, to attend Alfred Academy and University, five of the children of William F. Randolph; viz., Preston, Esther, Judson, Jethro, and Silas; together with their cousins Frank-

---

[1]. In 1801, Clarksburg had an academy in which about fifty pupils were taught. Isaac Van Meter's *Journal.* Cf. *Transallegheny Historical Magazine*, Vol. I, No. 1, p. 96.

Northwestern Virginia Academy.

THE DESIGN OF THE INSTITUTION is to afford the best possible opportunity for acquiring a thorough English, Classical, Mathematical, and Mercantile Education.

THE COURSE OF INSTRUCTION embraces every branch taught either in the Common School or College. Students will be furnished with every facility to prepare themselves for any of the professions or pursuits of life.

THE GOVERNMENT OF THE ACADEMY is mild, though firm—avoiding severity as far as possible, and yet requiring order industry, and obedience as essential to success in study, and to meeting the just expectations of friends and patrons. Diligent and constant care is used to induce and strengthen habits of pure morality and virtue.— No student will be allowed to continue in the school, whose conduct is found to be subversive of these, or of good order and government.

THE YEAR IS DIVIDED INTO TWO SESSIONS of twenty-two weeks each—beginning with the last Monday in April and October respectively. Each session is closed with a public examination of the various classes, at which all the students are required to be present, accompanied with such other literary exercise as usually pertain to the occasion after which there is a vacation of four weeks.

THE RATES OF TUITION PER SESSION are as follows, viz

Orthography Reading, Writing, &c.	$5 00
Geography, Grammar, Arithmetic, &c.,	7 00
History Chemistry, Philosophy, and other Studies in Mental Moral, or Natural Science,	9 00
Latin and Greek Languages, or the higher Mathematics,	12 00

ALL THE TEXT-BOOKS used in this institution can be had in town, on reasonable terms. Students are received at any time, but it is exceedingly desirable that they should be present at the opening of the session when the classes are first formed.

GOOD BOARDING can be had in private families, at about $1 50 per week. Provision is made so that those desiring it can board themselves at perhaps one-half of the above.

AN EXCELLENT SETT OF APPARATUS in the departments of Electricity, Philosophy, Astronomy, Optics, Magnetism, &c., belongs to the Academy, and affords great advantage to the student or those branches.

THERE IS A LITERARY SOCIETY in connection with the Institution whose exercises of Composition, Declamation, Oration, Criticism and Debate, are in many respects of great importance and utility to the student. It has a respectable and growing Library to which all the members have free access.

THE LAWS OF THE ACADEMY require each student to attend Public Worship on the Sabbath at such place as himself or parents may select. The Scriptures are daily read with prayer, at which all the students are required to be present. While nothing of a sectarian character is allowed in the instructions of the school, parents are assured that earnest efforts will be made to inculcate from the Bible those lessons of Duty and Moral Obligation which, no less than Mental culture, are essential to individual and social happiness and prosperity.

The undersigned would call attention to the claims of this Institution on the patronage and favor of the public. At almost every session since its organization it has sent out a greater or less number of well instructed and disciplined young men, some of whom are honorably and usefully employed in the various avocations and pursuits of life, others, with credit to themselves, have graduated at higher institutions, while perhaps a majority of the young men immediately on leaving us become actively and profitably engaged in Teaching. The low rates of tuition—the central location of the Institution in a region eminently healthy and easy of access from all points in connection with its superior educational facilities, all unite to commend it to the friends of sound instruction, and to young men especially who wish to be prepared for the worthy and intelligent performance of their parts in life. We have the pleasure of stating that the present attendance and future prospects of the Institution are altogether of the most encouraging character

ALEX. MARTIN, PRINCIPAL.
CHARLES LEWIS, Pres.
NATHAN GOFF, Treas. } Of the Board of Trustees.
R. T. MOORE, Sec.

FACSIMILE OF PROSPECTUS OF THE NORTH-WESTERN VIRGINIA ACADEMY.

lin, son of Jepthah F. Randolph; and Darius King, son of Eliona Davis; besides Andrew Judson, son of Dr. Lathrop R. Charter, a leading surgeon and physician of Doddridge County. Neither Dr. Lathrop R. Charter nor his son, Andrew Judson, was a Seventh Day Baptist. The first named of these, Preston F. Randolph, afterward became the most potent educational factor which has ever appeared in the counties of Harrison, Doddridge, and Ritchie, of West Virginia.

Born nearly thirty years before the organisation of the public school system in that locality, he was taught to read by his older brother Waldo, who in his time had, along with two sisters and a brother, been taught by their father, who often conducted a school in his own home during the winter for his own children and those of his neighbors. The last of his father's schools Preston was permitted to attend, but he was not allowed to take part in the class recitations, owing to a grave defect of speech. Nevertheless, he carried along his school work, especially that in arithmetic, so satisfactorily, that he was invited to teach a school in an adjoining neighbourhood, because it was understood that he had "ciphered through the Rule of Three" in *Pike's Arithmetic* —a text book much in vogue in western Virginia in those days. He next attended a school taught near home by his older sister Harriet. Soon after that, Stephen Thomas West Potter arrived to open the proposed academy at West Union, and Preston, with five brothers and sisters, was sent there. Here he was kept for two years, when a lameness developed, which he has carried ever since. In the hope of at least arresting, if not permanently curing, this trouble, he was taken out of school at West Union and kept at home, until April, 1855, when, in company with his brothers Judson and Silas, and his sister Esther, he started for Alfred, New York, to attend Alfred Academy. The first sixty miles of the journey was made in a road wagon to St. Mary's on the Ohio River. The remainder of the distance was travelled by steamboat and railroad. At Alfred the brothers and sister boarded themselves at a total expense of less than seventy cents a week. Here Preston applied himself with diligence, and despite the fact that he was heavily handicapped physically, in a year and a half had equipped himself for teaching district schools.

PRESTON FITZ RANDOLPH.

He taught for two consecutive winters at Hebron, Pennsylvania; and the following winter, that of 1859-60, he spent in the home of Rev. Azor Estee at Petersburgh, New York, teaching the latter's son James A., and pursuing his own studies. In the summer time he busied himself as a peddler in the New England States, especially Vermont, New Hampshire, and Maine. He then returned to Alfred, where he graduated in 1862. After graduation, he continued his studies at Alfred for a short time, when he went to Quincy, Franklin County, Pennsylvania, not many miles from Gettysburg, to teach school. The invasion of Lee's army closed the academy at Quincy, of which he was principal. Here he was visited at the home of Rev. Azor Estee, by Dr. Isaiah Bee, a surgeon in the invading army, who had been a fellow student at the West Union Academy when it was conducted by Azor Estee. Military operations decided him to return home, and through the kind offices of his friend, Dr. Bee, he was enabled to pass through the Confederate lines, and reach home by way of Cumberland, Maryland, over the Baltimore and Ohio Railroad, after an absence from home of nearly seven years.

For the next three years, he was engaged for the most of the time in teaching select, or subscription, schools in New Salem and vicinity. Free schools were now opening, as teachers could be found for them, and Preston F. Randolph was kept busy for nearly twenty years, sometimes teaching thirteen school months of twenty days each in a year.

Besides the select schools, previously referred to, he taught at New Salem for more than two years, and during one winter at the home of his brother-in-law, Richard Ford, on Long Run. After the establishment of the Free School System, he taught two years at West Union; three on Buckeye Run, and on Flint Run; all in Doddridge County: two and a half years at Berea and vicinity; two years at Pennsboro; and six months at Ellenboro; all in Ritchie County. The rest of the twenty years was spent in teaching at New Salem and near-by points in the western part of Harrison County. During all this time, he fondly cherished in his heart the hope that he might in some way be instrumental in realising for the Seventh Day Baptists in West Virginia, the object which had lain so near his father's heart for so many years; *viz.*, the successful establishment of a denominational academy. While the father's objective point for the location of such a school had been West Union, that of the son was New Salem. With the assistance of Rev. Charles A. Burdick, who was at that time labouring among the churches of West Virginia, under the auspices of the Seventh Day Baptist Missionary Society, and others, he succeeded in obtaining from the legislature of the state of West Virginia, a charter for an independent school district at New Salem, with the privilege of establishing an academy. A graded course of study was prepared for the new school, which was aided financially by the Peabody Educational Fund, then recently established for the aid of education in the south. Until a suitable school building could be erected, the New Salem Seventh Day Baptist church was, on two different occasions, used for that purpose. Of the school thus established, Preston F. Randolph had charge for several terms.

Nor were his efforts confined solely to secular work. He organised, and in some cases, personally conducted successfully, Sabbath Schools at New Salem and other Seventh Day Baptist points embraced in the localities where he taught.

He first introduced vocal music into the public schools of that part of West Virginia, and for several years he and the teachers whom he trained were the only ones who had singing in their schools.

Not the least important phase of his work was the training of teachers for public schools.

With the establishment of the state of West Virginia in 1863, a public school system was organised, and teachers for these schools were in great demand. Wherever a competent teacher was found, the school was crowded, not only with children, but with adults as well. It was not at all unusual to find, in a single school, pupils ranging from six-year-old children to men upwards of thirty years of age.

Preston F. Randolph's methods were not only novel and striking for his day and for his field of labour, but they were paedagogically good, even when compared with the best standards of modern education. His schools were normal schools in the truest sense. The work was spirited, the results substantial, and here young men and young women preparing for teaching learned, truly by precept, but more truly by the

SALEM ACADEMY

SALEM, HARRISON COUNTY, WEST VIRGINIA.

PRESTON F. RANDOLPH, - PRINCIPAL.
THREE ASSISTANT TEACHERS.

CALENDAR FOR 1872.

Spring Term of 12 weeks begins Tuesday, April 16th.
Vacation about 4 weeks.
Fall Term of 12 weeks begins Monday, August 5th.
Winter Term, November —

EXPENSES, IN ADVANCE.

Tuition in Common School branches, $3 per Term, or $1 25 per month.

In Higher English, Higher Mathematics, and Languages, $5 per Term.

Incidentals, 50 cents per Term.

Boarding in private families, $10 to $16 per month.

The Principal will take parental care of young pupils placed in his family for that purpose.

A NORMAL DEPARTMENT

Will be organized during the Fall Term, for the special training of those designing to teach. C. W. SMITH, the County Superintendent, and other educators, will assist in this Department, by lecturing, etc. An Examination of Teachers will be held by the Superintendent at the close of the session.

This Institution is chartered by the Legislature, in connection with the Graded Schools of Salem, which receive aid from the Peabody Educational Fund.

BOARD OF EDUCATION.

SILAS FITTRO, } *Commissioners.*
JOHN FLINT,
DR. J. L. F. RANDOLPH, *President.*
P. F. RANDOLPH, *Secretary.*
LLOYD F. RANDOLPH, *Treasurer.*

concretest of concrete examples, how teaching should be done. They in turn, went forth to their work as teachers in the spirit of their professional master.

Of the more successful of these teachers there may be mentioned, Luther F. Randolph, Davis N. Meredith, Thomas H. Lowther, Stillman F. Lowther, Thomas B. Pepper, John H. Benedum, and James A. Estee, the son of Rev. Azor Estee.

Among those of the pupils of Preston F. Randolph, who became teachers and then clergymen, were his brother Lewis F. Randolph, besides Gideon Henry F. Randolph, Experience F. Randolph, (now Mrs. Perie R. Burdick), Boothe Colwell Davis, and Samuel Hoffman Davis, all of whom are Seventh Day Baptist clergymen. Besides these, there were several teachers who afterward become clergymen of other denominations, particularly the Baptist.

NAMES OF PRINCIPALS AND STUDENTS.

The following is an incomplete list of names of students who attended West Union Academy under the following principals:—

STEPHEN THOMAS WEST POTTER, of Scott, N. Y.
REV. AZOR ESTEE, of Petersburgh, N. Y.
DANIEL MAXSON BURDICK, of Little Genesee, N. Y.

WEST UNION.

Names of Parents.	Names of Students.[1]	Post Office Address of Students at present, or at time of decease.
BEE.		
EPHRAIM and CATHARINE.	LOUISE (*l*), mar. John Smith,	Knight, W. Va.
BOND.		
ETHELBERT D. and MARY DAVIS.	WILLIAM (*l*),	Williamstown, W. Va.
	IRVIN, (*d*),	Parkersburg, W. Va.
	NATHAN (*l*),	Parkersburg, W. Va.
CHARTER.		
LATHROP R., M.D. and	ANDREW JUDSON, (*l*),	Ravenswood, W. Va.

---

1. *l*, living; *d*, dead; *u*, unknown.

THOMAS H. LOWTHER.   STILLMAN F. LOWTHER.
LUTHER F. RANDOLPH.
DAVIS N. MEREDITH.   THOMAS B. PEPPER.
(A group of Preston F. Randolph's students).

Names of Parents.	Names of Students.	Post Office Address of Students at present, or at time of decease.
DAVIS. ALFRED and REBECCA DAVIS.	FRANKLIN MAXWELL (*l*), TACY JANE (*l*), mar. Jeriel Sutton,	West Union, W. Va. Blandville, W. Va.
DAVIS. BENJAMIN L. and NANCY BROWN.	RACHEL (*d*), mar. — Boyles,	——, Lewis Co., W. Va.
DAVIS. ELIONA and SOPHIA DAVIS.	EHUD JOHNSON (*l*), DARIUS KING (*l*), IRVING PINDLE CHAPIN (*l*), DELILA CHAPMAN (*d*), AMY (*l*), mar. William J. Ott, ALPHEUS MARTIN (*d*), THOMAS BENTON (*l*), MARY TACY, (*l*), mar. Guy K. Butler,	Leroy, Kan. Milton Junction, Wis. Texarkana, Ark. Emporia, Kan. Gardner, Kan. Alton, Ill. Emporia, Kan. Vallego, Cal.
DAVIS. HEZEKIAH and STATIRA DAVIS.	EMZA JANE (*d*), mar. — Williams,	West Union, W. Va.
DAVIS. JOHN S. and ESTHER F. RANDOLPH.	LEWIS TOWNSEND (*l*), CAROLINE (*d*), ELISABETH (*d*), EMILY (*d*), mar. Hiram Jennings,	West Union, W. Va. West Union, W. Va. West Union, W. Va. Moberly, Mo.
DAVIS. PHINEAS and RHULANAH F. RANDOLPH.	CHARLES CHRISTOPHER (*l*),	Harrisville, W. Va.

Names of Parents.	Names of Students.	Post Office Address of Students at present, or at time of decease.
ESTEE.		
AZOR and BETSEY BROWN.	CHARLES B. (*l*),	Gibson City, Ill.
GARNER.		
JOHN and SARAH ANN WILLIAMS.	ISAIAH (*d*),	West Union, W. Va.
INGLE.		
JACOB, M.D. and MAHALA RACHEL.	SALINA (*l*), ARTHUR (*l*), WILLIAM (*d*),	West Union, W. Va. West Union, W. Va. West Union, W. Va.
JEFFREY.		
JOSEPH and TACY DAVIS.	ROBERT ALEXANDER (*d*), CONTENT ANN (*d*), BENONI ISRAEL (*d*), CLARISSA (*d*), mar. Michael Bush, SOPHIA ANN (*d*), mar. John Wesley Longacre, LOUISE (*d*), STILLMAN (*d*),	West Union, W. Va. West Union, W. Va. West Union, W. Va. Auburn, W. Va. West Union, W. Va. West Union, W. Va. West Union, W. Va.
KNIGHT.		
TALIAFFERO K. and ELISABETH HOLLIDAY.	BLACKWELL (*d*),	West Union, W. Va.
LEWIN.		
WILLIAM and ELIZA ——.	AMANDA (*d*), mar. Robert Alexander Jeffrey,	West Union, W. Va.
MACJUNKIN.		
JOSHUA and	ELISABETH (*u*),	

STEPHEN THOMAS WEST POTTER.
DANIEL MAXSON BURDICK.
AZOR ESTEE.

Names of Parents.	Names of Students.	Post Office Address of Students at present, or at time of decease.
MAHANY.		
WILLIAM and	CHARLES (d),	West Union, W. Va.
MANEER. (Keeper of the county jail).	—(a boy) (u),	——————
MAULSBY.		
LAWSON and TABITHA OGDEN.	AMELIA CHARLOTTE (l), mar. Noah Hetrick, MARY LETHE (l), mar. John Johnson,	Ada, O. West Union, W. Va.
RANDOLPH.		
SAMUEL PRESTON F. and HANNAH DAVIS.	VIRGINIA F. (l), mar. Alfred Jennings,	Parkersburg, W. Va.
SOUTHWORTH.		
ENOCH B. and MARY ANN CHILDERS.	SOPHIA (d), GEORGE WASHINGTON (l),	West Union, W. Va. West Union, W. Va.
STUART.		
CHAPMAN J. and ELISABETH.	ANNA (l), mar. Dr. Dougherty,	—————— Ill.

NEW SALEM.

RANDOLPH.		
JESSE F. and ELIZA GILLIS.	LLOYD F. (d), ELISABETH F. (l), mar. Rev. Samuel D. Davis,	Salem, W. Va. Jane Lew, W. Va.
RANDOLPH.		
PETER F. and MARIA MACVICAR.	MADISON MACVICAR F. (l), DANIEL F. (d),	Rockford, W. Va. Salem, W. Va.

Names of Parents.	Names of Students.	Post Office Address of Students at present, or at time of decease.
RANDOLPH.		
PHINEAS F. and MARVEL MAXSON,	PHINEAS CHAPIN F. (d),	Salem, W. Va.
RANDOLPH.		
JOHN LaFORGE F. M.D., and EXPERIENCE BROWN,	TACY JANE F. (d),	———————.

GREENBRIER.

RANDOLPH.		
WILLIAM F. and MARY DAVIS.	EZRA F. (d),	Greenbrier, W. Va.
	ESTHER F. (d), mar. LeRoy Burdick,	Hebron, Pa.
	SILAS F. (l),	Riverside, Cal.
	JUDSON F. (l),	Salem, W. Va.
	PRESTON F. (l),	Salem, W. Va.
	JETHRO F. (d),	Alfred, N. Y.
	ZIPPORAH ELISABETH, (d), mar. Leander Place.	Hebron, Pa.

NEW MILTON.

BEE.		
JOSIAH and PRISCILLA DAVIS.	ISAIAH (l),	Princeton, W. Va.
RANDOLPH.		
JEPTHAH F. and DEBORAH SUTTON.	FRANKLIN F. (l),	New Milton, W. Va.
	RACHEL F. (d), mar. Johnson J. Lowther,	New Milton, W. Va.

BUCKEYE RUN.

DAVIS.		
COL. DAVID D. and	JUDITH (l), mar. Jonathan Traugh,	Middlebourne, W. Va.
ANNA DAVIS.	MORRIS, N. (d),	Numan, W. Va.

| Names of Parents. | Names of Students. | Post Office Address of Students at present, or at time of decease. |

DAVIS.
   Lodowick Hughes   Silas Carder (*d*),   Salem, W. Va.
   and
   Margaret Davis.

FORD.
   Albert   Hamilton (*l*),   Numan, W. Va.
   and   Elisabeth (*l*), mar.
   Rhulanah Davis.   Elisha Stoneking,   Booker, W. Va.

TATE.
   William   Sarah (*d*), mar. A.
   and   J. Hickman,

ROCK RUN.

DAVIS.
   William Johnson   Gamble Shannon (*d*),   West Union, W. Va.
   ("Rock Run Billy")   Samull Preston (*d*),   West Union, W. Va.
   and   William Granville (*l*),   Sugar Camp, W. Va.
   Experience Thorp.

HUGHES RIVER.

BEE.
   Asa   Zebulon (*d*),   Bolair, W. Va.
   and   Abigail A. (*d*), mar.
   Hannah Maxson.   Daniel Nay,   Pullman, W. Va.
    Asa Jr. (*l*),   South Lancaster, Mass.

FLINT RUN.

DAVIS.
   William F.   Emily Virginia (*d*),
   ("Flint Billy")   mar. Rev. James
   and   B. Davis.   Salem, W. Va.
   Rachel Hughes.   Dudley Hughes (*d*),   Quiet Dell, W. Va.

MEAT HOUSE FORK.

DAVIS.
   Stephen Thorp   Francis Marion (*l*),   Buckhannon, W. Va.
   and
   Elisabeth Jeffrey.

Names of Parents.	Names of Students.	Post Office Address of Students at present, or at time of decease.
	LOST CREEK.	

DAVIS.
  JACOB
  and
  SARAH HOFFMAN.
	ABIGAIL HOFFMAN (*d*), mar. Reuben Hevener,	Roanoke, W. Va.

	ROBINSON'S FORK.	

BONNELL.
  CHARLES
  and
  ————
	LEHMAN (*d*),	————

	BONE CREEK.	

HALL.
  ELISHA
  and
  SUSANNAH THORP.
	LAWSON (*l*),	Auburn, W. Va.

	UNKNOWN.	

WILLIAMS.
  ————
  and
  ————
	EMILY (*d*),	————

XXVI.

SALEM COLLEGE.

EVER since the inauguration of the movement which resulted in the establishment of the ill-fated West Union Academy, it had been the dream of the Seventh Day Baptists of western Virginia to have a denominational school maintained in their midst.

After the final dissolution of the West Union Academy, the village of New Salem, by common consent, was fixed upon as the site of the future school; and many of those connected with the West Union Academy laboured and hoped, incessantly, for the realisation of this dream.

Preston F. Randolph, in all his educational work in West Virginia, held this thought uppermost in his mind, and Rev. Charles A. Burdick, from the time he began his duties as a general missionary among the West Virginia churches in 1870, looked forward with anxiety to the time when that hope would be fulfilled.

So confident was he of the success of such a movement, that after four years service as a missionary, he resigned that work and opened a select school at New Salem, doubting nothing that it would soon become a permanent school, of the grade of an academy. This school was opened in April, 1875.

At the annual session of the South-Eastern Association, held at Lost Creek, beginning May 28, 1874, the question of a denominational school had been especially prominent. But it was not deemed wise for the association to move in the matter. The select school started in the following spring by

Rev. Charles A. Burdick, was undertaken, however, upon the assurance of financial assistance from private sources. The business depression prevalent throughout the country, rapidly grew worse, and the expected aid failed to materialise, although the school was a distinct success in attendance and in the quality of work done; for it was well patronised by the Seventh Day Baptists throughout the association, with a generous representation of non-Sabbath-keepers.

Rev. Charles A. Burdick, with his wife, and Miss Adelle M. Whitford, of Utica, Wisconsin, composed the teaching staff. The meeting house of the New Salem Church was used as a school building, it being expected that in a short time a suitable building would be erected for the school. After conducting this school through the spring and summer of 1875, it was abandoned, for several reasons, principally for lack of funds for the erection of a school building. Mr. and Mrs. Burdick taught in the public school in the village of Rockford, on Lost Creek, the following winter, as they had done the preceding winter; and in the summer of 1876, assisted again by Miss Whitford, they taught a select school at Rockford. Mr. Burdick then abandoned his attempts to establish a denominationl school in West Virginia.[1]

Terence M. Davis, a son of Lodowick H. Davis, and afterward a professor in Alfred University, hoped that upon his graduation from Alfred, in 1881, he might establish an academy at New Salem. He carried his plans so far as the designing of the necessary buildings, to be erected on grounds adjoining his father's home in New Salem. But his disappointment was destined to be added to the growing catalogue of unsuccessful attempts to establish a Seventh Day Baptist school in West Virginia.

Nevertheless, events soon began to shape themselves so as to force the issue. The principal cause of immediate anxiety was due to the fact that of the rapidly increasing number of young people who were going away to Alfred University, very few returned to make their homes in West Virginia after graduation.

It should be remembered, also, that as already intimated

---

1. A history of this school, written by Rev. Charles A. Burdick, may be found in *The Sabbath Recorder*, under date of March 5, 1891.

(23)

TERENCE M. DAVIS. CORLISS F. RANDOLPH.
GIDEON HENRY F. RANDOLPH. LUTHER A. BOND.
(A group of Charles A. Burdick's students at New Salem).

in the preceding chapter on the *West Union Academy*, the essential cause of the decay of that institution was its failure to pay cash dividends on its stock, a failure which was not soon forgotten, and which, to a great extent, deterred men of means from investing money in a denominational school after that time. In other words, the financial side of such a school was considered in the light of the probable material profits which it would yield, and the failure of the West Union Academy was a very discouraging example.

Events now transpired which deeply interested several of the prominent business men of Salem, and the establishment of Salem College resulted.

In this connection, it may be interesting to note that at the annual session of the Seventh Day Baptist General Conference, held with the church at Salem, in August, 1890, the largest share-holder of the capital stock of Salem College, declared that up to that time his stock in the college had yielded the largest financial returns of any investment he had ever made.

The immediate events resulting in the establishment of Salem College may be briefly sketched as follows:—

The Methodist Episcopal General Conference of the state of West Virginia, at its annual session in 1886, determined to establish a seminary of learning for young people of both sexes somewhere within the state, and announced that it would be established in or near the city or town offering the most acceptable inducements, financial and otherwise.

In the hope of securing the location of the seminary at Salem, the citizens of that village and immediate vicinity, pledged for that purpose, a sum aggregating, in round numbers, forty thousand dollars ($40,000.00). Their efforts were not successful, however, as the Methodist Episcopal General Conference finally fixed upon the village of Buckhannon, as the site of the seminary.

This fruitless effort, however, showed that the opportunity to secure the long-desired Seventh Day Baptist secondary school was at hand; for if such a sum could be raised for the establishment of a Methodist school, surely enough could be raised to establish a good Seventh Day Baptist school upon a solid conservative basis.

At the session of the South-Eastern Association held with the Ritchie Church at Berea, beginning May 26, 1887, the association took the following action:—

"We would heartily encourage and seek to have a school within the bounds of our association, in which our young people may be thoroughly prepared to enter college."

In accordance with the spirit of this action, a committee, consisting of Rev. John L. Huffman, Jesse F. Randolph, and Rev. Henry B. Lewis, was appointed "to canvass the matter and take such steps as they may find practicable, looking to the establishment of a school in the bounds of the association, in which our young people may be thoroughly prepared to enter college."

At the next annual session of the association, held with the church at Lost Creek, beginning May 24, 1888, this committee reported as follows:—

"1. That we are fully satisfied that the time has come when the demand is such that we ought to have such a school.

"2. That Salem is a good place for its location.

"3. We are of the opinion that sufficient money could be raised within the bounds of this association to secure the grounds and erect such buildings as would be suitable for present use.

"4. We recommend that a committee be appointed which shall take steps at once to ascertain the amount that can be raised by subscriptions; and if a sufficient amount can be secured, so that no debts should be incurred, to make the needed arrangements, and secure a suitable location, and erect the buildings."

The report of the committee was adopted, and the committee which they recommended was appointed as follows:— Rev. John L. Huffman, Rev. Samuel D. Davis, Jesse F. Randolph, George W. F. Randolph, Charles N. Maxson, Ethelbert J. Davis, Franklin F. Randolph, Flavius J. Ehret, and Samuel D. Bond.

At its annual session held in connection with the Seventh Day Baptist General Conference at Leonardsville, New York, August 24, 1888, the Seventh Day Baptist Education Society adopted the following resolution:—

"RESOLVED, That we have learned with approval of the efforts of our people in the South-Eastern Association, to establish a college preparatory school at New Salem, West Virginia; that we recognise

SALEM COLLEGE.

the need of the special training which such an institution can furnish to the youth of that body; and that we earnestly trust sufficient accommodations will soon be provided for the favourable opening and the successful maintenance of this school."

In the meantime the committee appointed by the association was proceeding with its work, which moved along so satisfactorily that on the 28th of December, 1888, a charter for Salem Academy was issued by the secretary of the state of West Virginia, as will be observed from the following:—

"CERTIFICATE OF INCORPORATION.

"STATE OF WEST VIRGINIA.

"SALEM ACADEMY.

"I, HENRY S. WALKER, Secretary of the State of West Virginia, hereby certify that an agreement duly acknowledged and accompanied by the proper affidavits has been this day delivered to me, which agreement is in the words and figures following:—

"The undersigned agree to become a corporation by the name of SALEM ACADEMY to be subject to the regulations of the Seventh Day Baptist Educational Society, for the purpose of purchasing real estate in Salem, Harrison County, West Virginia, and erecting a building or buildings thereon in which to establish an ACADEMY, and so soon as the financial condition and circumstances will warrant, a COLLEGE; and for the purpose of teaching therein and thereat all the various branches of learning composing a thorough academic and collegiate course; and of awarding diplomas to students who may pass the requisite examination upon the various branches of learning taught therein; and for the diffusion of knowledge incident to institutions of like kind. Which corporation shall keep its principal office, or place of business, at Salem in the County of Harrison and State of West Virginia; and is to expire on the 20th day of November, 1938.

"And for the purpose of forming the said corporation, we have subscribed the sum of two thousand one hundred and fifty dollars to the capital thereof, and have paid in on said subscription, the sum of two hundred and fifteen dollars; and desire the privilege of increasing the said capital by the sale of additional shares from time to time to the sum of fifty thousand dollars in all.

"The capital so subscribed is divided into shares of twenty-five dollars each, which are held by the undersigned, respectively, as follows, that is to say:—

"By G. W. F. RANDOLPH, Salem, W. Va.   Forty shares,
"By JESSE F. RANDOLPH, Salem, W. Va.,   Twenty shares,
"By L. B. DAVIS, Salem, W. Va.,   One share,
"By F. M. SWIGER, Salem, W. Va.,   Two shares,
"By A. S. CHILDERS, Salem, W. Va.,   Four shares,

"By J. L. Huffman, Lost Creek, W. Va.,   Four   shares,
"By Chas. N. Maxson, Lost Creek, W. Va.,   Four   shares,
"By Ernest Randolph, Salem, W. Va.,   One   share,
"By Uric F. Randolph, Salem, W. Va.,   One   share,
"By Lloyd F. Randolph, Salem, W. Va.,   Four   shares,
"By C. M. Randolph, Salem, W. Va.,   One   share,
"By Jas. N. David, Salem, W. Va.,   Two   shares,
"By Hiram Wilson, Salem, W. Va.,   Two   shares.

"And the capital to be hereafter sold is to be divided into shares of the like amount.

"Given under our hands, this 20th day of November, 1888.
"G. W. F. Randolph,
"Jesse F. Randolph,
"L. B. Davis,
"F. M. Swiger,
"A. S. Childers,
"J. L. Huffman,
"Chas. N. Maxson,
"Ernest Randolph,
"Uric F. Randolph,
"Lloyd F. Randolph,
"C. M. Randolph,
"James N. David,
"Hiram Wilson.

"WHEREFORE, The incorporators named in the said agreement, and who have signed the same, and their successors and assigns, are hereby declared to be from this date until the 20th day of November, 1938, a corporation, by the name, and for the purpose set forth in said agreement.

"GIVEN under my hand and the Great Seal of the said State, at the City of Charleston, this the twenty-eighth day of December, eighteen hundred and eighty-eight.
"Henry S. Walker,
[L. S.]   "*Secretary of State.*"

The charter was amended afterward so as change the name from SALEM ACADEMY to SALEM COLLEGE, in accordance with a vote of the stockholders of the corporation, as will be observed from the following certificate of the Secretary of State:—

"State of West Virginia,
"Office of Secretary of State.

"I, WM. A. OHLEY, Secretary of State of the State of West Virginia, do hereby certify that J. F. RANDOLPH, President of SALEM ACADEMY, a corporation created under the laws of this State, has this day certified to me under his signature and the corporate seal of

JESSE FITZ RANDOLPH.

said corporation, that at a regular meeting of the stockholders thereof, held in pursuance of law, on the 10th day of June, A. D. 1890, and at which meeting a majority of the capital stock thereof was represented by the holders thereof in person or by proxy, the following resolution was unanimously adopted:—

"RESOLVED, That the corporation known as SALEM ACADEMY be changed to, and from this time hence, be known as, SALEM COLLEGE, and that any and all necessary legal steps be taken to constitute the same a college in conformity to the charter of said institution, granted by, and in conformity with, the laws of West Virginia, on the 28th day of December, A. D. 1888,—

"WHEREFORE, I do declare said change of name of SALEM ACADEMY to SALEM COLLEGE, as set forth in the foregoing resolution, to be authorised by law.

"GIVEN under my hand and the Great Seal of the said State, at the City of Charleston, this sixteenth day of August, 1890.

"WM. A. OHLEY,
[L. S.] *"Secretary of State."*

"STATE OF WEST VIRGINIA,

"Office of the Clerk of Harrison County Court, August 28, 1890.

BE IT REMEMBERED, That this writing was this day duly admitted to record in this office.

"Attest: JAMES MONROE, *Clerk."*

Acting under the provisions of the charter, the incorporators organised on the 21st of January, 1889, and arranged for opening the academy in the following spring, using the Seventh Day Baptist church at Salem, which had so often already served as a school building, as temporary quarters. At the annual session of the South-Eastern Association held with the church at Salem in May of that year, the committee appointed the previous year, to act in behalf of a school, reported that they had secured pledges to the amount of four thousand eight hundred and sixty-six dollars ($4,866.00), including a tract of five acres of land valued at one thousand dollars ($1,000.00), at the west end of the village of Salem, and that a contract had been let for the erection of a two-story frame building, forty-five feet by sixty feet, at a cost which would be covered by the subscriptions, the building to be completed by the middle of the following November; and that a term of school was already in successful operation, with Rev. John L. Huffman as acting principal.

The report of "Salem Academy and College" to the Seventh Day Baptist Education Society, at its annual session in August, 1889, announced that "It is the purpose of the institution to give instruction in Preparatory, Academic, and Collegiate courses."

The report further announced that Rev. Sanford Lafayette Maxson, A. M., B. D., was the principal, and that such assistants as might be needed would be engaged for the ensuing year.

Up to this time, the three men who had contributed most to the success of the enterprise, were Rev. John L. Huffman, George W. F. Randolph, and Jesse F. Randolph. Rev. John L. Huffman, by his spirited leadership and organising ability, created a most healthful spirit throughout the association in favour of the school, and served as the general promoter of the enterprise. George W. F. Randolph and Jesse F. Randolph, two prominent business men of Salem, besides devoting time without stint, contributed most generously to the treasury of the academy. The former was the largest subscriber, and the latter the second largest. Jesse F. Randolph was made president of the corporation at the time of its organisation and with the exception of but one year, he has served in that capacity continuously up to the present time.

In the fall of 1889, the term opened under the leadership of Rev. Sanford Lafayette Maxson, who had recently resigned a position as principal of the Albion Academy at Albion, Wisconsin, where he had won for himself an enviable reputation in secondary school work. He was re-enforced by two competent assistants in the regular work of the academy, besides one teacher in each of the three special departments of music, business, and art. To these were added two special lecturers in physiology, anatomy, and hygiene. The enrollment for the year was one hundred and sixty (160).

The next year, the name of the institution had been changed from that of Salem Academy to that of Salem College, and there were in attendance during the academic year, six or more young men who anticipated entering the the Gospel ministry.

At the close of the academic year of 1891-1892, Rev. Sanford L. Maxson retired from the presidency of the college, and Rev. Theodore Livingston Gardiner, A. M., B. D.,

GEORGE WASHINGTON FITZ RANDOLPH.

was elected to succeed him. President Gardiner, as well as President Maxson, was a graduate of Alfred University; the former of the class of '74, the latter of the class of '85.

President Gardiner, at the time of his election to his new office, was the pastor of the Seventh Day Baptist Church at Salem, and accepted the presidency with reluctance, because he had had no previous experience in such work, besides being very fond of his church work.

Nevertheless, he threw himself into his new duties with energy and enthusiasm, and with a perseverance born of a determination to succeed, however great the cost.

From the beginning, he succeeded, and it was but a short time until it was apparent that he was the right man in the right place.

In addition to his new and laborious duties of teaching in the class room, was added that of securing the necessary funds from year to year with which to make up the annual deficiency which averaged about two thousand dollars ($2,000.00). In this he was fully as successful as in his other work, although it was a great strain upon him.

In its report to the Seventh Day Baptist Education Society for the year ending June 17, 1902, the college reported a debt on a new building of a little upwards of seven hundred and fifty dollars ($750.00), with but two hundred dollars ($200.00) of unpaid bills besides. To offset the latter item, the college held unpaid subscriptions sufficient to cover it.

The resources of the college consisted of the college campus and adjoining grounds of five acres, with two good buildings, besides a valuable library, together with a generous equipment of apparatus for teaching physics and chemistry, and an extensive collection of specimens for work in natural history.

In addition, the college held permanent productive funds aggregating two hundred and fifty dollars ($250.00).

This was a magnificent showing for the thirteen years of the history of the college, ten years of which had been under the leadership of President Gardiner.

In recognition of his successful career in church and educational work, his *Alma Mater,* Alfred University, conferred the degree of Doctor of Divinity upon President Gardiner, at its annual commencement in June, 1899.

For a time, the special departments were as prosperous as any departments of the college. In 1890-1891, the subjects of telegraphy, and stenography and typewriting were added to the curriculum of the commercial department. After a few years, however, the interest in some of these departments began to decline. At the end of the year 1892-1893, several subjects were dropped from the commercial department, and a year afterwards, the department was wholly abandoned, the college taking the position that that department was detrimental to the best interests of the institution. At the same time that the commercial department was dropped, the art department was likewise abandoned, for similar reasons. The music department has continued, however, doing satisfactory work to the present time.

In order to accommodate the growing needs of the college a new building, twenty feet by thirty-four feet, was erected during the year 1900-1901 at a cost of eight hundred and nine dollars and twenty cents ($809.20).

The work to which Salem College has, for the most part, devoted itself since it was first established, has been that of equipping and training teachers for the public schools of West Virginia.

So successfully has this work been done, that now all students of Salem College completing the prescribed course for that purpose, are awarded a state licence to teach, upon the same basis as the graduates of the normal schools of the state, and of West Virginia University.

Moreover, the administrative officers of the public schools of the county of Harrison, and several neighbouring counties, have received their training in Salem College.

The gratifying success of the college has been dependent upon its normal work more than any other; and that, too, despite the fact that the state normal schools and the state university are maintained at the expence of the public treasury of the state, and consequently are able to offer free tuition as well as other attractive inducements; while Salem College, receiving no revenues, whatever, from public sources, and

ESLE FITZ RANDOLPH.
(A graduate of Salem College).

without an endowment fund, upon which it can lean, is dependent upon the private subscriptions of her generous friends from year to year, to cover the inevitable deficit in her treasury, and is compelled to charge a substantial tuition fee, besides.

The secret of the success of the college, then, is the fact that its normal work has been made strong and attractive in a way that it is difficult for a state institution to become strong and attractive, particularly if political influences are potent.

Salem College, wholly free from political taint and intrigue, maintains a certain steadfastness of purpose and firmness of discipline, while at the same time enjoying a certain desirable, if not necessary freedom, that state institutions do not enjoy in West Virginia at the present time.

Nor should it be forgotten that the spirit of sectarian competition has been strong. But fourteen miles away, at Clarksburg, is Broadus, a Baptist institution, very much older than Salem, and a powerful rival of the latter.

Even more powerful, but somewhat more remote, is the Methodist Episcopal seat of learning at Buckhannon, out of the village of Salem's efforts to secure which, Salem College grew.

Amid all these influences, nevertheless, Salem College has steadily progressed, and won respect and reputation.

In the last analysis, however, the real secret of the success of Salem College lies in the fact that her faculty consists of men and women possessed of the sacrificial spirit, and the catholicity of toleration of the true teacher,—men and women whose sheet anchor is a deep and abiding faith in the destiny of the institution.

With such a body of teachers, working in the atmosphere they naturally created about them, Salem College could not fail. It had to succeed.

Tabular statements showing the changes in the faculty, the attendance, as well as some other matters of interest to the college, and the financial history of the college, to the end of the academic year 1901-1902, are appended hereto. These statements are compiled from the annual reports of the college to the Seventh Day Baptist Education Society.

BOARD OF DIRECTORS.

PRESIDENT:—
    JESSE F. RANDOLPH, 1889-1891, 1893-1902,
    C. LATON FORD, 1892-1893.

SECRETARY:—
    LEVI B. DAVIS, 1889,
    WILLIAM JEFFREY, 1890,
    M. WARDNER DAVIS, 1891, 1895-1898,
    CORTEZ R. CLAWSON, 1899-1902.

CORRESPONDING SECRETARY:—
    FRANKLIN F. RANDOLPH, 1890, 1893.

TREASURER:—
    PRESTON F. RANDOLPH, 1889-1891,
    ASHER S. CHILDERS, 1892-1902.

FINANCIAL AGENT:—
    JOHN L. HUFFMAN, 1890, 1892-1895,
    THEODORE L. GARDINER, 1892, 1896-1902.

ASSISTANT FINANCIAL AGENT:—
    JOHN L. HUFFMAN, 1891.

DIRECTORS:—
    DAVID M. BOYER, 1889-1902,
    ASHER S. CHILDERS, 1889-1902,
    JAMES N. DAVID, 1889-1891,
    EDGAR S. DAVIS, 1889,
    GRANVILLE H. DAVIS, 1889-1891,
    HERMAN B. DAVIS, 1889-1891,
    FLAVIUS J. EHRET, 1889-1902,
    FESTUS P. FORD, 1889-1895,
    JOHN L. HUFFMAN, 1889-1896,
    CHARLES N. MAXSON, 1889-1891,
    GEORGE W. F. RANDOLPH, 1889-1900,
    JESSE F. RANDOLPH, 1889-1902,
    LLOYD F. RANDOLPH, 1889-1894, 1896-1902,
    FRED M. SWIGER, 1889-1902,
    JAMES TONGE, 1889-1891,
    WILLIAM B. VANHORN, 1889-1902,
    WILLIAM JEFFREY, 1890,
    MILTON DAVIS, 1891-1902,
    C. LATON FORD, 1891-1901,
    R. LLOYD TOWLES, 1892-1896,
    S. ORLANDO DAVIS, 1892-1902,
    HIRAM WILSON, 1892-1902,
    HENRY HAWKER, 1892-1898,
    M. WARDNER DAVIS, 1895-1902,

ALICE CLAWSON GARDINER. ELSIE B. BOND.
CORTEZ R. CLAWSON. SAMUEL B. BOND.
(A group from the Faculty of Salem College).

SALEM COLLEGE

Moses Huffman VanHorn, 1897-1902,
D. C. Louchery, 1897,
O. L. Rohrbaugh, 1898-1902,
Preston F. Randolph, 1899-1902,
William Corwin, 1901-1902,
Lucian D. Lowther, 1902.

FACULTY OF SALEM COLLEGE, FROM ITS OPENING IN THE SPRING OF 1889 AS AN ACADEMY, TO AUGUST 1, 1902.

PRESIDENTS:—

Rev. John L. Huffman, A.M., B.D., Acting Principal, and chief instructor for the first term, Spring of 1889.

Rev. Sanford Lafayette Maxson, A.M., B.D., 1889-1892.
Greek, Latin, Natural History.
Elected in the Spring of 1889, but did not begin service until August following.

Rev. Theodore L. Gardiner, A.M., D.D., 1892-1902.
English Literature, Logic, Rhetoric, Physics, Moral Science, Psychology, Civics.

INSTRUCTORS:—

William Marcellus Blair, B.P., 1889(Spring)-1894.
Principal of Normal Department, and Instructor in Mathematics.

(Mrs.) Flora Rust. Spring of 1889.
Assistant.

Alice Maude Hoard, A.M., Ph.B., 1889-1890.
German, French, Rhetoric.

Mary J. Haven, A.B., M.M., 1889-1891.
In charge of Music Department.

Charlotte D. Maxson, 1889-1892.
Assistant in Music, 1889-1891; in charge of Music Department, 1891-1892.

Silas B. Davis, 1889-1892.
Principal of Commercial Department.

Eda L. Crandall, 1889-1890.
In charge of Art Department.

D. C. Louchery, A.B., M.D., 1889-1891.
Lecturer on Anatomy and Physiology.

I. Scott Kennedy, M.D., 1889-1891.
Lecturer on Hygiene.

Emma A. Maxson, B.F.A., 1890-1891.
In charge of Art Department.

Elsie Belinda Bond, A.M., 1890-1902.
English, History, Latin.

G. O. Doak, 1890-1891.
Assistant in Commercial Department.

C. Laton Ford, 1890-1893.
   Telegraphy.
Clarence L. Bond, 1890-1893.
   Stenography and Typewriting, 1890-1892;
   Principal of Commercial Department, 1892-1893.
Ora James Davis, 1890-1891.
   Instructor in Physiology.
C. C. Morrison, 1890-1891.
   Instructor in Mathematics.
Alleyne Hamilton, 1891-1892.
   In charge of Art Department.
John H. Wolfe, 1892-1898.
   Practical and Ornamental Penmanship.
(Mrs.) Mary Hughes, 1892-1893.
   In charge of Music Department.
Gertrude Fitz Randolph, 1892-1894.
   In charge of Art Department.
Mary E. Muncy, A.B., 1893-1894.
   History, Greek. Assistant in Normal Department.
Buchannon White, 1893-1894.
   Principal of Commercial Department.
Frances E. Stillman, 1893-1899.
   In charge of Music Department.
Joseph Rosier, B.P., 1894-1896.
   Principal of Normal Department.
Cortez R. Clawson, Ph.B., Litt. B., A.B., 1894-1902.
   Greek, History, Assistant in Normal Department.
T. Francis Kemper, B.P., 1894-1902.
   Mathematics, College Chorister.
(Mrs.) Abbie M. Clawson, 1895-1896.
   Astronomy, Assistant in Normal Department.
J. Alice Clawson, 1896-1898, 1899-1902.
   German, French.
Flavius E. Ashburn, 1897-1899.
   Instructor in Normal Department.
Eugenia Marvin, 1898-1899.
   German, Rhetoric.
Samuel B. Bond, A.B., 1899-1902.
   Physics, Astronomy, Mathematics.
Nellie Eaton, 1899-1901.
   In charge of music Department.
Beatrice Lowther, 1901-1902.
   In charge of Music Department.

DEGREES CONFERRED BY SALEM COLLEGE, 1889-1902.

1891. Ora James Davis, Bachelor of Paedagogy,
   William Marcellus Blair, Bachelor of Paedagogy,
   Elsie Belinda Bond, A.B., Master of Arts.

PRESIDENT GARDNER AND A GROUP OF SALEM COLLEGE STUDENTS.

1892. C. L. BOND, Bachelor of Commercial Science,
G. O. DOAK, Bachelor of Commercial Science.
1893. CORA FITZ RANDOLPH, Bachelor of Paedagogy,
V. CURTIS SNODGRASS, Bachelor of Paedagogy.
1894. ERNEST FITZ RANDOLPH, Bachelor of Arts,
LELA DEW, Bachelor of Commercial Science,
W. HOWARD HOLMES, Bachelor of Commercial Science,
CECIL W. CUNNINGHAM, Bachelor of Commercial Science,
JOHN L. THOMPSON, Bachelor of Commercial Science.
JOHN J. CLAWSON, Bachelor of Commercial Science.
1895. JOSEPH ROSIER, Bachelor of Paedagogy,
T. FRANCIS KEMPER, Bachelor of Paedagogy.
1896. SAMUEL B. BOND, Bachelor of Paedagogy,
MOSES HUFFMAN VANHORN, Bachelor of Paedagogy,
ALDIS L. DAVIS, Bachelor of Paedagogy.
1897. XENIA E. BOND, Bachelor of Arts,
EDNA LOUCHERY, Bachelor of Arts,
MOSES HUFFMAN VANHORN, Bachelor of Arts,
JOHN H. WOLFE, Bachelor of Arts,
ALDIS L. DAVIS, Bachelor of Philosophy,
CHESTER R. OGDEN, Bachelor of Science,
CURTIS L. OGDEN, Bachelor of Paedagogy.
LELA M. POWELL, Bachelor of Music.
1898. CHARLES G. COFFMAN, Bachelor of Paedagogy,
MORTON B. NEWLON, Bachelor of Paedagogy.
1899. FLAVIUS E. ASHBURN, Bachelor of Paedagogy,
(Mrs.) EMMA ASHBURN, Bachelor of Paedagogy,
DAISY LOWTHER, Bachelor of Paedagogy,
VENIE HAGERTY, Bachelor of Paedagogy,
DORA GARDINER, Bachelor of Paedagogy.
1900. O. AUSTIN BOND, Bachelor of Paedagogy,
DELMA M. DAVIS, Bachelor of Paedagogy,
EVA L. YOUNG, Bachelor of Paedagogy.
1901. S. ORESTES BOND, Bachelor of Paedagogy,
JAMES A. CARDER, Bachelor of Paedagogy,
ORESTES W. FRUM, Bachelor of Paedagogy,
ROY F. RANDOLPH, Bachelor of Paedagogy,
CORA E. BOND, Bachelor of Paedagogy,
MABEL LOWTHER, Bachelor of Paedagogy.
1902. CHARLES M. BOND, Bachelor of Paedagogy,
ARTHUR T. POST, Bachelor of Paedagogy,
HAROLD C. STILLMAN, Bachelor of Paedagogy,
XENIA BOND, A.B., Master of Arts,
CORTEZ R. CLAWSON, Ph.B., B. Litt., Bachelor of Arts.

SUMMARY.

Bachelor of Paedagogy, 29,
Bachelor of Commercial Science, 7,

Bachelor of Arts, 6,
Master of Arts, 2,
Bachelor of Philosophy, 1,
Bachelor of Science, 1,
Bachelor of Music, 1,

Total degrees granted 47.

TABLE SHOWING ATTENDANCE AND FINANCIAL RECEIPTS.

Year.	Number of Students.	Receipts from Tuition.	Receipts from Subscriptions.	Receipts from Memorial Board.[1]	Receipts from all Sources.
1889	54	$ 345 28			
89-90	160	1,038 66	$1,947 59[2]		$3,331 53[3]
90-91	140	2,051 72	675 70		2,772 42
91-92	131	1,059 79	2,297 27		3,357 06
92-93	151	2,023 39	2,567 89	$ 100 00	4,691 28
93-94	181	2,615 59	1,676 78	16 05	4,308 42
94-95	138	1,897 06	2,317 24		4,214 30
95-96	175	1,937 27	1,303 44	100 00	3,340 71
96-97	141	1,890 43	1,311 61	1,100 00	4,302 04
97-98	159	1,903 00	729 57	1,201 04	3,906 78
98-99	140	1,363 44	520 90	1,425 00	3,444 34
99-1900	140	1,395 38	855 00	1,739 04	5,235 42
00-01	163	1,769 74	370 15	2,151 11	5,115 35
01-02	139	1,559 80	228 78	2,020 20	3,972 28

1. Trustees of the Seventh Day Baptist Memorial Fund.
2. From the beginning of the enterprise, and includes cost of site of the college.
3. From the beginning of the enterprise.

XXVII.

SLAVERY.

OF the western Virginia churches, but one, the Lost Creek Church, contained any slave holders. Within the bounds of the New Salem Church lived a man who regarded himself, in so far as he was religiously inclined, as a Seventh Day Baptist. He never joined any church, but was an active and sympathetic trustee of the West Union Academy.[1] But so far as available records and traditions show, the Lost Creek Church was the only one of this group of Seventh Day Baptist churches which enrolled a slave holder among its membership.

Deacon Abel Bond of the Lost Creek Church married, in Maryland, a wife, whose uncle made her a present of a slave girl. This slave girl, on reaching womanhood, married against the wishes of Deacon Bond, but nevertheless with his permission. She raised a family of children, who, according to the laws of slave-holding states, were born into bondage. Deacon Bond offered to set the family free and to pay their expences to a free state, but they preferred to remain with him, as he was a kind master exercising only such authority over them as the laws of the state and of humanity demanded at his hands. Deacon Bond provided in his will that they should be freed as soon as circumstances should warrant, but soon after his death all the coloured family died but the mother and one son, who was not physically strong. Deacon Bond's

---

1. Samuel Preston F. Randolph.

son, into whose care they were committed at the death of his father, again offered them freedom, but they still chose to remain where they were.[1]

At the session of the Eastern Association held at Shiloh, New Jersey, May, 1856, the New Salem and Lost Creek churches, made application for admission to that body, and Rev. Samuel D. Davis appeared as a delegate from both of these churches. These applications were referred, as usual in such cases, to the committee on petitions, consisting of P. L. Perry, B. F. Langworthy, and Enoch J. Davis, who reported to the association in favour of admitting both churches. This recommendation called forth considerable discussion, chiefly by Alfred B. Burdick, Sherman S. Griswold, Charles M. Lewis, David Clawson, Samuel D. Davis, James Bailey, Walter B. Gillette, and Halsey H. Baker, the discussion relating chiefly to the relation of these churches to slavery. The New Salem Church was finally admitted by a unanimous vote, and the Lost Creek Church with but a single dissenting vote, that of Alfred B. Burdick.

The Pawcatuck Church now took up the matter inde-

---

1. "Black Manuel was the husband of Lottie, a black woman who lived and died in the Bond family on Elk Creek, at the place now known as Quiet Dell. Lottie and her husband were both members of the Seventh Day Baptist Church on Lost Creek. Manuel was the slave of Thomas Bond of Lost Creek, who though not a member of the church, was a nominal Sabbath-keeper. When Manuel was well stricken in years, his master sold the farm on which they lived to two members of the Lost Creek Church, Eli and Moses Van Horn, and sold Manuel to a man keeping First Day, who moved him to a farm further away from the church.

"Being dissatisfied with his new home, he appealed to the men who bought his old master's farm, to buy him also, and bring him back to the humble cottage he had occupied so many years, that he might live among his church brethren.

"This they did, and became the legal owners of a brother in the same church with themselves.

"But they did this, and thus became responsible for Manuel's conduct and future maintenance, not for sordid money's sake, for Manuel was not now able to earn wages, but that they might make comfortable and happy a beloved brother.

"It was my privilege to pay pastoral visits to all three of these brethren when on their dying beds, and I have no doubt that it will be said in the judgment to these last owners of Manuel, 'Inasmuch as ye have done it unto one of the least of these my brethren, ye have done it unto me.'

"Should the reader question why Manuel's brethren did not set him free, let it be remembered that such was the law of the state of Virginia, that a freed slave could not remain in it beyond a stated number of days, without being sold again into bondage."

The foregoing statement made by the Reverend Samuel D. Davis now of Jane Lew, West Virginia, formerly the pastor of the Lost Creek Church, was placed in the hands of the author of this book, after the manuscript of the book was completed, ready to go to press.

pendently, and appointed a committee to investigate the subject. The committee accordingly addressed the following letter to the Lost Creek Church:—

'To THE SEVENTH DAY BAPTIST CHURCH AT LOST CREEK:

"*Dear Brethren*:—

"The undersigned by appointment of the Pawcatuck Seventh Day Baptist Church, in Westerly, R. I., are instructed to write you for the purpose of obtaining your views of the system of American Slavery, and also to ascertain what apology you have to offer for permitting some of your members to hold human beings in bondage. It is with feelings of deep regret that we learn the fact that slave holding is tolerated by you as a church, & we assure you that it is with no other than Christian & fraternal feelings, and an earnest wish for the purity and upholding of our common cause, that we address you.

"We hope you will respond fully and explicitly to these points by letter at your earliest convenience, that we may know your views as a church on these subjects, & thereby greatly oblige

"Yours fraternally,
"E. G. CHAMPLIN,
"JONATHAN MAXSON,
"CHARLES POTTER, JR."

The reply of the Lost Creek Church was not satisfactory to the Pawcatuck Church, and at the next annual session of the Eastern Association held at New Market, New Jersey, in 1857, the Pawcatuck and Greenmanville churches of that association presented formal protest against the reception of the Lost Creek Church into the association. On the other hand, the Lost Creek Church, in its annual letter, complained of the insinuations which had been made against it. In the meantime the North-Western Association had taken the following action:—

"RESOLVED, That we deeply regret the reception of the Lost Creek Church by the Eastern Association, as a member, while slavery nestles in its bosom."

This resolution was also presented to the Eastern Association, which referred the whole matter to a special committee consisting of William B. Maxson, Thomas M. Clarke, and James Bailey. This committee presented a report, which, after discussion by William B. Maxson, James Bailey, Sherman S. Griswold, George B. Utter, Lucius Crandall, Samuel D. Davis, Halsey H. Baker, and Alfred B. Burdick, was amended to read as follows:—

"The committee to whom was referred the letters of the Pawcatuck and Greenmanville churches relative to the reception of the Lost Creek Church into the association, and also the letter of the Lost Creek Church relative to the action of the North-Western Association upon the same subject, respectfully report: That they have had these letters under consideration, and have investigated the subject to which they refer, as far as time would allow. They find the facts in regard to the existence, real or supposed, of slavery in the Lost Creek Church, to be as follows: A member of the Lost Creek Church, who died several years ago, was the legal owner of two coloured persons—one a woman about sixty years of age, who had been a member of his family from childhood, and the other a son of the old woman, of feeble constitution, aged about twenty-five years. These coloured persons the deceased brother left by will to his heirs, with an injunction to take good care of them, and set them free when circumstances should favour. In the appraisement of the estate of the deceased, these persons were not considered as property, and no price was placed upon them. They now remain in the family of one of the heirs, who is a member of the church, and are technically slaves in the eye of the law, which requires that every coloured person shall either have a nominal master, or shall leave the state. The brother with whom they live has offered them their freedom; but they decline to accept it. He has also given public assurance of his willingness to set them free, and pay their expenses to a free state, if any resident in such a state will agree to take the guardianship of them; but no one has yet come forward to take that position. In these circumstances, the brother in question considers it his duty to allow the coloured persons to remain with him, subject to the regulations imposed by the laws of the state in which he lives.

"Having found such to be the facts in the case, and desiring to ascertain the views of the Lost Creek Church upon the subject of slavery, the committee propounded to Bro. Davis, the delegate from that church, four questions, which were answered as follows:—

"*1st.* Does your church have or hold any sympathy, in any sense, with American Slavery? Ans. It does not.

"*2nd.* Does the church hold that American Slavery ought to be abolished, as a sin against God and man? Ans. It does.

"*3rd.* In what sense, if not as slaves, are those persons, understood by some as such, held by a member or members of your church? Ans. If held at all, it is to shield them from the action of the laws of the state that would otherwise enslave them.

"*4th.* What would the church do with a member who should buy or sell or hold a person as property? Ans. It would exclude him.

"The committee also found, that the Lost Creek Church, by its delegates, adopted the following resolution, at an association held in Ritchie County, Va., Sept. 1854: 'That we regard American Slavery as a sin of great magnitude in the sight of God, and a flagrant violation of the rights of our fellow men, and that it is our duty to use all of our influence against it.'

"From these and other facts before them, the committee came to the following conclusions:—

"*1st.* That the relation of master and slave does not exist in the Lost Creek Church, in the proper sense of the phrase, and only technically, and that the church is not justly chargeable with sustaining slavery.

"*2nd.* That we deeply regret the acrimonious spirit, and the personal reflections and accusations, made against brethren, in the discussion had upon the subject in the denominational paper.

"*3rd.* With regard to the resolution of the North-Western Association, we think the language used is stronger than the facts warrant, and that the regret expressed by that association results from the manner in which the subject has been discussed, more than from the existence of slavery itself.

"W. B. MAXSON,
"J. BAILEY."

The minority report of the committee was as follows:—

"The minority of your committee begs leave to report, that in view of the technical and legal relations of the Lost Creek Church to American Slavery, he is unable to concur in the majority report of said committee; holding himself morally and religiously bound to sustain no relation to that institution but that of opposition as an essential evil.

"THOMAS M. CLARKE."

When these reports came up for action, they were laid upon the table. Several efforts were then made by various individuals to present something acceptable to the association for its favourable action, and the following preamble and resolution offered by Joseph W. Morton were adopted:—

"*Whereas,* Elder S. D. Davis, delegate of the Lost Creek Church to this association, has, in reply to certain questions proposed to him by a special committee of this body, assured us that that church considers American Slavery as a sin against God and man; that they would withdraw the hand of fellowship from any brother or sister who would hold a human being as a slave; and that no member of that church is known to him, who does actually hold any person as a slave, or claim any legal or other right to do so; therefore,

"RESOLVED, That we have entire confidence in the integrity of our brother Davis and fully believe that his statements are in perfect accordance with the facts as he understands them.

"RESOLVED, That we rejoice to hear that this, our younger sister, is heart and hand with us in opposition to the great crime of

American Slavery; and we bid her God-speed in her efforts to undo the heavy burdens of the bondman, as in every other good work.

"*Yet,* Inasmuch as many of our brethren desire to have in writing, from that church, a formal and authoritative statement of her sentiments and practise in relation to human slavery, that it may be spread out upon our records, as her testimony to all who may succeed us, therefore,

"RESOLVED, That the Lost Creek Church be respectfully requested, through the clerk of this association, to favour us with an official answer in writing, to the questions which have been so satisfactorily answered, verbally and unofficially, by her delegate.

"RESOLVED, That we earnestly entreat that all those of our brethren who may have felt aggrieved by any unpleasant remarks on this subject, either in private conversation, public debate, or written correspondence, to forgive and forget the same, and cultivate a spirit of mutual kindness and Christian confidence."

In accordance with the foregoing action, the corresponding secretary of the association, Rev. James Bailey, wrote the Lost Creek Church requesting the information desired by the association. His letter called forth the following reply:—

"Copy of a communication written and forwarded agreeable to Church order, made June 12th, 1857.

"DEAR BROTHER:—

"Your official letter of June 3d, sent under instructions of the Eastern Association, requesting of the Lost Creek Church official answers in writing to certain questions heretofore answered by the delegate of that church, was received in due time. You say we 'will see from the minutes of the meeting how the whole matter stands.' We have seen no minutes, except what is given in the *Recorder,* 28th May.

"This we suppose, however, contains the principal matter. The church, at a regular business meeting, held June 12, 1857, after fully deliberating upon the case as shown in that paper and prints elsewhere, together with all the attendant circumstances and bearings, came to the conclusion that it was not duty to fill the request, and I was instructed, at the same meeting, to inform you of this decision of the church and communicate to you some of the reasons why we decline answering. There are various considerations why the church thinks it not proper to answer the questions propounded, some of which we now proceed to notice.

"You say in your letter that "the statement of our delegate was satisfactory to most of the members of the association, but in a matter involving so much as the question of freedom and bondage, it is proper to have the official statement of the church.' Here, we ask, Is freedom jeopardised in our Church? Is a spirit and feeling for bondage shown there? Do the facts justify such a conclusion? Is what has been said by us to the contrary, time after time, repeated again and again by our delegate and through the press, over and over almost continually, for more than a year, all to go for nothing? If suspicion and incredulity are really so deeply rooted in the minds of brethren as to doubt the truth of all they have heretofore heard from us on this subject, it is not likely that anything we might say now would erase that distrust. This view alone of the subject might justify a refusal to answer, but there are other and perhaps more weighty reasons.

"It does seem to us that the act of propounding these questions is uncalled for, unequal, illegal, and imposing. Uncalled for, because the questions have been answered, all needful information on the subject has heretofore been abundantly given. Unequal, because no other church is thus interrogated about slavery or any other evil, although many gross ones exist and are more universal than slavery.

"A forward character in the association wrote thus in the *Recorder*, April 30th:— 'I believe war to be as great an evil and far more criminal than either rum-selling or slavery, and if either reform is most important, it is that of peace.'

"Here we have the published sentiment of one who stands apparently among the most officious members of our own body. He ranks war, rum-selling, and slavery somewhat together, but says decidedly that war is far the most criminal. Others of the body, all, for aught we know, may entertain the same views of the comparative magnitude of these evils, all of which are common. Now, although war, rum-selling, and many other great evils are prevalent, as must be admitted by all, yet of eighteen churches comprised in the body, one alone is singled out, and of the very many prominent evils, one only is inquired after. With a knowledge of all these facts, who can fail to see that inequality is practised?

"The second article of the constitution says 'The object of this association shall be to promote the piety, order, and increase of the churches belonging to it and the cause of our Lord Jesus Christ generally in the world.' This is as it should be. The letter of our covenant is right, intended doubtless to bear equally upon every church, for the good of the whole, but the present movement deviates from the rule laid down. It gives the appearance of partiality and is manifestly at variance with both the letter and spirit of the compact. Here the act is illegal. This will still be more fully seen by a little further examination.

"'What would the church do with a member who would buy or sell or hold a person as property?' is one interrogation put to us.

"Now, the thirteenth article of the constitution expressly forbids the exercise of ecclesiastical jurisdiction over the churches leaving each to 'manage its own concerns of all matters of discipline without being amenable to any other body.' This clause of the law of the body shows at once that it is illegal to press such questions as the one above quoted, this association having no province even over acts of church discipline past, much less a right to reach ahead after what perchance may be in the future.

"Was not such an act forbidden by covenant agreement? There is rather too strong a spirit and principle of aristocracy betrayed in it to be tolerated by a free people, especially the Christian church. The voice of inspiration cautions against 'being lords over God's heritage.'

"We now notice something of the imposing feature of the act of pressing these questions upon us. As before mentioned, it is admitted that the statements of our representative were satisfactory to most of the members of the association. This we fully believe (for enough has been said by the delegates and others, as may be seen by tracing the history of the matter) to satisfy every reasonable inquirer and we are glad to say that we are persuaded that reasonableness characterises a large majority of our brethren in the association. Much has come to our knowledge to raise and confirm this belief. For all these many sympathising brethren, we do now, and hope we ever shall entertain deep sentiments of kind Christian affection, though forced to a non-compliance of a resolution passed under their notice. Perhaps all did not sanction it. We trust they did not.

"Is this catechising system adopted and carried through in a consistent manner bearing equal on every church as it should? The church at Lost Creek and the sin of slavery is not all that is to be noticed. The association has much more to do. First inquire of this, that, and the other church; does it 'have or hold any sympathy in any sense with Sabbath breakers, profane swearers, those who go to 'war, rum-sellers,' high-way robbers, and so continue on until each church in the body is separately interrogated. Then again inquiring of each branch separately what it would 'do with a member' who was guilty of this, that, or the other sin, following on until every church and the whole catalogue of misdemeanors are gone over. In short, adopting the system, we enter a laborious uphill road, crossing the laws by which we profess to be governed, beating strongly toward usurpation and tyranny. The act of putting these questions is not only an encroachment upon liberties guaranteed, but imposing, because it gives the appearance of distrust of the truth of much that many have said before, amounting virtually and very near directly to a high impeachment upon the veracity of our representative, on whose feelings and reputation we place far too high an estimate to countenance or give strength to such a censure by answering the questions.

"We have, as a church, voted him our thanks for his services in attending the meetings of the association and an approval of his course as delegate, and although we may stand ever so ready to give the desired answers full and clear when justice and propriety demand, yet to answer now, under existing circumstances, would be an open foreseen act of ingratitude, to which it would be cruel to descend.

"These are some of the considerations that brought us to the conclusion that it is not duty to fill the request.

"Was it proper to extend such inquiries and that we should be disposed to answer them?

"We see no probability of good resulting, unless perhaps it might be a slight gratification to a few ultra-abolitionists, whose prejudices we suppose are so deeply set, that they perhaps will never know when they have said and done enough to defame and oppress southern dwellers, and such a good or gratification we think will have no tendency to promote the true interest of our Lord Jesus Christ, in the world, which agreeable to our profession, should be the prime motive of our lives and labour. To this duty we are solemnly bound by the social compact into which we have entered, as is explicitly stated in the constitution of the body. No self gratification or other sinister motive should be indulged in, most certainly not at the expense of the feelings and reputation of others.

"More might be added in justification of the position we take, but enough is said, perhaps, to give some idea of our views and feelings.

"We therefore leave this point with the brethren of the association, to be disposed of as their pleasure may dictate, and pass (as painful as the thought may be) to the subject of separation. While, as in the present case, sundering covenant relations is frequently a source of grief and tears, yet it is sometimes the most prudent course. How can any body of people walk together, with pleasure or profit, when peace and union are broken up by convulsions of useless strife and discord? A house divided against itself cannot stand. Was our church located in a more northern clime disclaiming, as we do, sentiments and practise of slavery, we think present difficulties might not have been raised. Existing facts lead us to this conclusion. We are slow to believe that it is the condition of the two coloured people with Brother Bond, that causes these ruptures, for it is well known that a remedy of any supposed wrong existing there has long since been spread out ready to the hands of any and every benevolent friend to change, at Brother Bond's expence, the condition of these people at their pleasure and that of their friends, if it can be done for the better; but great as the sound of sympathy and charity from the north for Mother Charlotte and her son has been, it all proves cold as winter in the region from whence it comes. Though the way is opened and made easy, no benefactor appears, leaving us to conclude that it is not the condition of these people, but a local dislike, a sectional prejudice, that keeps up dissatisfaction, which, though we believe it dwells in the bosoms of but few (perhaps very few) yet we have no disposition to contend further with the prejudices of these men, believing it would be fruitless, as well as unpleasant to do so.

"We therefore withdraw, that we no longer be a party in war among covenant brethren. The contest proves not only unpleasant and fruitless, but sadly disastrous; all this too with little or no visible cause, more certainly without any good reason; nothing new or more unfavourable as to the real facts in the case has come to light since our reception, yet variance and division enlarges. When we entered the compact, one individual alone raised the dissenting voice. Since that, a number of brethren, two churches, and one other association at least have raised the denouncing cry in high and degrading tones through the columns of our denominational organ, evincing to the world that neither gospel duty, weighty and sacred as it is, nor christian covenant, however solemn and binding, prevents brethren among us from defaming one another in the most public manner. Moreover, our own association, at its recent session, not only virtually refused to rebuke these things or give us redress in any form, but have shaped matters still more unfavourable by refusing to adopt the majority report of her own select committee, prepared for the purpose of alleviating the matter, and by an over-act adopted another in its stead, urging imposing superfluous duties upon us, such as are not required of any other church.

"Under this state of things, Christian sociability and fellowship is broken. Our usefulness to each other and to the cause as co-workers, paralysed if not destroyed. By the union, our hearts were lifted with the hope that by the blessing of our heavenly Father, we might labour together much for the edification and mutual benefit of each other as well as for the furtherance of our common cause in the world; but alas, these anticipations, bright and promising as they were, soon began to darken and now close in sad disappointment. Isolated, weak, and destitute as we are, we choose rather to retire than remain where prevailing contention wounds the feelings and reproaches the cause. The time and labour of our minister is too much appreciated, his feelings too much regarded, for us any longer to spend money in sending him away to meet with those whose manner of reception have already pierced his heart, as well as others with deep sorrows, unmerited affliction, as well as sad disappointment.

"Under the weight of the foregoing considerations, the church, June 12, 1857, resolved to request a release from the association, desiring no longer to be a member thereof. You will please, therefore, lay this communication before the association at the earliest opportunity. No further delegation or correspondence as an acting member of that body need be expected.

"Although thus withdrawing from the association, we feel under high and lasting obligations to many of its members, and desire cordially to tender to such churches and brethren as have favoured us with their friendship (and we believe they are many), expressions of deep and heartfelt gratitude for their kindness and brother-like deportment toward us.

"Written and forwarded agreeable to church order.

"WILLIAM F. RANDOLPH, *Special Committee*,
"To JAMES BAILEY, *Corresponding Secretary*,
"*of the Eastern Association.*"

The reply of the Lost Creek Church was received by the association at its annual meeting with the First Hopkinton Church in May, 1858, and was referred to a special committee consisting of Joseph Potter, William B. Maxson, and Walter B. Gillette.

The report of the special committee was as follows:—

"The special committee to whom was referred a letter from the Lost Creek Church, Va., stating that said church had voted to withdraw from the association, respectfully report, that they have duly considered the question, and recommend that the association take no other action upon the subject than to adopt the following preamble and resolution:—

"*Whereas*, The church at Lost Creek, Va., has given notice of its vote to withdraw from the association; and,

"*Whereas*, The letter from that church containing such notice, leads us to conclude that their withdrawal is based mainly upon a supposition that the association discredited the statements made last year by their delegate and that there was something inquisitional in the resolution adopted by the association, requesting from the church a formal and authenticated statement of her sentiments and practise in relation to human slavery; therefore,

"RESOLVED, That we hereby disclaim any intention in the resolution adopted last year, either to discredit the statements made by the delegate of the Lost Creek Church (which statement he informed us was not official), or to catechise that church discourteously or unnecessarily, assuring them that our only intention was to obtain from them such official information as seemed to us necessary in view of what had been written and spoken on the subject to remove the impression that was upon some minds, that the spirit of slavery existed in that church."

This report was discussed at length, and after an unsuccessful effort to have a substitute for it adopted, the whole matter was referred back to the special committee, and George B. Utter and William C. Whitford added to the committee. The committee re-presented its original report, which was adopted.

The New Salem Church, it should be observed, took no formal part in this controversy with the Eastern Association, of which it will be remembered the New Salem Church was a member also, although that church had joined with the Lost Creek Church in sending Rev. Samuel D. Davis as a delegate for two consecutive years to the annual sessions of the Eastern Association held at Shiloh and New Market, New Jersey.

It was perfectly clear, however, that the New Salem Church strongly sympathised with her sister church in what they both regarded as persecution of the latter, concerning slavery. From the date of the final action of the Eastern Association upon the withdrawal of the Lost Creek Church, the New Salem Church maintained an attitude of dignified silence as a member of that association, for a period of nine years, or until the year 1867, after the Civil War had been closed and slavery forever banished from American soil.

But the feeling engendered by so bitter and so intense a controversy could not die out all at once, and it was not until the occasion of the visit of Rev. Sherman S. Griswold at Lost Creek in May, 1881, that it was made entirely clear that peace and harmony were wholly restored, and that the slavery question among Seventh Day Baptists had become wholly a thing of the past. So far as records accessible at the present time show, not more than two members of the Seventh Day Baptist churches of western Virginia took up arms against the Government of the United States in behalf of slavery. With these exceptions the Union was upheld and loyally supported by the entire membership of all these churches.

Situated as they were on the very border line between the north and the south, where political feelings, always intense, were many fold so at that time, it was but natural that any and all persons not definitely known to have voted for the successful candidate for the presidency of the United States in the campaign of 1860, should be regarded with doubt, and many were arrested upon suspicion and confined in the county jails or carried away to Camp Chase or other government prisons. On one occasion, a posse of officers called at midnight at the home of the loyal clerk of the New Salem Church for the ostensible purpose of arresting him and taking him away to prison as a suspicious character. To their disgust, they found him at the Township Hall, performing his duty as a loyal citizen of the United States in helping to conduct a federal election, whose returns must be made out before the commissioners of the election were permitted to leave their post of duty for sleep. The churches of this association were all represented in the Federal Army.

BIOGRAPHICAL SKETCHES.

REV. JOHN DAVIS.

Rev. John Davis was the son of William Davis, whose biography appears in the first chapter of this book. He was born in or near Philadelphia, in the year 1692. Probably about the year 1710, he accompanied his parents to Westerly, Rhode Island, where he was baptized May 25, 1713, by his father, and admitted to membership in the Westerly Church on the 22d of the following June.

In the year 1715, he was married to Elisabeth Clarke, the daughter of Joseph Clarke, Jr.

On November 9, 1743, the Westerly Church called him to ordination as a Gospel minister, but he declined to accept ordination.

Soon afterward, he removed to Shrewsbury, New Jersey, in company with his father, and other members of the family.

On June 19, 1746, the Shrewsbury Church, of which he was a constituent member, called him to ordination, and arrangements were made at once to send him to Westerly to be ordained. Accordingly, five days afterward, taking a letter written by Joseph Maxson in behalf of the Shrewsbury Church, to the church at Westerly, making known the wishes of the former church, he set sail for Westerly, where he arrived safely after a week's voyage. Here the letter was read to the Westerly Church at the Sabbath service on July 12. The Westerly Church at once voted to grant the request, and on the afternoon of the following day, he was ordained. The ordination service was conducted by Rev. Joseph Maxson, assisted by Rev. John Maxson and Deacon Clarke.

He returned to Shrewsbury, but after serving the church about eight years as its pastor, he died at Manasquan, in the town of Shrewsbury, August 18, 1854.

REV. JACOB DAVIS.

REV. JACOB DAVIS, a son of James Davis, a grandson of Rev. William Davis, and a nephew of Rev. John Davis, was born at Shrewsbury, New Jersey, in 1748.

He was baptized and received into the Shrewsbury Church, by Rev. Jonathan Jarman, in the year 1772; and was afterward licenced to preach. On the 19th of June, 1774, the church gave him a formal call to ordination. The ordination service, which was conducted at the home of Thomas Babcock, by Rev. Jonathan Dunham and Rev. Jonathan Jarman, probably took place on February 27, 1775.[1]

The War of the Revolution claimed him as a chaplain, but he obtained frequent furloughs, and came home to minister to the wants of his flock. It was under his leadership that the church erected its first house of worship amid the perils and hardships of war, and it was to him that the deed for the church lot was entrusted for safe keeping.

When the Shrewsbury Church emigrated to western Virginia in 1789, he accompanied it to its new home, and amid all the vicissitudes and hardships of life in a wilderness, he never faltered in the path of duty. Often with his pack upon his back, amid constant danger from the Indians, he travelled on foot from New Salem to the West Fork River, thence on to White Day Creek, and finally to the Woodbridgetown Church in Fayette County, Pennsylvania. It was upon one of these journeys in July, 1793, that he was taken sick at Woodbridgetown, and died on the 17th of that month. He lies in an unnamed grave at Woodbridgetown.

His wife was Mary Davis, a daughter of William Davis, who in turn was the son of Rev. John Davis, the son of Rev. William Davis, the founder of the Shrewsbury Church.

To Jacob and Mary Davis were born the following children (order uncertain):— Jacob, Zebulon, Samuel, Crandall, Mary (Polly), Lydia, and Elisabeth.

There are reasons for believing that Jacob Davis studied at Brown University.

REV. JOHN DAVIS, 2D.

REV. JOHN DAVIS, 2D, was born May 1, 1754, in Shrewsbury, Monmouth County, New Jersey. He was the son of

---
1. *Vid.* pp. 18-19 *supra*.

William Davis, who was the son of Rev. John Davis, who, in turn, was the son of Rev. William Davis, the founder of the Shrewsbury Church.

John Davis, the subject of this sketch, was a brother of Mary Davis, wife of Rev. Jacob Davis, preceding.

He was elected a ruling elder in the New Salem Church, on November 16, 1799. On the same date the church licenced him to preach, and also voted that he should be ordained. Arrangements were made for the ordination service to take place on the 8th of the succeeding June, but owing to the absence of ministers who were expected to be present, the service was postponed. It took place, however, at some time between January 11 and May 10 of the following year, and was conducted by Rev. Samuel Woodbridge of the Woodbridgetown (Pennsylvania) Church, and Rev. John Patterson.

At once he began service for the New Salem Church as its pastor; and from the date of the organisation of the Lost Creek Church, in 1805, he was pastor of that church also.

With the exception of a short period about the year 1811, when, for a short time, he removed to the state of Ohio, where he was a member of the Mad River Church, he ministered to the wants of both the New Salem and Lost Creek Churches, until his death, which occurred June 22, 1842, in the eighty-ninth year of his age. He was buried in the graveyard on Broad Run, about two miles west of Jane Lew, in Lewis County, Virginia.

He established his home on the Brushy Fork of Elk Creek, some ten miles distant from the Lost Creek Church. He sustained an intimate relationship with the Baptists on Brushy Fork, as well as on Broad Run.

Abram VanHorn, Sr., a native of Holland, came from the vicinity of the Woodbridgetown Church, in Pennsylvania, and settled near the home of Rev. John Davis, on Brushy Fork. The former had a family of five children,—three sons and two daughters. Through the influence of Rev. John Davis, the oldest son of Abram VanHorn, Sr., Job, as well as several of his (Job's) family embraced the Sabbath, as follows:— His son-in-law, James Kennedy; his son William, who was married; his son Abram, Jr., who was unmarried; his daughter Abby, who married Abner Batten, afterward a deacon in the Lost

Creek Church; and Betsey (Elisabeth), who married Moses Hoffman, for several years clerk of the Lost Creek Church. Abram VanHorn, Sr., who was at first sadly disappointed at the course of his son and grandchildren, at length became reconciled to what they had done, and finally embraced the Sabbath himself.[1]

Rev. John Davis was a soldier in the War of the Revolution, and drew a pension for that service. For several years previous to his death, he was too enfeebled physically and mentally to preach. At the time of his death he was the oldest minister among the Seventh Day Baptists.

Some of his children were as follows:— Rev. Lewis A. Davis; Sarah, wife of Jacob Davis, 3d, and grandmother of Rev. Lewis A. Platts; Amy, wife of George Davis, and grandmother of Rev. Darius K. Davis, the son of Eliona Davis; Zippa, wife of Samuel F. Randolph, the son of Jesse F. Randolph; Mary (Polly), wife of William F. Randolph, and mother of Rev. Lewis F. Randolph, and grandmother of Rev. William L. Burdick.[2]

REV. LEWIS A. DAVIS.

REV. LEWIS A. DAVIS, a lineal descendant in the fifth generation, of William Davis, the founder of the Shrewsbury Church, was a son of Rev. John Davis, 2d, in this line, and was born in western Virginia, August 20, 1801.

When he was about eighteen years of age, he was baptized and became a member of the New Salem Church.

In his twentieth year, he visited the Seventh Day Baptist churches in New Jersey, Connecticut, and Rhode Island, and attended the annual session of the General Conference at Hopkinton, Rhode Island. He then visited Ohio, and pursued private studies for a short time under the tuition of a clergyman, whom he paid with a half month's labour. He was soon obliged to abandon his studies, however, when he returned to Virginia.

On February 18, 1821, he was granted licence to preach, and on January 15, 1824, he was ordained a Gospel minister.

---

1. For this information relating to Abram VanHorn, Sr., and his son Job and family, the author is indebted to Rev. Richard C. Bond.
2. For information relating to the children of Rev. John Davis, the author is indebted to Rev. Boothe C. Davis, and his father, Rev. Samuel D. Davis.

REV. LEWIS A. DAVIS.

The ordination service was conducted by Rev. John Green, assisted by Rev. John Davis and Rev. Peter Davis.

For some time, he engaged in general missionary labour in Virginia, Pennsylvania, Ohio, and Indiana, travelling from place to place on horseback.

Having decided to remove to Ohio for his home, a committee of the Lost Creek Church followed him after he had started, and induced him to return. He remained nearly a year longer in Virginia. He finally decided, however, to make his home in Ohio, and on August 16, 1833, the New Salem Church granted him and his wife, Rebecca, letters of dismissal to join the Pike Church of Ohio.

He soon devoted his entire time to the work of the ministry. To provide himself and his family with the means of sustenance, he sold his farm. When the proceeds of his farm were exhausted, he turned his attention to the study of medicine. After the necessary preparation, he practised medicine for a living, but continued to preach at the same time, achieving success in both professions.

His health failed, and he was obliged to relinquish his work for an imperative rest. After a vacation of a year or two, he resumed his professional duties.

After a term of service at Jackson Centre, Ohio, and then at Farmington, Illinois, he finally removed to Welton, Iowa, where he died October 12, 1867.

His ministerial activities extended over a period of forty-five years. Two weeks before his death, he concluded a series of sermons on the Lord's Prayer.

He compiled a volume of sacred hymns, which he called the *Sacred Lyre*.

REV. PETER DAVIS.

REV. PETER DAVIS was born in Shrewsbury, New Jersey, September 16, 1783, and was, consequently, about six years of age when he accompanied his parents in the emigration of the Shrewsbury Church to western Virginia.

He was a lineal descendant of Rev. William Davis, the founder of the Shrewsbury Church. His father was William Davis, known in Virginia as "Greenbrier Billy" to distinguish him from the several other William Davises, among whom were, "Jarsey Billy," "Bottom Billy," "Flint Billy," "Rock

Run Billy," *et al.* His mother was Elisabeth Johnson, a daughter, probably, of Elisha Johnson and Amy Davis, who were married in Monmouth County, New Jersey, October 28, 1755.

"Greenbrier Billy" was a cousin of "Jarsey Billy," whose first wife was a sister of Elisabeth Johnson, the wife of "Greenbrier Billy." His ("Jarsey Billy's") second wife was the widowed mother of Joseph Jeffrey, a prominent member of the Middle Island Church in the first period of its history.

"Jarsey Billy" was a brother of Captain Nathan Davis, a soldier of the War of 1812, on whose lands the present village of West Union in Doddridge County, West Virginia, was laid out.

"Jarsey Billy" and Captain Nathan Davis were sons of Nathan Davis, who was born May 9, 1740, and Anna Gifford, born January 7, 1742. They were married January 19, 1761.

Nathan Davis (born May 9, 1740) was, in turn, the son of William Davis, who was the son of Rev. John Davis of the Shrewsbury Church, who, in his turn, was the son of Rev. William Davis, the founder of that church.[1]

So that, doubtless, "Greenbrier Billy," the father of Rev. Peter Davis, was the grandson of William Davis, the son of Rev. John Davis, of the Shrewsbury Church.

Rev. Peter Davis, who was a soldier in the War of 1812, became a member of the New Salem Church, probably, on August 16, 1807; certainly, at some time previous to December 28, 1815. On June 19, 1819, he was chosen a deacon in the New Salem Church. He was licenced to preach November 21, 1819, and ordained a minister of the Gospel in December, 1823, at Middle Island (Lewisport), by Rev. John Greene, assisted by Rev. John Davis.

He at once engaged in pastoral labour in the New Salem Church, along with Rev. John Davis.

The soundness of his theological views was called in question at different times during his ministry. In 1825, his doctrine of the immortality of man excited some fears, which were soon shown be groundless. In 1834, his attitude toward church government, particularly toward open communion, was at variance with the views of a large number of the church.

---

1. From MSS. in possession of Lewis Townsend Davis, Esq., of West Union, West Virginia.

Again, at a period late in his active ministry, he startled the church by declaring that the purpose of the Lord's Supper had been fulfilled, and that it had passed away.

His life was replete with faithful, conscientious service. From his home at the head of Greenbrier Run, he was accustomed to walk to New Salem on Sabbath mornings to preach. On these walks, he was accompanied, frequently, by members of the church, whose homes were on the road to New Salem.

Reared amid privation and adversity, his life and character were naturally colored by his environment, and his career as a soldier added a modicum of influence. But his tender heart was as big and loyal, as he was rugged and uncompromising.

Although the Greenbrier Church was organised in 1870, he retained his membership in the New Salem Church to the end of his life.

His wife, Sarah, died January 24, 1868; and he, an invalid, partly blind, during the last years of his life was tenderly cared for by his dutiful daughter, Jemima, the wife of Rev. Jacob Davis. On the 4th of March, 1873, he passed to his eternal reward at the ripe age of eighty-nine years, five months, and sixteen days.

REV. JAMES BALL DAVIS.[1]

REV. JAMES BALL DAVIS, son of Jacob and Prudence (Maxson) Davis, was born in what is now Lewis County, West Virginia, October 1, 1814.

When he was about fifteen months old his mother died, and at the age of twelve years, he was left without a father. After the death of his father, he remained on the farm with his stepmother until he was in his seventeenth year, when he went to the state of Ohio.

He was married, May 17, 1833, to Jane Hopping. To them were born eight children, six of whom lived to reach adult life.

At the age of seventeen, soon after going to Ohio, he became a member of one of the Seventh Day Baptist churches there. In 1840, the Pike Church, of which he was a member, granted him licence to preach, and sent him as a delegate

---

1. The author is indebted to Mrs. George H. Trainor of New Salem, West Virginia, for material aid in the preparation of this sketch.

to the annual meeting of the South-Western Association, which met that year with the church at New Salem, Virginia. While in attendance at the association, he preached his first sermon as an accredited minister of the Gospel, at an evening service, held at the home of John Sutton, on Greenbrier Run.

In 1843, with some five other ministers, he organised a preaching circuit extending from Northhampton to the "Yankee Street" Seventh Day Baptist Church on the Sciota River, covering a distance of seventy-five miles, with eleven preaching stations, requiring four weeks for the trip. These six men took turns in covering this route, and gave their services free of charge.

His wife died in 1853, and his own health failing, he gave up preaching temporarily, and returned to Virginia, where he was married in 1854 to Emily Virginia Davis, daughter of William F. and Rachel (Hughes) Davis. He then returned to Ohio and resumed his labours as a minister.

In the summer of 1857, he removed with his family to western Virginia, and settled at New Milton, in Doddridge County. He and his wife joined the New Salem Church, but upon the re-organisation of the Middle Island Church, in 1866, he became a member of that church, by which he was at once licenced to preach. On March 1, 1867, the church called him to ordination; and in compliance with a request of the church, a council composed of delegates from the New Salem, Lost Creek, and Middle Island churches met with the Middle Island Church on September 5, 1867. The council recommended his ordination. Accordingly, early in the year 1868, he was ordained, Rev. Samuel D. Davis conducting the ordination service, assisted by Rev. Jacob Davis.

At various times he was formally invited by the Middle Island Church to serve as its pastor, but without waiting for such action, he preached with great regularity for the church, once a month, from the time of its re-organisation for a period of twenty years or more. The interests of the church he placed above everything else, and his hand was its ruling influence throughout this period.

Upon the organisation of the Ritchie Church in 1870, he was invited to become its pastor. But as the church was thirty

HOME OF REV. JAMES B. DAVIS, NEAR NEW MILTON.
(After a photograph taken in 1882).

miles away from his home, and his pastoral duties there placed him at a great disadvantage, for that reason he resigned the charge at the end of one year.

He established and maintained a preaching station on the Bear Fork of Cove Creek, where through his influence, a church was organised in 1881.

Compelled to maintain his family by labour upon his farm, and at his trade as a wagon-maker, he, nevertheless, made the most clear-cut personal impress upon the Middle Island Church, of any one man upon any one of the existing churches of the South-Eastern Association.

In 1889, he removed from his home near New Milton to Salem, and again united with the New Salem Church. Here he passed the remaining years of his life in restful peace. Although his activity in church work ceased about this time, he maintained the same deep interest that characterised his life, to the end.

He died at Salem, July 2, 1902, at the ripe age of eighty-nine years, nine months, and one day.

REV. SAMUEL DAVIS DAVIS.[1]

REV. SAMUEL DAVIS DAVIS was born at what is now Jane Lew, West Virginia, July 6, 1824.

He was the son of Jacob Davis, 2d, and Sarah (Hoffman) Davis. His great-great-grandfather was Rev. William Davis, the Welshman who founded the Shrewsbury Church. Rev. William Davis's sixth son, James, was the father of Rev. Jacob Davis, who was the father of Jacob Davis, 2d, who was the father of Rev. Samuel Davis Davis.

Rev. Samuel D. Davis was baptized by Rev. Peter Davis in March, 1837, and soon afterward, was received into membership in the Lost Creek Church, by Rev. Stillman Coon, who was engaged in missionary labour in western Virginia at that time.

His father died when he was but three and a half years old, and at an early age he became the mainstay of his widowed mother and four orphan sisters. His boyhood and early manhood were filled with poverty, hardship, and toil.

---

1. For much of the material for this biography, as well as those of Rev. John, 1st, Rev. John Davis, 2d, and Rev. Jacob Davis, 1st, the author is indebted to Rev. Boothe C. Davis, President of Alfred University.

In the year 1841, at the age of seventeen years, he was licenced by the Lost Creek Church to preach "within the bounds of the church," and was appointed to preach one Sabbath in each month for the church. This licence was renewed from year to year, until in 1840, when, under date of September 11, he was given a formal certificate of licence to preach, signed by the clerk of the church, and renewed from year to year as follows:—

"*This is to certify, to all whom it may concern,* That SAMUEL D. DAVIS is a member in good standing in the Seventh Day Baptist Church on Lost Creek, Harrison County, and State of Virginia; and as such, we do licence and authorise him to preach the Gospel for one year, wherever a door of usefulness may be opened.

"Done by order of the Church, this the 11th day of September, 1846.

"THOS. B. BOND, *Cl'k.*"

"*This is to certify,* That the Lost Creek Church has extended the licence of BRO. SAML. DAVIS to preach the Gospel one year.

"Sept. 10th, 1847.

"Done by order of the Church.

"THOS. B. BOND, *Cl'k.*"

"*This is to certify,* That the Lost Creek Church has extended the licence of BRO. SAMUEL D. DAVIS to preach the Gospel one year.

"Done by order of the Church, this the 8th day of September, 1848.

"JACOB DAVIS, *Clerk.*"

"*This is to certify,* That this licence is continued.

"Done by order of the Church, this the 7th day of September, 1849.

"JACOB DAVIS, *Clerk.*"

At a meeting of the church held on September 7, 1849, he was requested to take his ordination into consideration. This he was reluctant to do. Nevertheless, at the annual meeting of the South-Western Association, held with the church at Lost Creek, in the following October, the church asked that he be ordained. Rev. Peter Davis was the only ordained minister present, however, and his physical condition was such that on the second day of the session, he was compelled to resign his office as presiding officer of the association and consequently did not feel equal to the task of conducting an ordination service. Accordingly, the ordination was postponed.

On the 27th of the following January, the church

REV. BOOTHE COLWELL DAVIS, D. D., PRESIDENT OF ALFRED UNIVERSITY.

instructed Rev. Azor Estee, who was engaged in pastoral labour with the Lost Creek and New Salem churches, to make the necessary arrangements for the ordination.

Th ordination took place on May 11, succeeding, when Samuel D. Davis was solemnly set apart to the sacred duties of the office to which he had been called, at a service conducted by Rev. Azor Estee and Rev. Peter Davis, at Lost Creek. The certificate of ordination is as follows:—

"*To all whom it may concern*:—

"This may certify that our beloved brother SAMUEL D. DAVIS, of the Seventh Day Baptist Church of Lost Creek, Va., was solemnly set apart and ordained to the work of the Gospel Ministry, by prayer and the imposition of our hands at Lost Creek, Harrison County, Va., on the eleventh day of May, in the year of our Lord, one thousand eight hundred and fifty.

"Given under our hands at Lost Creek, this eleventh day of May, 1850.

"AZOR ESTEE,
"PETER DAVIS,
"*Elders.*"

Soon after his ordination, he was called to the pastorate of the Lost Creek Church, and with such brief intervals as ill health demanded for rest, he sustained that relation for more than a quarter of a century, resigning in 1875.

During this pastorate, aside from maintaining the appointments of the church, he devoted much time to evangelistic and revival meetings in western Virginia, such work extending to all the churches in that region together with their many outposts.

In 1867, the Lost Creek and New Salem churches sent him and Rev. Jacob Davis as missionaries on a visit to Shelbyville, Tennesee. Some two years afterward, he again visited Tennessee under the auspices of the American Sabbath Tract Society to labour with Rev. James Bailey, in the interest of Sabbath Reform. Although strongly urged by the American Sabbath Tract Society to go upon that field and remain indefinitely, he, nevertheless, declined, believing the interests there were too great to be served adequately in the time that he felt that he could spare from the West Virginia field, to which under the call of duty, he had pledged his life work.

Under his leadership and pastoral care, the Lost Creek

Church increased its membership from about sixty-five at the time he became its pastor, to upwards of two hundred when he finally resigned. It had also built and dedicated a new commodious brick house of worship.

When he became pastor of the Lost Creek Church, the only other active churches were the New Salem and South Fork of Hughes River (Pine Grove) churches. With the founding and organisation of every existing Seventh Day Baptist church now in the South-Eastern Association, except the New Salem, Lost Creek, and Middle Island churches, he has been intimately connected.

Perhaps the most trying experience in his pastorate at Lost Creek, was that of the events of the Civil War. The political views of the members of the church were widely divergent fundamentally, and there was every incentive to precipitate unguarded action, as well as great danger of arousing blind and unreasoning passions. Himself, an uncompromising abolitionist, he was diplomatic enough withal, not only to retain the confidence and affection of all his church, but likewise to prevent any outburst, or open rupture in it.

During more than half of his term of service with the Lost Creek Church, he received no stipulated salary, receiving only such contributions as individual members might offer him. In one year of this period, he travelled upward of six hundred miles on horseback, preaching in the church and in school houses, holding special meetings and visiting people in their homes, and receiving for the entire year, a financial remuneration aggregating six dollars ($6.00), a part of which was in merchandise.

During these years, he maintained his family upon his farm, which had to be paid for from his earnings, performing the labour, for the most part, with his own hands, and frequently toiling till the midnight hour.

During the latter part of his pastorate with the Lost Creek Church, it had become sufficiently prosperous to pay the pastor a small salary, which never exceeded three hundred dollars ($300.00) annually.

In the spring of 1876, after he had previously resigned the pastorate of the Lost Creek Church, he assisted Rev. Charles M. Lewis in a series of revival meetings conducted

REV. SAMUEL HOFFMAN DAVIS.

by the latter at New Salem. These meetings resulted in about fifty accessions to the church, and in his being called to the pastorate of the New Salem Church.

This pastorate continued for a term of three years, greatly to the good of the church, which was strengthened by growth of spiritual life, and by accessions to its numbers.

In the year 1879, he returned to his farm near Jane Lew, and engaged in evangelistic and missionary work, independently. In the following year, 1880, the Board of Managers of the Seventh Day Baptist Missionary Society, engaged him as a general field missionary, to labour in West Virginia under its direction.

For more than ten years he continued in this service, constantly visiting pastorless churches, conducting revival meetings in every church and Sabbath-keeping community within the bound of the South-Eastern Association, and calling upon the families from house to house.

Such labour as this he had performed lavishly during his long pastorate of the Lost Creek Church, and the results had been gratifying; but now that the opportunity to do such work was larger, the beneficent results were correspondingly greater. The membership of the churches was increased, converts to the Sabbath resulted, and new churches were organised.

The field of such activities was not limited to West Virginia. It extended to the church at Jackson Centre, Ohio, where he had visited at different times previously; to Salemville, Pennsylvania, where in 1885, he organised a prosperous Seventh Day Baptist Church; and to Cumberland County, North Carolina, where he found a strong prejudice against such work as he was engaged in doing. This prejudice he had the gratifying pleasure of seeing give way to a hearty welcome to Seventh Day Baptist home missionaries.

After the close of his labours under the direction of the Missionary Board, he continued to do missionary and evangelistic work independently, until recently, when the infirmities of advancing age have compelled him almost wholly to relinquish active ministerial labour.

He was three times married. First, to Elisabeth Ford, who died in 1851. His second wife died in 1861. His third wife, the daughter of Jesse and Elisabeth (Gillis) Fitz Randolph, who is still living has been his faithful, sympathetic companion for upwards of forty years.

Three sons were born to him by his first marriage, two of whom died in infancy. The oldest, S. Orlando, lives at Jane Lew, West Virginia.

Four sons were born to him by the third marriage. Boothe Colwell lives at Alfred, New York; Morton Wardner, at Salem, West Virginia, and Samuel Hoffman, in Boston, Massachusetts. Simeon Gillis died at six years of age.

It is not given many men to grasp the really great opportunities of life, and to fewer yet, to enjoy to its full, the fruit of the possibilities of such opportunities when once seized upon and wrought out.

To Rev. Samuel D. Davis came a magnificent opportunity, —an opportunity, however, that to most on-lookers must, at best, have appeared to be sadly obscured and doubtful. To him inviting as it was magnificent, it revealed no less surely its hardships and toil. But it was worth the effort. And to the work of cultivating the soil of the Seventh Day Baptist churches of West Virginia, he addressed himself. No spot was left unturned. There was no plant not watered, none so unpromising as not to receive the tenderest care, none so thrifty as not to need cultivation. He has literally been a pastor to every church in the association. The indelible impress of his personality is everywhere.

And he has wrought wisely and well. As he has seen western Virginia develop from the crude conditions of frontier life into conditions of civilisation, comfort, and it might almost be said, luxury, he has also seen the religious and spiritual life keep pace with the changing conditions of material things. He has seen the primitive meeting house give place to neat, attractive, and commodious houses of worship. He has seen the attitude of the church toward its pastor change so that the latter may expect a comfortable maintenance. from the former.

Was it worth the while? It has produced Salem College. It has given Alfred University a president. West Virginia has produced men who, scattered in different places, participate actively in the affairs that make for the destiny

HOME OF REV. SAMUEL D. DAVIS, NEAR JANE LEW.
(From a recent photograph).

of the Seventh Day Baptist denomination,—in the affairs of the Seventh Day Baptist Education Society, the Seventh Day Baptist Missionary Society, the American Sabbath Tract Society, and the Sabbath School Board of the Seventh Day Baptist General Conference, and other places of trust and responsibility.

To-day, besides all this, the fruits of his work may be seen in one of the healthiest and most promising groups of churches of the Seventh Day Baptist denomination. Surely, it was worth the while.

The highest academic honours paid for ecclesiastical service, as tokens of superiour merit, are awarded for either of two reasons; *viz.*, Scholastic attainments, or signal service to the church. No Seventh Day Baptist can lay claim to greater service to the church, than can Samuel Davis Davis, but his highest honour, his chiefest delight is to be called a Minister of the Gospel.

REV. JACOB DAVIS, 2D.

REV. JACOB DAVIS, 2D, the son of Jesse Maxson and Abigail (Hoffman) Davis, was born in Harrison County, Virginia, August 15, 1827. Jesse Maxson Davis was the son of Jacob Davis, the son of Rev. Jacob Davis, of the Shrewsbury Church.

In early life, Rev. Jacob Davis, 2d, was baptized by Rev. Richard C. Bond, and became a member of the Lost Creek Church, which he served for several years as clerk.

In the year 1858, he removed his membership from the Lost Creek Church to the New Salem Church, the latter church admitting him to membership on May 14, of that year.

On November 18, 1859, the New Salem Church upon motion of Rev. David Clawson, granted licence to Jacob Davis to preach for one year within the bounds of the New Salem and Lost Creek churches. The formal action was as follows:—

"We as a church, assembled for the transaction of business, at New Salem, Va., this 18th day of the 11th month in the year of our Lord 1859, do resolve that we extend a permission to Bro. Jacob Davis to improve his gifts in explaining the scripture, preaching and setting forth the doctrines of the Gospel of our Lord and Saviour,

Jesus Christ; hereby expressing our wish that in addition to his heretofore activity in leading in prayer and engaging in exhortation, he will freely go forward in the afore-mentioned duty as the Spirit may give him utterance, for one year from the above date in any of the meetings of this church for worship, when opportunity offers and circumstances justify.

And we also extend to him the privilege, if he should meet with the church at Lost Creek and be invited by them through their Elder, Deacons, or other efficient member, to use the privilege the same as in the meetings of this church; commending him to God and the word of his grace, praying that he may be filled with the spirit of his station, and become an able minister of Jesus Christ [to] spend and be spent in the cause,—be faithful until death and receive a crown of life."

On November 20, 1863, the church took action as follows:—

"RESOLVED, That Bro. Jacob Davis be licenced to labour as a Gospel minister whenever and wherever an opportunity may offer, and that the clerk write said licence and tender it to Bro. Jacob."

By joint action of the New Salem and Lost Creek churches, he was ordained to the Gospel ministry at New Salem, on August 19, 1865.

From this time for a period of a good many years, he served the Lost Creek and New Salem churches, one or both, in a pastoral capacity, preaching sometimes regularly, at other times at irregular intervals at the various preaching stations of these churches. After the organisation of the Greenbrier and Ritchie churches, he served them both, for a time, as pastor.

In the summer of 1867, he accompanied Rev. Samuel D. Davis upon a trip to Shelbyville, Tennessee, in the interest of the New Salem and Lost Creek churches.[1]

As his home was at the head of Greenbrier Run, he became a member of the Greenbrier church when it was organised in 1870.

Although he died at a comparatively early age, he left an indelible impress upon the churches of the South-Eastern Association. As a speaker, he was forceful and logical, deliberate in his delivery.

On June 5, 1850, he was married to Jemima Davis, the daughter of Rev. Peter Davis.

---

1. *Vid.* pp. 157-158 *supra*.

REV. JACOB DAVIS.

As the remuneration for his services to the church were very meagre, in accordance with the prevailing custom of the country at that time. he supported himself and his family upon his farm, which he cultivated himself.

He died April 4, 1885, at the age of fifty-seven years, seven months, and nineteen days.

REV. ENOCH DAVID.

REV. ENOCH DAVID was born near Dover, on Duck Creek, in the state of Delaware, March 6, 1715. His father, Owen David, was a native of Wales, and his mother was born in England. They were both Presbyterians, but Enoch became a member of the Baptist church at Welch Tract.

He afterward became a Seventh Day Baptist, and removed to Philadelphia, where he was an active preacher among the Seventh Day Baptists in and near that city. Here he conducted a thriving business as a tailor, also.

Under date of June 12, 1792, the church at Welch Tract gave him a letter directed to the Baptist church in Middletown, East New Jersey, certifying to his membership in good standing in the Welch Tract Church, as well as to his exemplary life, and commending him to the care of the Middletown Church so long as he might remain with them.

Soon afterward, however, he went to visit with some of his children living in Fayette County, Pennsylvania, in the vicinity of the Woodbridgetown Church. There he shared the care of the Woodbridgetown Church with Rev. Samuel Woodbridge, until, as a result of exposure while preaching, he contracted a pulmonary disease which ended in his death at the home of his son-in-law, John John, at Woodbridgetown, November 28, 1793, at the age of seventy-eight years, eight months, and twenty-two days.

He was married four times, and had eleven children. His oldest son, Ebenezer, was graduated from Brown University, in 1772. A year afterward, Ebenezer was licenced to preach by the Newport (Rhode Island) Church, which on May 31, 1775, ordained him to the Gospel ministry. He then returned to Philadelphia to visit his father and other friends, where he enlisted as a chaplain in the American Army in the Revolutionary War. He died in the army, March 19, 1778.

Apparently Enoch David never was a member of the Woodbridgetown Church, although the names of several of his children are found on its roll of membership.

There are reasons for thinking that his son, Owen David, at one time, may have been licenced to preach by the Woodbridgetown Church, but the church records are silent upon the question.[1]

REV. RICHARD CLAYTON BOND.

REV. RICHARD CLAYTON BOND was born April 11, 1813, at Lost Creek, Virginia. He was the son of Abel Bond, Jr., and Sarah (Powers) Bond.

On April 10, 1835, the Lost Creek Church granted him licence to preach. On March 8, 1840, his licence was renewed for an indefinite period. He preached once a month for the Lost Creek Church, which, on September 5, 1842, voted to request the South-Western Association to ordain him, at its annual session to be held with the church at Port Jefferson, Ohio.

His great-grandfather, Richard Bond, who was born in 1728, and died January 14, 1819, was the father of Major Richard Bond, a soldier of the Revolutionary War, who was born March 9, 1756, and died February 14, 1820.

Major Richard Bond was three times married: first, to Tamar Davis; second, to Mary Brumfield, the mother of his children; and third, to Mary Lewis. He was the older brother of Deacon Abel Bond, of the Lost Creek Church, whose home was at Quiet Dell, where the early missionaries to western Virginia were always first entertained on their arrival upon that field.[2]

Major Richard Bond's son Abel, the father of Rev. Richard Clayton Bond, was born in Cecil County, Maryland, May 20, 1787. On November 3, 1807, he was married to

---

1. Cf. MSS. of Rev. Enoch David, Daniel G. W. David, *et al.*

2. Abel Bond entered eighty-eight (88) acres of land on Elk Creek, in Harrison County, Virginia, in 1800. In 1838, the following entries were made on the North Fork of Hughes River:—
Benjamin F. Bond, one hundred (100) acres.
Ethelbert Bond, one hundred (100) acres.
Lewis Bond, one hundred and ninety-one (191) acres.
Lewis Bond, one hundred and sixteen (116) acres.
Cf. *Dyer's Index to Land Grants in West Virginia.*

REV. RICHARD C. BOND.

Sarah Powers, at Jane Lew, Virginia; and in 1845, with his family removed to Wisconsin.

Major Richard Bond was, also, the father of Levi Bond, whose son Brumfield was the father of Boothe Bond, who, in turn is the father of Samuel B. Bond and Elsie B. Bond, both of whom are members of the faculty of Salem College.

Richard Clayton Bond was baptized, in his eighteenth year by Rev. Lewis A. Davis, and became a member of the Lost Creek Church.

On April 10, 1835, the Lost Creek Church granted him licence to preach. On March 8, 1840, his licence was renewed for an indefinite period. He preached once a month for the Lost Creek Church, which on September 5, 1842, voted to request the South-Western Association to ordain him, at its annual session to be held with the church at Port Jefferson, Ohio.

The association referred the request to its Presbytery, which recommended that the petition be granted. Accordingly, on October 16, 1842, the ordination service took place, conducted by Rev. Lewis A. Davis, of the Port Jefferson Church, who preached the sermon, assisted by Rev. Peter Davis of the New Salem Church, who was in attendance at the association, and Rev. Joshua Hill, of the Port Jefferson Church.

During the year 1844, he represented the Seventh Day Baptist Missionary Society upon the western Virginia field, visiting the Woodbridgetown (Pennsylvania) Church also. He had four regular preaching stations, which he visited each once a month.

Under his ministrations, the church membership was increased, and the activity of church work quickened.

On October 19, 1839, he was married to Eliza Grant.

In the spring of 1846, he removed to Wisconsin, and engaged in farming, near Milton in that state.

At the date of this writing, August 1, 1905, his home is at Milton Junction, Wisconsin.

SAMUEL FITZ RANDOLPH.

SAMUEL FITZ RANDOLPH was born in October, 1738. His great-grandfather, Edward Fitz Randolph, came to America from Nottinghamshire, England, after the middle of the first half of the seventeenth century, and settled at Scituate, Plymouth Colony (now Massachusetts), where he married, May 10, 1637, Elisabeth Blossom, daughter of Thomas Blossom, the first deacon of the church in Plymouth. In the spring of 1639, in company with many of his neighbours, Edward removed to Barnstable, Plymouth Colony, where his several children were born. In 1669, he removed to Piscataway, East Jersey. His son Thomas, was born at Barnstable, August 16, 1659; and on November 23, 1686, Thomas married Elisabeth Manning of Piscataway. Thomas and Elisabeth's son Jonathan, was born at Piscataway, January 12, 1692, or 1693. In the year 1717, Jonathan married Mary ———, of Piscataway. Thomas and Elisabeth's son David, was born in Piscataway, January 1, 1690 or 1691. David married Sarah Molleson, of Piscataway, in 1712.

Samuel Fitz Randolph, son of Jonathan and Mary Fitz Randolph, married Margaret, the daughter of David and Sarah (Molleson) Fitz Randolph, March 25, 1761. Margaret was born in November, 1739.

Samuel and Margaret were members of the Piscataway Seventh Day Baptist Church, as their respective parents had been before them, as were also their grandparents, Thomas and Elisabeth Fitz Randolph.

Samuel enlisted as a soldier in the War of the Revolution, where he served as an ensign in the Second Regiment of Sussex County, New Jersey. His commission reads as follows:—

"THE STATE OF NEW JERSEY.

"To SAMUEL RANDOLF, GENT., Greeting:

"*Whereas*, It hath been certified to His Excellency, William Livingston, Esquire, Governor and Commander-in-chief of this State, that you have been duly chosen by the Company of Militia in the County of Sussex, (being the —— Company in the Second Regiment of the said County, whereof Aaron Hankinson, Esqr., is Colonel) to be ensign of the said Company; you therefore are to take the said Company of Militia into your charge and care as ensign thereof, and duly to exercise both officers and soldiers of the said company in arms; and as they are hereby directed to obey you as their Ensign, you are likewise to obey and follow such orders and directions, from time to time, as you shall receive from your Colonel or other, your superior officer or officers; and for your so doing, this shall be your commission.

(26)

APPENDIX

"*In Testimony Whereof* The GREAT SEAL of the said State is hereunto affixed:

"*Witness WILLIAM LIVINGSTON,* Esquire, Governor, Captain-General and Commander-in-chief in and over the State of New Jersey and Territories thereunto belonging, Chancellor and Ordinary in the same, at Haddonfield, the Sixteenth Day of May in the Year of our Lord, One Thousand Seven Hundred and Seventy-seven.

[L. S.]   "WIL: LIVINGSTON."

"*By His Excellency's Command,*
   "CHAS. PETTITT, Secry."

Some years after the close of the Revolution, Samuel Fitz Randolph in company with his family removed to south-western Pennsylvania, where he and his wife both became constituent members of the Woodbridgetown Church.[1] Subsequently, they removed to western Virginia, where he established the village of New Salem.[2] Here they became members of the New Salem Church, and remained so until their death. Samuel died, February 25, 1825; and Margaret, February 29, 1832.

Samuel and Margaret had the following children:— Mary, born October 16, 1761; Sarah, born November 8, 1763; Elisabeth, born May 13, 1766; Jesse, born May 21, 1768; David, born June 23, 1770; Rhulanah, born March 13, 1773; Jonathan, born March 20, 1775; Margaret, born February 4, 1777; Nancy, born February 19, 1781.

Mary married James Hill, November 14, 1795. She and her family removed to Ohio.

Sarah married, first, Daniel Sharpneck, and upon his death, John Rice. Her home was in south-western Pennsylvania, not far from the former home of her father, in Fayette County.

Elisabeth married William Brand, and with her husband, went to Ohio.

Jesse married, first, Delilah LaForge, and upon her death, Elisabeth Gillis. His daughter Elisabeth became the wife of Rev. Samuel D. Davis, and is the mother of Rev. Boothe C. Davis and Rev. Samuel H. Davis. Jesse's son John LaForge, was the father of Rev. Gideon Henry F. Randolph, and the grandfather of Rev. Experience F. Randolph (now Rev. Perie R. Burdick).

---
1. Cf. pp. 52, 74, *supra.*
2. Cf. pp. 52 *et seq., supra.*

David, upon his marriage, removed to Ohio, where he and his father owned a farm, jointly, probably not far from Cincinnati.

Rhulanah married John Bonnell.

Jonathan married Mary Davis, the daughter of William ("Greenbrier Billy") Davis and Elisabeth Davis. Jonathan's son William was the father of Rev. Lewis F. Randolph, and the grandfather of Rev. William L. Burdick.

Margaret married ——— Clayton, and removed to Ohio.

Nancy married Stephen Davis.

All of Samuel's children, except as stated otherwise, made their homes at or near New Salem after they were married.

JEPTHAH FITZ RANDOLPH.

JEPTHAH FITZ RANDOLPH, son of Jonathan and Mary (Davis) Fitz Randolph, and grandson of Samuel and Margaret Fitz Randolph, was born at New Salem, November 18, 1814.

He became a member of the New Salem Church at the time of the Quarterly Meeting in February, 1830. On February 7, 1836, he was married to Deborah Sutton, daughter of John and Rachel (Davis) Sutton, and grand-daughter of Cornelius and Elisabeth (?) [Applegate (?)] Sutton.

From May 15, 1836, to May 19, 1843, he served the New Salem Church as its clerk. During this period he devoted much time and labour to completing the records of the church from the time it had come to New Salem, down to the time he became clerk.

In the spring of 1845, he removed with his family to Milton, Wisconsin, travelling overland in a wagon, a distance of six hundred and fifty miles. Here he arranged to establish his home, and to that end he purchased a farm of James M. Burgess and wife for a cash consideration of three hundred dollars ($300.00). The deed is dated July 24, 1845, and calls for the east half of the north-east quarter of section 17, in township 4, north of range 14, east, in Rock County.

In the following fall, however, he returned to Virginia, and took up his residence at New Milton (a post office established through his influence, and named by him for Milton, Wisconsin, from which he had so recently come), on the Meat

THE HOME OF JEPTHAH FITZ RANDOLPH, AT NEW MILTON.
(From a photograph taken in 1877).

House Fork of Middle Island Creek. Here he lived until his death, July 19, 1879.

Although New Salem was ten miles away, he retained his membership in the New Salem Church.

On November 17, 1855, he was appointed a deacon, and after twelve years service, he was formally ordained to that office along with Lodowick H. Davis, and Judson F. Randolph, by Rev. Samuel D. Davis, assisted by Rev. Jacob Davis.

He served the church at different times as its moderator, and for many years immediately preceding his death, he was its treasurer. He represented the church, officially, at New Milton, where several families lived who were members of the New Salem Church; and for many of the last years of his life, he conducted religious services there, once a month, unless provision was made otherwise by the church.

He was one of the prime movers in the establishment of the West Union Academy, and when its doom was sealed, to his hands was committed the disagreeable, but responsible, task of closing up its business affairs.

Besides various other positions of public trust which he held, he represented his county (Doddridge) in the Second Constitutional Convention of the state of West Virginia, which convened in Charleston in 1872,—the only constitutional convention held in that state since the Civil War. Here he was excused from duty on the Seventh Day of the week, because of his religious belief and practise. Of this convention, a trustworthy historian asserts that it was "the most notable body of men, in point of legal ability, that ever met in the state."

FRANKLIN FITZ RANDOLPH.

FRANKLIN FITZ RANDOLPH, son of Jepthah and Deborah (Sutton) Fitz Randolph, was born at New Salem, November 9, 1836, On May 18, 1850, he became a member of the New Salem Church.

He received his education in the neighbourhood subscription schools in vogue at that time, at West Union Academy, and at Alfred University. He was one of the first to teach in the public schools of Doddridge County, when the free school system was established after the formation of the state of West Virginia.

He was clerk of the New Salem Church, and the keeper of its records, for a period of twenty-eight years continuously, the original appointment being made May 18, 1855, and his term of service closing November 16, 1883, because of having changed his membership to the Greenbrier Church on the 22d of September preceding. For two of the four years that he was a member of the Greenbrier Church, he was its moderator.

In March, 1887, he became a member of the Middle Island Church, and since December, 1889, he has been the moderator of that church.

For the last two years of its existence, he was secretary of the Board of Directors of the West Union Academy, and to his care were committed the records of the board, for safe keeping, when the corporation was dissolved and passed out of existence.

He was one of the first two recording secretaries of the South-Eastern Association, and for many years served the association in that capacity.

He has frequently been solicited by the church to permit it to make him a deacon, but he has uniformly declined that honour. His great service to the church has been as a keeper of records.

He was twice married. His first wife was Mary Catharine Rickard, to whom he was married November 9, 1858, and who died July 25, 1859. On January 10, 1861, he was married to Mary Elisabeth Fox, the daughter of George and Elisabeth (Burgess) Fox, who was born in Greenbrier County, Virginia, April 26, 1842.

Ever since he was first married, he has made his home at New Milton, West Virginia, his present home.

REV. AZOR ESTEE.[1]

Rev. Azor Estee was born in Shushan, Washington County, New York, June 30, 1803.

His early life was spent on his father's farm, and when he became a young man, he worked on the farm in summer, and in winter taught district school.

At twelve years of age, he became a member of the Bap-

---

1. The author is indebted to Mrs. Susan M. Estee, of Alfred, New York, for aid in the preparation of this sketch.

Franklin F. Randolph

tist church. After reaching manhood, he began to prepare for the ministry, by entering school at Bennington, Vermont. Here his religious views underwent a change, and he became a Seventh Day Baptist, afterward becoming a member of the Seventh Day Baptist Church at Petersburgh, New York. Upon the completion of his studies, he accepted a call to the pastorate of the Petersburgh Church. Here he made his home for a period of twenty-five years.

At one time during this period, however, he was pastor of the church at Shiloh, New Jersey. He was also frequently employed by the Seventh Day Baptist Missionary Society. In December, 1849, the Missionary Society sent him to visit the churches in western Virginia and Ohio. He remained with the Virginia churches during that winter and the following spring. In the summer of 1850, he made a visit to the Ohio churches, and then returned to Virginia. Here he took up the question of education, a subject which was being agitated throughout the Virginia churches at that time. This movement culminated in the establishment of the West Union Academy, at West Union. Rev. Azor Estee took no small part in this work. He was instrumental in procuring Stephen T. W. Potter as principal of the academy, and when the latter returned to his home at Scott, New York, the former succeeded him as principal, and conducted the school successfully, until the spring of 1852, when private business called him back to his home at Petersburgh.

The last five years of his life were spent in Quincy, Franklin County, near Snow Hill, Pennsylvania, as a home missionary among the German Seventh Day Baptists.

He was the son of Stephen and Abigail (Thompson) Estee. In 1828, he was married to Betsey Brown, the daughter of Elias and Betsey Estee Brown. She died in 1845, leaving two sons, Henry Estee, of Milton, Wisconsin, and Charles B. Estee, of Gibson City, Illinois.

He was married a second time, in March, 1847, to Susan Maxson, a daughter of Daniel and Susan Armsbury Maxson, of Petersburgh, New York. To them were born two sons, James Ayars Estee, now superintendent of public schools, of Gloversville, New York, and Daniel Maxson Estee, of Buffalo, New York.

Rev. Azor Estee died September 7, 1864, His second wife is still living at Alfred, New York.

STEPHEN THOMAS WEST POTTER.[1]

STEPHEN THOMAS WEST POTTER, son of Ezekiel G. and Abigail (West) Potter, was born in the town of Scott, New York, October 1, 1828. He was educated in the district schools near his home, and at DeRuyter Institute, at DeRuyter, New York, from which he was graduated in 1849.

On January 1, 1850, he was married to Cynthia Barber, daughter of John Barber, of Scott. In the latter part of the same year, he became principal of the West Union Academy, at West Union, Virginia.

The following summer, he relinquished his duties at the academy, and returned to his former home at Scott, where he embarked in the mercantile business. He subsequently studied medicine, and was graduated from the Homoeopathic Medical College at Cleveland, Ohio. He then practised medicine, successively, first at Terra Haute, Indiana; afterward in New York, at Spafford, Onondago County; Moravia, Cayuga County; and Friendship, Allegany County. In the meantime, he had invented several agricultural implements, and thus added materially to his prosperity.

He next removed to Brookfield, in northern Missouri. After ten years residence here, he removed to Illinois, where he remained for several years.

Finally, after spending some time in travel, he removed to Los Angeles, California. Here he continued the practise of his profession as long as his declining years would permit. He died at Los Angeles, April 28, 1904. In early life he became a member of the Seventh Day Baptist Church at Scott, New York, and maintained that relation with the church until his death.

DANIEL MAXSON BURDICK.

DANIEL MAXSON BURDICK, the son of Daniel O. and Betsey Burdick, was born at Lincklaen, Chenango County, New York, August 15, 1813. He received his education in the district schools near his home, and at Alfred Academy (now Alfred University), at Alfred, New York.

---

1. Acknowledgment is due Dr. Lehman H. Potter, of Homer, New York, for assistance in the preparation of this sketch.

REV. DAVID W. LEATH.

In the early history of Richburg Academy, at Richburg, New York, he was an instructor there. In the summer of 1853, he went to West Union, Virginia, to assume charge of the West Union Academy. Illness in his family soon called him back to Little Genesee, New York, and he did not return to Virginia. He began teaching at the age of twenty years, and continued until he was seventy-two. He was engaged for the most part, in district schools.

He lived for the greater part of his life at Little Genesee, New York, where he was married, in 1837, to Sally A., daughter of Zaccheus R. and Temperance Coon Maxson, of Little Genesee.

He was a member of the Seventh Day Baptist Church of Little Genesee.

He died May 5, 1898, at Little Genesee, New York.

MOSES HOFFMAN DAVIS.

MOSES HOFFMAN DAVIS, son of Jesse Maxson Davis, who was the son of Jacob Davis, was born February 27, 1833. He was married, April 14, 1857, to Julia A. Davis, daughter of Lodowick H. Davis, and lived on Flint Run, in Doddridge County, West Virginia, until the death of his wife, November 12, 1861, after which he returned to the home of his father on Lost Creek, in the adjoining county of Harrison.

On November 3, 1863, he was married to Emily V. Swisher. He died July 16, 1891.

Soon after the organisation of the state of West Virginia, he served on the county board of supervisors. For several years afterward, he was a justice of the peace; and in 1880, he was elected to represent his county in the lower house of the state legislature.

He was one of the leading spirits in the Lost Creek Seventh Day Baptist Church, of which he was a deacon for some twenty years. He was likewise one of the clerks of the South-Eastern Seventh Day Baptist Association at the time of its organisation, and for several years afterward.

REV. DAVID W. LEATH.

REV. DAVID W. LEATH was born in Fishomingo County, Mississippi, July 17, 1848. When he was eight years of age, his father removed with his family to Tennessee. He was educated at a small college at Milan, Tennessee, where he joined the Methodist Episcopal Church, South, in 1870. In less than a year, he entered upon active preparation for the ministry, which he had decided to enter. In due course of time this preparation was completed, and he was assigned to a circuit.

In 1875, his views changed upon the subject of baptism, and he became a member of the Baptist church. He subsequently became pastor of a Baptist church in Texas, after which he engaged in missionary work on the Pacific coast. In 1893, his religious views underwent another change, and he became a Seventh Day Baptist, and two years afterward, he joined the Seventh Day Baptist Church, of Chicago, Illinois.

He then engaged in evangelistic work for a time; and in 1899, he became the pastor of the Middle Island, Greenbrier, and Black Lick churches, in West Virginia, jointly. Here he remained for a period of two years, when he accepted a call to the pastorate of the Salemville (Pennsylvania) Church.

CLYDE FITZ RANDOLPH.

CLYDE FITZ RANDOLPH, son of Preston and Harriet (Meredith) Fitz Randolph, was born in February, 1875, and died at Morgantown, West Virginia, May 16, 1904.

He was prepared for college in the preparatory department of Salem College, and in evening school in Plainfield, New Jersey, where he was employed during the day, in the works of the Potter Printing Press Company.

In June, 1899, he was graduated from the West Virginia University, with the degree of Bachelor of Arts. He had specialised in mechanical engineering, and after a year's graduate study at Cornell University, he was graduated from that institution as a Mechanical Engineer.

Soon after his graduation, he was offered a position as an instructor in the department of engineering at Cornell; but he declined, having previously accepted an appointment as associate professor of mechanical engineering at the West Virginia University.

For a short time after his graduation, however, for the sake of acquiring experience in designing machinery, he

CLYDE FITZ RANDOLPH.

entered the employment of the Blaisdell Machinery Company, of Bradford, Pennsylvania. Here he achieved distinction by working out some hitherto unsolved problems in designs of gas engines and air compressors.

After about a year and a half of this kind of work, he entered upon the active duties of his position at the West Virginia University, where he remained until his untimely death. His work there was of a high rank for a young man, and promised him honour and distinction among his fellows, in the world of mechanical engineering, had he lived.

CLARKE'S ACCOUNT OF THE VIRGINIA CHURCHES.

Clarke's *History of the Sabbatarians,* pp. 57-58, has the following:—

"VIRGINIA CHURCHES.

"At the Sabbatarian General Conference, held at Hopkinton, R. I., Sept. 1808, there were letters, sent by Elder John Davis, from two churches in that quarter; one from Lost Creek, Virginia, then composed of 23 members, and the other in Salem, Virginia, composed of 38 members, and said Davis had the oversight of both of said churches. Their deacon was Abel Bond, and their clerk was Moses Huffman.

The distance of those churches is so great (although they were admitted in the Sabbatarian Conference) that I have no correct information from them since. And although I saw Elder John Davis, and heard him preach (who is esteemed by many as an able, entertaining preacher) yet as I had then no knowledge of my writing this history, I took no memorandum of the date of their organisation, or from what people they originated. I rather conclude they formerly went from the state of New Jersey. There was a letter from them at our last conference, in Oct., 1810. But as I took no minutes from it then, and the Conference Minutes have not got to me yet, I must omit giving further account of them.

"There is a number of societies or sections of churches, of this order, in several other places, as a church on the West Fork of the Monongahela River, in the state of Virginia, who also sent a letter to be admitted into the Sabbatarian General Conference. But as they admitted communion with first-day members, they were not admitted into Conference.

"I learn there is a society of this sect, at Red Stone, in Virginia. And I have heard something of one or two other societies of this order in our South-Western Territories, but am not able to give correct information about them."

On p. 27 he says:—

"I have seen, and heard preach several times, Elder Jacob Davis,—I expect of this church, since the late American War; and I understand, that church since I saw Elder Jacob Davis, generally removed into the remote parts of the state of Virginia, where Eld. Davis died. But what has become of that church, I am not able to ascertain with precision; as I have no correct account of them, I shall not give them a place distinctly in this narrative."

MINISTERS DESCENDED FROM WILLIAM DAVIS.

The following is a list of Seventh Day Baptist clergymen descended from William Davis, the founder of the Shrewsbury Church.[1]

Deceased.

1. WILLIAM DAVIS, (founder of the line),
2. JOHN DAVIS, (son of William),
3. JACOB DAVIS, (grandson of William, and first pastor at New Salem),
4. JOHN DAVIS,
5. LEWIS A. DAVIS,
6. PETER DAVIS,
7. SIMEON BABCOCK,
8. JAMES BALL DAVIS,
9. JACOB DAVIS, 2d,
10. MAXSON BABCOCK,
11. URI MORTON BABCOCK,
12. JOHN LIVINGSTON HUFFMAN.

Living.

13. SAMUEL DAVIS DAVIS,
14. DARIUS KING DAVIS,
15. LEWIS ALEXANDER PLATTS, D. D.,
16. LEWIS FITZ RANDOLPH,
17. SIMEON H. BABCOCK,
18. JOHN T. DAVIS,
19. GIDEON HENRY FITZ RANDOLPH,
20. DARWIN C. LIPPINCOTT,
21. BOOTHE COLWELL DAVIS, D. D.
22. THEODORE J. VAN HORN,
23. WILLIAM L. BURDICK,
24. RILEY G. DAVIS,
25. JAMES H. HURLEY,
26. SAMUEL HOFFMAN DAVIS,
27. CHARLES S. SAYRE,
28. ELI FORSYTHE LOOFBORO,
29. HERBERT C. VAN HORN.
30. EDGAR D. VAN HORN,
31. AHVA JOHN CLARENCE BOND.

---

1. This list was prepared by Rev. Boothe Colwell Davis, D. D., of Alfred University.

MARRIAGES.

MARRIAGE LICENCES.

BY AN ACT of the state of New Jersey, approved by the governor, March 27, 1719, all who so desired could procure a licence to marry from the governor of the state, which permitted a marriage without the usual formality of publishing the banns three times from the pulpit. As the licence method was by far the more private, that mode of procedure became quite prevalent; so much so, in fact, that it was greatly abused, and the licence law was finally repealed the 4th of March, 1795. The licence was not returnable to any public office, and was usually destroyed after the ceremony was performed. But the bridegroom was required by law, on making application for licence to wed, and before a licence could issue, to file a bond in the penal sum of five hundred pounds, colonial money, with two approved sureties.

These bonds were kept on file in the office of the secretary of state. About 1880, Henry C. Kelsey, at that time secretary of state, caused these bonds to be bound in thirty-two thick folio volumes. He also had two indexes of these volumes made, one of the men, and another of the women. These indexes, together with certain historical matter relating to marriage customs and laws in New Jersey, as well as certain other marriage records, have been published under the editorial supervision of William Nelson, Esq., in the *Archives of the State of New Jersey. Documents relating to Colonial History of the State of New Jersey. Volume XXII. Marriage Records, 1665-1800.* Paterson, N. J., 1900.

The following records of marriage licences are from this volume:—

(Any irregular spelling in the following lists may be accounted for by the fact that the exact spelling of the *New Jersey Archives* has been carefully followed.)

Names.	Date.
ALLGOR,[1] WILLIAM, Monmouth, and Elisabeth Havens, Monmouth	1763, Jan. 7.
AMOCK, APHAM, Monmouth, and Joseph Davis, Monmouth	1754, Sept. 14.

---
1. Auger, probably.

APPENDIX

ASHLEY, JOHN, Monmouth, and Prudence Maxen, Middletown	1765, July	1.
AYARS, DARKIS, Cumberland, and David Randolph, Cumberland	1775, Nov.	8.
BABCOCK, SIMEON, Monmouth, and Jane Greggory, Monmouth	1757, Aug.	20.
BARTLETT, JOSEPH, Monmouth, and Hannah Gifford	1766, April	5.
BRAND, REBECCA, Monmouth, and James Davis, Monmouth	1765, July	1.
BRAND, WILLIAM, Monmouth, and Deborah Lawrence, Monmouth	1767, Feb.	20.
BROWN, ELISABETH, Monmouth, and Nathan Maxson, Monmouth	1764, April	27.
BURDGE, DAVID, Monmouth, and Elisabeth Davis, Monmouth	1753, Aug.	22.
CAMPBELL, ANNE, Woodbridge, and Jacob Sutton, Piscataway	1756, Sept.	27.
COVENHOVEN, PETER, Monmouth, and Anne Davis, Monmouth	1749, Feb.	5.
CURTIS, JOHN, Monmouth, and Mary Davis, Monmouth	1746, March	31.
DARKIN, JALE, Salem, and David Fitz Randolph, Salem	1740, May	25.
DAVIS, AMY, Monmouth, and Elisha Johnston, Monmouth	1755, Oct.	28.
DAVIS, ANNA, Monmouth, and John Havens, Monmouth	1745, Jan.	21.
DAVIS, ANNE, Monmouth, and Peter Covenhoven, Monmouth	1749, Feb.	5.
DAVIS, BENJAMIN, Monmouth, and Mary Woolley, Monmouth	1749, Dec.	11.
DAVIS, ELISABETH, Monmouth, and David Burdge, Monmouth	1753, Aug.	22.
DAVIS, ELISABETH, Monmouth, and Ephraim Maxson, Monmouth	1764, April	27.
DAVIS, ENOCH, Monmouth, and Anna Swindon, Monmouth	1762, Oct.	20.
DAVIS, JAMES, Monmouth, and Rebecca Brand, Monmouth	1765, July	1.
DAVIS, JOSEPH, Monmouth, and Upham Amock, Monmouth	1754, Sept.	14.
DAVIS, MARY, Monmouth, and John Curtis, Monmouth	1746, March	31.
DAVIS, NATHAN, Monmouth, and Anney Gifford, Monmouth	1761, Jan.	20.
DAVIS, THOMAS, Piscataway, and Anne Smalley, Piscataway	1750, Aug.	24.

DUNN, ELISABETH, Piscataway, and Thomas Fitz Randolph, Piscataway	1755, May	26.
FITZ RANDOLPH, (see also Randolph).		
FITZ RANDOLPH, DAVID, Salem, and Jale Darkin, Salem	1740, May	25.
FITZ RANDOLPH, EPHRAIM, Piscataway, and Rachel Stelle, Piscataway	1752, July	11.
FITZ RANDOLPH, THOMAS, Piscataway, and Elisabeth Dunn, Piscataway	1755, May	26.
FRAZEE, STEPHEN, Monmouth, and Hannah Gifford, Monmouth	1765, May	16.
GIFFORD, ANNEY, Monmouth, and Nathan Davis, Monmouth	1761, Jan.	20.
GIFFORD, HANNAH, Monmouth, and Stephen Frazer, Monmouth	1765, May	16.
GIFFORD, HANNAH, and Joseph Bartlett, Monmouth	1766, April	5.
GIFFORD, MARGARET, Monmouth, and John Martin, Monmouth	1760, Feb.	5.
GILLMAN, LETITIA, Cumberland, and David Platts, Cumberland	1763, Jan.	4.
GREGORY, JANE, Monmouth, and Simeon Babcock, Monmouth	1757, Aug.	20.
HAVENS, ELISABETH, Monmouth, and William Allgor,[1] Monmouth	1763, Jan.	7.
HAVENS, JOHN, Monmouth, and Anna Davis, Monmouth	1745, Jan.	21.
HOFFMIRE, MENER, Middletown, and Benjamin Thorpe, Middletown	1761, Sept.	30.
JOHNSTOWN, ELISHA, Monmouth, and Amy Davis, Monmouth	1755, Oct.	28.
LANGSTAFF, MARY, Piscataway, and Henry Sutton, Piscataway	1751, Oct.	1.
LAWRANCE, DEBORAH, Monmouth, and William Brand, Monmouth	1767, Feb.	21.
MARTIN, JOHN, Monmouth, and Margaret Gifford, Monmouth	1760, Feb.	5.
MAXEN, PRUDENCE, Middletown, and John Ashley, Monmouth	1765, July	1.
MAXSON, EPHRAIM, Monmouth, and Elisabeth Davis, Monmouth	1764, April	27.
MAXSON, JOSEPH, Monmouth, and Hannah Osborne, Monmouth	1774, Oct.	14.
MAXSON, NATHAN, Monmouth, and Elisabeth Brown, Monmouth	1764, April	27.
OSBORNE, HANNAH, Monmouth, and Joseph Maxson, Monmouth	1774, Oct.	14.

---

1. Auger, probably.

APPENDIX

PLATTS, DAVID, Cumberland, and Lettitia Gillman, Cumberland	1763, Jan.	4.
RANDOLPH (see also Fitz Randolph).		
RANDOLPH, DAVID, Cumberland, and Darkis Ayars, Cumberland	1775, Nov.	8.
SMALLEY, ANN, Piscataway, and Thomas Davis, Piscataway	1750, Aug.	24.
STELLE, RACHEL, Piscataway, and Ephraim Fitz Randolph, Piscataway	1752, July	11.
SUTTON, HENRY, Piscataway, and Mary Langstaff, Piscataway	1751, Oct.	1.
SUTTON, JACOB, Piscataway, and Anne Campbell, Woodbridge	1756, Sept.	27.
SWINDON, ANNA, Monmouth, and Enoch Davis, Monmouth	1762, Oct.	20.
THORP, BENJAMIN, Middletown, and Mener Hoffmire, Middletown	1761, Sept.	30.
WOOLLEY, MARY, Monmouth, and Benjamin Davis, Monmouth	1749, Dec.	11.

MARRIAGE RECORDS: NEW JERSEY.

Several years ago there were found in western Pennsylvania the marriage records kept by Rev. Jonathan Dunham, while he was pastor of the Piscataway Seventh Day Baptist Church, 1745 to 1776, in Piscataway Township (now New Market), New Jersey. The following entries are copied from that record as published in the *New Jersey Archives, Vol. XXII*, from which the foregoing records of marriage licences have been taken:—

BLOOMFIELD, KEZIA, and Abraham Lufbery	1759, Nov.	28.
DUNN, ELISABETH, and Thomas Fitz Randolph	1755, May	27.
FITZ RANDOLPH, MARGARET, and Samuel Fitz Randolph	1761, March	25.
FITZ RANDOLPH, SAMUEL, and Margaret F. Randolph	1761, March	25.
FITZ RANDOLPH, THOMAS, and Elisabeth Dunn	1755, May	27.
LUFBERY, ABRAHAM, and Kezia Bloomfield	1759, Nov.	28.
OSMUN, CATHERINE, and Peter Sutton	1762, Dec.	21.
RUNYON, ELISABETH, and Jonas Sutton	1764, Sept.	27.
SUTTON, JONAS, and Elisabeth Runyon	1764, Sept.	27.
SUTTON, PETER, and Catherine Osmun	1762, Dec.	21.

MARRIAGES: WESTERN VIRGINIA.

The following marriages are from the records in the office of the Clerk of the County Court of Harrison County, at Clarksburg, West Virginia:—

By John W. Loofboro.
SAMUEL HARBERT to ABIGAIL LOOFBORO, January 3, 1784.
JOHN HARBERT to SARAH LOOFBORO, January 22, 1789.
THOMAS BARKLEY to MARY LOOFBORO, November 17, 1795.
JACOB BEARD to CATHERINE RANDOLPH, August 2, 1796.
JONATHAN DAVIS to PIETY MAXSON, November 17, 1796.

By Rev. Isaac Edwards, D. D.
JOHN KELLEY, to ANN DAVIS, SR., February 14, 1786.
WILLIAM DAVIS to ABBY DENHAM, April 15, 1788.

By Rev. John Patterson.
JOSEPH DAVIS to EXPERIENCE MAXSON, February 18, 1795.
GEORGE MAXSON to ANN HAVENS, September 3, 1795.
JAMES DAVIS to ELISABETH DAVIS, September 8, 1795.

By Rev. John Denham, D. D.
JAMES HILL to MARY FITZ RANDOLPH, November 14, 1795.

By Benjamin Webb, "D. N."
WILLIAM STROTHER to RUTH RANDOLPH, July 31, 1800.
WILLIAM RANDOLPH to ANN MACKIE, December 29, 1803.

By Rev. John Davis.
GEORGE MAXSON to ELISABETH REED, September 5, 1801.
PETER DAVIS to SARAH DAVIS, November 6, 1802.
JAMES BELL to ESTHER DAVIS, September 26, 1805.
CORNELIUS SUTTON to ELISABETH MAXSON, September 18, 1806.
SAMUEL CHANEY to ANN DAVIS, November 12, 1807.
DAVID DAVIS to LYDIA JEFFREY, March 10, 1807.
GEORGE J. DAVIS to CATHARINE DAVIS, November 10, 1807.
ELI BOND to AMELIA BOND, April 9, 1816.
SYLVESTER DAVIS to LOIS VANHORN, January 8, 1822.
JEPTHA DAVIS to MATILDA LOOFBORO, August 4, 1822.
WILLIAM F. RANDOLPH to MARY DAVIS, August 12, 1823.
WILLIAM BABCOCK to ASENETH DAVIS, October 14, 1823.
PHINEAS F. RANDOLPH to MARVEL MAXSON, February 27, 1823.
JOSHUA DAVIS to HANNAH BELL, February —, 1823.
GEORGE WILLIAMS to MARGARET F. RANDOLPH, November 6, 1823.
EPHRAIM BEE to CATHARINE DAVIS, June 19, 1823.
JOHN KELLEY to TACY DAVIS, June 23, 1825.
JONATHAN BONNELL to ELISABETH MAXSON, September 22, 1825.
JOHN L. F. RANDOLPH to EXPERIENCE BROWN, October 12, 1826.
CALVIN DAVIS to LYDIA MAXSON, April 21, 1823.
ETHELBERT BOND to MARY DAVIS, August 1, 1832.
LEVI SUTTON to SARAH BROWN, April 8, 1833.
THOMAS FORD to HANNAH DAVIS, May 22, 1833.
DAVIS W. SUTTON to LURANA DAVIS, September 16, 1834.
EVAN HUTSON to CHARLOTTE DAVIS, September 16, 1834.
WINTER HUTSON to SARAH DAVIS, October 13, 1834.

(27)

APPENDIX 433

By Rev. Joseph Cheuvront.

JESSE DAVIS to HANNAH DAVIS, May 11, 1806.
JOHN SUTTON to RACHEL DAVIS, December 2, 1807.
PHINEAS DAVIS to RULANA F. RANDOLPH, May 16, 1816.

By Rev. Thomas Maxson.

WILLIAM VANHORN to JANE MAXSON, August 13, 1812.
WILLIAM DAVIS to CATHARINE ASH, January 18, 1813.
ASA DAVIS to CONTENT DAVIS, July 15, 1813.

By Zebulon Maxson.

WILLIAM DAVIS to RACHEL HUGHES, November 20, 1813.
SEHABA DAVIS to SARAH DAVIS, June 14, 1815.
JAMES HILL to DEBORAH DAVIS, March 19, 1816.
NATHAN DAVIS to KEZIAH DAVIS, May 8, 1816.
JOSEPH JEFFREY to TACY DAVIS, April 24, 1817.
ASA BEE to HANNAH MAXSON, September 24, 1818.
JOHN DAVIS to PERMELIA MAXSON, ———
MARTIN HUGHES to ANN DAVIS, June 23, 1819.

By Joseph Morris.

REUBEN BOND to SARAH BELL, August 17, 1814.

By R. Smith.

JONATHAN BEE to PATTY HOWARD, September 5, 1817.

By Rev. Tho. M. Hudson.

JESSE F. RANDOLPH to ELISABETH GILLIS, March 23, 1826.

By Rev. Peter Davis.

SAMUEL P. F. RANDOLPH to HANNAH DAVIS, October 27, 1827.
REUBEN SUTTON to DRUSILLA MAXSON, February 27, 1828.
ELIONA DAVIS to SOPHIAH DAVIS, August 14, 1828.
ABSOLOM DAVIS to POLINA DAVIS, October 9, 1828.
HUGH TATE to ELISABETH F. RANDOLPH, August 2, 1831.
JOSIAH BEE to PRISCILLA DAVIS, August 11, 1831.
AMOS DAVIS to ASENETH DAVIS, March 23, 1833.
JESSE DAVIS to HULDAH DAVIS, May 2, 1833.
ZIBA DAVIS to JOSEPHINE DAVIS, January 22, 1834.
WILLIAM P. HALL to FATIMA DAVIS, February 10, 1834.
EHUD DAVIS to CATHARINE DAVIS, February 26, 1835.
JESSE M. LOWTHER to LUCINDA HALL, April 23, 1835.
JOHN D. BEE to INGABE DAVIS, June 14, 1835.
LODOWICK H. DAVIS to MARGARET DAVIS, July 2, 1835.
JEPTHAH F. RANDOLPH to DEBORAH SUTTON, February 7, 1836.
SUTTON MAXSON to VIENNA SUTTON, October 6, 1836.
ALBERT FORD to RHULANA DAVIS, March 16, 1837.
ALFRED N. DAVIS to REBECCA DAVIS, November 9, 1838.
NATHAN G. DAVIS to MARY ANN M. DAVIS, March 8, 1838.

By *Elias Brown*.
RICHARD C. BOND to ELIZA GRANT, October 19, 1837.
By *Rev. Lewis A. Davis*.
JOB VANHORN to PRUDENCE DAVIS, September 20, 1839.

MARRIAGE LICENCES RECORDED IN MONONGALIA COUNTY, VIRGINIA.[1]

Groom.	Bride.	Officiating Clergyman
	1795.	
JOHN DAVIS	MARY JONES	JAMES FLEMING.
	1797.	
LUKE DAVIS	SARAH BROWN	JOHN WILLEY.
	1799.	
JOHN DAVIS	ELISABETH COLE	JOHN WILLEY.
ROBERT DAVIS	MARY KOON	————

---

1. It is doubtful if any of these Monongalia County licences are of interest to Seventh Day Baptists. In the list of licences granted for the years 1799 and 1802, the name of John Patterson appears several times as that of the officiating clergyman. Cf. *Transallegheny Historical Magazine*. Vol. II., No. 1, pp. 56 *et seq*.

WILLS, ETC.

The following are references to the records in the office of the secretary of state at Trenton, New Jersey:—

NATHAN MAXSON, intestate,	Will Book No. 28 p. 293.
THOMAS BABCOCK, guardian of Jacob Covenhoven	Will Book No. 28, p. 296.
ZEBULON MAXSON, will,	Will Book No. 29, p. 326.
THOS. DAVIS, will and inventory,	Will Book No. 30, p. 80.
JOSEPH MAXSON, will,	Will Book, No. 38, p. 299.

On October 17, 1760, letters of administration were granted Isaac Rogers on the estate of William Davis, late of Monmouth County.

As the best available information pertaining to the manners and condition of life which prevailed among the members of the Shrewsbury Church, the will, with the annexed inventory of his personal property, of Zebulon Maxson is here given. It runs as follows:

"IN THE NAME OF GOD, AMEN. Know ye that I, Zebulon Maxson, of the Township of Shrewsbury, County of Monmouth, and Eastern Division of the State of New Jersey, Farmer, being in good health of body, and of perfect mind and memory, thanks be given to God for it, and calling into mind the mortality of the body and knowing it is appointed for all men once to die, do ordain this my last will and testament.

"Principally and first of all I give and recommend my soul into the hands of God who gave it; and as for my body I recommend [it] to the earth to be buried in a christian-like and decent burial at the discretion of my executors, nothing doubting but at the general resurrection I shall receive the same again by the mighty power of God; and as touching such worldly estates wherewith it hath pleased God to bless me in this life, I give and dispose of the same in manner and form following; *viz.*,

"That first of all my will is that all my just debts and funeral charges be paid out of my estate by my executors.

"*Item.* I give and bequeath unto my dear and loving wife the best bed and furniture, a cow and my Great Bible, Pot chest, and chest of drawers, the largest basin and platter, a woolen wheel and linen wheel, together with a privilege of the house during the time she remains my widow.

"*Item.* My will is that these my three children, Zebulon, Bethiah, and Experience, have their bringing up till they arrive to age, out of my estate, or till in a proper capacity to maintain themselves; and the remainder of my estate to be divided among my five children, Marvel, Elisabeth, Bethiah, and Experience, Zebulon.

"*Item.* I give and bequeath unto my beloved son all my lands when he comes to age, with a proper maintainance of his aged mother, to him and his heirs forever.

"*Item.* I give and bequeath to my four daughters all my moveable estate: Marvel and Elisabeth to have one feather bed apiece, and the other two daughters when they come to the age of eighteen years, and as much more of the moveable estate as to make them equal with the two oldest, and the remainder divided among my four daughters when my youngest daughter comes to age.

"*Item.* I also do appoint and ordain my loving wife executrix, and my loving brother Ephraim Maxson to be executor of this my last will and testament, ratifying, pronouncing, and declaring this and no other to be my last will and testament.

"In witness whereof I do hereunto put my hand [and] seal this Fifteenth Day of February in the Year of Our Lord One Thousand Seven Hundred and Seventy-nine.

"Signed, sealed, declared, and pronounced

'This to be my last will and testament.

"Ephraim Maxson   "Zebulon   [L. S.]
                                                      Maxson."

"Thos. Davis, Jr."

INVENTORY.

"October 31, 1787.

"A true inventory of the goods and chattels, rights and credits of Zebulon Maxson, late of the Township of Shrewsbury in the County of Monmouth and state of New Jersey, deceased, taken and apprised this day at the request of Experience Maxson, executor.

"Prised by Jacob Davis and William Davis:—

	£	s	d
To wearing apparel of the deceased (money of the State of New Jersey)	3	0	0
Flax in sheaf		12	0
Bilsted [*sic*] boards		15	
One yoke of oxen and yoke	18	0	0
One yoke of yearling steers	2	5	0
One yearling heifer	1	6	0
One cow bell		6	0
Two stacks of hay	4	0	0
To one bottom of rye	1	0	0

APPENDIX

To two beehives	1 10	0
To one hay tackling	10	0
To one wagon	6 10	0
To one wheelbarrow	10	0
To one corn plow	8	0
To one iron harrow	15	0
To two fattening hogs	4 0	0
To one dutch plow	1 5	0
To one cider barrel	3	0
To one small ox-chain	4	6
To one big clevis	2	6
To one wood sledge	5	0
To one shaving-horse	1	0
To corn in the crib	2 12	6
To oak plank for felloe stuff	6	0
To one large ox-chain	7	6
To one spade	3	0
To one pair of beetle rings	2	0
To two ax eyes	2	0
To one grubbing hoe	3	0
To two broad hoes	1	6
To offal corn	1 2	6
To one post ax	5	0
To one cutting knife	1	6
To carpenter's tools	7	0
To shoe-make tools and lasts	5	0
To one cider barrel in the Cambor [*sic*-chamber(?)]	3	0
To offal leather	5	0
To sundries of tubs and barrels	3	0
To old iron	1	0
To one bed and furniture	6 10	0
To one loom, warping bars, quill-wheel, and scarn and spools, about 20	1 10	0
To six slay [sleys]	1 4	0
To thirteen pair of gears	17	0
To one frying pan	4	0
To one copper kettle	10	0
To one iron tea kettle	5	0
To one iron pot	6	0
To one tin sieve		9
To two pair of shears	1	0
To one beaming knife and bark-shave	5	0
To one iron trammel and two hooks	10	0
To one grid-iron		6
To eleven turkeys	15	0
To pewter	10	0
To crockery ware on the dresser	2	0

To earthen [ware] and trenchers	3 0
To four jugs and two bottles	2 0
To three pair of pillow cases	8 6
To three sheets and table cloth	8 0
To 5 kegs	6 0
To foot wheel	7 6
To one old chest	3 0
To three scythes and two tacklings	12 0
To one bed in the back room	3 15 0
To one trundle bed and bedstead	2 10 0
To three trays, wooden bowl, and leaden dish	2 5
To one large cedar tub	1 6
To one small *ditto*	1 0
To one churn	5 0
To one half-bushel [measure]	1 0
To one stone pot	1 6
To one large table	1 6
To one *ditto*	1 0
To two meal bags	3 0
To eight chairs	4 6
To one plat [*sic*] iron	2 0
To knives and forks	2 0
To one Bible	6 0
To one psalter	1 6
To one Testament	1 0
To one spelling *ditto* [*sic*]	1 0
To one psalm *ditto*	6
To one water pail	2 6
To one basket (large)	1 6
To three ladles	1 6
To one slate	2 0
To loft hay	4 15 0
To one bed, bedstead and furniture	7 0 0
To one cow	3 15 0
To one foot wheel	10 0
To one wool *ditto*	8 0
To one pewter platter	4 0
To one iron pot	10 0
To one case of drawers	1 10 0
To old chest	1 6
To one Bible	10 0
To one pewter basin	2 6
To two pair of temples and two shuttles	5 0
To one iron kettle	6
To one tray, 2 pails, and two not [*sic*,-note or nut(?)] dishes	3 0
To one not [*sic*,-note or nut(?)] dish	3

To two shuttles		2	0
To one chopping ax		6	0
To one barrel		1	6
To one book debt at Thomas Babcock's	1	16	0
To one book debt against William Davis	2	1	6
Due from John Tilton		12	1
To one half of a loom	2	0	0
[Total	105	1	6][1]

---

1. About three hundred dollars ($300.00.)

TOMBSTONE INSCRIPTIONS.

THE FOLLOWING tombstone inscriptions have been gathered from the various graveyards named as follows:—

NEW JERSEY.

SHREWSBURY.

HANNAH, daughr. of Nathan & Anna Davis. Died March ye 3d, 1788, aged 20 years.

PISCATAWAY.

Here lyes ye body of ELISABETH, wife of Thomas Fitz Randolph. Died with smallpox, March ye 1, 1732, aged 63 years.

Here lyes ye body of ELISABETH Fitz Randolph, died March ye 19, 1732, aged 43 yrs. Daughr. of Thomas. Died with ye small-pox.

Here lyes THOMAS, son of Thomas & Margaret Fitz Randolph. Died March 21, 1732, aged 17 years.

PENNSYLVANIA.

WOODBRIDGETOWN.[1]

In memory of the REV. ENOCH DAVID, who departed this life Nov. 28th, 1793. Aged 78 years, 8 months, and 22 days.

Farewell, Good Man.
A faithful herald, thou, of Heavenly grace,
Thou couldst awake conviction on the soul
Where others touched not, and e'en thoughts control;
Full on the mind enforce each Gospel truth;
Nor didst deceive by noise, by art, by sound
The vacant minds of gaping crowds around.
Tho' science marked thee not, yet thou knew'st well
In plainest language noblest truth to tell,
And tho' thy page was not with learning fraught
Thy warfare so ended in a good old age
Has thou concluded well thy pilgrimage.
Adieu, good man, rewards await thee now,
Where men of greater fame
Shall to thy virtue bow.

DANIEL G. W. DAVID died May 7, 1861, in the 94 yr. of his age.

ELISABETH, wife of DANIEL G. W. DAVID, died Aug. 20, 1833, in the 61 year of her age.

MARIE E. DAVID died Aug. 22, 1854, in the 45 year of her age.

---

1. For copies of these inscriptions, the author of this book is indebted to Charles H. Greene, Esq., of Alfred, New York, who visited the graveyard at Woodbridgetown, in August, 1903.

THE SOLE REMAINING GRAVESTONE IN THE
GRAVEYARD AT SHREWSBURY.

APPENDIX

MARY WOODBRIDGE departed this, life, November the 26, A. D. 1811, aged 97 years, 8 months & 5 days.

In memory of the REV. SAMUEL WOODBRIDGE, minister of the Gospel, who departed this life July the 7, A. D. 1814, aged 8-[?] years, 10 months & 18 days.

In memory of ANNE WOODBRIDGE, consort of the late Rev. Samuel Woodbridge, deceased. She departed this life August the 18th, 1821, aged 59 years & 3 days.

In memory of COL. JOHN OLLIPHANT. Born Sep. 9th, 1759. Died Feb. 28th, 1836, aged 76 years, 5 months, & 10 days.

In memory of MRS. SARAH OLIPHANT, wife of Col. John Oliphant. Born Feb. 28, 1778; died Dec. 15, 1842, aged 64 years, 9 months, & 15 days.

In memory of SAMUEL WOODBRIDGE OLAPHANT, who departed this life December the 28, 1820, aged 25 years.

In memory of KEZIA DAVIS. Was the wife of James Davis, & departed this life June 20th, 1810, age 48 years.

In memory of JAMES DAVIS, who died Sept. 10th, 1850, in the 89th year of his age.

In memory of JOSHUA DAVIS, who departed this life Feb. the 20th, 1816, in the 29th year of his age.

In memory of JOHN STURGIS, who departed this life Feb. 11th, 1822, in the 73rd year of his age.

Here lays the body of LEAH STURGES, the wife of John Sturges, who died 12 of February, 1794, aged 42 years, 3 months, & 5 days.

In memory of RHODA STURGIS, who departed this life February 3d, 1816, aged 17 years & 11 months & 25 days.

Here lays the body of PHILLIS STURGES, who died July 6th, 1806, aged 22 years, 4 months, & 8 days.

WEST VIRGINIA.

WHITE DAY.

Careful inquiry has been made for graves at White Day, in Monongalia County, West Virginia, but none have been found of interest there. The old graveyards in that vicinity have been abandoned, for the most part, and very few gravestones are left standing.

SALEM.

WILLIAM DAVIS was born March 21, 1758; died January 6, 1845.[1]

ELISABETH DAVIS was born July 11, 1762; died January 6, 1845.

G. J. DAVIS, died Feb. 5, 1868, aged 78 years.

---

1. "Greenbrier Billy."

APPENDIX

ANN, wife of MARTIN HUGHES; born Sept. 25, 1800, died April 7, 1885.

ZEBULON MAXSON died Nov. 20, 1821, aged 40 yrs.

MARY, wife of ZEBULON MAXSON, died Mar. 30, 1868, aged 88 ys., 7 ms.

GIDEON MAXSON, born Oct. 30, 1815, died Feb. 7, 1890.

R: S:,[1] born July 25, 1792; died April 26, 1853. M. H.[2]

GRAVEYARD OVER BRANDY GAP TUNNEL, EAST OF SALEM.

CONTENT, wife of ASA DAVIS, born Jan. 21, 1797; died Jan. 10, 1887.

GRAVEYARD AT MIDDLE ISLAND CHURCH, NEAR NEW MILTON.

AMAZIAH BEE, born May 15, 1805, died Jan. 16, 1894, aged 88 ys., 8 Ms., & 1 D.

RHODA, wife of A. BEE, born Mar. 26, 1808; died Sep. 10, 1901, aged 93 Ys., 5 Ms., 14 Ds.

JACOB BOND, born Jan. 20, 1808; died May 9, 1902.

MANERVA S. BOND, born Jan. 6, 1815; died Nov. 12, 1884.

STEPHEN T. DAVIS, born Sep. 3, 1817; died Sep. 18, 1895, aged 78 Yrs. & 15 Ds.

ELISABETH DAVIS, died June 4,[3] 1897, aged 77 Ys., 8 Ms., 11 Ds.

NATHAN KELLEY, born Sept. 10, 1816; died Sept. 12, 1894, aged 78 Yrs., 2 Ds.

ELEANOR D. KELLEY, born Nov. 16, 1812; died July 15, 1892, aged 79 Ys., 2 Ms., 29 Ds.

ASA KELLEY, born May 26, 1826; died Dec. 29, 1901.

EMILY, wife of ASA KELLEY, born May 26, 1827; died Dec. 5, 1887.

A. B. PARKS. July 31, 1807—Feb. 20, 1892.

HANNAH PARKS. Nov. 13, 1806—Oct. 8, 1879.

JEPTHAH F. RANDOLPH, died July 19, 1879, aged 64 Ys., 8 Mo., 1 Day.

DEBORAH, wife of J. F. RANDOLPH, born Oct. 14, 1813; died Feb. 19, 1901, aged 87 Ys., 4 Ms., 5 Ds.

GREENBRIER.

REV. PETER DAVIS, died Mch 4, 1873, aged 89 Ys., 5 Ms., 16 Ds.

SARAH, wife of REV. PETER DAVIS, died Jan. 24, 1868, aged 72 Ys., 1 Mo., 8 Ds.

---

1. Rachel Sutton, wife of John Sutton.
2. The letters "M. H." are for "Martin Hughes," the stone cutter who made the tombstone.
3. Incorrect; it should be January instead of June.

NATHAN J. DAVIS, born Nov. 24, 1797; died April 15, 1891, aged 93 ys., 4 ms., 21 ds.

KEZIAH, wife of N. J. DAVIS, born Sept. 15, 1796; died May 14, 1862, aged 65 Ys., 8 Mo., 29 Ds.

In loving remembrance of ASENATH, wife of AMOS DAVIS. Born Sep. 26, 1811; died Sep. 1, 1888, aged 77 ys., 25 Ds.

REV. JACOB DAVIS, died April 4, 1885; aged 57 Ys., 7 Ms., 19 Ds.

DAVID R. PLATTS, born Mar. 29, 1805; died Feb. 26, 1878.

OLD FRAME MEETING HOUSE GRAVEYARD, AT LOST CREEK.

WILLIAM BATTEN, born Sept. 7, 1807; died Oct. 13, 1881, aged 74 Ys., 1 Mo., 6 D.

ELISABETH BOND, wife of WM. BATTEN, died Feb. 26, 1870, aged 53 Yrs.

ELISABETH BATTEN, wife of T[?] BATTEN, born April 27th, 1781; died June 10th, 1850.

ABLE BOND, died Jan. 23, 1852, in his 89 Yr.

ELISABETH, wife of ABLE BOND, died Feb. 18, 1863, in her 89 Yr.

LEWIS BOND, born Feb. 16, 1779; died Apr. 14, 1867.

LYDIA BOND, born Oct. 29, 1788; died July 8, 1880.

ELI BOND, son of S & E BOND, died March 22, 1850, aged 61 Yrs.

AMELIA, wife of ELI BOND, born Oct. 29, 1790; died July 27, 1880.

EDY BOND, daughter of ELI & AMELIA BOND, died Sept. 25, 1845, aged 21 years.

ELI BOND, JR., born July 6, 1827; died Sept. 1, 1901.

MARY E., wife of ELI BOND, JR., born Jan. 15, 1832, died Oct. 3, 1899.

BRUMFIELD BOND, born Dec. 15, 1809; departed this life Jan. 27, 1890, aged 80 Y's, 1 Mo., and 12 Ds.

DAVID CLAWSON. Born New Market, N. J., July 19, 1801. A 7th day Baptist Minister; ordained Alfred, N. Y., Sept., 1836; pastor Marlboro, N. J., 19 years; missionary in Va. 3 yrs. Died March 6, 1860.

JESSE M. DAVIS, born Dec. 24, 1796; died Mar. 10, 1871.

ABIGAIL H., wife of J. M. DAVIS, born Sept. 6, 1801; died Nov. 12, 1863

JOSHUA S. DAVIS, died March 21, 1869, in the 64 year of his age.

HANNAH, wife of JOSHUA S. DAVIS, born Dec. 26, 1802; died Apr. 7, 1884.

WILLIAM KENNEDY, born Jan. 2, 1805; died Sept. 1, 1876.

BELINDA H., wife of WM. KENNEDY, died Sept. 25, 1872, in her 48 Yr.

APPENDIX

NAOMI DAVID, born Feb. 20, 1804, was married to John Kildow, July 10, 1834; died Oct. 7, 1881.

AI VAN HORN, died Feb. 11, 1854, aged 64 Yrs.

HANNAH VAN HORN, died Jan. 7, 1832, aged 52 Yrs.

CATHARINE, wife of JOB VAN HORN, born Oct. 25, 1829; died June 15, 1852.

BROAD RUN.

ELD. JOHN DAVIS, Pastor of the S. D. B. Church at New Salem. Born May 1, 1754. Died June 22, 1842.

WEST UNION.

NATHAN DAVIS,[1] born June 21, 1772; died May 23, 1866, aged 93 Yrs., 11 Mo's., 2 D's.

JANE, wife of NATHAN DAVIS, died April 27th, 1857, aged 86 years, 6 Mo's., & 20 d's.

WILLIAM [J.] DAVIS, died July 15, 1878, aged 89 Ys., 4 Ms., 15 Ds.[2]

EXPERIENCE, wife of W. J. DAVIS, died Jan. 6, 1866, in her 76 Yr.

Our mother, ESTHER F. DAVIS, wife of J. S. DAVIS,[3] born Oct. 31, 1810; died Feb. 7, 1894.

JOSEPH JEFFREY, born June 8, 1794; died April 23, 1874.

TACY, wife of JOSEPH JEFFREY, died Feb. 9, 1872, aged 70 Ys., 7 Ms., 24 Ds.

CORNELIUS SUTTON, died Sep. 31, 1850, aged 99 yrs., 11 mo's., 1 day.

CHILDERS GRAVEYARD, NEAR NEW MILTON.

GEORGE FOX, died Aug. 4, 1860, aged 54 ys., 6 ms. 19 Ds.

ELISABETH, wife of GEORGE FOX, died June 19, 1890, aged 80 Ys., 22 Ds.

PINE GROVE GRAVEYARD, NEAR BEREA.[4]

EZEKIEL BEE, died Feb. 20, 1893, aged 92 Yrs. 5 Ms., 23 Ds.

MARIAH, wife of EZEKIEL BEE, died Aug. 9, 1865, aged 56 Ys., 1 Mo., 8 Ds.

Z. DAVIS, died Feb. 4, 1887, aged 70 Yrs. 8 mo., 12 ds.

DORINDA, wife of Z. DAVIS, died Nov. 7, 1885, aged 71 Yrs., 4 Mo., 23 ds.

---

1. Popularly known as Captain Nathan Davis, from his having served as a captain in the War of 1812.

2. "Rock Billy," or "Rock Run Billy."

3. John S. Davis was buried at Peakeville, Clarke County, Missouri.

4. The author of this book is indebted to Mr. Erlow Sutton, of Berea, West Virginia, for copies of these inscriptions.

Jesse M. Lowther, died Nov. 15, 1855, aged 46 Yrs., 6 mos., 13 ds.

Priscilla, wife of B. W. Bee, born Feb. 14, 1825; died Dec. 17, 1888.

Harriet Brissey, born Dec. 25, 1811; died Dec. 5, 1885, aged 73 Yrs., 11 Mo., 10 Ds.

Asa Fitz Randolph, died Sep. 3, 1903, aged 70 Yrs., 6 Mos., 18 das.

A LIST OF STUDENTS WHO MATRICULATED IN ALFRED UNIVERSITY FROM WEST VIRGINIA.

Names.	Year of Matriculation.	Residence.
	1855-1856	
Esther Fitz Randolph *Burdick*,[1]		Greenbrier Run,
Judson Fitz Randolph,[1]		Greenbrier Run,
Preston Fitz Randolph,[1]		Greenbrier Run,
Silas Fitz Randolph,[1]		Greenbrier Run.
	1856-1857	
Darius King Davis,[1]		New Salem.
	1857-1858	
Franklin Fitz Randolph,[1]		New Milton,
Jethro Fitz Randolph,[1]		Greenbrier Run.
	1862-1863	
Andrew Judson Charter,[1]		West Union.
	1865-1866	
George Washington Fitz Randolph,		New Milton,
Lewis Fitz Randolph,		New Salem.
	1871-1872	
Abraham Wolfe Sullivan,		Lost Creek.
	1874-1875	
Arthur Bond,		Lost Creek,
John Edwin Meatherell,		Clarksburg,
Calphurnia Fitz Randolph *Meatherell*,		Berea,
Experience Fitz Randolph *Burdick*,		Berea.
	1875-1876	
Gideon Henry Fitz Randolph,		New Salem.
	1876-1877	
Terence McGuire Davis,		Long Run.
	1881-1882	
Emza Fitz Randolph *Coon*,		Berea.
	1882-1883	
Virgil Fitz Randolph,		Berea.
	1883-1884	
Ermine Basil Davis,		New Milton,
Hannibal Hamlin Davis,		New Milton.
	1884-1885	
Ora James Davis,		New Milton,
Herman Ceberry Ford,		Salem,

---

1. Formerly students at the West Union Academy, at West Union, Virginia, now West Virginia.

Corliss Fitz Randolph, New Milton,
Ellsworth Fitz Randolph, Berea.

1885-1886

Boothe Colwell Davis, Jane Lew,
Crede Hammond Davis, New Milton,
Emily Virginia Davis, Salem,
Morton Wardner Davis, Jane Lew,
Stillman Forest Lowther, Salem,
Florence May Fitz Randolph *Townsend*, Salem.

1886-1887[1]

Columbus Franklin Davis, Lost Creek,
Belle Langfitt *Summers*. Morgansville.

1887-1888

Aurelius Grantham Davis, New Milton,
Martha Lelia Davis *Brown*, Salem,
Rosa Davis, Lost Creek,
Samuel Hoffman Davis, Jane Lew,
Silas Benton Davis, Salem,
Tressie May Davis *Trainor*, Lost Creek,
Virginius Leonidas Davis, New Milton,
Herbert Lewis Ford, Long Run,
Amanda Ethel Hall *West*, Auburn,
Gertrude Fitz Randolph, Lost Creek,
Delbert Edwin Smith, Morgansville.

1888-1889

Elsie Belinda Bond, Aberdeen,
Thomas Marsden Bond, Aberdeen,
Arthur Clarence Davis, New Milton,
William Ernest Davis, Lost Creek.

1889-1890

Alva Fitz Randolph, Berea.

1890-1891

Cleora Fitz Randolph *Jordan*, Berea.

1891-1892

Cora Davis, Salem.

1892-1893

Joshua Ledona McWhorter, Quiet Dell.

1893-1894

Charles Gilbert McWhorter, Quiet Dell.

1896-1897

Samuel Brumfield Bond, Aberdeen.

1897-1898

Alva Lucien Davis, New Milton.

---

1. For the names since 1885-1886, in this and the following lists, acknowledgment is due Professor Alpheus B. Kenyon, Registrar of Alfred University, and to Mr. Silas G. Burdick, recently Principal of Alfred Academy.

REV. DARIUS KING DAVIS.

APPENDIX

1898-1899
Maleta Haseltine Davis,   Jane Lew.

1899-1900
Harvey Evans,   Jane Lew.
Delvinus Fitz Randolph   Berea.

1900-1901
Beatrice Lowther *Clarke,*   Salem.

GRADUATES OF ALFRED UNIVERSITY FROM WEST VIRGINIA.

Name.   *Residence*

1862
Preston Fitz Randolph, E. M.,   New Salem.

1869
Darius King Davis, A. B.,   New Salem.

1874
Darius King Davis, B. D.,   New Salem.

1878
Abraham Wolfe Sullivan, A. B.,   Lost Creek.

1879
Calphurnia Fitz Randolph, A. L.,   Berea,
Experience Fitz Randolph, A. B.,   Berea.

1881
Terence McGuire Davis, A. B.,   New Salem.

1885
Experience Fitz Randolph, B. D.,   Berea.

1888
Corliss Fitz Randolph, A. B.,   New Milton,
Gideon Henry Fitz Randolph, A. B.,   Salem,
Virgil Fitz Randolph, Ph. B.,   Berea.

1890
Elsie Belinda Bond, A. B.,   Aberdeen,
Boothe Colwell Davis, A. B.,   Jane Lew,
Herman Ceberry Ford, Ph. B.,   Salem.

1893
Alva Fitz Randolph, B. S.,   Berea.

1897
Samuel Brumfield Bond, A. B.,   Aberdeen.

1900
Maleta Haseltine Davis, Ph. B.,   Jane Lew,
Delvinus Fitz Randolph, A. B.,   Berea.

SEVENTH DAY BAPTIST SOLDIERS.

THE REVOLUTIONARY WAR.

ASA BEE,
RICHARD BOND, Major,
REV. JACOB DAVIS, Chaplain,
REV. JOHN DAVIS, (2d),
SAMUEL LIPPINCOTT,[1]
SAMUEL FITZ RANDOLPH, Ensign in Second Regiment of Sussex County, New Jersey.
CORNELIUS SUTTON,
WILLIAM DAVIS, a brother of Rev. Jacob Davis, was in the British Army.[2]

WAYNE'S WAR.[3]

JONATHAN FITZ RANDOLPH, (son of Samuel, the founder of the village of New Salem.
DANIEL DAVIS, a private in the 1st Troop of Dragoons,
DAVID DAVIS, Surgeon's mate,
JAMES DAVIS,
JAMES DAVIS, private.

WAR OF 1812.

NATHAN DAVIS, Captain,
REV. PETER DAVIS.

CIVIL WAR.[4]

Names.	Regiments.
Arthur G. Bee,	Co. G, 14th Reg., Infantry,
Ephraim W. Bee,	Co. C, 6th Reg., Infantry,
Ephraim W. Bee,	Co. H, 4th Reg., Cavalry,
Joel Bee,	Co. M, 6th Reg., Infantry,
Joel Bee,	Co. F, 1st Reg., Light Artillery,

---

1. Cf. *The Davis Families.* By James B. Davis, p. 9.
2. *Ibidem,* p. 10.

3. Diligent inquiry has failed satisfactorily to establish any connection between the settlers in the village of New Salem, Virginia, and any of these five soldiers in the army of General Anthony Wayne, in the campaign in which he defeated the Indians at the Maumee, except that of Jonathan Fitz Randolph, who was the son of Samuel Fitz Randolph, the founder of the village of New Salem. The other four names are courteously supplied by C. M. Burton, Esq., of Detroit, Michigan, who copied them from Wayne's *Orderly Book.* They are offered in the hope that by a bare possibility, they may prove of value.

4. This list has been compiled, largely, from the *Annual Report of the Adjutant General of the State of West Virginia, for the year ending December 31, 1864.* Wheeling, 1865. The report for the following year, states that Ritchie County furnished, in all, six hundred and twenty-five (625) men for the Federal Army during the war; Doddridge County, five hundred and ninety-five (595); Harrison County, twenty-one hundred and eighty-eight (2188); and Lewis County, seven hundred and forty-five (745).

APPENDIX 451

Josiah H. Bee,[1]   Co. C, 6th Reg., Infantry,
Obediah Bee,   Co. M, 6th Reg., Infantry,
Richard Bee,   Co. M, 6th Reg., Infantry,
William Bee,[2]   Co. H, 7th Reg., Infantry,
Camden Bond,   Co. C, 6th Reg., Infantry,
Henry C. Bond,   Co. H, 4th Reg., Cavalry,
Nathan C. D. Bond,   Co. E, 3d Reg., Cavalry,
Richard E. Bond,   Co. K, 6th Reg., Cavalry,
Thomas Bond,   Co. A, 14th Reg., Infantry,
Charles B. Bonnell,   Co. G, 6th Reg., Infantry,
Jonathan Bonnell,   Co. B, Independent,
Leeman Bonnell,   Co. B, Independent,
Enoch Childers,   Co. E, 3d Reg., Cavalry,
Abner J. Davis,   Co. A, 17th Reg., Infantry,
Austin M. Davis,   Co. A, 14th Reg., Infantry,
A. S. Davis,   Co. K, 6th Reg., Infantry,
Benjamin F. Davis,   Co. A, 14th Reg., Infantry,
Daniel T. Davis,   Co. E, 3d Reg., Cavalry,
David Davis,   Co. M, 6th Reg., Infantry,
Eastburn A. Davis,   Co. A, 14th Reg., Infantry,
Eli Davis,   Co. A, 14th Reg., Infantry,
Eli F. Davis,   Co. A, 14th Reg., Infantry,
Ezra Davis,   Co. H, 4th Reg., Cavalry,
Franklin Davis,   Co. H, 4th Reg., Cavalry,
Granville H. Davis,   Co. A, 14th Reg., Infantry,
Hezekiah S. Davis,   Co. K, 6th Reg., Infantry,
James M. Davis,   Co. K, 6th Reg., Cavalry,
James W. Davis,   Co. K, 6th Reg., Infantry,
Joshua F. Davis,   Co. E, 3d Reg., Cavalry,
Lewis Davis,   Co. C, 6th Reg., Infantry,
Lewis Davis,   Co. H, 4th Reg., Cavalry,
Owen Davis,   Co. M, 6th Reg., Infantry,
Riley G. Davis,   Co. A, 14th Reg., Infantry,
Stephen C. Davis,   Co. G, 14th Reg., Infantry,
Sylvanus Davis,   Co. G, 6th Reg., Infantry,
Timothy K. Davis,   Co. G, 6th Reg., Infantry,
William Davis,   Co. E, 3d Reg., Cavalry,
Wm. E. Davis,   Co. M, 6th Reg., Infantry,
Wm. H. H. Davis,   Co. E, 3d Reg. Cavalry,
Wm. R. Davis,   Co. A, 14th Reg., Infantry,
Richard Ford,   Co. H, 4th Reg., Cavalry,
Thomas N. Gribble,   Co. C, 6th Reg., Infantry,
Thomas E. Holiday,   Co. A, 14th Reg., Infantry,
John Hutson,   Co. A, 14th Reg., Infantry,
Peter F. Hutson,   Co. E, 4th Reg., Cavalry,

1. Captain of the company.
2. Re-enrolled in Co. C, of the same regiment.

Peter F. Hutson,   Co. A, 14th Reg., Infantry,
A. W. Jeffrey,   Co. K, 6th Reg., Infantry,
William Jett,   Co. G, 14th Reg., Infantry,
William Jett,   Co. K, 6th Reg., Infantry,
Daniel D. Kildow,   Co. E, 3d Reg., Cavalry,
Francis M. Kildow,   Co. E, 3d Reg., Cavalry,
John McClary,   Co. A, 14th Reg., Infantry,
W. F. McWhorter,[1]   Co. E, 3d Reg. Cavalry,
Cornelius Maxson,   Co. A, 14th Reg., Infantry,
David F. Randolph,   Co. G, 14th Reg., Infantry,
Samuel F. Randolph,   Co. K, 6th Reg., Cavalry,
Jabez Spurgeon,   Co. M, 6th Reg., Infantry,
Enoch M. Sutton,   Co. H, 1st Reg. Cavalry,
Israel W. Sutton,   Co. A, 14th Reg., Infantry,
Taylor Sutton,   Co. E, 3d Reg., Cavalry,
Thadeus Sutton,   Co. E, 11th Reg., Infantry,
Wm. Wildman,   Co. E, 4th Reg., Cavalry.

1. Sergeant.

PURCHASERS OF TOWN LOTS AT NEW SALEM.

Deeds executed by Samuel Fitz Randolph and his wife, Margaret, for lots in the village of New Salem are on record in the office of the County Clerk at Clarksburg, Harrison County, West Virginia, as follows:—

"IN" LOTS.[1]

No. of Lot.	Name of Purchaser.	Date of Deed.	
1.	Matthew Parremore,	January 15,	1796,
2.	Simeon Maxson,	January 13,	1796,
3.	Jacob Davis's Heirs,	January 13,	1796,
4.	Matthew Parremore,	January 15,	1796,
6.	Enoch Betts,	January 15,	1796,
7.	William Maulsby,	January 15,	1796,
8.	James Davis, Sr.,	February 13,	1796,
9.	James Davis, Sr.,	February 13,	1796,
10.	William Fraser,	March 25,	1814,
11.	Enoch Betts,	January 15,	1796,
12.	Ann Davisson,	February 15,	1796,
13.	Jacob Davis's Heirs,	January 13,	1796,
14.	Thomas Clayton,	January 14,	1796,
15.	Matthew Parremore,	January 15,	1796,
16.	John Davis, Sr.,	January 13,	1796,
17.	William Davis, Jr.,	February 13,	1796,
17.	Thomas Davis,	November 13,	1810,
18.	John Hinton,	February 6,	1798,
20.	Zebulon Maxson,	February 13,	1796,
21.	John Hinton,	February 6,	1798,
22.	Zebulon Maxson,	February 13,	1796,
23.	Zebulon Maxson,	February 13,	1796,
24.	Nathan Davis,	September 5,	1803,
26.	William Davis, Trustee for New Salem Church,	September 5,	1803,
27.	Nathan Davis, Sr.,[3]	February 13,	1796,
29.	Jacob Davis's Heirs,	January 13,	1796,
—.	John Kidd,	September 10,	1799.

1. The name of "New Salem" as a postoffice, became "Salem," by order of the Post Office Department, in March, 1884.

2. The "in" lots contained eighty-four square rods each.

3. Conveyed to the New Salem Church, by Nathan Davis, and Ann his wife, by deed under date of March 14, 1811.

"OUT" LOTS.[1]

No. of Lot.	Name of Purchaser.	Date of Deed.	
1.	Nathan Davis, Sr.,	February 13,	1796,
2.	Zebulon Maxson,	February 13,	1796,
3.	Zebulon Maxson,	February 13,	1796,
4.	Thomas Babcock,	February 14,	1796,
5.	John Davis, Sr.,	January 13,	1796,
6.	Jacob Davis's Heirs,	January 13,	1796,
7.	Jacob Davis's Heirs,	January 13,	1796,
8.	Matthew Parremore,	January 15,	1796,
9.	Thomas Babcock,	February 14,	1796,
10.	Simeon Maxson,	January 13,	1796,
11.	James Davis,	February 13,	1796,
12.	Thomas Clayton,	January 14,	1796,
13.	Enoch Betts,	January 15,	1796,
14.	Enoch Betts,	January 15,	1796,
15.	William Maulsby,	January 15,	1796,
19.	Thomas Babcock,	January 15,	1796,
16.	Enoch Betts,	January 15,	1796,
17.	Enoch Betts,	February 14,	1796,
18.	Thomas Babcock,	January 15,	1796,
19.	William Maulsby,	February 14,	1796,
20.	William Maxson,	September 5,	1803,
21.	Thomas Babcock,	February 14,	1796,
22.	Enoch Betts,	January 15,	1796,
23.	Enoch Betts,	January 15,	1796,
25.	Enoch Betts,	January 15,	1796.
25.	James Davis,	February 13,	1796,
26.	Thomas Babcock,	February 14,	1796,
27.	Enoch Betts,	January 15,	1796,
28.	Matthew Parremore,	January 15,	1796,
29.	Enoch Betts,	January 15,	1796,
30.	Enoch Betts,	January 15,	1796,
34.	William Maulsby,	January 15,	1796.

---

1. The "out" lots contained from two to three acres each.

INDEX.

Aberdeen, W. Va., 448, 449.
Ada, Ohio, 363.
Adams, Mary E., 242.
Adams Centre, N. Y., 216.
Ailes, Moses H., 167.
Albion Academy, 99, 374.
Albion, Wis., 99, 374.
Alexander, Robert, 129, 130, 179.
Alfred, N. Y., 102, 197, 218, 258, 315, 320, 356, 357, 364, 410, 420 note, 422, 440, 444.
Alfred Academy, 97, 356, 422, 448.
Alfred Church, 172.
Alfred University, 97, 249, 292, 294, 308, 309, 310, 329, 335, 368, 375, 405 note, 410, 419, 422, 427 note, 447, 448 note, 449.
Allegany County, N. Y., 265, 422.
Allegheny Mountains, 44, 48 note.
Allen, Pamela, 196.
Allgor, William, 428, 430.
Alton, Ill., 361.
America, 245.
American Army, 413.
American slavery, 385. (See Slavery, also).
American Missionary Association, 328.
American Revolution, 40. (See Revolutionary War, also).
American Sabbath Tract Society, 106, 193 note, 275, 289, 292, 294, 296, 297, 303, 306, 307, 308, 309, 310, 311, 331, 407, 411.
American Seventh Day Baptists, 201.
American War, 426.

Amock, Apham, 428.
  Upham, 429.
Arkansas, 7.
Arminian, 325.
Armitage, Thomas, 2 note.
Armstrong Township, Westmoreland County, Pa., 52.
Arnold, David, 59 note.
Arnolds Creek, 60.
Asbury Park, 10.
Ash, Catharine, 433.
Ashburn, Emma, 381.
  Flavius E., 380, 381.
Ashaway, R. I., 218.
Ashley, John, 429, 430.
"Association in New Jersey," 101 and note.
Auburn, W. Va., 362, 366, 448.
Auger, 428 note, 430 note.
Auger, Elisabeth, 26, 33.
Auger, Joseph, 26, 33.
Auger, William, 33.
Ayars, Darkis, 429, 431.
  L. D., 271.
Awful Sentence of Excommunication, 26, 84.

Babcock, Amy, 34.
  Asenath, 131, 179.
  Eamy, 34.
  Elisabeth, 22, 32, 33, 38.
  Emma, 34.
  Experience, 22, 32, 33.
  H. W., 279.
  John, 270.
  Joshua G., 274, 277.
  Judith, 21, 32, 33, 34.
  Maxson, 427.
  Rowse, 277.
  Ruth, 12, 31, 37.

Babcock (Continued)
  Simeon, 29, 158, 270, 273, 427, 429, 430.
  Simeon H., 287, 288, 293, 427.
  Thomas, 12, 16, 18, 21, 24, 29, 31, 33, 34, 35, 38, 39, 84, 85, 104, 105, 124, 398, 435, 439, 454.
  Thomas E., 105, 279.
  Uri M., 98, 114, 289, 293, 427.
  William, 112, 128, 131, 179, 432.
Babcocks, 61.
Backus, James E. N., 296.
Bacon, Job, 74, 79.
  Rhoda, 74, 79.
Baker, Halsey H., 384, 385.
  Joshua, 54.
Bailey, James, 121, 267, 286, 327, 333, 384, 385, 387, 388, 392, 407.
Bald Eagle, 54.
Ball, Elisabeth, 125.
Baltimore & Ohio R. R., 357.
Barber, Cynthia, 422.
  John, 422.
Barbour County, W. Va., 47.
Barkley, Thomas, 432.
Barnstable, Mass., 416.
Bartlett, Joseph, 429, 430.
Baptists, 36, 399.
Baptist Church, 262, 413, 420, 424.
  Clergyman, 353.
  Denomination, 360.
  Institution, 377.
Bassell, "Mr.", 153, 160.
Batten, Abner, 169, 316, 399.
  Abraham, 348.
  Elisabeth, 444.
  Elisabeth Bond, 444.
  John M., 214.
  T., 444.
  William, 156, 170, 348, 444.
Battens, 61.
Battle of Brandywine, 246 and note.
  Fallen Timbers, 46, 55.
  Monmouth, 27.
Beach Lick, 43.
Beard, Jacob, 432.

Bear Fork of Cove Creek, 189, 241, 405.
Bear Fork Church, 252, 293, 294, 295, 298, 311, 340. (Also see Conings Church).
Bear Fork Sabbath School. (See Conings Sabbath School).
Bear Track, 43.
Bedford County, Tenn., 157 note.
Bee, Abigail A., 365.
  Albert, 210.
  Allen, 210.
  Almira, 210.
  Amaziah, 113, 120, 121, 129, 175, 176, 177, 180, 181, 182, 183, 184, 185, 187, 188, 190, 191, 192, 193, 338, 348, 443.
  Angelina, 210.
  Arthur G., 210, 226, 450.
  Asa, 112, 113, 121, 128, 131, 182, 200, 201, 202, 205, 206, 209, 210, 279, 339, 365, 433, 450.
  Asa, widow of, 182.
  Azor Estee, 210.
  B. Wilson, 210, 340, 446.
  Catharine, 360.
  C. R., 210.
  Charles W., 210.
  Cordelia, 210.
  Elisabeth, 210.
  Elisabeth Ann, 210.
  Elma, 210.
  Ephraim, 128, 130, 174, 177, 179, 182, 360, 432.
  Ephraim W., 450.
  Eudolpheus, 210.
  Eudolpheus J., 220.
  Ezekiel, 87, 93, 112, 113, 120, 122, 129, 174, 175, 176, 177, 178, 180, 182, 185, 202, 205, 206, 210, 269, 278, 279, 345, 445.
  Hannah, 210.
  Hannah Maxson, 365.
  Ingaby, 132, 180, 210.
  Ira, 210.
  Isaiah, 54, 55, 133, 180, 353, 357, 364.
  Jeremiah, 210, 215.

INDEX 457

Bee (Continued)
  Jerusha, 210.
  Joel, 210, 450.
  John D., 128, 178, 180, 182, 189, 210, 433.
  John Nelson, 210.
  Jonathan, 131, 433.
  Josiah, 128, 175, 177, 178, 180, 182, 210, 215, 230, 278 note, 364, 433.
  Josiah H., 451.
  Kosannah, 210.
  Laomi, 210.
  Lear V., 210.
  Louise, 360.
  Luhama, 210.
  Mariah, 445.
  Martha, 131.
  Mary, 210.
  Mary A., 210.
  Obediah, 451.
  Olive E., 210.
  Ozina M., 210, 219.
  Perdilla, 210.
  Priscilla, 180, 210, 446.
  Priscilla Davis, 364.
  Rhoda, 129, 187, 188, 443.
  Richard, 451.
  Sally, 210.
  Sedilla, 210.
  Stephen, 210.
  Tacy Jane, 215.
  "The Elder", 205.
  William, 451.
  Zebulon, 206, 210, 291, 365.
  Family, 87, 182.
Bees, 61.
Beissel, Conrad, 245, 246.
Bell, Hannah, 432.
  James, 432.
  Sarah, 433.
Benedum, John H., 360.
Bennington, Vt., 421.
Berea, W. Va., 76, 216, 248, 357, 370, 445 and note, 447, 448, 449.
Berkeley County, Va., 44.
Berlin Church, 265, 313.
Bertly, John, 125.
Betts, Enoch, 453, 454.
Besontown, 75.
Big Steer Creek, 30 note.
Bingamon Creek, 48 note.
Black Lick, 43.
Black Lick Church, 219, 304, 305, 306, 307, 309, 310, 311, 312, 342, 424.
  History of, 261.
  Clerks, 263.
  Constituent members, 263-264.
  Deacons, 263.
  House of worship, 262.
  Licenced to preach, 263.
  Membership in superior bodies, 262.
  Moderators, 263.
  Organisation, 261-262.
  Pastors, 262.
Black Lick Run, 261, 262.
Black Lottie, 384 note.
Black Manuel, 384 note.
Blair, William M., 379, 380.
Blaisdell Machinery Co., 425.
Blandville, W. Va., 46, 361.
Blennerhassett Island, 55.
Bliss, William, 39.
Bliven, Eliza, 196.
Block-house, 58, 85.
Bloomfield, Kezia, 431.
Blossom, Elizabeth, 416.
  Thomas, 416.
Blough, Leannah, 250.
  Noah B., 247, 248, 250, 341.
Blue Ridge Mountains, 43.
Bolair, W. Va., 365.
Bond, Abel, 91, 93, 109, 110, 146, 148, 149, 150, 151, 154, 159, 163, 164, 165, 169, 171, 314, 315, 316, 317, 318, 319, 320, 323, 324, 338, 383, 414 and note, 426, 444.
  Abel D., 168.
  Abel P., 345, 348.
  Ahva John Clarence, 240, 306, 308, 311, 340, 427.
  Alfred J., 196.
  Amelia, 149, 432, 444.
  Anna, 320.

Bond (Continued)
Ann E., 237, 239.
Arthur, 447.
Austin O., 169.
Benjamin F., 76, 77, 80, 94, 196, 271, 272, 414 note.
Betsey, 237.
Boothe, 160, 162, 163, 170, 338, 415.
Brumfield, 338, 415, 444.
Camden, 451.
Cassandra, 196.
Charles M., 381.
Clarence L., 380, 381.
Cora E., 381.
Deacon, 169.
E., 444.
Ebenezer, 170.
Edy, 444.
Edwin Passmore, 196.
Eli, 93, 149, 230, 274, 338, 432, 444.
Elisabeth, 149, 239, 444.
Elisabeth S., 239.
Elsie B., 379, 380, 415, 448, 449.
Emeline, 210, 215.
Ethelbert, 343, 345, 349, 352, 414 note, 432.
Ethelbert and wife, 197.
Ethelbert D., 196 and note, 197, 360.
Florin L., 239, 242.
Frances, 80.
Mrs. Frances W., 80.
Henry C., 451.
Irvin, 360.
Jacob, 443.
Jane C., 238.
John C., 237, 238.
Jonathan, 77, 79, 271, 315, 321.
Joshua, 262.
Joshua S., 220.
Levi, 170, 171, 317, 338, 415.
Levi D., 160.
Levi H., 93, 169, 171, 266, 267.
Lewis, 94, 113, 130, 169, 170, 179, 196, 197, 198, 200, 266, 267, 269, 273, 324, 414 note, 444.

Bond (Continued)
Lewis and wife, 154, 197.
Luther A., 170, 171, 289, 298, 302, 304, 338.
Luther H., 211, 215, 242.
Lydia, 196, 198, 444.
Manerva S., 443.
Margaret, 149.
Martha, 211.
Mary, 126, 146, 149, 316, 318.
Mary Ann, 196.
Mary Davis, 360.
Mary E., 444.
Mrs., 320.
Naomi, 79.
Nathan, 360.
Nathan C. D., 451.
N. Clayton D., 253.
N. C. D., 252.
O. Austin, 381.
Prudence, 149.
Rachel, 320.
Rebecca E., 196.
Reuben, 149, 433.
Richard, 126, 146, 149, 160, 167, 215, 216, 414, 415, 450.
Richard C., 76, 78, 80, 132, 168, 171, 196, 267, 270, 271, 272, 273, 327, 400 note, 411, 414, 415, 434.
Richard E., 210, 211, 451.
S., 444.
Samuel B., 118, 169, 304, 305, 306, 307, 308, 310, 337, 380, 381, 415, 448, 449.
Samuel D., 237, 238, 239, 240, 299, 340, 370.
Sarah, 149.
Sarah Powers, 414.
Simeon, 196.
S. Orestes, 169, 311, 381.
Thomas, 149, 196, 348, 384 note, 451.
Thomas B., 171, 196, 317, 406.
Thomas M., 448.
Widow, 317.
William, 360.
William P., 163, 196.
Xenia E., 307, 308, 309, 381.

Bonds, 61, 86, 147.
Bond's Mills, 159.
Bone Creek, 366.
Bonnell, Charles, 366.
   Charles B., 235, 451.
   John, 418.
   Jonathan, 432, 451.
   Leeman, 451.
   Lehman, 366.
   Rhulanah, 235.
Booker, W. Va., 365.
Boone, Daniel, 46.
Boston, Mass., 45, 56 note, 410.
Bowen, Joseph C., 298.
Boyce School House, 241, 243.
Boyer, D. M., 378.
Boyles, —, 361.
Braddock's Road, 48 note.
Bradford, Pa., 425.
"Branches," 10.
Brand, Elisabeth, 12, 16, 22, 31,
   John 22, 32, 33, 74, 79.
   Rebecca, 32, 38, 429.
   William, 12, 16, 17, 22, 31, 32, 33, 34, 417, 429, 430.
Brands, 61.
Brandy Gap Tunnel, 443.
Braxton County, W. Va., 47, 251, 299.
Brick Church, 163.
Bridgeport, W. Va., 56 note.
Bridge Town, (N. J.), 148.
Bright, John, 86, 151, 159, 315, 316, 323.
Brisley, Elisabeth, 4, 6.
Brissey, George Amos, 219.
   George W., 243.
   Harriet, 446.
   Luther, 340.
British Army, 450.
British Central Africa, 309.
Broad Run, Va., 399, 445.
Broadus College, 377.
Brookfield, Mo., 422.
Brookfield, N. Y., 78, 194, 262, 266, 321, 327.
Brookville, Ind., 196.
Brown, Betsey, 421.
   Betsey Estee, 421.

Brown (Continued)
   Elias, 421, 434.
   Elisabeth, 81, 429, 430.
   Experience, 128, 432.
   Ezekiel, 127.
   Herbert C., 309.
   Lydia, 127.
   Martha L. Davis, 448.
   Nancy, 131.
   Sarah, 432, 434.
   Tacy, 127.
   Thomas B., 94, 154, 165, 272.
   William H., 218.
Brown University, 398, 423.
Brownfield, William, 76 note.
Brownsville, Pa., 52 note, 56.
Brumfield, Mary, 414.
Brushy Fork, 399.
Brunswick, N. J., 150.
Buckeye Creek, 60, 85, 333.
Buckeye Fork, 60, 262.
Buckeye Run, 60, 85, 96, 108, 132, 337, 339, 357, 364.
Buckhannon, W. Va., 365, 369, 377.
Buffalo, N. Y., 421.
Buffalo Calf, 43.
Bull, Captain, 54.
Bulltown, 54.
Burcher, Tillman H., 278 note.
Burdge, David, 429.
Burdick, Alfred B., 281, 384, 385.
   Betsey, 422.
   Charles A., 97, 110 note, 114, 121, 122, 158, 161, 166, 193, 195, 220, 238, 283, 285, 286, 287, 288, 328, 329, 335, 358, 367, 368 and note.
   Clayton A., 302, 308.
   Daniel Maxson, 352, 353, 360, 422.
   Daniel O., 422.
   Esther F. R., 447.
   Experience R., 300.
   Experience F. R., 447.
   George W., 292, 300.
   Hiram P., 190, 193, 233, 252, 253, 255, 293.

Burdick (Continued)
  Judson G., 188, 297, 306, 310, 330.
  Leon D., 310.
  LeRoy, 364.
  Perie R., 360, 417.
  Silas G., 448 note.
  Stephen, 288, 296, 303.
  Susie M., 306.
  Willard D., 306, 308.
  William L., 159, 167, 261, 262, 305, 307, 400, 418, 427.
Bureau of Ethnology, 41.
Burgess, James M., 418.
Burnsville, W. Va., 254.
Burr, Aaron, 55, 56 note.
Burton, C. M., 450 note.
Bush, Michael, 362.
Butler, Guy K., 361.

California, 7.
Calvin, John, 322.
Calvinism, 151, 316, 322.
Calvinist, 325.
Calvinists, 322.
Camp Chase, 394.
Campbell, Alexander, 78, 88, 110, 159, 163, 164, 195, 197, 200, 265, 278 note, 293, 321, 322, 323, 324, 325, 326, 331.
  Mrs. Alexander, 323.
  Anne, 429, 431.
  Orson, 265.
Capuchins, 246.
Carder, Dennis, 184.
  James A., 381.
Carpenter, Nicholas, 50 note, 53, 56, 58.
Carpenters (Nicholas) Camp, 50 note, 54, 56.
Carpenters Run, 56.
Cat Fish Camp, 48 note.
Cayuga County, N. Y., 422.
Cecil County, Md., 86, 147, 196, 414.
Celibacy, 246.
Central Association, 267, 285, 286, 287, 288, 289, 290, 292, 293, 294, 295, 296, 297, 298, 302, 303, 304, 305, 306, 307, 308, 309, 310, 311.
Ceremonial Law, 213.
Champlin, E. G., 385.
Chana, Samuel, 186.
Chaney, Samuel, 432.
Charleston, W. Va., 30 note, 372, 373, 419.
Charter, Andrew Judson, 356, 360, 447.
  Lathrop R., 356, 360.
Chautauqua Normal Course, 290.
Cheat River, 30, 47, 48 note, 52 note, 56 note.
Chedester, Marshall L., 115, 124.
  Presley, 115.
Chenango County, N. Y., 422.
Cherry Camp, 85.
Cheuvront, Joseph, 433.
Chicago, Ill., 424.
Chicago Church, 424.
Childers, Asher S., 371, 372, 378.
  Enoch, 451.
  Jane, 278 note.
  Mrs., 55.
China Mission, 274, 289.
Church, Bethuel C., 168, 270.
Church of England, 4, 26, 141.
Churches (Seventh Day Baptist) in England, 5.
Cincinnati, O., 418.
Circuit Court of Doddridge County, W. Va., 258, 346.
Circuit Court of Harrison County, W. Va., 45.
Civil War, 97, 103, 156, 209, 327, 353, 394, 408, 419, 450.
Clarence Church, 266.
Clark, Charlotte, 235.
  Effilee, 235.
  Fenton R., 235, 241, 340.
  G. Wise, 252.
  Jesse, 108, 109, 191, 193, 214, 233, 235, 340.
  Lucy A., 235.
  Marvel, 235.
  Milton, 234, 235, 340.
Clarke, Beatrice Lowther, 449.
  Deacon, 38, 397.

INDEX 461

Clark (Continued)
 Elisabeth, 397.
 Herman D., 294, 308.
 J. Bennett, 289, 295, 296, 297, 333.
 Joseph, 397.
 Joshua, 290, 302.
 Thomas M., 385, 387.
Clarke County, Mo., 445 note.
Clarksburg, W. Va., 44, 45, 55, 56 and note, 60, 61, 135, 149, 150, 159, 161, 331, 353, 354 and note, 377, 431, 447, 453.
Clawson, Abbie M., 380.
 Cortez R., 337, 378, 380, 381.
 David, 96, 103, 106, 113, 121, 155, 156, 165, 327, 384, 411, 444.
 J. Alice, 380.
 John J., 381.
Clauson, John, 76.
Clay Pit Creek, 9, 29, 31, 35.
Clayton, Elisabeth, 125, 126.
 John, 79.
 Thomas, 58, 104, 125, 453, 454.
 ———, 418.
Claytons, 61.
Clement, Benjamin, 274, 276.
Clendennon, James, 320.
Clermont, The, 46 note.
Cleveland, O., 422.
Coburn, Captain, 45, 55.
Cocalico River, 246.
Cochran, James H., 266, 267.
Coffman, Charles G., 381.
Cohansey, N. J., 2, 18, 101, 102, 147, 148, 151.
Cole, Elisabeth, 434.
Collins, Cynthia, 211.
 Sylvester, 211.
Colts Neck, 27.
Confederate lines, 357.
Congress, 52.
Conings Church, 15 note, 189, 252, 301, 304, 309, 310, 311, 340. (Also see Bear Fork Church).
 History of, 241.
 Clerk, 244.

Conings Church (Continued)
 Deacon, 244.
 House of worship, 243.
 Membership in superior bodies, 242.
 Moderator, 244.
 Name, 242.
 Organisation, 241.
 Pastors, 243.
Conings Sabbath School, 340.
Connecticut, 265, 400.
Conotoway Baptist Church, 79.
Consolidation of the South Fork of Hughes River, or Pine Grove, Church with the Ritchie Church, 205.
Cookman, Samuel, 161.
Cooley, Samuel, 82.
Coon, Adelia, 196.
 Amos W., 218, 287.
 Daniel, 88.
 D. Burdette, 307.
 Stillman, 78, 88, 89, 91, 152, 196, 269, 326, 405.
Copen Church, 299, 301, 304, 311, 312, 341.
 History of, 251.
 Membership in superior bodies, 253.
 Officers, 254.
 Organisation, 251.
 Records, 254.
Copen Sabbath School, 341.
Copen Run, 251.
Corbly, John, 76 note.
Cornell University, 424.
Cornstalk, 54.
Cornwall, ———, 315.
Corwin, William, 379.
Cottrell, George M., 294.
 Ira Lee, 115, 293.
 Libbeus M., 247.
Cottrille, Addie, 264.
 Gertrude, 262, 263, 264, 342.
 Sarah E., 264, 342.
County Clerk of Harrison County, W. Va., 453.
County Court of Harrison County, W. Va., 431.

Court of Record of Doddridge
County, W. Va., 346.
Cove Creek, 405.
Covenhoven, Jacob, 435.
  Peter, 429.
Cranberry Bog, 10.
Crandall, Eda L., 379.
  George J., 226, 294.
  Lucius, 385.
Cresap, Michael, 54 note.
Cross Creek, 48 note.
Crofoot, Asa G., 302.
Cumberland, Md., 357.
Cumberland County, N. C., 409.
Cumberland County, N. J., 429, 430, 431.
Cunningham, Cecil W., 381.
Curtis, John, 429.
Cussewago (Pennsylvania) Church, 170.
Cutright, John, 54.
Daland, William C., 298, 311.
Darkin, Jale, 429, 430.
David, Daniel, 80.
  Daniel G. W., 80, 414 note, 440
  Daniel W., 82.
  Ebenezer, 80, 413.
  Elisabeth, 79, 80, 196, 440.
  Enoch, 75, 78, 155, 196, 413, 414 and note, 440.
  Isaac and wife, 80.
  James N., 372, 378.
  Jane, 80.
  Joseph, 80.
  Marie E., 440.
  Mary Ann, 80.
  Mrs., 317.
  Naomi, 79.
  Owen, 77, 79, 413, 414.
  Penelope, 80.
  William, 80.
Davis, Abigail Hoffman, 366, 411, 444.
  Abner J., 188, 339, 451.
  Absolom A., 128, 132, 214, 433.
  Adolphus A., 235.
  Alcena J., 235.
  Aldis L., 118, 310, 381.
  Alfred, 361.

Davis (Continued)
  Alfred N., 176, 178, 180, 433.
  Almeda, 236.
  Alpheus Martin, 361.
  Alva L., 448.
  Alvin H., 230.
  Alvin M., 191, 262, 263, 264.
  Alwilda, 259.
  Amos, 128, 433, 444.
  Amy, 125, 133, 146, 361, 400, 402, 429, 430.
  Ananias, 264.
  Ananias R., 264.
  Anderson, 260.
  Anderson H., 339.
  Ann, 22, 33, 34, 130, 432, 433, 453.
  Anna, 37, 127, 364, 429, 430, 440.
  Anne, 429.
  Arthur, 264.
  Arthur Clarence, 448.
  Artilla, 264.
  Arzander, 211.
  Asa, 433, 443.
  Aseneth, 129, 432, 433, 444.
  Austin M., 451.
  A. S., 451.
  Benjamin, 131, 429, 431.
  Benjamin F., 451.
  Benjamin L., 361.
  Bethiah, 12, 31, 37.
  Betsey, 127, 134.
  "Billy Buckeye", 192 note.
  Boothe Colwell, 36 note, 115, 307, 308, 309, 310, 360, 400 note, 405 note, 410, 417, 427 and note, 448, 449.
  "Bottom Billy," 401.
  "Bottom William," 127.
  Calvin, 129, 130, 179, 432.
  Caroline, 361.
  Catharine, 34, 127, 131, 180, 432, 433, 442.
  Cecelia, 259.
  C. C., 259.
  Charles Christopher, 361.
  Charles Compton, 339.
  Charles G., 131, 132.
  Charlotta, 132.

INDEX

Davis (Continued)
  Charlotte, 129, 131, 264, 432.
  Clementina M., 339.
  Clinton H., 162.
  Columbus F., 448.
  Comfort, 16, 32.
  Content, 125, 128, 133, 433, 442, 443.
  Cora, 448.
  Cornelius R., 234.
  Cornelius S., 234, 262, 263, 264, 337.
  Crandall, 398.
  Crede H., 448.
  Daniel, 450.
  Daniel T., 451.
  Daniel W., 211.
  Darius King, 285, 289, 305, 356, 361, 400, 427, 447, 449.
  David, 34, 129, 432, 450, 451.
  David D., 343 note, 348, 364, 442.
  David H., 289, 302.
  Mrs. David H., 302.
  Deborah, 433.
  Delia G., 235.
  Delilah, 129, 264.
  Delila Chapman, 361.
  Delma M., 381.
  Dorinda, 132, 211, 215, 445.
  Dudley H., 159, 163, 287, 336, 338, 365.
  Eastburn A., 451.
  Ebenezer, 265.
  Edgar S., 378.
  Edith, 129, 131, 180.
  Edward, 6.
  Ehud, 128, 132, 433.
  Ehud Johnson, 361.
  Elhanan W., 278 note.
  Eli, 451.
  Eli F., 451.
  Eli R., 260.
  Elias B., 129.
  Elias L., 130, 179.
  Elijah, 264.
  Eliona, 128, 345, 348, 349, 350, 353, 356, 361, 400, 433.
  Elisabeth, 6, 12, 16, 31, 32, 37,

Davis (Continued)
    125, 126, 127, 130, 132, 179, 180, 361, 398, 418, 429, 430, 432, 441, 443.
  Elisabeth A., 263.
  Elisabeth F., 132.
  Elisabeth Jeffrey, 365.
  Emily, 132, 361.
  Emily Virginia, 365, 404, 442, 448.
  Emma, 341.
  Emma J., 256.
  Emza J., 361.
  Miss E. J., 259.
  Enoch, 429, 431.
  Enoch J., 384.
  Ermine B., 447.
  Esther, 129, 432.
  Esther F., 445.
  Esther F. R., 361.
  Ethelbert J., 234, 235, 252, 261, 299, 340, 370.
  Experience, 32, 127, 130, 179, 256, 445.
  Experience Thorp, 365.
  Ezra, 451.
  Hannah, 34, 37, 79, 125, 128, 185, 186, 211, 264, 432, 433, 440, 444.
  Hannibal Hamlin, 447.
  Harmon, 259.
  Hermon, 256.
  Herman B., 378.
  Hezekiah, 361.
  Hezekiah S., 451.
  Hiram N., 157, 171.
  Hulda, 128.
  Huldah, 235, 433.
  Gamble S., 256, 259, 341, 365.
  George J., 113, 119, 121, 122, 126, 127, 278, 316, 317, 319, 320, 347, 348, 349, 432, 441, 442.
  Gladie, 264.
  Granville H., 191, 192, 214, 230, 238, 378, 451.
  "Greenbrier Billy", 54, 134, 401, 402, 418, 441.
  Fatima, 433.

Davis (Continued)
"Flint Billy," 365, 401, 442.
Francis M., 211, 235, 365.
Franklin, 451.
Franklin Maxwell, 361.
Ichabod, 318.
Ingabe, 433.
Ira, 132.
Ira C., 132.
Irving P. C., 361.
Isaiah B., 211.
Jacob, 18, 19, 22, 27, 28, 29, 30, 32, 33, 34, 35, 38, 58, 59, 73, 84, 98, 113, 119, 120, 122, 124, 126, 133, 149, 156, 157, 158, 165, 166, 169, 171, 191, 214, 215, 217, 220, 230, 231, 232, 234, 235, 238, 276, 278, 286, 288, 289, 291, 294, 296, 316, 340, 366, 398, 399, 400, 403, 404, 405, 406, 407, 411, 412, 419, 423, 426, 427, 436, 444, 450, 453, 454.
James, 12, 18, 22, 27, 29, 31, 32, 33, 34, 37, 58, 124, 125, 127, 129, 130, 137, 179, 180, 317, 398, 405, 429, 432, 441, 450, 453, 454.
James B., 181, 183, 187, 189, 190, 191, 192, 193, 213, 214, 217, 220, 230, 241, 242, 243, 255, 288, 293, 338, 339, 365, 403, 427, 442, 450 note.
James M., 130, 179, 451.
James W., 451.
Jane, 127, 130, 132, 215, 343 note, 445.
Mrs. Jane, 316.
Jane Eliza, 128.
"Jarsey Billy," 55, 133, 401, 402.
Jean, 264.
Jemima, 131, 132, 215, 235, 403, 412.
Jeptha, 127, 432.
Jesse, 105, 123, 127, 133, 316, 317, 319, 320, 338, 433.
Jesse D., 131.
Jesse J., 121, 123, 128, 235.
Jesse Maxson, 411, 423, 444.

Davis (Continued)
Joel, 125, 132, 133, 442.
Joel H., 131.
John, 12, 14, 16, 17, 18, 22, 29, 31, 32, 33, 34, 35, 37, 38 and note, 39, 58, 59, 76, 84, 85, 86, 96, 102, 104, 111, 112, 119, 120, 124, 125, 126, 127, 128, 133, 136, 137, 147, 148, 150, 151, 159, 163, 164, 173, 273, 313, 315, 316, 317, 323, 326, 338, 397, 398, 399, 400 and note, 401, 402, 405 note, 426, 427, 432, 433, 434, 445, 450, 453, 454.
John J., 234, 263.
John S., 129, 343 and note, 344, 345, 347, 348, 349, 350, 352, 353, 361.
John T., 298, 310, 427.
Johnson, 211.
Jonathan, 5, 125, 432.
Joseph, 6, 12, 16, 22, 31, 32, 33, 34, 37, 38, 61, 84, 107, 111, 124, 125, 126, 136, 142, 178, 182, 185, 186, 187, 428, 429, 432.
Joseph and wife, 126.
Josephine, 433.
Joshua, 123, 125, 127, 131, 180, 317, 319, 338, 432, 441.
Joshua F., 451.
Joshua G., 90, 91, 93, 133, 442.
Joshua J., 175, 176, 185, 187, 211, 235.
Joshua S., 93, 128, 168, 171, 201, 206, 211, 339, 344, 444.
Judith, 12, 31, 32, 37, 364.
Julia A., 423.
Kate, 256, 259.
Katharine, 180.
Kezia, 441.
Keziah, 127, 130, 179, 433, 444.
Laban, 129.
Loverna Beatrice, 264.
Leander, 211.
Leda, 264.
Lemuel, 133, 180, 211.
Levi, 128.

(29)

Davis (Continued)
- Levi B., 162, 170, 171, 238, 294, 371, 372, 378.
- Lewis, 127, 128, 129, 130, 180, 451.
- Lewis A., 78, 86, 111, 128, 131, 165, 168, 266, 267, 269, 270, 271, 273, 275, 277, 319, 320, 326, 400, 415, 427, 434.
- Lewis Townsend, 361, 402 note.
- Linville B., 188, 194, 339.
- Lodowick H., 93, 95, 114, 120, 121, 122, 130, 191, 230, 337, 343 and note, 344, 347, 348, 349, 350, 351, 365, 368, 419, 423, 433.
- Lora, 264.
- Louisa Bell, 253.
- Lucinda, 131.
- Luke, 434.
- Lurana, 129, 432.
- Luther, 129, 130, 179.
- Lydia, 6, 34, 127, 129, 130, 179, 398.
- Madison, 129.
- Maggie E., 260.
- Maleta H., 449.
- Maria, 264.
- Marcellus Berkeley, 171, 172, 338.
- Margaret, 125, 131, 132, 365, 433.
- Martha, 6, 22, 33, 129.
- Martin VanBuren, 120.
- Marvel, 34, 126, 146, 264.
- Mary, 6, 22, 32, 33, 34, 38, 126, 129, 131, 180, 336, 398, 399, 400, 418, 429, 432.
- Mary Ann, 235.
- Mary Ann M., 433.
- Mary D., 259.
- Mary Josephine, 129, 133.
- Mary Tacy, 361.
- Melissa, 256, 259.
- Milton, 378.
- Milton S., 290, 337.
- Morris N., 364.
- M. Wardner, 120, 299, 301, 304, 305, 308, 337, 378, 410, 448.

Davis (Continued)
- Moses H., 122, 162, 170, 171, 191, 238, 278, 279, 283, 284, 285, 286, 288, 289, 290, 291, 292, 295, 338, 423.
- Nancy, 125, 126, 264, 442.
- Nancy Brown, 361.
- Nancy E., 264.
- Nancy I., 264.
- Nancy J., 342.
- Nathan, 22, 24, 25, 32, 33, 34, 37, 61, 89, 90, 104, 105 and note, 107, 123 note, 125, 127, 130, 133, 174, 178, 180, 196, 258, 315, 316, 317, 319, 320, 343 note, 348, 349, 350, 402, 429, 430, 433, 440, 445, 450, 453, 454.
- Nathan G., 433.
- Nathan J., 337, 444.
- Newton, 260.
- Okey S., 260.
- Ora James, 380, 447.
- Owen, 451.
- Owen T., 171.
- Penelope, 22, 32, 33.
- Peter, 78, 86, 87, 90, 91, 95, 96, 105, 107, 111, 112, 113, 120, 121, 126, 131, 133, 141, 165, 168, 199, 205, 213, 231, 266, 267, 271, 276, 277, 286, 319, 324, 401, 405, 406, 407, 412, 415, 427, 432, 433, 443, 450.
- Peter W., 130.
- Phiathata, 129, 130, 179.
- Philip, 125.
- Philotheta, 211.
- Phineas, 127, 361, 433.
- Phineas R., 211.
- Phoebe, 132.
- Polina, 128, 132, 433.
- Polina A., 132.
- Polina S. W., 264.
- Polly, 398, 400.
- Priscilla, 128, 433.
- Prudence, 434.
- Prudence Maxson, 403.
- Rachel, 127, 134, 361, 433, 442.
- Rachel Hughes, 365, 404.

Davis (Continued)
Randolph, 157.
Rebecca, 33, 86, 131, 361, 401, 433.
Rebekah, 22, 124, 125.
Rhoda, 133, 180, 211.
Rhulana, 433.
Rhulanah, 127.
Rhulanah F. R., 361.
Riley G., 118, 219, 220, 233, 234, 244, 252, 261, 263, 306, 307, 308, 340, 427, 451.
Robert, 434.
"Rock Run Billy," 175 note, 365, 401, 445.
Rosa, 448.
Salla, 442.
Sally, 125, 133.
Sally C., 235.
Sabrina, 211.
Salathiel, 236.
Samuel, 34, 86, 125, 126, 137, 314, 398.
Samuel D., 98, 103, 113, 114, 115, 120, 122, 123, 141, 154, 156, 157, 158, 161, 165, 166, 168, 191, 193, 214, 215, 218, 220, 230, 232, 237, 238, 239, 241, 244, 247, 248, 252, 253, 254, 255, 256, 257, 274, 276, 277, 278, 279, 281, 285, 287, 288, 295, 297, 299, 302, 305, 310, 330, 333, 363, 370, 384, 385, 386, 393, 400 note, 404, 405, 412, 417, 419, 427.
Samuel H., 117, 309, 360, 410, 417, 427, 448.
S. Preston, 256, 259, 365.
Sapphira, 131, 180.
Sarah, 126, 132, 149, 400, 403, 432, 433, 443.
Sarah Ann, 180.
Sarah Hoffman, 366, 405.
Sehaba, 433.
Silas B., 379, 448.
Silas Carder, 337, 365.
Simeon Gillis, 410.
Sophia, 129, 361.
Sophiah, 433.

Davis (Continued)
"Squire," 129.
Statira, 361.
Stephen, 127, 133, 211, 320, 418.
Stephen C., 214, 215, 442, 451.
Stephen T., 175, 177, 178, 180, 183, 184, 191, 192, 193, 242, 347, 348, 349, 350, 351, 365, 443.
Sylvanus, 230, 259, 262, 263, 342, 451.
Sylvester, 127, 130, 179, 432.
S. Orlando, 171, 378, 410.
Tacy, 21, 32, 33, 128, 133, 432, 433.
Tacy Jane, 361.
Talitha, 211.
Tamar, 414.
Taysey, 133.
Terence M., 337, 368, 447, 449.
Theodore, 132, 133, 263.
Thomas, 6, 12, 21, 22, 29, 31, 32, 33, 37, 39, 429, 431, 435, 436, 453.
Thomas A., 163.
Thomas B., 170, 361.
Thomas Edgar, 338, 339.
Timothy K., 451.
Victoria, 264.
Vienna, 127.
Virginius L., 448.
Waitman T. Willy, 252, 253, 341.
Wardner, 162. (Also see M. Wardner).
William, 6, 12, 16, 21, 22, 29, 30, 31, 32, 33, 34, 37, 39, 54, 55, 58, 59, 61, 83, 84, 100, 105, 107, 123, 124, 125, 126, 127, 133, 134, 137, 142, 178, 260, 317, 319, 397, 398, 399, 400, 401, 402, 405, 418, 427, 432, 433, 435, 436, 439, 441, 450, 451, 453.
William, of Wales, 1.
  Ancestry, 1.
  Applies for membership in the Newport Church, 4.
  Arranges to go to England, 5.

INDEX 467

Davis (Continued)
    Banished from Pennepek Church, 2.
    Becomes a Baptist, 1.
    Becomes a Seventh Day Baptist, 2.
    Becomes a follower of George Keith, 1.
    Becomes a member of the Westerly Church, 5.
    Becomes a Quaker, 1.
    Born in Glamorganshire, Wales, 1.
    Conflict with Keith, 4.
    Death, 7.
    Descendants, 7.
    Educated at Oxford University, 1.
    Emigrates to America, 1.
    Invited by the Westerly Church to preach, 5.
    Marriage and children, 6.
    Organises a Seventh Day Baptist Church, 2.
    Publishes a book, 2.
    Removes back to Pennsylvania, 6.
    Removes to Monmouth County, N. J., 7.
    Returns to the Westerly Church, 6.
    William B., 123, 129, 132, 192, 214, 230, 337.
    William E., 448, 451.
    William F., 134, 365, 404, 442.
    William G., 130, 179, 365.
    William H. H., 278 note, 339, 451.
    William J., 129, 130, 174, 175, 176, 177, 178, 179, 180, 185, 348, 349, 365, 445.
    William L., 191, 311, 339.
    William R., 451.
    William S., 129, 130, 131, 179, 180.
    W. Franklin, 122.
    Z., 445.
    Zania, 264.
    Zebulon, 131, 133, 398.

Davis (Continued)
    Ziba, 128, 133, 211, 213, 214, 215, 219, 220, 230, 433.
    Zippa, 400.
    "Davis disabled", 2.
    Davis (town of), W. Va., 56 note.
Davises, 61.
Davisson, Ann, 453.
    Daniel, 55.
    Hezekiah, 50 note.
    Samuel, 275, 276.
Dawson, Henry, 33, 38.
Day, Gideon, 34, 39.
    Lois, 79.
Deal, N. J., 9, 14.
Delaware Indians, 2.
Delaware River, 46 note.
Denham, Abby, 432.
Denham, John, 432.
Dennis, Anna, 34.
    Catharine, 34.
    William, 34.
DeRuyter, N. Y., 88, 152, 159, 167, 316, 319, 321, 325, 422.
DeRuyter church, 314.
DeRuyter Institute, 422.
Detroit, Mich., 450 note.
Dew, Lela, 381.
Dicks, Mrs., 320.
Dinwiddie, Governor, 44.
Doddridge County, W. Va., 47, 61, 176, 178, 328, 332, 343, 351, 357, 402, 404, 419, 423, 450 note.
Doddridge County Court, 187.
Doddridge, Joseph, 63, 64, 67, 68, 69, 72.
Doak, G. O., 379, 381.
Dougherty, Dr., 363.
Dover, Delaware, 413.
Drake, 55.
    Rachel, 79.
Duck Creek, Delaware, 413.
Dunaway, John, 146, 319.
    Mary, 146.
Dunham, Jonathan, 18, 32, 38, 398, 431.
    Stephen, 73, 74, 77, 79.

Dunkards (see Dunkers).
Dunkers, 245, 246.
Dunlap's Road, 48 note.
Dunn, Charlotte, 80.
  David, 80.
  Elisabeth, 430, 431.
  Elston M., 290, 301.
  James, 74, 77, 79.
  Manning, 148, 150, 313.
  Sarah, 80.
Duvall, John P., 50 note.
Eastern Association, 103, 172, 265, 281, 285, 287, 288, 289, 290, 292, 293, 294, 295, 296, 297, 298, 301, 302, 303, 304, 306, 307, 308, 309, 310, 311, 327, 333, 384, 385, 392, 393, 394.
East Jersey, 150, 416.
East New Jersey, 413.
  Province of, 12, 14.
Eastern Division of New Jersey, 28.
Eaton, Nellie, 380.
Eberbach, 245.
Eckerling, Israel, 7.
  Samuel, 7.
Edwards, Isaac, 432.
  Morgan, 30.
Ehret, Clyde, 340.
  Elisabeth, 211, 215.
  Flavius J., 118, 120, 224, 226, 227, 295, 296, 299, 301, 304, 305, 306, 308, 309, 310, 337, 370, 378.
  Hannah M., 211.
  Jacob, 215.
  Joanna, 215.
  John, 206, 211, 215, 219, 220, 226.
  Sarah A., 215.
  William F., 211, 214, 215, 220, 224, 339.
Eggleston, D. Q., 59.
Elberon, 9.
Election Commissioners, 156.
Elk Creek, 44, 45, 55, 60, 109, 147, 159, 338, 384 note, 399, 414.
Elk River, 43.
Ellenboro, W. Va., 357.
Emporia, Kansas, 361.

England, 4, 5.
Envelope system, 293.
Ephrata, Penn., 7, 246.
Episcopalian Church, 4.
Etruscan Characters, 41.
Erie County, N. Y., 266.
Ernst, William H., 296.
Estee, Abigail Thompson, 421.
  Azor, 96, 121, 154, 165, 168, 178, 276, 277, 278, 327, 343, 344, 349, 352, 353, 357, 360, 362, 407, 420.
  Betsey Brown, 362.
  Charles B., 362, 421.
  Daniel Maxson, 421.
  Henry, 421.
  James A., 357, 360, 421.
  Stephen, 421.
  Susan M., 420, 421.
Evans, Evan 4.
  Harvey, 449.
  Col. John, 50 note.

Fall Run, 30 note.
Farmington, Ill., 401.
Fasting, 14.
Fast Days, 17, 40, 101.
Fayette County, Pa., 47, 50, 53, 58, 59 note, 84, 196, 268, 398, 413, 417.
Federal Army, 394.
Feet-washing, 14, 15 and note, 16.
Ferris, W. H., 163.
First Brookfield Church, 266.
First Day Baptist Church, 78.
First Day Baptists, 80, 138, 140, 141, 151, 216, 325.
First Hopkinton Church, 4, 265, 393.
Fishomingo County, Miss., 423.
Fiske, Byron E., 301.
Fitch, John, 46 note.
Fittro, Silas, 359.
Fleming, James, 434.
Flesher, Eliza Jane, 340.
  J. L., 340.
  Rebecca Ann, 242, 340.
  Sigourney, 340.
  William H., 242, 243, 244, 340.

INDEX

Flint, Amaziah, 235.
  John, 359.
  Mary, 236.
Flint Run, 60, 85, 108, 357, 365, 423.
Ford, Albert, 365, 433.
  C. Laton, 256, 259, 378, 380.
  Elisabeth, 132, 365, 409.
  Emily, 131, 132.
  E. Jane, 256, 259.
  Festus P., 256, 259, 290, 301, 303, 340, 341, 378.
  George, 121, 122, 131, 132, 191, 230, 337, 348, 349.
  Hamilton, 365.
  Herbert L., 448.
  Herman C., 447, 449.
  Irene Belle Davis, 259.
  James, 256, 259, 337.
  Laura, 255.
  Laura A., 256, 259, 341.
  Lillie M., 256, 259, 341.
  Polina, 131.
  Rhulanah Davis, 365.
  Richard, 114, 131, 132, 191, 337, 348, 349, 353, 357.
  Samuel A., 190, 191, 233, 261, 342.
  Samuel L., 256, 258, 259, 341.
  Septimius Ardvern, 256, 259, 341.
  Talitha W., 256, 259.
  Thomas, 132, 432.
Ford, Reed and, 30.
Forsythe, Eli, 272, 273, 274, 277.
  John, 149, 169, 171, 270, 316.
  Sarah, 149.
Forsythes, 147.
Fox, Elisabeth, 445.
  Elisabeth Burgess, 420.
  George, 1, 420, 445.
  Mary Elisabeth, 420.
Frame Church, 153, 160.
France, 46 note.
Franklin County, Penn., 421.
Fraser, William, 453.
Frasure, Elisabeth, 131.
Frazee, Stephen, 430.
Frazer, Stephen, 430.

Free Methodists, 36.
Free school system, 357.
Freehold, 27.
French and Indian War, 44.
French Creek, Penn., 315, 320.
French Creek Church, 77.
Friendship, N. Y., 422.
Frontier life described, 63.
  Housewarming, 67.
  Labour and its discouragements, 69.
  The Mechanic Arts, 70.
  Wedding Customs, 64.
Frum, Orestes W., 381.
Fulton, Robert, 46 note.
Furby, Melvina Davis, 259.

Gaelic Characters, 41.
Gamble, James L., 307.
Gardiner, Dora, 310, 337, 381.
  Theodore L., 99, 110, 116, 117, 118, 219, 249, 292, 300, 301, 303, 308, 309, 310, 311, 374, 375, 376, 378, 379.
Gardner, Kansas, 361.
Garner, Isaiah, 362.
  John, 362.
  Sarah Ann Williams, 362.
General Assembly of Virginia, 48 note, 56, 58, 89, 178, 196 note, 258, 344, 345, 347, 351, 354.
General Conference, 78, 88, 98, 101, 135, 137, 138, 147, 148, 152, 163, 164, 172, 194, 195, 197, 202, 205, 216, 231, 239, 243, 247, 254, 258, 262, 265, 266, 268, 273, 293, 313, 314, 326, 327, 369, 370, 400, 411, 426.
Georges Camp, 43, 182.
Georges Creek, 73, 315.
Georges Township, Fayette County, Penn., 73, 81.
German Baptist Brethren, 245.
German Seventh Day Baptists, 246, 247, 284, 285, 421.
German Seventh Day Baptist Cemetery at Ephrata, Penn., 246.

German Seventh Day Baptist
    Church, 245, 249.
Germantown, Penn., 245, 246.
Germany, 245.
Gettysburg, Penn., 357.
Gibson, William, 5.
Gibson City, Ill., 362, 421.
Gifford, Ananias, 34.
  Anna, 402,
  Anney, 429, 430.
  Elisabeth, 34.
  Hannah, 429, 430.
  Joseph, 34.
  Margaret, 430.
  Mary, 34.
  Sarah, 34.
Gillette, Walter B., 78, 97, 113, 121, 122, 157, 161, 213, 214, 215, 229, 230, 247, 274, 323, 328, 337, 339, 384, 393.
Gillis, Elisabeth, 417, 433.
Gilhman, Lettitia, 430, 431.
Gilmer County, W. Va., 47, 241, 328.
Girty, 54.
Gist, Christopher, 44.
Glades, The, 74.
Glendola, N. J., 36.
Gloversville, N. Y., 421.
Gochenauer, William Alonzo, 252, 253.
Goodwin, E. A., 211.
  Henry H., 211, 224.
Gordon, William J., 157 and note, 158.
Goss, Hamilton, 150, 164.
Government of the United States, 56.
Grant, Eliza, 415, 434.
Graves, James, 316.
  Thomas, 2, 4.
Great Kanawha River, 43, 44.
Great Branch, 10, 28, 35.
Great Miami, 52.
Greathouse, Daniel, 54.
Greek Characters, 41.
Greenbrier, 119, 127, 166, 217, 218, 319, 325, 340, 352, 364, 443.

Greenbrier Church, 97, 108, 113, 118, 123, 190, 193 note, 219, 238, 241, 252, 261, 262, 263, 287, 288, 289, 290, 291, 292, 293, 295, 297, 301, 303, 304, 305, 306, 307, 309, 310, 311, 328, 403, 412, 420, 424.
  History of, 229.
  Church clerks, 234.
  Constituent members, 235.
  Deacons, 233.
  House of worship, 231.
  Licenced to preach, 233.
  Membership in superior bodies, 231.
  Moderators, 234.
  Organisation, 229.
  Pastors, 232.
Greenbrier Sabbath School, 340.
Greenbrier County, 70, 420.
Greenbrier Run, 54, 60, 85, 87, 96, 106, 107, 108, 109, 121, 133, 205, 229, 230, 231, 239, 324, 403, 404, 412, 447.
Greenbrier River, 48 note.
Greene, Charles H., 440 note.
  Joel, 77, 78, 88, 94, 152, 164, 173, 265, 266, 267, 273, 320, 321, 323, 326, 327.
  John, 86, 109, 159, 316, 317, 318, 320, 323, 401, 402.
  Sister, 323.
Greenmanville Church, 385, 386.
Greenville, 54.
Greggory, Jane, 429, 430.
Gribble, Talitha C., 215.
  Thomas N., 215, 451.
Griffin, Eliza, 317.
  Isaac, 76, 316, 318, 320.
  Mary, 74, 79, 80.
  Mrs., 317.
Griswold, Sherman S., 293, 384, 385, 394.
Growden, Barbara, 250.
  Jeremiah, 250.
Hacker, William, 54.
Hackers Creek, 46 note, 54, 61, 86, 147, 159, 160.

INDEX

Haddonfield, N. J., 417.
Hagerty, Venie, 381.
Halbert, Prine, 211.
Hall, Mary, 80 .
  David, 28.
  Elisha, 366.
  Lawson, 366.
  Lucinda, 433.
  Peter, 125, 126.
  Susannah Thorp, 366.
  William P., 433.
Halle, 245.
Halls Run, 85, 106, 108, 121.
Hamilton, Alleyne, 380.
Hammond, Louisiana, 118.
Hampton, Elisabeth, 26, 32.
  John, 32.
Hankinson, Aaron, 416.
Harbert, Calvin, 34.
  John, 432.
  Samuel, 432.
Harrison County, W. Va., 30 note, 44, 45, 46, 47, 58, 178, 196, 314, 328, 356, 357, 373, 376, 411, 414 note, 423, 431, 450.
Harrisville, W. Va., 361.
Haven, Mary J., 379.
Havens, Anna, 22, 32, 33, 37.
  Elisabeth, 428, 430.
  Jacob, 33.
  John, 37, 429, 430.
  Lydia, 22, 33.
Hawker, Henry, 378.
Hayfield, Penn., 321.
Haymond, John, 59.
  William, 50 note.
Hays, H. T., 353.
Haystack Knob, 48 note.
Hebrew Religion, 201.
Hebrews, 201.
Hebron, Penn., 357, 364.
Heckewelder, 2 note.
Hersey, Thomas, 76 note.
Hetrick, Noah, 363.
Hevener, Abigail H., 237, 238, 240.
  Amanda J., 239.
  Ina, 340.

Hevener (Continued)
  John J., 237, 238, 239, 240.
  Mansfield M., 237, 240, 242, 340.
  Mary E., 237, 238.
  Reuben, 237, 238, 239, 366.
Hickman, Andrew Jackson, 365.
Hildeburn, Charles R., 2 note.
High School at West Union, 278.
Hill, James, 125, 272, 273, 417, 432, 433.
  Joshua, 132, 168, 270, 271, 272, 273, 274, 415.
Hills, George W., 311.
Hinton, John, 453.
Hitt, Sarah Catharine, 253.
Hoard, Alice Maud, 379.
Hodgson, Mary, 52.
Hoff, Eri, 211.
  Malinda, 211.
Hoffmire, Mener, 430, 431.
Holiday, Thomas E., 451.
Holland, 399.
Holmes, W. Howard, 381.
Holtz, Xenia Davis, 259.
Home Department of Sabbath School, 303.
Homer, N. Y., 422 note.
Hopkinton, R. I., 38 note, 86, 89, 102, 137, 138, 147, 152, 159, 326, 400, 426.
Hopkinton Church, 313.
Hopping, Jane, 403.
Howard, Patty, 433.
Howell, Elisabeth, 127, 130, 179.
  George W., 130, 179.
  John, 317.
  Jonathan, 126, 130, 179, 320.
  Lucinda, 129.
  Maria A., 129, 130.
  Mariah A., 179.
  Mary, 130.
  Washington, 129.
Howell, Town of, 9.
Hubbard, J. Frank, 328.
Huddy, Joshua, 27.
Hudson, Tho. M., 433.
Hudson River, 46 note, 265.
Huffman, Elisabeth, 146, 149.

Huffman (Continued)
  John L., 99, 115, 117, 118, 159, 162, 167, 190, 193, 219, 227, 252, 255, 261, 262, 288, 296, 298, 299, 300, 301, 370, 372, 373, 374, 378, 379, 427.
  Moses, 146, 148, 150, 167, 171, 400, 426.
Huffmans, 147.
Hughes, Abigail, 127, 133.
  Ann, 236, 443.
  Asenath, 126.
  Betsey, 319.
  David, 128.
  Dudley, 126, 133.
  Elisabeth, 127.
  Hannah, 126.
  Jesse, 54.
  Jonathan, 126, 127, 133.
  Leah, 126.
  Martin, 127, 443.
  Mary 129, 131, 180, 380.
  Rachel, 433.
  Sally, 132.
  William, 126.
Hughes Fork of Buckeye Creek, 189.
Hughes River, 365.
Hull, Nathan V., 88, 265, 287.
Hunters Fork, 43, 286, 333.
Hurley, James H., 427.
Hursey, Elmore B., 109.
Husted, N. Victoria, 256, 259.
Hutson, Charlotte, 235.
  Delia L., 264.
  Evan, 432.
  John, 451.
  May M., 264.
  Peter F., 451, 452.
  Winter, 432.
Hyatt, James, 132.

Ideographic characters, 41.
Illinois, 7, 363, 422.
Independence, N. Y., 279, 326.
Indiana, 275, 315, 318, 320, 326, 401.
Indians, 28, 41, 45, 46, 47 and note, 54, 55, 56, 60, 85.

Indians,
  Delawares, 43.
  Mingoes, 43.
  Northern Confederacy, 54.
  Shawnees, 43.
  Six Nations, 43, 44, 47, 53.
Ingle, Arthur, 362.
  Jacob, 362.
  Mahala Rachel, 362.
  Salina, 362.
  William, 362.
Inspirational views, 245.
Irish, James R., 289.
Iowa, 7, 80.
Irish Baptists, 2 note.
Issues of the American press in Pennsylvania, 2 note.

Jackson, Benjamin W., 347.
  George, 58.
Jackson Centre, O., 94, 158, 401, 409.
Jackson Centre Church, 271, 272, 273, 274, 275, 276, 277, 284, 287, 288, 289, 311, 312.
Jane Lew, W. Va., 141 note, 248, 363, 384 note, 399, 405, 410, 415, 448, 449.
Jansen, Reynier, 2 note, 3.
Jarvis, James, 128.
Jefferson, Thomas, 46.
Jefferson County, W. Va., 45.
Jeffrey, A. W., 452.
  Benoni, 352.
  Clarissa, 362.
  Benoni Israel, 352, 362.
  Columbia, 336,
  Content Ann, 362.
  Delia Ann, 180, 256, 259.
  Joseph, 131, 175, 176, 177, 180, 181, 186, 187, 192, 343 note, 345, 347, 348, 349, 351, 352, 362, 402, 433, 445.
  Louise, 362.
  Lydia, 432.
  Neely, 133.
  Neely D., 176, 180, 347.
  Robert Alexander, 352, 362.
  Sophia Ann, 362.
  Stillman, 362.

INDEX 473

Jeffrey (Continued)
  Tacy, 131, 180, 445.
  Tacy Davis, 362.
  Tamar, 445.
  William, 183, 378.
Jennings, Alfred, 363.
  Hiram, 361.
Jesses Run, 54.
"Jesus the Crucified Man" etc., 2 and note, 3.
Jett, Leonard F., 221.
  Sophronia E., 215.
  William, 211, 213, 214, 215, 221, 223, 227, 339, 452.
Jew, 325.
John, Elisabeth, 79.
  Jehu, 79, 82.
  John, 196, 413.
  Louisa, 196.
  Lydia, 196.
Johnson, Elisabeth, 402.
  Elisha, 402.
  Fred F., 300.
  John, 363.
  Joseph, 56 note.
Johnston, Elisha, 429, 430.
Jones, Albert R., 338.
  Henry, 131.
  Hester, 131.
  Jane, 80.
  Joshua E., 211.
  Mary, 434.
Jordan, Cleora F. R., 448.
  Jacob B., 248, 249, 250.
  Jennie, 250.
  Jerome, 249, 341.

Kagarise, George B., 248, 250, 296, 298, 300, 341.
  Susan, 250.
  Wilson, 248, 341.
  Wilson S., 250.
Kansas, 7, 183.
  Leroy, Kansas, 361.
Keith, George 1, 4.
  Governor of Penn., 6.
"Keith, George, Disabled," 4.
Keithians, 2.

Kelly, Abigail, 131.
  Ai G., 211.
  Archibald W., 192, 261, 339.
  Asa, 182, 338, 443.
  Catharine L., 211.
  Eleanor D., 443.
  Emily, 443.
  Estella, 211.
  Ezekiel, 211, 215.
  Ezekiel B., 188.
  Festus, 340.
  Jemima, 180.
  John, 129, 131, 182, 432.
  Mary Ann, 131.
  Mordecai B., 304.
  Nathan, 182, 252, 338, 443.
  Ruanna, 211.
  Sophia, 129.
Kelleys, 61, 87.
Kelsey, Henry C., 428.
Kemper, T. Francis, 380, 381.
Kennedy, Belinda H., 444.
  I. Scott, 379.
  James, 149, 318, 399.
  Lloyd R., 162.
  Loman J., 163.
  William, 156, 169, 170, 191, 280, 289, 338, 444.
  Zurah, 149.
Kennedys, 61.
Kenyon, Alpheus B., 448 note.
  George P., 303.
Kidd, John, 453.
Kildow, Daniel D., 196, 542.
  Francis, 76.
  Francis M., 230, 242, 452.
  John, 80, 445.
  Naomi, 154.
  Naomi David, 445.
Kile, Luther E., 187.
Killingworth, Thomas, 1, 4.
King, John S., 246.
Kinney, Benjamin, 259.
Kirby Farm, 36.
Knight, Blackwell, 362.
  Elisabeth Holliday, 362.
  John, 129, 130, 179.
  Mary, 130, 179.
  Taliaffero K., 362.

Knight, W. Va., 360.
Koon, Mary, 434.
Lake Superior, 43.
Lafferty, Elisabeth, 34.
  Henry, 34, 38, 39.
  (also see McLafferty).
LaForge, Delilah, 417.
Lamberts Run, 60, 83, 106, 135.
Lancaster, Penn., 44.
Langstaff, Mary, 430, 431.
Langworthy, B. F., 384.
La Salle, 43.
Lasure, Andrew J., 242, 340.
  Ary, 242.
  Emily E. Spurgeon, 242.
Lawrence, Alphonso, 303.
  Deborah, 429, 430.
Leath, David W., 188, 190, 219, 233, 249, 263, 309, 423.
Lederer, John, 43.
Lee, (General), 27.
Lee's Army, 357.
Leeson, John, 192, 340.
  Mary Ann, 340.
  Nancy Ellen, 340.
  Thomas, 340.
Leonardsville, N. Y., 370.
Levenston, Charity, 127. (See Livingston).
Lewin, Amanda, 362.
  Eliza, 362.
  William, 362.
Lewis, Abram Herbert, 106, 161, 193, 283, 288, 292, 306, 307, 308, 309, 310, 331, 332, 338.
  Charles M., 114, 121, 122, 223, 329, 384, 408.
  George W., 118.
  Henry B., 218, 289, 298, 299, 370.
  Mary, 414.
Lewis county, 47, 178, 361, 399, 403, 450 note.
Lewisport, Va., 87, 105, 106, 107, 109, 121, 123 note, 173, 175, 178, 182, 185, 319, 325, 402.
Lick Run, 181, 189.
Lincklaen, N. Y., 422.

Lippincott, Amy, 124.
  Darwin C., 118, 188, 190, 219, 233, 234, 248, 249, 261, 262, 263, 304, 306, 307, 310, 427.
  Increase, 22, 33.
  Lemon, 270.
  Samuel, 58, 120, 124, 125, 450.
Lippincotts, 61.
Little Brushy Neck, 28.
Little Genesee, N. Y., 352, 360, 423.
Little Genesee Church, 423.
Little Kanawha River, 43, 53, 54.
Little Miami, 52.
Livermore, Leander E., 293, 296.
Livingston, Charity, 127, (see Levenston).
  William, 416, 417.
Logan, 54.
London, 4, 5.
Long, David C., 246, 247, 285.
  George C., 250, 341.
  Jacob, 247, 285.
Long Branch, 9, 10.
Long Island Sound, 7.
Long Run, W. Va., 60, 108, 189, 304, 337, 447, 448.
Long Run Station, W. Va., 261.
Long Run Sabbath School, 337.
Longacre, John Wesley, 362.
Loofboro, Abigail, 432.
  Davis, 167, 316, 318.
  D. W., 149.
  Eli F., 427.
  John, 127.
  J. W., 149, 432.
  Mary, 149, 432.
  Mrs. Mary, 318.
  Matilda, 432.
  Sarah, 432.
Loofboros, 61, 66, 147. (See Lufbery, also).
Los Angeles, California, 422.
Lost Creek, 61, 86, 94, 100, 143, 147, 157, 162, 226, 266, 267, 271, 280, 284, 287, 290, 314, 315, 316, 317, 321, 324, 326, 327, 331, 332, 333, 335, 338,

INDEX 475

Lost Creek (Continued)
  366, 367, 368, 372, 407, 414,
  423, 444, 447, 448, 449.
Lost Creek Church, 87, 88, 90, 91,
  92, 93, 96, 100, 102, 103, 110,
  112, 113, 118, 126, 137, 142,
  191, 195, 198, 200, 214, 216,
  219, 229, 230, 232, 237, 238,
  240, 242, 249, 252, 254, 261,
  266, 267, 269, 270, 271, 272,
  273, 274, 275, 276, 277, 278,
  279, 280, 281, 283, 284, 286,
  287, 288, 289, 290, 291, 292,
  293, 294, 295, 297, 298, 299,
  301, 303, 304, 305, 307, 309,
  310, 311, 313, 316, 318, 319,
  323, 324, 327, 329, 330, 332,
  336, 338, 370, 383, 384 note,
  385, 386, 387, 388, 393, 394,
  399, 400, 401, 404, 405, 406,
  407, 408, 409, 411, 412, 414,
  415, 423, 426.
Lost Creek Church, History of, 143.
  Controversy over Calvinism, 151.
  Deacons, 169.
  Graveyards, 162.
  Letter to General Conference, 147, 148.
  Licenced to preach, 167.
  Meeting houses, 160.
  Membership in superior bodies, 172.
  Mission to Tennessee, 157.
  Moderator, 170.
  Organisation, 146.
  Parsonage, 163.
  Pastors, 163.
  Quiet Dell and Hackers Creek, 159.
  Records, 143.
  Second Lost Creek Church, 152.
  Troubles arising from the Civil War, 156.
Lost Creek Sabbath Schools, 338.
Lost Creek Station, 160, 163.
Louchery, D. C., 379.
  Edna, 381.

Lower Dublin, Penn., 2 note.
Lower Squankum, 9.
Lowther, Beatrice, 306, 307, 337, 380.
  Catharine R., 211.
  Celina, 211.
  Daisy, 381.
  Decatur, 199, 200, 211.
  Dorinda, 199, 200, 211.
  Elias, 211.
  Emza M., 211.
  Jesse M., 206, 211, 212, 433, 446.
  Johnson J., 192, 255, 261, 339, 364.
  Jonathan C., 199, 200, 211, 212, 291, 339.
  Lucian D., 379.
  Lucinda, 211.
  Mabel, 381.
  Mandane, 212.
  Margaret, 199, 200, 212.
  Mary, 199, 200, 212.
  Rebecca, 199, 200, 212.
  Similde J., 212.
  Sophronia, 212.
  Stillman F., 120, 212, 337, 338, 360, 448.
  Thomas H., 212, 360.
  Varnum B., 188.
  William I., 174.
  William W., 212.
Lowther Family, 325.
Lufbery, Abraham, 431. (See Loofboro, also).
Mack, Alexander, 7.
  Andrew, 245.
Mackie, Ann, 432.
MacJunkin, Elisabeth, 362.
  Joshua, 362.
Mad River Church, 150, 164, 314, 318, 399.
Madison (Jay County, Ind.) Church, 271, 272, 273, 274, 275.
Mahany, Charles, 363.
  William, 363.
Mahoney, James G., 309.
Main, Arthur E., 117, 226, 247, 290, 294, 295, 296, 302, 311.

Maine, 357.
Manasquan, 10 note, 12, 18, 32, 37, 397.
Manasquan River, 6, 7, 9, 10, 35, 38 note.
Maneer, ——, 363.
Manning, Elisabeth, 416.
Manufacture of Salt, 9.
Marlboro, N. J., 232, 444.
Marietta, O., 53, 56.
Martin, Abraham, 79.
  Ann, 79.
  John, 430.
  Marcus E., 190, 205, 206, 212, 228, 233, 239, 240, 241, 242, 243, 244, 257, 261, 262, 263, 301, 305.
  Mrs. Marcus E., 340, 342.
  Margaret, 34.
  Nathan, 76.
  Nathaniel, 79.
  Robert, 52.
Marvin, Eugenia, 380.
Maryland, 43, 48 note, 61, 147, 383.
Matthew, Levi B., 128.
  John W., 128.
Maulsby, Amelia Charlotte, 363.
  Lawson, 363.
  Mary Lethe, 363.
  Tabitha Ogden, 363.
  William, 453, 454.
Maumee River, 46, 55, 85, 450 note.
Maxson, Anna, 135, 142.
  Annetta, 133.
  Bethiah, 12, 31, 34, 435, 436.
  Catharine, 131, 132.
  Catharine L., 235.
  Charity, 125.
  Charles N., 162, 170, 171, 290, 292, 294, 295, 296, 298, 299, 301, 338, 370, 372, 378.
  Charlotte D., 379.
  Cornelius, 235, 452.
  Daniel, 421.
  Deacon, 73, 124.
  Drusilla, 433.
  Elisabeth, 12, 21, 22, 31, 32, 33,

Maxson (Continued)
  34, 126, 128, 432, 436.
  Elisha J., 220, 242, 252.
  Elva, 220.
  Emma A., 379.
  Ephraim, 22, 29, 32, 33, 34, 35, 39, 133, 135, 429, 430, 436.
  Experience, 21, 28, 33, 34, 133, 432, 435, 436.
  George, 34, 84, 124, 432.
  Gideon, 128, 132, 235.
  Hannah, 433.
  Holly Welcome, 170, 171, 295.
  Jacob, 120, 127, 130, 179, 318.
  Jacob D., 320.
  James, 34, 84, 124, 125, 129, 130, 136, 142, 179.
  Jane, 433.
  Jesse, 34, 84, 125, 128.
  John, 22, 29, 33, 34, 37, 38, 125, 128, 344, 397.
  Jonathan, 385.
  Joseph, 6, 12, 21, 24, 31, 32, 33, 37, 38, 39, 397, 430, 435.
  Judith, 16.
  Lydia, 129, 432.
  Marvel, 22, 33, 126, 432, 436.
  Mary, 22, 33, 38, 125, 126, 128, 131, 180, 443.
  Mosher, 16, 17, 32, 34, 84, 85, 111, 123, 124.
  Nathan, 22, 33, 429, 430, 435.
  Parmelia, 126.
  Permelia, 433.
  Piety, 432.
  Prudence, 34, 429, 430.
  Rebekah, 127.
  Ruth, 22, 32, 33.
  Sally A., 423.
  Sanford L., 99, 115, 116, 301, 309, 374, 375, 379.
  Simeon, 16, 18, 22, 24, 29, 32, 33, 34, 35, 38, 119, 120, 124, 126, 127, 130, 133, 136, 179, 315, 316, 317, 319, 320, 453, 454.
  Susan, 421.
  Susan Armstrong, 421.
  Susanna, 34.

INDEX

Maxson (Continued)
  Sutton, 433.
  Tacy, 16, 32.
  Temperance Coon, 423.
  Thomas, 22, 26, 33, 84, 120, 125, 135, 137, 138, 142, 433.
  Timothy, 135, 142.
  Widow, 317.
  William, 22, 29, 33, 34, 35, 85, 124.
  William B., 88, 313, 315, 321, 385, 387, 393.
  Zaccheus, 86.
  Zaccheus R., 423.
  Zebulon, 22, 28, 29, 33, 34, 35, 37, 58, 59, 84, 111, 119, 120, 125, 126, 433, 435, 436, 443, 453, 454.
Maxsons, 61.
  Shipbuilders, 9.
Maxwell, Franklin, 256.
Mayberry, ——, 76 note.
McClary, John, 452.
McLearn, Alexander, 297, 302.
McCleery, William, 50 note.
McLafferty, (see Lafferty).
McWhorter, Joshua L., 448.
  Charles G., 448.
  Walter Fields, 170, 191, 192, 339, 452.
Meat House, 325.
Meat House Fork, 43, 55, 69, 85, 87, 96, 108, 109, 121, 133, 175, 176, 181, 182, 187, 189, 205, 277, 279 note, 325, 365, 418.
Mediterranean people, 41.
Meatherell, Calphurnia F. Randolph, 340, 447.
  John E., 447.
Meek, Alfred N., 233, 261, 262, 263, 342.
  Lucetta, 263.
Menallen (Township of), Penn., 59 note.
Meredith, Alpheus A., 202, 206, 207, 212, 291.
  Davis, 81.
  Davis N., 212, 222, 360.
  Edith Pepper, 212.
  Elmina, 212.
  Hannah, 81.
  Harriet, 212.
  Jane, 212.
  Job, 206, 207, 212.
  John, 212.
  Marshall, 212.
  Mary Ann, 212.
  Obed, 74, 79.
Methodist Camp Meeting, 314.
Methodist Episcopal Church, 200, 285, 324.
Methodist Episcopal Church, South, 424.
Methodist Episcopal clergyman, 331.
Methodist Episcopal General Conference, 369.
Methodist Episcopal Seminary, 377.
Methodist Protestant Church, 36.
Methodist School, 369.
Methodists, 325.
Miami Rivers, 50.
Middle Association, 265.
Middle Fork of Ten Mile Creek, 47, 56, 60.
Middle Island, 85, 86, 100, 123 note, 201, 290, 319, 402.
Middle Island Church, 15 note, 47, 86, 88, 102, 107, 108, 109, 122, 130, 131, 169, 213, 214, 216, 217, 219, 220, 225, 229, 230, 233, 238, 239, 242, 243, 247, 252, 256, 258, 261, 263, 277, 278, 279, 284, 285, 286, 287, 288, 289, 290, 292, 293, 294, 296, 297, 299, 301, 303, 304, 305, 306, 307, 309, 310, 311, 333, 338, 402, 404, 405, 408, 420, 424, 443.
  History of, 173.
  Clerks, 193.
  Deacons, 177, 191.
  Division in, 174.
  Graveyards, 189.
  Licenced to preach, 190.
  List of early members, 179.
  Meeting houses, 178, 182.

Middle Island Church (Continued)
   Membership in superior bodies, 194.
   Moderators, 192.
   Organisation, 173.
   Parsonage, 188.
   Pastors, 178, 189.
   Preaching stations, 189.
   Re-organisation, 180.
   Treasurer, 178.
Middle Island Sabbath School, 338.
Middle Island Creek, 48 note, 60, 85, 107, 133, 173, 182, 325, 419.
Middle Tennessee, 157.
Middlebourne, W. Va., 364.
Middlesex County, N. J., 50.
Middletown, N. J., 9, 10, 14, 17, 18, 20, 24, 29, 30, 31, 32, 35, 37, 39, 99, 413, 429, 430, 431.
Middletown Church, 413.
Mifflintown, Penn., 76, 81.
Milan, Tenn., 424.
Mill Creek, Penn., 44, 246.
Miller, Elisabeth, 343 note.
   Henry M., 343 note.
   Margaret, 22, 33.
   Peter, 7, 246.
Mills, Orpheus S., 218, 244, 298, 300, 307, 340.
Milton College, 294.
Milton, Wis., 182, 183, 247, 415, 418, 421.
Milton Junction, Wis., 361, 415.
Minute Men, 45.
Missionary Association, 272, 327.
Missionary Board, 197.
Missionary Society, 148, 320, (also see Seventh Day Baptist Missionary Society).
Missionary Work, History of, 313.
Missions, 197.
Missouri, 218.
Moberly, Mo., 361.
Molleson, Sarah, 416.
Monmouth County, N. J., 6, 7, 9, 10, 27, 28, 398, 402, 428, 429, 430, 431, 435, 436.

Monmouth Court House, 27.
Monongalia County, W. Va., 30 and note, 46, 47, 48 and note, 50 note, 63 note, 434 and note, 441.
Monongahela River, 31, 43, 45, 47, 48 note, 53, 315, 426.
Monroe, James, 373.
Monroe County, O., 324.
Moravia, N. Y., 422.
Morgan, Morgan, 44.
Morgan Park Theological Seminary, 303.
Morgan's Spring, 45.
Morgansville, 448.
Morgantown, W. Va., 45, 63 note, 424.
Morris, Isaac, 84, 111, 124, 135, 136, 142.
   John, 74, 79.
   Joseph, 433.
Morrison, C. C., 380.
   H. Homer, 215.
   Mary, 215.
Morse, Jedediah, 56 note.
Morton, Joseph W., 387.
Mosaic Ceremonial Law, 141.
Mosaic Law, 201, 203.
Mound Builders, 41.
Moundsville, 41.
Mount Moriah Baptist Church, of Fayette County, Penn., 75 note, 79.
Mumford, George W., 347.
Muncy, Mary E., 380.
Mundy, Ann, 79.

Navesink, N. J., 9.
Nay, Daniel, 365.
Neal, James, 50 note.
Neeley, Thomas S., 186, 187.
Negley, George E., 341.
Nelson, William, 428.
Neptune, Town of, 9.
New England States, 357.
New England, 12, 14, 18, 32, 43.
New Enterprise, Penn., 285.
New Geneva, Penn., 315, 316, 322.
New Hampshire, 357.

INDEX 479

New Jersey, 4, 5, 7, 15 note, 25, 27, 30, 31, 43, 44, 52, 53, 54, 59, 63, 73, 75, 83, 101 note, 103, 104, 109, 120, 147, 164, 167, 265, 313, 315, 318, 400, 426, 428, 440.
New London, Conn., 32.
New Market, N. J., 286, 385, 393, 431, 444.
New Milton, W. Va., 98, 181, 183, 217, 239, 247, 258, 279, 284, 285, 288, 296, 301, 331, 333, 352, 364, 404, 405, 418, 419, 420, 443, 445, 447, 448, 449.
Newport, R. I., 5.
Newport Church, 4, 5, 413.
New Salem, Penn., 59 note.
New Salem, W. Va., 31, 35, 39, 47, 50 note, 53, 54, 55, 59, 60, 61, 63 note, 64, 83, 85, 89, 97, 98, 101, 104, 106, 109, 110 and note, 112, 119, 121, 124, 132, 133, 147, 152, 181, 182, 225, 269, 284, 286, 290, 292, 316, 317, 319, 321, 324, 325, 332, 333, 335, 336, 337, 343, 344, 348, 352, 354, 357, 358, 363, 367, 398, 403 and note, 409, 417, 419, 445, 447, 449, 450 note, 453 and note.
New Salem Church, 15 note, 35, 45, 79, 135, 136, 137, 147, 150, 153, 154, 155, 157, 163, 164, 165, 166, 168, 169, 172, 173, 175, 176, 178, 179, 182, 183, 184, 185, 191, 205, 214, 216, 229, 230, 231, 232, 233, 238, 241, 249, 252, 256, 258, 261, 266, 267, 269, 270, 271, 272, 273, 274, 275, 276, 277, 278, 279, 281, 282, 286, 287, 288, 289, 290, 292, 293, 294, 295, 313, 315, 318, 319, 324, 326, 327, 328, 337, 358, 368, 383, 384, 393, 394, 399, 400, 402, 404, 405, 407, 408, 409, 411, 412, 415, 417, 418, 419, 420, 426, 427, 453 and note.
History of, 83.

New Salem Church (Continued)
Arrival at New Salem, 83.
Baptisms, 132.
Church discipline, 84.
Clerks, 122.
Communion service, 99.
Deacons, 119.
Death of Jacob Davis, 84.
Deaths, 133.
Fast Days, 101.
Incorporated, 99.
Internal Dissensions, 87.
List of early members, 124.
Meeting Houses, 85, 97, 99, 104.
Membership in superiour bodies, 101.
Ministers, 110.
Moderators, 120.
Organisation of West Fork River Church, 83.
Parsonage, 109.
Quarterly Meetings, 99.
Ruling Elders, 119.
Settlements within bounds of, 85.
Yearly Meetings, 99.
New Salem Sabbath School, 336.
New York City, 9, 101 note.
New York State, 7, 43, 53, 56 note, 166, 314, 316, 318, 319, 327.
Newlon, Morton B., 381.
Newman, Bartine, 36.
  Hannah, 34.
  Margaret, 34.
  Samuel, 34.
Nicholson, Frances, 196.
  Francis, 80.
  Mrs., 316, 318.
  Nancy, 80, 323.
Noble, Abel, 2.
  Eva, 339.
  Keziah, 188.
  Thomas W., 188.
Norse Characters, 41.
North America, 41.
North Carolina, 44.
North Fork of Hughes River, 60, 196, 197, 200, 266, 324, 414 note.

North Fork of Hughes River Church, 154, 169, 170, 267, 269, 270, 271, 272, 273, 274, 275, 276, 277, 324.
History of, 195.
North Hampton, O., 274, 404.
North Hampton Church, 269, 270, 271, 272, 273, 274, 275, 276, 277.
North Shrewsbury River, 9.
Northumberland, Penn., 52.
North-West Territory, 52 note.
North-Western Association, 288, 289, 290, 292, 293, 294, 295, 296, 297, 298, 301, 302, 303, 304, 305, 306, 307, 308, 309, 310, 311, 312, 385, 386, 387.
North-Western Virginia Academy, 353, 354, 355.
Nottinghamshire, England, 415.
Numan, W. Va., 364, 365.

Ocean, Town of, N. J., 10.
Ocean County, N. J., 10.
Ocean Grove, N. J., 10.
Ogden, Chester R., 381.
  Cora F. Randolph, 337.
  Curtis L., 381.
Ohley, William A., 373.
Oliphant, Colonel, 321.
  John, 82, 441.
  Julit, 81.
  Mrs. 321.
  Samuel Woodbridge, 441.
  Sarah, 81, 441.
  Woodbridge, 81.
Ohio, 7, 50, 53, 75, 80, 86, 102, 164, 169, 183, 266, 268, 270, 273, 274, 275, 276, 277, 313, 315, 318, 320, 326, 400, 401, 403, 404, 417, 418, 421.
Ohio Association, 103, 176, 198, 204, 277.
Ohio Company, 44.
Ohio County, W. Va., 48 and note, 50 note.
Ohio River, 43, 44, 47, 53, 55, 56, 60, 103, 272, 273, 276, 277, 356.
Old Dominion, 209.
Old Erse Characters, 41.

Old Frame Meeting House, 96, 161, 162, 444.
Onondaga County, N. Y., 422.
Order of the Solitary, 246.
Osborne, Hannah, 430.
Osmun, Catharine, 431.
Ott, William J., 361.
Otter Slide, 216, 217, 224.
Oxford University, 2, 354.
Pacific Coast, 424.
Pacific Slope, 7.
Palatinate, 245.
Palmborg, Rose, 310.
Parker, John, 22, 24, 25, 33, 37, 38.
Parks, A. B., 187, 188, 443.
  Hannah, 443.
Paris, France, 46.
Parkersburg, W. Va., 360, 363.
Parremore, Matthew, 453, 454.
Paterson, N. J., 428.
Patterson, John, 34, 58, 74, 75, 77, 79, 84, 111, 124, 137, 399, 432, 434.
  Sally, 34, 74, 79.
  Sarah, 124, 137.
Pattersons Fork, 60.
Paugh, George, 230, 338.
Pavior, Elisabeth, 6.
Pawcatuck Church, 384, 385.
Peabody Educational Fund, 358.
Peakeville, Mo., 445 note.
Peirman, Mary, 79.
Pelasgi, 41.
Penn, William, 1.
Pennepek, Penn., 2.
Pennepek Baptist Church, 2.
Pennepek Seventh Day Baptist Church, 4.
Pennsboro, W. Va., 60, 196, 200, 324, 357.
Pennsylvania, 4, 5, 6, 7, 12, 30, 31, 43, 47, 48 note, 52 and note, 53, 55, 61, 69, 75 and note, 275, 277, 313, 315, 316, 318, 319, 401, 417, 431, 440.
Penyfay Church, 1.
Pepper, Thomas B., 360.
Perry, P. L., 384.

INDEX 481

Petersburg, N. Y., 154, 265, 276, 321, 327, 357, 360.
Petersburgh Church, 314, 421.
Peterson, Frank E., 304.
Pettitt, Charles, 417.
Pharisee, 325.
Philadelphia, Penn., 2 and note, 3, 4, 397, 413.
Phoenician characters, 41.
Pietistic views, 245.
Pike Church, 86, 131, 267, 268, 269, 270, 271, 272, 401, 403.
Pike Township Church, 271.
Pike's Arithmetic, 356.
Pine Grove Church, 177, 202, 214, 215, 217, 220, 221, 225, 226, 227, 228, 282, 289, 291, 292, 293, 294, 335, 339. (Also see South Fork of Hughes River Church).
Pine Grove Meeting House, 228.
Pine Grove Sabbath School, 225, 290. (Also see South Fork Sabbath School).
"Pines," The, 28.
Pirates, 28.
Piscataway, N. J., 18, 30, 38, 50, 61, 75, 314, 416, 429, 430, 431, 440.
Piscataway Church, 7, 38, 73, 79, 313, 316, 320, 335, 416, 431.
Pitcher, Molly, 27.
Place, Leander, 364.
Plainfield, N. J., 106, 327, 328, 424.
Platts, David, 430, 431.
  David R., 444.
  J. Allison, 306.
  Lewis A., 286, 287, 288, 294, 335, 400, 427.
Plymouth (Mass.) Church, 416.
Plymouth Colony, 416.
Pocahontas County, W. Va., 48.
Polan, Charles L., 192, 193, 293.
  Experience Davis, 259.
  John A., 192, 193, 194, 230, 242, 252, 261.
  Keziah, 180.
  Manville, O., 339.

Polan (Continued)
  Samuel, 176, 180, 182, 183, 193, 338.
Port Jefferson, Ohio, 168, 270.
Port Jefferson Church, 168, 271, 272, 273, 274, 275, 276, 277, 414, 415.
Post, Arthur T., 381.
Potomac River, 45, 48 note.
Potter, Abigail West, 422.
Potter, Charles, Jr., 328, 385.
  C., Jr., & Co., 328.
  Ezekiel G., 422.
  Joseph, 393.
  Lehman H., 422.
  Stephen Thomas West, 343, 344, 349, 350, 352, 356, 360, 421, 422.
Potter Printing Press Co., 424.
Powell, Lela M., 381.
  J. W., 41.
  Sylvester S., 305.
Powers, Sarah, 415.
Prentice, Asa B., 286, 304.
Presbyterians, 413.
Presbytery, 168, 269, 270, 271, 415.
Preston, Jonathan, 74, 79.
Princeton, W. Va., 54, 364.
Pritchard, Mary, 212.
Providence (Penn.) Church, 2.
Pullman, W. Va., 365.
Puritanism, 204.

Quakers, 1.
Quarterly Meeting, 100, 113, 114, 115, 116, 128, 129.
Quiet Dell, W. Va., 61, 109, 110, 159, 160, 163, 198, 200, 290, 323, 336, 338, 365, 384 note, 414, 448.
Quiet Dell Sabbath School, 338.
Quincy, Penn., 357, 421.

Raccoon, 43.
Randolph, Alexander F., 124.
  Asa F., 220, 226, 227, 242, 252, 253, 278 note, 289, 339, 446.
  Belle F., 337.
  Calphurnia F., 449.

Randolph (Continued)
  Catherine, 432.
  Charles A. F., 171.
  Clyde F., 424.
  Cora F., 381.
  Corliss F., 294, 295, 339, 448, 449.
  C. M., 372.
  Daniel F., 337, 363.
  Daniel Fillmore F., 114, 339.
  David F., 125, 416, 417, 418, 429, 430, 431, 452.
  Davis F., 442.
  Deborah F., 132, 187, 188, 443.
  Deborah Sutton F., 364, 419.
  Delilah F., 126.
  Delvinus F., 449.
  Edmund, 354.
  Edward F., 415, 416.
  Elisabeth, 132.
  Elisabeth F., 129, 363, 416, 417, 433, 440.
  Elisabeth Ann, 235.
  Elisabeth Gillis F., 410.
  Elisabeth Jane F., 235.
  Eliza Gillis F., 363.
  Emily F., 336.
  Esle F., 339.
  Ellsworth F., 220, 221, 340, 448.
  Emza F., 221, 447.
  Ephraim F., 430, 431.
  Ernest F., 307, 337, 372, 381.
  Esther F., 132, 352, 354, 364.
  Experience F., 219, 360, 417, 449.
  Experience Brown F., 364.
  Ezra F., 132, 352, 364.
  Fenton F., 191, 336.
  Franklin F., 98, 123, 183, 188, 189, 193, 230, 234, 241, 283, 285, 286, 288, 289, 290, 293, 295, 296, 297, 299, 301, 303, 338, 339, 352, 354, 364, 370, 378, 419, 442, 447.
  George W. F., 299, 370, 371, 372, 374, 378, 447.
  Gertrude F., 380, 448.
  Gideon Henry F., 298, 360, 417, 427, 447, 449.

Randolph (Continued)
  Hannah Davis F., 363.
  Harriet F., 132, 356.
  Harriet Meredith F., 424.
  Isaac F., 132, 273, 344, 348, 353.
  Iseus F., 339.
  Jane F., 128, 133.
  Jepthah F., 105, 108, 109, 114, 120, 121, 122, 123, 129, 132, 181, 182, 183, 184, 185, 187, 188, 201, 214, 230, 269, 277, 278 and note, 279 and note, 285, 287, 288, 338, 347, 348, 349, 351, 353, 356, 364, 418, 419, 433, 443.
  Jesse F., 106, 109, 114, 126, 127, 292, 295, 297, 298, 299, 315, 316, 317, 319, 320, 337, 348, 349, 353, 363, 370, 371, 372, 374, 378, 400, 410, 417, 433.
  Jethro F., 354, 364, 447.
  John F., 234, 236, 340.
  John LaForge F., 121, 319, 344, 349, 359, 364, 417, 432.
  Jonathan F., 89, 95, 101, 105, 107, 120, 127, 129, 133, 235, 319, 348, 349, 353, 416, 417, 418, 442, 450 and note.
  Judson F., 98, 113, 120, 122, 214, 233, 234, 235, 241, 340, 354, 356, 364, 419, 447.
  Lester C., 310.
  Lewis F., 98, 113, 156, 161, 166, 189, 193, 214, 217, 218, 229, 230, 232, 234, 235, 239, 241, 242, 285, 289, 291, 293, 296, 303, 328, 340, 360, 400, 418, 427, 447.
  Lloyd F., 120, 122, 191, 214, 230, 336, 359, 363, 372, 378.
  Luther F., 114, 339, 360.
  Madison MacVicar F., 363.
  Margaret F., 74, 79, 126, 336, 416, 417, 418, 431, 432, 440, 442, 453.
  Maria F., 442.
  Maria MacVicar F., 363.
  Marvel F., 336, 442.
  Marvel Maxson F., 364.

INDEX

Randolph (Continued)
 Mary, 132.
 Mary F., 125, 416, 417, 432, 442.
 Mary Ann F., 132.
 Mary C. F., 442.
 Mary Davis F., 364, 418.
 Mary E., 235.
 Mary E. F., 442.
 Melissa F., 236.
 Mrs., 319, 320.
 Nancy F., 337, 417, 418.
 Peter F., 348, 353, 363, 442.
 Pheneas F., 442.
 Phineas F., 336, 364, 432.
 Phineas Chapin F., 336, 364.
 Preston F., 114, 124, 255, 285, 286, 289, 292, 294, 296, 297, 301, 303, 335, 336, 337, 340, 354, 356, 357, 358, 359, 360, 364, 367, 378, 379, 424, 447, 449.
 Rachel F., 364.
 Rachel B., 442.
 Ray F., 303.
 Rhulanah F., 417, 418.
 Roy F., 309, 339, 381.
 Rulana F., 433.
 Ruth, 432.
 Samuel F., 30, 31, 50, 52, 58, 59, 61, 74, 75, 79, 105 and note, 124, 125, 127, 136, 315, 319, 400, 415, 418, 431, 442, 450 and note, 452, 453.
 Samuel Preston F., 187, 343 and note, 347, 348, 349, 350, 351, 352, 353, 363, 433.
 Sarah F., 416, 417.
 Silas F., 354, 356, 364, 447.
 Tacy Jane F., 364.
 Thomas F., 416, 430, 431, 440.
 Uric F., 372.
 Virgil F., 447, 449.
 Virginia F., 363.
 Waldo F., 356.
 Walton F., 337.
 William, 432.
 William F., 90, 91, 92, 93, 94, 95, 107, 120, 127, 143, 145, 154, 269, 270, 272, 274, 276, 280,

Randolph (Continued)
 343, 344, 345, 348, 349, 350, 352, 353, 354, 364, 392, 400, 418, 432, 442.
 Zipporah Elisabeth F., 364.
Randolph Academy, 354.
Randolphs, 61.
Ravenswood, W. Va., 360.
Record Book of Shrewsbury Church, 17.
Red Lick Run, 181, 182.
Redemptioners, 25.
Redstone Country, 52 and note, 53.
Redstone Old Fort, 48 note.
Redstone, Penn., 50, 56.
Redstone, Va., 426.
Reed, ——, 30.
 Elisabeth, 432.
 Francis, 30 note.
 John, 30 note.
Reed and Ford, 30 note.
Revolutionary War, 45, 50, 54, 400, 413, 414, 450. (Also see War of Revolution.)
Rhode Island, 4, 39, 234, 265, 400.
Rhode Island Colony, 14.
Rice, Barbara, 250.
 David E., 249, 250.
 John, 417.
Richards, ——, 55.
 Isaac H., 212.
 John W., 212.
Richburg, N. Y., 423.
Richburg Academy, 423.
Richmond, Va., 59, 344, 345, 347.
Rickard, Elisabeth, 442.
 Mary Catharine, 420.
 William, 442.
Ritchie Church, 15 note, 97, 120, 167, 202, 203, 204, 209, 230, 242, 244, 248, 252, 261, 262, 287, 288, 289, 290, 292, 293, 294, 295, 297, 301, 302, 303, 304, 305, 306, 307, 308, 309, 310, 311, 328, 331, 339, 370, 404, 412.
 History of, 213.
 Clerks, 221.

Ritchie Church (Continued)
　Consolidation of the South Fork of Hughes River and Ritchie churches, 221.
　Deacons, 219.
　Licenced to preach, 219.
　Meeting houses, 216.
　Membership in superior bodies, 216.
　Moderators, 220.
　Organisation, 213.
　Parsonage, 216.
　Pastors, 217.
Ritchie County, 47, 178, 228, 328, 356, 357, 386, 450.
Ritchie Sabbath School, 225, 290, 339.
Riverside, California, 364.
Roadstown, N. J., 2.
Roane County, W. Va., 47.
Roanoke Church, 162, 242, 284, 294, 297, 298, 301, 303, 304, 305, 306, 307, 309, 311, 329, 340.
　History of, 237.
　　Clerks, 240.
　　Licenced to preach, 240.
　　Meeting house, 239.
　　Membership in superior bodies, 239.
　　Moderators, 240.
　　Name, 240.
　　Organisation, 237.
　　Pastors, 239.
Roanoke, W. Va., 238, 262, 366.
Roanoke Sabbath School, 340.
Robinson, James E., 47 note.
Robinsons Fork, 60, 366.
Rock County, Wis., 76, 80, 418.
Rock Run, 175, 177, 180, 182, 189, 365.
Rock Run School House, 256.
Rockford, W. Va., 363, 368.
Rogers, Benjamin F., 296, 305.
　Isaac, 435.
　James C., 287.
　Lester C., 247.
　Nathan, 32.
Rohrbaugh, O. L., 379.

Rosier, Mrs. Iva Randolph, 306.
　Joseph, 380, 381.
Ruling Elders, 164.
Rumsey, 46.
Runner, Elijah, 54.
Runyon, Elisabeth, 431.
Rust, Mrs. Flora, 379.
R. : S., 443.

Sabbatarian General Conference, 426.
Sabbatarian Valley, 162, 237, 284.
Sabbath Reform, 407.
　History of, 331.
Sabbath School Board, 286, 287.
Sabbath Schools, History of, 335.
　Bear Fork. (See Conings).
　Black Lick, 342.
　Buckeye Run, 337.
　Conings, 340.
　Copen, 341.
　Greenbrier, 340.
　Long Run, 337.
　Lost Creek, 338.
　Middle Island, 338.
　New Salem, 336.
　Pine Grove. (See South Fork).
　Quiet Dell, 338.
　Ritchie, 339.
　Roanoke, 340.
　Salemville, 341.
　South Fork, 339.
　West Union, 341.
Sabbath Tract Society, 277.
Sacred Lyre, 401.
Sadducee, 325.
Salem, N. J., 61, 182, 314, 429, 430.
Salem, W. Va., 44, 50, 56, 59, 106, 113, 115, 116, 133, 249, 258, 294, 299, 359, 363, 364, 365, 405, 410, 441, 443, 447, 448, 449, 453 note. (Also see New Salem).
Salem Academy, 99, 300, 302.
Salem Church, 24, 83, 167, 184, 193 note, 221, 297, 301, 303, 304, 305, 306, 307, 309, 310, 311, 373, 375. (Also see New Salem Church).

Salem College, 99, 116, 117, 159, 190, 219, 249, 301, 302, 303, 304, 305, 308, 309, 310, 410, 415, 424.
  History of, 367.
    Attendance, 382.
    Board of directors, 378.
    Degrees conferred, 380.
    Faculty, 379.
    Financial statistics, 382.
    Incorporation, 371.
Salem Settlement, 84.
Salemville, Penn., 246, 247, 249, 285, 297, 298, 306, 341, 409.
Salemville Church, 7, 296, 306, 307, 309, 310, 311, 424.
  History of, 245.
    Clerks, 250.
    Constituent members, 250.
    Deacons, 249.
    German Seventh Day Baptists, 245.
    House of Worship, 248.
    Licenced to preach, 249.
    Membership in superior bodies, 247.
    Organisation, 247.
    Pastors, 248.
Salemville Sabbath School, 341.
Sammons, Lewis, 78, 80, 269.
Satterlee, William, 313.
Sauer, Christopher, 245.
Saunders, Edward B., 249, 306, 308, 329.
Sayre, Charles S., 427.
Sayres, Solomon, 129, 130, 179.
Schenectady, N. Y., 265.
Schwartzenau, 245.
Sciota Church, 271, 272, 273, 274, 275, 276, 277.
Sciota River, 404.
Scituate, Mass., 416.
Scott, Jacob, 54.
Scott, N. Y., 327, 343, 360, 421, 422.
Scott Church, 314, 422.
Sea Girt Inlet, N. J., 10.
Seager, Lely D., 118, 159, 167, 217, 219, 244, 248, 303, 304.

Second Alfred Church, 266.
Second Constitutional Convention of West Virginia, 419.
Second Hopkinton Church, 218, 232.
Second Lost Creek Church, 152, 160, 326.
Seine River, 46 note.
Select Schools, 335.
Seventh Day Adventists, 202, 228.
Seventh Day Baptist churches in United States, 265.
Seventh Day Baptists, 6, 9, 41, 43, 47, 55.
Seventh Day Baptist Education Society, 296, 300, 307, 309, 310, 311, 370, 374, 375, 377, 411.
Seventh Day Baptist hymn books used for wadding in Battle of Brandywine, 246 note.
Seventh Day Baptist Missionary Society, 113, 117, 188, 213, 248, 249, 267, 274, 275, 289, 294, 295, 296, 297, 298, 301, 302, 305, 306, 307, 308, 309, 310, 311, 358, 409, 411, 415, 421.
Seventh Day Dunkers, 246.
Shacklett, Elisabeth, 79.
  John, 76, 77, 79.
Shanghai, China, 298, 302, 310.
Shannon, Content, 129, 130, 179.
  Gamble, 127, 130, 174, 177, 179.
  James, 129, 130, 179.
Shark River, 9, 12, 27, 32, 35, 36.
Sharpneck, Daniel, 417.
Shaw, George B., 311.
Shelbyville, Tenn., 157, 407, 412.
Shepardstown, W. Va., 46.
Sherman, Oliver D., 226, 290, 294, 303.
Sherwood, S. Todd, 46.
Shiloh, N. J., 18, 76, 86, 102, 103, 110, 159, 164, 321, 384, 393.
Shiloh Church, 7, 151, 314, 316, 421.
Shipbuilders' yard, 9.
Shock, Albert, 169, 191, 251, 253, 254, 286, 339, 341.
  Cinderilla, 251, 253.

Shock (Continued)
  Clara, 252.
  Clara Ethel, 253.
  Iva Virginia, 253, 341.
  Virginia, 252.
  Uriah C., 251, 253, 341.
Shrewsbury, N. J., 10, 12, 14, 28, 29, 30, 31, 35, 39, 54, 59, 100, 135, 286, 397, 398, 401, 435, 436, 440.
Shrewsbury Church, 7, 19, 20, 24, 44, 47, 52, 59, 61, 63, 83, 122, 124, 141, 182, 397, 398, 399, 400, 401, 402, 405, 411, 427, 435.
  History of, 9.
  Articles of faith and practise, and church covenant, 20.
  "Awful Sentence of Excommunication," 26.
  Battle of Monmouth, 27.
  Church Meeting, 39.
  Clerk, 39.
  Communion service, 39.
  Constituent members, 31.
  Deaths, 37.
  Discipline, 18, 24.
  Doctrine of feet-washing, 14, 15.
  Fast Days, 40.
  Meeting House, 29, 35.
  Ministers, 37.
  Moderator, 39.
  Notes concerning members, 31.
  Ordination of pastor, 18.
  Organisation, 10, 12.
  Record book, 17.
  Redemptioners, 25.
  Removal to New Salem from White Day, 31.
  Removal to Virginia from New Jersey, 29.
  Ruling Elders, 39.
  Settlement at Shrewsbury, 9.
  Settlement at White Day, 30.
  Short articles of faith and practise, 22.

Shriner, Charles F., 250.
  Nancy, 250.
Shushan, N. Y., 420.
Simpson, James, 276.
  John, 44, 55.
Sindall, Martin, 307.
Slavery, 103, 154, 172.
  History of, 383.
Smalley, Anne, 429, 431.
Smith, C. W., 359.
  Delbert Edwin, 448.
  Hannah, 22, 32, 33.
  John, 360.
  Mr., 167.
  ———, 164.
  R., 433.
  Zebulon, 32.
Snake Run, 43.
Snodgrass, V. Curtis, 381.
Snow Hill, Penn., 246, 421.
Society for the Propagation of the Gospel in Foreign Parts, 4.
Socwell, Eugene H., 304.
South Branch, 28.
South Branch of Little Brushy Neck, 10.
South Branch of the Potomac River, 44.
South Carolina, 43.
Southampton, Ill., 231, 239.
South-Eastern Association, 7, 104, 106, 115, 158, 162, 170, 172, 194, 202, 204, 216, 225, 231, 237, 238, 239, 241, 242, 246, 247, 249, 253, 257, 258, 262, 326, 329, 330, 333, 336, 367, 370, 373, 405, 408, 409, 412, 420, 423.
  History of, 281.
South Fork of Hughes River, 60, 216, 217.
South Fork of Hughes River Church, 175, 177, 213, 214, 222, 223, 224, 267, 269, 270, 271, 272, 273, 274, 275, 276, 277, 278, 279, 282, 289, 325, 331, 335, 336, 339, 408.
  History of, 199.
  Clerks, 207.

South Fork of Hughes River Church (Continued)
  Deacons, 206.
  Distinctive tenets of faith and practise, 203.
  Internal dissensions, 202.
  Licenced to preach, 206.
  List of members, 209.
  Meeting houses, 208.
  Membership in superior bodies, 204.
  Moderators, 207.
  Organisation, 199.
  Pastors, 205.
  Perplexing questions of polity and doctrine, 201.
  School, 209.
  Union with Ritchie Church, 204, 221.
South Fork of Hughes River Sabbath School, 339.
South Lancaster, Mass., 365.
South-Western Association, 78, 90, 94, 96, 102, 103, 168, 172, 176, 194, 195, 197, 198, 204, 205, 301, 305, 307, 308, 309, 310, 311, 327, 404, 406, 414, 415, 426.
  History of, 265.
Southworth, Enoch B., 363.
  Mary Ann Childers, 363.
  Sophia, 363.
  George Washington, 363.
Spafford, N. Y., 422.
Spottswood, Governor, 43.
Spring Hill Township (Fayette County), Penn., 48 note.
Springer, Cornel Zeadock, 82.
Spurgeon, Charles, 340.
  Charles J., 242, 244.
  Christina, 242, 340.
  Emily, 340.
  Jabez, 242, 243, 252, 340.
  Joshua C., 242, 244, 252, 340.
Squam, incorrect form of Squan, 10 note.
Squan, 10 and note, 14, 27, 28, 30, 37.
Squan River, 10.

Squankum, 9, 14, 17, 32, 37.
St. Margaret's, Westminster Abbey, 46.
St. Mary's, W. Va., 356.
Stalnaker, Dorinda, 215.
  Levi, 113, 169, 212, 214, 215, 217, 219, 230, 339.
Starkey, George, 199, 200, 212.
  John C., 199, 200, 212.
  Rebecca, 212.
  Sarah, 199, 200, 212.
Starkey Family, 325.
State Church of Germany, 245.
Steamboat, The first, 46 note.
Steele, Jennie, 253.
Stelle, Rachel, 430, 431.
Stevenson, Captain Hugh, 45.
Stillman, Frances E., 380.
  Harold, 311.
  Harold C., 381.
  Henry R., 269.
  Horace, 218, 295.
  Joseph, 16, 18, 32.
  Mrs. Marcella, 306.
  Mary, 12, 31.
  Mazzini G., 159, 240, 249, 306, 307, 309, 311.
Stites, Benjamin, 50, 52.
Stokes Church, 271, 272, 273, 274, 275, 276, 277.
Stone, ———, 76 note.
Stoneking, Elisha, 365.
Stonington, Conn., 6, 7, 12.
Stout, Hezekiah M., 158, 284, 287.
  Lloyd, 162.
  Milan, 320.
Strother, Daniel P., 234, 235.
  James E., 233, 235.
  Love C., 235.
  Lucinda, 235.
  Mary J., 235.
  Oliver C., 235.
  Resella, 235.
  William, 432.
Stuart, Anna, 363.
  Chapman J., 363.
  Elisabeth, 363.
Sturgis, John, 441.
  Leah, 74, 79, 441.

Sturgis (Continued)
  Phyllis, 441.
  Rhoda, 441.
Stuttler, Leah, 128.
  Lewis B., 340.
  Oris O., 234.
  Sarah, 236.
Sugar Camp, W. Va., 365.
Sugar Camp Run, 175, 181, 182, 183.
Sullivan, Abraham W., 447, 449.
  Ollie, 256, 259.
Sussex County, N. J., 50, 416, 450.
Sutton, Cornelius, 124, 418, 432, 445, 450.
  Davis, 128.
  Davis W., 432.
  Dorinda, 212.
  Deborah, 128, 418, 433.
  Drusilla, 128.
  Eleanor, 128.
  Elisabeth, 133.
  Elisabeth Applegate, 418.
  Elva, 340.
  Enoch M., 452.
  Erlow, 219, 340, 445.
  Francis M., 212.
  George J., 128.
  Henry, 430, 431.
  Hannah J., 212.
  Hezekiah D., 212, 226.
  Israel W., 452.
  Jacob, 429, 431.
  Jane, 131.
  Jeriel, 361.
  John, 107, 108, 120, 123, 127, 404, 418, 433, 443.
  Jonas, 431.
  Lafayette, 337.
  Levi, 128, 432.
  Lovey J., 212.
  Martin, 212.
  Peter, 431.
  Rachel, 126, 443 note.
  Rachel Davis, 418.
  Reuben, 433.
  Reuben D., 128.
  Taylor, 452.
  Thadeus, 452.

Sutton (Continued)
  Vienna, 433.
Suttons, 61.
Swearingen, Catharine, 48 and note, 50, 58.
  John, 48, 50 note.
  Joseph, 47, 50 note, 58.
Swiger, Frederick M., 120, 371, 372, 378.
Swindon, Anna, 429, 431.
Swinney, Lucius R., 116, 158, 167, 217, 232, 289, 290, 291, 292, 293, 294, 296, 303, 336.
Swisher, Emily V., 423.
Symmes, John Cleves, 52 and note.

Tate, Hugh, 433.
  Sarah, 365.
  William, 365.
Taylor, Barbara, 79.
Tecumseh, 54.
Ten Mile Creek, 30 note, 31, 47, 48 note, 50 note, 53, 54, 83, 135.
Ten Mile Settlement, 54.
Tennessee, 423.
Tennessee River, 43.
Temperance Reform Pike Church, 267, 269.
Terra Haute, Ind., 422.
Texarkana, Ark., 361.
Texas, 424.
Thompson, John L., 381.
Thorp, Benjamin, 35, 58, 59, 124, 133, 430, 431.
Threlkeld, Charles W., 218, 295.
Tichnell, Rev. Mr., 200, 324.
Tilton, John, 439.
Titsworth, Isaac D., 286, 335.
Todd, Julius M., 288, 292, 297.
Toll Gate, W. Va., 196.
Tomlinson, George E., 285, 333.
Tonge, James, 378.
Towers, George, 354.
Towles, R. Lloyd, 378.
Townsend, Florence M. F. Randolph, 448.

Trainer, Mrs. George H., 403 note.
Tressie M. D., 448.
Traugh, Jonathan, 364.
Trent, William, 47.
Treaty of Lancaster, 47 note.
Trenton, N. J., 18, 435.
Trough School House, 261, 342.
Truxton, N. Y., 86.
Turkey Run, 43.
Turkey Track, 43.
Turtle Tree, 43.
Tygarts Valley River, 48 note, 56 note.
Tyler County, W. Va., 178.
Union Army, 353.
Union Chapel, 36.
Uniontown, Penn., 81, 321.
United States, 103, 270.
United States Government, 394.
Universalists, 36.
Upper Providence, Penn., 2.
Upshur County, W. Va., 47, 328.
Utica, Wis., 368.
Utter, George B., 287, 385, 393.

Vallego, California, 361.
Van Horn, Abby, 399.
  Abram, 399, 400.
  Ai, 445.
  Austin, 230.
  Betsey, 400.
  Catharine, 445.
  Edgar D., 427.
  Eli, 384 note.
  Elisabeth, 153, 400.
  Hannah, 445.
  Herbert C., 427.
  Jacob, 158.
  Job, 399, 400 note, 434, 445.
  John J., 170.
  Lois, 149, 432.
  Moses, 384.
  Moses H., 169, 303, 305, 310, 337, 379, 381.
  Sally, 320.
  Sarah, 146, 149.
  Theodore J., 307, 427.
  Thomas, 149, 320.

Van Horn (Continued)
  Virginia, 135, 142.
  William, 135, 142, 146, 149, 150, 160, 169, 316, 320, 399, 433.
  William B., 161, 170, 378.
Van Horns, 61, 147.
Van Matre, John, 44.
Van Meter, Isaac, 354.
"Verginey," State of, 36. (See Virginia).
Vermont, 357.
Virginia, 15 note, 27, 29, 30, 35, 38 note, 43, 75, 78, 102, 266, 268, 270, 274, 275, 276, 277, 313, 398, 399, 400, 401, 404, 405, 407, 414, 418, 421, 431, 444.
Virginia Association, 78, 103, 172, 176, 194, 195, 197, 198, 201, 204, 277, 281, 311.
  History of, 277.

Wade, A. M., 216.
Wales, 5, 413.
  Cardiff, 1.
  Glamorganshire, 1.
  Penyfay, 1.
  Swansea, 1.
Walker, Henry S., 371, 372.
Washington, General, 27, 44, 45.
Washington County, N. Y., 420.
War of American Independence, 24.
War of Independence, 27.
War of the Revolution, 45, 246, 416. (Also see Revolutionary War).
War of 1812, 402, 450.
Watkins, Joseph, 80.
  Sarah, 80.
Watts, John, 2.
Wayne, General ("Mad Anthony"), 45, 46, 53, 55, 85, 450 note.
Wayne's Orderly Book, 450 note.
Wayne's War, 45, 450.
Webb, Benjamin, 432.
Webster County, 47.
"Weeling" Creek, 43.

Welch Tract, 413.
Welch Tract Church, 413.
Wells, Abraham, 79.
  Amos R., 86, 159, 164, 265, 313, 314, 318.
  Ann, 79.
Wellsburg, Va., 63.
Welton, Iowa, 401.
Welsh Baptists, 2 note.
West, Amanda E. Hall, 448.
  Jacob, 148.
West Augusta, District of, 48 and note.
West Fork Church, 162, 242, 284, 286, 287, 288, 289, 290, 292, 293, 298, 311, 329. (Also see Roanoke Church).
West Fork River, 30 note, 31, 44, 45, 46 note, 47, 50 note, 53, 60, 83, 135, 159, 398.
West Fork River Church, 83, 84, 102, 111, 120, 124, 426.
  History of, 135.
West New Jersey, 148.
West Union, W. Va., 60, 61, 85, 87, 105, 106, 173, 178, 181, 183, 185, 189, 196 and note, 255, 256, 258, 278, 319, 332, 341, 343, 354, 360, 361, 362, 363, 365, 402 and note, 421, 422, 423, 445, 447 and note.
West Union Academy, 97, 154 note, 165, 196 note, 258, 279, 327, 329, 367, 369, 383, 419, 420, 421, 422, 423, 447 note.
  History of, 343.
  Building erected, 350.
  Charter, 344.
  Fundamental weakness, 354.
  List of stockholders, 348.
  Modeled after the North-Western Virginia Academy, 354.
  Names of principals and students, 360.
  Organisation completed, 348.
  Preliminary organisation, 343.
  Property sold, 351.
  Teachers of, 352.

West Union Church, 181, 185 note, 261, 262, 300, 301, 303, 311, 312.
  History of, 255.
  Clerk, 259.
  Deacons, 256.
  Dissolution of, 258.
  House of worship, 256.
  Membership in superior bodies, 258.
  Moderator, 259.
  Names of members, 259.
  Organisation, 255.
  Records, 258.
West Union Sabbath School, 341.
West Virginia, 15 note, 41, 156, 209, 228, 300, 409, 410, 423, 424, 441, 447, 449, 450 note.
West Virginia churches, 213.
West Virginia University, 376, 424, 425.
Westerly, R. I., 5, 6, 7, 14, 31, 32, 37, 249, 385, 397.
Westerly Church, 4, 5, 6, 14, 18, 38, 397.
Western Association, 102, 172, 194, 197, 265, 266, 267, 271, 273, 279 and note, 285, 287, 288, 289, 290, 292, 293, 294, 295, 296, 297, 298, 302, 303, 304, 305, 306, 307, 308, 309, 310, 311.
Western Virginia, Description of, 41.
  Boone, Daniel, 46.
  First explored, 43.
  First settled, 44.
  Indians, 43, 53.
  Indian names, 43.
  Mound-builders, 41.
  New Salem established, 58.
  Political boundaries, 47, 48 note.
  Represented in Revolutionary War, 45.
  Settlement on Ten Mile Creek, 47.
  Stone Tablet, 41, 42.
Westminster Abbey, 46.
Westmoreland County, Penn., 52.

Weston, W. Va., 161.
Wheeler, Samuel R., 288, 303.
Wheeling, W. Va., 43, 450 note.
Wheeling Creek, 43. (Also see Weeling Creek).
White, Buchannon, 380.
　Joshua Judson, 293.
　William, 54.
White Day, W. Va., 133, 441.
White Day Creek, 30, 31, 47, 83, 398.
White Friars, 246.
Whitford, Adelle M., 368.
　John, 88.
　Oscar U., 116, 249, 289, 301, 305, 307, 308, 309.
　William C., 311, 393.
Wilcox, Martin, 88.
Wildman, Bird, 251.
　Cora Bird, 252.
　Emily A., 251.
　Emily A. Nettie, 252.
　Mary, 253.
　Mary E., 251, 252.
　Sally C., 251, 252.
　William, 452.
　William L., 251, 252, 253, 341.
Willey, John, 434.
William and Mary's College, 354.
Williams, Cornelius, 74, 79, 146, 148, 150, 167, 316, 318, 320.
　Elijah, 318, 320.
　Emily, 366.
　Fenton, 340.
　Frank W., 340.
　George, 432.
　John, 107.
　Orville D., 296.
　Thomas R., 288.
　William, 149, 151, 153, 167.
　Williams, ——, 366.
Williamses, 61, 147.
Williamstown, W. Va., 360.
Willis, James E., 193, 339.
Wilson, Hiram, 372, 378.
Wisconsin, 7, 80, 415.
Withers, (Alexander), 55.
Witter, Ellis A., 99, 119, 310, 311.
Wittgenstein, 245.

Wolf Pen Run, 43, 181, 278, 325.
Wolfe, Amos D., 250, 341.
　Charles C., 249, 311, 341.
　John, 249, 341.
　John H., 249, 306, 380, 381.
Wood County, W. Va., 47.
Woodbridge, Anne, 74, 79, 81, 82, 441.
　Mary, 79, 81, 441.
　Mrs., 316.
　Samuel, 73, 74, 75, 76, 77, 78, 80, 81, 82, 84, 111, 321, 399, 413, 441.
Woodbridge, N. J., 429, 431.
Woodbridgetown, Penn., 76, 84, 103, 147, 316, 317, 318, 319, 321, 323, 398, 413, 440 and note.
Woodbridgetown Church, 47, 58, 124, 136, 147, 155, 159, 196, 267, 269, 270, 271, 272, 273, 274, 275, 277, 278, 279, 289, 315, 321, 322, 398, 399, 413, 414, 415, 417.
　History of, 73.
　Clerks, 77.
　Constituent members, 74.
　Deacons, 77.
　Deaths, 80.
　List of members, 78.
　Meeting house, 76.
　Membership in superior bodies, 78.
　Organisation, 73.
　Records, 73, 76.
　Will of Samuel Woodbridge, 81.
Woodsfield, Ohio, 324.
Woolley, Mary, 429, 431.
Wreck Pond, 10.
Wright, Joshua, 278 note.
Wyoming, 39.

Yankee frame, 108, 184.
Yankee Street Church, 404.
Yearly Meeting, 5, 14, 100, 101 note.
Yellow Creek, Penn., 52.
Yohogania County, 48 and note,

50 note.
York County, Penn., 246.
Young, Eva L., 381.
Young People's Society of Christian Endeavour, 301.

Zinn, Adeline, 212.
  Angelina, 212.
  Elisabeth, 212.
  Nancy, 212.
  Otho Preston, 212.

ADVANCE SUBSCRIBERS.

The following is a list of advance subscribers to *A History of Seventh Day Baptists in West Virginia,* whose names have been received up to the time of going to press:—

ALABAMA.

Attalla.

W. L. Willson.

Tuscumbia.

Rev. David W. Leath, 2 copies.

ARKANSAS.

DeQueen.

Mrs. Lillie Fillyaw Grace.

Fouke.

Rev. Gideon Henry F. Randolph,
Morton S. Wardner.

Gentry.

Rev. D. Burdette Coon,
A. M. Furrow,
Rev. J. H. Hurley,
L. A. Hurley,
Mrs. Frances Lanphere.

CALIFORNIA.

Bakersfield.

Mrs. George S. McKee.

Riverside.

Rev. John T. Davis.
L. R. Davis,
Silas F. Randolph,
B. F. Titsworth.

COLORADO.

Boulder.

Mrs. Roanna McWhorter.

CONNECTICUT.

Lebanon.

Rev. Leander E. Livermore.

New London.
A. B. Burdick,
Mrs. Thomas W. Rogers.
Stamford.
B. Frank Whitford.

FLORIDA.

Daytona.
William A. Langworthy.
Tampa.
J. Belle Witter.

ILLINOIS.

Chicago.
Alfred S. Burdick,
William M. Davis,
B. F. Langworthy,
Ira J. Ordway,
George W. Post,
Mrs. A. R. Sheppard,
Mrs. R. M. Thompson,
Rev. Wayland D. Wilcox.
Farina.
A. C. Bond,
Rev. Charles A. Burdick,
Mrs. Thankful C. Childs,
Mrs. Lura P. Persels,
Ernest F. Randolph,
Rev. Lely D. Seager,
Mrs. O. C. Wells,
C. H. West,
Thomas Zinn.
Stone Fort.
Oliver Lewis,
Rev. Robert Lewis.

INDIAN TERRITORY.

Tiawah.
Lloyd Bond, 2 copies.

IOWA.

Welton.
J. O. Babcock,
A. E. Forsythe,
H. R. Loofboro,
J. W. Loofboro,
L. A. Loofboro.

KANSAS.
Americus.
P. B. Maxson.
Elmdale.
Elsworth W. Jeffrey, 2 copies.
Nortonville.
T. C. Davis,
Rev. George W. Hills.

MINNESOTA.
Dodge Centre.
Rev. George W. Lewis.
Minneapolis.
P. C. Maxson.
New Auburn.
Rev. Perie R. Burdick,
Mrs. James W. Crosby,
Mrs. John Ritchie.

MISSOURI.
Moberly.
John B. Jennings.
Summerville.
Rev. T. G. Helm.

NERBASKA.
Lincoln.
Mrs. Rachel David.
North Loup.
Rev. M. B. Kelley,
H. C. VanHorn.

NEW JERSEY.
Belmar.
Bartine Newman.
Hoboken.
Thomas B. Stillman.
New Brunswick.
Alfred A. Titsworth.
New Market.
Rev. Henry N. Jordan,
Iseus F. Randolph.
Nutley.
William R. Clarke, 2 copies.
Plainfield.
Mrs. George H. Babcock, 5 copies,
William E. Bond,
Rose Davis,

Plainfield (Continued).

Mrs. Charles H. Dunham,
   Helen T. Ford,
   Mandella Ford,
   Frank J. Hubbard,
   *J. Frank Hubbard, 2 copies,
   Joseph A. Hubbard, 2 copies,
   William C. Hubbard,
   Irving Hunting.
Rev. Abram Herbert Lewis,
   Henry M. Maxson,
Mrs. Henry M. Maxson,
   John P. Mosher,
   Asa F. Randolph,
   Ida F. Randolph,
   A. C. Rogers,
   Orra S. Rogers,
   Friedrich Schreiner,
Rev. George B. Shaw,
   J. Dennison Spicer,
Mrs. D. R. Stillman,
   William M. Stillman, 2 copies,
   Arthur L. Titsworth,
   David E. Titsworth,
   *Joseph M. Titsworth,
   Lewis T. Titsworth,
Mrs. Valentine Utzinger,
   Nathan S. Wardner,
   Frank S. Wells, 2 copies.

Shiloh.

   Micajah Ayars,
   George Bonham,
   Albino W. Davis,
   Irene C. Davis.

NEW YORK.

Adams Centre.

Mrs. W. T. Colton,
   Levi A. Crandall,
   Grant W. Davis,
   DeChois Greene,
   O. DeGrasse Greene,
   A. J. Horton,
Rev. Sylvester S. Powell.

Alfred.

   Alfred University Library, 2 copies,
   Vernon A. Baggs,
   Lyle Bennehoff,

ADVANCE SUBSCRIBERS

Alfred (Continued).

Rev. Ahva J. C. Bond,
Asa C. Burdick,
Silas G. Burdick,
William H. Crandall,
Rev. Boothe C. Davis, 3 copies,
H. Eugene Davis,
W. E. Drummond,
Rev. James L. Gamble,
Charles H. Greene,
Rev. Walter L. Greene,
Alpheus B. Kenyon,
Rev. Arthur E. Main, 2 copies,
Alfred T. Randolph,
Mrs. Loisanna T. Stanton,
Charles Stillman,
Edward M. Tomlinson,
Rev. Edgar D. VanHorn,
Rev. Herbert C. VanHorn,
A. E. Webster,
Rev. William C. Whitford.

Allentown.

H. L. Hulett.

Andover.

Rev. Stephen Burdick.

Berlin.

P. O. Lamphier,
Sabbath School.

Bristol.

Mrs. Eunice L. Noble.

Brookfield.

Mrs. Annetta A. Clarke,
Jennet T. Rogers.

Brooklyn.

Frank L. Greene,
John B. Cottrell.

Cuba.

Mrs. William W. Kingsbury.

DeRuyter.

*Rev. Lucius R. Swinney.

Great Kills P. O.

Esle F. Randolph.

Hamilton.

Virginia A. Willson,
(for Colgate Collection of Baptist History),

Independence.

Rev. Asa G. Crofoot,
Mrs. Abbie Berry.

Leonardsville.

H. D. Babcock,
Mrs. S. E. Brand,
Rev. Ira Lee Cottrell,
Alva L. Davis,
Mrs. Rebecca E. H. Wheeler, 2 copies.

Little Genesee.

Rev. Simeon H. Babcock,
Mary E. Bowler,
Ormond E. Burdick,
H. B. Clark,
Rev. J. L. Hull.

New Rochelle.

Edna J. Brown,
Lena M. Greene.

New York City.

Stephen Babcock, 2 copies,
Samuel F. Bates,
L. K. Burdick,
Kate M. Clarke,
Rev. Samuel H. Davis,
Bernard Login,
Rev. Eli F. Loofboro,
Anna F. Maltby,
Alfred C. Prentice,
L. Adelle Rogers,
Herbert G. Whipple.

Nile.

L. Burdick,
Rev. Willard D. Burdick.

Oneida.

William E. Witter.

Scott.

Rev. William H. Ernst,
Mrs. Sarah W. Richardson,
Mrs. D. D. L. Burdick.

Syracuse.

E. S. Maxson.

Utica.

Holly W. Maxson.

Yonkers.

Charles C. Chipman, 2 copies.

OHIO.
Ada.
Mrs. C. A. Hetrick.
" *De Graff.*
Mary A. A. Davis, 2 copies.
Jackson Centre.
Rev. Judson G. Burdick,
A. H. Davis,
Linville B. Davis,
J. D. Jones,
Charles L. Polan,
Charles Sutton.
Lake View.
J. S. Van Horn.

OKLAHOMA.
Kingfisher.
Rev. Sanford L. Maxson.

OREGON.
Bellewood.
Willard D. Stillman.
Erskineville.
Ralph G. Junkin.

PENNSYLVANIA.
Coudersport.
*Mrs. LeRoy Burdick.
Erie.
Mrs. Angeline Abbey.
Philadelphia.
Sherman E. Ayars.
Salemville.
Lewis P. Berksheimer,
Rev. Riley G. Davis,
Simeon E. King,
Abraham W. Walter,
Amos D. Wolfe,
Charles C. Wolfe.
Shadeland.
John H. Wolfe.

RHODE ISLAND.
Ashaway.
George B. Carpenter,
Mrs. Asa S. Briggs,
Rev. William L. Burdick,
Matthew I. Kenyon,
Thomas Turnbull.

Hopkinton.
Sarah A. Langworthy,
Rev. Lewis F. Randolph.
Potter Hill.
Mary G. Stillman,
George N. Burdick.
Providence.
Albert W. Brown, 3 copies.
Westerly.
William L. Clarke,
Hannah Crandall,
J. Irving Maxson,
Joseph H. Potter,
C. Latham Stillman,
Eugene Stillman,
George H. Utter,
*Rev. Oscar U. Whitford, 2 copies.

TEXAS.

Port Lavaca.
D. S. Allen.

WEST VIRGINIA.

Aberdeen.
Levi D. Bond.
Berea.
G. W. Brissey,
Mrs. M. A. Maxson Davis, 2 copies,
T. N. Gribble,
Minerva Kildow, 2 copies,
John E. Meatherell,
*Ellsworth F. Randolph,
Erlow Sutton.
Blandville.
C. P. Davis,
E. B. Kelley,
John A. Polan,
W. E. Sutton,
S. B. Sutton,
A. W. Willis.
Bolair.
Ozina M. Bee, 2 copies.
Bridgeport.
Samuel S. Faris.
Burnsville.
Iva Virginia Shock.
Cascara.
M. W. Bonnell.

Clarksburg.

Mrs. Perry Williams,
P. M. Long.

Craigmoor.

J. B. Paugh.

Fairmont.

Mrs. Joseph Rosier.

Jane Lew.

Rev. Samuel D. Davis,
S. Orlando Davis,
U. B. Davis.

Long Run.

James Kelley, 2 copies.

Lost Creek.

John E. Batten,
Luther A. Bond,
T. M. Bond,
H. N. DAVIS,
J. Lewis Davis,
Levi B. Davis,
M. S. Davis,
Scott F. Randolph,
William F. Randolph.

Miletus.

Neely Davis,
Cornelius Maxson,
*Daniel P. Strother,
Oris O. Stutler,
Fenton W. Williams,

New Milton.

William H. H. Davis,
Franklin F. Randolph,
Roy F. Randolph.

Nina.

Marcellus Clark,
Mrs. Marvel Davis.

Numan.

C. G. Davis,
M. Van Buren Davis, 2 copies.

Parkersburg.

Virginia Jennings.

Princeton.

Isaiah Bee.

Pursley.

Mrs. W. T. Ford.

Ravenswood.

Andrew Judson Charter.

Roanoke.

C. A. Bond,
J. C. Bond,
Mrs. Lenora M. Bond.

Salem.

Elsie B. Bond,
Samuel B. Bond,
C. B. Bonnell,
Sarah C. Bonnell,
Asher S. Childers,
Fenton R. Clark,
Cortez R. Clawson,
Burdick Davis,
Clementina M. Davis,
Earl W. Davis,
Ernest O. Davis,
Ethelbert J. Davis,
Guy Davis, Jr.,
L. Dow Davis,
Mrs. Mollie B. Davis,
Okey W. Davis,
M. Wardner Davis,
W. Franklin Davis,
Flavius J. Ehret,
Laura Ford,
Samuel A. Ford,
S. W. Ford,
Rev. Theodore L. Gardiner, 2 copies,
Daisy L. Kemper,
I. Scott Kennedy,
Mrs. B. W. Kinney,
Lucian D. Lowther,
Stillman F. Lowther, 2 copies,
Ella Meek,
Mrs. Cora R. Ogden,
Charles A. F. Randolph, 2 copies,
Colwell M. Randolph,
Daniel Fillmore F. Randolph,
Ernest F. Randolph,
Mrs. George W. F. Randolph, 2 copies,
Gillette F. Randolph,
James F. Randolph,
Jesse F. Randolph,
John F. Randolph,
Judson F. Randolph,
Preston F. Randolph,
Ray F. Randolph,

Salem (Continued).
O. W. Swiger,
Salem College Library,
Mrs. George H. Trainer, 3 copies,
Moses H. VanHorn,
William B. VanHorn,
Rev. Ellis A. Witter, 2 copies.

Shinston.
S. Orestes Bond.

Spurgeon.
Joshua C. Spurgeon.

Sugar Camp.
Johnson J. Lowther.

Peel Tree.
Mrs. Erene R. Bond.

West Union.
F. M. Davis,
Herbert T. Davis,
Lewis Townsend Davis,
Samuel L. Ford,
Mrs. J. E. Trainer.
Ida J. Warner.

White Oak.
Festus Kelley.

WISCONSIN.

Albion.
Fred Davis,
Lester Kelley,
Nathan Kelley,
Paul Palmiter,
Rev. Theodore J. VanHorn.

Clinton.
Mrs. M. G. Townsend.

Drummond.
W. R. Rood.

Milton.
Albert R. Crandall,
Rev. William C. Daland,
Benoni I. Jeffrey,
Rev. Lewis A. Platts,
Albert Whitford.

Milton Junction.
Rev. Richard C. Bond,
Rev. Darius K. Davis.

Utica.
James H. Coon.

Walworth.
Mrs. W. L. Hibbard,
Rev. Mazzini G. Stillman.

CANADA.

Petitcodiac, New Brunswick.
Rev. George Seeley.

WEST AFRICA.

Ayan Main, Gold Coast.
E. G. A. Ammokoo.

Milton Keynes UK
Ingram Content Group UK Ltd.
UKHW051106250324
439991UK00007B/797